ABSOLUTELY EVERYTHING
A *TEEN* SHOULD KNOW

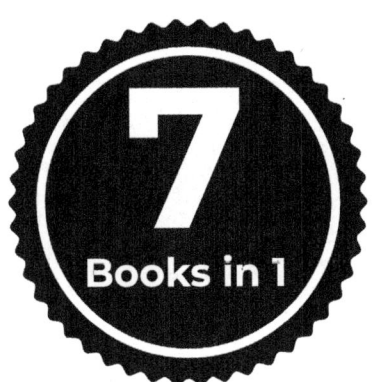

7 Books in 1

Life Skills
Money Skills
Social Skills
Career Planning
Self-Regulation
DBT and
Coping Skills Workbook
for Teens

EMILY CARTER

© Copyright 2025 Emily Carter - All rights reserved.

The content contained within this book may not be reproduced, duplicated or transmitted without direct written permission from the author or the publisher.

Under no circumstances will any blame or legal responsibility be held against the publisher, or author, for any damages, reparation, or monetary loss due to the information contained within this book, either directly or indirectly.

Legal Notice:

This book is copyright protected. It is only for personal use. You cannot amend, distribute, sell, use, quote or paraphrase any part, or the content within this book, without the consent of the author or publisher.

Disclaimer Notice:

Please note the information contained within this document is for educational and entertainment purposes only. All effort has been executed to present accurate, up to date, reliable, complete information. No warranties of any kind are declared or implied. Readers acknowledge that the author is not engaged in the rendering of legal, financial, medical or professional advice. The content within this book has been derived from various sources. Please consult a licensed professional before attempting any techniques outlined in this book.

By reading this document, the reader agrees that under no circumstances is the author responsible for any losses, direct or indirect, that are incurred as a result of the use of the information contained within this document, including, but not limited to, errors, omissions, or inaccuracies.

TABLE OF CONTENTS

Your Free Gift vi

THE BIG BOOK OF ADULTING LIFE SKILLS FOR TEENS

Introduction 2
Part 1: Living Away From Home 4
Chapter 1: Renting and Moving 4
Chapter 2: Cooking and Meal Planning 8
Chapter 3: Cleaning and Organization 11
Chapter 4: Home Maintenance and Repairs 13
Part 2: Financial Literacy 17
Chapter 5: Healthy Finances Are the Foundation of a Happy Life 17
Chapter 6: Credit Scores, Credit Cards, and Debt 21
Chapter 7: Investing and Planning for the Future 24
Part 3: Relationships and Communication 28
Chapter 8: Different Relationships, Same Foundations 28
Chapter 9: Developing Healthy Communication Skills 32
Part 4: Health and Wellness 36
Chapter 10: Physical and Mental Health Go Hand-in-Hand 36
Chapter 11: Self-Care and Healthy Habits 40
Chapter 12: Medical Matters 45
Part 5: Personal Development 48
Chapter 13: Time Management and Goal Setting 48
Chapter 14: Growth Mindset, Self-Confidence, and Resilience 54
Conclusion 57

MONEY SKILLS FOR TEENS

Introduction 60
Chapter 1: Understanding Money 61
Chapter 2: Making Money 65
Chapter 3: Banking and Financial Services 71

Chapter 4: Budgeting 78
Chapter 5: Spending and Paying Bills 84
Chapter 6: Credit, Credit Cards, and Debt Management 91
Chapter 7: Investing 95
Chapter 8: Insurance 100
Chapter 9: Big Purchases and Paying for College 102
Chapter 10: Retirement 104
Conclusion 105

SOCIAL SKILLS FOR TEENS

Introduction 108
Chapter 1: Self-Awareness 110
Chapter 2: Self-Confidence 118
Chapter 3: Social Skills 124
Chapter 4: Social Anxiety 131
Chapter 5: Connection 138
Chapter 6: Handling Difficult Social Situations 144
Chapter 7: Social Sustainability 151
Conclusion 157

CAREER PLANNING FOR TEENS

Introduction 160
Chapter 1: Understanding Yourself 163
Chapter 2: Exploring Career Options 167
Chapter 3: Developing Essential Skills 172
Chapter 4: Seeking Guidance 179
Chapter 5: Planning for Education and Training 183
Chapter 6: Gaining Practical Experience 188
Chapter 7: Making Informed Decisions 193
Chapter 8: Taking Action 198
Chapter 9: Transitioning to the World of Work 204
Conclusion 209

SELF-REGULATION WORKBOOK FOR TEENS

Introduction 212
Part 1: CBT Cognitive Techniques 214
Chapter 1: Introduction to Cognitive Behavioral Therapy (CBT) 215

Chapter 2: Understanding Thoughts, Feelings, and Behaviors............................220
Chapter 3: Challenging Negative Thinking Patterns............................223
Chapter 4: Building Positive Self-Talk............................229
Chapter 5: Mindfulness and Acceptance............................239
Part 2: CBT Behavioral Techniques............................252
Chapter 6: Understanding Behavior Patterns............................253
Chapter 7: Developing Coping Skills............................263
Chapter 8: Behavioral Activation............................266
Chapter 9: Assertiveness Training............................283
Chapter 10: Problem-Solving Skills............................287
Chapter 11: Relapse Prevention............................299
Conclusion............................303

DBT WORKBOOK FOR TEENS

Introduction............................306
Part 1: Mindfulness............................308
Part 2: Distress Tolerance............................334
Part 3: Emotional Regulation............................355
Part 4: Interpersonal Effectiveness............................376
Conclusion............................407

COPING SKILLS WORKBOOK FOR TEENS

Introduction............................410
Chapter 1: Understanding CBT and DBT............................412
Chapter 2: Understanding Your Emotions............................416
Chapter 3: Building Emotional Awareness............................428
Chapter 4: Cognitive Behavioral Strategies............................451
Chapter 5: Dialectical Behavior Therapy Strategies............................467
Chapter 6: Building Healthy Coping Skills............................480
Chapter 7: Building Healthy Relationships............................492
Chapter 8: Long-Term Emotional Regulation Strategies............................506
Conclusion............................524

Thank You............................526
About The Author............................527
References............................528

YOUR FREE GIFT

To really make the most out of your life, and to succeed in it, it's crucial to never stop learning. To further develop your knowledge of important life skills, I've got something for you... something you can really be excited about!

As a way of saying thank you for your purchase, I want to offer you some BONUSES completely FREE of charge:

To get instant access, just go to https://lifeskillbooks.com

Here's just a glimpse of what is included:

BONUS 1

Unleashing Your Potential: A Teenager's Guide to Developing a Growth Mindset and Opening Your Path to Success

Inside the book, you will discover...

- ✧ The differences between a fixed and growth mindset, how your mindset impacts your personal growth and success, and why a growth mindset is the one you should adopt.
- ✧ Practical strategies to cultivate a growth mindset, from daily habits to overcoming obstacles.
- ✧ How to utilize a growth mindset to supercharge your academic and career success.
- ✧ And much more!

BONUS 2

The Anxiety Handbook: Understand the Types, Triggers and Symptoms of Anxiety to Effectively Cope With It

Inside this comprehensive guide, you will discover...

- ✧ Insights into different types of anxiety disorders, so you can understand and identify specific triggers.
- ✧ Overview of the symptoms of each anxiety type so you can learn to recognize them better.
- ✧ Proven techniques to manage and reduce anxiety, helping you regain control over your life.
- ✧ And more!

BONUS 3

Printable Self-Regulation & Coping Skills Worksheets: Practical Tools for Managing Stress, Anxiety and Emotions

Inside this comprehensive workbook, you will discover...

- ⬥ **Step-by-Step Coping Strategies**: Gain access to structured exercises that help you identify, challenge, and reframe negative thoughts, leading to a more positive mindset.
- ⬥ **Personalized Mood and Habit Tracking**: Utilize detailed trackers to monitor your mood and daily habits, allowing you to identify patterns and make informed changes for better mental health.
- ⬥ **Self-Care and Mindfulness Practices**: Engage in a 30-day self-care challenge and explore various self-soothing techniques to promote relaxation and reduce stress.
- ⬥ **Interactive and Easy-to-Use Worksheets**: Enjoy a user-friendly layout with guided prompts and questions designed to support your journey toward improved mental well-being and personal growth.
- ⬥ **And more!** Everything is in easily printable form.

Now, go to the website below for instant access to these and several other amazing bonuses. Completely free of charge.

https://lifeskillbooks.com

THE BIG BOOK OF ADULTING LIFE SKILLS FOR TEENS

A Complete Guide to All the Crucial Life Skills They Don't Teach You in School for Teenagers

EMILY CARTER

INTRODUCTION

For in every adult there dwells the child that was, and in every child there lies the adult that will be.

–John Connolly

The moment my parents drove away after dropping me off at my college dorm was a shock to my system. It was at that moment that I realized I was alone. I was responsible for myself, from what and when I'd eat to what time I'd go to bed at night. It was at that moment that I realized I'd made it. I was an adult with adult responsibilities.

In my sophomore year, when I opted to rent an apartment with a friend near campus, I realized that I'd been wrong. Living in a dorm is like adulthood on training wheels. You have a meal plan and dining halls. There are Resident Assistants (RAs) there to help with conflicts with roommates or other problems. In your own apartment or house? You're responsible for it all, from cleaning and cooking to making sure all the bills you've never had to think about before are paid.

Moving away from home for the first time is a big deal. Whether you're leaving the nest for a dorm for the school year or choosing an apartment, it's a big responsibility. From renting and moving to keeping yourself fed and your home organized, there's enough to consider to make your head spin, and don't worry—that's normal. This is your first major step into independence and adulthood. Once you move, you'll be responsible for feeding yourself, keeping your home clean, and doing maintenance on your home and car. You won't have your parents to fall back on the second something goes wrong, and while you may be able to call them to ask for help, they probably won't be cooking and cleaning or doing your laundry for you.

The first time my apartment sink backed up, I had no clue what to do. It wouldn't drain, no matter how much I ran the garbage disposal. It wouldn't budge. I was equally clueless the time my car's tire blew out mid-winter one year until I was informed that the tire pressure was well under what it should have been.

There were so many things I didn't know about adulthood that, looking back, should have been taught in school. After all, if school is meant to prepare us for the world, why are we spending time memorizing the Pythagorean theorem instead of how to handle debt? Why aren't we taught how to take care of ourselves and our homes?

Ultimately, now as an adult, I understand the importance of teaching children how to *be* adults. That begins with an understanding of all the things you'll need to do living away from home.

That's why I put together this book. It's all about the skills I wish I'd learned sooner. I'm sure they would have saved me a lot of time learning via trial by fire. I don't regret the past or the struggles I faced growing up—they certainly taught me valuable life lessons that I've used to thrive later on. However, if I can save even one teen from making all those same mistakes or going into adulthood blindly, I've done my job.

As you read this book, you'll get a preview of what it takes to be an adult. This means being able to manage your own household and finances to managing your relationships and conflicts. You'll learn about keeping yourself healthy and also what it takes to have a mindset that will set you up for success.

Before you dive in, there's one thing I want to emphasize. You never stop learning, growing, or changing. Even if these things seem tough to remember or do at first, that doesn't mean you won't be able to do them later. You may be an adult or approaching adulthood, but that doesn't mean that you'll suddenly have all the right answers. You don't magically get any brand new insight the moment you hit adulthood. But, you do get handed a whole lot of new responsibilities as you prepare to set off on your own.

Approach these skills with an open mind and a willingness to learn, even if it takes you several tries to get something done. As long as you keep on trying, you'll get to where you want to go. After all, you haven't failed unless you've decided to give up or not participate at all!

PART 1

LIVING AWAY FROM HOME

Never underestimate the power you have to take your life in a new direction.

–Germany Kent

CHAPTER 1

RENTING AND MOVING

When it's time to move on to your own place, it's normal to feel nervous, excited, and maybe even a little bit scared. As you say goodbye to your parents and shut your door on them for the first time, it's strange. It's like shutting that door breaks a tether that's held you to them for your entire life. You entered this world knowing only them. You held their hand as you grew, watched them as they taught you, and lived with them your whole life, and now? You've left the nest.

It's a bittersweet moment for you and probably your parents too. They're probably brimming with pride as they drop their precious baby off for the last time, but they're probably also a little bit afraid, sad, and not quite ready to let go.

Whether you're moving into a dorm, a rental, or buying a house, there's always a huge transition shift when you finally walk out the door of your parents' home for the last time. There's a finality to it, but that doesn't have to be a bad thing. It just means you've grown up, and you're ready to start your own life. That's normal. It's only natural.

Of course, this comes with a little caveat—you suddenly find yourself responsible for all the things you probably took for granted growing up. Bills being paid, chores getting done, milk magically appearing in the fridge… These things take time and mental labor. And now? That's all yours. Congratulations!

But, before it's time to say goodbye and start your new life, you have to get somewhere to live first. Moving into a dorm is relatively simple for most people. You put in the application, you get assigned a room on campus, and you pay for it for the year. However, moving into an apartment on your own requires a lot more thought. From knowing lease terms to how to avoid a scam, there are some things to keep in mind.

Don't forget that your parents or guardians can be a major support during this process. They might cry when you get your first set of keys, but they can be just the people to turn to if you have specific questions. After all, they want what's best for you and they've got the experience to boot.

Everything You Need to Know

Before renting and moving, you'll want to familiarize yourself with several steps in the process. What are the terms of your lease? What utilities does the rent cover, if any? What about furniture and appliances? Why do you have to pay two or three months' rent upfront? Does renter's insurance really matter? Why? What is it? For a brand-new apartment hunter, there's a lot that you need to know that you may never have considered before, and that's okay! We all start somewhere and this is the perfect starting point.

Lease Terms

Leases are the contracts you sign when renting an apartment that grants you exclusive use of an apartment, room, house, or any other rental unit in exchange for an agreed-upon price. They're more than just that, though. They also list out the rules and guidelines that you need to abide by while renting, and if you violate the terms of the lease, you may break the contract and lose your right to remain in the unit.

Each lease will be different, so you'll want to read it all prior to signing it and ask any questions about terms you're unsure about or don't understand. The leasing agent will be able to walk you through it all.

Keep in mind that leases will also vary around the world. While in the US, it's standard for leases to include appliances; other countries may give you an entirely empty unit without a fridge, cabinets, or counters. While in the US, you can expect to have a background check run, be required to verify your income, and provide valid identification; other countries may also have additional requirements. You may be required to provide structural repairs in other countries as well.

Another thing to remember is that your lease will likely dictate whether you're allowed to have long-term guests to prevent unintended residencies. In many places, someone residing in a unit for longer than a month is enough to establish tenancy, even if they're a guest, and that can create a lot of legal headaches for the landlord if they refuse to leave. Even without a valid lease for that long-term guest, they may be forced to legally evict them if they can prove they've been there long enough.

Are Utilities Included?

Sometimes, utilities are included in your rental costs. This is especially common if you rent a room in a house. However, most rentals in the US will require you to have utilities in your own name, including electricity, gas, water, sewer, and garbage. You'll also likely have to pay for your own internet costs. Verify what's included in your lease beforehand to avoid any surprises, such as having to have the utilities transferred prior to moving in.

Deposits and Move-In Costs

Before you move in, you'll usually be responsible for the first month of rent. This seems pretty straightforward, right? Well, there are other expenses that will likely come into play too. Most rentals will charge a security deposit for any damages beyond normal wear and tear, which is any expected damage accrued by regular use, such as a wobbly doorknob or scuffs and wear on flooring.

The exact amount of your deposit will depend on what the state or country allows. For example, in Seattle, where I live now, a landlord can't charge more than one month's rent for a security deposit or nonrefundable fees, and renters have up to six months to pay off the security deposit, nonrefundable fees, and the last month's rent in a payment plan. This is a city-specific regulation, while the state of Washington has no such cap. Colorado has no caps on security deposits. Connecticut allows two months' rent for most tenants, but for those 62 or older, that number is halved to the equivalent of one month.

Make sure you know what's considered a legal deposit in your location prior to signing a lease and remember, if the deposit doesn't seem to align with what the law allows, there's a chance you're walking into a scam.

Beyond the deposit and last month's rent, you may also be required to pay a pet deposit or pet rent, deposits to begin utility services in your name, or other fees that may be dictated in your lease. You may also have to pay for movers, rent a moving truck, or pay someone to help you to get your belongings where they need to go.

Renters Insurance

Your lease may or may not require that you keep a renters insurance policy, but even if it's not obligatory, it's still a good idea to have. Renters' insurance typically covers unexpected events, which in the insurance world are known as covered perils. Each policy will vary in both coverage and cost, so make sure you speak with an agent who can help you understand which plans will work best for you. It typically comes with three types of coverage:

- **Personal Property:** This covers the cost to replace or repair any of your belongings that have been damaged, including furniture, electronics, and other items, up to the limit of your policy.
- **Liability:** This covers the cost of repairs if you accidentally damage the property or the cost of medical bills for a guest if they are injured on the property and you're found responsible, up to the limit of your policy.
- **Additional Living Expenses:** This covers any costs you may incur if your rental is damaged and you have to stay in a hotel.

Of course, there will be additional terms that will vary from company to company and state to state, such as what your deductible (the amount you pay before insurance pays out) will be, your premiums (the amount you pay monthly), and any covered perils.

Pet Policies

Pet policies can vary wildly, from allowing any and all dogs or cats to restricting you to specific sizes or prohibiting certain breeds. If you have a pet, this is probably one of the first considerations to make. Be sure to check your lease for pet policies, including a pet deposit, monthly pet rent, and any restrictions the property may have.

If you think you can get around the pet fees by hiding your pet, think again. This is a violation of your lease and you can be evicted and charged fees for pet damage. Likewise, if you have an apartment that doesn't allow pets at all, don't try to hide them.

Do You Need a Cosigner?

As a young adult, you'll likely start out without much credit unless your parents have been actively building it for you (more on this later). This means that you won't always look like the most attractive prospective tenant to landlords and they may be hesitant to rent to you since you won't have any sort of rental history. That's where cosigners come into play.

A cosigner is someone who co-signs your lease and agrees to be responsible for any fees, unpaid rent, or damages if you don't pay them. Typically, your cosigner will be someone with a much more established credit history and financial position, like your parents. Just remember that the cosigner is also on the lease and will have the same access to the property as you will. An alternative to a cosigner is a guarantor, who promises to pay the rent if you don't but does not have access to the apartment.

Choosing a Rental

If it's time to begin your rental search, hold your horses. Before you get too excited and start circling all the chic rentals with a million amenities and upgraded features, you've got some planning to do. I know how tempting it is to scroll through available units and dream of your new life in the best of the best, but the reality is most of us start small and work our way up. Choosing a rental takes a whole lot of planning, research, and time, and even then, you may not get the first one you apply for.

What's Your Budget?

The biggest factor in the entire apartment search is your budget. After all, you have to be able to afford your new place. Getting in over your head, even if you may qualify for an apartment that is, on paper, unaffordable, is a good way to start on the wrong foot.

Generally speaking, your budget should be less than 30% of your monthly income. This is where things get tricky, especially with the housing and rental markets skyrocketing. If you're making the U.S. minimum wage of $7.25 per hour while working a full-time job, that puts your annual pay at $15,080, or an average of about $1,257 per month. Using the 30% rule, you can only afford to pay about $377 per month in rent.

If that's looking bleak to you, you understand exactly what problem so many young adults of today face, and that's being unable to afford to live alone. If your pay alone is not enough to cover the average cost of rent in your area, you have some options. The most popular one is to rent with friends or roommates and everyone contributes to the monthly cost. This can make rent more affordable.

Alternatively, you may need to consider living with parents or family members while gaining work experience, going to college, or pursuing a trade to boost your earning power.

To calculate your budget, take your hourly pay and multiply it by the number of hours you work per week. Then, multiply that number by 52 (for 52 weeks in the year to get annual pay). Divide that number by 12 to get your monthly average income. Then, multiply your monthly average income by 0.3 to see what the most you should be paying for rent is.

What Do You Want or Need?

Once you know how much you can pay, you can start considering amenities that matter to you. Start with a list of all the things you need out of your home, such as the distance to where you work or go to school and non-negotiable amenities.

- **Parking:** If you drive, you probably want somewhere that has available parking. Some apartment complexes may have assigned parking spots. Others may not offer any parking at all and require you to park on the streets.
- **Neighborhood:** Do you have a particular neighborhood you're partial to or neighborhoods you'd like to avoid? Check out crime statistics in the area you're considering, and spend some time looking around the area in person if you can to get a good feel for it.
- **Amenities:** Are there any amenities that you absolutely must have? For many, appliances like dishwashers and washers and dryers are required. Others may consider having an on-site gym or pool essential.
- **Closeness to work or school:** What is the farthest you're willing to move from your work or school? Remember, even if prices are cheaper for you to live further away, you may be spending so much more on transportation that it's actually more expensive than living closer.

Make a Short List

With your list of wants and needs and with your budget, you can then go searching for vacancies. Make a list of three to five rentals that you'd like to check out, that you can afford, and that meet your list of needs. You can search for rentals through word of mouth, asking around if anyone knows of vacancies, or online. Check out local property management companies to see if they have anything that will work for you.

View Apartments

Contact the apartments on your shortlist and ask if you can schedule a tour. It's strongly recommended that you never rent a place sight unseen because there may be problems that aren't obvious in photographs online. Take the time to tour the units and neighborhoods, and if you can, bring a trusted, experienced adult to take a look at everything, too.

Apply

Once you've decided on an apartment in your budget that meets your needs, it's time to apply. Be aware that most places will have non refundable application fees to cover background checks, and applying isn't a guarantee you'll get the place, especially in areas with a lot of competition. If your application is accepted, make sure you review the lease carefully before signing it.

Chapter Summary

Getting your first place is probably going to feel a little overwhelming at first. After all, you have to figure out what you need and can afford and then find somewhere with the availability that works for you. It might be with roommates, or you may truly be on your own for the first time. Either way, these tips are meant to try to smooth out the process. Don't forget that you can always ask for help from people around you!

And, once you've got your very own place to call home, you get to experience something new—managing your diet. From cooking to meal prepping, the next chapter will dive into everything you need to know.

CHAPTER 2
COOKING AND MEAL PLANNING

We all need to eat at some point. Once you've settled into your new place, that responsibility falls firmly on your plate. Or, you might have roommates and decide to split up the responsibilities. Either way, there's no more Mom or Dad taking care of this for you, so it's time to get comfortable in the kitchen if you're not already.

I had roommates at one point and we rotated between cooking and cleaning on various nights. I've also had roommate situations where we were each responsible for feeding ourselves and cleaning up our messes after using the kitchens. You'll want to hash out expectations with your roommates before moving in together so you're on the same page. Will some items be free for everyone to use? Will you have different shelves in the fridge and cabinets for your food? These are all considerations to make.

Then comes meal planning, shopping, and keeping yourself satisfied, hopefully with healthy foods.

Dive Into Meal Planning

Meal planning is one of those things that sounds intimidating but is far easier than most people think. It's all about setting up a calendar with what you'll eat and when and making sure you have all of the ingredients on hand. This can really help you if you're the kind of person who gets overwhelmed with choices and doesn't know what to make, so you end up choosing to order out or buy something easy, which can be a big drain on your budget.

Meal Planning Steps

Meal planning really is as easy as following four simple steps that will keep you on track and help you to stretch your budget while still eating healthy foods that will keep your body running. If you reach for empty carbs and snacks like potato chips when you're busy and hungry, you aren't doing yourself any favors. You'll be hungry again a short while later. With meal planning, especially if you prep your meals in advance, you'll always know what's available and have something easy to eat.

Step 1: Take the Time to Plan

Each week, dedicate an hour or two to planning your meals for the next week. Try to plan breakfasts, lunches, and dinners. If you know there are days in your schedule when you're busy, make sure you have quick meals for them. Write down the meals and ingredients you'll need to make them.

While you're at it, choose meals that use similar ingredients so you can buy in bulk and lower costs. For example, maybe you make a chicken stir fry one night and then chicken fajitas the next. This lets you use up everything without waste.

Step 2: Check What's Already in the Kitchen

Once you have a list of ingredients, check your kitchen to see what you already have. Make sure that you check the use-by dates to ensure everything is still good, and if you have any ingredients that are about to expire, consider altering your meal plan to include those foods to avoid waste.

Step 3: Make Sure You Like the Meals

The key to sticking to a meal plan is making sure you're excited to eat the food. If you decide on recipes to use up items that you don't really like much, you'll be more tempted to ignore them and order in.

Step 4: Cook in Bulk and Use Your Leftovers

Choosing meals that make multiple servings can help make your meal-planning process easier. Even better, you can use the leftovers for lunch the next day. Just make sure that any meals that you choose to cook in bulk will reheat easily.

If you like big casseroles or dishes that usually result in a lot of food, you may be able to freeze them too. Foods like pot pies, casseroles, lasagna, spaghetti sauce, and stews all tend to freeze well, and you'll be able to pull out servings for lunches or dinners on busy days.

A Well-Stocked Kitchen is Key

Part of meal planning successfully is relying on some essentials in the pantry and fridge. When you first move to your first place, there are some things you should just keep stocked if they're part of your usual rotation of foods. These include:

Pantry Goods	Refrigerator Goods	Freezer Goods
Rice and grains, Pasta, Canned meats, Potato flakes, Snacks, Veggie and chicken broth, Jarred peppers and olives, Cream soups, Oils, Flour, Sugar, Salt, Baking soda, Baking powder, Seasonings, Dried herbs	Milk, Butter, Cheese, Eggs, Yogurt, Fresh fruits and veggies, Meats, Condiments	Frozen meats, Frozen vegetables, Frozen potatoes, Frozen fruits

A good way to help build up this stockpile is to buy in bulk when there are good sales and put items in your freezer. For example, maybe there's a good sale on chicken, so you buy more than you'd normally need and vacuum seal the extras to put in your freezer. This is a great way to cut down your costs.

Sprucing Up Cheap Meals

While ramen is hardly a balanced meal on its own, it's also one of those go-to foods that young adults eat regularly. After all, it's cheap, filling, and can be pretty tasty, too. I get it! I've had more than my fair share of instant noodles over the years.

When you go for cheap meals, there's no reason you can't spruce them up a bit. Toss in some frozen mixed veggies, a hard-boiled egg, and some chicken, and you've got a full meal. You can do this with other meals, too, like tossing vegetables into pasta or making fried rice with leftovers.

Meal Planning Tips for Young Adults

If you're planning out your weekly meals and trying to keep to a strict budget, you've got some options. These are some of my tried-and-true tips that I use to keep my food costs down without sacrificing much in the quality department.

Shop With Weekly Ads and Coupons in Mind

When you sit down to meal plan, review all the weekly ads and coupons at the store or stores you plan to shop at. You might notice that certain meats go on sale at certain points in the month or catch some killer deals on produce that you can use to implement into your meal plan. You might even be able to add some meat to your stockpile if you plan accordingly.

Stretch the Proteins

Especially in the US, there's this idea that protein has to be the main part of a meal. While planning around a protein can be helpful, it doesn't have to be the main dish. For example, instead of making burritos with lots of ground beef, you can cut the beef with a can of whole black beans to make it go further.

Throwing proteins into casseroles or pasta dishes can also help them feel like they go farther. Meat, in particular, is expensive, but by mixing it with other foods, you may be able to get more out of it.

Reach for Filling Foods

Foods that fill you up should be the bulk of your diet. When you shop, that means looking for whole foods that are on the perimeters of most grocery stores. The center aisles tend to be full of other foods that won't be as satisfying. Stick to the produce, meat, dairy, and whole grain areas as much as possible.

When you're hungry, grab satisfying foods like nuts, whole veggies, and fruits. Pair a carb with a healthy fat to boost feelings of fullness. After all, when you're satisfied with healthy foods, you're not going to be reaching for so many snacks, which can get expensive.

Cook at Home Whenever Possible

Just because you decide to meal plan doesn't mean that you can't eat out from time to time. But you'll want to focus on your meals at home, giving you healthy meals without breaking the bank.

Have Easy-to-Grab Foods Available for Those Busy Mornings

I get it—mornings are busy. I skipped my morning meals way too much when I was younger. Why bother eating if I need to rush out the door when having breakfast means waking up earlier? Why not just pick up a coffee and pastry at my favorite cafe on my way? Why not just pick up something from one of the dining halls? Well, the problem with this is that it gets expensive quickly.

Breakfast is the most important meal of your day. It stabilizes your blood sugar, which can help you feel more alert and energetic throughout the day, which also reduces the chances you'll be tempted by that afternoon's unhealthy snack.

I recommend keeping some easy grab-and-go foods on hand so you can have a complete breakfast any time you're in a rush. I love keeping DIY breakfast burritos and sandwiches in my freezer, so all I have to do is pop it onto a plate and warm it up for a minute while I get my coffee going. It saves my wallet and keeps me satisfied and full throughout my morning.

Chapter Summary

As one of the most basic needs that you require, food and thinking about food will probably be a pretty major part of your life for the foreseeable future. That's why implementing meal planning can be so useful—it takes thinking about food out of the equation. With minimal time spent handling and planning your food, you'll be able to free up time for other important things, like chores and staying organized.

CHAPTER 3

CLEANING AND ORGANIZATION

One of the biggest shocks to my system when I moved into my own place was just how much work goes into maintaining it. A good, solid cleaning schedule is key to keeping a clean environment, and that requires discipline. When I first got my own apartment, I realized that my parents did a lot more than I initially thought. They kept the floors vacuumed and mopped. They kept the bathrooms clean and the living room organized. While I had chores that I was responsible for, they paled in comparison to the regular upkeep of a home.

The best way for you to maintain your home is to have a schedule for daily, weekly, and monthly chores so you know what you're doing and when. This helps to keep you accountable and builds a routine where the cleanup is completed.

A Place for Everything

Any time you bring something home, it needs to have a dedicated place. This is one of the easiest ways to keep clutter down. If you don't have room for something, then it probably shouldn't be brought home. When you finish using something, return it back to its designated spot.

If it Takes Five Minutes, Do it Right Away

How often do you make a small mess and then tell yourself that you'll get to it later? This is an easy trap to fall into, but all those quick, little jobs can build up over time until what should have been easy tidying up becomes needing a deep clean or a more extensive scrub-down of an area. For example, if you spill something on the counter, you might tell yourself that you'll clean it when you do the dishes. Sure, it's not a big deal, but if you do that with all the little messes you make throughout the day, they all add up to a longer cleaning session.

The rule I use and that I teach my children is that if a cleanup task only takes five minutes or less to do after making a mess, then do it right away. If you spill your coffee, wipe it up right away. By doing the little tasks as soon as they pop up, you help maintain the cleanliness of your home so your cleanup routine stays consistent.

Develop a Regular Cleaning Schedule

Setting up a regular cleaning schedule can feel a little too reminiscent of chore charts for some new adults, but that's kind of the point. The chore chart helps keep everything done on time and makes sure nothing slips through the cracks. In my home, we divide chores into three categories.

Daily	Weekly	Monthly
Make your bed Do the dishes Wipe counters Tidy up clutter Take out trash/recycling	Scrub bathrooms Mop Vacuum Wash bedding Clean out fridge Dust surfaces	Wipe baseboards Wipe light switches Deep clean appliances Replace filters Vacuum underneath furniture Clean windows and tracks Scrub out trash cans

Of course, you might have other chores that you need to take care of, too, like cleaning out cat boxes, water changes for aquariums, watering plants, or yard work. Fit those in as needed as well.

From there, you have a few options. You can designate one day per week as your deep cleaning day or you can choose to do one or two weekly chores each day. For example:

- Sunday: Clean bedding and empty fridge
- Monday: Monthly chore
- Tuesday: Monthly chore
- Wednesday: Monthly chore
- Thursday: Dust surfaces
- Friday: Mop and vacuum
- Saturday: Scrub bathrooms

By adding in a few monthly chores on days you don't have weekly chores to complete, you can spread them out throughout the month so you don't find yourself overwhelmed on one or two days trying to get to everything on the list.

Chapter Summary

Keeping a tidy home can do wonders for your mental health, and it doesn't take much. Following these tips and setting a schedule can help you keep your home in tip-top shape—until something goes wrong and you have to fix it, that is. That's why the next chapter's here to prepare you with everything you need to know about maintaining your home—and which repairs to leave to the pros.

CHAPTER 4
HOME MAINTENANCE AND REPAIRS

The first time I had an apartment, I thought everything would be taken care of. After all, that's what maintenance is for, right? Well, there are a lot of maintenance things that the apartment isn't responsible for. Yes, they'll repair major issues with plumbing, dead appliances, and make sure that the environment is livable. You'll need to know what your responsibilities are and what your landlord is responsible for. Most of this is going to be dictated in your lease, outlining what you need to do.

Beyond when not to do your repairs, there are several common issues that you'll likely run into at one point or another that you'll need to be able to repair on your own.

When Not to Do Your Own Repairs

Some repairs are major and aren't your responsibility. In particular, these are habitable issues, problems with safety, or emergency requests.

- **Habitable issues:** If you have an issue that makes the environment uninhabitable, like issues with the electrical system, heating, air conditioning, or plumbing, these are usually concerns that maintenance will handle. Other issues include faulty appliances and pest infestations.
- **Safety problems:** Safety problems may include issues with smoke alarms, locks, or carbon monoxide detectors. While you may need to do battery replacements in alarms, your landlord has to make sure these devices function properly. Likewise, the entire property needs to be maintained. If there are trees outside that appear unstable, for example, the property owner has a duty to keep them safe.
- **Emergency requests:** Some emergency issues also warrant a call to maintenance for help. These include gas leaks, flooding, water leaks, or mold. If you notice these issues, you should contact maintenance and have them handle the situation.

How to Unclog a Drain

A clogged drain can really bring your daily routine grinding to a halt, especially if it's in your kitchen. However, other clogs can also occur, like in your toilet or bathtub. Thankfully, there are a lot of easy ways you can fix a clog without having to wait for maintenance.

Use a Plunger

A plunger is most commonly used for a toilet but can also be useful in other drains as well. Just be sure that any plunger used in your kitchen isn't shared with the toilet or make sure that it's thoroughly sanitized before using it. These work by forcing water down into the drain pipe to push the clog through and work well in many cases.

Use a Drain Snake

A drain snake or an auger is a long, flexible cable that you can use to push down a drain to pull out major clogs that you can't force through the plumbing with a plunger. With most of these, you simply put the coiled end into the drain and then turn the handle until it catches on something. Then, rotate it around to either catch the clog or break it apart. Recoil the snake and see if you pulled anything out, then flush the drain with hot water. If it's still draining slowly, you can repeat the process with the snake or move on to a liquid drain cleaner to chemically break down the clog.

Use a Liquid Drain Cleaner

Liquid drain cleaners are products you buy from the store that are poured down the drain to chemically break it down. They're great for breaking down clogs in drain systems, like hair or grease, especially in areas you can't easily reach the plumbing, like in a bathtub, but that also means that they can be dangerous if they get on your skin too. Make sure you follow the directions on the product's packaging to remove the drain and take care to avoid getting it on you.

Cleaning a Sink Trap

You may also be able to remove a clog by removing a sink's p-trap and then manually removing whatever is blocking it up. However, this can be messy, too, and you'll need to be careful to have a bucket or some other large container ready to catch any water stuck inside.

The p-trap is the u-shaped pipe underneath a sink and is designed to keep smelly sewer smells from coming through the pipes. This is usually done with a water seal, which means as soon as you remove it, water will spill.

To clean your p-trap, you'll need a flexible wire brush as well as pliers or an adjustable wrench, depending on the setup of your pipe. If you have a hard time visualizing the steps listed below, there are dozens of videos online that can also walk you through the repair step by step.

1. Turn off the water faucet and remember, even if the faucet is off, water will still leak once you remove the trap.
2. Many p-traps can be removed by hand. Twist the big nuts holding the p-trap onto the rest of the plumbing until it loosens. If it's tight, use a wrench or pliers. Be ready to catch the water because it'll start spilling as soon as the nut is loosened.
3. Once you've removed the p-trap, you can clean it out by pulling out any clogs. If needed, use a wire brush to force any clogs through the other end.
4. Put the pipe back into place and tighten the nuts again. Use the wrench or pliers if necessary to get a solid seal. Then run the water for 15–20 seconds to make sure there's no leakage from the nuts. If water leaks, turn off the faucet and tighten the nuts before testing it again.

Cleaning the Garbage Disposal

Is your garbage disposal getting smelly? This is one of those appliances that you'll want to clean out at least monthly, but every week or every other week is often preferred. While garbage disposals see a lot of water pumping through them, there are areas that aren't easily rinsed clean when used, and that's what you'll need to clean.

It might seem daunting to stick your hand inside an appliance that exists just to break down foods, but you can remove the risk simply by turning off the power to the device at the breaker box. Before you begin, make sure you flip the switch to see if the disposal has been disabled. If it doesn't turn on, flip it off again, and then you can begin the cleaning process.

You'll need:

- a kitchen sponge
- a sink stopper
- dish soap
- ½ cup baking soda
- 1 cup vinegar
- ice cubes
- 1 cup rock salt
- water
- rubber gloves (if you want them)

Once you've got your tools handy and the power is off (this is important enough to repeat!), it's time to scrub.

1. Put on the gloves if you want to keep your hands clean, and then take the sponge and add dish soap to it. First, you'll want to scrub the baffle, which is the rubber part that leads down into the drain and keeps food from flying back up and out of the drain when using the disposal. Scrub it thoroughly, rinsing the sponge regularly to get rid of all the built-up gunk.

2. Use the sponge to clean out the grinding chamber, scrubbing the walls around the top and sides, and once again rinsing frequently until you stop seeing gunk come up on your sponge. This is enough for a weekly scrub of your disposal, but if it's extra stinky or it's been a while since you cleaned it thoroughly, you'll want to keep cleaning.

3. Dump the baking soda down the drain, then slowly follow up with the vinegar. Place the drain stopper over the drain to keep all the foam inside the garbage disposal, where it'll do its work. Leave it for at least 10 minutes. While waiting, go switch the power back on to the garbage disposal, and after the time is up, rinse the drain with hot water while running the disposal.

4. Turn off the disposal and fill up the drain with ice cubes. Dump in the cup of rock salt, then run the disposal to grind up the ice and salt. This will get any last bits of gunk left behind. Once the ice is ground up, run some hot water to wash everything through, and your garbage disposal should smell fresh.

How to Clean Washers and Dryers

Washers, in particular, can start smelling dank if you don't take good care of them. The care for these will change based on whether you have a top-loading or front-loading washer. Front-loading washers tend to build up mold inside the door. The easiest way to prevent them from stinking is to remove wet clothes from them promptly and make sure you leave the door open when not in use to dry them out.

If your front-loading washer is starting to stink, you can wipe it down with a mix of 1:9 bleach to water solution and a small scrubber like a toothbrush. From there, the process of cleaning out any residue buildup is the same in both top- and front-loading appliances.

To clean it, you'll want to run a hot cycle with a cup of bleach on the long cleaning cycle. Then, run a second cycle with hot water and two cups of vinegar. Let it sit, then run another long cleaning cycle. Finally, run a long cycle with just hot water.

To be safe, you'll want to make sure the first load of laundry you do after bleaching your washer is just whites. I've learned this the hard way after turning my favorite pink shirt into a shell of what it once was, covered in bleached spots.

Dryers don't need as thorough of a cleaning since there are only clean clothes going into them, but lint can build up. Make sure you remove the lint trap and clean it out before every load of laundry to make sure that lint doesn't build up in the duct. This can be a fire hazard!

Try fitting a vacuum hose into the lint trap to suck out the remaining lint, then wipe out the drum with a mild detergent. You'll also want to clean the exhaust on the back of the dryer if you can. Loosen up the clamp on the back and use your hands to take out as much lint as you can. You'll want to shove your vacuum hose into this as well to suck out any remaining lint.

How to Clean Dishwashers

You might not know this but your dishwasher *also* needs to be cleaned frequently. Yes, the device that sanitizes your dishes can get dirty! If you've noticed that your machine isn't washing as well as it used to or you're getting funky smells coming from it, there's a good chance that the filter needs to be cleaned out. The good news is this is usually an easy cleaning process and with maybe ten minutes of active work, you can have it working as good as new.

You'll either want to have dishwasher cleaning products or baking soda and vinegar so you can break down any grease or soap scum stuck in the appliance.

1. Remove the racks, utensil holders, and the filter from the dishwasher. If you're unsure how, look up the model online or consult the instruction manual. The filter, in particular, will probably look

pretty gross if you haven't cleaned it in a while. Scrub out the filter to remove any food, scum, or mold that may have built up, then soak it in vinegar and warm water while you finish the rest of the scrubbing.
2. Wipe down everything you can see, including spray arms, side walls, and corners where gunk may have gotten stuck. Use a toothbrush or toothpick to get stubborn bits out.
3. Place the filter, racks, and utensil holders back into the machine and either use a dishwasher cleaning product on its own according to the instructions or set a bowl with a cup of vinegar into the bottom of the dishwasher. Run the cycle (sanitation cycle if you have it!).
4. After the vinegar cycle, remove the bowl and toss in a cup of baking soda across the bottom. This will deodorize the dishwasher and also remove any stains that may have gotten stuck. Run an express cycle with the baking soda and you're done!

How to Replace an Air Filter

Air filter replacements should happen frequently, every other month or so, or more often if you have pets or live somewhere that's dry and dusty. This is often a part of maintenance that you're expected to do on your own. You may have a reusable filter that needs to be vacuumed out from time to time, or you may need to replace it on your own. To change it, follow these steps:

1. Find the location(s) of your air filter. There may be more than one that needs to be changed.
2. Make sure you know the right size and get a new one. You'll need the right length, width, and thickness.
3. When you have the new filter, open up the housing and remove the old one. Wipe out any dust or grime from the housing and then place the new filter into the duct, paying attention to the arrows. Then, close the grille and secure it in place.

How to Replace Lightbulbs

If you have a lightbulb that doesn't turn on or is flickering a lot, it's probably time to replace it. Before you crack a joke about how many young adults it takes to change a bulb, know it's really simple. All you have to do is make sure you have the right light bulbs on hand, make sure the light is switched off and that the lightbulb is cooled off, then unscrew the old one and place the new one in.

If you have light fixtures, you may have to remove those first by unscrewing them to gain access to the bulbs. That's okay too! While you're changing your bulbs, consider picking up LED bulbs, which last much longer and are also energy-efficient and can lower your overall energy bill.

Chapter Summary

Doing basic maintenance on your home can be really intimidating if you were never taught to do it before, but it's not so bad after practicing it. Even better, knowing how to maintain appliances can actually help you to keep some money in your pocket instead of rushing out to replace them at the first sign of a problem or if you get a clog somewhere in your drain. Practice, check out tutorial videos online, and trust that you can learn and do these things just like other adults. After all, the handiest person around the house that you know once knew nothing about maintenance too.

With that money you save on repairs, you can throw it toward your savings. The next section of the book talks all about how to manage your finances and keep your spending under control while saving for the future.

PART 2
FINANCIAL LITERACY

Financial literacy makes it okay for you to make small or big mistakes. On the other hand, being financially illiterate only makes those mistakes dire and regrettable

–Anas Hamshari

CHAPTER 5
HEALTHY FINANCES ARE THE FOUNDATION OF A HAPPY LIFE

One thing I regret never being taught as a child and a teen is the value of saving money. It's easy to spend when it's sitting in your pocket or bank account, which makes saving all the more difficult when you know you have enough money to buy that new video game, phone, dress, or whatever else has caught your eye. As we'll talk about a few chapters from now, though, saving money, especially when you're able to grow it with interest, is one of the best things you can do for yourself, even if you have to give up a little bit for now to have it later.

While money can't buy happiness in the truest sense, in my experience, it's incredibly difficult to be happy *without* it. That doesn't mean that you need to strive for lavish vacations, designer brands, and partying it up without a care in the world to be happy, but feeling secure is difficult if you're scraping every last cent together to pay your bills or buy that cheap pack of ramen to have something to eat for the day. Having your finances in order means that you can alleviate some of that stress, and it all begins with budgeting. Through budgeting, you can save money and manage it better. The result? Less stress and more time to enjoy yourself, even if you're skipping out on that fun event everyone else is doing or not eating out as often as before.

The Basics of Budgeting

Budgeting is as simple as meeting three simple steps: Tracking your income, your expenses, and managing what's left over. The hard part is finding the willpower to stick to your budget. I personally manage my budget weekly and monthly using a spreadsheet with all of my family's expenses against the income we receive. Once per week, I tally up all of my expenditures and check them against my budget to make sure I haven't gone over.

Sure, my family gets by well enough that I don't have to count every last dollar or worry about whether I can buy something, but I've found that the only way to grow and *maintain* any wealth is through avoiding lifestyle creep and living well within our means. That means that sometimes, I tell my children no, we won't be going out to a restaurant for dinner when they request it. Could we? Sure. Should we? Not if we've already used our fun money for the week. Staying accountable and true to the budget is the best way that I've found to really help my family financially, and it's a skill I learned a decade later than I should have.

Your budget will help you understand exactly how much money you have for different things. If you decide to spend less in some categories, you may be able to free up additional cash to use elsewhere. For example, if you budget $100 for clothing every month but only spend $50, you've got $50 free that you can use on something fun or to put into savings.

Track Your Income

Income is any money that you have coming in that you can spend from all sources. Whether we're talking about money from a job, royalties, money you get refunded from student loans for living expenses, cash from your parents, or any other source, it's important to count it here so you'll know how much usable money you have. Start writing down all the sources of money you have, the amount you get, and how frequently you get it.

Make sure that, when counting money from jobs, you rely on the after-tax (net) income amounts since the taxes will likely be deducted immediately if you work a traditional job, or if you freelance, you'll have to pay those taxes at some point.

Once you have that number, hold onto it. It might not be as much as it looks like at first when you realize how much money you're spending. That's why it's so important to track your income.

Track Your Expenses

Next, it's time to track your expenses. Either write them down or put them into a spreadsheet for easy access. This will include recurring expenses, like any streaming subscriptions, credit card bills, rent, utilities, and car costs. It should also include a set amount that you spend on living necessities like food, clothing, haircuts, and similar budget lines.

Part of your budget should also include savings for emergencies, car repairs, or other unforeseen expenses. It should also include a line for money that you can use for fun.

With your spreadsheet ready to go, you can now track your expenses. Every week or two, you should sit down and check out all of the expenses from your bank account to see where you're spending money and then deduct that from the monthly allotments for those categories.

Once your budget of expenses is done, you can also begin a plan to save cash.

Pay Yourself First and Build Savings

No matter who you are or what your life plans are, having savings helps bring those goals to life. If you want to buy a house, you'll need healthy savings to do so. If you want to travel the world? You'll need money for that. Starting a business, paying off student debt, and generally just living life require money. Getting into good saving habits now means that it'll be easier to get to a comfortable position later.

One way to see this play out is in a 1960s psychology study by Stanford professor Walter Mischel. He studied the reactions of hundreds of children to determine their ability to delay gratification. The test involved setting a child in a private room with a marshmallow. The child was then told that the adult would leave the room and if the child didn't eat the marshmallow, they'd get two marshmallows later, but if they decided to eat the marshmallow while the adult was out, they wouldn't get the second marshmallow.

Some children ate the marshmallow immediately in the 15 minutes they were alone. Many others tried to wait but gave in a few minutes after. A few children were able to delay their urge to eat the marshmallow and got the second one. This is called delayed gratification—these children wait to enjoy more later.

Even more interesting, the children who were able to delay gratification also tested to have higher SAT scores, lower levels of substance abuse and obesity, and scored better in several other categories than their peers who didn't, including better stress responses and social skills. You can do the same thing with money.

Saving Money Now to Have It Later

If you learn to delay gratification, you get a wealth of benefits, and one of those is in your financial life. If you can turn down the invitation to that concert or choose to eat at home instead of going out, you can quickly build up cash savings that other people squander away on instant gratification.

The sooner you start saving, the less of your income you'll have to save just because your money will have more time to grow and accumulate interest, especially if you choose to invest it. It's recommended that you save 10–15% of your income for retirement if you start in your late teens or early 20s.

Emergency Savings

An emergency fund should be considered fully funded when you have enough in it to cover six months of expenses. Yes, this is probably a lot more than you'd expect, but it's important to have on hand. You never know if you'll get sick or hurt and need to take time off work, or you could lose or leave a job and need time to get a new one. This can also cover major expenses, like buying a new car if you suddenly need to replace it or covering the cost of medical expenses. Try to place at least 10% of your income into emergency savings.

Money Management Tips for Young Adults

Looking for some ways to manage your money and stick more into savings? These are some of my tried and true tricks to free up extra cash.

Skip the Debt. Pay with Cash

You pay a lot in credit card interest, which we'll discuss in the next chapter. Even if you only pay a minimum payment on a credit card, the final price of your purchases are inflated by interest. Pay with cash. If you can't afford it with cash now and it's not a necessity, don't buy it.

Stick to Your Budget

Your budget helps allocate every dollar you have so you know what's available to spend and what's already earmarked for something else. By making sure you stick to your budget, you can make sure that you hit your savings goals each month.

Manage Your Grocery Budget

Groceries are one of the biggest expenses we have. According to the U.S. Department of Agriculture, the average cost for groceries for one person is between $300 and $540 per month, but this can vary widely based on where you live and what kind of diet you eat. Make sure that you keep a close eye on the budget line and plan your meals to help manage your costs.

Consider Generic

Generic brands can help cut out a lot of extra costs. Those few cents between items can add up quickly, and often, generic food is just as good as the name brands. Figure out which foods you're happy to have the generic versions of and buy them to save money.

Coupons and Grocery Store Memberships

Coupons and memberships can help cut the cost of food as well. Make sure you're checking weekly ads and digital coupons to see what you can save, as well as signing up for grocery store loyalty discount memberships where you shop the most.

Cut Out the Subscriptions and Memberships You Don't Need

Do you really need three video or music streaming subscriptions? Are you actually using your gym membership or online gaming? These little subscriptions can be easy to sign up for since they're pretty cheap on their own, but they can quickly add up if you're not careful. Double-check any subscriptions you currently have and see if any of them can be cut out.

Transfer Money to Savings Automatically

Did you know that a lot of banks will allow you to transfer money to your savings account automatically? This is an easy way to put money out of sight immediately before it ever hits your checking account. Consider setting this up with your direct deposit if that's how you get paid.

Be Wise With Unexpected Income

Any time you get a sudden windfall, whether it's some cash for a holiday or birthday or you managed to win a sum of money. You could also wind up inheriting money, depending on your family setup, or getting a bonus at work. Be wise when you get unexpected income. Instead of running out to spend it, consider putting it into savings or investing it instead.

Pay Attention to Taxes

Part of being an adult is paying taxes. If, when you file your taxes, you receive a large tax refund, there's a chance your taxes aren't set up properly.

Spending Freeze

Have you ever heard of a spending freeze? It's a sort of challenge where you don't spend any extra money at all. Don't buy anything nonessential for a month and see how much cash you save.

DIY

While there are some things best left to the professionals, a lot of things can be done yourself, from sewing up minor tears in clothing to refurbishing furniture to give it a nice facelift.

Choose Secondhand Items

Buying things you need secondhand is a great way to pocket the extra cash that would otherwise go toward buying a boxed or brand-new item. While some things should be bought new for sanitary reasons, most things can be bought on secondhand marketplaces like Facebook Marketplace or Craigslist.

Chapter Summary

Making the most of your money is all about stretching your dollar as far as you can and building up savings so you're ready to cover any expenses that may arise. By managing your money, you can better get a handle on any potential debt you may accrue. In the next chapter, we'll be discussing how to safely use credit cards in ways that are beneficial to your financial health.

CHAPTER 6
CREDIT SCORES, CREDIT CARDS, AND DEBT

Credit—it's one of those things that you can't live without but building it can be dangerous. Part of building it requires you to take out loans and credit cards, but if you're not smart about how you use them, you'll do more harm than good.

As a young adult, you most likely won't have any credit, or if you do, it'll probably be pretty bad unless your parents helped you build it by adding you to credit accounts while you were younger to help you piggyback off their scores. Unfortunately, that makes it difficult for you to get housing, rent an apartment, or buy a car if you plan on using a loan. It can be hard to get credit cards, too, unless you know where to look.

This can make a loop where you can't take out lines of credit that won't put you at risk of serious interest payments, which means you can't build your credit easily. If you're like me, you'll fall into the trap of using credit cards as a sort of bridge between what you want and what you can afford. Don't do this! One of the worst things you can do is put yourself in debt over wants.

Credit Scores

If you live in the US, you have a credit score that's tracked by Experian, Equifax, or TransUnion. Many other countries have similar programs used to track creditworthiness that use similar factors in calculating a score.

In the US, this credit score is determined by considering several factors, including:

- **Debt owed:** The amount you owe versus how much available credit you have is a major component of your credit score. If you use most or all of your available credit, the assumption is that you are making ends meet with your credit because you don't have enough money to cover your monthly expenses, making you a higher risk for defaulting on future credit accounts.
- **New credit:** This considers how many accounts have been opened recently. People who have recently opened several credit accounts are usually considered a higher risk, so multiple new accounts can lower your score.
- **Length of credit history:** This is a tough one for young adults, but it's going to be helpful later. Credit scores are calculated in part by how long you've had credit, the age of your oldest account and newest account, and how long it's been since you've used accounts. The length of your credit history plays a part in calculating your score.
- **Credit mix:** This refers to the types of credit and loans you have, such as credit cards, installment loans (like cars or student loans), mortgages, and finance company accounts.
- **Payment history:** This is one of the biggest factors considered. All payments you make to your credit lines and loans are reported, and if you make them 30 days late or longer, they will be negative marks on your credit.

How to Judge Your Credit Score

Most credit scores range from 300–850, and those scores are divided into several categories that can give you a good idea of how your credit looks. These are:

- **Excellent:** 720–850
- **Good:** 690–719
- **Fair:** 630–689
- **Bad:** 300–629

We don't start out with a credit score—the first one is calculated based on your credit usage once you open your first line of credit. For many young adults, this is a student loan, but it may also be a credit card. Your first credit score will be calculated after having at least one credit account open and reporting to one of the three major bureaus for six months. Once you get your first account set up, make it count! Don't run out to celebrate that shiny new Visa card if you can't afford to pay it off.

What if You Miss a Payment?

If you miss a payment, a few things happen. One, you'll probably have some late fees associated with missing it. Two, if it's not paid within 30 days of the due date, it may be marked on your credit report as a missed payment, which will negatively impact your score. Some lenders don't report late payments until after 60 days past due, but you should still always pay your bills on time. Your late payments will remain on your credit report for seven years, which is why it's so important to avoid them whenever possible.

Credit Cards and Debt

Credit cards work by loaning you money to make purchases. In exchange, you owe the lender a debt that has to be repaid with interest. The interest amount will vary based on the terms of the card that you select. The vast majority of credit cards have a pre authorized limit based on your credit score. Many new cards start out with just a few hundred dollars but can go up into the thousands as your credit improves.

Carrying a balance on your credit card means that you owe money even after making the assigned payment, and that balance will be charged interest based on the annual percentage rate (APR) that you agreed to when taking out the card. Many cards use a variable APR that changes over time, and being 60 days late on your card can trigger a penalty APR, which will dramatically increase what you owe.

Some credit cards also come with fees, such as monthly and annual membership fees. While these cards often are easier to get with little or no credit, they're also incredibly expensive and you're essentially paying for the privilege of having it.

Other potential fees you may accrue include balance transfer fees, where you move the balance of one card to another, over-limit fees when you go over the card's credit limit, or late fees for missing the payment.

Credit cards aren't all bad, though. Many of them have perks that can make them worth using—wisely, of course. Credit cards tend to be safer than cash, coming with liability guarantees. It's often easier to dispute a credit charge than it is to fight a debit. Other benefits include:

- They're easy to use.
- Some offer rewards and cash back.
- They boost credit scores when used correctly.

On the other hand, before taking out a credit card and using it, be aware of the cons:
Interest and fees add up when you carry a balance.
They can harm your credit score if you carry a high balance or miss payments.
They make it easy to spiral into debt.

When Should You Use a Credit Card?

As dangerous as credit card usage can be, that doesn't mean that you should never use yours. Learning to use credit cards responsibly is the best thing that you can do for your credit score.

To Access a One-Time Bonus

Some credit cards will offer incentives for you to use them, such as offering a one-time bonus if you spend a set amount of money in the first few months the account is open. If you have an offer like this, using a credit card for your monthly expenses, like food and bills, allows you to then pay it off in full with the cash you'd normally use, avoiding the interest and earning access to the reward.

For Cash Back

Some cards also offer cash back for your purchases. If you have one of those cards, like with the one-time bonuses, you can build up cashback points. Some cards may offer up to 5 or 6 percent cash back on certain purchases, though they often have spending caps.

For Rewards Points or Frequent Flyer Miles

Other cards opt for rewards points or frequent flier miles when you use them. The more you spend, the more points you rack up, which can be used up later.

To Prevent Fraud

As we already discussed, credit cards are much easier to work with to fight fraudulent charges than when you pay with a debit card or cash. Because of this, your credit card offers a safe option for paying for your purchases.

This can also be used for making large payments toward vendors or handymen. If someone does a shoddy job, if you've paid with a credit card, you can get the charge reversed and have access to the money sooner rather than later. If subpar work is done after you've paid for it and you paid in cash, you run the risk of having to spend months fighting to claw back your money through legal avenues.

For Hotels or Car Rentals

If you plan to rent a car or stay at a hotel, you'll be required to use a credit card. This is just in case you cause damages.

Debt and Interest

Loans and credit card balances are considered debts, and they typically accrue interest. Interest rates on credit cards can vary wildly, with the average somewhere around 24 percent. That might not sound that bad, but it can get scary quickly.

Let's say you buy a new gaming console and accessories for $500 on a credit card with an average 24 percent APR. If you make your minimum monthly payment of $35, do you know how long it'd take you to pay it off?

By the time you pay it off in full with minimum payments, it will take 17 months. By the end, you'll have paid $82 in interest, adding that to the cost of the purchase. Is it worth it?

Interest is the cost of debt. It can be simple or complex, and most credit cards use compound interest, allowing it to accrue daily.

Simple Interest

Simple interest assigns the interest at the beginning of a loan at a set percentage. For example, a $100,000 loan with a 3 percent interest rate would have $3,000 in interest charged to it if the whole loan is paid off in a year. This is calculated by multiplying the principal (the amount of the loan) by the interest rate and by the number of years you'll be paying it.

Compound Interest

More commonly, especially with credit cards, you'll pay compound interest. This means that you'll pay interest on accruing interest as well as the principal. When you have to pay compound interest, you pay more over the long run because your balance owed grows while you pay it off. Some of each payment you make goes toward the principal, but the rest goes to pay off interest, meaning you're not paying it off as quickly as you'd probably think.

Chapter Summary

Credit cards might seem like a sudden windfall of fun money, but racking up debt is never a good idea. Even if you really want something, if you can't pay it off in full, you should wait until you can. Save on interest and save your credit score by using your credit wisely. This will help you to invest and plan for your future, which we'll discuss in the next chapter.

CHAPTER 7
INVESTING AND PLANNING FOR THE FUTURE

When you're just getting started in adulthood, it's easy to think that you've got plenty of time before you need to start worrying about retirement. After all, you have a whole career to build up money for your future financial security, right?

Well, the years go by much faster than you'd expect, and the sooner you start investing in yourself and your future, the more money you'll have, thanks to the very same interest you learned about in the previous chapter. When you invest and save, you can gain interest, allowing your money to work for you and grow while it sits. Having a savings account isn't enough to keep your money growing quickly enough to outpace inflation, either. Each year, your money has less buying power just because each year inflation pushes costs up. On average, the U.S. inflation rate is around 3.8 percent, though the COVID-19 pandemic caused it to increase significantly.

What that means is that your $100 one year is worth $96.20 the next, on average. If you leave your money sitting in a savings account, it loses value year after year, and the average interest rate in a savings account is around 0.39 percent. That's only 1/10 the inflation rate, meaning the longer your money sits, even in a savings account, the less spending power you'll have.

There are ways to get around this, and while I'm not delving deeply into these subjects, this will give you an overview of the options that you have. These options can help you safely build up money over time, and the sooner you set them up, the longer that interest can build. Remember this—a dollar that you save early will generate you more than a dollar saved later in life, thanks to the power of compounding interest.

For example, let's say you invest $1,000 right now in an account that has a 5% growth rate. This is how it will compound over the next 60 years:

Year	Total value of investment
0	$1,000
1	$1,050
2	$1,102.50
3	$1,157.63
4	$1,215.51
5	$1,276.28
10	$1,628.89
15	$2,078.93
20	$2,653.30
30	$4,321.94
40	$7,039.99

50	$11,467.40
60	$18,679.19

Looking at these numbers, you can see that they start to jump quickly. Look at the growth in terms of decades:

Period (years)	Growth
0–10	$628.89
10–20	$1,024.41
20–30	$1,668.64
30–40	$2,718.05
40–50	$4,427.41
50–60	$7,191.76

If you were to retire 50 years from now and invest $1,000 today, you'd have $11,467.40 with an annual compounding interest rate of 5%. If you were to wait 30 years from now and then invest $1,000, you'd only have $2,653.30 50 years from today in comparison. The initial investment would be the same, but that extra 30 years of compounding growth makes a big difference. This is why investing early is so important. The longer your money grows, the larger the growth becomes. Three of the best ways to grow your money are through life insurance (but only the right kind), investments, and retirement accounts.

Life Insurance

While life insurance is commonly seen as a way to provide for families in the event that someone dies, it's also a great way to grow money that you can use during your lifetime as well. It's a slower form of investment, but it's also the safest way to grow your money if you set up a policy correctly with the help of a licensed insurance agent.

Life insurance comes in two forms: term and permanent. Term policies are good for a set period of time and are cheaper. You pay into them, but they usually don't build cash value and they only pay out a death benefit if you die during the term you have them. This is great for families worried about making ends meet if they die while a spouse raises children because it provides a safety net while minor children are in the home.

Permanent life insurance is often more expensive, but it can also work to grow cash value that you can then borrow or withdraw while you're still alive. Because the cash value doesn't usually get added to the death benefit that pays out, the money that you invest and grow can be pulled out and used as a way to pay for retirement, investments, or other expenses. Even better, you can take that money out as a loan to avoid paying taxes on this money.

One consideration to make, though, is that if you overfund these life insurance policies, they can convert into a modified endowment contract by the IRS, which can create tax liabilities, meaning that you would owe tax on withdrawing cash value.

According to a 2023 Nerdwallet article, the types of life insurance policies that you can use to invest your cash are whole life insurance or universal life insurance policies.

Whole Life Insurance

Whole life insurance policies are pretty straightforward. They have fixed premiums (the amount you pay per month) and permanent, guaranteed death benefits to your designated beneficiaries. This means that when you die, the beneficiary listed will receive a payout equivalent to the policy value. Your cash value will grow at a fixed rate set by your policy, meaning it won't fluctuate with the market.

Universal Life Insurance

Universal life insurance is more flexible and can grow more, but the death benefit, premiums, and cash value are not guaranteed. They may change with the market, making this a slightly riskier way to grow cash value. On the other hand, you can increase or decrease premiums and death benefits within certain parameters if you realize you want to pay more or you need to reduce them.

Variable Universal Life Insurance

Variable universal life insurance is a type of universal life insurance that allows you to adjust your premiums and death benefits while also giving you control over how to invest any cash value through subaccounts. Cash value grows based on the sub account options and their performance on the market, or the insurance policy may offer a fixed interest rate based on the policy.

Indexed Universal Life Insurance

As another type of universal life insurance, indexed universal life insurance gives similar flexibility in the types of coverage and values. However, cash value earns interest differently with these policies. In this case, the growth is based on how the stock indexes perform. It's kind of like investing in the stock market, so during good market conditions, the cash value grows quicker.

Unlike the stock market, however, an indexed universal life policy typically has an interest floor, meaning cash value will never grow less than a set amount, which is often 0%. What that means is that when the stock market crashes, your cash value is protected. This also comes with interest caps, meaning that your cash value can never accrue interest at a higher rate than whatever is set, even if the stock market sees better performance.

Other types of life insurance exist as well, but these are the main ones used for their cash value. Make sure that you speak with your insurance agent before making any decisions. They will be able to help you understand the terms, answer questions you may have, and recommend the right kinds of coverage for you.

Investments and Retirement Accounts

Investing money is risky and isn't guaranteed, but it is commonly used to grow cash value. By investing smartly, you can increase your chances of seeing growth in your money. Some are tax-advantaged, meaning that they help save you money that would otherwise be spent on taxes or allow you to invest pre-tax income into them, lowering your overall tax obligation.

Types of Investment Accounts

Investing your money will help it grow, and there are plenty of options that you can choose from. Financial planners, brokers, and investment advisors can help you review your options and help you make the best decisions for you and your unique situation.

- **Annuities:** These are insurance products you can use to create regular income during retirement. Some can be tax-deferred.
- **Mutual funds:** Mutual funds are managed by a professional who pools together bonds, stocks, and other investments that then get divided into shares and sold to people who want to invest.
- **Stocks:** Stocks represent a share of ownership in a specific corporation. Their value rises and falls based on the performance of the market or the specific company.
- **Bonds:** When investing in bonds, you pay to loan money to an issuer, like the government or a business, and you receive interest payments on top of the face value.
- **ETFs:** An exchange-traded fund (ETF) is an investment that trades like a stock on an exchange but may also include sector indexes or collections of assets.

- **Dividend reinvestment plans:** DRIPs let you reinvest your cash dividends into more stock instead of receiving cash dividends.
- **Cash investments:** Certificates of deposits (CDs) and money market deposit accounts allow you to invest income short-term in low-risk settings while allowing you to receive interest.

Types of Retirement Accounts

Retirement accounts allow you to invest your income to use specifically for retirement. They can be used effectively, but there are often penalties if you try to withdraw income early. These are the most common ones you'll encounter:

- **Defined benefit plans:** Also referred to as pensions, these plans are funded by employers, guaranteeing specific benefits based on how much you made and how long you worked with a company. However, they're not very common if you don't work for the public sector.
- **401(k)s:** 401(k)s are sponsored by employers that employees pay into. The money is usually taken out of your pay automatically and then invested, and sometimes even matched up to a certain amount each year.
- **Traditional IRAs:** IRAs are retirement accounts that allow you to defer taxes on your contributions. This allows you to invest more upfront because you can put what would have gone to taxes toward the account. Then, when you withdraw the money in retirement, you're taxed at your income rate.
- **Roth IRAs:** Unlike traditional IRAs, Roth IRAs are not tax deductible. However, other than that, they work the same as a traditional IRA (Folger, 2022).

Especially if you have an offer from an employer to match your contributions into these retirement accounts, you should try to max them out each year as often as possible to get the most out of them.

Chapter Summary

Investing now will set you up in the future. The sooner you start, the more your money can grow into what you will eventually need. It's never too soon to start thinking about retirement, and when you free yourself from financial stress, you can start thinking about other things, like your relationships.

PART 3
RELATIONSHIPS AND COMMUNICATION

> *Communication to a relationship is like oxygen is to life. Without it, it dies.*
>
> *–Tony A. Gaskins Jr.*

CHAPTER 8
DIFFERENT RELATIONSHIPS, SAME FOUNDATIONS

We all crave relationships in our lives. Friendships, familial relationships, romantic partners, and even workplace relationships help meet our social needs and can make us feel fulfilled and confident in ourselves. I don't know where I'd be in life without my family or friends, and I'm sure you feel the same way.

But relationships aren't easy to maintain, and knowing how to spot and leave a bad relationship can be even harder. Knowing how to navigate relationships is one of the most important skills you can learn. Part of being able to navigate is knowing how to communicate, which we'll discuss in the next chapter. Part of it is also knowing what goes into fostering and maintaining those connections. After all, they're two-way streets.

No matter what kind of relationship you're talking about, they all should be based on mutual trust, honesty, open communication, and respect. Remember that you deserve to be treated well, and respect is a basic human decency, not something that needs to be earned.

Relationships should make you feel good. They should make you feel heard and seen, and you should feel like you can be yourself in them. Those that don't make you feel good or those that show signs of red flags can be harmful to your mental health. I've had toxic friendships and I know how much they can mess with your mind. I know what it's like to feel like I was the problem and that if I changed, I could enjoy the relationship that I wanted with the other person. The truth was, the foundation for a healthy relationship just wasn't there with them.

The Foundation of a Healthy Relationship

Relationships of all kinds are hard work. Yes, it seems like this is something that should be simple, but the reality is they aren't. They take a lot of effort to maintain, but in the end, the effort is worth it. There will be times that you fight with those you care about, and we'll talk about solving those conflicts in a healthy manner in the next chapter. No matter what is going on in your relationship, however, these four factors should be present. You should always feel like there is a foundation of honesty, trust, open communication, and respect, even in conflicts.

Honesty

Honesty is where transparency and authenticity shine through. It is what allows you to tell the other person anything without fear of judgment or backlash and what allows the other person to come to you as well. It's easy to feel tempted to slip into dishonesty to avoid hurting someone's feelings, but this isn't a good way to approach the situation. It can be harmful to the relationship because you aren't being straightforward.

Honesty involves being able to share what you feel and trust the other person with that information, building intimacy. Intimacy isn't limited to just romantic relationships, either. To be intimate with someone is to be *close* to them. It's to be connected and supported and comfortable with the other person, and it's present in most personal relationships to various degrees. Yes, you're usually the most intimate with your romantic partner if you have one, but sharing your thoughts and secrets with your best friend or a parent is another way to be intimate.

Trust

Trust in relationships allows you to feel safe and confident with the other person. You know that they will not hurt or betray you. As a result, you can be vulnerable and honest with that other person. Friends, family members, and romantic partners can all be some of our most valued confidantes, allowing us to connect and show our truest selves to them.

Trust brings so much to our relationships. It fosters positivity, forgiveness, and closeness. It helps us to navigate and reduce conflict because when you trust someone, you feel more compelled to find solutions and common ground or to give them the benefit of the doubt when (not if!) they mess up.

Trust is a beautiful thing, but it's also something that has to be built and fostered. It's fragile and easy to destroy, and once you damage trust, rebuilding it is even harder. To foster it, you need to communicate honestly and be on the same page with the other person.

Without trust, you can harm your relationship, eroding it with secrecy and pushing away your loved one. Trust can be hurt by insecurity, which can make you even more insecure in your relationship with the other person.

Open Communication

Open communication builds upon the previous two foundations, helping to secure the relationship by discussing anything that may get in the way of it. Problems and fights happen. In fact, according to John Gottman, a relationship researcher, the magic ratio between positive and negative interactions is 5:1, meaning that for every one negative interaction, there should be five positive ones. That sounds like a lot more negative interactions between people than would be expected, but it just goes to show how common conflict really is.

That's why it's so important to have open communication. Not only will it build trust in a relationship, but it will also help solve those conflicts in a constructive manner, which will help you to strengthen your connection with the other person.

Respect

The problem with respect is that so many people see it differently. You've got a whole group of people who believe that respecting someone is listening to them, while other people say respect is treating someone with basic human decency. The respect you need in any relationship is the kind where you regard them with kindness. You treat them well like you'd want to be treated.

Mutual respect forms the foundation of relationships of all kinds and is shown through giving consideration to the other person's feelings, thoughts, and boundaries. To respect someone is to show you care about them through how you act and speak toward them. It can also involve being accountable for your actions when you make a mistake or hurt someone's feelings. No relationship is perfect, but respecting the other person should be a common pattern.

Relationship Red Flags

Red flags can pop up in just about any relationship, from romantic partners to coworkers. When you see red flags waving, it's your sign to run like the wind, or at least consider the relationship heavily because there's something toxic going on. Some of these red flags may not be obvious if you're not looking for them, but they are a sign that the other person isn't likely to be in a healthy relationship of any kind.

Violent Or Abusive Actions

While violence is straightforward, abuse can take several different forms, all of which are red flags. You can experience abuse in more than just romantic relationships too. Friends, family, and coworkers can be abusive. Some types of abuse include:

- **Physical abuse:** This is any type of physical violence or threats used to keep control of a situation. It includes throwing, breaking, or destroying objects.
- **Emotional abuse:** Emotional abuse is a lot harder to identify because it's non-physical. It's any behavior designed to isolate, control, or scare you, like name-calling, insults, possessiveness, trying to get you to cut off your friends or family, monitoring your behaviors, humiliating you in front of others, gaslighting, and blaming you for their abusive actions. It could also include threatening you or damaging your belongings.
- **Financial abuse:** When a partner limits access to finances or actively hinders your ability to earn money, they are financially abusive. This isn't the same as expecting adherence to a budget—it involves actively preventing access to funds, maxing out your credit cards, a refusal to contribute while expecting you to work for everything, or refusing money for necessary expenses.
- **Sexual abuse:** Sexual abuse happens when a partner or other person takes control of physical and sexual intimacy without consent. It includes manipulating or guilting into having sex, nonconsensual sexual actions, ignoring how you feel about sex, or intentionally attempting to give you a sexually transmitted infection. Sexual abuse can be present in any kind of relationship or even without a relationship with the other person.
- **Digital abuse:** Digital abuse uses the internet to bully, intimidate, or control a partner, often through emotional abuse.
- **Stalking:** Stalkers follow, harass, or watch their target despite being told to stop, causing them to feel uncomfortable, unsafe, or afraid.

Mismatch in Goals

This is more of a romantic relationship red flag than any other kind. When you and your partner want vastly different things, it's a red flag for the relationship because it means someone will have to give up their wants for the other party. For example, if you want children but your romantic partner doesn't, you have to grapple with whether you're willing to forego having kids to keep your partner or if you're both simply too incompatible for each other. It could also involve career goals, how to handle finances, or irreconcilable political or religious differences.

Jealousy

When someone is constantly jealous when you spend time with other people, regardless of what your relationship with them is, it's a sign of insecurity. That insecurity can be incredibly damaging to your relationship and cause issues down the road. It can also be a sign of possessiveness.

Lack of Trust

Trust is the foundation of all relationships, and without it, there's no real healthy relationship.

Lying or Infidelity

Both lying and infidelity involve dishonest behaviors and can be major red flags in any relationship. People comfortable with lying to you often continue to lie, and without being able to trust the other person, it's hard to maintain any kind of relationship.

Controlling

People who attempt to control you by limiting access to other people, telling you what to do, or otherwise attempting to monitor your behavior are usually not respectful of your autonomy. While, especially at work, there's some expectation that your supervisors will tell you what to do, it shouldn't get to the point where it's controlling you outside of work as well.

Stories of "Crazy Exes"

This goes for friends, bosses, coworkers, and romantic partners. If the person you are speaking to has a bunch of stories about how other people are all problematic for a bunch of reasons, there's a good chance that you're not getting the whole picture. For example, if your new romantic partner has a whole slew of exes that all are terrible, dishonest, and controlling, there's a chance that your partner actually has unresolved issues that will make it difficult to have a meaningful, healthy relationship with them and they perceive healthy boundaries, conversations, and expectations as wrong.

Inability to Maintain Friendships

People who have no friends or struggle to maintain friends or relationships often have a reason for it. This is especially true if you hear a lot of deflection and refusal to take personal accountability for any part in their situation.

Gaslighting

Gaslighting can be a huge problem in many relationships, causing you to think that you are wrong. It happens when someone says or does things that make you question your own perception of what happened. For example, they might say they don't know what you did with your phone when you notice that it's not on the counter anymore and mention how you often lose it when, in fact, they have it in their pocket. They can use other tactics to manipulate you and make you feel like you're the problem instead in an attempt to control you and your behavior.

Love Bombing

Love bombing is the attempt to gain love and trust quickly by showering someone with praise and affection. They may tell you how much they love you, how you're different from everyone they've ever known, or give you plenty of gifts in an attempt to make you feel good. By making you feel good, adored, and desired, they essentially create an addiction to those feelings, but it usually fades over time. Once you're hooked, you get less affection and adoration, so you chase after getting back to that pedestal, which is how the person love bombing gets control.

Breadcrumbing

Breadcrumbing is another way to play with your feelings by giving you just enough affection or encouragement to keep you hooked on the relationship. However, as you try to get closer, they'll pull back. If you start to lose interest, they'll give you more. There's no commitment with this type of hot-and-cold behavior.

Chapter Summary

While you're not defined by the people around you, they do influence you. Healthy relationships of all kinds need healthy foundations, and as you gain more experience in life, you'll learn to spot the red flags and know when something isn't quite right. This will help you to communicate better in your relationships, too, because you'll be able to articulate what you see that's wrong and make moves to fix the problems. The next chapter is all about learning healthy, effective communication techniques.

CHAPTER 9
DEVELOPING HEALTHY COMMUNICATION SKILLS

Communication can be *hard*. You can say one thing and the other person can hear something completely different from what you intended to convey. Back when I was dating my husband, I remember a conversation we had when we just weren't on the same page. We had an argument that was so unimportant I can't even remember what it was about. I just remember feeling frustrated, unheard, and unloved. We weren't on the same page, and I really thought it'd be the end of our relationship.

Nowadays, we have much better skills regarding our communication. We're capable of talking through our issues and finding common ground that will help us to get past our conflicts. Don't get me wrong, those arguments still suck. It's never fun to fight with someone you care about, but it's much easier to get back on the same page and keep moving forward when you have the right tools in your toolbox.

Communicating Effectively

The best thing you can do for your relationships of all kinds is learn how to communicate clearly and effectively. These are strategies that I've implemented and dedicated myself to teaching my own children to better prepare them for adulthood and I think that anyone could benefit from them. If you put these tools to the test, especially if your loved ones do them with you (remember, communication is a two-way street, after all!), then you'll probably see improvements in how you interact and get along with each other too. It all begins with learning how to listen actively, and then begin putting these strategies to good use.

Active Listening

When you listen actively, you do more than just hear the words the other person has to say. It's about really understanding the meaning of the words being told to you before you ever begin formatting a response. All too often, people get so caught up in trying to respond as quickly as they can or thinking of how they'll respond instead of paying attention to what's being conveyed.

To listen actively, you need to:
- Be present in the conversation, giving it your complete focus.
- Hold eye contact and open body language to convey interest in the conversation.
- Pay attention to body language cues.
- Instead of responding, ask open-ended questions to encourage the other person to elaborate.
- Before responding, paraphrase what you have heard to make sure that you're both on the same page.
- Listen without judgment or without giving advice unless it's asked for.

How to Communicate Effectively

Being able to listen only helps with half of the communication. After all, it takes two to communicate; otherwise, it's just a lecture. Communicating effectively requires you to be comfortable with not only listening but also with responding.

Choosing to speak concisely is a great way to help improve communication skills. Stick to the basics, especially when emotions run high. I've experienced arguments that quickly devolve because we get stuck on tangents instead of focusing on what matters the most, and it's never fun. To avoid this, if you have to have a heavy conversation, try planning it ahead of time.

While sometimes, these conversations pop up when you least expect them, there's nothing wrong with stopping in the moment, saying you need some time to think, and coming back to the conversation when you and the other person are calmer and able to tackle it on with a level-headed approach. Some other great ways to keep your communication clear include:

- **Pay attention to body language:** Your body speaks just as much as your mouth does, and if you're not careful, you may send off cues that disrupt what you actually want to say. For example, if your body language comes off as angry, the other person may get defensive, which will shut down any effective communication.
- **Be careful with your tone:** Like body language, how you speak and your tone of voice will also influence what you're trying to say. Would you want to listen to someone tell you how to be confident if they stuttered and stumbled over their words in the most timid voice you've ever heard? Probably not! Speak calmly, especially during important conversations.
- **Avoid judgment:** You don't necessarily have to agree with what the other person has to say, but you should hold off on judgment. When you communicate with someone, you need to be open to what they have to say and hear them out to truly understand what they're saying.
- **Pause before you speak:** This goes back to taking the time to communicate clearly. While you don't necessarily have to take a break mid-conversation, you should take a moment to breathe before responding to make sure you've thought out what you want to say.
- **Use "I" statements:** Especially when emotions are high, you should stick to "I" statements. For example, "I feel like you don't have time for me" is a much more effective phrase compared to "You never make time for me." Instead of making it an attack or a judgment, you're discussing your feelings instead. This stops defensiveness or arguing over whether that's actually the case or just your perspective on it (which is valid, too!).

By learning to communicate better, you can help avoid conflicts, but not all of them can be dodged. It's only natural for there to be disagreements sometimes, and that's okay! You and the other person, no matter who they are to you, don't have to see eye to eye on every single thing. You're both unique people with your own thoughts, feelings, and experiences guiding you.

Conflict Resolution

As natural as conflict is in every relationship, it's still a big drag, and it can be something that a lot of us try to run away from. Running from conflicts and constantly people-pleasing to avoid them can both be huge detriments to your relationships and your mental health. As tempting as it can be to ignore them, all this does is let them continue to fester and worsen, and when they finally explode, the results can be disastrous. But conflicts are also opportunities for growth and bettering your relationships with other people. They let you build trust and feel secure that you and the other person can work through your disagreements.

Because conflict triggers such strong emotions that can get the best of us sometimes, it's important to stay ahead of your stress level when you face one. To handle a conflict healthily, sometimes you need to put a pin in it for later to calm down, which is absolutely valid, as long as you come back to it later instead of ignoring it.

Solving your conflicts will require you to:

- manage your stress without getting distracted.
- stay grounded and control your behavior while managing your emotions.
- listen to the other person's feelings.
- respect your differences.

Sounds easy enough, right? Well, like all things worth doing well, it's easier said than done. Try implementing some of these strategies to help defuse your conflicts.

No Interruptions

Take turns speaking instead of constantly trying to butt in. Let one person have the floor to speak their mind while the other listens actively. Once you confirm you understand what the other person is saying, you can formulate your response.

Discuss From a Place of Curiosity

A lot of times, conflicts arise because you and the other person aren't on the same page. Approaching the conversation from a place of curiosity and without judgment allows both of you to better understand each other. You may learn something new about the other person, which can be useful in avoiding future conflicts over the same issue.

Use Repair Attempts

Repair attempts are ways that we try to reconnect with someone after a conflict arises. They can help assure the other person that you see that there's a problem and that you want to de-escalate. Some people turn to humor (but make sure the other person won't get more upset!), say you understand, and show positive, open body language. You could even offer a hug or hold their hand to show that you care and don't want to continue fighting.

Apologize—The Right Way

Genuine apologies are more than just saying, "I'm sorry." They should also say what you did wrong, why it was wrong, and what you'll do in the future to avoid the problem. They should also include some sort of restitution—an offer to make it right. Apologies should never be followed by "but" or other words that immediately imply you're going to deflect or justify your actions.

For example, "I'm sorry I broke your laptop. I really wasn't paying attention to where I was walking, and I didn't mean to knock it off the desk. I'll be sure to pay more attention in the future to avoid this. Is there anything I can do to make it up to you?"

Ask What They Need

This is a point that should go both ways. You should tell the other person what you need while also asking them what they need to find some sort of resolution. Don't be afraid to vocalize what you need from them to prevent this from being an issue again in the future. They aren't mind readers, and neither are you. This helps boost communication and keep you both on the same page.

Find a Compromise

In many conflicts, a compromise can be a great way to put an end to the argument. While it's not always right (or fair) to expect a compromise, such as if you have a roommate who never cleans up after themselves (been there, done that!) and you're sick of playing maid, in many cases, compromise can be one of your most valuable tools.

For example, imagine that you and your best friend both have vastly different ideas for a fun night. Your friend wants to go out to the club or hang out at a party while you prefer staying in. A valid compromise is that you go out one night and stay in the next. Or, let's say you like to sleep with a TV on but your college dorm roommate prefers to sleep in the dark and silence. A good compromise here could be you watching videos on your phone with the screen dimmed and a set of headphones so you both mostly get what you want.

Sometimes, compromises may seem unreasonable to you, especially if they push you past certain boundaries that you have. It's okay, and even healthy, to have boundaries, and that means you also need to know how to enforce them.

Boundary Setting

Boundaries are the lines you draw in relationships that you do not tolerate being crossed. It could be something like don't take food off your plate or that you want to be called a certain name. Your boundaries are a form of self-care that help you to feel safe and secure in your relationship. They should be communicated clearly and protected as long as they're healthy.

Unhealthy boundaries can be dangerous and tend to either harm or hold you back or attempt to exert control over someone else. Some common unhealthy boundaries (which are also red flags in relationships!) are:

- putting yourself down or letting someone else put you down.
- attempts to control someone else's behavior, such as saying that the other person can't have any friends other than you.
- attempts to change someone else, telling them how to act or what to do.

The boundaries you'll enforce in your life will be related to you and your wishes. Healthy ones create a sort of reflection of your lifestyle, showcasing the rules, principles, and guidelines that you have for your relationships. Some common healthy boundaries you may choose include:

- refusing to be manipulated or blamed for someone else's actions.
- expecting to be treated with respect and kindness.
- asking for space when you need it and expecting the request to be respected.
- communicating what makes you uncomfortable and expecting the request to be respected.
- expecting a certain degree of privacy with journals, passwords, or certain feelings or events.
- expecting your time to be respected.
- expressing sexual boundaries and expecting them to be respected.
- expecting your religion (or lack thereof) to be respected.
- protecting your material possessions and what will and won't be shared.

Your exact boundaries may deviate from these, such as saying that if someone leaves you hanging and doesn't respect your time, then you'll stop waiting for them. It's okay to protect your boundaries, and although it might feel like you're retaliating against the person who broke them, you aren't. If your boundaries are broken, especially repeatedly and after many attempts at communicating them clearly, then you are well within your rights to remove yourself from the situation.

Setting Your Boundaries

Establishing your boundaries shouldn't be difficult in a healthy relationship, especially if you put your good communication skills to the test. It's all about communicating them and it's often best to do so in a moment of calmness. After a boundary has been crossed, handle the natural anger you feel first and then write down what's bothering you so you won't forget it.

When you've calmed down, you can go to the other person and calmly and clearly state what happened and how it made you feel. You can then assert your boundary, stating exactly what that boundary is, that you will not tolerate it being crossed or ignored, and why it's a problem.

This should come from a place of love and kindness, explaining that you trust the other person not to violate your boundaries, and you should follow up by asking the other person if there are any boundaries that they need enforcing. They should have some things that they state are their non-negotiable points. You can model good boundary respecting as well by following theirs and apologizing whenever you make a mistake.

Setting and enforcing your boundaries is part of keeping yourself healthy. Your mental health and self-care are just as important as feeding yourself or sleeping. Remember that your boundaries are what allow you to feel safe and secure, and in healthy relationships of all kinds, people respect those boundaries.

Chapter Summary

Healthy communication will take you far in life. It'll help you to relate to others, express your own boundaries, and solve conflicts. Skills like active listening and learning not to interrupt others can all help you to be more successful in your communication, and when you can communicate well, you can work better with the people that surround you, whether they're coworkers, classmates, or your friends and family, reducing stress, and increasing positive feelings. All of this can have an overall impact on your general health too.

Moving into the next section of the book, we're taking a closer look at your physical and mental health, which go hand in hand.

PART 4
HEALTH AND WELLNESS

Self-care is not selfish. You cannot serve from an empty vessel.

–Eleanor Brown

CHAPTER 10
PHYSICAL AND MENTAL HEALTH GO HAND-IN-HAND

Your body and mind might seem like two separate things, but the truth is, they're more connected than most people would think. From the gut-brain axis influencing the neurotransmitters that make you think and feel to exercise being a fantastic way to boost energy levels and mental health, the two are highly linked. The best way to take care of your mind is to take care of your body and vice versa. After all, how good will you feel mentally if your body aches or is too tired to do anything? Or how good do you think you'd feel physically if you're stuck in anxiety or depression?

By taking care of both your body and mind, you'll feel your best. That means getting enough sleep, eating healthily, and keeping hydrated. It also means being able to guard your mental health with healthy boundaries and good mindsets. When both your body and mind are healthy, you have more energy and mental bandwidth to take care of the things you need to do, like work, keep stress levels down, or maintain good relationships.

The Connection Between Physical and Mental Health

Our bodies react to our perceptions of the world around us that our minds generate. When you think something is scary, your body responds in kind, entering the fight, flight, or freeze response. While your college final is a far stretch from being as dangerous as a lion staring you down, your body still reacts the same way to stress-inducing events, regardless of the actual threat level they may pose.

Now, imagine that you constantly live with stress. You're busy with school and work, and you want to spend time with friends. Or you're having a hard time somewhere. What do you think your body does? Those stress hormones prepare your body to fend off the potential threat, causing your heart to race, inducing anxiety, and building up cortisol. This redirects your body's energy and efforts to survival instead of maintenance processes that usually happen at rest.

While short bursts of these hormones aren't a big deal for your body; when you live under a constant state of stress, cortisol, a stress hormone, can cause inflammation throughout your body. Extended periods of exposure to this can lead to depression and constant feelings of fatigue while also weakening your immune system. In other words, people who are stressed often get or feel sick, and it can also increase their risk of several diseases.

Much of what you need to do to stay healthy uses this connection between body and mind. Exercise, for example, is great for you and boosts your mood. Eating healthy foods encourages a healthy gut biome, which also leads to having more energy and feeling better overall.

Maintaining a Healthy Body and Mind

Your body is the only one you get, so taking care of it is important. Yeah, you're young and your body can bounce back from a lot more than mine can. You can probably eat that extra slice of pizza without a care in the world, whereas I have indigestion if I so much as think about indulging. Just because you're young doesn't mean that you should neglect your health, even if your body can take it.

When I was in college, I lived off cheap ramen, pizza, and microwave meals. Let me tell you, if I tried to make that my diet today, it wouldn't be a fun time. I also rarely bothered with exercise and lived by the motto of "Sleep is for the weak! I'll sleep when I'm dead." It's a wonder my body never gave out on me from the years of abuse in my young adult years.

Nowadays, I make sure I walk the dogs for at least an hour most days. I eat healthy, well-balanced meals. I'm that boring old lady that goes to sleep at 10 each night when before, I'd still be getting ready for that night out. And you know what? My body feels so much better for it. I've noticed the slip in my mood and energy levels when I'm not taking care of myself the way I should be.

Taking care of yourself might feel like a huge time sink, but like saving for the future, it's an investment in yourself and your long-term health.

Sleep

While teens need an average of 8–10 hours of sleep per day, including potential naps, adults need around 7. I know, I know. If you're in college and have a job and a semi-healthy social life, it's more likely that you'll live off of copious amounts of coffee, energy drinks, and the occasional quick nap between classes in the library. Here in Seattle, I've walked through the campus at the University of Washington to enjoy the cherry blossom blooming and have seen students sleeping in the grass under the trees!

When we're busy, it's easy to make sleep the first thing we cut, but your body needs it consistently. Getting those 7 hours of sleep each day should be a major priority for you whenever possible. This is best done by consistently sleeping and waking at the same time. Of course, young adults have lives to live and people to see, but your sleep quality will have a major impact on your overall health and well-being.

Try keeping your room dark, comfortable, and relaxing. If you're able to, avoid electronics from the bedroom and try to skip large meals, caffeine, or alcohol before bed. All of this helps foster healthier sleep, which can leave you feeling better overall. Exercise can also help you sleep easier at night.

Exercise

Exercise helps you to maintain a healthy weight, but it also does more than that. It can improve your mood, brain health and keep you energetic, as well as strengthen your body and reduce the risk of many diseases. Ideally, you'd be active at least 150 minutes per week, which sounds like a lot but it is really just 30 minutes five days per week. Part of getting your exercise in for the day should include two days of strength training, making sure to focus on all major muscle groups at least once.

If this is tough to schedule in, there are plenty of ways to change up your daily schedule to stay active and still reap the benefits. Try implementing some of these:

- If you work at a desk often, use a standing desk.
- Walk to work, class, or on errands instead of driving if possible.
- Park in the back of parking lots and walk inside instead of parking as close to the store as possible.
- Take the stairs instead of the elevators.
- Implement a daily walk after work to decompress.

- Wake up 30 minutes early to get a quick workout in from home.
- Use an under-desk bicycle for some extra exercise.
- When you're watching TV, get a quick bit of exercise in during commercials.
- Have some basic small exercise equipment at home or easily available for at-home workouts.
- Use the weekend to catch up on missed exercise during the work or school week.

The more consistently you exercise, the easier it will become, and soon, you may find that you feel much better than you did before.

Diet

Eating healthily can be a challenge. From healthy whole foods often being more expensive than processed foods to needing to find time to meal plan and prep, it can be tough to squeeze it in. We've already addressed plenty of ways to implement a good, healthy meal plan, but now's the time to dive into what makes a healthy meal and how it'll benefit you.

Eating healthy meals can improve overall wellness by providing everything your body needs to thrive. It's associated with benefits such as longer lives, healthy skin, teeth, and eyes, and a lower risk of heart disease, type 2 diabetes, and cancer. It's also a major component in maintaining a healthy weight.

On the mental health frontier, a healthy diet full of nutrient-rich foods decreases mood swings and improves your ability to focus for longer periods. Some studies also suggest that clean diets can improve the symptoms of depression and anxiety, as opposed to unhealthy diets being associated with an increased risk of dementia or stroke.

Healthy diets often are fiber-rich, which helps keep your blood sugar (and energy) steady to avoid sugar crashes. Antioxidants in healthy foods fight inflammation, which can help counteract the effect of long-term stress. Probiotic-rich fermented foods improve your gut bacteria biome, which can leave you feeling better as well. Folate, a B vitamin, manages dopamine production, while vitamin D, which you get from sunlight and foods like mushrooms, can boost serotonin and moods. Magnesium is crucial for nerve and muscle function while also keeping your gut bacteria healthy. Mineral deficiencies can set your biome off-kilter, which can lead to anxiety and depression symptoms.

Implementing a wide range of whole foods is one of the easiest ways to get everything your body needs. It can be tempting to just pop multivitamin supplements, but keep in mind that the nutrients in food are often much more bioavailable than in supplement form, meaning that your body can better benefit from them in food sources.

I know how hard it is to get a rainbow on your plate every day, a way that many people rely on to get a range of vitamins in their diet. However, there are little changes you can make that will taste great and help keep your body healthy. This is what I do to make sure I get most of what I need in my diet.

Add More Fiber

Fiber keeps you full and your blood sugar stable. I keep prepped veggies available in my fridge to grab whenever I need a quick snack. Celery and carrots do great in jars of water! They last much longer than if you just left them in a bag. Reach for whole grains, beans, and lentils when you really need some staying power in your diet.

Vitamin D and Calcium Go Hand in Hand

When eaten together, vitamin D and calcium have a synergizing effect. Many foods are fortified with these nutrients to boost their bioavailability. Foods like milk, salmon, and dark, leafy greens will give you the boost you need. Remember, we get a lot of our vitamin D from sunlight, so don't forget to get outdoors!

Skip the Added Sugars

Added sugar may taste good, but all it does is prepare you for some serious sugar crashes. Instead of soda, opt for water with fruit slices, or use fresh fruit to sweeten your yogurt instead of buying the sweetened stuff.

Healthy Fats

We need fats to function, but only if they're the right kind. Ditch the saturated fats for unsaturated ones, like olive oil, instead of canola oil or margarine. Limit red meats in favor of seafood or vegetarian meals, and when you do choose pork or beef, try to choose leaner cuts.

Be Careful With Salts

We need both salt and potassium in balance with each other for our nerves to work. However, it's really easy to get too much salt and not enough potassium, which can leave you feeling unwell and raise your blood pressure. Cut out food from restaurants and processed sources and make your own food and rely on herbs and seasonings instead of salt.

An ideal plate will be half fruits and veggies (ideally of different colors), a quarter whole grains, and a quarter protein. Especially if you live in the United States, you probably have the idea that your meal is built around protein, but really, it should be built around the plant-based foods you choose.

Food is expensive, but it's also an important way to keep your body healthy. It's another way of self-care. Another way to look at it is that if you eat healthy foods, you may save money on medical expenses.

Chapter Summary

Your health is one of the biggest investments you'll ever make in yourself. Yes, it can be expensive to take care of yourself well with rising food costs, but this is one where you shouldn't skimp if you don't have to. You can still be mindful of expenses and eat well if you put together good meal plans and keep a healthy diet, and having a healthy body is one of the best ways to make sure that you have a healthy mind as well. In the next chapter, we're going to discuss just how important self-care is and what you need to do to keep your mental health in good shape.

CHAPTER 11
SELF-CARE AND HEALTHY HABITS

Skipping out on self-care is another thing we tend to do to maintain our busy schedules. Why take that mental health time when you have to study and write that paper or you have overtime for the week and still have chores to do? Well, the answer is simple: You can't be on the go constantly and worrying about everything but yourself. Taking time to implement self-care can be one of the best ways to avoid burnout and improve your mental health. Some aspects of self-care are meeting your basic physical needs, like we talked about in the last chapter. Eating good foods, sleeping well, and keeping your body in shape with exercise are all forms of self-care.

I've been hit by burnout before, exhausted and feeling like I didn't have the mental energy to do *anything*. I didn't want to do chores and they piled up. I could barely drag myself out of bed to work or get to class. I had chosen a particularly heavy course load for the quarter and was maxing out the number of credits I could take as a full-time student. I also worked to pay my bills and support myself at the time. I was up at 6 a.m. to get ready for school, had classes from 8–3 most days, with small breaks between them that I spent working on homework and studying. I worked from 6–10 p.m. most days, got home at 10:30 p.m., and did homework til close to 2–3 a.m. most days. I threw out exercise, time with friends, and my hobbies, telling myself it was temporary and I'd be fine.

Halfway through the quarter, midterms came around, and I had two long research papers and two exams to study for, plus my usual work. Of course, most of my coworkers were also college students and had asked for extra time off, which led to me being scheduled for longer shifts than usual. I was eating nothing but processed garbage when I could spare a few minutes and awake through the magic of caffeine.

One evening, on my way to work, I found myself feeling completely drained. I drank another energy drink and went on my way, only to start feeling jittery and lightheaded, like I'd pass out if I didn't sit down. Long story short, I got sent home from work by my manager because he was afraid I'd genuinely pass out at work and had the longest sleep I had for weeks.

My dear husband, who was my long-term boyfriend at the time, fussed over me and babied me for the rest of the evening, giving me that "I told you so" look without actually saying the words out loud. And sure enough, he *had* told me so. He'd tried to discourage me from taking so many classes or accepting so many hours. He'd encouraged me to ask for time off that week well in advance, but I was convinced we needed the money. He'd begged me to take time to myself to rest and relax when he'd catch me dozing off on my textbooks at my desk, but I told him I couldn't. Long story short, he was right. He loved me and wanted me to take care of myself. I had assumed that I'd have time to rest later.

Why Self-Care Matters

Self-care matters because it keeps us from burning out, it relieves the pressures of daily life, and lets us rest. Without rest, it's hard to maintain high levels of productivity for long. You might get a quick burst out of foregoing the self-care, but it's not sustainable, and you can very quickly end up like me, exhausted and feeling like utter garbage. I burnt the proverbial candle from both ends and by the time it was completely gone, I was in need of some serious rest.

I could have completely avoided the problem with self-care, which is proven to reduce anxiety, depression, and stress. As a result, it makes us more able to concentrate, feel happier, and have more energy. Speaking purely physically, self-care has been shown to reduce heart disease, cancer, and stroke. It can also greatly improve our quality of life by encouraging us to follow our passions and remain rooted in what we want and need the most in life.

Types of Self-Care

Self-care can take many different forms, from taking care of our bodies to finding things we love to do and making time for them. I like to break down self-care into three categories, depending on what it does for us at the time: physical, emotional, and spiritual.

Physical Self-Care

Physical self-care is all about taking care of your body and involves most of what we talked about in the previous chapter.

Emotional Self-Care

Emotional self-care emphasizes how we take care of our mental health. It can involve our self-talk, setting boundaries to protect us from unnecessary stress, or taking time to ourselves to rest and enjoy ourselves. Try setting up a coffee date with a friend or a weekly movie or game night that you can count on to unwind. Remember, you have permission to unwind and rest. Protect that. You work to live, you don't live to work, and that's a lesson I learned far too late in life.

Emotional self-care comes in several forms, with my favorites being:

- accepting and allowing yourself to feel what you feel
- learning your emotional triggers and how to work with them
- putting your needs first and tending to them
- maintaining your boundaries
- avoiding negative people and places
- using self-compassion and not being too hard on yourself
- asking for help when you need it
- resting when you need it
- finding time each day to do something you love

Spiritual Self-Care

Spiritual self-care is very personal. For some, it's focusing on their religion. For others, it's finding ways to care for themselves deeply through meditation or regular acts of kindness, or a gratitude journal. It's all about developing a deeper sense of meaning within yourself, fostering and nurturing a sense of your beliefs and values. Some ways I practice spiritual self-care include:

- practicing yoga
- meditating
- finding ways to connect to the greater community, such as joining clubs or volunteering
- taking time to get into nature
- practicing forgiveness and letting go of grudges or negative emotions

Starting a Self-Care Routine

Building a self-care routine can be tough if you've gotten into the habit of putting your needs last or ignoring them. It can feel selfish or like you're putting too much time into yourself when there are other things you could spend your time on. It can also be tough to get into the habit of taking the time for yourself. Making self-care your habit is one of the best ways you can support yourself. Getting into the habit can be broken down into several steps that can make it easier to implement.

Identify What Makes You Feel Centered

As much as everyone needs self-care, it also looks different for everyone. While you might think spending an hour at the gym lifting weights is a great way to spend your time, someone else might think it's brutal. Self-care is all about what you can do to feel centered and good about yourself.

Make a list of the things that you love that make you feel centered and fulfilled. Maybe you like to read and write or ride horses. Or, you could be the kind of person who loves cooking or gardening.

Think of How to Implement These Into Your Life

Once you have your list of things that help you feel centered, you need to start implementing them. Let's say your list is:

- listening to music
- writing
- jogging
- yoga
- spending time with friends

Now, it's time to slide those into your regular schedule. Listening to music is easy—you can pop in a pair of headphones or listen to music on your commute or while doing chores. Jogging and yoga can fit into your exercise regimen. The hard part would be fitting in writing and spending time with friends into your life, but it's important to do so. Maybe you opt to write for ten minutes before bed each night and schedule a regular weekly meetup with your friends.

Set Goals for Daily Self-Care

In two chapters, we'll be diving into how to set goals so you can achieve them, so we'll hold off on going in depth here. Setting goals to meet your self-care daily is a great way to prioritize that care, as long as you choose SMART goals. These are goals that are specific, measurable, achievable, relevant, and timely (Boogaard, 2021). Maybe you set goals to go to bed at a set time, eat a healthy diet, and get your exercise time in.

It's okay to work your goals in slowly, starting with one or two easier ones until they develop into habits. Then, you can start implementing more self-care and better address your needs.

Create a Support System

One of my favorite ways to stick to my goals, especially in self-care, is to set up a support system. This is more than just having people who cheer you on and encourage you. It's also a good idea to have people who use the same self-care activities for themselves, allowing you to both work together. If you want to exercise more to care for yourself, you can have accountability buddies that you jog or go to the gym with. Writers can write concurrently with their buddies to keep going even when they feel like writer's block is overwhelming.

Having a support system of people who self-care like you do means that you can talk together and work together to meet your goals. They'll understand your struggles and be able to talk through problems. Plus, it's always satisfying to do something with someone else and get that social interaction in too!

Take the Trial and Error Approach

The most important part about putting together your self-care routine is to remember that it's all about trial and error. What works for someone else may not work for you, and vice versa. You might also try to set up a routine that just isn't working for you. Instead of trying to browbeat yourself into being able to do it and creating negative associations, remember that it's totally valid to take a new approach.

Your needs will change over time. Your schedule will, too. That means that self-care has to be flexible to fit into your schedule. After all, you wouldn't forego a great job that overlaps with your scheduled gym time—you'd probably shift your gym time to accommodate your work schedule. Other self-care practices can be shifted around too.

Don't be afraid to mix things up if you need to find a better schedule for you. What's most important here is that you get your time for self-care and make it enjoyable.

Self-Care and Stress Relief Tips

A lot of what we've already talked about throughout the book falls into self-care. Eating well, staying hydrated, sleeping, and exercising all help your body. Setting goals and priorities can help too. There's more to self-care than just that, and many stress relief tips can also help with your practice. Here are some of my tried and true stress relief and self-care tips and tricks.

Set Up a Gratitude Journal

Gratitude journals remind you of the positives in your life and improve your mindset to be more positive. Each night before bed, I stop and write down at least three things that I'm grateful for. Even on the worst of days, there's always something I can appreciate. Some days, I've written that my husband, children, and I are alive and mostly well. Others, I've written about a sweet thing someone did for me or about the beautiful view I saw.

This helps to reframe your mindset to be something more positive just because it has you thinking about good things that happened throughout your day.

Pick Up a Self-Care Book

There are so many good books out there about self-care. We've touched upon some subjects, but this is really just an overview. Especially if you like to read, picking up a dedicated self-care book may be just what you need to get inspired and fix up your routine. They can also offer insight into areas you struggle and how to overcome them. If you're busy, you can choose an audiobook to listen to during commutes or chore time.

Enjoy a Pet Companion

Did you know that pets, particularly dogs, can reduce stress and anxiety and even lower blood pressure? There's a reason they're used as emotional support animals and service animals for people with disorders like PTSD—they're great at it. You might not be able to get a pet of your own, especially if you're still in college or you live somewhere that isn't pet-friendly, but there are still ways you can take advantage of this. Volunteering at a pet shelter, choosing to moonlight as a pet sitter on the weekends, or spending time with friends or family members with dogs can all help you reap the benefits of a quick puppy snuggle and assuage your frayed nerves.

Get Outside

Being outside is so good for us. Remember, we evolved to be outside, working, hunting, and farming. Nowadays, we spend so much of our time indoors, at school, or sitting at a desk at work, and it can really be draining. Getting outside can improve energy levels and help with burnout while also improving sleep quality. Your circadian rhythm, which regulates your sleep and wake cycles, relies on natural sunlight to manage your hormone levels, so getting out there is a great way to reset them. Go hiking, plant a garden, or just take a nice walk and bust that stress.

Breathing and Grounding

Having tools and tricks that can ground you help when your emotions run haywire. There are always times when we feel overwhelmed. Even the most organized of us, the ones who seem the most put together, have times when something seems impossible, or they're blinded with anger or burnt out so much that they just want to give up.

Various grounding techniques exist, from mindful meditation to yoga. One of my favorites is a trick that's easy to implement anywhere you go. It's called square breathing and you can do it in a meeting, driving your car, or just about anywhere else. All you have to do is a few quick deep breathing exercises and feel the benefits. It's discreet and suitable for those moments when you're out and about and just need to reset your mind.

To begin, you breathe deeply through your nose for four seconds. You hold your breath for four seconds, then exhale through your mouth for four seconds. Finally, hold it for four more seconds before starting over. It's called square breathing because it's paced out with four seconds per step. As you do this, you activate your parasympathetic nervous system, which is the part that controls your fight-or-flight response. By breathing calmly, you send messages to that part of your nervous system that says there's no danger here and it calms you down.

Chapter Summary

Being in control of yourself and your mind can be difficult at times, and without self-care, you can find yourself quickly burning out. Implementing a solid self-care routine is one of the best ways you can keep yourself grounded and feeling good about yourself. Grounding techniques, in particular, like deep breathing exercises, can help you when emotions run high and you find yourself feeling out of control. These can be particularly useful when you find yourself in stressful situations, like when you go to a doctor's office.

The next chapter focuses on handling medical matters of all kinds, including what to expect with health insurance, how to set up doctors' appointments, and when you need to be seen.

CHAPTER 12
MEDICAL MATTERS

One of the biggest changes that happen when you reach adulthood is that suddenly, you're responsible for your own health. You have to consent to treatments, you have medical privacy from your parents, and you get to make all the decisions. Depending on your agreement with your parents, you may also be responsible for paying for your care. This can feel like a pretty big responsibility, especially if your parents handled everything before.

When I turned 18, the revelation that I had to schedule my own appointments *terrified* me. Looking back on it, I'm not sure why it was such a problem for me, but I think a part of it was that I was intimidated by having to make the phone call, get myself to the appointment, and then be on my own for the appointment. While it had been years since my parents went into the room with me for most of my annual checkups, they still were present and could handle if any treatment was needed. It was far easier to pretend that I was healthy and therefore didn't need the appointments.

There's a problem with this line of thinking, though—when you don't get regular screenings and checkups, you can miss something important that would have otherwise been detected earlier. There are all sorts of symptoms that you might not be conscious of that can be detected in a blood test or physical exam. Missing preventative care can mean dealing with costlier care in the future.

Health Insurance

In the US, young adults can remain on their parent's health care plans until they turn 26, meaning that even if you're an adult and responsible for yourself financially, your parents can still keep you on their own insurance plans through work or that they pay for themselves. This is good news, too, because health insurance can be expensive. Even being on their plans, you still have to deal with deductibles, copays, and other costs associated with them.

In other areas of the world, health insurance may look different. Many countries have a nationalized health system where the cost of care is covered by the country. In Canada and several European countries, for example, public health care is free to everyone. The same goes for Australia and Brazil.

Important Terms in Health Insurance

Whether you have your own health insurance plan or rely on your parents', there are some terms you'll want to know in advance:

- ⬥ **Deductible:** A deductible is an amount you have to cover for your health care before your insurance plan begins to pay. For example, if your plan has a $2,000 annual deductible, your health insurance won't start paying out on treatment until you've already spent and paid $2,000 out of pocket.
- ⬥ **Copayment:** Even when insurance is covering the bill for your appointment, you may have a copayment (copay). This is the amount you pay as your portion of the bill. They can vary based on your plan.
- ⬥ **Coinsurance:** Coinsurance refers to the share of the cost for covered services that you are responsible for. It's usually a set percentage in your plan.
- ⬥ **Premium:** Each month, you or the policyholder have a premium. This is the amount you pay to keep your plan active.

- **Network:** Not all medical facilities accept all insurance, especially if you're in the United States. When a facility or doctor is in network, they accept your insurance.
- **Out-of-pocket maximum:** This is the most you'll pay out of pocket for your care for a calendar year. Once you reach the out-of-pocket maximum, your health insurance will cover the rest of the bills until the end of the year. You'll still owe your regular premium, but anything else should be covered if it's in network.

What if I Don't Have Health Insurance?

If, for whatever reason, you don't have health insurance, you can still go to the doctor if you need to be seen. However, you'll have to pay the office yourself for the services. This can be especially stressful for young adults who usually don't have a lot of money and can be a big reason for not going in for routine care. If you don't have insurance, you can be seen in the emergency room. You can't be turned away due to a lack of money if you truly need care.

Another consideration, if you don't currently have insurance, is looking into your state's Medicaid program or seeing what the cost for sliding scale insurance looks like. You might be able to get assistance with health care coverage this way.

Making a Doctor's Appointment

If you move for college, you may need to set up new health care local to you. Many college campuses have on-site health care available, or you can set up appointments around the area. When it's time to make a new appointment, find a doctor that accepts your insurance and meets your personal preferences. For example, if you're a woman and would prefer a woman treating you, or vice versa, for men, you can do that.

Then, you just follow some simple steps:

1. Call the office and inform them if you're a new patient. You may have to wait a week or two for a new patient appointment. If you're requesting care with a specific doctor, this is the time to bring it up.
2. Let the receptionist know why you need the appointment. It could be a checkup due to specific concerns like an illness or to have tests run.
3. Provide your insurance information.
4. Ask if you need to bring anything to the appointment, like records or a list of your prescriptions.

Sometimes, you'll have an appointment scheduled within a day or two, or it could be weeks or months, depending on the reason for the appointment and the doctor's availability. However, not all conditions can wait.

What to Do if the Problem Can't Wait for an Appointment

If you have to wait for a new patient appointment but have a pressing medical concern, you've got other options. Urgent care offices often allow you to be seen on the same day, which can be a great help if you think you have a minor infection or need antibiotics. Some common reasons people go to urgent care include:

- urinary tract infections
- a persistent cold or flu
- a minor injury like a sprain or strain
- stomach bugs or food poisoning
- sudden rashes or insect bites
- burns, cuts, or scrapes that need treatment but don't warrant going to the emergency room

Sometimes, going to the emergency room is the right answer for more serious conditions or injuries:

- sudden severe pain
- uncontrollable bleeding
- vision changes
- pain or pressure in the chest or upper abdomen
- altered consciousness, confusion, or disorientation, especially after a head injury
- vomiting or coughing up blood
- bright red blood in bowel movements
- shortness of breath or difficulty breathing
- severe headaches, especially with slurred speech or difficulty speaking
- dizziness, fainting, or weakness in half the body
- having a seizure for the first time, or for people who are known to have seizures, one that lasts longer than five minutes
- feeling like you want to hurt yourself or others
- severe injuries, including broken bones, head injuries, deep cuts, and severe burns
- severe, persistent vomiting or diarrhea

If you're not sure if something is ER-worthy, the best thing to do is call the hospital. They often have triage nurses available to speak to about whether you need to be seen immediately or if you can wait for an appointment.

Attending a Doctor's Appointment Alone

When appointment day rolls around, you might be nervous if you've never been responsible for getting yourself there alone before. With a bit of preparation and planning out what to expect and what to do, it's not so bad! It gets easier after the first few times, especially if you're prepared.

Be Early and Prepared

Make sure that you arrive at the office 10–15 minutes before your scheduled appointment time. You may need to fill out intake paperwork or you might get lost trying to get there. This 15-minute buffer helps in case of traffic or you get lost. Bring your ID, insurance card, and anything else the receptionist said that you needed when you scheduled your appointment, too.

Have Questions Ready

If you have any particular concerns before your appointment, write them down, along with any questions you may have. The appointment probably won't be very long, so you'll want to be able to efficiently go down the list and address all concerns.

Be Specific

When you describe symptoms and concerns to your doctor or nurse, be as specific as possible. It's best if you're able to tell them when the symptoms started, where the pain is, and anything you've done to try to alleviate them.

Chapter Summary

When you become an adult, you also inherit the responsibility for your health and well-being, something that, before this point, your parents were responsible for. As scary as it can be the first few times, it gets easier with practice! This is true of many things in life as you learn to readjust your expectations and keep pushing yourself out of your comfort zone.

The next section of this book focuses on personal development, including being able to learn and grow as a person. Personal development is all about learning, resilience, and recognizing that it's okay to be uncomfortable sometimes.

PART 5

PERSONAL DEVELOPMENT

> *Everyone thinks you make mistakes when you're young. But I don't think we make any fewer when we're grown up.*
>
> –Jodi Picoult

CHAPTER 13

TIME MANAGEMENT AND GOAL SETTING

We never get our time back. Once it's gone, it's gone for good. If you waste that time endlessly scrolling through TikTok or Facebook, that's time squandered that you may one day wish you had spent differently. Did you know that the average person uses social media for 2 hours and 31 minutes per day? How much is that in a year? Well, it's nearly 919 hours annually or the equivalent of 38.3 days around the clock. If we count just waking hours, averaging 16 per day, that number nearly doubles to 57 days. That's right, nearly two months of time each year is spent on social media on average.

What would you do with all that time if you had it? That's enough time to spend on hobbies, studies, or passions, and instead, it's wasted scrolling through things that you probably won't remember a few days later.

Social media, silly videos on the internet, and other time wasters sap away at what time we have, wasting it away. Wouldn't you rather do something productive with it instead?

Learning to balance your time is one of the most important parts of being an adult. As kids, we had our parents there to tell us what to do and when to do it. They could limit screen time and wasted hours by setting rules, but as soon as you enter adulthood, your time is your own and no one else's. What will you do with it?

Time is Money—Don't Waste It!

We've all heard people say that time is money, but it's actually quite true. Every hour you have is one that you can use to potentially earn or save money. A freed-up hour can be used to cook yourself a nutritious meal, saving money on eating out. An hour could be spent doing chores instead of outsourcing or working on your passion projects that could one day become your livelihood.

The worst thing you can do to yourself is waste your time. Sure, you can have fun and do things that you enjoy, but when you're constantly letting the little things eat away at your time, you're quite literally wasting your life away. The good news is that you can reclaim your time. You can put down the phone and stop doom-scrolling and instead direct your efforts to things that will be more productive.

Time Sinks to Avoid

Ready to figure out how much time you waste? We're going to go over a list of the most common time-wasters people in college tend to fall into. How many of them apply to you? How much time do you spend each day doing each of these activities? One or two little time wasters might not seem like a big deal, but if you're not careful, you can build habits that waste more time than you use to be productive. That's not to say that you have to be active and productive all the time—you need downtime to rest, too! But as they say, everything in moderation. Check out these common time wasters:

Binging TV Shows or Online Videos

Watching an episode of your favorite show is a great way to unwind after a long day. Watching hours of it while you try to do other things, on the other hand, can really just distract you. This is especially true if you're trying to study while watching a show. Stick to playing instrumental background music if you don't want to study in silence.

Studying Without a Plan

If you study without some sort of plan, you can find yourself wasting a lot of time. It's not enough to just read the textbook from start to finish, and when you have several classes to study for, you have to be intentional with your time.

Develop a study plan that outlines what you will do and when so you'll know how to tackle it all and best spend your time. For example:

- Take notes on the assigned chapter for psychology for 45 minutes.
- Study for the upcoming chemistry midterm for an hour.
- Spend half an hour working on a philosophy paper.

When you study with an intentional plan, it's much easier to make good progress.

Social Media

With so many social media platforms to browse, it can be easy to underestimate how much time you're actually spending on them. You might spend 20 minutes on Facebook, 30 minutes on Instagram, and another 30 minutes scrolling through TikTok and not realize just how much time you're spending. Then, add in notifications popping up and sucking you back in, or the time that you spend chatting with people on the platform and the amount of time balloons up pretty quickly.

Instead of using social media all day, disable the notifications and set specific times when you'll use the apps. You don't have to cut social media out cold turkey and it can be a great way to stay in touch with friends, but you shouldn't let it consume your life.

Procrastination

We all procrastinate from time to time, but if it's a habit for you to say that you'll do something later or tomorrow, you're probably wasting a lot of time while also putting some pretty stressful time crunches onto yourself as well. If you say you'll study later, you lose out on study time that you might have now and you may find yourself staying up later to get to it all. Or, if you say you'll do the dishes after work instead of before like you normally do, you may find yourself in a position where you don't have anything clean to make dinner with. Beating procrastination can be tough, but learning to do so is one of the most valuable tools you can teach yourself. If you have to do something that will take less than five minutes, do it immediately instead of putting it off.

Schedules, tools like the Pomodoro method (more on this later!), and breaking down tasks into smaller steps so they don't feel so overwhelming can all help you beat procrastination.

Overplanning

Are you an overplanner? A lot of us are—we spend inordinate amounts of time trying to make sure that every last detail of our plans are going to go off without a hitch that we run out of time to actually properly execute it. Or, all that overplanning can lead us to give up when whatever it was doesn't go exactly according to plan.

Trying to Make Things Perfect

If that last point resonated with you, you might also spend a lot of time agonizing over the tiniest details of whatever you're doing. If it's not exactly right, you might focus endlessly on a small detail that really isn't very important.

There's no such thing as perfection, meaning it's useless to waste your time trying to achieve it. Instead, focus on setting realistic standards and let go of the small details. No one cares if the sandwich you make doesn't look perfect if it still tastes good.

Unclear Goals

Setting goals that aren't efficient is another way that a lot of people waste their time. We'll be talking about setting effective goals later in this chapter. When your goals are unnecessarily vague, like "I want to lose weight" or "I want to eat more vegetables," you don't really give yourself something concrete to work toward, and we'll talk about addressing that shortly.

Multitasking

We often think that multitasking is the perfect way to squeeze more into a short period of time, but the truth is this is incredibly inefficient. Your brain can only really focus on one thing at a time, which means when you're multitasking, you are constantly forcing your brain to shift gears, which can quickly draw things out and cost you time.

It's better to focus on one task at a time, giving it your full attention, rather than trying to do several things at once. If you're in a position where you feel like you have to multitask, try breaking down the task into something more manageable. The more you streamline your process, the quicker you'll get things done, and the more time you'll save!

How to Manage Your Time

As you start saving time, you'll better be able to manage it. For most young adults, college is the first real test they get at managing their time by themselves, and that freedom can be addictive. There's no one telling you what to do, when to study, or how to live. The problem is, if you've never had the experience of managing your time yourself or facing the consequences of poor time management, you're at risk of completely dropping the ball.

It took me a solid two weeks after I moved into my dorm to realize that my time management was *horrible*. I'd put off my studying or homework assignments until the last minute, which meant my first few grades in my classes were much lower than what I was used to. I'd prioritize having fun and making friends rather than getting to the tasks I needed to handle. By the end of my second week, I was exhausted and staring at a whole mess of studying, chores, and other responsibilities.

Part of the reason I struggled so much was that when I lived with my parents, they had me on a structured schedule. I had to complete my homework before I could go out with friends. I had to do my chores beforehand, too. All the structure they built into my life felt like a big drag when I was a teen, but once I got to college, I realized that they were really just trying to help me out and set me up for success.

While my first semester of college ended with grades lower than I was used to, it also gave me a solid understanding of what it's like to be an adult. I needed to manage my time because no one else would do it for me. I had to take responsibility for those lower grades, and by the time the second semester rolled around, I had the solid schedule and foundation I needed to succeed.

My recommendation for time management is to have a predictable schedule and stick to it. Anything that you need to do should be prioritized in the level of importance to you, which means that you'll have to make those major decisions for yourself.

For example, you might really want to go to that party, but you have to be up early the next morning for your weekend job. What's more important to you? You may decide that you still want to go to the party, but you also don't want to be exhausted, so you decide to go home early instead of partying into the wee hours of the morning.

Prioritize Your Work

Prioritizing your work is all about figuring out what needs to be done immediately and what can wait or be eliminated entirely. When it feels like you're drowning in work, make a list of all the tasks you're trying to squeeze in. Then, start rating them by their urgency.

Unimportant tasks, like endless time scrolling through social media, can be put off or don't matter to you.

Important tasks matter to you or need to be done. These could be your hobbies, studying, working, or completing your chores. They need to be scheduled somewhere during your day and completed in a timely manner.

Urgent tasks are things that have to be done to avoid issues. This could be completing an assignment for school, studying for an impending test, or getting car maintenance done to keep your car running. Many of these tasks could be things that were once important that you decided to push off until you couldn't any longer.

One of the best solutions to having a buildup of tasks is to avoid procrastinating. We'll have some tips for time management and beating procrastination shortly.

Don't Overcommit

Saying no when you're asked to do something can be difficult, especially if you fall into people-pleasing habits. The problem with this comes when you start getting overwhelmed with commitments. Life is busy enough on its own, with work, school, and maintaining a social life. There's no need to make it worse by taking on every little favor that people ask you to do.

Or, maybe you're already overcommitted because you thought you'd have the time to do everything, only to find out that it all piled up on you. I get it—as a busy parent, I'm constantly inundated with all the things needed from me for work, my children, and my husband. There's always laundry to do, homework to complete, extracurriculars to drive to, and more. In college, it seemed like there was just as much going on. I had to study, work, and still find time for my friends.

It's okay to say no to things that you don't have the time or bandwidth to complete. Let go of the things that don't matter to you or that you simply can't dedicate your time to. Yes, this might mean letting go of some things that are important, like foregoing a favorite club on campus to go to work sometimes or not going out with friends every night, but it'll help you to balance your schedule.

By avoiding the trap of overcommitting, you free up time that can better be utilized doing important and urgent things on your list. All you'll need to do is use that time wisely and efficiently.

Pomodoro Technique

One of my absolute favorite ways of being efficient with time is using the Pomodoro Technique to manage my time without feeling like I'm overwhelmed or like I don't have time to relax. As a fun aside, the technique got its name from the Italian word for tomato because the person who mainstreamed it used a kitchen timer shaped like a tomato to break up his time.

With this technique, you are breaking up your time into 25-minute stretches of working on something with a 5-minute break. After four intervals, you get a 15- or 30-minute break to unwind.

This helps by breaking down what otherwise feels like a long, unbearable task and turning it into smaller chunks that feel more manageable. That means less time dwelling on how long it will take, feeling overwhelmed and procrastinating, and more time doing what you need to do.

Get started by choosing a task you need to complete, like a paper, or choosing to study something or a chore. Set a timer for 25 minutes and work the whole time. Don't get distracted, leave your phone somewhere you won't be tempted by it, and get going. When the timer goes off, give yourself that quick break. I like to write down my progress as I go so I can see how productive I've been while I use this method. If I'm reading or writing, I jot down my word count or how many pages I got through and then unwind. After your short break is over, set up the timer and start again. I'd bet this will help save time by keeping you on task!

Time-Saving Tips

Still feel tight on time after implementing these changes? These are some of my favorite tips I used in college and still use today to make the most out of my time:

- **Pay attention to your time:** I like to keep track of my time by making sure I'm conscious of how long I spend on my biggest time wasters. For me, checking my phone is absolutely one of the worst. When I feel like my time is getting out of control, I take a look at my phone's apps to see just how long I spend on it. The number can be pretty scary sometimes and it reminds me to set it down and focus on what's going on around me instead.
- **Use downtime to your advantage:** Do you commute to work or school? Whether you walk, ride a bus, or drive, you can always boost your productivity with audiobooks. Or, if you take the bus or carpool, you can use the time you spend traveling to study, catch up on work, or tend to some of your planning for the week. Instead of just waiting around, get productive instead!
- **Separate work and pleasure:** We associate our spaces with what we do most in them, so separating where you work from where you sleep or enjoy yourself can help put you into the productive mindset by association. This could be tough if you have a dorm, but you could choose to do most of your studying in the library on campus. Dedicate a set office for yourself in your home if you've got the luxury to do so.
- **Outsource if you can:** This might be kind of hard, depending on where you are in your life. Some things can be outsourced, and if you have the ability to do so, you should. For students, a major source of outsourcing is eating in the school dining halls. You don't have to cook or clean up after yourself.
- **Find tools to help you:** Let me tell you—when I first heard about robot vacuums, I thought it was a ridiculous luxury and a waste of time and money. Now, with children and pets? I couldn't imagine it any other way. These tools are my livelihood and keep me grounded. If there are tools that will boost your productivity and they're affordable to you, they're probably worth the investment.

As you implement these tools, you can remain focused on what matters the most. Then, you just have to make sure you have the goals to roadmap your plan forward.

SMART Goals Keep You Focused

We already introduced the topic of SMART goals earlier when talking about self-care, but now it's time to go in-depth with them. As stated earlier, SMART goals are specific, measurable, achievable, relevant, and timely.

The reason I like these goals is that it keeps me focused. When writing goals in this format, it's much easier to see exactly what needs to be done by which date or time to stay on track. As a result, I'm able to focus so much more on what needs to be done without getting stuck with tasks that suddenly become urgent or necessary to complete quickly to meet requirements.

- **Specific:** Goals should be very specific. For example, if your goal is to get good grades in college, you don't really have a metric that tells you what you're aiming for. What's a good grade to you?
- **Measurable:** By making your goal measurable, you give yourself something that has a definitive ending. This could be getting a 3.5 GPA or not getting below an 80% on an assignment for the semester.
- **Achievable:** Goals need to be achievable, too. You can't, for example, say you want to graduate with a 4.0 GPA when you already have below that, or you want to run a marathon in a week when you're currently living a relatively inactive life. Make sure you're realistic about what you can and can't do when you set your goal. It should be something that's a bit of a stretch and

makes you work for it, but not something you can never do. How will you achieve it? If you want to get that 3.5 GPA, what's your study plan? How many classes will you take at once?

- **Relevant:** Your goal also needs to be relevant to you. Is it something you'd willingly do? Do you have an interest in doing it? If you genuinely don't care about college, for example, because you plan on going into a career that doesn't require a degree, are you really going to give it your all?
- **Timely:** Finally, your goal needs to have some sort of finality to it. There has to be a deadline on it so you know whether you've succeeded or failed. This could be graduation if you want that high GPA or an arbitrary date you've set. This will help keep you accountable and working toward your goal.

When you set up your goal, start by writing down each step. What do you want? How will you achieve it? Why does it matter to you? When do you need to be done with your work toward it? These things matter, and writing them all down will help paint a clearer picture of what you'll need to do and how to schedule it all into your plan.

Chapter Summary

A major part of personal development is being able to stick to schedules and manage your time wisely. When you can mitigate time sinks and focus on SMART goals, you can push yourself forward, learning more and working toward being more successful. From there, it's all about resilience and remembering that it's okay to be a work in progress. It's okay to not be able to do everything right the first time, and developing a growth mindset, which we'll introduce in the next chapter, is all about getting back up when we fall.

CHAPTER 14
GROWTH MINDSET, SELF-CONFIDENCE, AND RESILIENCE

With tools for managing your time in place, you can start tackling your goals and bringing them to fruition. It's so fulfilling to see all your hard work bear fruitful results! As you achieve your goals, you'll likely find yourself feeling more confident and capable in your life. The key here, though, is recognizing that when you do fail at something (and it will happen, I promise!), you can keep moving forward.

One of the hardest things in life to learn is to be resilient. Resilience requires you to be confident and recognize that failing at something isn't the worst thing in the world. In fact, failure is what propels growth. If you didn't fail at something, how do you know that what you were doing wasn't too easy for you?

Something I had to learn with my kids is that praising them for every single thing they did right wasn't the right path to building confidence. In fact, the more I praised them for getting things done correctly, the more resistant they were to try new things. When I talked to them about it, what they said surprised me: They were afraid that if they messed up, I wouldn't give them the praise, and I'd be disappointed in them. In other words, they were afraid of failure and what I'd do if they struggled, so they resisted trying new things and challenging themselves. Instead of teaching them to be confident, bold children who wanted to tackle everything life had to offer, they wanted to stay firmly in their comfort zone.

Your Brain Never Stops Growing

If staying in your comfort zone resonates with you, you're not alone. Looking back on it, I was the same way when I was younger. I was afraid of making mistakes because mistakes meant I was wrong, and being wrong meant I wasn't right and I hated not being right. It was a dangerous thought spiral. I thought that if I just didn't try, I couldn't fail, but this is the wrong way to look at it. You don't fail at something until you give up on it. By never being willing to try something, I was inadvertently failing by default, but somehow convinced myself it wasn't the same thing.

Developing a Growth Mindset

Part of what builds resilience is to develop a growth mindset. Resilience is the ability to bounce back from failure and keep moving toward your goal. It's okay to be disappointed that you didn't succeed, but what's more important is recognizing that you can keep working in the future to see better results.

In other words, just because you didn't succeed today doesn't mean that you won't succeed in the future. This is because your brain never stops growing. It's like a muscle in the sense that the more that you work it, the stronger it becomes. It's never too late to learn a new skill or achieve new goals, and it's only natural not to be very good at something when you first start.

Imagine if we all gave up the first time we tried and failed something. Babies would never crawl or walk. We'd never talk or read or write because all of these are learned skills that have a lot of failure at the beginning. Doctors would never perform surgery or help heal people. Lawyers would give up in law school the first time they misremembered something.

We all fail from time to time. We all get things wrong every now and then. And that's okay.

When we focus on a growth mindset, we don't look at the results as much as we look at the effort put into it. After all, it's the effort that really deserves the praise—it's all the hard work you put into getting to that end goal that really matters. Yes, it's great that you succeeded, but that success is meaningful and satisfying because you worked for it.

If you shift your mindset to focus on the effort you put into a situation instead of the end result, you find that it's easier to bounce back after getting an undesired result. Instead of thinking that where you're at in that moment in terms of skill level is it, you'll see that you can keep learning and growing. In other words, you become resilient, and that resilience will help keep you moving forward with your life.

Tips to Develop a Growth Mindset for Resilience

If you're the kind of person to crumble at the thought of failure, don't worry—you can change your mindset. After all, that's what this is all about, right? Developing a growth mindset both requires and develops resilience. The more you practice, the easier it will become, just like with any other type of exercise. Only this time, you're exercising your brain.

Embrace Your Imperfections

You don't have to be perfect. In fact, your imperfections are valuable parts of who you are and how much room you still have to grow. When you get something wrong, it's not a ding against who you are as a person. It's not a sign that you're useless or stupid. It's just a sign that you don't know that information or skill *yet*. You see, the "yet" is important here.

Just because you don't know something today doesn't mean you won't know it in the future. Remind yourself of this when you make mistakes. Instead of beating yourself up, say, "I don't know this yet, but I can learn."

See Challenges as Opportunities

When something is difficult, it's not a sign of you being inadequate, either. It's actually a really good opportunity for you to begin learning and for you to grow. Every challenge, every mishap along the way, is a way you can move forward and develop as a person. I'll bet you didn't know algebra when you stepped into class for the first time, but by the time you left, your skills had grown dramatically. Everything is like that. It's not raw talent that makes us successful—it's how we handle the challenges and use them to grow along the way.

Focus on Positive Language

So much of what makes up our mindsets is how we speak, both about ourselves and about the world around us. When you use negative language, like "I'm never going to figure this out," you're putting yourself in a precarious position. How much effort do you think you'll really put into figuring out whatever it is if you don't think you can actually do it? You might make a halfhearted attempt, but to really put your all into something, you have to believe that you can do it.

Get rid of absolutes in your language. There's no "always" or "never" or black and white. The world is more than shades of gray, too. We live in a vibrant world filled with spectrums of color, just like we ourselves have spectrums of abilities. You add or take away a little light to a color and what you're left with changes. Likewise, your abilities are the same way. They aren't stagnant and they can change based on what you put into them.

The more you make yourself comfortable with positive language, the better you will feel. Even better, the more confident you can grow. Growth mindsets and positive mindsets leave us feeling better about ourselves, granting us the key to success.

Self-Confidence and Success

Self-confidence is what gives you faith that you can succeed. It's what allows you to keep on trudging through the hard times and to trust yourself enough to know that you'll make the choices that are right for you. It also assures you that even if you don't have the answers now, you'll be able to come up with the answers with a little bit of effort.

In other words, self-confidence is having trust in yourself. It's not the same thing as being overconfident, where you overestimate your abilities. Rather, when you're self-confident, you're well aware of what you can do. This comes with all sorts of benefits that will help you through your life and take you on the pathway to success.

Self-confidence shows in how we present ourselves to others, how we hold our bodies, and how we approach problems. That inner confidence tells people they can put their confidence in you too. The result? People with self-confidence are more likely to get raises and promotions when they interview. They're also, as a result, more likely to be successful.

The good news here is that self-confidence is something we learn. Some people might be naturally more self-confident than others, but that doesn't mean that you can't grow it too. Growth mindset, remember?

Trial and Error and Trial Some More

Self-confidence is all about being able to pick yourself back up again when you fall. It's being able to trust your abilities. That doesn't mean that you trust that you're perfect already—it's about being aware of what they truly are and what you can do to continue learning and growing.

If you're not confident yet, all you need to do is to keep on trying, even in the face of challenges. This is a cycle of trial and error. Each error brings you another step closer to finding your solution. It's like being a scientist—you know what you want to do, and then you have to experiment to find the answer. Every time you try something that doesn't work, you know that it's time to try something different. Eventually, you'll get it right.

The more you work at this, remembering that you have a growth mindset and that you can continue to learn as long as you live and keep trying, the more confident you'll become. You'll become comfortable with making mistakes or failing, recognizing the silver lining of learning that comes with it. As you become more comfortable, you'll also be able to explore more, opening up doors that you never knew existed in your future.

Step Out of Your Comfort Zone

Self-confidence helps us step out of our comfort zone because we know we can trust ourselves to navigate through it, no matter what happens. It's the ability to trust that there are more things to learn and that sometimes, the learning and growing process is uncomfortable. However, resilience helps us through.

I've had to step out of my comfort zone countless times throughout life, applying for jobs, deciding to have children, making moves across the country... It can be intimidating or even terrifying when you face the unknown. But, it's only unknown for as long as you let it be.

The funny thing about stepping out of your comfort zone is that the more you do it, the easier it becomes and the more confident you feel. That's why I like to try new things all the time. I might try cooking a new meal with a technique I've never tried before or going to a new activity. There's something awe-inspiring about facing something brand new and slowly but surely learning how to actually do it. It's like being a child again, growing and learning.

Just because your body finishes growing doesn't mean your mind has to, and the more you try new things and stick to them, even when they're hard, the more likely you are to succeed. After all, you miss 100% of the shots you don't take. Your chances are infinitely higher just by trying, even if they're still low. And the more you practice, the easier those shots will get over time.

Chapter Summary

Developing a growth mindset and having the self-confidence and resilience to continue in the face of failure are the keys to success. When you learn to pick yourself up after you fall, you grow as a person, and that growth is priceless. You'll be able to step out of your comfort zone and thrive. Remember that failure isn't concrete until you give up. Until then, any mistakes and mishaps along the way are just speed bumps on your path to success.

CONCLUSION

Relax. You will become an adult. You will figure out your career. You will find someone who loves you. You have a whole lifetime; time takes time. The only way to fail at life is to abstain.

–Johanna de Silentio

The thing no one ever tells you about growing up is that it's not about knowing everything there is to know or being right all the time. There's never going to be a time when you feel perfectly equipped to take on everything the world has to throw your way. No—growing up is learning how to navigate through it all, even when you don't have the solutions. It's about learning to stand on your own two feet as an independent adult, but that doesn't mean that you have to face the world alone.

Rely on your loved ones. Build a social safety net of people you trust. Keep on learning, even when things are tough at first. Foster that growth mindset until the idea of failing isn't scary anymore. Put all these skills to the test and keep on practicing them.

You'll make mistakes. You'll probably miss a bill or two by accident (but I really hope you don't!). Things won't always work out as planned, but that's life. As you work on yourself and your skills, you'll keep learning. You'll grow. You'll *thrive*. All you have to do is remember not to give up.

Adulthood can be scary. After all, there's a lot riding on you that you'll have to figure out. However, I know that you can do it. We all can. Keep up the good work. Don't be afraid to ask questions or for help. And most importantly, have the confidence in yourself that you can, and will, succeed in this life, no matter where it takes you. Whether you enter the workforce immediately, decide to run your own business, go to college, or pursue a trade, you can do it. You just have to remember to pick yourself back up again when you fall. If you can do that, you're already halfway there. Good luck and happy adulting!

MONEY SKILLS
FOR TEENS

*These Are The Things About
Money Management and Personal Finance
You Must Know But They Didn't Teach You in School*

EMILY CARTER

INTRODUCTION

You are at a stage in your life where you need to learn as much as you can and prepare yourself for what is coming. Finances and financial literacy, in general, are very important parts of being an adult, and making the right financial decisions can set you up for a great life. Being financially literate will teach you important lessons that many adults only learn later in life after they've already made a few mistakes. This is not to say that these mistakes cannot be reversed, but they take time and effort, and you certainly want your adult life to go as smoothly as you possibly can. While there are many different aspects of life that we can't control, finances aren't one of them. We can act on them and turn things around.

By understanding finances, you can learn the differences between your needs and your wants, the real value of money, how money can work in your favor, and how you can avoid crippling debt. Your future and your financial independence are coming, and it's always best to be prepared for them.

The main goal of this book is to encourage you to take control of your finances from the very start so you can build enough wealth to live a peaceful life (at least when it comes to your finances) and to prepare you for what's coming. This book is structured in a way to make you understand the very basics first, such as what money is or how to make money as a teenager. Then, once you know the basics, I'll move on to more complex subjects such as banking and financial services; what is budgeting and how can it help; what is credit or debt management; the intricacies of insurance and how it can provide security for you, and your loved ones; and how caring about retirement now can help you later in life.

This is the beginning of your journey, but if you make good decisions now, you will have a much easier life in the future.

CHAPTER 1

UNDERSTANDING MONEY

> *A wise person should have money in their head, but not in their heart.*
> –Jonathan Swift

When we think about money, we think about notes and coins and, more recently, numbers in our banking apps that allow us to pay for products or services that we want or need. But in a sober way, money is a system of exchange that allows us to get services or goods for a certain value in money. The monetary system was created to replace another, older system that you might have heard about called barter trading, which was used thousands of years ago. In this system, money wasn't involved, so if you wanted a service or good, you'd have to exchange it for another service or good. Let's say you lived during those times and you wanted someone to come fix your fence; in return, you'd give him goods, which at the time could be eggs, a cow, or milk. Or, if you could perform a service such as shoemaking, maybe you'd fix or even make new shoes for the person fixing your fence.

So, in other words, money is an asset, in this case, a liquid asset (because it can easily be transformed into cash; for instance, if you withdraw $10 from an ATM, you're turning money into cash), that allows us to make transfers of value in an easy way between two people or organizations.

In this chapter, we are going to understand the role of money in our lives, what exactly the value of money is and its impact on our personal finance decisions, and how we can develop a healthy money mindset and set attainable financial goals.

The Role of Money in Our Lives

In our lives, money is important because it allows us to have a better quality of life by enabling us to have options in the things we do in our day-to-day activities, both short- and long-term. Having enough money allows us to have more security and freedom. It's safe to say that the amount of money we have can dictate our lifestyle.

It's also true that money, at times, can have negative effects on people, but it largely depends on their actions. In fact, our actions regarding the money we collect are crucial; whether it is how we spend it, save it, or invest it, these actions have an impact on our lives. The store value of money is crucial, allowing us to keep it and use it later on. This ability allows people and businesses to plan for the future, such as retirement, purchasing a property, or buying a car. Money can also be used as a medium to account for and give value to services and goods. If a pair of shoes costs $100, this is money being used as a unit of account to allow us to understand the value of the pair of shoes compared to other things. It's extremely easy for us to compare different items and services and make financial decisions.

Besides that, money can also be used in more complex contexts, such as a vital part of financial markets or financial institutions such as banks. In the case of banks, their business is solely based on money, especially the loan and the store of money, while investors use the money to purchase financial instruments such as bonds or stocks.

Money allows us to pay for the most basic things, such as healthcare, food, and housing. But it can also be a source of stress, happiness, status, or power. Whether we like it or not, even though we often hear that money is not everything (and it certainly isn't), it's a crucial part of our lives and our society, and without it, the world would be a completely different place.

Moreover, money can also have an impact on emotional, mental, and even physical well-being. This often stems from a lack of it rather than an abundance. Stress-related money issues can come from difficulties in paying bills or providing basic needs to us or our families, which can lead to anxiety, stress, and even depression. The constant pursuit of money can have an effect on our happiness, even if we have enough of it. It comes down to a never-ending cycle of permanent desire and chasing material things. And so having a good balance between what we want and what we have is essential for our own health. At the end of the day, money is simply a tool; it can't buy happiness or fulfillment, and it can only fulfill these momentarily. While the scope of this book is about money and all the things we can accomplish with it, it's important to understand that there's more to life.

How to Develop a Healthy Money Mindset and Set Up Your Financial Goals

Now that this is out of the way let's get down to what this book is about. Developing a healthy money mindset and setting financial goals is the first step to understanding money and being able to manage it.

Did you know that one in five people says they are overwhelmed by debt? This is according to a survey done by the Money Advice Service, which can have a negative impact on people's health. This comes from the constant worry that occupies our minds, which in turn can inflate the issue, making it look like it's impossible to resolve (FarmWell, n.d.). Ignoring the problem is probably our first reaction. I know it was mine before I learned the hard way that we shouldn't simply ignore these issues, as oftentimes, they simply don't go away and come back way worse than before. As hard as it might seem, we need to look the problem in the eye and try to understand what we can do to overcome it. What are the steps that you need to take to make this problem go away? Everybody's different, and so we have different issues, but by developing a healthy money mindset, you become a lot less scared of these problems, and you will have a clear head on what you need to do next.

Some of the most common barriers when it comes to developing this mindset are how to properly manage money. This can stem from a lack of knowledge, a lack of confidence, or even debt. Although all of these can be worked out. One other problem when establishing a healthy money mindset is the too-often limiting thought about money and finance in general. The problem here is that these thoughts often limit the things we can do. You might not even realize it, but things such as "I don't make enough money to be able to save" or "I will never be able to get out of debt." Even if you don't actively think about them, they live in your subconscious. You need to get rid of these limitations, or you will never be able to develop a healthy money mindset. The first thing you have to do is identify when these thoughts come and push them back. This might take a little getting used to because we've been living with these thoughts for a while, and it's hard to break the habit, but when you feel them coming, try to hold them by looking at the evidence. For instance, how is it even possible that you will never be out of debt? It doesn't make sense, especially if you have a plan to pay off that debt. Looking at the real evidence in these cases, you'll find that many limitations are quite absurd. The most important aspect of developing a healthy money mindset is to have control. If you feel overwhelmed or out of control, then you feel more stressed.

In the following section, I will talk about many different techniques, such as setting financial goals and others that will make you more open to the development of your healthy mindset. One that I tend to recommend is to make a plan and create a budget. There are many different tools that can help you do that, and you can even find free templates online. But tools like apps will do most of the work for you and help you take control of your finances. Sometimes simply talking to someone can help you manage your financial stress too. Most of us try to keep everything for ourselves, which is often not a great solution. Communicating with someone that you trust can have a calming effect on you and put things into better perspective. Taking inventory of your finances might be a boring job to do, but it can really help you understand where your money is going and get control over your finances. Again, there are many different tools and apps that can help you track your expenses automatically, such as Mint, Personal Capital, or PocketGuard.

Steps to Develop a Healthy Money Mindset

One of the hardest things someone has to overcome when developing a healthy mindset is forgiving their past financial mistakes. It's way too easy to get hung up on the mistakes we've made and constantly think about what we should have done instead. But the past is the past, and there's nothing we can do to change it. We need to stop wasting our mental focus on things that we can no longer control and focus on the things we can, such as future financial decisions. Focus your money decisions on things that you can control and not on things of the past. Your success is ahead of you.

It's also important to be able to identify the emotions you usually have when it comes to money. This way, you can try to change that emotional state as well as the thoughts that might trigger those negative emotions. A good exercise to identify these thoughts and emotions is to write down what you're feeling after each transaction for a week. At the end of the week, take a look over, and you'll find the necessary purchases and those that aren't. For instance, if you buy a pair of shoes and at the moment of purchase you believe this will bring you joy, at the end of the week, you might feel differently and know that the purchase might have been an impulse purchase. This is also a great way to understand your spending habits and how emotionally connected you are to your purchases. Don't let your purchases be guided by your emotions; think rationally when it comes to financial decisions.

We often compare ourselves to others, and it's not only in financial terms. Either way is a losing game, and it's something that we should try to steer away from. These types of comparisons are never accurate, especially because we often compare ourselves with someone who is apparently much better off than we are and that we know nothing about. This is even more abundant in our social media-filled lives, where often people just post their highlights or only the things they want you to see. Looking at social media posts, for instance, you might see someone enjoying a beach day in the Caribbean, but you don't know how much debt they might have incurred to be there or if they owe money to family or friends. Chances are you will never find out the truth because they won't post it on their social media. Now, when you do these comparisons, you know everything about you, the good and the bad, and that makes it an unfair comparison to make. Even when you compare yourself with people that you know, it's still an unfair comparison because the circumstances aren't similar, even though you might know them a little. After all, even if you realize that they are better off than you are, what do you have to gain from that? You will likely become quite discouraged with yourself, which doesn't help anyone. You should be developing a healthy mindset, which you can't do if you focus on all the negative sides of it. In order to build a healthy money mindset, you have to solely focus on yourself and on achieving your goals. What others do or don't shouldn't be on your mind.

Forming good habits, in general, is not something that will happen overnight, so you have to work on them continuously. This is exactly the same when trying to form good financial habits. You should take some time to do your budget every week, or at least every month, and go over the bills and your spending habits too. This is the only way you will be able to find out what can be improved. Avoiding doing this is probably the worst thing you can do because if there are any problems, they won't go away anyway. Make sure you create good financial habits and work on them, such as making a budget. These habits are the foundation of your personal finances today and in the future.

However, when creating a budget, don't restrain yourself too much, at least not at the beginning. You have to create one that brings you happiness and that you're comfortable with. This often means not restricting yourself from enjoying life. Although you might have to limit this. For instance, instead of dining out every day, you might have to cut it back to twice a week. However, all budgets are different, and we are going through the different budget strategies in the chapter dedicated to budgeting later in the book.

Setting Financial Goals

While the way you set financial goals will differ as you grow, there's always a structure that you might want to follow. For instance, if you're just starting out, your main concern should be focusing on quick wins so you get the feel for it and understand that financial goals are indeed attainable. Starting slowly is important to keep your motivation levels high and pursue other, more ambitious goals. When starting anything, sometimes we have the fear of failing, which often prevents us from reaching certain goals. However, if you're not going to try, you will certainly not accomplish anything at all. For instance, while saving $1000 might seem like a daunting goal, it's much easier to save $200 or $300, and this is where you should start. This will also help you steer away from procrastination and continue to set more goals as the current ones get accomplished.

Having the freedom to set your own goals is great, but you also need to understand the costs and benefits of the goals you want to set. For instance, if you want to take a summer course that will cost you money, how will taking that course benefit you in the long run? Are you going to be able to improve your financial situation because of that course? If so, it's certainly a good investment. Also, it's important to remember that not all costs are monetary; some of them take up some of your time. You have to consider all of the pros and cons associated with those.

Financial goals come in three distinct lengths: short, medium, and long. To determine the length of your goals, you have to look at the cost of the goal, or how much you will have to save, the resources you have to use, and your motivations, since the higher the motivation, the more likely you are to accomplish your goals. But, as a rule of thumb, a short-term financial goal is anything that takes a maximum of a month to accomplish, a medium-term goal is anything between one and three months, and a long-term goal is anything over three months. When setting your goals, it's important that you have a mix of these three so you always have something to look forward to and keep you motivated, but I will develop this in the chapter about budgeting.

Understanding money is the first step to acquiring the necessary skills that will help you as you go from your teenage years into your young adult years, and you will have to rely more on how you manage your money. As we've seen, money is an integral part of everybody's lives, and so making the right decisions is absolutely essential for you to continue to prosper financially. For that, starting with developing a healthy money mindset and understanding how to set attainable financial goals is essential.

In the following chapter, I'll go through the different ways you can start making money and how you can develop skills that will be useful to you later on in your career.

CHAPTER 2
MAKING MONEY

> *Opportunity is missed by most people because it is dressed in overalls and looks like work.*
>
> —Thomas Edison

Now we get to the good part: how can you make money as a teenager? Well, I can tell you right away that there are many different options you can take, and I'm certain you will find some that you will be happy with.

The Different Ways You Can Make Money

Usually, there are three types of work you can do to earn money as a teenager: part-time jobs, freelancing, or entrepreneurship. You might wonder what exactly the difference is between freelancing and entrepreneurship, and while there are definitely some similarities, there are some crucial differences. I believe the main difference between these two is that a freelancer is hired to work or do some tasks by other companies, while entrepreneurs create companies and manage them. While entrepreneurs come up with an idea and develop it into a business model, freelancers give more value to their skills and try to hone them as best they can. While entrepreneurs can sell products and services behind a business to customers, freelancers sell their services and skills to other businesses. Let's delve into it a little more.

Part-Time Jobs

While you're under the age of 18, you can't apply for every single job, but there's quite a lot to choose from, especially if you're looking for a part-time job. Whether you want to work after school, during the weekends, or throughout the summer, I'm going to give you some of the most common part-time jobs you are allowed to do.

For example, babysitting is a very common job for teenagers. I understand it's not for everyone since you might not have the patience to take care of younger kids, but either way, this is a very well-paid job. I'm sure you're familiar with what the job requires you to do, such as looking after young children while their parents are away. To apply for these jobs, while it is not strictly necessary, I always recommend having first aid training because little accidents happen, especially with kids, and you want to make sure you have that covered. If you have a younger sibling, then I'm sure you have some experience taking care of kids; if not, you don't have any previous references to give. I suggest you go around the neighborhoods to find families that you know and talk to them to understand if they would be interested in getting a babysitter.

A sales assistant, sometimes called a sales associate or a shop assistant, is also a job that many teenagers can do, and the advantage of these types of jobs is that you can choose to work in many different industries. Maybe you're interested in fashion, and so working in a clothes shop might be an interesting experience for you, or maybe a video game shop or a pet shop. The options are many, and that's the beauty of being a shop assistant. There's usually some manual work alongside customer service, but it gives you a lot of great experience interacting with people, and it's usually a lot of fun. Many businesses in the retail industry staff teenagers, so you might also find interesting people your age. If you like to interact with customers, then becoming a shop assistant can be something that you will really enjoy.

Barista is another great first job if you want to earn some money. If you already know how to make any type of coffee, that's great, but in most coffee shops, that's not a requirement, and it's a skill you might be able to learn within a week or two. However, the most important skill to have as a barista is your customer service skills. If you are a natural at talking to people and are cheerful, you will love working as a barista. Most of those places also give you some training if you're not proficient at talking to people but want to learn how to interact and be skilled at customer service.

If you enjoy working outdoors, then perhaps you might want to find a part-time job as a gardener. Now, there are many different things to learn when you become a gardener, but as a teenager starting your first job, you won't need to know everything professional gardeners do, plus, you are likely to work with a more experienced gardener, so you can learn. There are also easy gardening jobs that you can do, such as trimming edges, mowing lawns, clipping bushes, watering, or planting. Again, perhaps the easiest way to start making money as a gardener is to go around your neighborhood and ask if they need a gardener for small jobs. While your parents might already have some of the most basic tools, as you progress and continue to do the job, you might want to add a few more tools or upgrade the ones you use to make your job easier.

Being a fast food worker is a very cliche job for a teenager, but it's an easy one to find, and you can make great money even working part-time. Now, most employees in these types of jobs have to be on their feet all day, and that's perhaps the hardest part of the job. But if you can do it, fast food restaurants tend to have very flexible hours that you can accommodate with the other things that you do throughout your day.

If you love animals, dog walking might be the right job for you. In fact, it may not even feel like a job at all. It's quite a popular job for teenagers who like the outdoors and feel confident around dogs. Many dog owners simply don't have the time to walk their pets, but they deeply care about them and have no problem spending money to give their furry friends the best treatment. For you, it all comes down to establishing some good clients, and you can even walk more than one dog, which will increase your income exponentially. This is also a job that is quite flexible, so you can manage your time better.

In recent years, the food delivery industry changed its way of delivering, which allowed teenagers who didn't yet have a full driver's license to do the job by riding bicycles or mopeds. This type of transportation is more evident in large cities with a lot of traffic, where bike couriers have become the norm. While earning money, you might also get a chance to exercise if you ride a bicycle. The amount of money you can make in these jobs is dependent on the number of hours, of course, but also on how efficient you are in quickly getting the food to the customers, where you are then rated. If you do a great job, you are more likely to get tips, which increase your income.

Nowadays, there are many car drivers who use an automatic car wash to clean their cars, but there's still money to be made as a car washer if you do it by hand. This is especially true in smaller cities, where many don't have access to automatic car washers. Alternatively, you can work in these places as a car wash attendant, where you don't have to wash the cars but are there to collect the money and do other smaller tasks when needed.

A quick search online will show you many other options when it comes to looking for part-time jobs; these are far from being the only ones out there. Try to search for things that interest you and that you know you will enjoy doing. Try job search platforms such as Indeed, Glassdoor, FlexJobs, LinkedIn, or Getwork to see who's looking.

Freelancing Jobs

There are a lot of different jobs you can do when it comes to freelancing, but before we get into them, freelancing requires you to take care of how you're going to get paid and to set your own prices. Besides that, because you are your own employer, you need to be far more organized in how you do things. For instance, you need to keep track of the things you need to do, such as tasks and responsibilities, that will help you become more successful at what you do. Freelancing jobs are the most flexible type of work you can find because you can literally work whenever you want or can. However, many of us, especially throughout our teenage years, are far from organized, but you don't have to worry because this is a skill that can be learned and will be very useful for you in the future. There are many tools that you can use, such as online calendars, other tracking apps, and to-do lists. For example, Google Calendar, TimeFree, and Timepage are excellent calendar apps. When it comes to tracking and to-do list applications, some of the best ones out there are Google Tasks, Things 3, or Todolist. Whatever you choose to use, what is important is that you keep everything in order so you know what tasks you should be doing.

Creating an online portfolio is crucial to bringing in clients, and this is not only for visual artists. These are important for any type of freelancing job, from writers to voice actors or transcriptionists. Your potential clients want to know what your level of skill is before hiring you, and this is the only way for them to know. You will also need to know how you're getting paid, and this is something that should be done before you accept your first job. While some jobs might pay directly to your bank account, this method of payment is not very common in freelancing. Usually, online services such as PayPal or Payoneer are far more common and secure to use. You also need to discuss this with the client beforehand to understand the best way for them to pay you. When it comes to actually getting paid, don't deliver any work until at least some of the payment has been transferred to you. The best way to do this and to ensure that no one gets scammed is by getting paid in two tranches: one before the start of the work and one at the end.

Becoming great at marketing is also important because you will find that there's quite some competition, so it's crucial that you understand your target market and spend some time creating your marketing plan. However, nowadays, it has become a lot easier to do this through social media platforms and your dedicated website.

Now, onto the most common freelancing jobs for you. Online tutoring is a great job if you're interested in pursuing any academic field and like to teach. Obviously, you need to teach grades below yours, or if you know a foreign language, you might find yourself getting a great income. Some of the most sought-after subjects are mathematics and science, such as physics or chemistry. When doing this type of work, you need to be extremely organized and have excellent communication skills. Of course, you don't have to be a master at it, but you need to want to learn and become better at it.

Digital artistry is also a job where you can earn a great income, but you need to have a particular skill and be interested in the genre. If you like to create anything through the digital medium, you can sell your art online. Alternatively, you can also work as a digital artist through an agency, but here, you're more likely to have to create art that clients require instead of creating your own and selling it. The requirements for this job differ depending on the type of digital art you want to create, but being good at drawing and understanding at least the basics of animation software can go a long way in this field.

Freelance writing is a job for those who are quite creative with written content, and it's perhaps one of the freelancing jobs where you have the most subgenres to choose from. You can become a ghostwriter, a social media writer, write commercial slogans, etc. There are many different types of writing to choose from. It requires you to have a great knowledge of the written word as well as grammar, and if you want to increase your income, you might want to specialize in a certain industry, such as finance or business.

A virtual assistant, often simply called VA, is a job where you work directly with clients and help them with their daily routine, such as answering emails, doing online research, or keeping track of their meetings and deadlines. Like freelance writing, you can work in many different industries and pick the one that interests you more. You have to be extremely organized since it's a big part of your job, but you also have to be proficient at working with a computer and have great communication skills.

Voice acting is not for everyone, but it's certainly a great job to do if you like it and can. Often, these jobs require you to record readings, such as from a book or other texts, or be a voice actor. However, you might need to purchase some equipment beforehand, such as a microphone or recording software, so you can record your material at home.

If you love video games, you can become a game tester, and it won't even feel like work! Basically, the job is to test new video games to find bugs, typos, or any other type of error before the game comes out to the public. Depending on the platform the games are on, you might have to have that specific platform to test the game, but the majority of these might be done on a computer. A great ability to write reports and good attention to detail are essential for these types of jobs.

Transcriptionists are a common job in the freelancing world, and it often consists of listening to a recording and writing it down. You might also have to proofread your written text or simplify the transcribed text. Much like freelance writing, you need to have a good grasp of the written language.

Regardless of what you want to do as a freelancer, creating accounts on some freelancing platforms is always a great idea, especially if you want to start building your portfolio. For instance, Upwork, 99Designs, ZipRecruiter, or Toptal are great places to start. Again, quick online searches will point you to many other reputable websites and sources on how you can get started.

Entrepreneurship Jobs

Perhaps you want to not only have control over your hours but also start your own business, grow it, and eventually do it full-time (or not). Coming up with your own business allows you to develop different types of skills that freelancing or working part-time doesn't, but you also have quite a few more responsibilities. Obviously, the first thing you have to do is choose what you want to do, such as the industry and the company you want to create.

One of the things many teenagers have, even when they might not have a lot of experience, is knowledge of technology and the online world. And this is certainly something that you can take advantage of since you probably understand the current trends and what people will be willing to use or buy. So, becoming an online marketer might be where your knowledge of the online world and entrepreneurship align. Couple your internet and online knowledge with your social media knowledge, and you can establish your own online marketing company.

Your creativity doesn't have to be bound to digital art; in fact, you can make it big through custom crafts if that's what you like to do. It's quite frequent to see teenagers and others selling things on Etsy; however, you don't have to only sell that, and you shouldn't if you want your business to grow. These crafts can be anything, really, from jewelry to decorations or anything in between, depending on what you want to do. The start is the hardest part, but you can do it by selling your crafts to family and friends and advertising them online.

If you want to run a business in a physical place (as opposed to being at home), something like being a snow cone shop owner might be interesting for you. This is actually one of the easiest ways to start your entrepreneurial career. There are a lot of things that you need to think about, such as what kind of storefront you'd like or what you want it to look like.

If you've washed cars before and want to continue in the same industry, perhaps automotive detailers are exactly what you are looking for. If you think that you don't have the necessary experience, you can start working in the detailing business in another company, but many, after getting the necessary experience, prefer to start their own mobile detailing company.

If you're really great with computers and you believe you have an excellent idea and know how to program, then starting your own tech business might be the single best thing you'll do. Many tech giants started this way, and you can even start working for other tech companies that accept teenagers, such as Vivint.

Obviously, these are just some ideas, and there are many other different things you could be doing. But one thing that I've learned is to first understand what you're good at and what you like to do, and then start from there to try and find what you are going to do.

How to Develop the Necessary Skills for Your Career Ahead?

There are many different skills you will have to learn that will have to do with your career and others that won't, but some of these that will help you progress in your career later in life are general and necessary.

For example, money and budgeting skills are essential, regardless of what career you might follow. Understanding how to make a budget and remain focused on it, how you can open a bank account, transfer money online, apply for a credit card, or write a check. Or how to maintain financial records, understand and assess basic market values, or how to save, purchase, or invest. We will go through this particular subject more in-depth later in the book.

Social skills and manners are also things that will probably help you in your career. This is how you are going to portray yourself in different social settings and will determine the impression you will have on others. Some of the things that might help you with that are learning how to make friendships and maintain them, exploring hobbies and interests, and meeting people with similar interests. Understand the value of the people in your life, and respect their views regardless of how against them you might be. Lastly, learning party etiquette, how to be a good guest, and how to host can help you meet new people and maintain those with whom you've formed a good relationship.

As I've mentioned, organizational skills will come in handy in any career you pursue, so learning as much as you can will make your life much easier. There's a great rule that I always like to mention called the rule of Kaizen, which essentially says "a place for everything and everything in its place." Besides that, there are other little things that you can do, such as declutter your space and reorganize so you know where everything is at any given time.

Communication skills are essential in any job where you have to communicate with others, which is practically all of them, at least to a certain extent. You have to get the message you want people to hear across as cleanly as you possibly can. There are many ways you can practice this, such as being aware every time you have to relay some information to someone on a daily basis. However, there are other things that you need to pay attention to, such as understanding who you are talking to. Everybody is different, and people have the most diverse temperaments, so you might have to communicate in a different manner. Being empathic and trying to understand the other person's perspective can also help you formulate the way you are speaking to them.

Behavioral skills are a way to show your character. Obviously, you build a strong personality, but you have to work on it, not simply wish for it. For instance, admitting your mistakes or taking responsibility for actions you've taken instead of hiding or blaming someone else. Apologizing when you're wrong is also important, and I understand that sometimes it is not an easy thing to do. Always being polite to anyone, regardless of who they are, or understanding the concept of morality so you can rightfully stand up for the things you believe in. Asking for help when you're in need can be a great thing to do. Many of us are too proud to ask for help, but often, that simply makes things worse.

You might also want to develop skills for coping with your emotions. We live in a stressful place where emotions often run high. Camping with these emotions can help you make better decisions or even strengthen ties with other people. For instance, chances are that when you go to college, you might experience loneliness if you leave your parents behind and go study in another city. Self-management allows you to be in control of what is going on in your head. This can be done in many different ways, but meditating or taking time for yourself to let those emotions run through you can help you get through those difficult times. It will also allow you to avoid making impulsive decisions that can have negative consequences.

You will face problems in your career that you will need to solve, and here, problem-solving skills will really come in handy. While your parents might have helped you solve some of your issues, you can't expect them to continue to do that once you grow up and start taking on more responsibilities. While you will get more experience the more problems you solve, this is really a self-learning skill. The first thing you have to do is start facing your problems and stop running away from them. Then, you have to identify the problem correctly so you can start looking for solutions. It's crucial that you analyze the different solutions you've come up with and understand the different outcomes. When you've gone through all of that, you can apply the solution with the best outcome.

Goal setting is essentially understanding how to prioritize the things you have to do. Understand where you want to go and come up with a plan to do it. Here, it's also important that you identify the resources that can help you achieve the goals you've set, and at times, you might even have to change or adjust your goals to suit your needs. The main thing here is to focus on the ultimate goal and devise a plan with smaller goals to get there.

Do you perhaps think that you don't have time to do everything you'd like to? While you might be very busy, there's a chance that your time management is not developed enough to carry out all the tasks you have. There are only 24 hours in which you can try and fit everything you have to do in, and having great time management skills can really help you do that. Using a calendar, a timetable, or even a planner where you can write down all the things you need to do throughout the day is a simple way to keep tabs on everything you have to do. You also have to become good at scheduling and sticking to the things you plan because if you take a little longer on certain things, your time might not be enough to go through everything. Here, it's also relevant that you learn how to prioritize certain tasks over others since some of the things that you might have scheduled might be more urgent or time-pressing. The most important thing, however, is to develop routines so it becomes easier for you to manage your time.

Lastly, another set of skills that will help you in your career are employability skills. These encompass some of the sets of skills I've already mentioned, such as communication, decision-making, and critical thinking. But others, such as work ethic, adaptability, leadership, or teamwork, will make you more likely to be employed in better positions.

As you can see, there are a myriad of jobs that you can take on, depending on what interests you. I've taken on my share of different jobs throughout my teenage years so I could have a solid base of different skills to work with in the future. Obviously, you don't have to work in every industry, but trying out different types of work, such as freelancing, part-time work, or entrepreneurship, might be helpful to learn skills that will stay with you for life. Besides that, you will also have to develop some other skills that you might learn by working and getting experience, but also by practicing them. These are crucial not only to increase your employment rate but also if you want to choose an entrepreneurial path to becoming a great boss.

A Few Words About Taxes

Taxes are mandatory payments to the government and are paid not only by individuals like you and me but also by businesses and corporations. These are used to fund government activities such as services or public works like schools or roads, but also to fund governmental organizations and other programs such as Social Security. Essentially, the taxes that we all pay serve as income for the government to pay for the most varied things. Income taxes are what most individuals pay, and they are automatically taken out of your monthly income, which you can see in your pay stub. But another common tax we pay is capital gains, which are taken out of any interest received from our investments, such as dividends. It's a crime to try and avoid taxes, and it's called tax evasion. However, there are certain things that an individual can do to alleviate the tax burden within the laws, and that's called tax avoidance. Governments use an agency to collect these taxes. For example, in the US, this is called the Internal Revenue Service, or IRS. What you pay in taxes is usually proportional to what you earn, so the more you earn, the more you pay.

While if you work for a company, you don't have to do anything to pay taxes since the company's account does everything for you, and the taxes are taken directly from your pay stub if you are self-employed, then you have to do your own taxes. There are many ways to do this, and many different third-party companies that can help you do this easily, such as TurboTax. However, if you think you can file it yourself, you can go to the IRS website and do it for free. This is for the US; of course, other countries have other entities that collect taxes. For instance, in the UK, it's HMRC. The process is the same; you can do it yourself, which takes some time, or you can find a company that simplifies the process for you. Every other country works more or less the same way; you just need to look for the entity that collects taxes in that specific country. If you need help on how to actually file the forms in the US, you can use the USA.gov website, where they tell you exactly what forms you have to file and how to do it. Every tax collector's website should also have a step-by-step guide on how to file the tax and fill out the form for that specific country.

In the next chapter, I will go through the financial part of things, such as how to open a bank account, what the different bank accounts are and their main functionalities, and many other things that will be useful for you to make the right decisions.

CHAPTER 3

BANKING AND FINANCIAL SERVICES

> *A big part of financial freedom is having your heart and mind free from worry about the what-ifs of life.*
>
> –Suze Orman

Understanding how the banking system works is fundamental to your money skills. There's no other way around it than to open a bank account and be able to manage it. It's actually quite easy, and many teenagers already have some sort of bank account opened by their parents. If you don't, it's alright; simply follow the steps I'll list below.

Opening Your First Bank Account

To open a bank account, first, you need to choose a bank to open with and give them some of your information. If you're under the age of 18, you might need your parents to open it for you, but you will still have access to it. However, there are also teen bank accounts, which are similar to other accounts with only a few features missing. For example, you can't have an overdraft or a credit card, and if you're over 16, you won't need a guardian or a parent to open it for you. Besides that, you can do everything you want with the account, such as setting up direct debits, making bank transfers, etc. However, to register a debit card yourself, you also need to be over 16 years old; otherwise, a parent or guardian will have to authorize it first.

Whether or not you need a parent or guardian to open an account, there's information that needs to be passed on to the bank, such as proof of address, contact information, and proof of identity, which can be a birth certificate, passport, or a driver's license if you already have one. If you have opened a teen bank account, once you turn 18 years old, it usually turns into an adult account right away so you can have all the features that were currently missing, but sometimes the bank provider might request that you authorize this change.

While I'll be talking about the different accounts you can apply for later in this chapter, when you're opening your first bank account, there are a few things that you need to take into account. For example, some bank providers have a minimum opening amount, which means that you need to add some money right away to the account when you open it. The amount differs, and it could be as little as $1, but you need to make sure what the minimum opening amount is before you apply for one. Another thing that you have to take into consideration is the monthly fee. While these often don't happen on teens' accounts, they might once you turn 18. Interest is also something worth checking because the money you have in your account grows depending on the interest rate; however, in regular checking accounts, there's usually no interest rate (we will talk more about this later on in the chapter). Some accounts (especially teen accounts) have limits such as withdrawals or spending limits, so you can't use more money if you reach a certain amount. While it might be a little annoying, it's a great way for you to learn how to handle and manage your money properly. Lastly, when thinking of opening a bank account, make sure it has a robust online banking app where you can track everything from your phone as well as make bank transfers. This makes things a lot easier.

The Different Types of Bank Accounts

There are a few different types of accounts that you can open; however, as a teenager, you can only open a checking account. Besides that, other bank accounts include savings, money market accounts (MMAs), and certificate of deposit accounts (CDs). Understanding the differences is crucial so you can make better decisions.

Checking Accounts

These types of accounts are the most basic ones and are essentially deposit accounts that you can first open. You can hold funds, transfer them, withdraw money at ATMs, or use paper checks. These can also be linked to other accounts (usually through the same bank institutions), such as savings accounts. Banking institutions have many different types of checking accounts, such as teen checking, student, senior, rewards, or interest (since the basic checking account doesn't have interest associated with it). But to start with, a basic checking account is fine as long as you understand the minimum deposit requirements (if any), the minimum balance requirements (if any), if there are monthly maintenance fees, if there are ATM fees, and the ATM network size (this allows you to know how many ATMs you can withdraw money from).

Setting up an account is easy. As a teen, you might need a parent or guardian to do it, but usually, you can do it online or by visiting a branch, and the process is usually immediate. Obviously, you will have to provide some important and personal information, such as an ID and Social Security number. Depositing cash can usually be done through a check or cash, and you will get a debit card linked to that account that you can use to pay for things or withdraw money. Like in many other accounts, your funds are protected up to $250,000 by the Federal Deposit Insurance Corporation or FDIC. This means that if there's any error by your bank or something happens to your money while it's in your bank account, you are covered as long as it's below the threshold. You can usually opt to have an overdraft or not in your account. I personally don't recommend it since this allows for debts where the fees are quite high. Besides allowing you to use an ATM and debit cards, other services used with a checking account include wire transfer, which is essentially moving money from one account to another electronically, or direct deposit, where, say, your employer pays your income directly into your account, which becomes immediately available to you.

Savings Account

The main difference between savings and checking accounts is that with savings, you have an interest rate, which means that for as long as you hold money in the account, the amount is increasing. In other words, the savings account pays you interest on the amount of the deposit you have in the account. All the things that you have to check when opening a checking account, such as the minimum balance, etc., are also relevant when you open a savings account. But while checking accounts usually allow you limitless withdrawals, savings accounts don't because they are not designed for everyday use. They also usually don't have a debit card, which is usually linked to your checking account, so any transfers are usually conducted from there.

These accounts are created to hold your money there and withdraw from it as little as possible because, as I've mentioned, the interest you earn is based on the money you have deposited there. The more money you have there, the more you earn in interest. But the most important thing to look for when opening a savings account is the annual percentage yield (APY), which is essentially the percentage you earn on the money deposited. The higher the APY, the more you earn. Every bank offers different percentages, and while you might think the higher, the better, these high-yield savings often have more conditions that you need to abide by, for instance, fewer withdrawals, withdrawals that take longer, or higher maintenance fees. If you want to have a savings account but don't want to have limited withdrawals, you can choose an easy-access savings account that allows you to withdraw money whenever you want, but these usually have a lower APY. It really all comes down to your needs. If you think you won't need the money, it's best to place it in a high-interest savings account; if not, it might be best to deposit it in a lower-interest account where you have easier access to your money.

There are other accounts that I will just briefly mention, such as a money market account (MMA) or a certificate of deposit account (CDs). MMAs can be seen as a mix of checking and savings accounts where you can deposit money in them, earn interest, have a debit card, and even have paper checks. However, with these accounts, you still have a withdrawal limit, but you can set up direct debits. Some of the main differences with these accounts include, for instance, a higher minimum balance requirement if you want to keep the account open. These are great when you want to earn interest but still want all the convenient features a checking account has to offer, such as the use of a debit card. CDs are time deposit accounts, which means that these mostly work as savings accounts where you leave your money there for a certain amount of time, which in the financial world is called "maturity term." During the maturity term, your money is increasing, or you're earning interest on the balance you have there.

When looking to open a bank account, it's also important that you not only look at the different brick-and-mortar bank providers but also at credit unions and online banks. Credit unions are customer-owned institutions that have many of the same services a big bank has and may even offer you better interest rates (although not always), mainly because they are non-profit organizations. Online banks often offer fewer fees because they don't have branches that they have to pay for, which means they might offer you better rates as well. However, because they don't have physical branches, all contact with the bank is done online through a computer or mobile phone.

To sum up the steps of opening a bank account, first, you need to choose how to apply (whether in branch, online, or through the phone), gather all the necessary information, such as your Social Security Number, ID, and proof of address, provide contact details, select the type of account you want, read and accept the terms and conditions, submit the application, and fund your account.

Managing Your Account

Usually, when you open any type of bank account, you will have to sign a document (usually the terms and conditions, which you have to read thoroughly). While sometimes you might have to sign and mail the documents, more often, you can sign the documents online before you can start using the account.

Checking and savings accounts need to be funded before you can start using them, which can be done in different ways, such as by depositing cash, depositing a check (which usually takes a couple of business days to reach your account), setting up a direct debit from your employer, which is nowadays the most common way to get your income, or transferring funds electronically from another bank account that you might already have.

After that, if you're expecting a debit card, this should arrive at your address in a couple of days. From then on, you can pay bills online, make remote check deposits, and even sign up for alerts on your phone or email when your balance is low or when you withdraw money. Apart from that, the only thing that you should keep an eye on is your balance to see if there are fees incurred or if you need a minimum balance on the account.

Using Online Baking

Online banking, also known as internet banking, allows you to do pretty much everything banking-related online as opposed to going to a banking branch, which might include deposits, payment of online bills, or transfers. Nowadays, every banking institution has online banking in one way or another, where you can access your account through the banking app or through your computer. This makes things a lot easier, especially if you're quite proficient with new technology, and it saves you plenty of time. It's also a lot more convenient because it allows you to make transactions or pay bills anywhere you are, simply from your phone or computer, and all you need is one of those devices connected to the internet. Some financial institutions even allow you to open savings accounts and other accounts linked to your main account online, as well as set up direct debits or report changes in your account.

This advance in technology allowed us to have online-exclusive banks, which offer much lower costs or free banking features and better gains in terms of interest. And even though they don't have branches or ATMs of their own, you are still able to withdraw money from your online bank accounts from any other bank ATMs, so there's little change for you here if you decide to go for an online-only bank.

Advantages and Disadvantages of Online Banking

As I've mentioned above, convenience is certainly the best advantage of online banking, and you can perform the most common things from the comfort of your home on your phone or laptop. Transactions are extremely efficient, can be done almost instantly, and can open and close accounts just as easily. Besides that, you also have a lot of options when it comes to the different types of accounts to open, from high- or low-interest savings accounts to fixed deposits, etc.

Monitoring your finances also became a lot easier since you don't have to go to the nearest ATM or branch to check your funds and can simply do it anywhere on any device. Because of this, you have access to your account 24/7, which wasn't always the case when you had to wait for bank branches to open in the morning.

While I believe online banking makes banking accessible for everyone, including people who are just starting out in the financial world, it also comes with some disadvantages that you need to be aware of. In this case, the disadvantages I'll be listing target online-only banking institutions. For instance, if you are a new banking customer, not having someone to talk to face-to-face might be a little daunting at first, and customer service is only available over the phone or through chat. Online banking depends entirely on access to the internet, and if for any reason you don't have it, you become quite limited. Lastly, while online banking security is constantly improving, accounts are still subjected to hacking, but this refers to any type of online banking, even those belonging to brick-and-mortar banks.

Staying Safe With Online Banking

As I've said, online banking security is constantly improving, and it's quite secure, but it's still susceptible to hacking and other scams if you don't pay attention. There are a few things that you can do to make your accounts more secure and prevent your information from falling into a hacker's hands. One of the easiest things you can do is choose a strong password, as you'd normally do with any other online account. You can also enable two-factor authentication or, if you're on your phone, face identification, which allows you to only access the banking app after your face is scanned.

Alternatively, you can also sign up for banking alerts, so if there are any strange movements in your account, you will be notified right away, and you can then contact your bank to know more or to freeze your account. Steering away from public Wi-Fi connections is also a good way to prevent your information from spreading to other people. Use only private or well-secured Wi-Fi connections. Hackers can get your information through malicious hotspots, through malware and spyware on the Wi-Fi, or through data transmissions over unencrypted networks.

Other than that, simply pay attention to any phishing scams so you don't give your personal information away. There are many different ways these scams operate, but they all have the same finality: you giving your information away. This can be in the form of SMS texts or emails that usually look like they come from your bank. However, they often urge you to insert personal information on the website or to change your information and then redirect you to a website that often looks like your bank. Paying attention to the sender's email address is important, and you can check if that's actually your bank's email address. Alternatively, you can call your bank and ask them if they've sent an email from that email address. Hovering over the links on an email sent to you often allows you to see the webpage it is addressing you to. And lastly, your bank almost never asks you to share your personal information. When in doubt, contact your bank to make sure before you share any personal information.

Understanding Bank Cards, ATMs, and Fees

There's quite a lot more to know when it comes to all these financial services and products than you might think. Things like debit and credit cards might sound and look like the same thing, but they can be very different. The same goes for all the different fees these services and products might charge. So, let's go through all the most important things you need to know to use them with confidence.

Credit Cards vs. Debit Cards

When you look at both a debit and a credit card, there's not much difference, right? They have 16-digit numbers on them, as well as expiration dates, magnetic strips, etc. You can use both in the same way and use them to purchase things, but this is where things get a little different. When making purchases, a debit card draws money that you have in your bank account, while credit cards draw borrowed money from your bank and have a limit. So, in other words, a debit card uses your money, and a credit card uses the bank's money that you will need to pay back eventually. This is not to say that credit cards are bad; they are not. The way you use it might have negative implications for your finances. A credit card offers you security, but you need to know how to use it. Let's get down to it.

Credit Cards

As I've mentioned, a credit card is usually issued by a financial institution where you already have an account. The institution allows you to borrow money from them with the condition that you pay them back with interest, so you will always pay them back more than what you've spent. However, there are many different types of credit cards that might offer you different perks.

Regular credit cards are easy to understand, allow you to pay with borrowed money, make balance transfers, and are usually free (meaning no annual fees). Premium credit cards often have perks for their customers, such as access to special events, airport lounge access, and other things, but they incur an annual fee. Then, there are the specific rewards credit cards that give you travel points, which give you discounted airline tickets, cash back, and other rewards. Balance transfer credit cards usually have extremely low-interest rates as well as low fees from another credit card's balance transfer. Secured credit cards are for those people who can't get standard or any other type of credit card, and they have to pay an initial deposit as collateral to be able to use a credit card. Lastly, there are charge credit cards that do not have a limit, but usually, you'd have to pay the balance within a month before you could use them again.

There are quite a few benefits to using a credit card besides the security and rewards it gives you. For example, they help you build your credit history, which appears on your credit reports. Credit reports are important documents that allow banks and other financial institutions to check if you're financially trustworthy when you're asking for loans or a mortgage for your property. Credit cards help you build a stronger credit report because they show if you have been paying your credit card back on time, for instance. If you use your credit card properly, you can raise your credit score, get higher chances of getting accepted for loans, and get lower interest rates on those loans.

Most credit cards also allow purchase protections and warranties on items that you purchase, besides whatever retail warranty the company producing the item gives you. For instance, if you buy a TV with your credit card, you usually have a warranty that lasts a year or two, but if the TV stops working after the retail company's warranty, you can check if your credit card offers an extended warranty and has you covered. Some credit cards might also offer price protection, which allows you to replace any item that might have been lost or stolen or even get a refund.

Credit cards also have fraud protection in case of theft or loss, and if you report it in a timely manner, this is not exclusive to credit cards and debit cards. The Electronic Fund Transfer Act can give you the same protection, but again, you have to report it within 48 hours of finding out you've lost your card. But with a credit card, you are far more protected. For example, you can dispute an unauthorized purchase if the goods are lost during shipping or are delivered damaged under the Fair Credit Billing Act. If you have bought goods that have been lost or damaged during shipping with a debit card, you can only get a refund if the merchant wants it. Another example of credit cards being more secure is if you were to rent a car. Many credit card providers (but not all) allow a waiver for any collisions you might have.

But of course, there are cons when it comes to using credit cards, and you've probably heard some of them. For instance, the unhealthy use of credit cards can lead to large debts. As I've mentioned, when you're using a credit card, you're not using your money but the bank's money, which you will have to pay back with interest at some point. You have to at least pay the minimum payment every single month, but the more you spend, the harder it becomes to pay at least those minimum payments. Plus, you should only pay the absolute minimum if you can't pay more because if you keep on paying the minimum, you will never finish paying your debt because of the rise in interest rates.

If you fail to make the minimum payments, that will have a negative impact on your credit score, but keeping the balance on your credit card at a low level will help your credit score. But if you do the opposite and fail to make credit card payments, max out your credit cards, or apply for too many credit cards, you will see your credit score decrease.

You can think of a credit card as a short-term loan, and these can get really high-interest rates, which are calculated using your annual percentage rate (APR). The higher the interest and APR, the more you pay in interest when you're paying back the money you've spent with your credit card. Also, keep in mind that the higher the interest, the harder it is for you to pay and the more it will cost you to pay what you owe. Besides the interest on your credit card, there are other fees that might also be applied and that you have to be aware of, such as a late payment fee, a cash advance fee, an annual fee (but not always), a balance transfer fee, or a foreign transaction fee. We will go deeper into credit later in its own dedicated chapter.

Debit Cards

As I've mentioned above, when you're paying with a debit card, you are not using anyone else's money but your own, which comes straight from your checking or savings account. With a debit card, you can only use as much money as you have deposited in the account. Like credit cards, debit cards can also offer some consumer protections, but credit cards usually offer more when it comes to fraud. While most debit cards are linked to a bank account, this is not strictly necessary. In fact, there are two types of debit cards that don't require you to have a savings or checking account: Prepaid debit cards and electronic benefits transfer (EBT) cards. The first is used by people who don't have a bank account but want to make electronic purchases and be able to use all the features a debit card allows. However, as the name indicates, you'd have to preload your card with the amount of money you'd like to have on it. So, for instance, if you wanted to have $300 in the prepaid debit card, you'd have to transfer that money first, and you cannot use more than what you've deposited. EBTs are issued by federal and state agencies, but only qualifying people can use them and have the benefits that come with them. Such benefits can include, for instance, food stamps or cash. Because these are essentially debit cards with a PIN number and a magnetic strip, they can be used in ATM machines and other point-of-sale terminals. The way it works is that once the recipient gets accepted or approved for benefits, the state they are in creates an account, and the Supplemental Nutrition Assistance Program (SNAP) benefits are placed in the account for them to use every month. By federal law, there are no processing fees or sales taxes on these purchases. These systems exist in the US, but other countries have their own that often work similarly.

When you use a debit card, you don't have the issue of incurring debt since all the money you spend with it is yours, and you don't have to pay it back to anyone. And it is known that people tend to spend more money when using a card (debit or credit) than when using cash, so if you use a debit card, you don't have the issue of racking up large debts. While credit cards still offer better fraud protection, debit cards are becoming better and better when it comes to this subject, and so they have become quite safe. As I've said, the quicker you report the missing card or any unusual activity, the better chances you have of getting the money back. There's also no annual fee on debit cards, unlike many credit cards. You also don't have a withdrawal fee with a debit card, which you do with a credit card.

Now, when it comes to the disadvantages of debit cards, they are not free from some. For instance, there are no rewards, with the exception of rewards checking accounts, but these are not as good as the perks from credit cards. Debit cards don't help you build credit like credit cards do. Essentially, when you pay back your credit card, you are telling lenders that you are financially trustworthy and that you will pay your money back. With a debit card, you don't have to pay it back, so you're not proving that you can be financially trustworthy. Lastly, even though debit cards don't have annual fees like credit cards do, you might have to pay other fees such as maintenance fees, overdraft fees, or even foreign ATM fees.

So, while credit and debit cards might look similar, their advantages and disadvantages are quite different. You need to understand your priorities when thinking about using one or the other. While it's recommended that you have both before you make a purchase, you need to understand if you want to start building your credit or getting rewards or if you prefer to have your finances totally under control. Obviously, using a bit of both might be the wisest thing you'd do, but when using your credit card, make sure you have enough money to pay your debt.

How Do You Use an ATM?

You probably know what an ATM is, and even if you've never used one before, you know it's a machine that allows you to withdraw money from your bank account. Out of curiosity, do you know what ATM stands for? I didn't for a long time after I started using it, but it stands for Automated Teller Machine, and it has many more different uses than simply withdrawing money from your bank account. It also allows you to make basic transactions without having to go to a bank and talk to a teller (hence the automatic teller). While most people use a debit card when withdrawing money, you can also use a credit card, although these usually come with a higher fee. ATMs are spread across the country and other countries and make it easier for you to use financial systems anywhere, which makes them quite convenient even nowadays, where financial services are dominated by the internet and mobile banking.

When it comes to fees, these are usually charged by the ATM operator, your bank, or both; however, if you use an ATM that is operated by your bank, these fees can be avoided. If you use an ATM in a foreign country, you are always likely to pay fees, even if they are only exchange rates.

There are two main types of ATM machines, with the most basic of the models only allowing you to check your account's balance and withdraw money. These are the most common ones seen anywhere. But there is another type that is often inside bank branches, and you hardly see them on a high street, for instance. These allow you to perform more services such as transfers, access account information, accept deposits (often cash), and aid you with a line of credit payments. Obviously, you have to have an account at that same bank to be able to use these more complex ATM machines.

Apart from that, the common design of ATM machines is pretty straightforward. There's a card reader where you insert your card, so the ATM knows your bank details. The keypad allows you to enter your PIN or the amount you want to withdraw or send; there's also a cash dispenser from where the ATM "gives" you the money. ATMs also have a printer in case you want to have a copy of the receipt of whatever service you've just performed, and of course, a screen where you can see what is happening and allow you to guide yourself through the process.

When it comes to using it, it's also quite simple. You will have to insert your bank card, and it will prompt you to type your PIN. From there, you will see on the screen some options, such as withdrawing money or checking your balance. As I've mentioned, if you don't want to be charged for any transactions, you should use the ATM operated by your bank since ATMs operated by other banks or other ATM operators will incur a fee upon transaction. This is especially important if you withdraw money quite often, which might add up at the end of the week or month. There's usually a certain amount that you can withdraw per day, week, or month, but these differ depending on your bank and bank account. While some might limit your daily withdrawal to $300, others might allow a $1500 daily withdrawal. However, if you need to withdraw more than the limit, you can usually get around this by calling your bank and asking for permission, or you can go directly to a branch and talk to a teller.

Opening your first bank account is quite exciting since it will allow you to have a little more financial freedom. It's important that you shop around and check out the best banks for your first account. This should align with the purpose of your bank account—what are you using it for, etc.? Then, you have to choose your account type, and the first one is almost always a regular checking account. In fact, you can't open a savings account without opening a checking account first. Then you have MMAs and CDs, but these can come later. Because you might be tech-savvy, you will have a much easier time managing your account through your phone via mobile or internet banking. The advance of this technology allows us to simplify how people manage their accounts, which has become fairly easy. Lastly, understanding the differences between credit and debit cards is crucial so you don't end up accumulating a lot of debt. To start with, chances are you won't need a credit card, and if you're working part-time, as a freelancer, or even as an entrepreneur but still living with your parents, I don't think you will need a credit card. However, if you do take one, make sure you understand the terms and conditions, the APR, and everything else that is involved when it comes to spending money with a credit card.

In the next chapter, I will talk about budgeting, which is oftentimes linked to your capacity to spend only the money that you have (as opposed to using credit cards). Here, I'll introduce the concept of budgeting, why it's so important, how you can create your own personal budget by tracking your income and expenses, how you can allocate funds to the different categories, how you can manage irregular income (if you're a freelancer or an entrepreneur), and talk about some of the most common strategies when it comes to budgeting.

CHAPTER 4

BUDGETING

> *A budget is more than just a series of numbers on a page; it is an embodiment of our values.*
>
> *- Barack Obama*

Budgeting is the only way we can understand if we are on the right path in terms of finances. Sure, you've heard of a budget and budgeting before, and you might even have a faint idea of what it is exactly. But having a budget is one of the most fundamental things we can do to understand how our finances work and how to be successful when it comes to money. Essentially, with a budget, you can tell where the money is coming from and where it's going, and that's the only way to get absolute control of your money. Now, if we want to get a little more technical, a budget allows you to track your income and expenses and establish a balance of what you can and can't spend throughout a month (or more).

There are several ways to create a budget with more or fewer variants, but a budget always has to have three fundamental things: it has to have an identity, which in this case is you (although there are also budgets for companies, governments, households, etc.). There has to be a defined time period, for instance, a month (businesses tend to do longer budgets). And it has to have detailed information on where the money is coming in (such as from your employer or freelancing work) and where the money is going (where you spend the money, etc.).

Let me give you an example of what the personal budget of a teenager might look like. Say you started working part-time on the weekends, and you're earning $500 a month. Because you are still living with your parents, you are not paying rent, bills, etc. But instead, you're saving a part of it, and the rest is for expenses such as a night out every week and traveling to work on the weekends. Everything else goes to savings.

	Income		Expenditures
Salary	$500	Night outs	$200
		Traveling	$20
Total (savings):	$280		

This is a pretty easy budget since you don't have to pay for groceries, bills, etc., but once you start doing that, things get a little more complex, and you will need to allocate certain amounts to certain places and not exceed them. For instance, if you wanted to save $380 instead of $280, you'd have to cut your nights out in half.

Why Should You Care About Budgeting?

Well, if I haven't convinced you yet about starting to budget, I can come up with a few more reasons as to why you should be budgeting, especially if you want to save as much as possible. First of all, starting to budget at a young age will teach you the basics of money habits and mindset that we've discussed in the previous chapter. This alone should be reason enough to convince you, but there's more.

Budgeting allows you to set and reach your long-term goals, regardless of what they are. For instance, there's this trip that your friends are planning to do, and, obviously, you want to go with them, but while you have money for the flight, you don't have enough for the accommodation. Because the trip is a year away, you might still have time to save some money to go, but I know that when you're a teenager, one year is very far away. Either way, the logic is the same. The accommodation is $1000 for five days, and using the example from above, you are saving $280 a month. This means that in about four months, you'll be able to pay for the accommodation. However, your friends are only willing to wait three months for you to book the accommodation because they say that particular place gets full rather quickly. So, you have to go back to your budget and relocate some of the money so you can save more. Looking at it, the only thing that you can really change is the nights out because you need to pay for travel if you want to continue to have an income. So, if you cut the money you spend on your night outs in half, you'd have $380 saved a month. This means that in three months, you'd have enough time to book the accommodation. Without a budget, you wouldn't know exactly where you'd have to cut and how much you could spend on certain things. It essentially forces you to plan your goals and to know exactly how much you can spend and how much you need to allocate to the different expenses and savings. You have a great overview of money coming in and money coming out, which allows you to know how much you have progressed and how far your goal is.

Budgeting can keep you from overspending, especially on money that you don't necessarily have. Assuming you have a credit card, overspending can become a really bad situation because you are spending money that is not yours, you have to pay it back, and you don't have that money. With a budget, you know exactly how much you can spend and when you should stop. As a teenager, this is easier to understand because you have fewer expenses and, most likely, don't have a credit card yet. However, this will change in the future, and you have to be prepared to plan a budget and stick to it. Before, when people used cash instead of cards, things were also simpler because the fact that you visualized money coming out of your wallet made you think about it. Nowadays, you don't see that money, and so it's easy to simply type a PIN or even touch your card (with contactless payments), and that's it; you don't think about it anymore. This is also one of the reasons budgeting is important: it can keep you in line and make sure you don't spend without thinking.

Budgeting can make your retirement savings a lot easier. I know that retirement is a long way from where you are now, and we will talk about it later in the book. But once you get there and have been budgeting all those years, you will be thankful you've done it. Budgeting doesn't only make retirement savings easier, but all savings in general. It's crucial that you build regular savings and make contributions to your retirement accounts so you don't have to worry about not having enough once you retire.

I've briefly mentioned emergency funds, which are quite necessary if, well, an emergency appears. Budgeting allows you to save, which means that it also allows you to build a financial cushion in case of an emergency. Obviously, as a teen, you might have your back covered by your parents, but as soon as you start your young adult life, you might be on your own, so you will want to save as much as you can to start your adult life and have no issues navigating it.

Budgeting can also reveal your spending habits. For instance, if we use the example above, you know you'd be spending $200 a month on nights out. That's a big chunk of your income. However, when you start your young adult life, you will have far more expenses. Things like TV or streaming subscriptions might add up and take a big chunk of your income. Without a budget, you might not even notice any of that. Only once you list all your expenses do you start to understand how much you usually spend on things that you probably shouldn't. Not only that, but it might also reveal bad spending habits such as purchasing too many clothes, unnecessary food, etc., that you might be able to stop.

How Should You Create a Personal Budget?

While budgets can be created in different ways and also depend on each person's lifestyle, there are a few steps that you can follow to make this right. The small changes you will be able to figure out as you gain more experience creating budgets.

The first step is to create your net income. This might be a new word for you, but it simply means your take-home income. So, if you're only working part-time, you probably are not paying any taxes yet. But once you move to a full-time job, some expenses, such as taxes and retirement programs, will be deducted from your pay. Usually, you don't have to worry about it, and the accountant of your employer does that. The important aspect here is finding out how much you're actually making or how much is entering your account each month. Calculating your income gets a little harder if you have an irregular income, for instance, if you are a freelancer or an entrepreneur; however, you can write down and find out how much you're making.

The next step is tracking your spending, and this is where you might find some revelations about your spending habits. First, you should list your regular spending, such as bills, mortgage, rent, etc. In the example I've used, your regular spending would be your traveling (and not your night outs!). Other things, such as utilities or car payments, are also part of your regular payments. Then, you have to list your variable expenses, and these are a little harder to find out because, well, they are irregular. Your night outs would fall into this category because even though you might spend more or less the same every time you go out, there might be times when you spend a little less or a little more. Other variable expenses would be groceries or gas. This is also the best area where you can reduce your overall expenses because most of them might not be necessary (yes, night outs are not as necessary as paying your rent). But obviously, fixed expenses can also be cut; for example, you could change your phone provider if you think you're paying too much or your energy provider. To help you find all of this information, credit and debit card statements are your best resources because you will have a detailed list of where your money came from and where it went.

When doing your budget, you need to set goals, but it's important that these goals are realistic. Before you even analyze all the information you've tracked, you should write down a list of your goals: short-, medium-, and long-term goals. In the short-term goals, things like setting up an emergency fund should be listed, as well as any other short-term goal you want to achieve, such as going on a trip with your friends. Long-term goals should be things that will take some time to achieve, such as saving for a down payment on a property or retirement. Of course, these goals can change over time, which will change the way you set up your budget, but what's important is that you have them so you can keep yourself motivated.

When that's done, it's time to make a plan. This is where you take all the information you've gathered and bring everything together. The first thing is to look at what you're actually spending and compare it with what you actually want to spend. When you have those side by side, then you have to start looking for ways to cut down on some of the expenses. It's easier to cut down on variable costs such as going out, TV or streaming subscriptions, etc.

Again, you have to do your budgeting at least every month because it will need constant adjustments. But you also have to adjust your spending so it stays within your budget. Once you've followed all the steps until now, you'll have a much clearer idea of the things you need to adjust and where you can't overspend. Here, I like to make two columns of my expenses, one with my wants and another with my needs. The first thing that you can cut is anything in the "wants" column. For instance, do you really need to go to the movies once a week? Or can you have movie nights at home? Either way, movie night is not a need; it's a want. Food, rent, mortgage, transport, etc. Those are needs, and even for those, you might find a solution on how to decrease spending. The main thing to take from here is that even small decreases and changes can add up at the end of the month.

The last step is to regularly check on your budget, ideally every month because expenses and even income might change. The hard part is starting, but once you have a budget, you can simply adjust it every month. This is a habit that you should try to incorporate into your routine, and you will see the difference that will make.

Budget Allocation

While right now you might not have as many sections in your budget as you will once you have your independence, it's important that you understand what budget allocation is. There are many different categories that you can make when setting up your allocation, which might be a little daunting, but there are a few that should always be incorporated. It all comes down to how much more control you want over your money, your spending habits, and your goals. All of this will allow you to organize your money and reach your financial goals faster.

When you're just starting to budget, I find it easier to first catalog the different sections as "essential" and "non-essential." As we've discussed, essential spending has to do with the things that you have to spend money on regardless, such as rent or mortgage, groceries, travel, etc. Non-essential is everything else that doesn't fall into the first category.

There's a very popular budget rule called the 50/30/20 rule, where you allocate 50% of your income to your needs (essential), 30% to your wants (non-essential), and 20% to savings. Of course, this is just a guide, and you might have to adjust it. Also, there are many other budgeting strategies that I will talk about later in this chapter. Now, once you get independence, there will be many other categories in your budget, and I like to divide it into five different categories: Housing that encompasses rent or mortgage; transportation that involves public transportation tickets, gas, car maintenance, car loan payment, etc.; utilities such as electricity, water, mobile, internet, and cable; food and supplies, such as groceries, household items, cleaning supplies, and savings. These categories might expand if or when you have a child or a pet, or both, in which case you'd add another category, childcare, where you'd insert babysitting, nursery, and daycare, and a pets category, where you'd add pet food, vet bills, flea treatments, toys, etc.

This is quite a basic budget category, but obviously, there are other things that you will need to add as you get better at budgeting, such as healthcare, insurance, personal care, or clothing. You can add more categories as you see fit for your lifestyle, as these are just simple ideas.

Now, you might be asking, "How much money should I be allocating to the different categories?" Well, that depends on your needs. I've already given you an example with the 50/30/20 method, but it really depends. One thing is certain: your needs have to be met, and that's a great way to start your budget. But the different categories you add simply have to work for you. After all, it is a personal budget and a personal process. Everybody has a different income, different expenses, needs, and goals, and it's hard to give the right number.

What If I Have an Irregular Income?

If you have an irregular income, then things get a little more complicated, but nothing that you can't overcome. Here, you need a different approach. You might not know your income for sure, but you know your expenses, at least the fixed ones. This is where I would start when budgeting on an irregular income. For instance, you'd still have rent or a mortgage, bills, groceries, and maybe travel costs. While these can also vary, they are easier to predict. When you've written down the fixed expenses, you need to make sure that you can at least cover them every month.

Another thing that you can do is budget for the lowest monthly income you can have. It might be tempting to budget for a good month when your income is irregular, but you should budget for your lowest income so you know for sure you can make it. Here, it's also important that you think ahead since different months and seasons could mean more or less income. This is especially true if you're self-employed. There are certain industries where certain seasons, such as Summer or Christmas, might bring in more money while others might bring in less. You should try to save more during the higher income periods so you can then pay for those months when business is less stable.

Different Budgeting Strategies

As I've said before, there are many different budgets, but they simply serve as a template from which you have to make your own adjustments so they fit your lifestyle. In any case, I'll show you some of the most popular budgeting strategies used in personal finance so you can have a better idea of where to start.

Again, I like to emphasize that when you start budgeting, it might be hard to stay on track, and that's one of the reasons you should start now when you have fewer expenses so you can create the habit. But let's get to the strategies.

I've already mentioned the 50/30/20 formula, sometimes known as the balanced money formula, but I want to explain some of its benefits. This is an easy budget to start with because it only has three simple categories, which means less calculation and fewer worries. However, overspending can happen when using this strategy because there's more leeway, and it's not as strict. This comes from the fact that you are not budgeting for every category, like food or gas, which might mean that if you don't pay attention, you might overspend. If you follow this budget, I recommend that you overestimate a little so you have some room for overspending.

Cash-Only Budget

This strategy is exactly as the name indicates: You only use cash (if you still remember what cash is, of course). This strategy is also called envelope budgeting because you place the cash in different envelopes, and on each one of those envelopes is written the purpose of that money. This means you wouldn't be using your bank cards. Nowadays, using this method is not as easy as it once was because most things we pay are standing orders, but there are certain categories where you can only use cash. For example, you can add $200 to an envelope named "groceries." So, you would withdraw $200, write "groceries" on an envelope, and place that cash on that envelope. That's all you can spend on groceries. Once that money is gone, you can't purchase more. You can also do this for gas, clothing, etc.

This is a great strategy if you overspend often. It's quite simple: once there's no more cash in that specific envelope, you can't spend more. To make this method more efficient, make sure you leave your bank cards at home. One thing that you should pay attention to when using this budgeting method is to be extra careful since you're using cash and can lose it. Make sure all the money you carry is in a safe place.

Zero-Based Budget

The zero-based budget, which many refer to as the budget where you "give every dollar a job," is exactly that. Every income money has a purpose, meaning that your income matches every money outgoing from your account. Obviously, this doesn't mean you spend all your money, but instead, at the end of the month, you shouldn't have any money in your checking account because you've also transferred some to an external savings account. Essentially, all your money has a purpose, and you shouldn't have money in your regular checking account because it's not bringing you any benefits.

Some of your income has the job of paying the bills, paying rent or mortgage, while another portion goes for savings, groceries, etc. You should use this budget technique if you want absolute control of your money, where you essentially micromanage everything. In other words, you wouldn't spend any money unless it had been planned before. However, this is quite a time-consuming budget because it involves a lot of planning, and you'd be recording every single transaction. So, while it gives you total control over your income, you need to have time to actually make it work.

The 60% Solution Budget

This budget strategy is in many ways similar to the zero-budget one in the sense that you use every single dollar of your income somewhere. Essentially, 60% of your income goes to committed expenses, and this includes both fixed and non-fixed expenses, so you can have a mortgage or rent, but also gas, cable, streaming services, etc. In other words, every expense that comes every month falls into this 60%. The rest (40%) is then divided into four 10% groups, such as long-term savings, short-term savings, retirement, and wants. Long-term savings include emergency funds and any investments you might want to make. Short-term savings is any goal that you want to save up for that is coming soon, such as vacations. The retirement allocation is the money that goes to retirement accounts such as 401(k)s (which I will discuss later in the "Retirement" chapter). If these are done through your employer, then you don't have to do them. Then, the want is anything that you want to do with the remaining 10%, such as going out for dinner, going to the cinema, etc.

This is a less intensive budget to follow while still using every dollar of your income for something. The issue with this method is that you might lean on percentages quite a lot and forget to track your expenses. You should still track everything so that you know that you're on the right path. Another thing to take into consideration is whether you're in a good financial position to actually follow this budget since not everybody is.

Value-Based Budget

This budget strategy works best if your income is high, so if you don't think you're in the higher-income bracket, this budget strategy is not for you. Also, this budget requires you to actively think about yourself and the things you want to do. In sum, this budget allows you to spend money on things that you give value to (which you still have to track) instead of making sure a certain percentage of your income goes towards a certain allocation. Here, you have to write down the things that you value most. So, for instance, if you value going out for dinner or traveling, that's what you should be writing down. Anything else that is not on your list, you shouldn't be spending money on.

This budget is also better suited for those who have some level of discipline and already have some savings. It also saves you more time since you're not trying to track every single dollar of your income.

If you don't have the discipline, this strategy is not for you because chances are that you will get off track easily. If you tend to spend money on things that are not really of any value to you, then this is also not for you. But this soul-searching when writing about the things that you value can be a way to really understand the things you like. For instance, you might think that you like to go watch an NBA game every month or so, but after some thinking about it, there might be many other things that you value more, so you don't add NBA games to your list.

Again, these are just guidelines that will help you come up with your own budget that will suit your needs. The most important thing is feeling comfortable with the budget you are creating every month. And don't forget that your income changes, as do your priorities, so make sure you adjust your budget accordingly.

Budgeting is a crucial thing to do when we are handling money. Without a good budget, you simply can't save enough money for the things you want to do and for your future. For this, you need to analyze how you spend your money and what your income is. Once you know exactly how these things work, you need to be able to properly allocate your income to things that matter to you, and that will help you reach your goals. However, budgeting is not an easy thing to do, and that is why it is so important to start now so you can create healthy habits that you will bring with you into adulthood. It is also not something that you do once; it needs to be constantly changing and adapting to fit your needs and your lifestyle, but it needs to be done.

The next chapter is like a continuation of this, where I will be talking about your spending and paying the bills. I'll dive into how you can make informed purchasing decisions, how you can differentiate between needs and wants, how to practice smart shopping, such as comparing prices, and other tips on saving money on bills.

CHAPTER 5
SPENDING AND PAYING BILLS

> *Do not save what is left after spending, but spend what is left after saving.*
> –Warren Buffet

Once you reach adulthood and independence, you will find that you have more freedom when it comes to the things you want to purchase. However, if you have not developed control over your finances as a teenager, in the form of budgeting, for instance, you will have a much harder time making the right financial decisions. This will then have consequences for your overall spending and needs, such as paying bills, etc.

There are other things that during your teenage years you can develop and become better at, such as differentiating between your needs and your wants, how to practice smart shopping and using other techniques such as comparing prices, and many other things I'll talk about in this chapter.

How Can You Make Informed Purchasing Decisions?

As the name indicates, to make better buying decisions, you need to be informed. So, the key here is to understand what you're buying so you can choose the best product or service over others.

The first thing you should do is ask yourself some questions. For instance, "If I buy this, how will it improve my life?" or "Do I really need this?" If whatever you're buying does improve your life significantly and you do need it, then you can ask, "Is a purchase the right thing to do? Couldn't I borrow it instead?" This often happens when what you are buying might be important and essential, but it's something that will only be essential once. And so, it begs the question, "How often will I use it?"

If it will make your life better, you cannot borrow it, and you might use it more than once; the questions don't end here. You should ask yourself, "Is now the best time to buy it?" These are the types of questions you should ask yourself before any purchase you make so you can determine if you should make one or not.

You also need to consider your current savings, especially if it's an expensive thing. Imagine that you need that, but it's quite expensive, and you don't have the savings for it. Is it worth it to take out a loan for it? Is this a planned purchase? If this is planned and you have savings, then by all means; however, if it was planned and you don't have the savings, perhaps you might consider holding off on the purchase until you can afford it. Taking out a loan to purchase something should be your last resort, especially if what you're purchasing won't bring you any income.

What I like to do when facing some purchases is look at the cost-per-use. Here, you will be calculating the value of the good or service you are thinking of purchasing, and with that, you will have more information about the potential purchase. It is also quite simple to calculate; all you have to do is divide the total cost of the item or service by the estimated number of times you will use it. You also have to think about the benefits of what you're buying. Here, you have to consider all its advantages and disadvantages. Will it bring in more money? Will it boost your productivity? If you purchase a new computer and work from home, perhaps in the long run, it will bring you some advantages, such as performing jobs quicker. If you invest in solar panels, in the long run, they will save you more money. On the other hand, purchasing a car is almost always a necessity if you live in an area where there's no public transport or it takes too long to get you where you want to be. This is because a car decreases in value from the moment you purchase it, plus you have to pay for maintenance, gas, insurance, etc. So, unless a car is the only way you can get to work and make some income, it is usually a bad investment.

Needs vs. Wants

I think one of the hardest things to do when you get financial independence is to distinguish between needs and wants, which is the basis for creating a good budget and making the right financial decisions. This is something that you have to do yourself. Of course, there are basic needs that we all have to prioritize, and I've mentioned most of them, such as rent or mortgage, groceries, or utility bills. Essentially, there are basic requirements that you must fulfill to live properly. They are things that you must have; they tend to remain constant over time, and their non-fulfillment can have serious consequences. Wants, especially in this context, can be described as services and goods that you might like to have, but they don't represent a necessity like needs do and are often a desire that is non-essential for you to live. They tend to change over time, unlike needs, and the non-fulfillment of these does not result in any tragedy, but it might result in disappointment for some time.

If you want to get a little more technical about needs and wants, I will give you another definition. Needs are requirements that are necessary for you to live and survive. If we go back to ancient times, humans had three needs: food, shelter, and clothing. But as time went on, our needs increased to encompass healthcare and education, not so much to survive as to improve our lives.

Wants, from an economic point of view, are things that you might wish to possess, often now but also at some point in the future. Most goods and services stem from wants and not needs, and that's one of the reasons many businesses are extremely wealthy because people really crave their wants. For instance, why would you want to buy the iPhone 14 when you bought the iPhone 13 last year? Your current iPhone 13 still works perfectly fine, but your desire to have that, for various reasons, will make you buy the new iPhone. This lack of control over our wants can really have a negative impact on our finances, and that's why it is so important to understand the difference between these two definitions and develop control over our wants.

How Can You Shop Smart?

While fixed expenses are hard to modify, you can save some money by reducing the price you pay for variable expenses, and this often comes in the form of smart shopping. There are many different ways you can reduce the cost of things, and I'm going to give you some ideas on how you can do that. While you might use many of these throughout your adulthood, it is important that you practice these methods and strategies so that when the transition to adulthood comes, you will be more prepared.

I think we can all agree that consumerism is a long-lasting trend nowadays, and people just want to buy and buy without even thinking if they actually need what they are purchasing. This is also a fast way to increase debt, especially if you don't have a budget. Just to give some actual research, the average person spends about $161 on clothes monthly, and the average child in the U.S. has about $6,000 worth of toys by the time they reach their teenage years (Bowling, 2019). That's a lot of wasted money, in my humble opinion, and this also reveals the lack of budgeting skills most people have. Many of these come from impulse purchases and bad spending habits. But let's look at some ways you can shop smarter.

Let's first look at online shopping, which is something that has been growing over the last few decades with the advent of technology and some companies such as Amazon. However, online shopping made it far easier to compare prices with other online retailers. And this is exactly the first thing you should do. You can quickly go to other websites, search for the same or similar items, and check their prices. This is a great way to get a bargain on certain items. Reading the reviews is also important, which is also something that online shopping makes easier. When reading the reviews of a certain item, if they are simply bad, you tend to give up on the product and move on. If you don't usually read reviews and you like what you see, chances are that you are going to purchase it and possibly be disappointed. Reading reviews stops many people from making purchasing mistakes. Sometimes the reviews don't need to be all that bad, but they might point out the capabilities of that item, which you might find to be of no use to you.

The world of coupons is gigantic, and more people should use it. Coupons allow us to get cheaper prices on certain things. But you have to be careful and only use coupons on things that you were looking for before because many people tend to buy things with coupons that they wouldn't even think about buying if they hadn't seen the coupon. For that, make sure you know what you want, and don't let yourself be persuaded by these marketing tricks. Waiting for a sale, especially an internet sale, might be quite convenient since you can simply sign in and order the items once the sales start, which is far easier than offline shopping. If this is something that you can purchase later, then by all means, you should wait for a sale if you know one is coming.

Always double-check the return policy when you shop online because, especially with clothes, we often purchase the wrong size. However, if you don't know how the return policy works, you might find yourself unable to replace the item. Some return policies last only two weeks, while others might last a month, two, or even three. Either way, you need to make sure you check it and know when you have to send it back. Imagine that you buy a jacket, and the policy states that you have 15 days to return it. The jacket takes eight or nine days to arrive, so chances are that you're not going to be able to return it in time.

Let's move on to purchasing clothes since this is where many people spend a lot of money. The first thing you should do is refer back to your budget and understand how much you can spend on clothes. Without this, chances are that you are going to overspend. Knowing exactly what you need is also important because it stops you from purchasing things that you might like but don't need. If you go to the mall with no clear idea of what you need to buy, you are probably coming back home with too many things and sometimes without the things you need. When shopping for clothes, you need to take your time, especially if you are in a shopping center or mall, and go around other shops to check on prices. If you're looking for a shirt, don't buy the first one you like because it might happen that later on you will find another one that you like more at a cheaper price. So, shop around and come back to the one that you liked more.

Buying clothes off-season tends to be a little cheaper. This can be better done after the season ends because merchants tend to lower their prices so they can sell the remnants of the previous collection and have more space to place the new collection. Alternatively, you can go to thrift stores. I do understand that not everybody likes to purchase clothes at the thrift store, but if you don't mind, it's a great place to find good brands at lower prices. Lastly, you should always go for quality over quantity. It's better to buy one pair of high-quality jeans than four pairs of lower-quality jeans because chances are that those cheap jeans will all wear out faster than the single high-quality one, and you will be back to shopping faster.

Groceries are a necessity but are not a fixed expense, so you could apply strategies and methods that will reduce their cost. The first thing that I would recommend is to always have a grocery list with you when grocery shopping. Planning ahead is fundamental so you don't get caught up in purchasing things that you weren't meant to purchase. It's also important so you don't forget to purchase important goods. It's important that you buy fruits and vegetables locally, not because they are necessarily cheaper (although they might be), but because they are certainly fresher than those you can find in a supermarket. Before you head out to go grocery shopping, have a look at your fridge and cupboards so you don't buy goods that you wouldn't need, and that would eventually be thrown away. Here, you should always plan to avoid wasting food. To do that, everything you buy should have a planned purpose. For instance, don't buy tomatoes if you're not planning on using them next week since chances are they will expire, and you will have to throw them away.

It's always better to buy groceries for the whole household since it's cheaper to buy in bulk instead of going grocery shopping every few days. Bigger packs are usually cheaper than smaller ones. However, you should always check expiration dates as well as prices so things don't go to waste or you buy alternative products that will cost you more.

Once in a while, we need to make big purchases, and these require more thorough planning. I'm talking about cars, fridges, tables, TVs, etc., things that you buy once every few years. And exactly because of that, you need to think more about them. Here, you should be researching as many options as you possibly can and even asking for professional advice if possible. When you are divided about what to purchase, you should know everything you can, from the model to the consumption, reviews, etc. It is even worth talking to friends or family members who have made similar purchases before to help you make a decision and talk to you about the item. But I'll leave the different strategies about big purchases for a dedicated chapter later in the book.

I've mentioned this before briefly, but when making big purchases, you should go for functionalities over big-name brands. The first thing that comes to mind is mobile phones. There might not be any point in purchasing the latest version of an iPhone if you can find another phone that has the same or even more functionalities but whose brand is not as recognizable. Here, it's also important that you look at reviews before purchasing, of course. Usually, with big brands, you rarely pay for how good the item is and pay more for its name. If you can, you should consider purchasing in installments; this is especially true if there's no interest on the items you are purchasing. If the interest is minimal, you can still consider it since you might not be able to purchase the whole amount in one sitting or if this would disrupt your budget and take from your savings.

While you might not really think about having kids, it's important to understand that they will be a sizable part of your budget. This also has to be thought out thoroughly. When shopping for kids, one thing that you should often keep in mind is that, in most cases, you probably don't need to buy anything. I'm mostly talking about toys and other things to spoil your kid. They will probably throw a tantrum, but that's fine; they are kids, after all, and they will get over it. You have to be reasonable and explain to them that they can't have everything they want. However, it's also important that you consider their opinion on certain things. If you want to buy something for them, you should probably take them with you, as it is more likely that they will use it or play with it for longer periods, and you won't need to purchase something else in a short period of time.

How Can You Compare Prices?

As I've noted above, purchasing online or in-store items is a little different, and as such, you should use slightly different ways of comparing prices. Let's start with comparing prices online.

The easiest way to compare prices online is to use a comparison tool. These are usually websites where you can compare online products side by side. There are many different ones that you can use, and amidst so many to choose from, you have to actually use some of them to see which ones you prefer. I tend to use more than one so I can have more information and make a better choice. Some of the most popular ones are Google Shopping, Shopzilla, and Shopping.com. Bear in mind that these are popular ones in the US, there might be different ones in different countries.

A quick Google search will allow you to check out many different comparison websites. Some are better at comparing prices in specific stores, while others are really good at checking certain types of items, so do your research and decide which ones you want to use. Alternatively, you can also use mobile apps if you find them more convenient. Then, once you've decided on what websites or app comparison tools to use, you can go on and type the product in the search bar. Here, you will find that different tools display items and prices differently. You can also look for the type of item or for specific brand products. Usually, the tool will give you some other options to look at. If you don't have any specific brand in mind, you can also search for different categories or departments and browse through the different items.

Then, all you have to do is browse through the different results that appear. Some of these tools allow you to see the number of stores selling a certain product, but you can filter it to look for other results or list them in different orders. Then, you can click on the item that interests you, and a list of different merchants selling the same item will appear. Here, you can filter for the best or lowest price. Keep in mind that the lowest price might not be the best deal you will find. Sometimes the merchant might be more reliable, and you will know you won't have any issues with the product or the delivery. If there's not much of a discrepancy, or if there's a discrepancy between a reputable seller and one that doesn't have a good reputation, I always go for the one with the best reputation. Researching the seller is something that you should always aim to do, especially if you don't know them, regardless of how reputable they are. Usually, you can purchase right from the price comparison page; other times, you might have to go to the merchant's website.

Of course, some people still prefer to compare prices manually, even though they use computers. Here's what you can do: First, you need to make a list of stores that you know are reliable. Before this, you should have a product in mind, and depending on the product you want to purchase, the type of stores you will be listing will be different. Then, you should visit each store's website. Even if you don't know the website, this can easily be found by Googling the name of the store. Every merchant's website has a search bar where you can simply type the name or the kind of product you want, and it will appear. You then proceed to write down the price and the brand. It's always wise to check shipping policies since a product might be cheaper at one merchant than at another, but the shipping price might be a lot higher, which makes the whole item more expensive. Ideally, if you can find a merchant that ships the product for free or you pick it up in-store, that would definitely be the cheapest option. Then, as you do your research and write everything down, you can compare it at the end and check out the best options for you.

Now, when it comes to comparing and calculating prices at the store, it might take a little longer than when done online. This is especially true when you're looking at bigger packages and trying to figure out if the overall price is really that much better than smaller packages. Usually, checking the unit price of the item can give you a better idea of how much you are actually saving. When we talk about unit price, we are usually referring to its cost per quantity. However, here this can mean that the quantity is per item or per unit of measurement, but don't worry, I'll go through all the processes.

In order to calculate the unit price, all you have to do is divide the cost of the product by its quantity (what you are actually receiving by purchasing the package). There are two ways of doing this. The first is, as I've said, calculating the unit price. The first thing to do here is to check the item's total price, which is usually a smaller percentage of the total cost of the packaged product. This can usually be found on the product's label at the store. You might have a coupon, and if you want to calculate the unit price with the coupon, you need to subtract the coupon's value from the overall price before you calculate the unit price. Then, you have to find the quantity that the package has. You can find this on the label of the product. While some goods are sold by item, such as pencils or toilet paper, others will have a unit of measurement, such as liters, ounces, or gallons.

When comparing, it's important to make sure that the two products you are comparing are in the same units of measurement when not compared by item. It is very common that two products you are comparing might be in different units of measurement, which makes it harder to compare. If this is the case, then you will have to convert the units of measurement so they are the same. You can simply use a measurement unit online to figure this out. Let's look at milk, which is sometimes measured in gallons and sometimes in quarts. If a quart of milk is priced at $2 and a gallon is $8, then these two products cost the same because a gallon is four quarts of milk, so $2 x 4 = $8.

You can then divide the total price by the quantity of the item to figure out the unit price. Here, I would say using a calculator would be faster. For instance, if you are looking at a 4-roll pack of toilet paper at $5 and you want to know the unit price, you'd have to divide $5 by 4, so the unit price is $1.25 per roll of toilet paper. Again, most stores have the unit cost on their label, so you don't have to make any calculations, but it is always better to know how it works in case some products don't display that.

The second method is comparing unit prices. Here, to calculate the unit price of the goods you want to purchase, you need to divide the total cost of each good by the quantity in the package they are sold in. So, for example, one package of 4-roll toilet paper is priced at $5, and another package has 6 rolls and is priced at $6.30. Which one do you think has the cheaper unit price? First, you need to calculate $5/4, which is $1.25 a roll. Then you need to divide $6.30 by 6, which is $1.05. The 6-roll package of toilet paper is cheaper. In general, the product with the lowest unit price is the best value, but you also have to look at the quality. If the quality is similar, then you should go for the cheaper one, but if not, you need to try and understand if it's worth it to pay less for worse quality. While these two methods have the same results, the first allows you to calculate unit prices to understand the price of each unit, and the second allows you to take two items with the same function but different prices and figure out which one has the best value.

How to Save Money on Bills and Other Purchases?

The best way to increase your savings is to make a budget, but there are other ways you can retain more of the money you earn and add it to your savings, such as by cutting your energy bills. You might have heard your parents talking around the house about the incredibly high cost of bills at the moment. While this might change by the time you have to pay your own bills, you can always try to save as much as you can. One thing that you might not be aware of is that usually, energy bills such as electricity and gas are paid through direct debit from your card, and this can be changed. What energy companies usually take is an estimate to cover what you have spent. This is because we use more energy in certain months than we do in others; for instance, in the winter, we tend to use more energy so we can warm our houses. However, while some months you might have a debt on your energy account, other times you might have credit. But you need to keep checking that to make sure you are not overpaying your energy bill or falling into a large debt. Sometimes, the energy company increases the direct debit on your card, and this might be for some reason, such as if you've moved on to a more expensive bill or if your contract with them has expired. They usually put you on a higher tariff. You need to contact them to renew your contract or look for a new energy provider. It can also happen that you are in a variable tariff contract, in which case the rates have increased. If you don't want that to happen, you would have to get into a fixed tariff, which might look more expensive but is often better since you know exactly how much you will be paying per unit of energy. If your energy use has increased, this could also be another reason why your direct debit has gone up too. If you're not sure why the direct debit has increased, you should always contact your energy provider to make sure there's no mistake on their behalf.

Now that this is out of the way let's get into the real tips. Heating your home is where most people spend the most energy. So, you might ask, What is the most energy-efficient way to heat a room? Well, central heating is definitely the most efficient way to do this, but not all properties have it. This is especially true if you're renting and you don't have another choice but to use what is provided to you. However, if central heating is not an option and you only need to heat the room you are in, then a portable heater is definitely the second-best choice. However, you need to pick one that is cost-efficient. You can use the price comparison tips I've mentioned above to pick the best one. Ideally, you'd pick a portable heater that has a timer and a good thermostat so it doesn't overheat and you don't spend too much energy and money on it.

Cooking is another thing where a lot of energy is consumed. Here, electric ovens are far more efficient than gas ones. The same is true for electric hobs. However, here, more efficiency doesn't mean cheaper since gas tends to be cheaper than electricity. However, air fryers and microwaves (for small things) tend to save you more money in the long run. Apart from that, there's not much you can do when it comes to cooking besides trying not to have your oven on for too long and preparing everything before so you can cook as fast as you can. However, if and when you have your own property, purchasing energy-efficient appliances can really make a difference in your energy bill. Again, when doing this, make sure you compare all the appliances so you can have the most energy-efficient and not the cheapest appliance since, in the long run, you'd be paying more.

Insulating your home is also a good way to save energy. Once again, if you're renting, there's not a lot you can do. But when you're looking for properties to rent, you should keep in mind that properties that are better insulated tend to waste less energy. So, properties that have the attic insulated, have draft proofing installed, and have double-glazing tend to be more energy efficient.

Not everything is gas and electricity when it comes to bills, and there are other things such as cellphone contracts, broadband, and insurance where you can also reduce costs. When it comes to an internet connection, unless you are out of contract, in my experience, there's no point in changing because you most certainly have to pay an early opt-out fee. However, if your contract runs out, this is an excellent opportunity to get a cheaper and faster internet connection. If you don't have fiber yet, then this is the best time to upgrade. While it usually costs the same as standard broadband, it is a lot faster and more reliable. When it comes to your cell phone, you should keep an eye on your data and check if you are really using all the data you are purchasing every month or if you can reduce that data and the price you're paying for it. While many providers offer high amounts of data and sometimes even unlimited data, most people use between 5 and 10 GB, so there's no need to purchase all that data most of the time.

One thing that I had to learn with time and experience is that when it comes to cell phones and broadband, you can haggle the price. Yes, nothing is really set in stone, and if you've been a customer with them for quite some time, your chances are even higher to get a better price. If you think that negotiating can be overwhelming, you can do it over a text chat or email. But to be prepared, you should compare the services with those of other providers so you can back up your negotiations.

At some point in your adult life, you will have home and car insurance. These are needs because you need your valuables protected. The best way to reduce them is when it's time to renew them. Obviously, when you got them the first time, you should have gone through comparison websites and checked out the best available deal for you. But this insurance industry is always on the move, and when it is time to renew, chances are that you will find a better deal. You do the same thing you've done before and do your research with the help of comparison websites. Even if you're not near renewal, you can always check with other insurance companies, and perhaps an early switch might be able to save you some money. Here, you have to take into account the cost of early cancellation, of course, but if the rival's prices are that much better, you should consider switching. The way you pay is also important. These usually come in monthly or annual payments, and annual payments are almost always cheaper. But this is a calculation that you can do quickly; simply divide the total amount of the annual insurance payment by 12 and check if it's cheaper than paying monthly. It's also important to have a close look at the extras insurance companies often add to the contract; most of the time, you won't need those extra covers, and you can save money that way. A good piece of advice that I would give and that you could probably follow is to put the name of someone with more driving experience if you don't have that much experience because young and inexperienced drivers tend to pay more.

Fuel is a necessity if you, like many people, rely on your own method of transportation. The question that should be on your mind when the time comes is, How can I drive and spend less on fuel? Well, the first thing that comes to mind here is to drive as smoothly as possible, try to preserve momentum, and don't accelerate if there's no need to. This might not be much of a tip, but trust me, in the long run, it will save you a lot of fuel. For instance, if you have a good idea of what's ahead of you when you drive, you will better control your acceleration or know when you should and when you shouldn't. Essentially, anticipating what is ahead and not using braking and acceleration for no reason. By the way, breaking also wastes fuel since you then have to use more fuel to accelerate. While in the U.S., manual gears are not very common, if you do ever drive one, shifting gears as soon as possible will ease the work the engine will have to do and, with that, consume less fuel too. In fact, if you drive a new-ish car, they already indicate when it is best to shift gears. Plus, new cars have other modes where you can switch to Eco, for instance, which will allow you to consume less fuel too.

Perhaps you've seen your parents use the car on cold days, and they run the engine while staying stationary so the engine heats up. This is hardly needed with new cars because the engine is designed to heat up way faster. Only use air conditioning when strictly necessary since these waste quite some energy, but using it once in a while will also prevent it from having issues more often. Heated seats are hardly ever necessary unless you live in a very cold place. These seats also consume a lot of energy, most of the time unnecessarily. Also, checking your tire pressure can often help you save some fuel since the more deflated the tires are, the more energy the engine wastes.

Reducing your overall spending as well as your bills can have a huge impact on your savings. It all starts with making informed decisions when purchasing goods or services. Understanding how to shop smartly and how to compare prices is fundamental to all of this. There are many comparison websites where you can find the most varied goods to do your research. You also have to have a clear idea of your needs and wants, and when shopping, it is best to bring a list with you so you don't forget anything and don't spend unnecessarily. With the tips I talked about on how to save money, while I don't expect you to memorize everything or even apply all of them, it is important that you are aware of them and that when the time comes, you know the things you can do to increase your savings.

CHAPTER 6

CREDIT, CREDIT CARDS, AND DEBT MANAGEMENT

> *Don't let your mouth write no check that your tail can't cash.*
>
> –Bo Diddley

Credit, credit cards, and debt might be something that scares you. Perhaps you don't fully understand it, but you've probably heard your parents talking about it, someone in your family, or even on TV. The truth is, while debt and credit cards can have a negative effect on your finances, they also have a positive side. I've briefly talked about it before, but now I'm delving more into the topic.

What Is Credit, and Why Is it Important?

While the word "credit" might have different meanings in the financial sector, it often means an agreement where an individual, also called a borrower, gets money but at the same time states that they will give it back at a later date, usually with interest. But credit can also refer to the credit score or credit history of someone, so you can have good or bad credit. Don't worry; I will get to that.

There are many different forms of credit, but the most common one is a credit card; however, there are also mortgages, car loans, and personal loans. With a credit card, you have a line of credit where you have a certain amount that you can spend on that specific card. There are two main types of credit, and all of the forms of credit I've mentioned above fall within one of them. These are revolving or installment loans. Revolving credit is, for instance, a credit card where you can continuously borrow more and more money as long as you pay the minimum balance at a certain date. An installment credit is, for example, a mortgage where you have fixed amounts to pay every month, and you don't continuously take out money. Usually, this comes as a lump sum. Both of these usually have interest.

When somebody says that credit is important, it usually refers to your credit score or history. This is what banks and other financial institutions refer to when deciding if they should lend you money or not. They often look at your credit report, which often states things like payment history, which tells them how often you make credit payments on time; credit utilization, which means how much of your credit in your credit cards you have used (usually the less, the better); length of credit history, which refers to the amount of time you have had credit, whether it is a credit card or a car loan (where usually the longer, the better); credit mix, which is how diversified your credit is, such as credit cards, mortgages, car loans, etc.; and new credit, which tells them how often you take on a new credit card (opening too many credit accounts throughout a small period of time is usually not good).

The health of your credit is important because it opens the doors for many things, such as applying for a credit card, purchasing a house, renting a house or apartment, applying for a job, buying a car, or even starting a business. This is because, for most of these, you need to borrow money, and the lender is going to look at your credit score and credit history to understand if it is safe for them to actually lend you the money. It's also important to note that even with a bad credit score, financial institutions can still lend you money, but oftentimes this will have a higher interest rate. This is something that you want to avoid because it means you'd be spying on a lot more than what you are borrowing.

So, as you can see, having a credit card is not so bad and allows you to build your credit score and credit history. However, you have to manage it properly.

How Can You Manage Your Credit Properly and Responsibly?

Managing your credit responsibly is the important part. You want to get a high credit score so you can borrow higher amounts and pay less interest. If you miss payment dates, default, or file for bankruptcy, your credit score will decrease. This is also true if you, as I said, use too much of your credit or open too many credit card accounts in a short period of time.

So, in order to manage your credit responsibly, I have a few tips for you. Always make your credit card payments and other credit payments on time. While paying more than the minimum payment is better because it means in the long run, you will be paying less, you have to at least pay the minimum amount. In fact, if you don't make a single payment on time, this can stay on your credit report for years to come. Another thing you should not do is spend more than you can afford to repay. It seems easy enough, but many people fall for this mistake. You should never live off your credit card unless you have absolutely no money for your basic necessities. What I like to do to ensure I never miss a payment is to set up a reminder or a direct debit.

Credit cards should strictly be used to build credit, so you should pay small amounts with them and not big amounts unless you have the money ready to pay them. One last thing: you should keep your old credit card accounts open even if you don't use them because they count toward your length of credit history.

How Can You Build a Good Credit Score?

Some of the things you can do to build or maintain a great credit score have already been mentioned. But there are other things. For instance, getting on your electoral roll is an easy way to get some points on your credit score. This is often used by lenders to check your address as well as your name and to verify if everything is up-to-date.

Getting credit, as I've mentioned, is also a great way to improve your score. But remember to take out a small and manageable amount so you can pay it back on time and fully, and don't get overwhelmed by the amount of debt. Sometimes, you can get a score boost too. The three major credit bureau companies are Experian, Equifax, and TransUnion, and sometimes all you need to do is link your current account to one of the credit bureau companies. This is an easier way for those companies to know how well you manage your credit. When it comes to credit score levels, what you want to achieve is "excellent," but a "very good" or even a "good" level of credit score points can give you quite some rewards. Here's a table of the credit score range for your credit level:

Poor	300–579
Fair	580–669
Good	670–739
Very good	740–799
Excellent	800–850

Here's a summarized list of things you can do to increase your credit score, besides some of the things I've already mentioned before:

- Setting up automatic bill payments
- Paying down credit balances
- Getting a credit-builder loan
- Disputing credit report inaccuracies
- Keeping old credit card accounts open
- Limiting the number of lines of credit you get
- Paying off credit card balances every single month

- ✧ Keeping track of your credit score
- ✧ Adding to your credit mix
- ✧ Adding rent payments to your credit score report
- ✧ Asking for an increase on your credit card limit

How Can You Manage Your Credit Card Debt?

Although most people understand the risks of taking on large amounts of debt, there are times when they fall into these debts and struggle to pay them. It's important that you don't shy away from or try to ignore this problem. In fact, you have to face it and look for solutions. While it might look bad, and it is, it's not the end of the world, and there are things you can do. But first, let me explain to you the process if you fall into overwhelming amounts of debt and can't pay them.

Every credit card is covered by the Consumer Credit Protection Act, which means that lending companies such as banks and other financial institutions have to follow some rules if the debtor (you) is struggling to pay. So, it all starts by not paying the minimum amount in a month, after which your bank will contact you and demand that you pay that month's amount. If you don't, then they will put your account in default. If you still don't pay, then they might bring in a debt collection agent to recover the money you owe. It sounds a little scary, but at this point, you've had enough time to do something about it, as I'll explain below.

Banks and other financial institutions, to help their customers that are struggling, can do a few things: they can give you a credit card payment "holiday," which means you are "off the hook" for three months (obviously, you still have to pay it). They often make sure that your credit score is not affected during this three-month period. And they can also increase your credit card limit; however, you should be careful about this because it means that later on, you can incur more debt.

Now, onto things that you can do to pay off your credit card. The first thing you have to do is really try to understand your finances. This means fully understanding what you can afford every month. You have to budget! If you have been forgetting to budget, you will have to do it because this is the only way you can understand how much you can spend. When doing your budget, make sure you set aside a part of your income so you can pay your debt. You have to absolutely stop using your credit card. You can't afford to incur more debt than you already have.

You can also negotiate your credit card debt by contacting your bank and explaining everything to them. Here, you can also tell them how much you can pay each month, and believe it or not, many banks agree to some of the terms you might bring up and even agree to an affordable repayment plan.

How Can You Deal With Debt Collectors?

Hopefully, this will never happen to you, and if you ever have an overwhelming amount of debt, you will follow the steps I've written above to avoid it. But if you are ever in a situation where you have to deal with debt collectors, there are also a few things that you can do. Usually, debt collectors will contact you about an unpaid debt. Remember, you have to face your problems here, and hiding is never the solution because it can get much worse. While you have to deal with them, it's important that you understand your rights under the Fair Debt Collection Practices Act (FDCPA). For instance, debt collectors cannot threaten you, lie to you, or insult you in any way (they can't even say they will sue you if they don't intend to do so). They can't add interest to your debt unless it is written in the contract on your credit card or other agreement, and they can't threaten to take your property (or even take it) unless the property is served as collateral when you take out a loan.

They have to first notify you in writing (this could be by mail or online) at least within five days of any contact you've had with them. And they have to give you 30 days from their notification to ask for any more information about the debt. Also, there have been some recent rule changes where debt collectors can't call you more than seven times in a single week, and they can't talk to you from any social media platform.

You can also check if your debt is actually valid. This means that you need to check the notification the debt collector gave you and make sure that it is yours. It could be that the amount is wrong, or perhaps you've already paid the debt. Understanding your statute of limitations is also important. This means that debt collectors have a certain amount of time to claim the debt, but this amount of time differs depending on the state you are in. If they come after you after that statute of limitations has expired, you don't have to pay, and in fact, you can sue them.

Of course, you can always consider negotiating with a debt collector. This is after you've checked your statute of limitations and know for sure the debt is yours, but you can't afford to pay everything right away, you can try and negotiate with them. For instance, you can try to get an agreement where you pay back the debt in installments, or you can propose a settlement where they will have to agree not to pay the full amount of debt. However, if the debt is legitimate, you should always try to pay it in full, even if it is in installments, because this will hurt your credit score.

If you believe that a debt collector is harassing you, you can send a cease and desist letter, which basically tells them to stop contacting you. This can be done if the statute of limitations has run out or you don't have any assets, which means you won't be able to pay anything even if they sue you and you lose.

Credit is quite important to understand and to build as soon as we possibly can. Having good credit allows us to borrow money for large expenses such as buying a car or a house. However, credit can also be quite dangerous if we don't pay attention to it. We could become overwhelmed with the amount of debt we accumulate, which would make our financial lives quite complicated. It's important that we always pay back whatever we have borrowed and don't borrow more than we can pay; that's how debts get out of hand. But again, we need to use our credit cards to build a good credit history. If, for some reason, you accumulate more debt than you can pay, you should never try to hide from it, as it will always find you. This is one of those problems that don't go away until we face them. As I've explained in this chapter, there are ways that you can actively work to reduce your debt, such as by fully understanding your finances, creating a budget, or, in extreme cases, contacting your bank.

CHAPTER 7

INVESTING

> *Invest for the long haul. Don't get too greedy, and don't get too scared.*
>
> –Shelby M.C. Davies

Investing is another one of those things that people get a little scared of when mentioned. Many believe it's a way to lose all your money. But I assure you that those people have never invested in their lives. Yes, it is true that you can lose money if you don't have the faintest idea of what you're doing, but you can also make a lot of money just by understanding the basics.

The Basics You Need to Know

People have been investing for many years, and it is a tried and true way to put your money to work for you. You should be able to invest at regular intervals as you get your income, and once you know the basics and have the possibilities, it should be a part of your budget to set aside some money to invest. This is also the reason why investing as soon as you possibly can might allow you to make a lot of money. The thing is, you don't need a large amount of money to start; you can simply begin with $10, $25, or even a single dollar. But of course, you need to know what you're doing, and while many people feel daunted about the stock market and investing in general, the basics are not that hard to grasp.

Now, before we get into it, I want to talk about the three most common ways of investing: stocks, mutual funds, and bonds. You've probably heard about these but don't know exactly what they mean.

Let's start with what I believe to be the most popular of them all: stocks. These are often referred to as equity, and essentially, they are a small part of a business or corporation. Every time you purchase a fraction of such an organization in the stock market (where they are sold), you are buying what is called a share. This officially tells you that you are the owner of a portion of a corporation. In case your head is still wrapped up in what you might have heard about stocks, the trading of these is regulated by the government to protect investors like you from fraud. Now, businesses and corporations issue these shares or stocks to raise funds for their businesses so they can operate. Now, to buy stocks, you have to get them through stock exchanges, or more commonly, the stock market, such as the New York Stock Exchange (NYSE) or the Nasdaq. However, you don't have to physically go there, and nowadays, buying and selling stocks is easier than ever. There are many mobile applications that you can download, sign up for, and use from your mobile phone. For instance, a popular one is called Robinhood. You have to be over 18 years old to hold an account and trade stocks, plus you have to give ID proof and proof of address, as well as have a bank account. Although you might be asking, How do I earn income from owning stocks? There are two ways you can do this. The first, and probably simpler, is when the stock increases in value. Say you buy a single share of Microsoft for $100, and after a year, the value has risen to $150. If you sold at that time, you would take $150 or a $50 profit. Another way is through dividends, but this is only specific to some stocks. In fact, Microsoft also offers dividends on its stocks. Dividends are a small percentage of the value of the stock paid to shareholders or investors. This is usually paid every quarter, and you can check how much the corporation pays to the investors by looking at the dividend yield (also, most of this information can be looked up online or through your brokerage app). For instance, using the same example above, if you have a share of Microsoft valued at $100 and the dividend yield is 1%, you'd get paid $1.

Getting Started

Before you get started trading stocks, you need to learn the basics, of course, but there are other things that you need to establish. The first thing you should do is define your tolerance for risk. In basic terms, tolerance for risk is what you can afford to lose when investing. There are many categories within stocks that can tell you more or less about their risk (obviously, investments are never 100% sure); for example, you have large, medium, and small capitalization stocks, meaning the larger the capitalization, the smaller the volatility of the price, but also the fewer chances you have to make big money. Then you have value stocks and aggressive stocks, and all of these have different levels of risk. Once you know your risk tolerance, you can start really looking at the types of stocks to buy.

You also have to understand what your investment goals are. For most people, investments mean the long term. This means that you usually purchase some stock that you believe will go up over a long period of time (say five years, for instance. Other, more professional investors, like to invest in the short- or medium-term. This is something that I wouldn't recommend, especially if you're just starting out. Of course, your goals could also change over time; for instance, you might start by simply trying to increase the amount of money you have, while later on, you could try to get an income from your investments through dividends. Other more concrete investments could be purchasing a car or a house, saving for retirement, or paying for tuition.

Then, you have to determine your investment style, which basically means how you want to manage your portfolio (all your stocks). Many people prefer to purchase something and forget about it, meaning that they are not constantly checking it. You believe that they will continue to slowly go up. Others prefer to be more thorough, check their portfolios more often, and tweak here and there for maximum profitability. There's also something called the robo-advisor, which is an automated tool where you insert your goals, and add money to them (often through a stockbroker's app), and the robo-advisor tweaks your investments to align with your goals. Lastly, you can also pay for a financial advisor to give you some tips. However, these can be quite expensive, and unless you have a lot of money invested, they are probably not worth it.

Then, you will have to choose your investment account. Here, you have retirement plans usually sponsored by your employer, such as a 401(k), where you can choose from stocks, bonds, mutual funds, etc. However, I'll talk about all of this later. You can also choose to open a taxable account or IRA with a brokerage instead of an employer-sponsored one. These can also be retirement accounts, and you can have your own as well as employer-sponsored ones. Robo-advisors also have a specific account.

Lastly, you have to really learn the basics and learn how to diversify so you can reduce the risk. Diversification is perhaps the most important thing when it comes to investment. Let me give you an example of diversification. Say, you have $1000 invested in the stock market, but all the money is on Microsoft stocks. Here, your portfolio has zero diversification because everything is in one single stock. What happens if Microsoft has a bad quarter or some negative news? All your portfolios will suffer. But now, you have put only $250 on Microsoft, $250 on Nvidia, $250 on Apple, and $250 on Facebook. There's some more diversification, without a doubt, because even if Microsoft goes down momentarily, you have the other three stocks to keep your portfolio from free-falling. However, as you might have noticed, all of these stocks are in the technology sector. What if this specific sector is having a rough time for whatever reason? What if you put $250 on Microsoft, $250 on Apple, $250 on Coca-Cola, and $250 on Fiat? Your diversification would be a lot better, and you'd reduce the risk of losing a lot of your investment money.

Mutual funds are managed funds that use money from several investors to invest in stocks. This way, you don't have to manage it yourself. It's also important to understand that in these mutual funds, there can be stocks as well as bonds (which I will mention later in the chapter). These funds are managed by professional money managers, and their goal is to try and maximize gains for the investors, although every mutual fund has a different way of investing, such as being risky or risk averse, and the securities (both stocks and bonds) can be tailored depending on the mutual stock. For instance, you might choose a mutual fund whose premise is to invest in green stocks and bonds. This means that the companies the manager invests in are environmentally friendly. This also means that when you gain or lose money, so do all the other investors in the mutual fund.

However, you must be thinking, How are mutual funds priced? After all, they must have a price since you have to invest a certain amount of money, right? Well, you can look at it as if every time you invest in a mutual fund, a share of it is the average of the prices of all stocks and bonds within the fund. So, for example, if you invest in a mutual fund with two stocks (which is impossible since they usually have more, but bear with me for the sake of explanation) and one stock is currently priced at $200 and the other at $100, a share of the mutual fund would be $150. So, in other words, when you invest in a mutual fund, you are investing in many different stocks and bonds, which is good for diversity. You can also get income from dividends when investing in a mutual fund that holds stocks that distribute dividends.

As I've said, there are many different types of mutual funds, but I'll give some examples of the most common ones. Stock funds, as the name indicates, invest almost exclusively in stocks. Of course, here you will have many more subcategories, at least as many as there are subcategories of stocks and companies. For instance, you might have growth funds that invest in companies that focus on growth, but they usually don't pay dividends. However, you are more likely to gain from the increase in stock price.

Index funds also exclusively invest in stocks but focus on index stocks. These are like mutual funds that you can purchase straight away from the stock market, which can also be called ETFs. One of the largest ones is the S&P 500, which tracks the value of the 500 largest companies in the U.S. ETFs are also an excellent option if you want to diversify your portfolio, and there are many different types.

Balanced funds are a hybrid type of mutual fund that has stocks, bonds, and sometimes even other investment vehicles.

Bonds can be seen as fixed-income investments. They are loans made by a part of a government (for instance, a local government) or a corporation to raise funds. In this particular case, you are the one loaning the money to these entities, and in return (after some time), they will give you back the money plus interest. As you might have guessed, bonds have an end date, which is the date the loan (called the principal) has to be paid back to you. These are called fixed-income because you know for sure they will be paid back, and you know when. Bonds are also much more risk-averse than stocks in mutual funds; however, they are not risk-free, especially bonds from corporations, because they can default. However, this is rare, and even more rare, if you purchase a government bond since these almost never default. Government bonds are issued at literally all levels, so you can have, as I said, local governments, but you also have federal government bonds. Because these are a lot safer, the profit is usually a lot less than in stocks, for instance. Governments usually issue bonds to pay for infrastructure such as schools, hospitals, roads, etc. While corporations might do it to expand their business or raise capital for a new product launch. When you purchase a loan, you have all the necessary information, such as the expiration date, principal per bond, and interest rate (called the coupon rate), so you can clearly understand what the benefits are and how much you can actually receive back. However, after you've purchased a bond, you can resell it at a higher price, or you can also buy bonds from other investors and not directly from the source.

There are other types of bonds. I've already mentioned corporate bonds that are issued by companies. Governmental bonds are solely issued by the U.S. Treasury, and municipal bonds are issued by municipalities and states. Then, you can also have agency bonds, which are issued by government-affiliated organizations.

What Is Compound Interest When Investing?

Compound interest is a very interesting concept that you should be fully aware of because it can allow you to increase your money and wealth. Compound interest can be seen often in savings accounts but also when investing. Many savings accounts only earn interest on the initial deposit. For instance, if you deposit $100 and the interest rate is 5%, after a month, you will have $105. The next month, you will have $110 because the interest is only applied to the initial deposit of $100. However, if that savings account had compound interest, the second month's interest would be applied to the $105, so, you'd have $110.25, and in the third month, you'd have $115.76 instead of $115. While this might not look much, it actually is because if you leave the money for a long time, you're incrementally increasing your money.

This, added to the large amount, makes a massive difference in your earnings. Compound interest is often referred to as having interest in the interest. In other words, with compound interest, your money grows faster than if you had applied simple interest.

In investments, you can choose to have a broker's account with a dividend reinvestment plan, also known as DRIP. This automatically reinvests any dividend you receive. This is why, even though you might prefer growth stocks, dividends can really boost your returns.

The "magic" about compound interest is that because it accumulates interest from the previous month (or periods), it grows exponentially, meaning that the accelerating rate is always increasing. These periods, we call compound interest periods, are the intervals of time between when interest is added to the investment or your account. Now, this can come in different ways: annually, semi-annually, quarterly, monthly, or daily. Even if the account you have accrued compound interest daily, often you get paid monthly, and while it's daily, the additional interest is added to when the previous interest gets to the account. So, as you might imagine, the more frequent the compounding interest is, the better for you. But, as you probably figured too, if you are a borrower, compound interest works against you, and when it comes to the frequency of compound interest, you want as sparsely as possible. So, when looking at the benefits of compounding interest, it can help us build wealth in the long term, whether it is through investments or savings, and it mitigates inflation. However, if you are the borrower, compounding interest is not beneficial. It's also important to note that the returns you earn are taxable. Let's look at a table illustrating how much you'd get with compound interest. Here, your initial investment is $5000, and it has a 3% monthly interest for one year (12 months).

Month	Interest	Accrued Interest	Balance
0			$5,000
1	$150	$150.00	$5,150.00
2	$154.50	$304.50	$5,304.50
3	$159.14	$463.64	$5,463.64
4	$163.91	$627.54	$5,627.54
5	$168.83	$796.37	$5,796.37
6	$173.89	$970.26	$5,970.26
7	$179.11	$1,149.37	$6,149.37
8	$184.48	$1,333.85	$6,333.85
9	$190.02	$1,523.87	$6,523.87
10	$195.72	$1,719.58	$6,719.58
11	$201.59	$1,921.17	$6,921.17
12	$207.64	$2,128.80	$7,128.80

As you can see, the accrued interest as well as the interest increase exponentially which by the end of the year has grown quite significantly. If you were to have only simple interest at the exact same rate, your interest would always be fixed at $150 a month. By the end of the twelve months with compound interest, you're earning $207.64 by simply not touching your money.

Long-Term Investment Strategies

There are quite a few strategies to invest in; some are short-term, others long-term, but as you're starting out, I'm going to talk about long-term ones because they require less knowledge of the market and are far safer.

The "ride a winner" strategy means that in your portfolio, you'd have a really good winner," meaning that one of your stocks was really increasing, and you'd only consider selling it after it increased tenfold. However, you have to be quite disciplined and do your due diligence because even if a stock is going to increase ten times, there will be periods where it will go down before going back up, and you need to resist the temptation to sell it. In other words, you have to believe in the stock you've bought and not sell it because it went down a little.

Selling a loser is another long-term strategy where you essentially have to come to terms with the fact that a stock is not going to go back up (at least not any time soon) and cut your losses before it does more damage to your portfolio. I'm talking about drastic or continuous losses, not simply losing a few dollars. Also, you need to understand what is going on in the market to understand the reason behind some stocks losing value before deciding to sell.

Again, don't panic if the stock goes down for a little bit; these are short-term movements, and they are part of the market. You have to zoom out and take a look at what is happening in the big picture of the stock. Also, you should never chase a stock that has increased exponentially within a week. For instance, you see a stock that has increased 50% in the last week, and you have the urge to buy it because it's going up so fast. But chances are that you already lost the ride, and once you buy it, it might come crashing down or won't increase that much anymore. Stick to your strategy and do your due diligence on the stocks you've bought.

Dollar-cost averaging is quite a common strategy in the investment world, and it's often used to manage the price risk of your investments. You apply this strategy every time you're purchasing investments such as stocks or ETFs, and instead of purchasing five shares of a certain stock at one time and at a single price point, you purchase them at different times. So, you're buying that same investment at regular intervals and in smaller parts, independent of the price. Let me give you an example: if you buy two Microsoft shares at $100, your average cost per share is $100, but in the next month, the shares drop 50%, and your share value drops from $200 (since you had two shares) to $100. But what if you bought one share of Microsoft for $100, and the next month you bought it for $50? A month went by, and there was no significant price change; this would be because your average cost per share was $75, and so your investment only dropped 25% instead of 50%. Essentially, you are averaging the cost of your investments by diluting the price point and making them more secure. At the end of the day, you still have the same number of shares, but you bought them, on average, at a cheaper price.

Lastly, you have to focus on the future. You have to study the companies and try to understand where they will be in 5 to 10 years. Understand their business model, read the news, and look at their quarterly and annual reports so you have a better chance of making money.

Investing is a very important part of your finances, and fortunately, people are starting to be more involved in it than other generations were. It is not a place where you lose money; it can happen, but if you know what you are doing, it is often a place where you can make quite a lot of money. As I've mentioned, there are many different options when it comes to investing, such as stocks, bonds, and mutual funds, but a mix of them will make your portfolio more diverse and give you a much better chance at creating returns for you. I would advise you to start with mutual funds because they are more risk-resistant, and you don't have to pick your investments yourself; instead, you have a professional do it for you. Then, I would move on to stocks once you understand the market better and how everything works and have more confidence in your skills. Compound interest is a great way to make returns, and you should use it as often as you can, whether it is in your savings accounts or through your investments, because in the long run, it can make you a lot more money than using simple interest.

In the following chapter, I'm going to talk about insurance, what it is, why it is so important, and the different types of insurance you can have.

CHAPTER 8
INSURANCE

> *Because of the risks, the insurance premium may not be.*
>
> –Dwayne Brown

Insurance is an important aspect of life as well as finances if you're looking to protect your assets, your property, or even your family from financial risks. We tend to have a greater peace of mind when we have insurance that can protect us and maintain us financially secure from many risks that life might bring us.

For instance, without car insurance, we would have to bear the burden of paying for all the expenses of the car in case we had a car accident. The same with health insurance which can really cripple our finances. It's quite simple to understand how insurance works. You pay a fee, whether it is monthly or annually, it depends, and the insurance covers the majority of the things that can happen. Of course, this depends on the insurance you have and the many add-ons you might want to have.

Understanding Insurance

As I said, insurance is quite easy to understand, but its benefits are far greater than you might think. For instance, insurance plans might help you pay medical bills, emergencies, hospitalizations, and any medical care you might need in the future. If you don't have that, and with the lack of free healthcare in the U.S., you and your family can be really drained of savings. There's also life insurance that gives money to the surviving members of the family. This is especially good if the person who passed away was the sole earner of the household. This way, the family can pay any debts, mortgages, or anything else. It might not be something that you think too much about now, but once you have family and kids, you will definitely try to inform yourself about it.

Life insurance can also help you with retirement planning and stay financially independent throughout your retirement. Property insurance allows you to get paid in case of a natural disaster or any other kind that might destroy your property or if someone gets in and steals valuable things. Your insurance has coverage for that. It is a really good thing to have because life is unpredictable, and you don't know when something might happen. It is always best to be prepared.

What are the Types of Insurance Out There?

There are quite a lot, but I'm just going to name a few. While some of them I've already mentioned, I'll just go a little deeper in explaining what they are.

Life insurance, as I've said, is what can safeguard your family in the event of death. In simple words, it can help the family financially, usually with a lump sum of money that is paid to them if something happens. Health insurance covers medical expenses in many different ways. As I've mentioned, treatments, hospitalization, or any other treatments you'd need afterward. Child plans are great because they work as a sort of savings for when the child is ready to go to college or university.

Home insurance covers any damages to your property caused by accidents, natural calamities, mishaps, and pretty much anything else. And auto insurance is for vehicles, and these are mandatory.

These cover accidents with other vehicles as well as natural disasters. They also protect damages to third parties during an accident where you might have hurt somebody while driving your car.

Evaluating Your Options Before Purchasing Insurance

Like many other things when it comes to finances, it's important that you properly evaluate insurance before purchasing it. The first thing to do is assess what you need. Having a look at your requirements is key to fully comprehending the policies you need. Usually, the most important thing is to protect yourself and your family financially. For instance, if you want to save money for your kid's education or buy a property, you should perhaps look into a unit-linked insurance plan or ULIP. An insurance pension account, on the other hand, will give you an income once you retire.

However, purchasing your insurance is not something that you should do and forget. You have to review it throughout your life and change it as your needs change. Essentially, you should try to protect yourself and your family from all financial liabilities. For example, if you are purchasing life insurance, you need to make sure it is big enough to cover any debts.

As with many other things, comparing plans will give you a much better idea of the insurance you are purchasing. There are many different solutions out there, and it is important that you take your time to choose the best one, as well as the one where you pay the lowest premiums. However, I believe that the benefits of a plan are more important than its pricing. I know many of us don't read the terms and conditions, but when it comes to insurance, it's crucial that you do. Not only read them but understand them fully.

Buying insurance is not as hard as it seems, but you need to be absolutely sure of what you are buying and that you are making the best possible decision for you and your family.

In the next chapter, I'll be talking about big purchases, whether material or to improve ourselves and others, such as paying for college. I'm going to go through how you can plan for significant purchases, understand the financing options and explore the different strategies you can use.

CHAPTER 9

BIG PURCHASES AND PAYING FOR COLLEGE

> *Education is the most powerful weapon which you can use to change the world.*
> –Nelson Mandela

Big purchases don't always mean buying properties and cars (however, I will start with those); they also mean investing in our future. For that, you need to plan carefully so you don't end up making mistakes that might affect you in the future.

How Can You Plan For Big Purchases?

When planning for big purchases (yes, I'm talking houses or cars), you know that you will need significant funding. For that, you really need to think about how you are going to actually do it. You need to think about how much money you can put up front and all the consequences that entail.

The first thing to do is assess your needs, goals, and timeline. The latter is especially important because you might have to pay it for quite a few years, such as on a property through a mortgage. Determining the true cost of what you have to pay is also important. For example, if you are thinking about purchasing a property, you need to determine the down payment; if you are purchasing a car, you need to figure out the upfront money. So, for that, you also have to think about how long you have to save (a budget with this in mind is your best tool). For instance, you need to save $20,000 in the next two years so you can pay the down payment for a property. How much do you need to be saving every month? You have to save roughly $850. From there, you have to budget and make changes so you can reach your goal.

One thing that I like to do is set up a separate account. This means staying away from your regular savings, your checking account, and your emergency fund. Ideally, you could put it to work earning interest in a savings account. But the goal is to have it separate so you can clearly see it growing and know that you are getting closer to your goal every month.

However, it's important that you don't ignore your other financial goals, so don't make unrealistic goals for large purchases. It's crucial that you build yourself a good and strong financial foundation before taking on large purchases.

Financing Options When Making Big Purchases

If you're buying a property, the best financing option is definitely a mortgage through a bank. Again, you have to shop around and talk to several banks and financial institutions so you can get the best possible mortgage with lower interest rates.

Now, if you're purchasing another big purchase that is not a property, there are options. For instance, if you want to purchase a car, car financing is possibly the best option. There are different options when it comes to this particular financing option. For instance, you have a car loan where you choose the loan amount that you need and for how long you need it. If approved, this money will be paid into your account, and you will purchase the car. Then, you pay this loan in installments. Having a great credit score will ensure you have the best possible interest rates and that you are approved.

You also have a hire purchase, or HP, where you have to also pay in installments (both the loan and the interest), but unlike a car loan, usually, you have to pay something upfront (usually 10% of the car);

however, the larger the upfront money, the lower the interest rates are. Here, you can also choose the length of time that you want to pay it back.

For other purchases, you have other options. For instance, you could use your credit card. Of course, this should be done if you can pay the balance off as quickly as possible or if, by any chance, the interest is at 0%. You can also take out a personal loan. These require a great credit score and usually have fixed interest, but you can use them for many different purchases, such as home renovations. At times, it might also require collateral, which means you have to put something where if you can't pay the loan back, they will take it from you, for example, a car.

Depending on what you are buying, the merchant might offer an installment plan where you pay for the purchase over several months. These are usually quicker to get approved, but you still need to have a good credit score. They obviously come with interest when you pay them back.

The Different Ways You Can Save for College

College is important for your future. Nowadays, while there are alternatives, people who go to college usually earn more throughout their lives. However, it's expensive, and if you haven't been saving, it can become difficult to pay for it. Although there are many different ways that you can pay for your college expenses. The examples I will give below are exclusive to the US, but most countries have similar options available.

The first one that comes to mind is the 529 Education Savings Plan. This is a state-sponsored investment account that helps save for college expenses. Any money in here can be invested in many different investment vehicles, such as mutual funds or ETFs. But it gets better: any earnings from this are not taxed, unlike other investment accounts. However, you can only use these funds for anything related to education, such as the cost of tuition, transportation to college, or educational materials. In fact, there are high penalties if you use it for anything else but education-related things and your portfolio is usually a lot more limited than other investment accounts.

Another savings account you can use for your education is the Coverdell Education Savings Account. Usually, your parents have to open these because they are custodial accounts before you are 18 years old. Like the 529, you don't pay taxes on earnings, but your parents have to have a low annual income to apply for it, and they can only contribute $2,000 per year.

Another option is scholarships, grants, or work-study programs. Before talking more about it, you can visit studentaid.gov to check all the options for grants, scholarships, and other financial aid for your education.

Let's start with grants. These are financial aids that don't need to be paid back unless you withdraw from school. The Department of Education has many different grants that can help students pay for their education. Some of them are the Federal Pell Grants, the Federal Supplemental Education Opportunity Grants, and the Teacher Education Assistance for College and Higher Education. While eligibility changes, grants are only given to students who actually need financial aid to pay for their tuition.

Scholarships are offered by private and nonprofit organizations to help students pay for their education. Eligibility depends on many factors, such as talent or academic merit, but some are also based on financial need. Each scholarship has its own requirements, but a quick online search will give you all the websites you can visit to check on particular scholarships.

Work-study jobs are programs that allow you to earn money that you can then use to pay for your education. Usually, this work is part-time, so you can attend your education. While you can earn more than the minimum wage, this is not guaranteed. What you get from these work-study jobs depends on your level of financial need, the funding level of the organization, and when you apply for them.

Alternatively, you can also apply for a loan to pay for your education, but as you already know, this has to be paid back with interest, so it's important that you plan everything properly before doing it.

Big purchases and paying for college are things that might seem daunting, but they are part of life, and we need to go through them. In fact, with enough planning, they are not so hard to achieve. There are many different things that you can do and many different strategies that you can follow to reach these goals faster.

In the next and last chapter, I will talk about retirement, how to plan for long-term financial goals, explore retirement saving options that you can start right away, and the different strategies available.

CHAPTER 10

RETIREMENT

> *Retirement from work, but not from life. – M.K. Soni*

Yes, I know it's a long way until you retire; after all, you haven't even started to work, right? However, planning for retirement starts right now. In this last chapter, I'll be talking about retirement plans and the many different strategies you have, as well as the benefits of starting to plan this early in life.

How to Start Planning for Retirement?

When it's time to retire, you have worked all your life for yourself and your family. Now, you want to spend some quality time with your family and do what makes you happy—if you've planned properly, of course.

A retirement plan simply means that you have followed the right steps to live a comfortable life when it's time to stop working. There's not a single formula to plan for retirement, but there are guidelines. A retirement plan is important because you will have a regular income after you stop working, but you are also ready for any emergency and prepared to live a long, healthy life.

You have many investment options that will allow you to properly plan for when you retire. But like all kinds of investing, there are some with higher risks and higher rewards and others that help you protect your wealth. Let's take a look at the most common ones.

The Different Retirement Options

Before I get into the different retirement options, the examples I'm going to talk about below are specific to the US, but other countries have similar options available. The two most common retirement investment options are 401(k)s and IRAs. A 401(k) is a retirement savings plan that you often get through your employer, and it has tax advantages for you. When you are working, your employer will offer you a 401(k) that you have to sign up for if you want, and here, you are agreeing to give a percentage of your monthly income to your 401(k) savings plan, which is just like an investment account. Then, your employer usually matches what you have contributed. While you don't have all the options you'd have in your personal investment account, you can still pick from several investment options, but these are usually mutual funds because they are safer. In a traditional 401(k), any contributions you make are pre-taxed, which essentially means that you are not taxed on them now but will be when you eventually withdraw the money in your retirement. A Roth 401(k) works the same way, but it's after-tax, which means that your contributions are taxed right away but not when you withdraw the money in your retirement.

Then, you also have an Individual Retirement Account or IRA. This type of account also has tax benefits like a 401(k), and you can also contribute with pre- or after-tax money. This is a long-term savings account that works similarly to a 401(k), but it's not done through your employer. This is what self-employed workers use more often, and you can open it through your bank or even a brokerage. Here, you have four different types of IRAs: the traditional, Roth, Simplified Employee Pension (SEP), and Savings Incentive Match Plan for Employees (SIMPLE).

The differences between them have to do with the contribution limits. For instance, with a traditional IRA and a Roth IRA, you can contribute a maximum of $6,500 or $7,500 if you are 50 years old or older (however, these limits change every year). With a SEP, you can contribute a maximum of $65,000 or the lesser of 25%, and with a SIMPLE retirement account, you can contribute a maximum of $15,500 or $19,000 if you are 50 years old or older.

CONCLUSION

That's it! That's all you need to know to start your financial journey on the right foot and prepare for what's coming. I know, at times, it might seem a little overwhelming, but once you know how things are done and you allow yourself to create routines, everything becomes a lot easier.

Starting with the basics and understanding what money is and how to make money is fundamental. A good foundation will allow you to prosper in all the other areas of your personal finances. When it comes to making money, there are many different ways you can do it as a teenager, as you have seen in Chapter 2. Just pick whatever you are most comfortable doing or something that you believe you will be doing in the future. Gaining experience at this stage of your life will make it easier for you in the future. If you can, open a bank account (if you don't already have one) since understanding the basics here and how you can manage your account will make you more comfortable with these services. Understanding the two basic accounts—checking accounts and savings—will allow you to not only get paid but also grow your money effectively. Nowadays, everything is gamified, and bank accounts are no exception. With mobile and internet banking, it is a lot easier to understand what you are doing.

I cannot emphasize this enough: budgeting allows you to reach your financial goals, and you should make it a habit. Regardless of the type of budgeting you follow, it's important to have one so you have your finances under control at all times. The more you know and the more you are in control, the better purchasing decisions you will make. This brings us to the different techniques when it comes to purchasing goods or services: practicing smart shopping and comparing prices can save you a lot of money in the long run and is one of those things that you want to have in your routine. Credit, credit cards, and debt can all sound scary, but as you've seen, credit can actually help you with your finances as long as you keep it under control. It can build your credit score and allow you more opportunities.

While savings are important, so is investing. In fact, investing, when done properly, can increase your wealth exponentially. Having savings goals is important, but having investment goals is also crucial so you can create a good financial foundation and be prepared for any financial emergencies that might come your way. Preparedness is everything. And don't forget compound interest, which can exponentially increase the value of your savings and investments even without adding any more money to them.

You might never have associated insurance with money or savings, but as we've seen in Chapter 8, it can be a great protection for your wealth, yourself, and your family. There are all types of insurance, such as health or auto, and while some are mandatory, others are recommended. This is especially true for health insurance in the US since these are mostly not covered by the government, and any minor medical emergency can become very expensive. It's important that you know how to evaluate insurance policies and coverage so you know you are properly protected, but you can also save money.

There's always a point in our lives where we have to make big purchases or have big expenses, such as purchasing a car, a home, or paying for our education. It's crucial that you plan properly and in advance, know how to evaluate your options, and explore the different strategies on how to save for these big expenses. Lastly, retirement might seem very far away, but we've seen the importance of starting early. This is probably the longest-term financial goal you will have, but even at your age, there are things that you can do to start planning for it.

However, I believe the most important thing you can do is apply the knowledge you have acquired in this book on a daily basis. There are many concepts here that might take a while for you to make a habit of, but with practice, everything is possible. Taking control of your financial future is something that many of us adults didn't have the chance to do, mainly because we didn't have the knowledge, but you do. If you apply everything you've learned in this book, you will not only have total control of your finances, but you will also live a stress-free life.

SOCIAL SKILLS
FOR TEENS

A Simple **7 Day** *System for Teenagers*

to Break Out of Shyness, Build a Bulletproof Self-Confidence, and Eliminate Social Anxiety to Excel in Social Interactions

EMILY CARTER

INTRODUCTION

> "
> No one can make you feel inferior without your consent.
> –Eleanor Roosevelt

◆◆◆◆

While it's a good quote—a great one even—I have some notes. First of all, as much as we try to deny it, we are not in control of our thoughts and emotions. Sure, there are a lot of mental exercises and practices that can improve our self-awareness and emotional intelligence, which might lead us to better understand (and control) our reactions to the world around us—and to what goes on in our minds when life happens.

However, to say that we can choose not to be offended, hurt, or made to feel inferior to others' words and actions is implying we should deny or ignore our thoughts and emotions altogether. And honestly, I'm offended by that. We can learn how to respond to our emotions in a way that's healthy, but there's no magical switch you can flip to suddenly not care; this isn't *The Vampire Diaries*.

Now, you might be thinking, what do our emotions have to do with building confidence and self-esteem in social interactions? And the answer is: Probably more than you might realize. You see, your emotions shape your perspective on life, and perspective controls your thoughts, and your brain will believe everything it tells itself because it's biased.

Each and every one of us have what are called "automatic thoughts." These are thoughts that are influenced by things like past experiences, perspectives, and emotional triggers. If your automatic thoughts are negative by nature, they can wreak havoc on the way you see yourself, especially if you're still getting to know who you are and where you fit into the world as a teenager.

"I'm just introverted," your brain might say. And that might be true, but there's a difference between preferring to be alone and feeling like you're not socially capable of building meaningful relationships. Introverts are still confident in their ability to interact with the world; they just don't feel the need to.

If the only reason you don't like talking to other people is because it feels hard, you never seem to know what to say, you believe they don't like you based on zero evidence, you feel you're too awkward, you assume they're judging you, or you believe they're better than you, then you might not actually be an introvert after all.

Your inner monologue can make you believe things so strongly that you don't even question them. And it's only when you make a conscious effort to challenge your own beliefs, values, and perspectives that you start the process of rewiring your brain to be kind and more accepting of your flaws and perceived shortcomings. Becoming aware of your self-sabotaging thought processes and tendencies is the first step to a healthier self-image.

Building and practicing social skills in your teen years are important for a few reasons. Mainly because, as an adult, it's necessary to be willing and able to communicate effectively in unfamiliar circumstances. Whether it's for work, friendships, or romantic relationships, social skills are the foundation of any meaningful interaction. It helps avoid miscommunications, resolve conflict, build trust, set boundaries, and so much more.

If you think about it, the absolute best time to work on these skills—and practice using them—is during your teen years. Sure, you might make a fool of yourself once or twice, but everyone is so focused on themselves and their own presence in the world at this age that your mishaps go unnoticed most of the time. When you compare how many cringeworthy moments you've had to what you remember your peers having, it paints a clear picture.

The thing is, you don't remember their awkward moments because they've had less of them; you just don't think it's worse than yours. And that right there is a prime example of how powerful the brain can really be. It would be foolish to assume that they're watching and waiting for you to do or say something embarrassing as much as they're trying not to do or say something embarrassing themselves.

But let's say they do make a big deal of something you did or said. Oftentimes, when others are inflating your misgivings, it comes from a place of low self-esteem and a lack of confidence in themselves. It's a way to redirect attention away from themselves, so they can feel secure and lower their guard—even if just for a moment. It's never fun to be in a situation like that, but how you respond to it (regardless of how you feel) can make a world of difference to how others perceive you and your self-confidence.

The anxiety that comes with low self-esteem and social interaction is not going to go away on its own. Unfortunately, you're going to have to face your fears at some point or another, and it all starts with rebuilding the foundations of a positive self-image and finding your voice.

You might be thinking, "It's impossible to build confidence and overcome social anxiety in only seven days." And, of course, you'd be absolutely right. The idea—or my idea, at least—of the seven-day system is to build a habit. When you know exactly what to do every single day, and you have a clear strategy and plan in place, you're not left wondering what you should be doing.

Week after week, you follow the same steps of doing something small and seemingly insignificant every day until you've built up enough tolerance to face your fears (or hesitation) surrounding social interaction. Only once you're able to go through every exercise comfortably do you move on to more advanced or intimidating situations.

Throughout this book, we'll be doing just that. You'll learn effective and easy ways to work on personal growth, communication skills, and handling difficult or awkward situations using a seven-day system that will kickstart your journey to self-discovery and self-acceptance.

And remember, social skills—just like any other skill—require practice and perseverance (even when it's hard). By taking one tiny step at a time, you'll build tolerance and maybe even realize that it's not half as bad or difficult as you may have thought.

CHAPTER 1
Day 1 — SELF-AWARENESS

> "
> We don't see things as they are, we see them as we are.
>
> —Anais Nin

The term "self-awareness" gets thrown around a lot, and I believe that a lot of people don't truly understand what it means. Everyone is technically aware of themselves, but an overused profound quote that gets posted alongside a selfie with a grayscale filter on it isn't exactly the epitome of self-awareness.

Don't get me wrong; I hold cheesy philosophical quotes very near and dear to my heart. A lot of them inspire creative thinking, ideas, introspection, and new perspectives. The way that everyone can look at the exact same piece of art, for example, and come up with their own unique interpretations of what's happening based on their own unique set of brainwaves, the emotions they think it's meant to conjure, and the general "vibe" or meaning they personally look for behind it will forever fascinate me.

Levels of Self-Awareness

You are not born self-aware; it's something that develops over time—much like self-image. It's how you make sense of the things you do based on your opinions, emotions, values, and belief systems. There are five key elements (or levels) of self-awareness:

1. **Consciousness.** By the age of five, you'll have the basic understanding that you're a person with your own thoughts, emotions, and experiences. You can recognize your own reflection and identify yourself in a picture or video.
2. **Self-knowledge.** You know your current likes, dislikes, and preferences. It also includes your motivations, beliefs, and opinions.
3. **Emotional intelligence.** This is your ability to understand, manage, and express your emotions in a healthy way.

4. **Self-acceptance.** You're able to recognize your flaws and admit mistakes while still showing kindness and compassion for yourself.
5. **Self-reflection.** You reflect on your emotions and behaviors and whether or not they align with who you believe yourself to be. You use this feedback for self-improvement rather than self-hatred.

Furthermore, there are two distinct types of self-awareness: public and private. Public self-awareness is when there's a lot of attention on you from other people, like when you're delivering a speech or presentation—you have the spotlight. You're, therefore, hyper-aware that you're being watched and evaluated. This pressure usually causes us to behave in ways that are considered to be more socially acceptable. If you have social anxiety (or even something akin to "stage fright"), you're focused and concerned about what everyone might think of you–especially if you were to do something embarrassing or "wrong."

Private self-awareness is when you become aware of certain aspects, features, or traits about yourself privately. The way you feel or what you think when you look in the mirror, when you realize you forgot to study for a test and your stomach drops, when your crush walks into the classroom and your heart starts beating faster. These are all examples of private self-awareness. You can feel and recognize what's going on in your mind and body.

Being self-aware is a good thing; it allows us to put the things we do and feel into perspective. It allows us to become better people. However, it's possible to be overly self-aware—it's called being self-conscious.

Most—if not all—people experience bouts of self-consciousness every now and again. Honestly, it's impossible not to in the era of social media, unachievable societal expectations, and impossible beauty standards. But it's not normal to be experiencing excessive amounts of self-consciousness. If it's to the point where it's affecting your quality of life on a daily basis, it might be worth speaking to a mental health professional about.

Limiting Beliefs and Self-Sabotage

As part of your self-discovery journey, you'll have to come face-to-face with the fact that it was you holding yourself back all this time. Now, you might not be ready to hear that just yet, and that's okay.

The brain is biased, and it will convince itself that something is true even when it isn't based on facts. These are called limiting beliefs, and while some limiting beliefs are necessary to keep us safe and to form a productive and healthy society (like believing you can't fly so you don't try to jump out the window of a ten-story building or believing that stealing is wrong so you stop yourself from hotwiring a car).

However, some of these limiting beliefs keep us from achieving goals, experiencing new and exciting things, or taking advantage of great opportunities. For example, you might think you don't have what it takes to be a doctor, so you settle for being a teacher. You might think you won't get into the college of your dreams, so you don't even apply. You believe no one finds you interesting, so you sit alone at lunchtime.

There are unhelpful limiting beliefs, and they keep you stagnant, unable or unwilling to move forward, take on new opportunities, and grow as a person. Whether you have limiting beliefs about yourself, the world, or life in general, the first step is to identify them. And you do that by thinking about a goal you have had stored in the deepest pits of your medulla oblongata that never seemed to leave despite how many times you've shot it down.

This could be anything from learning a new skill to making new friends. Now, ask yourself why you aren't actively working on it. I can guarantee you there's a limiting belief somewhere surrounding it. For example, let's say you're into DIY and you've flipped furniture pieces for your own room. The idea of turning it into a side hustle has popped up in your head a couple of times, and even though it gets you excited every time, you haven't taken it further.

The limiting beliefs here can be that you don't think you have enough skill, knowledge, or creativity, or that no one would buy second-hand furniture from a teenager. See how none of these beliefs are rooted in reality? How none of them are based on evidence or facts?

If you're still having trouble identifying your limiting beliefs, here are a few alternative ways (besides thinking of a goal you're not working toward and why) that might bring more clarity:

- ◆ **Get rid of mind clutter.** Your mind, just like your desk or your bedroom floor, can get cluttered if you don't make an effort to get rid of all the unnecessary thoughts. Unnecessary thoughts are things that stick around in your mind and can be hard to get rid of: Fears and worries, wants and desires, the upcoming test you haven't studied for, your to-do list, negative experiences, lingering emotions, things you can't control, and so on. Either way, having too much going on upstairs makes it harder to think clearly or focus on anything. The easiest and most effective way to reduce and prevent mind clutter from accumulating to an overwhelming level is to write it out. The act of putting your thoughts onto paper (or even typing it out in your notes app) helps you let go of these unnecessary and negative thoughts. You could also try meditating, taking a nap (and making sure you're getting enough sleep in general), decluttering your physical environment (i.e., cleaning your room), spending some time in the sun, limiting external distractions and stimuli for a bit, or adding ten minutes of physical activity to your daily schedule. Keep what works; leave what doesn't.

- ◆ **Be curious.** Limiting beliefs are often associated with being closed-minded, and closed-mindedness is synonymous with having a fixed mindset (the idea that we can't change who we are or improve ourselves to any degree). You can start working on moving toward a growth mindset by adopting an "everything is figure-outable" mentality and being curious about yourself, your past experiences, and your current sense of reality (and whether it's possible that it might be warped). So be curious, doubt your mind's intentions for you, ask questions, and challenge yourself.

- ◆ **Work on self-improvement.** Self-improvement is kind of the entire goal of this book. And by admitting change is needed, being willing to change, and being open to the words written on these pages, you have already taken the first step! But self-improvement isn't a one-and-done type of deal; it's a life-long journey—one that is continuously changing who you are for the better. As part of the first step in self-improvement, you'll need to dig deep and identify your personal values. This is a list of what's most important to you in life. To identify your core values, start by answering the following questions:

    - Think of a time (or times) when you felt most at peace, happy, or fulfilled. Who were you with, and what were you doing?
    - Think of a time (or times) when you felt hurt, angry, or unhappy. What happened?
    - What inspires you the most?
    - What are you most proud of?
    - If you could change anything about the world, what would it be?

    Based on these answers, you should be able to see certain themes pop up. Maybe a majority of the moments when you were most happy were with family—you value family. Your worst moments were when someone betrayed or lied to you—you might value honesty, trust, and loyalty. If music inspires you, you could value creativity. And so on. By the end of this exercise, you should have a good idea of what your core values are. You can then do some soul-searching and define them better, add new ones, and remove ones you don't strongly identify with—until you're left with just a handful. This doesn't mean they can't change over time as you grow and gain new perspectives, but it's a pretty good starting point. You might also discover you have some unhelpful or negative core values, such as valuing money a bit too much, being dishonest at times, the need for attention or being liked all the time, being rude, superiority, entitlement, and so on. If you do find you have a couple of negative core values, these are the ones you focus on correcting while on your journey to self-improvement.

- ◆ **Counseling.** There comes a point where all the self-help books in the world won't help you break free from the shackles of your own mind. If you think you might already be too far down the rabbit hole, rest assured there's still hope. I can only give you so much advice and cheesy philosophical quotes from here. Sometimes you need someone right there with you on your self-discovery journey that can give you personalized support and course correct you when you veer too far from the path. Therapists and counselors can help, and there's nothing wrong with needing support until you can take the reins and continue on your journey alone.

Self-Acceptance 101

Self-acceptance doesn't mean making excuses for your bad habits or bad behaviors; it simply means acknowledging them, being aware of them, and admitting you need to work on them without creating resentment toward yourself. It also means being proud of your accomplishments, your progress, your contributions, and your skills.

Someone who is self-aware is able to view themselves realistically. They know what their strengths are and don't feel insecure about their weaknesses. For example, they don't look at a video of Tony Hawk skateboarding online and think they're useless because they can't perform at that same level.

Someone who accepts themselves will see themselves as a whole person with flaws, quirks, emotions, traits, and past experiences instead of defining themselves based on a certain or singular incident, ability, characteristic, or weakness. They believe they are worthy of respect and love because their sense of value comes from within—they respect, value, and love themselves unconditionally.

The good news is, you can become this person too!

Once you've identified your core values, you can adjust your actions accordingly. This strengthens your sense of identity so you feel more grounded and able to challenge negative self-talk and distorted thoughts.

Practice self-compassion and standing up to yourself, for yourself. Negative self-talk and distorted thoughts are a result of those pesky cognitive biases we talked about earlier. The more you entertain negative self-talk and allow them to go unchallenged, the stronger they get. Then, just like Mario when he eats a mushroom, they grow into distorted thoughts. When this happens, the constant negative self-talk has done its job and the distorted thoughts and beliefs take on a life of their own.

Distorted thoughts and beliefs can make spotting negative self-talk more challenging, but with a bit of practice and conscious effort, you'll be able to deconstruct your entire self-image and build it back up stronger and more accurately.

Self-Assessment

You can't accept yourself if you don't know who you are. Not only is knowing who you are necessary for self-acceptance and self-improvement, but it also plays a huge role when it comes to setting goals for yourself in every aspect of life. If something isn't important to you, if you're not good at it, or if it goes against who you are, you're not going to make progress in a way that's meaningful to *you*. And that defeats the whole purpose of life.

Let's start with something simple: What do you like to do? Keep it as broad and general or as detailed as you want. Look at your day-to-day life; what do you look forward to every day? Maybe you enjoy the bike ride home from school, the earthy smell when it just starts to rain, reading, listening to indie music, cosplaying, playing video games, rearranging your room, roller skating, watching movies, ASMR. Maybe you actually like pineapple on pizza!

Nothing is insignificant; even the small things—that many other people might also like to do—are what make up who you are.

Now ask yourself the opposite: What do you not like or not like doing? Start with the biggest, most obvious things like maybe school, homework, chores, and vegetables, if applicable. Once these are out of the way, go deeper. Maybe you don't like the color red, going into direct sun, taking a bath (because in your mind it's like making human soup), exercising, wearing jeans, the taste of artificial grape flavor, and so on.

The next question you're going to ask yourself is: What are you good at? You may find that the things you're good at are closely related or overlap with the things you enjoy doing. You like playing chess because you rarely lose. You like baking because it always turns out great. Maybe you actually enjoy school because you love learning new things, and you get good grades. You get the point. Evaluate the things you're good at to find the soft life skills that often lurk beneath the surface: Creativity, patience, kindness, curiosity, determination, and many more.

You probably saw this coming, but the next question is obviously: What are you bad at? The answers to these might also be in relation to the things you don't like doing, or it might be because you simply have no interest in them. For example, you might tell yourself that you're bad at socializing because you have no interest in it when in reality, you're just bad at socializing. So be honest with yourself here. Because being bad at something can be fixed, having no interest in it is a different story.

You can write down your answers to all of these questions separately and keep it as a reminder that you are a whole person—which includes the good and the bad. Try to approach your answers from an analytical standpoint (no judgment, just curiosity). Come back to it every now and then to add to the lists, take things away that no longer apply, or just read through it for fun.

If it helps, you can also find self-assessment tests online, which include personality tests. Though, I would advise using personality tests as rough or inspirational guidelines only since they tend to be anecdotal (not to mention your own bias can influence the results greatly). Don't take them at face value, is all I'm trying to say.

Once you know your true strengths, weaknesses, interests, values, and beliefs, you have a pretty good idea of who you are—in theory. Now, you might not be ecstatic about what you discovered about yourself in the process. No one is 100% happy with who they are. But again, self-acceptance isn't about whether you like who you are; it's about acknowledgment.

"Am I flawed?" Yes. "Do I still deserve love, compassion, empathy, and respect?" Yes, just like everyone else.

Self-acceptance means to treat yourself the way you would a close friend or loved one. You'd never tell someone you love that they're not good enough, not pretty enough, not talented enough, or not smart enough. And if you would say something like this to someone you care about, you need to acknowledge that your values and behavior toward others are bad and toxic, and take accountability for it.

But either way, the call is coming from inside the house. Whether you treat yourself badly or treat others badly, it's your responsibility to see the light, see that it doesn't serve you, and willingly choose to do the work in order to change for the better.

Self-Actualization

There's a lot of debate around what the term "self-actualization" really means. Some say it's the act of becoming who you were meant to be as a person; others say it's about reaching your fullest potential. But for the sake of our purposes, I'm going to define it as becoming the best possible version of yourself.

However, while self-actualization can be interpreted in a lot of different ways, none of the definitions involve being perfect. Unrealistic expectations, perfectionism, or anxiety about making the "right" choice can actually hinder your progress when trying to live authentically.

Becoming the best version of yourself is about living your life in a way that takes full advantage of your strengths while also taking your limits (or weaknesses) into consideration.

People who are actively being who they were meant to be (or self-actualized individuals) don't let what other people think of them get in the way of their reality and truth; they don't depend on external approval or validation. They let their creativity, intuition, and spontaneity guide them, they don't pretend to know things to impress others, and they are comfortable with uncertainty and constructive criticism. They don't take themselves too seriously, and they can admit when they've made a mistake and take responsibility for their actions and behaviors. They dedicate themselves to doing things that bring purpose, happiness, and fulfillment to their own lives while not harming others in the process. They consider the bigger picture while also being able to appreciate the smaller things in life.

Self-actualization goes hand-in-hand with self-awareness and self-improvement. In fact, working toward being more self-aware and wanting to improve yourself will most likely put you on the path to self-actualization, whether you like it or not. There's no endgame here; all of it is a lifelong journey without a destination.

Self-Awareness

Daily Task

Becoming self-aware takes practice and time. It's not going to happen after just one self-assessment session. It's not a possession; it's a skill. It's the ability to analyze your thoughts, habits, actions, and emotions—without judgment—and determine whether they are true to who you really are or who you want to become. And then gradually and consciously working toward positive change until the changes become subconscious or automatic.

This is why your first daily practice or task will be to start journaling. Regardless of whether you think it's silly, intimidating, or embarrassing—just try it. Challenge yourself: Journal every day for a week, and then stop for a week. Pay close attention to how you felt during the week you were journaling versus the week when you weren't.

Document the results by giving your mental clarity or general state of mind a rating (out of 5 stars, or 0–10, for example) every day during the two weeks of the challenge so you can compare your findings accurately.

If there's a visible improvement in your ratings during the week you were journaling and then a steady decline during the week you weren't journaling, you should continue the habit (and you owe me $5). If there's no improvement, or your rating gets worse when journaling, then journaling probably isn't for you, and you should maybe look into different ways to improve self-awareness—there are plenty to choose from, so don't panic.

And to prevent you from backing out because you don't know where to start or what to write about, I'm going to walk you through a few ideas and prompts to inspire your one-week daily writing challenge:

- **Day 1: What are three things that challenged me today, and how did I handle it?**

    This could include physical, mental, or emotional challenges of any degree of difficulty or significance. You couldn't find your socks this morning, you missed the bus, you messed up your verbal assignment, your dad was in a bad mood when he got home, the batteries in your controller dead, you have to work in a group for a project with someone you don't like, PE class, the girl you liked rolled her eyes at you. Anything goes!

    Then write down how you handled it, what you did before, during, and after, how it made you feel, and any further information that's relevant (or not relevant, it's your journal). Now, write how you think you should've handled it based on your ideal values and beliefs—only if how you handled it in reality doesn't align with who you want to be. And what you can do to realize these changes if you were to ever be in that situation again.

    You can also write about life challenges you face in general, not just for the day.

- **Day 2: What are my three most recent limiting beliefs, and why are they not true?**

    It might help to think about recent situations where you found yourself holding back or avoided doing something. For example, you avoided showing your art to someone, you held back when doing a presentation, or you avoided having a discussion with your parents about something that's bothering you.

    Now dig deeper. Try to remember the thought that came to mind or the reasoning behind why you didn't do something. The personal reasons you have for not doing something are, more often than not, due to a limiting belief. Sure, there are instances when holding yourself back from doing something is valid, for instance, when it involves hurting other people unnecessarily in any way.

    But when it involves you doubting your experience, abilities, or value, it's a limiting belief that doesn't serve you. Once you have your three recent limiting beliefs, challenge them. It might help to not think about them as your own limiting belief but rather something someone you care about said to you about themselves. What reasons or assurances would you give them in order to convince them it's not true?

- **Day 3: What is something nobody knows about me?**

    Again, it could be something small and superficial or deep and profound. It could be the first thing that comes to mind, maybe you already know the answer, or maybe you need to sit on it for a couple of minutes.

It could be anything that you haven't told anyone yet for whatever reason: a skill you taught yourself, a unique experience, a quirk or trait, a preference, a hobby, a hidden talent, or liking something controversial (like butter pecan-flavored ice cream). It could be as many things as you can think of or only one example. Take a second to let whatever it is resonate. You can expand on what you wrote down—the why's, what's, when's, and where's—or not.

The goal of this prompt isn't to justify, debunk, or prove anything but rather to appreciate yourself and acknowledge that you are a whole person regardless of what other people might think or say about you.

⬥ Day 4: What things have I avoided doing because of fear?

It might help, once again, to think of a recent example since you might not remember specifics or details about something that happened years ago—but feel free to still write about a distant past experience.

This prompt in itself might help you uncover deeper or stronger self-limiting beliefs. Don't be scared to dive into it and give all your thoughts, emotions, and theories on the fear itself, what caused it, how it has impacted you now, and how it can potentially hinder your growth in the future.

⬥ Day 5: What do I need to let go of?

Let me be clear: Letting go of something and forgiveness is not the same thing. You can let go of something and move on while still holding someone accountable for their hurtful actions against you. Letting go of negative, debilitating thoughts, emotions, and experiences is about and for you. Forgiveness is for those who deserve it, but it's not necessary for healing.

With that in mind, think of a negative feeling or thought you've been holding onto for a long time. Write as much detail as you can remember about the incident. Don't hold back; let your emotions take over and spill out over the pages. Write until there's nothing more to write about, until every last drop of resentment, frustration, regret, or devastation has been captured in ink.

Feel the weight of having to hold on to this burden for so long slip off your shoulders, feel the negative emotions seeping out of your pores and vaporizing, feel the hold it has had on your heart loosening. Take the deepest breath you've taken the entire day, breathe as if it's the first time your lungs are filling with oxygen, and let go—whatever that means to you.

⬥ Day 6: What would my ideal life look like?

What would your ideal life look like right now with regard to yourself, your habits, your accomplishments, and your skills? Yes, it would be nice to live in a mansion, be driven (or drive) to school in the newest Mercedes, and have more money than you know what to do with. But that's not what I'm referring to with this question.

The more specific you are, the better. For example: "I would exercise and make my bed every day, I wouldn't freeze or stumble over my words when having a conversation, I wouldn't care what other people say or think about me, I wouldn't doubt my place in the world, I would get into that program," and so on.

This prompt is about self-discovery. But instead of saying everything you think you aren't or can't do and getting down about it, you're reframing it a bit. It might reveal things about you that you might've not considered, and it might make you aware of things you didn't know you wanted to do or become. And at the very least, it gives you an idea of future goals relating to self-improvement that you can start working on.

⬥ Day 7: If I had to choose a mantra or quote to live by, what would it be and why?

Feel free to search for inspirational or meaningful quotes from philosophers, inventors, or whoever else tickles your fancy for ideas. Choose one that has a lot of meaning to you and explore why.

For example, my favorite quote that I live by is from Joshua J Marine: "Challenges are what make life interesting and overcoming them is what makes life meaningful" (2022).

The way I interpret this quote—and the reason why it's so meaningful to me—is that there will always be challenges in life, some bigger than others. Some mildly derail your plans or ruin your mood for the day, and others bring your entire world to the brink of collapse. There are a lot of things in life you can't change, but you can change your perspective. You can choose to overcome and learn from it. You can look back one day and see that everything turned out okay in the end anyway. You can admit that while it sucked at the time, it put into motion a butterfly effect that has gotten you to where you are today; it opened new doors and shut ones that you were too afraid to shut yourself.

The fact that I'm still here means that, so far, I have a 100% success rate at overcoming the biggest obstacles and challenges that I have faced. And that counts for something!

The seven prompts I provided above are for if you are the type of person who needs a guideline to follow or you don't know where to start. You can absolutely rearrange the order, make adjustments, or discard all of it and just write whatever comes up when the pen hits the paper—or your thumbs hit the screen. You can look up different prompts or ideas on what to write about, and you can create your own. There are no rules!

One suggestion I do have is that you stop here, do the first journaling prompt, and only continue on to the next chapter tomorrow. But keep journaling every day as you proceed with the daily tasks of the upcoming chapters. Doing this will prevent information overload.

CHAPTER 2
Day 2

SELF-CONFIDENCE

> *You're never as good as everyone tells you when you win, and you're never as bad as they say when you lose.*
>
> –Lou Holtz

♦♦♦♦

As with many things in life, everyone has their own thoughts, feelings, and ideologies on what self-confidence actually means and what it looks like. Some people think it's good to be confident since it's connected to self-esteem, success, and good mental health; others think it's bad because they confuse it with vanity or narcissism.

According to the Merriam-Webster dictionary, the word "self-confidence" is defined as "Confidence in oneself and in one's power and abilities." Thanks, that's... revolutionary information.

Let's clear things up. Self-confidence means believing you have inherent value regardless of your mistakes; feeling worthy despite your flaws; respecting and loving yourself; having the courage to stand up to others and defend yourself; living in a way that feels true to who you are; and loving yourself as a whole.

As you can see, it can mean a lot of things—and all of them are accurate descriptions. But what being self-confident *doesn't* mean is that you're perfect or you need to be perfect; that you're better than others; that you should have and achieve high standards, goals, and expectations; that you won't have problems or struggles in life; that you can't be humble; or that you should be selfish.

Developing A Growth Mindset

"You can't teach an old dog new tricks." A common saying implies that once a dog has reached a certain age, they are set in their ways and can't improve their behavior, skills, or abilities. Except, it's not true. One study that was published in 2016 shows that while older dogs might take longer to learn new tricks, it's still possible to teach them (Wallis et al., 2016). And this is only one of many.

But this phrase is also used amongst people, usually the older generations. In my opinion, using this term is a way to justify being stuck or stagnant. It's a way to get out of having to put in the work or effort to improve yourself. It's a way to absolve yourself of any responsibility regarding a need for change. It's lazy and outdated.

But this kind of mindset can happen to anyone at any age. It's called a fixed mindset and it will hold you back for your entire life. You have a fixed mindset if you believe that people are born with talent instead of having worked hard for years to develop it. You have a fixed mindset if you think there's a cap on what you're destined to become. You have a fixed mindset if you believe that not being good at or not knowing something is a permanent state of being.

People with a fixed mindset will avoid challenges because it could lead to failure, and since they believe that their attributes and skills can't be improved upon, failing at something means they are automatically a failure. It becomes so much more intense. They will also avoid or ignore constructive feedback from others (because they view it as a personal attack), feel threatened by others who achieve success, hide their flaws or mistakes, and give up easily.

When you believe that trying is futile, you become hopeless, and this only feeds into the narrative of someone with a fixed mindset. "I can't be better or do better, so why even try?" This black-and-white perspective of "you either *are* something or you're not" has a snowball effect on your self-confidence, self-esteem, self-image, and self-talk.

Getting out of a fixed mindset can be tricky because in order to do so, you first have to believe that change or improvement is possible—which literally goes against everything that someone with a fixed mindset believes. However, this is an instant where, once you've taken the first step, the most difficult part is already over.

What It Is

Now that you know what a fixed mindset is—and whether or not you have one—let's talk about the alternative. A growth mindset is basically the complete opposite of a fixed mindset. Even if you don't have a fixed mindset (or you're not really sure and haven't given it much thought), you can still benefit from strengthening and developing a growth mindset.

So, what even is a "growth mindset?"

Well, a growth mindset means you view setbacks and failures as valuable—a necessary part of the learning process. Someone with a growth mindset recognizes that learning and the ability to learn has no expiration date. They are open to constructive criticism because it might bring forth ideas and perspectives that they might not have considered. They get inspired by the success of others and see challenges as opportunities to grow, learn, and improve.

Having a growth mindset has a huge positive impact on your motivation and academic performance and achievements. And that's a fact! (Yeager et al., 2019).

Here's another fact: You can change your mind. Even if you're stuck in the negative feedback loop and thinking patterns of a fixed mindset, you can rewire your brain to be more open to growth and learning.

How To Change Your Mind

Don't get me wrong, changing your entire outlook on life will take time and practice, as most things do. But in my humble opinion, it's worth doing. What you need to understand is that if you believe anything, your brain will interpret and warp any information to prove itself to be right. There's that internal bias again.

And while there are certain things that will help you overcome a fixed mindset (like challenging your limiting beliefs and thoughts), I want to be even more specific about how you can go about changing your perspective—and, as a result, your mind.

- ⟡ **Know that, scientifically speaking, it's possible.** Your brain might not believe you if you simply tell it that developing, learning, and growing is possible. Luckily, there are studies that prove—without a doubt—that it is possible to change your mindset from negative (fixed) to positive (growth).
Neuroplasticity refers to the brain's ability to change, modify itself, and adapt its physical structure, as well as how it functions throughout your lifespan in response to various internal, external, and environmental factors (Voss et al., 2017). What this means is that your experiences and environment during childhood plays a huge role in how your brain's neural pathways form.

These neural pathways are how your brain makes sense of the world around you and your pathways are different and unique to everyone else's—but they can also be changed or "rewired." We see this with people who have lost one or more of their senses all the time. In someone who has undergone sensory loss, their remaining senses compensate for it. This is a prime example of neuroplasticity in the works. In order for their other senses to strengthen, their brain structure physically changes (Merabet & Pascual-Leone, 2009).

It's also proven that your thoughts have an effect on your emotions, and the stronger the emotional reaction to a thought, the more your brain believes it to be true. And since beliefs have the ability to change your brain structure (your neural pathways), it stands to reason that the only thing you need to do is change your beliefs. Sounds simple enough, right? However, it's exactly the "changing" part that many people struggle with. But again, just because it's going to take time and effort doesn't mean it won't happen or it's not worth it. So, in essence, the first and most important step in this journey is to convince yourself (through research and facts) that it is possible to change your mind.

- **Reward your efforts, not your results.** Remember, growing is a journey without a destination, which means that, oftentimes, you never get to see the end result. Stepping away from only feeling good about what you manage to accomplish and giving yourself a pat on the back for simply trying and making progress can be extremely validating and motivating.

    For example, reward yourself when you manage to spot a limiting belief or negative thought, not just when you manage to successfully challenge or reframe it; reward yourself for recognizing that your body language might be telling people you're unapproachable, not just after you've fixed it.

    Rewarding yourself could come in the form of anything you enjoy doing or what makes you feel good such as spending time in the sun, playing with a pet, having a movie night, taking a bubble bath, spending time on your favorite hobby, fixing yourself your favorite snack, and so on.

- **Relabel, reattribute, refocus, revalue.** Relabel negative thoughts as soon as you recognize them. If you did poorly on a test, for example, and your first thought is, *I'm so stupid*, pause and relabel it as anything other than true. Because it isn't. You can call it a brain glitch, a false message, an impulsive thought, a mental invasion, or anything else that questions the validity of the thought. Reattribute the reason for having the thought in the first place to something that's out of your control. Because it is. Remind yourself that your mind is still stuck in a negative feedback loop based on old beliefs, experiences, and emotions. And that it's going to take a while to reprogram and get used to the new features and commands.

    Refocus your attention to actively and consciously change your recurring negative thought patterns. This is when you replace the negative thought with one that's more realistic and accurate based on the evidence you have. Think of it as a manual override—since the automatic system is not doing what you need it to do. Using the example of automatically thinking you're stupid when you get a bad grade, you can counter it by following it up with, "Now hold on a second, since when does failing one singular test mean that a person is stupid in general? That doesn't seem like a fair analysis of overall intelligence." Go over the evidence and reality of the situation; maybe the truth is that you failed because you simply didn't study, studied the wrong material, or misunderstood a lot of the questions on the test. But again, none of the reasons for failing a test means you're not capable of passing the class in the end.

    If you consistently follow the first three steps when negative thought patterns emerge, eventually, your brain will revalue them as mere distractions and untruths. Your mind catches up and drifts away from negative automatic responses because they don't hold as much weight anymore. Through practice and persistence, your relabeling, reattributing, and refocusing of negative thoughts will become easier and more automatic. You will have trained your brain to react with more positive and reality-based thoughts, which will also change your limiting beliefs.

- **Pay attention to what you're being exposed to.** This is especially true in the era of social media. The algorithms dictate what's on your feeds and "for you" pages. But the thing is, negativity is more popular than positivity—because it generates a stronger emotional reaction. You're more likely to react to, comment on, and stay tuned (or read) to the end of a post that talks about all the bad stuff that makes us lose faith in humanity.

But when you do this, you'll only be fed more of the same stories! I'm not going to go into how social media is all marketing and engagement, but just know that your mind will grow off of whatever you feed it. So be wise about the content that you consume.

But this also counts in real life. You can't control what other people do, say, or think, but you can remove yourself from certain situations or take steps to protect yourself and your mental health.

- **Tap into the power of "yet."** The word "yet" is a great subtle reminder that improvement and growth are possible. "I'm not able to identify and challenge all my limiting beliefs and thoughts—yet." "I'm not as confident in myself—yet." "My skill isn't on the level that I want it to be—yet," "I'm not very good at social interactions and situations—yet." It changes the narrative from hopeless to hopeful. It opens up a small window of possibility, and that's all you need to cram a crowbar in there and break it right open.

- **Build mental resilience.** Mental resilience refers to one's ability to adapt or recover from things like stress, emotional dysregulation, or other mentally exhausting challenges. And one thing you'll need on your journey to self-improvement through self-awareness is mental "toughness." Mental resilience doesn't mean you should suppress or ignore your emotions or that you shouldn't have emotional reactions at all. It simply allows you to be courageous despite your doubts and fears, to stay in control of your thoughts and actions despite involuntary emotional responses, and to get where you want to be in life regardless of your past or current hardships.

    How do you build mental resilience? By living life. By practicing and giving it time. By taking care of yourself, finding a purpose, establishing realistic goals and working toward achieving them, being mindful of how you talk to yourself, keeping things in perspective, and building meaningful connections. By accepting the things you can't change and finding a way to push through them anyway, you're proving to yourself (and strengthening the idea) that you're capable enough.

Believing in yourself—as corny as it might sound—really has a big role to play in self-confidence. In order to raise your confidence, you have to change the way you think of yourself and your true abilities. You do this by getting used to correcting your knee-jerk assumptions and automatic thoughts and slowly turning them around until they cave in on themselves.

Building Self-Confidence

There's a reason why the majority of this chapter is filled with developing a growth mindset and setting goals. It's because believing that you are capable of improvement and achieving the goals you have been wanting to achieve (but might not have thought were possible) improves your self-esteem, and healthy self-esteem warrants self-confidence.

Self-esteem and self-confidence are a packaged deal; you can't authentically have one without the other—but they're separate concepts. Self-esteem is how you treat and value yourself in private and isn't always obvious from an outsider's perspective. Self-confidence is how you present yourself to the outside world and other people (and is typically based on self-esteem).

However, people with low self-esteem might present themselves as having a lot of self-confidence in order to make up for the former. In essence, "fake it 'till you make it." And while that sentiment might be helpful in many different, unrelated aspects of life, pretending to be confident in yourself only leads to a deeper identity crisis because you're living in two different realities where what you think and what you do doesn't line up—which may cause imposter syndrome (feeling like you're a fraud or you don't belong). It could also fuel anxiety and create mental exhaustion from always having to put on an act or a show—leading to eventual and complete social withdrawal and isolation.

Here's a fun fact: Opinions are not facts at all—not even when they're your own.

Your self-image is influenced by things such as your appearance, personality, the opinions of others, or past experiences. In a nutshell, your self-image is your opinion of yourself. It affects your behavior and how you interact with the world and other people. And most importantly, it affects your happiness, relationships, and overall well-being.

A negative self-image will impact the quality of your relationships. Whether that's because you doubt their intentions, aren't communicating your needs effectively, take constructive criticism personally, or feel like you can't be yourself around them, it all comes down to what goes on in your own head.

Expanding on that, people with low self-esteem might tolerate unhealthy or even abusive relationships because they will do mental gymnastics to excuse or defend the other person's behavior. They might even go as far as blaming it on themselves.

The inability to fully trust someone and open up to them will make it hard to connect on a deeper level, which will eventually lead them to believe that you're the one who's unwilling to build a relationship. As a result, they will withdraw, leaving you feeling confused and hurt once again, watering that now flourishing tree of doubt even more.

It's a vicious cycle, one that keeps you from living up to your potential, having people around you who care for you, and enjoying all the wonderful experiences that life has to offer.

Since self-esteem is the building block upon which self-confidence is built, it's easier to start there. So what can you do to work on improving your self-esteem?

First of all, stop comparing yourself to others. And yes, it's one of those things that's easier said than done. When the negative thoughts and emotional reactions start to creep in when looking at other people's lives, achievements, or success, do that thing where you challenge it. "I started my YouTube channel at the same time as [insert classmate's name here]. How come they have way more subscribers than me? That must mean I'm [insert limiting belief or cognitive distortion here]."

Now you follow up with the facts, but be careful not to assume things that you can't possibly know or verify. Sure, you may have started your respective channels at around the same time, but your niches and content are different; they post much more frequently than you and on a consistent schedule; they have better equipment and software, so their sound, lighting, and editing results in an overall better viewing experience. Maybe I could actually talk to them and find out what they're doing differently to me in terms of tags, titles, and all the other technical stuff.

See how the narrative changes? How it doesn't have to be so self-sabotaging and self-imposed?

It's normal to want to be extraordinary, and seeing others in a position that we want to be in right now can be demotivating. It rips our time and attention away from ourselves and our own goals and leaves us feeling defeated. Instead, compare yourself *with* yourself. But not in a mean, resentful type of way. Think of what you do differently today than you did yesterday. Did it improve your life? If not, think of what you can do today that your future self will thank you for.

Be your own hype man or woman. You can't always count on validation or acknowledgment from others, so tell yourself what you want to hear, be on your own side, comfort yourself, and reassure yourself—even if you don't believe it yet. Some additional small things you can do that will accumulate interest over time and build up your self-esteem—and inadvertently, your self-confidence—are:

- ✧ Make a list of things you're good at (big and small) and be proud of yourself for it.
- ✧ Stop focusing your attention on people who make you feel bad about yourself and gravitate toward people who are actually nice to you.
- ✧ Stop trying to convince people that you are cool, smart, chill, or whatever you think they want you to be or don't want you to be.
- ✧ Stop trying to please everyone with your words or actions; say "no" more often.
- ✧ Challenge yourself to step out of your comfort zone every day with small things and build up to bigger things.
- ✧ Stand up for yourself.

Daily Task

Positive self-talk is advised to patients by licensed therapists as a way to combat negative or distorted thoughts, limiting beliefs, anxiety, stress, and even depression. It's a form of dialectical behavioral therapy (DBT) and it can have a huge impact on your overall mental and physical well-being and performance.

There are many ways to implement positive self-talk into your daily life, and the more you practice it, the easier and more natural it becomes. Negative thinking usually comes in four forms and can even overlap each other or occur simultaneously. The four forms of negative self-talk are:

- **Personalizing:** Blaming yourself for everything.
Example thought: It would be so disappointing and inconsiderate of me if I change my mind.
Corrected thought: I have the right and power to change my mind, even if others might not understand.

- **Magnifying:** Focusing so much on the negative—or even blowing them out of proportion—that you ignore any and all the positive aspects.
Example thought: I completely embarrassed myself by doing that; I failed.
Corrected thought: It was hard to put myself out there like that, and I'm proud of myself for even trying, even if it didn't turn out the way I expected it to.

- **Catastrophizing:** Always expecting the worst despite logic or reason.
Example thought: There's no way I'm going to be able to accomplish that, so why even try?
Corrected thought: I will try my best; this is a great opportunity to learn something new.

- **Polarizing:** You categorize everything as either all good or all bad with no middle ground.
Example thought: I didn't clean my room; I am the laziest person in the world.
Corrected thought: I needed that hour of rest today; I'll get to it tomorrow.

Something you can do every day that ties in with positive self-talk is words of affirmation. I've mentioned this earlier on, but positive affirmations are a set of affirming statements that you tell yourself every day. They could be the same or different every time, and it can form part of your self-care routine.

With that being said, taking care of yourself is very important for your self-esteem and will contribute to building unshakable self-confidence. In order to feel good about yourself, you need to take care of yourself. It reinforces the idea or belief that you are important—which you are—and that your well-being is important to you—as it should be.

And that is why today's task will be to say some positive things *about* yourself *to* yourself. It's going to feel awkward, but push through the cringe and try to really take them in. You can craft your own positive affirmations or choose the ones you like the most from the following list:

- I'm strong enough and capable of reaching my goals.
- I will grow and learn from my mistakes.
- I don't need to be perfect.
- I am worthy.
- I am enough.
- There is no shame in being wrong or making mistakes.
- I'm patiently changing into the person I want to become.
- Getting to know myself is exciting.
- What others think of me is not my responsibility.
- I get to decide what's best for me.
- It's okay that I don't have all the answers.
- I'm proud of myself.
- I give myself permission to be myself.
- I am allowed to feel my emotions.
- I am open to opportunities and challenges.

Please don't dismiss the power of positive affirmations until you've tried it. You can combine it with the journaling challenge or do it on its own. Choose different ones every day or recite the same ones. There's no wrong way to approach it; whatever works for you. But don't resist doing it because you're afraid of how it *might* make you look or feel—for starters, no one has to know that you're doing it; it's for you, not them. But also, stop assuming things and just give it a go for a couple of days. See how you feel then. Keep doing the things that help you, leave the things that don't—but at least do them first.

Remember, the journey isn't linear; you don't know what the future holds. It's okay to reassess your goals or methods for achieving them if things aren't working out or if you come to find that you want something completely different. You have the right to change your mind.

CHAPTER 3
Day 3

SOCIAL SKILLS

> *Be courteous to all, but intimate with few, and let those few be well tried before you give them your confidence.*
> –George Washington

♦ ♦ ♦ ♦

You might find you know most (or all) of the "rules" regarding socializing already based on common sense and experience alone, but it can't hurt to go over the principles and theoretical aspects of how to build rapport with others.

However, the last thing I want is for you to find yourself in a situation that's upsetting or severely uncomfortable before you're ready, which is why this chapter is going to go over the basics of socializing, social skills, and social cues. The goal of this chapter is to arm yourself with knowledge, that's all.

Knowing what to say, when to say it, and how to say something; knowing whether a conversation or interaction is going good or bad; and reading non-verbal cues and body language are all important factors to consider. But before you get overwhelmed, our subconsciousness picks up on most of this stuff already. The issue is that your subconscious mind might not always interpret things correctly. By being aware of social cues and how to respond to or interpret them, you ditch the guessing game altogether.

And by improving your social skills, you'll not only experience less social anxiety and be able to build stronger, more meaningful relationships, but it also raises your self-esteem and self-confidence as well as improves overall mental and physical well-being.

The Basics

I find it ironic that social skills are so important, and yet we don't know exactly what they consist of. It's not like we're born grasping a pamphlet explaining this stuff, and it's also not something that's actively taught to us. I mean, the info is there; it's just not really presented to us in the same way as math or biology is. Okay, sure, the mitochondria are the powerhouse of the cell, but how much eye contact do I give before it's considered creepy?

Social skills and etiquette are necessary and important, especially once you enter the realm of young adulthood and beyond (which will come a lot sooner than you realize). One minute you're calling your mom "bro," and the next, you're getting excited in the home appliances aisle for 45 minutes.

My point is that humans are social creatures, and a lack of social skills can hold you back both from a personal and professional standpoint. Poor social skills might, for instance, ruin platonic and romantic relationships and be the cause for you not landing your dream job.

Social skills are how we express our feelings, communicate our thoughts, and relate to those around us. But being aware of how we do this is also important. It's not the easiest concept to wrap your head around. It's a lot to be aware of and pay attention to, and it's not like you've had much experience or time to polish these skills. So try not to feel bad about not having mastered the art of social interaction yet.

Before I go into detail on what individual skills make up "social skills," there are a few things I think are worth keeping in mind. First is that you don't need to get everything *just right* in order to build good and lasting relationships. You don't have to focus intently on just one factor or skill; they all work in unison. And you will mess up from time to time—even the most charismatic people can sometimes come across as rude or uninterested.

There are two main forms of communication, namely verbal and non-verbal. Verbal communication happens when you verbalize your thoughts, feelings, opinions, and ideas, either through talking or writing them down. Non-verbal communication happens through things like eye contact, gestures, facial expressions (including micro-expressions), and body language. Let's break that down.

Verbal Communication

Many argue that your tone and volume of voice don't (or shouldn't) fall under verbal communication. For one, you can't really discern tone or volume through written text—unless they're typing in all caps, then it's safe to assume they are, in fact, shouting. Nonetheless, I do feel like the way you say something does affect how it's received.

A simple example of this is when you look at what happens to the underlying implication of the sentence when you place emphasis on certain words:

"**I** didn't say you should do it." Someone else said it.

"I **didn't** say you should do it." I explicitly told you not to do it.

"I didn't say **you** should do it." I said someone else should.

It's the exact same sentence, but it means something different depending on where you place the stress. Here are the most important individual elements that form part of effective (or ineffective) verbal communication:

- ◆ **Form of language.** Knowing when and how to use either informal or formal language. This doesn't necessarily mean having a large vocabulary with big fancy words. A simple example of this is not cursing or swearing when talking to an elderly lady or your principal.
- ◆ **Clarity.** Pronouncing words correctly and articulating sentences so you're coherent and easy to understand. Stating your thoughts or ideas with confidence.
- ◆ **Tone.** Where you place emphasis changes the meaning or intention behind a sentence. This influences how your words are received by others.
- ◆ **Pitch.** Raising or lowering the pitch in your voice for effect. An example of this is when you're being sarcastic or trying to imitate someone else.
- ◆ **Pace.** Talking slowly might indicate that you're bored or uninterested, while talking fast can mean you're excited or angry. It speaks to the energy you're exerting while in conversation.
- ◆ **Volume.** Talking loudly or softly. Again, talking loudly might mean you're fired up, excited, passionate, or angry. Talking softly can mean the conversation is more intimate or even private—or that you're just shy.

The way you combine all these elements will depend on the situation you're in, your mood, the environment, the people you're talking to, and so on. The way you talk to your sibling is different from the way you talk to your parents or a teacher, for example.

Verbal communication, simply put, is the physical act of conscious communication—you turn your internal dialogue into an external one. The type of language you use, along with clarity, tone, pitch, pace, and volume, are just tools you can use to effectively drive forth the intended meaning behind your words. The way you use these tools can also differ depending on who you're talking to and the circumstances surrounding the interaction.

Misunderstandings happen when the message you're trying to convey gets lost in translation somehow. This most often happens when there's a discrepancy between what you're saying and how you're saying it—or how you're using the different elements.

There are a lot of other things that affect how you present yourself to the world verbally, but this is the basics of verbal communication.

Non-Verbal Communication

Non-verbal communication is how we send messages or convey information—either about ourselves or in reaction to others—through things like eye contact, body language, facial expressions, gestures, and even our appearance.

Did you know that 80% of communication happens non-verbally (Hull, 2016)? This means that the actual words that come out of your mouth only account for 20% of overall interaction. You could effectively have full-blown conversations with others without saying a single word.

Before we break down the elements of non-verbal communication, I want to talk a bit about first impressions. There's a famous quote from both Oscar Wilde and Will Rogers that you've likely heard by this point already: "You never get a second chance to make a first impression." (1966)

I mean… yes and no. From a literal standpoint, sure, you only get one shot at a first impression—unless the person forgot they met you in the first place. However, I think first impressions are overrated. You're going to tell me that you've never met someone, immediately didn't like them, but after spending some time with them, thought, *They're actually pretty cool*?

First impressions are a thing, but they don't hold nearly as much weight in casual everyday settings as people imply they do. Humans have a natural tendency to judge, and first impressions are a prime example of this. You can't possibly pretend to know me based on the first two minutes of meeting me (the average time "experts" say a first impression lasts). You can make judgments, assumptions, and form opinions, but once again, none of these are based on facts and all of it is subject to change over time.

I only bring this up to shed light on the fact that even if you mess up a first impression due to social anxiety, low confidence, or any other reason, you're not irredeemable; you're not doomed.

Here are the most important elements of non-verbal communication:

- **Facial expressions.** You can tell a lot about what or how someone is feeling simply by looking at their face. Facial expressions for emotions can differ between cultures around the world, but the main ones (happiness, sadness, anger, and fear) are pretty universal and usually hard to hide.
- **Gestures.** These are any deliberate movements you use to add emotion or more influence behind your words, such as pointing, waving your hands around, rubbing your eyes, pinching the bridge of your nose, and so on. But it can also include things like giving someone a thumbs up, high-fiving, and so on.
- **Body language.** Your posture and subconscious body movements also signify your reaction or emotions. For example, crossing your arms is said to be a defensive gesture, fidgeting with something could indicate nervousness, and so on.
- **Eye contact.** Facial expression and emotion rely heavily on our eyes—they are the windows to the soul, after all. But they also play a big role in non-verbal communication through eye contact. Eye contact is important for establishing a connection.
- **Physical appearance.** It's not something we as a society should be proud of, but the way you look does have an impact on how people view and judge you. Your style is an extension of your personality, and by no means should you alter the way you dress or how you style your

hair based on what other people may or may not think of you. The implication here is more on neatness and cleanliness. However, everyone has a different idea of what a neat and tidy appearance looks like—or should look like.

You don't need to be an expert on the theory of communication to communicate effectively. However, knowing the basics of verbal versus non-verbal communication can open up a whole new world where you're able to tell whether someone is authentic (their words match up with their behaviors) or being deceptive with malicious intent.

Conversation Skills

My mom always said, "There's a difference between hearing and listening." And while I used to roll my eyes at the time, as an adult, I get it. What she really meant was there's a difference between simply listening to respond and listening to connect.

A conversation can be superficial. You don't have to form a deep and meaningful connection with the person who happens to be seated next to you on the bus or the guy who asks you if you know where the nearest bathroom is at the doctor's office. But if you are looking to start any type of long-lasting relationship with anyone, communication will be a big part of that.

There are four types of conversation:

- **Discourse.** A one-way cooperative conversation where the purpose is to deliver information. A teacher presenting a lesson or presentation is a good example of this.
- **Diatribe.** A one-way competitive conversation where the purpose is to inspire or express emotions (usually negative ones). An example of this is when your parents express concern over your latest test results.
- **Dialogue.** A cooperative two-way conversation where the purpose is to exchange information and build a relationship. For example, two friends discussing what they did over summer break, there's a back-and-forth exchange of questions and answers that spawn from genuine curiosity and interest.
- **Debate.** A competitive two-way conversation where the purpose is to win an argument or convince someone. You and your sibling disagree over which fast food restaurant has the best fries. You're arguing each other's reasonings and opinions in a way that's non-aggressive.

There's a time and place for each of these types of conversations; in fact, all of them are necessary depending on what you're trying to accomplish. They allow you to express your emotions, connect, and even disagree with people respectfully. That's the key word here: Respectfully.

I tend to agree with the phrase, "Respect is earned," but you can still lead with it and react accordingly. A rule I follow is that if I'm the one initiating contact or starting a conversation, I'm always respectful. Most of the time, people return the same energy, but I'm not going to continue being respectful if my respect is met with disrespect. And if someone comes up to me and doesn't lead with respect, I'm not wasting time or energy on the conversation because they clearly don't value me as a person.

There are some soft skills that come into play when engaging in conversation, most of which fall under verbal and non-verbal communication skills, such as eye contact, tone of voice, body language, yada, yada. But there are also things like active listening, reciprocity, social cues, and a host of other things that are important for engaging in a conversation and keeping others engaged as well.

We went over what verbal and non-verbal communication is—most of it is pretty straightforward and you probably understand and do most of it without trying already—but now we're going to break down the less obvious aspects of having a conversation and establishing a relationship.

Social Strategies

Maybe your problem isn't actually with reading social cues but with initiating conversation and actually getting to a point where the interaction means something. You grasp the mechanics behind social interactions and have a good idea of how to participate, but it never seems to get past the small talk phase.

A good conversation is one that's pleasantly memorable; you wish you could've stayed longer, talked more, and can't wait to talk to them again. And yes, it's possible to feel all these feelings in regard to someone you don't necessarily want to pursue romantically.

You'd obviously feel more connected to someone who shares the same values, morals, and interests with you than you would with someone who doesn't. But that doesn't mean you can't form deep connections with someone who thinks differently than you. In fact, it's usually the people who bring up a different perspective that we might not have thought of that intrigues us.

Granted, if someone says something that you wholeheartedly disagree with, you might not want to be friends with them—and if they have extremely negative beliefs and values that are objectively immoral, you definitely shouldn't be. However, sometimes a good debate with someone who sees things in a different light is exhilarating and refreshing. If you only surround yourself with people who agree with you and never engage with people who don't, you risk being trapped in an echo chamber where you'll never be challenged to question yourself at all.

With that being said, there are some things that might be the cause for you not being able to hold a conversation or make it evolve into something deeper over time. Now, you might not even be aware that you're falling into these potholes, or it might not be something that's in your control, but keep in mind that you can work on improving them, which is the entire premise of this book:

- ⬥ **Social anxiety.** Yes, yes, this isn't exactly new information. You've known about your social anxiety for a long time. But this *is* the most prominent reason for not being able to build or advance meaningful relationships.

    Building a relationship with someone relies on your willingness to open up and be vulnerable. And with the probability of saying or doing something embarrassing being so high, you avoid it at all cost, which means avoiding social interaction altogether. The issue isn't in the act of doing or saying something embarrassing; it's in the fear surrounding it. You think you won't be able to redeem yourself after.

- ⬥ **Fear of rejection.** Awkward moments and silences are a natural part of communication between one topic and the next—it's a turning point. No one likes awkward silences, but in your mind, it's a sign of rejection. And rejection is humiliating to most people.

    Whether your cognitive distortions make you believe that someone is going to scoff in your face or flat-out ignore you when you try to talk to them, the fear of rejection is very real and can lead to social anxiety and, by extension, social withdrawal.

- ⬥ **Lack of social skills.** Whether it's you not pulling your weight or them, a lack of social skills is a conversation extinguisher. It's hard to participate in a conversation when it seems like one of the participants is totally disengaged or uninterested.

    Because that's what it looks like from the outside. Someone who lacks social skills may come across as rude when in reality, they just don't know what to say or how to reciprocate. Either way, it will lead to an abrupt end of any dialogue.

In order to have productive conversations that gradually evolve from generalized small talk to heart-to-heart personal deep dives, there are a few things to keep in mind. You're aiming for dialogue (from the four types of conversation), meaning that it's a two-way street, give and take. But how much is too much to give? How much is not enough?

Here are a few strategies and general guidelines to keep in mind and follow when talking to someone you really want to establish a continued relationship with:

- ⬥ **Actively listening.** I don't mean just processing what someone is saying; I mean taking their facial expressions and body language into consideration as well as paying attention to what they're *not* saying. This prevents you from judging, jumping to conclusions, and assuming what other people are thinking or feeling.

    For example, if someone says, "Your hair looks different today," unless there's something in their tone of voice or body language that suggests they're trying to mock you, don't just assume they are. They simply made a statement.

Actively paying attention to what someone is saying also includes not getting distracted by your phone or anything else and not interrupting them. This will help you remember what they're saying for future reference. You can also ensure you really understood what they were saying by rephrasing their words and asking clarifying questions if you're not sure that you're understanding correctly.

- **Ask open-ended questions.** Questions that can only be answered by a simple yes or no answer aren't the plague, and you don't have to recast or avoid asking a question entirely just because the answer is closed-ended. But you can follow it up with a question that requires a more elaborate answer. If someone says they've never heard of the band you like, ask them what type of music they're into and recommend a few songs from the band that fit that vibe.

    And when someone asks you a yes or no type of question, try to add some additional yet relevant information. For example, if someone asks you if you like a certain band, instead of saying just yes or no, add on why you do or don't like them.

- **Be genuinely curious.** This kind of ties in with the previous bullet point, just on a much deeper level. Asking questions is a great way to get to know people, but showing genuine curiosity about other people's lives is more than that.

    What I mean by being genuinely curious is, when they reveal something about themselves that you find interesting, don't just nod and say, "Oh, that's cool." Be curious! For example, let's say someone mentions that they dabble in music production; ask them if you can listen to some of their stuff, ask them how they got into it, what software they're using, how long they've been doing it, or if it's just a hobby or something they're serious about. Be excited for them, hype them up, and tell them if you're impressed.

    However, don't force it. People can tell when you're being insincere. So this should only be done if and when you come across someone whose hobbies or skills you're truly fascinated by. Just make your curiosity apparent.

- **Relate.** Being able to relate to others is the most powerful way to form a connection. And this can happen in many aspects, but most commonly, it's similar or shared interests, hobbies, opinions, experiences, beliefs, and values. However, relating to someone doesn't guarantee a healthy, strong, or long-lasting relationship.

    But it is a good way to open up a dialogue or initial conversation in order to figure out whether or not you are compatible. You might see someone drawing a character from your favorite anime series and you compliment them on their artistic talents. Maybe you become best friends, or maybe you realize after a while that besides having something in common, you don't really enjoy their company. But the only way to find out is to take that initial leap of faith.

- **Keep it light.** Don't reveal your deepest secrets or your entire life story in the first five minutes of introducing yourself. Small talk, although tedious and sometimes dull, is necessary. It can actually reveal a lot about you and the person you're talking to.

    For instance, it can reveal whether someone has a good sense of humor, their communication style, or personality traits, and oftentimes provides us with useful information. So while small talk is usually about trivial, unimportant, or light-hearted topics, it lays the groundwork for future interactions.

    You don't know them well enough to decide whether it's worth investing more time into the relationship. Small talk is limbo, in this case, a period of uncertainty as well as discovery.

    And while you certainly can comment on the weather, there are also plenty of other menial topics to discuss: Movies, TV shows or series, music, and books; sporting events and championships, your favorite sports teams, exercise routines; favorite food, restaurants; culture; travel; celebrity gossip; hobbies and interests; family, where you grew up, the list goes one.

- ◆ **Go with it.** You don't—and shouldn't—do all the heavy lifting. Give the other person a chance to speak, ask questions, and reciprocate. Don't force abrupt subject changes and don't come on too strong with rapid-fire interrogational questions about their lives, hobbies, interests, and so on.

  Let the conversation unfold naturally, and if a pause or awkward silence does inevitably happen, allow it to. Nothing is going to happen other than your brain making you hyper-aware that things are awkward right now. Building your tolerance to a point where you're able to endure the occasional awkward moment is a superpower!

  Additionally, if you do get the vibe that someone might not be open to a conversation, don't take it personally, and don't force them into one. Don't keep on talking to someone if they aren't actively contributing for whatever reason.

- ◆ **Reflect.** Reflecting on the type and "quality" of the conversations you're currently having will help you improve your conversational skills and strategy. Think back on the conversations you've had over the past couple of days. How did you feel directly afterward? How did it start, and where did it end up? At which moments did it seem to be going well? What happened? Were there any moments where it seemed like it wasn't going well, and why do you think so?

  The information from these questions might be able to give you an idea of what you're doing right, as well as areas that need improving. Be careful not to answer them with assumptions or negative beliefs, and be rational and realistic—look for evidence to confirm or deny your answers.

Daily Task

There are many resources available that will help you improve your social skills, including books (like the one you're reading right now), podcasts, blogs, and worksheets. Your task for today is going to be broken up into a few simple steps that you might have to do over a period of time.

First, you're going to do some observing. Without changing anything about what you're doing during conversations today (or tomorrow if you're reading this late in the afternoon or right before bed), you're going to simply pay attention. Make notes after every social interaction if you're afraid you might forget things, such as others' reactions to something you did or said, your own reactions and body language, and so on.

At the end of the day, write down each area of social interaction that you believe you struggle with based on what sticks out to you (or your notes). Maybe it's reading and interpreting body language, active listening (or constantly interrupting people), taking part in group conversations, conflict resolution, and so on. It might help to ask for honest feedback from people who know you well, but try not to get discouraged or defensive when they list things you didn't even think or realize you do (or don't do). Though, you can also phrase the question as if you're asking for advice since some people might be afraid to offend you with a list of things you're doing "wrong."

Next, you're going to remind yourself that socializing is a skill and that you will improve with time and practice. Isolate one thing from your list of social skills that you can benefit from improving, and think of ways to do so. For example, if you find that you generally don't pay attention to people's facial expressions, challenge yourself to scan their faces every now and then and take in their expression at that specific moment (their eyebrows are raised, they're smiling, etc.). Even if you don't consciously know what it means, just noting or becoming aware of their facial expressions will give you a certain vibe.

Once you've improved that one area, then move on to the next one. Set small milestones and give yourself a pat on the back when you reach them.

You might have to do some additional research on social skills, cues, norms, and etiquette since I can't possibly cover everything there is to it in a single book, let alone a chapter, but you'll at least be able to get somewhere with what's covered here. And remember, perfection is overrated, not to mention subjective—aim for progress and you'll never fail.

CHAPTER 4
Day 4 — SOCIAL ANXIETY

> *Courage is resistance to fear, mastery of fear, not absence of fear..*
>
> –Mark Twain

✦✦✦✦

Humans are social creatures; we need connection and interaction to live a fulfilling life. Being afraid of rejection or embarrassment can definitely form part of social anxiety, but in its most severe form, it's a debilitating phobia that can present itself as physical symptoms like dizziness or full-blown panic attacks even during low-risk, casual, or fleeting interactions.

Common Triggers

Social anxiety doesn't just randomly happen one Tuesday morning. There are lots of catalytic reasons for someone experiencing severe social anxiety, such as meeting new people, having to perform in front of a crowd, or fear of being embarrassed or humiliated. However, there's a difference between just experiencing nervousness and having social anxiety.

Social anxiety goes beyond being shy or feeling nervous in group settings or around people you don't know. Someone with a more severe form of social anxiety might go so far as to skip school, avoid grocery shopping, or cross the street when someone is about to walk past them on the sidewalk—they fear social situations *so* much that the mere thought of someone potentially greeting them is too much to bear.

Unsurprisingly, the root cause of severe or debilitating social anxiety is trauma (either domestic or social) related to negative past experiences such as having been bullied, teased, rejected, ridiculed, abandoned, and abused. Typically, the symptoms of social anxiety start in early childhood, but it's also possible to develop it later in life as a teenager or even as an adult.

Having social anxiety usually interferes with every aspect of a person's daily life and their ability to function normally. They don't simply get jittery right before they give a speech; they have sleepless nights about it for weeks or even months in advance. They worry about potentially being in a situation where they have to communicate with others—and they will go out of their way to avoid it at all costs.

It is possible to overcome social anxiety, but know that it will require you to face your fears (in small, manageable increments) and build up a tolerance to your triggers and reactions. And that is exactly what we'll be going over in this chapter. And even if you don't have social anxiety, these techniques could still be useful for putting yourself out there if you struggle with nervousness or shyness.

Managing Symptoms

The whole reason why social anxiety makes it so hard to function is because of the symptoms. A trigger sets off your fight or flight response, which makes your body pump out adrenaline like it's going out of style. This leads to physical symptoms such as shortness of breath, upset stomach (nausea or an intense feeling of "butterflies" that doesn't go away within seconds), shaky voice or hands, tight chest, fast heart rate, sweating or hot flashes, and feeling dizzy or faint. All of these symptoms, stacked on top of the mental aspects of social anxiety, could cause a full nervous system meltdown, resulting in a panic attack.

It's automatic and unavoidable; every fiber in your being is screaming at you to run because the situation is dangerous—even if you consciously know that's not true most of the time. By re-regulating your nervous system when the involuntary fight or flight response kicks in, you reduce the symptoms. And by reducing the symptoms, you're better able to face the fear and eventually even overcome it.

A few ways you can re-regulate your nervous system and manage the physical manifestations of social anxiety in the moment are as follows:

- **Breathing and relaxation exercises.** This is arguably the most effective way to relieve the uncomfortable and alarming symptoms of social anxiety quickly. All there is to it is taking a big breath in (the deepest you can manage) and slowly breathing out. Try to elongate the time it takes to breathe in and out with each breath, so start with two seconds per breath and work your way up to ten seconds or longer. While you do this, try to become aware of some areas or muscle groups where the tension might be residing (the jaw, shoulders, hips, etc.), and focus on releasing it. Picture the tension leaving your body as you exhale.
You might have to excuse yourself if you're feeling really overwhelmed and do this in a bathroom or somewhere else that's private, but you can also do it on the spot if you feel comfortable enough to do so.

- **Grounding.** A common tactic usually used in people who are on the verge of an anxiety or panic attack, but it works for social anxiety as well. It's called the 5-4-3-2-1 coping technique and it requires you to (when you feel dysregulated or overwhelmed) name five things you can see, four things you can touch, three things you can hear, two things you can smell, and one thing you can taste.
The goal of this exercise is to bring you back to the present moment instead of letting the panic or fear take over and progressively worsen.

- **Challenge your thoughts.** Break down your thoughts and fears and, using logic and objectivity, debunk them or challenge them. In the case of social anxiety, negative thoughts and fears are usually rooted in doing or saying something that you believe others might judge or ridicule you for. More on this later.

- **Acknowledge your symptoms.** Admitting to yourself what you're feeling and how these emotions are physically showing up in your body can bring comfort and relief in and of itself—to some degree. This could look like thinking something as simple as, "I am feeling really anxious right now because I'm about to talk to someone I don't know," or "There's a pit in my stomach and I feel dizzy because of my social anxiety."
You could also pair this with some form of reassurance phrase or affirmation like "I'm not in danger" or "This feeling will pass; just breathe."

Relieving symptoms of social anxiety in stressful situations is very helpful, but there are also some lifestyle changes you can make that will reduce your social anxiety in general and in the long term:

- **Diet and exercise.** Dietary changes don't have to be drastic or restrictive. Even small changes like limiting caffeine while making sure you're adding protein, fiber, and fruits or vegetables to most daily meals can make a difference.

Exercise includes any form of movement, bonus points if it's actually something you enjoy doing, like hiking (or just taking a walk), totem tennis (swingball), or jumping on a trampoline. It doesn't have to include repetitive movements, weight lifting, or excessive sweating. Increased activity not only takes your mind off of the things making you anxiously overthink, but it also decreases long-term muscle tension and encourages the production of stress-relieving hormones. It even helps you manage future nervous system reactions to perceived threats, meaning that it literally helps you deal with triggers relating to social anxiety (Ratey, 2019).

- ⬥ **Sleep.** It's hard to get a good night's sleep if you have social anxiety, and ironically, a lack of sleep (or sleep deprivation) actually worsens your symptoms of social anxiety—it also takes a toll on your general mental and physical health.
  Sleep deprivation or difficulties with sleep that persist and don't improve when you're taking measures to reduce overall anxiety should always be taken seriously and checked out by a medical professional.

- ⬥ **Meditation.** There's a lot of debate about what meditation really is and how it should be done. I'm here to tell you that, once again, there are no rules. If the way you approach it works, it's worth doing.
  Now, there are many ways to meditate, some more serious than others. But you don't have to be sitting cross-legged, eyes closed, with your thumb and middle finger touching on your knees for hours to benefit from it. Meditation is simply the act of focused concentration and staying in the present moment. You pick something neutral to focus on (like your breathing, a phrase or mantra, the texture on the wall, or your movements) and you stay there for a bit—as long as you need to.
  Your mind will get bored and wander; when this happens, you gently nudge it back to whatever your neutral focal point is. You can also adapt this so you're focusing intently on whatever mundane tasks you're doing, like walking, brushing your teeth, packing the dishwasher, and so on. Feel the pebbles crunching under your feet, the smell of the rose bush you're passing, and hear the wind rushing past you. Feel the coolness of the minty toothpaste in your mouth, taste it, the circular motions of the bristles. Just pay attention to life!
  Meditation works to reduce symptoms of anxiety by reducing or eliminating mind clutter and slowing your thoughts so you can process emotions and experiences better. It puts you into a deep state of relaxation which results in a feeling of peace and harmony between mind and body. And this state of practiced tranquility becomes almost like muscle memory which you can pull from during stressful times. It's a healthy and effective long-term coping mechanism.

- ⬥ **Therapy.** If your social anxiety is severe and nothing you try to implement or do is helping in any capacity, seeking professional help is the only remaining option. A licensed therapist or counselor will provide more specialized and personal insight into your situation. They will work with you to build the tools and skills necessary to overcome social anxiety and even help you find the right medications if needed.

- ⬥ **Positive affirmations.** Yes, I know I've mentioned this before; I'm telling you again for good reason. Positive affirmations are a popular cognitive behavioral therapy tool used to treat mental disorders such as depression and anxiety. It involves looking in the mirror and rehearsing a list of nice things about yourself. And while it sounds silly and embarrassing, it has a surprisingly high success rate—the mind is a very powerful thing.
  Do you know why positive affirmations work so well? Because if you tell yourself something over and over again, eventually, you'll believe it. But this works in reverse, too. Meaning that negative voice in your head that has been there since you can remember has been bamboozling you this entire time!
  This is also how your brain creates biases. When you don't see yourself as worthy of love, respect, friendship, or support, you're less likely to value your existence and your contributions. You don't see why there's a need to look after yourself, so you don't. You think no one would value you, not because of their actions, but because, in your mind, you're not worth the effort in the first

place. Every small and potentially innocent gesture from someone else gets twisted in your mind and serves as further evidence that you're simply not enough.

Overcoming Social Anxiety

I don't know if you've ever looked at a word and thought you misspelled it. And then you look it up and you actually didn't, but it still looks wrong. It's called "wordnesia" and the psychology behind it is interesting. When we read, we don't focus on the individual letters; rather, our brains automatically interpret it as a unit (i.e., a word). But when you become hyper-focused on the individual letters, you temporarily lose the ability to see the word as a whole. So, in your mind, it's no longer a word you recognize, if that makes any sense.

My hypothesis is that this is more or less what happens when you hyper-focus on a specific trait, attribute, or feature of yourself. Your brain blows it out of proportion and you're left with the result: anxiety.

The first step to overcoming social anxiety is to identify your triggers, and the second step is to find the techniques that help reduce the symptoms in both the short and long term. But in order to overcome it, you will have to face it. Unfortunately, there's no way around this one. In fact, the more you avoid your triggers, emotional reactions, and physical symptoms, the stronger they get.

Avoiding the things that cause an adverse negative physical and emotional response within us is encoded into our DNA. It's as much a part of you as the color of your eyes and the thickness of your fingernails are. It's a survival instinct.

Challenge Your Beliefs

The only constant in life is change. Your thoughts, beliefs, assumptions, and expectations are always changing. Or at least, it should. That's why public opinion, laws, legislation, and the status quo have continuously changed over the course of human history. Because we are constantly learning and discovering new information through studies, philosophers, and medicine. Because it's good to question things, consider alternative perspectives, outcomes, impacts, and decide to do better–be better.

We can look at some ideologies of our ancestors, the beliefs and behaviors that were considered "normal" in those times and grimace. We use that knowledge and information to change the way we do things, the way we see things, and we use it to literally change the world!

But won't actively challenging every thought and belief you have cause even more self-doubt and therefore lower your self-esteem even further? No, but it is a slippery slope. *Challenging* your beliefs (if you're going about it the right way) can strengthen and change your opinions and worldview for the better. *Overthinking* it can lead to mind clutter and self-doubt.

This is why I'm going to tell you how you should go about challenging your thoughts in a way that stops the cycle in its tracks instead of just branching off, making everything worse.

What is the difference between knowledge and belief? Knowledge requires evidence; it's rooted in reality; it's objective. Belief is conceptual knowledge, a strongly held opinion, meaning that even though something might be true, it can't be backed up with proof, and—more often than not—it's subjective (it can be influenced by thoughts, emotions, and assumptions).

An example that might help differentiate the two can be as simple as this: Imagine you're at a store, and you know this store very well. Based on your *knowledge*, you know they have cool ranch Doritos because you physically see it on the shelf, you can pick it up, and you can rip open the bag and eat it (assuming you're going to pay for it). However, that's not to say they're going to have it in stock the next time you come to this exact store. You may *believe* they have it based on your past experiences of buying it, but that doesn't necessarily make it true.

Being able to identify whether a thought is actual knowledge or just a belief is important because it will help you sift through your inner dialogue to find the limiting or negative beliefs that should be challenged in the first place.

Let's take a singular limiting belief that you may or may not have on a regular basis and go through the process of challenging it together. You can obviously swap out the context of the belief if you already have a different one in mind at this moment.

The limiting belief is: "No one likes me; that's why I have no friends."

Step 1: Pause. Let the thought resonate for a second. Really consider the words, the implications it has had on you, and the consequences.

Step 2: Determine whether it's knowledge or belief. Correlation doesn't equal causation. Ask yourself questions about your belief, such as: What proof do you have that this thought is objectively true? Can you read minds? Has every person you've ever met outright told you that they didn't like you, or is it merely a conclusion you drew based on their behavior? Just because you have no friends doesn't automatically mean it's because no one likes you.

Step 3: Consider the alternatives. Could it be possible that maybe people don't interact with you as much because you seem standoffish due to your belief that no one likes you? Could it be possible that other people are unsure of you because your fear of judgment makes it so you never reveal who you truly are? Could it be that your unwillingness to be vulnerable makes you look unapproachable?

Step 4: Gather new evidence. Now that you're considering alternative reasons for your belief, determine which ones are actually true. Think back to when you were in a setting where your belief seemed to be stronger than ever and find proof that supports the alternative reasons for the belief. Using our example, you can try to remember (in as much detail as you can) what your body language was like. Were you huddled in a corner, too scared to join the conversation? Were there opportunities to join the conversion that you didn't take? Did others maybe try to get you to join in by asking questions but your responses were short and detached? Did you maybe seem disinterested and only gave one-sided responses without throwing questions back at them?

Step 5: Experiment. You can test out your new-found beliefs and theories to solidify them. The next time the opportunity presents itself, change one small thing in the way you approach the situation and see if it makes any difference or supports your alternative belief. With our example, you can be more engaged in a group conversation by nodding along, expressing opposing opinions, and asking questions. Even if you're not in a group discussion, maybe you overhear someone say something to someone else that interests you and you—politely—pipe in with a question, statement, or simply agree with the person.

Step 6: Move on to the next limiting belief. Don't try to conquer all your limiting beliefs at once, as this can be overwhelming. It might take some time, practice, and courage, but one by one, you'll discover, debunk, and rectify the limiting beliefs that are holding you back in life. And even make a few friends along the way.

Focus on breaking down complex thoughts into one sentence and then deconstruct them using the steps outlined above. Write down your limiting beliefs as well as the process of dissecting and rationalizing them; when you try to do it in your head, things can get jumbled or spiral into different directions resulting in overthinking and additional mind clutter.

It could also help to start with thoughts that are a little less triggering and also do it while you're in a neutral headspace. Trying to change your perspective is hard on a good day, so make sure you're able to confront uncomfortable truths that come from challenging your thoughts. It could also help going over this process with someone you trust and who won't judge you; they could even answer some questions you may be stuck on or help you uproot personal biases (we all have them and it can be hard to spot them ourselves).

In the beginning, challenging a thought can feel forced or inauthentic. Like you're gaslighting yourself. But that's the thing; the whole reason challenging your thoughts is necessary is because you gaslit yourself into a limiting belief in the first place!

Try to give your mind some time to process all the new information and epiphanies that come up after challenging a belief. Do something that temporarily distracts you, like playing a video game for a couple of hours, helping your mom with dinner, or playing with a pet.

Exposure Therapy

How do you overcome a literal disorder that makes you believe and react as though making small talk with a stranger is equivalent to coming face-to-face with a grizzly bear? You slowly convince your brain that the threat is not as severe as it thinks or believes it to be.

It's called gradual exposure therapy or systematic desensitization. What it does is build your tolerance to triggers and emotional reactions by facing something, starting with the least fear-inducing situation and working your way up once you're ready and comfortable.

Basically, taking itty-bitty steps at a time and making gradual progress. Gradual exposure therapy is used in conjunction with relaxation techniques to help you stay regulated during the entire process.

The goal of gradual exposure therapy is to condition you or to help you build resilience so you're able to eventually face your fears—or in this case, social anxiety—without getting overwhelmed or inducing a panic attack which can be very traumatic and worsen your fear.

When implementing this desensitization technique, it helps to think of your fear in terms of levels. A level one fear is something that makes you feel the least amount of discomfort or anxiety, and obviously, a level ten fear would be something that causes the most adverse reaction.

The first step is to identify your personal level one and level ten fear. For example, a level one fear might be raising your hand in class, and a level ten fear is being at a party surrounded by mostly strangers and not knowing what to do with yourself (just the thought of it makes your stomach flip).

The next step is to identify all the levels of fear between one and ten. So level two could be seeing someone you know in public, level three is meeting someone new, and so on. The levels of fear get progressively more anxiety-inducing. Once you have your list, phase two can commence. Phase two is when you start exposing yourself to those fears in a controlled way.

What I mean by facing your fears in a controlled way is imagining a scenario of your fear taking place and then keeping yourself calm with your preferred breathing or relaxation technique as you do it. Rinse and repeat until the thought of your level-one fear no longer induces a physical or emotional reaction anymore.

Only once you're able to visualize or imagine yourself doing the thing you fear while being able to stay calm do you move on to real life. Using the example of a level one fear being raising your hand in class, the next time the opportunity presents itself, try to calm your nerves and do it. If the anxiety gets too bad and you're unable to keep calm and actually do it in the moment, it's okay! Go back to simply visualizing it while practicing your calming technique. Try again when you feel ready to.

Eventually, you'll do your level one fear for the first time. Then you'll do it more confidently, and then you'll do it without fear at all. At that point, you're done; you've overcome your level-one fear. Now you'll repeat this process for your level two fear until you reach level ten.

Some fears, however, might be hard or illogical to try and face or recreate in real life. For example, falling down or tripping in front of people. Please don't purposely trip or fall. Instead, what you can do is stick to the visualization practice while practicing staying calm, and if it does happen at some point, try to remember your training. Just breathe; it's going to be fine.

Daily Task

Gradual exposure therapy is, as the name suggests, gradual. Meaning it can take weeks—if not longer—until you're able to face a single fear in real life. So your task for today is to graze against the boundaries of your comfort zone in other areas of your life that may not be directly related to your social anxiety.

Stepping out of your comfort zone will translate or bleed into other areas and build your confidence and self-esteem. Get creative with it. Here's a list of things you can do to push the boundaries of what you're comfortable with (in a good way). Challenge yourself to do one of them today, or pick a few and do all of them over the span of a month:

- ⬥ Take a cold shower.
- ⬥ Change the route you take to school.

- Visit a new place (park, street, shopping center, etc.).
- Write using your non-dominant hand.
- Listen to a song you've never heard before (or don't like).
- Try out a new recipe.
- Go vegan for the day (if you're not already).
- Film yourself dancing or practicing a skill.
- Take a picture of yourself every day for a month.
- Change up your morning, evening, or workout routine.
- Ditch social media for a day.
- Start that creative project you've been meaning to do.
- Rearrange your room furniture.
- Sit in a place you've never sat before (a different couch, an ottoman, or a specific spot on the floor).
- Pick up a new skill or interest.
- Do something differently from how you've been doing it before.
- Change the scent of your shampoo, deodorant, lotion, body spray, or perfume.
- Order something you've never had before from a restaurant or fast food joint.
- Introduce yourself to a stranger (who you'll likely never see again).
- Reach out to someone you've fallen out of touch with or haven't spoken to in a while.
- Take on volunteer work that has to do with interacting with other humans.
- Eat at a restaurant by yourself.
- Ask someone for a recommendation (their favorite book, movie, or video game, for example).
- Sign up for a group class or extracurricular activity that you think you might enjoy.
- Give someone a compliment.
- Tell someone you know how much you appreciate them.
- Invite a classmate you don't know that well over to your house.

Get comfortable with change, tension, awkwardness, and the unknown. Someone once said, "If it doesn't challenge you, it doesn't change you." The only certainty in life is uncertainty; once you're able to laugh in the face of discomfort, you can take on the world!

CHAPTER 5
Day 5 — CONNECTION

> *Be who you are and say what you feel, because those who mind don't matter and those who matter don't mind.*
>
> –Bernard Baruch

All the small talk in the world isn't enough to establish a genuine, deep, and meaningful connection with someone. That's because the connection is based on mutual respect, trust, commitment, interest, and value. All of these are difficult to accomplish when you have social anxiety, lack certain social skills, or have some form of past trauma or negative experiences that you feel you need to actively protect yourself from.

Again, it's not your fault, but it is your responsibility to improve yourself, learn, and heal from your past. You can't force deeper connections with people, but you can place yourself in a position where it's more likely to happen.

Empathy and Understanding

Empathy is an interpersonal skill that involves being able to recognize, understand, and relate to others and their emotions and behaviors, even if you may think they're being dramatic or overreacting. It allows you to support others through certain situations and make them feel better.

Just because you're not afraid of frogs doesn't mean there aren't people who find them terrifying. A person with empathy isn't going to shame or belittle someone else for reacting differently than they themselves would've.

The difference between empathy and sympathy is understanding and shared experience. You feel sympathy if you see a stranger crying and empathy if you can relate to why they're crying (and you feel the need to support them in some capacity). So while sympathy can certainly turn into empathy, ultimately, they are separate things.

There are three stages of empathy:

1. **Cognitive empathy.** When you can identify someone else's emotional state (you see them crying and recognize that they are sad).

2. **Emotional empathy.** The ability to share or engage with the emotions of others (their emotions affect your own).

3. **Compassionate empathy.** When you actively try to reduce the emotional turmoil of others (you ask what's wrong or try to cheer them up).

There should obviously be some boundaries around the amount of empathy you are capable of showing at certain times. If you are going through a rough time, you can't always be there and support others to the best of your abilities. But empathy, along with body language awareness, does play a big part in human connection—and it should be reciprocated.

Body Language Awareness

I feel like it's appropriate to start with being able to read someone's body language or at least be aware of it and what it might indicate. It's important to note that reading body language is not an accurate way of determining someone's thoughts or feelings. Many people take reading body language way too seriously.

Reading body language is subjective, and a lot of the meanings overlap or even contradict each other. What I mean by this is that someone could scratch their nose, which, in body language lingo, means they're being insincere or dishonest when in reality, they just had an itchy nose at the wrong moment. For this reason, you should never 100% rely on body language alone to try and figure out what others are thinking or feeling.

Here's a breakdown of the most common body language cues and what they could potentially mean when they happen during a conversation:

- **Eye contact.** There's no correct amount of eye contact to give or receive. Too much eye contact can leave you or the other person feeling uncomfortable, and too little might mean you or the other person is distracted, uncomfortable, uninterested, or trying to hide true thoughts or feelings. The eyebrows are also typically pretty involved with emotions. For example, upturned eyebrows (think cartoon-style sadness) only happen during genuine sadness, empathy, or concern and are hard to replicate without real emotion tied to it (unless you're Amelia Clark, she manages to pull this off quite flawlessly).

- **The mouth.** Pursed lips usually signal disagreement, disapproval, or disgust. Lip biting could mean the person is stressed or anxious, and covering one's mouth can be a way to hide certain emotions from showing. Then there's the obvious: smiling. A genuine smile is one that "reaches the eyes," which is just code for when the eyes are engaging in it as well (narrowing and creasing in the outer corners). When the eyes are not actively participating in the smile, it could mean that the person is just trying to be polite; it doesn't mean that they're being fake—especially if they do this when they don't really know you very well.

- **Hands, arms, and legs.** Crossed arms or legs can be an indication that someone is defensive, dismissive, or disinterested. While clasping one's hands behind the back could signal boredom. Fidgeting is typically a sign that someone is nervous, frustrated, or impatient. Clenched fists signify unity or anger. Personal space also goes hand-in-hand with this; the more space a person takes up, the more confidence they tend to have. But if they're invading your personal space, it could mean they're trying to intimidate you.

- **Posture.** This is how a person holds themselves in a general sense. A closed-off posture (hunched over, taking up the least amount of space possible, crossed arms or legs, avoiding eye contact) could mean someone is generally an anxious or anti-social person (or they're just shy and uncomfortable), while an open posture (body takes up the necessary space, arms and legs are relaxed, the torso is exposed, not avoiding eye contact) typically indicates that someone is more confident and willing to engage in friendly conversation.

Again, I want to reiterate that body language is not the end-all-be-all of dissecting what someone might be thinking or feeling. However, if someone's words are not lining up with their body language, that is—more often than not—a sign that they are not really someone to be trusted. Chances are your subconscious will pick up on this anyway and your instincts will warn you of this to some degree.

The body language or "social cues" explained above are only the metaphorical tip of the iceberg. Don't get too caught up in learning everything there is to know about body language and using only that to figure people out. Body language is just too complicated, ambiguous, and multifactorial to rely on accurately.

Healthy Relationships

Relationships, whether it be romantic, platonic, or familial, enrich our lives and fulfills our need for belonging, support, and love. But not all relationships are created equal, some look, feel, and function differently than others. The important thing is that any relationship you cultivate should be healthy and happy.

This doesn't mean that you'll never argue, disagree, or unintentionally hurt each other, but it does mean you're able to respectfully and reasonably work it out and return to equilibrium.

But how do you know whether a relationship is healthy or not?

A healthy relationship is one where both or all parties involved are mutually supportive, trusting, accepting, supportive of personal growth, and adaptable to change. Overall, it *feels* good. You're never left questioning whether or not this person's intentions or behaviors are real and virtuous.

How To Spot a Toxic Person

The best cure is prevention. Toxic people will drain the life out of you, and while it isn't always possible to avoid interacting with toxic people, you definitely want to avoid giving off the impression that you're open to it.

General signs that someone might be toxic include selfish, hostile, and manipulative behavior. But here are a few more specific traits or behaviors that a toxic person might exhibit:

- always negative
- quick to judge
- lies and deceives
- general rudeness
- lack of empathy
- always thinks the worst of others
- being reckless
- argumentative
- gets aggressive or goes on the offense very easily
- controlling
- self-centered
- arrogant
- greedy
- disruptive or spiteful
- impulsivity
- apathy
- selfishness
- perfectionistic

It's important to remember that our actions don't always define who we are, but recurring negative themes and behaviors from people without taking accountability usually means they lack self-awareness. And without self-awareness, they won't change—or even admit that they're the problem in the first place.

Bear in mind that toxic traits can also exist within ourselves, so if you relate a bit too much to some of what was mentioned here, you're not a bad person. As long as you're willing to take accountability for it and work on changing for the better, you're already doing more than most people are!

How To Build Healthy Relationships

If you're someone who's particularly withdrawn, shy, or has social anxiety, building true, deep, and meaningful relationships has probably been a struggle for as long as you can remember. The truth is relationships of any nature are hard to grow and take effort to maintain, like a well-manicured garden.

Your garden might look sparse and overgrown right now, but once you take care of the soil (build self-esteem and social skills) and trim back the weeds (overcome social anxiety or fear), something is bound to sprout if you sow the right seeds and remember to water it every now and then.

Here's how to cultivate relationships and build connections that last:

- ◆ **Be authentic from the start.** If you're the type of person who is always looking for validation or approval from others (in other words, a people pleaser), it might be challenging to break out of this behavior. But pretending to be someone you're not so others would like you is simply not sustainable. Eventually, you'll burn out. Not to mention the other person might feel confused or betrayed because your behavior is inconsistent, which leads to distrust and suspicion on their end.

    Fight the urge to pretend you like something, know something, or believe something you don't. Avoid acting in a way that doesn't feel true to who you are.

- ◆ **Be thoughtful and empathetic.** It can be awkward or uncomfortable when someone shares something deeply intimate or personal with you. Unless they specifically ask for advice, don't give any. Sometimes people just need to vent, and someone venting to you is usually a good sign that they trust you. Simply acknowledging their feelings with a "that sucks, I'm so sorry" or "I don't know what to say, but I'm here for you" is all that's necessary. Thank them for sharing their feelings with you because it usually takes a lot of courage to do so.

    Being thoughtful can look like a lot of things, but paying attention and being present in a conversation to pick up what they might like or dislike is a good start. Not only can it give you a pretty good idea of what to get them for their birthdays, but it shows you really care about what they're saying and that they're important to you.

- ◆ **Be reliable.** Following through with promises or commitments you make to someone lets them know you're someone who can be trusted, and trust is a very important element of any relationship. This doesn't mean there won't be times when you have to cancel plans or tend to something urgent that came up instead, but being upfront and honest about it when it happens is key to maintaining any trust you've built.

- ◆ **Set boundaries.** Boundaries are like invisible lines—usually regarding behavior, but they can also apply to more ambiguous aspects—that you enforce in any relationship. It's like personal expectations and limitations.

    Boundaries allow all parties to feel safe and comfortable, and adhering to each other's boundaries is a sign of mutual respect. Having boundaries is non-negotiable, and being able to both communicate your own and respect the other person's is the epitome of a healthy relationship.

    Someone might question your boundaries, and you can certainly discuss why you have that boundary in a respectful way (if you feel comfortable doing so), but if someone judges, protests, or outright ignore it the first chance they get, that's a telltale sign that someone is toxic.

- ◆ **Communicate.** Okay, duh! Obviously, if you want to build a relationship with someone, it will require some form of continued communication. But bonding with someone isn't going to happen at a constant rate. Some moments will be raw and vulnerable, and others might be more superficial.

Enjoy the good moments because those make the best memories, lean into the vulnerability when it happens, and communicate openly when there are issues or tension for whatever reason.

It goes without saying that all of the points mentioned above should be reciprocated or mutual. Relationships are give-and-take, sometimes compromises are warranted and life happens. Don't be afraid to be vulnerable and express your feelings; in the grand scheme of things, it's unlikely that you'll ever regret it.

Respectful Expression

Everyone has their own idea of what respect means. The official definition of respect as a noun in the Merriam-Webster dictionary is: "To consider worthy of high regard." And, not surprisingly, that description is pretty spot on.

The way I define respect for myself is by treating others like human beings regardless of their age, race, culture, health, or status because we all have intrinsic value. The only thing that can influence my respect for others is a lack of reciprocity thereof.

I once saw a Tumblr post (yes, I'm that old) where someone compared the respect of personhood to the respect of authority. What it basically said was that people share this ideology of respect, meaning: If you treat me like a person, I'll treat you like a person. But there are some people—usually people in power—who, when they talk about mutual respect, really mean: Only if you treat me like an authority will I treat you like a person. And that has really stuck with me.

Entitled people aside, respect is a virtue that we all have the ability to grant to others. It builds trust, prevents conflict, and shows emotional intelligence and maturity. This doesn't mean that you'll never be in situations where someone is disrespectful to you or that you should never disagree with someone. But disagreeing with someone and being able to express your thoughts and feelings in a respectable way is an important skill to have in all forms of relationships.

Unless someone is just an awful or immature person, being respectful when setting boundaries, calling them out for their behavior, and disagreeing will actually strengthen a relationship. And knowing how to deal with receiving disrespect can help you feel more confident and assertive—you deserve respect, don't settle for less.

Here's how to express your opinions, thoughts, needs, and emotions in a respectful manner:

- ⬥ **Be assertive.** You can express yourself confidently and respectfully at the same time. And yes, this will take practice. You have to believe that you're worth standing up for and realize that the only person who's going to stand up for you *is* you. People can't read your mind, which is why you have to tell them when they've said or done something that has hurt you, or when you disagree with them, or when they're being unfair or rude.

  Being assertive doesn't mean you should be aggressive, rude, confrontational, or disrespectful. It means you value yourself and your rights while also acknowledging the rights of others. It's about being fair to yourself and others regardless of how they might react to it.

- ⬥ **Reframe the statement.** When you want to express your needs, thoughts, opinions, or emotions, outright telling someone that they are the reason you feel a certain type of way can cause them to feel attacked. This might lead them to become defensive or even start an argument, and that will not yield productive results. Your goal isn't to argue but to resolve.

  Instead, you can reframe your statement. So, instead of saying, "You always expect me to drop everything and clean my room when you tell me to," you can say, "I feel frustrated when you tell me to clean my room when I'm busy. I know it needs to be done; can I do it later?"

- ⬥ **Understand their point of view.** We're quick to disagree with someone if they're doing or saying something we don't approve of. But unless they're being rude or disrespectful, take a moment to process whatever it is that you don't agree with. Try to see things from their perspective, taking into consideration what information is or isn't available to them.

If you still can't understand where they're coming from, you can tell them how and why you disagree without attacking or making fun of them for their views and opinions.

- ❖ **Be considerate.** Talk to people the way you want to be talked to. Again, this doesn't mean that others will return the favor. However, a hallmark sign of being emotionally mature and respectful is leading by example. By considering the other person's feelings, you can prevent them from lashing out and causing an argument.

There are ways to go about expressing your feelings, thoughts, or opinions without being rude or judgmental. Some people will defend their direct rudeness or disrespect by saying they're "brutally" honest. I find that to be a lame excuse; you can be honest while still being kind and considerate.

For example, let's say someone you're talking to has something stuck in their teeth; the only options here are telling them or ignoring it. Not telling them isn't the kind thing to do, in my opinion. Think of it this way, if you had something stuck in your teeth, would you prefer it if someone told you or left you to go the whole day without knowing?

Being considerate is all in the delivery. Saying, "Oh, you have something in your teeth," without making a big deal out of it versus pulling a face and saying, "Ew, what's in your teeth?" Both scenarios display honesty, but only one is being considerate.

Daily Task

I get it. It seems daunting and scary to meet new people. Not every person you meet will become a permanent or important fixture in your life, and there's no way to know which relationships are built to last. But that's the name of the game; life is just one big gamble, really.

But you can't let the uncertainty stop you from trying, and you can't let the fear of wasting your time and effort stop you from participating at all. And you can't let your fear of rejection, embarrassment, or awkward moments dictate everything you do for the rest of your life. So here's what you're going to do today:

You're going to make micro-commitments. These are low-risk, medium-reward actions that might or might not result in an opportunity to get to know someone just a bit better, such as:

- ❖ Add someone from your friend recommendation lists to Snapchat, Facebook, or Instagram.
- ❖ Greet someone when they walk past you.
- ❖ Give someone a genuine compliment (their shoes, an accessory, their outfit, or skills are all safe options to go for).
- ❖ Ask to borrow something, but remember to give it back (an eraser, a pencil, white-out, etc.).
- ❖ Make that comment, either on social media or in real life, given that it's polite and appropriate (bonus points if it's funny).
- ❖ Ask someone for their opinion or recommendation.
- ❖ Agree (or disagree) with someone—respectfully, of course.

A lot of things can be an opportunity to start or join in on a conversation; you just have to take a chance sometimes. People are like flavors, some complement each other, and some don't mix, but it takes a certain level of risk and experimentation to figure it out.

CHAPTER 6
Day 6
HANDLING DIFFICULT SOCIAL SITUATIONS

> *I am not afraid of storms for I am learning how to sail my ship.*
> –Louise May Alcott

No matter what you do, there will always be conflict in any relationship. In fact, conflict is a sign of a healthy relationship. People have this idea that conflict is a bad thing that should be avoided. But that's simply not true. No two people are going to see eye to eye on everything all the time. It highlights the beautiful uniqueness that exists within all of humanity.

That being said, conflict isn't a sign that two people are incompatible, and it's how you handle the conflict that matters. It can strengthen and help the relationship grow, or it can burn it to the ground.

Conflict resolution is a necessary soft skill that is unimaginably important in most areas of your life, both now and in the future. You will use it with your future romantic partner, your colleagues, your boss, your friends, and even your children (if you decide to have them).

What Is Conflict?

Conflict is more than a disagreement. However, disagreements can certainly turn into conflict if it's not resolved properly. Conflict is a situation where someone feels threatened or becomes emotionally triggered due to the actions or words of someone else (usually someone they consider a friend, but can also be an acquaintance or stranger).

It doesn't go away when you ignore it. In fact, unresolved conflict will only become worse over time. And as crazy as it sounds, conflict is an opportunity to build trust and security in the relationship, but that will depend on your (and the other person's) ability to overcome it.

Your perception of conflict will tell you a lot about your conflict resolution skills. For example, if you're the type of person who avoids arguments, doesn't uphold your own boundaries, or defends or ignores others' negative actions toward you instead of bringing it up to them, you're probably not very good at it—no offense.

But you have to admit it makes perfect sense; if a person avoids conflict at all costs, then that means they haven't had much (if any) experience dealing with it. Hence, their problem-solving abilities go down the drain or never develop fully in the first place.

The good news is it's never too late to learn.

Conflict Resolution

How you handle conflict comes down to your ability to stay calm and alert when emotions are running high. This means that even when someone has said or done something that has triggered an adverse emotional response, you're able to re-regulate and continue to engage and even face the conflict head-on.

There are two main skills of conflict resolution: Emotional awareness and emotional regulation.

Staying calm during a stressful time allows you to still be aware of social cues and body language so you can assess the situation properly. It's important to regulate your emotions during conflict, so you're able to communicate your needs and feelings in a way that won't escalate things but rather resolve them.

Strategies

There are five main strategies for resolving conflict, but they're not all equal and the method you choose will depend on the importance, impact, and consequences it will have on everyone involved. The five conflict resolution strategies are:

- **Avoidance.** This is when you try to sidestep or ignore the issue at hand. And while it's not recommended in most situations, there are some cases in which this strategy can be effective. Avoidance can be used in cases where whatever conflict exists isn't really important to anyone involved and doesn't impact you or the other party in any major way (has no consequences).

- **Accommodation.** Resolving conflict with accommodation usually means you'll try to satisfy the other person's wishes, concerns, and needs—usually with some level of effort on your part. The thing to remember with this strategy is that it should only be used if the consequences (or effort you're putting in) don't infringe on your personal boundaries or requires you to ignore your emotions.

  An example of this would be to make a commitment to do something that you don't really want to do, say, go to a concert of an artist you don't like with a friend, but you value their friendship, so you're willing to accommodate their desires so you can still spend time together.

- **Compromising.** This strategy focuses on finding a way to partially satisfy the needs or concerns of everyone involved. Compromising is usually the best resolution in situations where it's impossible to meet everyone's needs, so each person has to be willing and able to compromise on or forfeit certain things.

  For example, you're working on a project with a classmate, the due date is in two days and you're not going to be done in time. You want to ask for an extension but your classmate wants to pull an all-nighter and get it done in time. A potential compromise here could be to meet up after school for the next two days to work on the project more than you were planning to and then decide if it's necessary to ask for more time.

- **Competing.** This is the opposite of accommodation. Someone who uses this strategy will do everything they can to satisfy their own needs and desires without considering the needs and feelings of those around them—it's usually done at the other party's expense.

  A clear-cut example of this is when you get mad at your friend and give them the silent treatment for not doing what you want to do.

- **Collaboration.** Collaboration includes finding a way to fully meet the needs of everyone involved (similar to compromising, only it's a win-win situation for all involved instead of needing to give up in some aspects).

An example of this would be if you want to go see a movie and your friend wants to go ice skating, instead of choosing one, you do both (either on the same day or not, either way, everyone gets what they want in the end).

There are many ways to quickly re-regulate your emotional state, such as breathing and grounding exercises. Emotional awareness can be improved by working on your emotional intelligence, which allows you to accept your emotions in real time instead of ignoring or suppressing them. It also allows you to understand yourself, your needs and emotions, as well as those of others, so you're in a better position to negotiate or mediate a resolution.

Emotional Intelligence

Emotional intelligence is one's ability to understand, use, and control your mental state in order to relieve stress, understand where others are coming from (even if they might be going about it in the wrong way), and empathize with them, as well as communicate effectively to avoid misunderstandings.

It's an important aspect of building strong and healthy relationships, achieving personal and professional goals, and making constructive choices with regard to what's most important to you.

You can improve your emotional intelligence by working on self-management, self-awareness, social awareness, and relationship management.

Emotions are like little blocks of information that help us understand ourselves better. But at times, it can also overwhelm us and make us lose control over ourselves. There's a fine line between managing your emotions and suppressing them. Managing your emotions (or self-management) involves accepting and processing them without letting your actions be controlled by them; suppressing your emotions means avoiding them altogether.

Take a moment to think of the relationship you have with your emotions, and this will give you an indication of how well you handle them. Ask yourself the following questions:

- ✧ Do your emotions flow?
- ✧ Do you pay attention to your emotions?
- ✧ Do you sometimes feel your emotions physically in your body?
- ✧ Do you experience individual emotions, and can you name them effectively?

If your answer to any of these questions is "no," it most likely means that you're not aware of or in touch with your emotions. There are many potential reasons for avoiding strong feelings, such as past trauma, extreme negative experiences with emotions, and the inability to self-regulate.

Dealing With Disrespect

As mentioned in the previous chapter, your peers or even authority figures (such as your teachers, guardians, elders, or even your parents) might treat you disrespectfully at times. Which is quite honestly ridiculous since they're the ones who should be modeling what it looks like to treat others with kindness and respect. Some people are truly so delusional that they believe they deserve respect without having to respect others in return.

But what exactly is disrespectful behavior? What does it look like? How do you know if someone is being disrespectful?

Disrespect can come in many forms. Disruptive behavior such as angry outbursts, threats, throwing objects, swearing at someone, or even physically hurting someone. Demeaning behavior such as shaming or humiliation, degrading comments, censorship, insults or inappropriate jokes, condescension, or faultfinding (nitpicking everything one does). Intimidation tactics like abuse of power, controlling behavior, arrogance, intentionally ignoring or overstepping boundaries, or bullying. Passive aggression or any insidious behavior such as staring, pointing, rude gestures, lying, belittling, taunting, or exclusion.

The circumstances don't matter. No one has the right to disrespect others, no matter how bad of a mood they're in. One could argue that sometimes disrespect is justified. Being disrespectful to someone who was disrespectful first can feel righteous, moral even. But where does it end? All you're doing is creating a perpetual cycle where you feel justified in disrespecting them back, and then they feel justified in continuing to disrespect you.

By refusing to participate in this snowball effect, you give the perpetrator a chance to think about their actions. Retaliated disrespect is expected. So at the end of the day, everyone focuses on defending their actions instead of reflecting on them and becoming a better person. Granted, some people are so stuck in their ways that no amount of self-reflection will help them be a better person. Don't let that be you.

Here's what you can do when dealing with disrespect from others instead of feeding into their narrow-minded delusions of grandeur:

◇ **Give them the benefit of the doubt.** Disrespect has to be intentional to count as such. So, it's possible that someone's actions might seem disrespectful when it's not actually meant that way. Some forms of disrespect are way less obvious than others. For instance, if someone yells at you, that's obvious and intentional disrespect, but someone not waving back at you when you could've sworn they saw you is less obvious.

   It might be possible that they did see you and chose to ignore you; however, if you're friends and have no reason to believe that they don't want to talk to you, chances are they just didn't see you (even if it looked like they did). Giving someone the benefit of the doubt might sometimes mean you let it fly without much thought until it happens again and only then start to investigate or deduce whether they are being disrespectful or just ignorant. If it does continue to happen, or you start to recognize other ways in which they're being disrespectful, you should bring it up and have a discussion about it.

◇ **Call them out.** Another thing someone who is actively and intentionally disrespecting you is not going to expect is someone calling them out on it. "What do you mean by that?" is a simple, non-confrontational question that's pretty effective.

   The beauty about this is that it's so low profile; if someone makes a rude remark about you or even about someone else, ask, "What do you mean by that?" This almost forces them to admit that they're being a walking red flag. Ask the question in a way that makes it seem that you're really curious as to what they are trying to say, don't come across as accusatory. You can ask them to elaborate by repeating the question or saying you don't understand, especially when someone is making a joke at your expense.

   But it also works to clear up misunderstandings; if they didn't mean something in a bad or disrespectful way, they'd have no issue explaining themselves. And watching them stumble over their words when they realize that they are, in fact, being a soggy pop tart is just an added bonus. It's really a win-win situation; either they clarify what they meant and you realize they were not actually trying to be disrespectful, or they're forced to tell on themselves.

   Other ways you can directly call out someone for being openly disrespectful is by saying, "That's a rude thing to say," "Why did you feel the need to say that?" or "That's not that funny though, is it?"

◇ **Try not to take it personally.** Impoliteness of disrespect is more common than you may realize, especially coming from strangers. Someone who's known for their bad attitude isn't going to change their stripes just for you, and a random person pushing past you without so much as an "excuse me" isn't a personal attack on you. So try not to put too much weight behind their rotten personality. Don't let someone who's insignificant to your existence ruin your day or take up mental energy that could be spent doing something more productive.

   This will also prevent you from taking your bad mood out on others who don't deserve it. It makes sense; when someone is rude or disrespectful to you, it might disrupt your mood for the whole day leading to you being unfriendly or even rude to others. It might help to think of strangers' disrespect as an isolated incident. Don't let an event that lasted a couple of minutes throw you off for hours.

Now, when it's someone you do know or that you have to deal with every day, like a parent, guardian, teacher, or teammate, and you can't avoid interacting with them, and their behavior is causing you distress, that's when you take matters into your own hands by looking at everything else on this list—and decide on a plan of action.

- **Remain calm.** This is where many people fail, myself included, sometimes. It's a perfectly reasonable response to lose your cool when someone is continually disrespecting you. But sometimes that's exactly what they want. They want to get a rise out of you. However, this doesn't mean you should just roll over and take it, either.

  Staying calm when someone is being disrespectful accomplishes a few things. It shows them that they're not in control of your behavior and that they can't phase you. Even if this is the furthest thing from the truth, even if you're on the verge of throwing hands, try to stay composed. Yes, this is easier said than done, and you might even have to excuse yourself to calm down elsewhere, but the disappointment they will feel afterward when they realize that they were the immature one is worth its weight in gold!

  When you do respond or engage (because you have a right to defend and stand up for yourself), don't raise your voice or resort to insulting them. Simply act with tact. Respond with clarifying questions or the classic "What do you mean by that?" Repeat their words back to them and ask them if you understand correctly. Tell them how or why you disagree with what they're saying.

  And if you need to, remove yourself from the situation and take some deep, calming breaths—or punch a pillow. Whatever you need to do to let out the frustration (in a healthy, controlled, non-vandalizing way) so they don't get the satisfaction of knowing they'd upset you.

- **Vocalize boundaries, and follow through with consequences.** There are certain behaviors that are simply not acceptable. What you deem as unacceptable will vary, but someone screaming and cursing at you is one fairly universal boundary, I feel. So we'll use this as an example.

  When someone oversteps a boundary of yours, in this case by yelling or cursing at you, you are well within your right to demand—not ask—them to stop, regardless of who they are. "If you don't stop yelling at me, I'm going to remove myself from this situation," or some variation of this. And if they do continue, be prepared to follow through with the consequences.

- **The power of intentionally misunderstanding.** This kind of ties in with asking them to clarify what they meant by whatever they said. When someone is being sarcastic, passive-aggressive, or gives you a backhanded compliment, take it at face value. Thank them or agree with them and move on. If they correct you by saying it wasn't a compliment or that they meant something else, they look like a bad person, and you can then call them out for it. If they ignore it, they are less likely to engage in that behavior around you.

- **Snip snip.** In some cases, it won't be possible to cut contact with someone who's constantly disrespectful toward you, but minimizing your interactions (or cutting them off completely) where possible will save you so much mental energy. And staying around people who are disrespectful is never worth it, no matter how cool you think they are.

  One thing I've learned in life is that if people tell—or show—you who they are, listen up. It's not exactly a big jump in moral ethics for someone to talk badly about someone else to you and then talk badly about you to whoever is willing to listen. Rudeness is contagious, and it's up to you to decide if it's worth getting infected.

  Surround yourself with people who are respectful, and your chances of being disrespected decrease exponentially.

I want to reiterate that it's not possible to avoid being disrespected, especially from people who believe they're superior and deserve respect, simply because they're an adult and you're still a child. And even as an adult, you'll still encounter disrespect from time to time, so getting comfortable with calling it out in a mature way (and even acknowledging and apologizing when you might be the disrespectful one) is an essential life skill.

Daily Task

Emotional intelligence is an important element in fostering strong connections with people, but it's also necessary for conflict resolution and expressing your emotions, needs, and boundaries in a respectful way—and also respecting the emotions, needs, and boundaries of others.

It allows you to stay calm in times of high stress, take responsibility for your own actions, express your emotions rather than simply unloading them, make others feel heard, and genuinely care about other people and the impact you have on them.

Practicing self-awareness will automatically improve your emotional intelligence, but here's another approach to take on a more proactive role in it:

- **Allow yourself to be bored.** Get rid of all the distractions for a bit, even if it's just ten minutes a day. Sit with yourself in the present moment without having something to do. It's a scary thought, but it will allow you to connect with and understand your thoughts and feelings better. Just be part of life for a short while every day, no screens, no music, no internet, no games, no hobbies, just you and your brain.

- **Pay more attention to your emotions.** When simply going about your day, pay attention to how your emotional state changes, and embrace and acknowledge the emotional rollercoaster. It might be unsettling to discover that you feel more sad, angry, or anxious during everyday life than you may have realized—and it can be shameful to admit that sometimes we're not very nice to the people we care about because of it. But it's only through admitting our anger when mom asks us to unload the dishwasher, our anxiety when walking past a group of our peers, or our sadness when thinking of an ex who broke our heart that we understand what makes us tick. And react accordingly.

- **React accordingly.** Here's a hard truth to swallow: we can't control our emotions; we can only control how we react to them. So what many people really mean when they say you should learn how to control your emotions is that you should learn how to control your reactions to your emotions.

- Recognize what you're feeling and decide if the emotion is warranted or appropriate for the situation, and then react to that emotion accordingly. This doesn't mean the feeling is going to go away. It simply means you're not hurting yourself or others because of it.

- **Redirection.** It's easy to look for scapegoats when trying to pinpoint the reason for our emotions. No one wants to be blamed for something, especially when it doesn't feel like it's our fault, but your emotions—regardless of who or what caused them—are your responsibility to deal with. Yes, they're acting like an a-hole, but you can choose to walk away and redirect your emotions elsewhere (in a healthy, non-harmful way).

Your task for today is going to be meditating. Don't worry; it sounds more intimidating than it actually is. You can choose to set a timer for at least five minutes (with a soft and gentle ring to let you know when you're done) or just meditate for as long as you need to. You're simply going to be in the present moment and do a body and mind check-in following a few simple steps:

Step 1: Get comfortable. Either sitting or lying down, settle into a position where your body can relax and be comfortable for the next few minutes. It may help if it's somewhere where you feel at ease and won't be disturbed until you're done.

Step 2: Focus on something. You can keep your eyes open (but your gaze softened, not focused on any particular object in front of you) or shut. A common thing many people who meditate choose to focus on is their breathing, but you can also focus on a sound or smell.

Step 3: Stay in the present. Your mind may drift away; it's normal. Don't get frustrated; simply redirect your attention back to whatever it is you are focusing on (your breathing, a taste, a smell, etc.).

Step 4: Feel. Pay attention to any sensations that may be happening in your body and acknowledge them. Feel the way your clothes are touching your skin, feel the couch you're sitting on (or the bed under you). Maybe a soft breeze makes its way through the window and causes your hair to tickle the back of your neck or your face. Maybe you're a bit hungry or thirsty. Maybe your hands are cold. Accept any emotional reaction that might be making its presence known, lean into it and feel your body react to it, allow it to happen. Invite it all in and then submit to it.

Step 5: Return. Start by bringing your attention back to your breath, and slowly open your eyes. Move your fingers and toes, then your arms and legs. Do a light stretch if it feels good. You can choose to say a few affirmations or journal your experience. Or just move on with your day from here.

Emotions are neutral, and there's no such thing as good or bad emotions. Yes, anger doesn't feel good, while happiness does, but that doesn't mean anger is inherently bad or that joy is inherently good. They all need to be experienced, processed, and accepted.

CHAPTER 7

Day 7 — SOCIAL SUSTAINABILITY

> *Confidence doesn't come out of nowhere. It's a result of something... hours and days and weeks and years of constant work and dedication..*
> –Roger Staubach

♦♦♦♦

It's a lot to take in—everything we've discussed so far. I want to remind you that building your social skills, working on self-awareness, establishing connections, and improving your self-esteem is going to take time. Much longer than seven days. However, this book is meant to guide you so you can isolate each of these things and work on them separately.

And while some of them do complement each other or interlace at certain points, if you stick with the program, you will create momentum and stay on track for making progress. Because that's the true goal: progress, no matter how slow.

Maintaining Momentum

If you've been following along and doing all the daily tasks since day one, you might've already gotten into a slightly different routine than usual. You might still be journaling every day, saying your affirmations, working on improving your social skills in certain areas, stepping out of your comfort zone, making micro-commitments, and having done your first ten-minute "no distractions" exercise.

You're doing the most here. Sticking to a routine that incorporates all of this to some degree—as well as taking care of your physical and mental well-being—is key to sustaining your progress in the long term.

Basically, you need to make habits out of it. I'm sure you know what a habit is; it's a set of actions that—the more you do them—the more ingrained they get and eventually become automatic. Meaning you don't even pay attention to doing them anymore; you just kind of do them without much thought.

There is a three-system loop that's responsible for creating a habit: the cue, the action, and the reward. Once your brain has made a strong connection between the cue and the reward, the action becomes automatic. And while it's hard to form a habit, it's even harder to break out of one (or rather replace it, since established habits don't ever really go away, they get replaced).

So yes, if you're in the habit of avoiding uncomfortable social situations, it's going to take some work to replace that habit with one that's completely new and scary to you. But it's necessary if you want to improve your social skills and connect with people.

The Routine

A good routine is one that incorporates activities that maintain self-care and promotes personal growth on a daily basis. Remember, the actions you take don't have to be big for results to occur. And whatever your current routine is (even if you don't think you have one), you should never try to change everything all at once because you will lose motivation and fall behind. This will leave you feeling defeated, which will further demotivate you, leading to you giving up on the whole thing entirely.

Self-Care

There's a lot of debate as to what self-care means. But, if you take it at face value, it means taking care of yourself, as the word itself implies. It's things you do to ensure your future self is well—which includes your mind, body, and spirit.

You take care of your body by leading a healthy lifestyle, eating a balanced diet, getting regular exercise, getting enough sleep, getting annual checkups with a doctor, and having healthy hygiene practices (like taking a shower semi-regularly, brushing your teeth daily, etc.).

You take care of your mind by doing things that bring you joy and get rid of stress and mind clutter, such as journaling, art, music, and other hobbies or activities. This can also include things like spending time with friends, being supported and surrounded by people who mean a lot to you, and even playing video games or watching a movie.

You take care of your spirit by doing things that make you feel like you're a part of something greater, something that makes you feel like you have a purpose. This could be helping others in need, volunteering, practicing mindfulness, connecting with nature, or praying to whichever higher power you believe in.

Self-care can also include things that you might not enjoy doing in the moment, but it makes you feel good about yourself afterward. Exercise is a great example of this. You don't enjoy sweating and being out of breath, but you feel a sense of accomplishment and fulfillment knowing every time you do it, you get just a little closer to your fitness goals.

Personal Growth

This includes things you wish to improve about yourself, whether it's your self-esteem, your social skills, your emotional intelligence, or all of the above. You need to implement and practice it as much as you can—preferably on a daily basis as part of your self-care routine where possible.

Life can get pretty crazy; everything happens so quickly in the era of the internet that our minds sometimes have trouble keeping up. Personal growth can mean a lot of things; it's up to you to decide what your goals are and how you're going to achieve them.

Goal Setting and Tracking for Personal Growth

Your self-discovery and self-improvement journey will look different depending on what exactly you would like to achieve. There's no communal list where everyone progresses at the same rate or even starts at the same level, which is why it's important to define your goals early on so you can work out a plan of action for achieving them.

Making progress is what gives you the motivation and encouragement to continue, and since self-improvement is very subjective and happens so gradually, you'll need a way to track your progress.

Think of it like this: You need to demolish a house; that's your goal. But not just any house, a brick house. It's a humongous task, so you focus on one thing at a time. You were only given a hammer, so you start chipping away at the mortar, and inch by inch, the bricks underneath get exposed. It feels like you're getting nowhere. Only after an entire day's work do you step back and see that you managed to complete an entire room. After a month, all the mortar on the walls of the entire house is gone, just by you repeating the same action day after day, by being consistent.

The house is still standing, and you still have a long way to go before you achieve your goal, but the work you have done so far was both necessary and meaningful. You might even stumble upon another tool that can get the job done quicker, or at the very least easier, but that doesn't minimize your previous efforts. Similarly, there might be days where all you have is a toothpick and can't get anything done, but again, that doesn't take away the progress you've already made so far.

But determining progress on something that can't physically be observed or quantified is a bit different than simply stepping back and having a looksie. And relying on your subjective memory or intuition to confirm or deny whether you're objectively moving forward or improving is not reliable.

Goal Setting

Look, the SMART method is a good guide for setting goals: Your goals *should* be specific, measurable, achievable, realistic, and time-bound. And if you want to use the SMART system, be my guest. I'm just personally very bored of it. It's everywhere!

This is why I want to introduce you to a slightly different approach. Starting with determining what your ultimate self-improvement goals are. Think of three of the most prominent challenges in your life right now (that you have control over) and write them down, for example:

- I don't have friends.
- I don't take care of myself.
- My GPA is 2.0.

There might be more, but we're going to focus on three of the challenges that affect you the most first. You're going to look at each of these and conjure up a unique goal based on what you want the end result to look like. Based on the above-mentioned examples, let's go with the following:

- Become part of a friend group.
- Get into a consistent self-care routine.
- Raise my GPA to 3.0 (so I can at least get into college).

This is your metaphorical brick house. You're going to craft a plan of action for the most important one and make a start. In my opinion, a self-care routine is the most important goal to achieve out of all three on the list. Because when you're taking care of yourself, you feel better, and when you feel better, you'll have the mental and physical capacity to tackle the rest of your problems.

I'm going to start by evaluating my current self-care routine: Doom scrolling social media until two a.m. in the morning, yes. Haven't had a glass of pure water in six months, check. Forgets to brush teeth—oh, don't you dare judge me! This is a safe space, remember?

So, it's not... ideal, but we know what we're working with now; we have a starting point. I would do some research and figure out what a healthy self-care routine generally looks like. Getting enough sleep, eating a balanced diet, drinking enough water, keeping up with personal hygiene, and moving your body are the bare basics of self-care. Simple enough.

What I'm *not* going to do is completely up-root my daily life and overwhelm myself by trying to change every single unhealthy habit at once until I inevitably give up and go back to square one. Instead, I'm going to isolate one factor, in this case, increasing my water intake.

My initial goal is to drink a single glass of water every day for at least a week. I'll set a reminder if I have to, or combine it with another task so I don't forget (like drinking a glass of water right after I take a hot shower since that is when I usually feel thirsty—and I would ignore it). I would reward myself every day that I manage to drink a glass of water and be kind to myself if I do happen to miss a day here and there.

After I have taken to the habit of drinking a full glass of water every day, I would move on to the next milestone: Drinking two glasses of water a day. Once that habit has been established, I have significantly increased my water intake from what it was—which was zero. By this point, I'd be pretty chuffed with myself, call it a win, and move on to a different factor of building a healthier self-care routine.

Your goal is your desired result; your milestones are how you get there. Jumping from drinking no water a day to the recommended amount, which is eight, is unrealistic. And honestly, even if you stick to two glasses of water a day for months before you try to increase it again, it's still an improvement!

You should also only focus on one, maybe two, manageable milestones per goal at a time. For example, drinking one glass of water a day and going to sleep half an hour earlier than I normally would. Only once I've gotten my water intake and sleep to where it needs to be would I move on to the next ones: Diet and movement. Again, small changes and milestones that are sustainable are the way to go.

Instead of only having chocolate as a snack, I'd have chocolate-covered strawberries; instead of only having Cheerios for breakfast, I'd also have some full-cream yogurt alongside it. A healthy, balanced diet is more about adding beneficial foods rather than taking 'unhealthy' stuff away, but I digress. For more movement, I'd add a five-minute walk around the block to my daily routine, obviously while listening to music, an audiobook, or my favorite podcast.

After months of consistent effort, I'd have gotten to a point where my self-care routine was solid. Sure, there might be days where I skip breakfast or don't take a walk, or still forget to brush my teeth, but 80% of the time, I nail it. I'm happy with a B minus, and you should be, too!

Now, whatever goal you choose to start with next will depend on the priority, importance, and effect it has on your life. Let's say I have less than a year before I need to start applying for colleges or universities. And I'm definitely going to need a scholarship. In this case, I would prioritize my goal of raising my GPA over my goal of becoming part of a friend group.

While still maintaining my new self-care routine, I would brainstorm what I could do to raise my grades. Summer school, online classes, and getting a tutor are all feasible options. On top of this, I can revise my textbooks (maybe going over previous chapters and highlighting what I'm struggling with) and ask for extra-credit assignments. I might do weekly study reviews to make sure I understand the work that was covered and make notes as I go so I have summaries of the important stuff when studying for tests. I would put more effort into homework, assignments, and projects and ask for help if I needed it.

There are plenty of YouTube channels dedicated to breaking down the high school curriculum content for any class so it's easier to memorize and understand. I would take full advantage of this resource, too. But I would also schedule rest or off days, days where I do the bare minimum, and make sure I have time for self-care as well as things I enjoy, like hobbies. Burnout takes years to recover from; you don't want that before you even start college or enter the workforce.

Last but certainly not least, I would sprinkle in small steps toward making friends while pursuing my other milestones relating to self-care and raising my grade. For example, my first milestone would be to do some introspection (as discussed in the previous chapters) and figure out who I am, what's important to me, the type of friendships I want, and the type of people who I want to be surrounded with.

Then, I'd observe my peers and identify who I'm most interested in being friends with, the kind ones, the non-judgmental ones (they're rare, but they exist), the ones who have the same interests and values as me, the ones who are applying to the same colleges as I am. This information will help establish an initial connection—albeit a rather superficial one. It will take time and effort to nurture the connection so a friendship can grow from it.

In the meantime, I'd also work on my self-confidence and self-esteem so I'm better able to showcase who I really am and not be so afraid to open up to and trust other people.

Goal Tracking

We are constantly changing, whether we're actively trying to or not. Our experiences, thoughts, and emotions create our perspective. A simple example of this is to think about something you didn't know when you were younger and how it has changed or shaped your current understanding of the world.

For example, when I was younger, I thought turning the car light on while driving was illegal because, well, my dad told me so. As an adult, I know that it's not actually illegal; it just drains the battery. My dad told me it was illegal because I wouldn't have been able to understand the consequences otherwise. He was just trying to avoid being stranded on the side of the highway with a dead battery.

We don't keep track of these little changes and bits of information we learn or figure out on our own. Until one day, you take a general knowledge quiz at 12 a.m. out of boredom and you realize that you didn't even know a lot of the things you know or remember where you learned them from. Personal growth is just like that, you hoard and implement little changes and habits until you're a completely different person, and yet, you didn't even notice it while it was happening.

How do you keep track of a concept such as self-improvement? How do you measure whether your self-confidence has leveled up? It's not like you have a stats menu where you can see your progress on a bar. Maybe Elon Musk can add that as a feature or app for his brain chip once it passes human trials.

Tracking your personal growth is as simple as finding a way to document it. Journaling can be a good way to do this, but while it can give you an overall idea of how your inner monologue and perspective have changed, it's not very specific.

You'll need to look at your goals and determine what the best way to track them would be—using my three goals from before, I'd say that for my self-care goal, a daily habit tracker is a good idea. For improving my grades, a spreadsheet that documents my progress in a line graph is straightforward and sufficient. And for building and tracking personal relationships, I'd add it to my daily habit tracker and put a symbol or draw a little smiley face every time I initiate a conversation with someone.

With regard to a timeline, I'd be lenient with it and not be too hard on myself if I don't complete milestones within the given timeframe. You really can't put a time limit on personal growth since you can't possibly know how long it's going to take. In most cases, with regard to personal growth, a due date is more so to keep yourself accountable. The only thing on my list that will need a set timeframe is raising my GPA before college applications open.

Your emotional health or mood can be tracked through a week/month/year in pixels: That's where you give all your feelings a color key and color in one square per day based on your most prominent mood for the day (red is anger, yellow is happy, blue is anxious, and so on). Your skills can be tracked by means of having a sketchbook for tracking art skills, recording yourself practicing, or anything else that allows you to physically see your improvement over time.

Another, more "out there" way to track your progress is by putting yourself to the test and seeing whether you would fare better now than you would've previously. This is for things like social skills, where there really is no other way to track your progress and new knowledge other than to just go out and try it out.

And obviously, you'll record your milestones and goals so you can celebrate once you've reached them!

Motivation

Your goals, milestones, and the approach you take to achieve them will look completely different to everyone. But any goal has to be important to you because if it isn't, you don't have any reason or motivation to complete it or make progress with it. So go ahead and ask yourself why, "Why is this goal important to me?"

Using my three example goals of being part of a friend circle, improving my self-care, and raising my GPA, the reasons are pretty self-explanatory. Having friends who support me is important for my mental health and it would make me feel less lonely. Self-care is equivalent to self-love, which will raise my self-image and ensure I stay healthy. Raising my GPA means I get into the college of my choice, which will allow me to pursue my dream job.

However, even when your goals are important to you, it doesn't mean your motivation will last. Motivation is just excitement rebranded. And since excitement is just an emotion, it's not enough to keep you going in the long term. I'm telling you now that you will inevitably lose motivation, probably quicker than you realize. Whether it's because you forget your motive behind them or get bored or distracted, it's how the cookie crumbles.

This is why you shouldn't rely on motivation to fuel you. Don't get me wrong, motivation is a great thing to have, but it shouldn't be the driving force behind your actions. If you wait for motivation to show up in order to take action, you will go long periods of time without making any effort toward progress at all.

It might help to think of motivation as the effect and not the cause, meaning that motivation isn't necessary for action but rather the result of action. And sure, in some cases, you might see something online or even in real life that inspires or motivates you, but I would say that's the lowest form of motivation that exists.

No, what's truly motivating is seeing the fruits of your labor—sticking to the plan even though you don't feel inspired or motivated to do so. The feeling you get when you realize you have been severely underestimating yourself all this time. Motivation *is* the reward. It's a release of dopamine—the feel-good hormone.

So, what *should* you then rely on to stay consistent?

Commitment.

Yes, it's hard. Losing sight of a goal, taking longer to reach a milestone than you anticipated, and backtracking by skipping multiple days are all things that will make you feel bad about yourself and just revert back to your old ways, giving up on the whole idea of self-improvement. It all comes down to commitment.

The journey to self-improvement is not linear. And what many people fail to understand is that commitment doesn't guarantee success. It means staying committed to a goal even when you regress or fail altogether. It means trying again no matter what others might say or think, or even what you might say or think of yourself.

Have the commitment of a toddler. It takes roughly two years before a child starts walking confidently, without support, and without falling down every two minutes. At no point has any physically-abled toddler decided that walking isn't for them because they have stumbled one too many times. It takes even longer for them to start talking fluently, but they don't give up. Why? Because they don't judge themselves—mainly because they don't yet have the mental capability to do so yet, but that's beside the point.

What would happen if you let go of the shame, guilt, or judgment that comes with perceived failure? What would happen if you completely redefine what failure and success mean to you?

Is failure the act of not meeting your own or others' expectations, or is it the lack of taking action in the first place? Does failure determine your value and worth, or does it simply mean that you need a different approach? Is failure a destination? And if it is, wouldn't that mean that you can only fail when you stop trying?

Failure can't be measured. Not in a way that's substantial or objective, anyway. It's purely based on opinions and imaginative social constructs. Your own included! Change the way you determine and view failure because nothing destroys commitment quite like the belief that you have already failed.

Daily Task

Your daily task for today is going to be about your daily routine and what small changes you can make so you can achieve your goals. You're going to start by mapping out your current routine. Think about what you do on most days from the moment you wake up to when you get back in bed, don't worry about time stamps; just keep it as detailed and accurate as you can.

Can you identify anything you're doing (or not doing) that's holding you back from achieving your goals? Maybe you try your best to fly under the radar at school, have no hobbies or extracurriculars, the only two places you go are to school and back home (even on weekends), and you spend more hours on your phone than the amount of sleep you get per night.

Now you're going to find one small thing you can do differently that will result in a slightly better outcome in the future. For example, sacrifice ten minutes of your screen time every day to do something that either includes self-care or self-improvement, like sitting in the sun, going for a short walk, or self-reflection. Or having a breakfast meal that consists of something other than a single cup of coffee. Or blocking out time to spend with people in your life who you value and care about.

You'll continue to accumulate all these little habits one at a time that make you feel better about yourself, and eventually, you'll be resilient enough, confident enough, and strong enough to face and recover from all the discomfort and curveballs that life throws at you—because sometimes life is simply unavoidable.

CONCLUSION

One thing that you learn quite quickly as you grow up is that no one—regardless of your social or economic status—makes it through life without getting a few scars along the way. In the hypothetical war zone that is life, some may lose limbs while others only end up with bruises, but getting hurt to some extent is inevitable.

We can't control our emotions, but we can learn to control what we do about them and how we express them. And how you react to your emotions will change your perception of the world in the long run by rewiring your brain. This is why every journal entry, every thought you challenge, every positive affirmation, and every milestone you achieve counts. Every effort and any amount of progress is worth celebrating.

Low self-esteem (and, as a result, low confidence and social anxiety) has many roots and can take on many forms. But I can tell you this: It's never your fault. Having unsupportive parents with unrealistic goals, narcissistic friends, having gone or are going through a stressful period, exhibiting signs of a mental health disorder, or doing poorly in school are all circumstances that are not in your control—and they create the perfect breeding ground for self-doubt and resentment.

Maybe you avoid conflict because it never ends well and leaves you triggered and emotional for days. It never feels like you're wanted or included, so it's easier and less painful to simply remove yourself from the discussion before others make the decision for you. You're so scared of failing and what the consequences would be that you can never take accountability for your mistakes or learn anything from them—because the fear of punishment overpowers the lesson behind it. You never seem to do anything right, so you avoid doing it at all, or you lack the motivation to even try because every time you do, you hear that little voice in your head telling you you're not good enough, not smart enough, not funny enough, not talented enough.

You look at what others your age have been able to accomplish and you feel angry, jealous, or spiteful. You're being compared to others by the people who are supposed to love and encourage you. How can you be happy for them if their success is being used against you? How can you be friends with them if they're a constant reminder of your incompetence?

It doesn't always take extreme circumstances to affect your self-image. And while a lot of it comes down to how you were raised, that's not always the case. The seed of doubt can be planted by a random comment from a teacher, a disappointed sigh from your father, or a bad grade on a test you actually studied for. If enough of these seeds are sowed, eventually, one will break through the soil. From then on, you'll look for any and all justifications as to why you keep on watering it:

"Why would they want to talk to me?"

"It's not even worth trying."

"I'm the only person I can trust."

It happens so gradually that you don't even realize it until one day, someone asks you why you're always so quiet and withdrawn, why you never come out of your room, or why you choose to be alone. It's because the world is a scary place for an impressionable young mind. It's because your assumptions and past experiences keep you hidden and scared to show the world who you really are. As a result, no one will know who you really are—not even you.

This unstable sense of self will follow you around until you've addressed it. You're at the age now where you're expected to know what your ultimate goals and dreams are in life. Only, you've been so focused on what you're *not* that you forgot to pay attention to what you *are*.

Here's the thing, though, when your brain has convinced you that no one likes you, you avoid others to avoid the emotional turmoil. When you don't practice social skills, they don't develop or strengthen.

So, you don't see yourself as worthy; you assume others think the same, and you don't know what to say or how to react in certain social situations. You're afraid you're going to embarrass yourself, and you're overthinking others' reactions, doubting their intentions, and going above and beyond to avoid spending time out in public. You might even break out in a sweat, experience heart palpitations, or have full-blown panic attacks during social events, or even while talking to someone you know well.

It's hard to connect with someone when it feels like you're fighting for your life. But by taking small steps at a time, using my version of the seven-day system, you can overcome your insecurities and build your confidence until nothing anyone does or says can shake the ground beneath your feet.

And as much as none of this is your fault, it's your life we're talking about here and, ultimately, your responsibility to take the reins. But do me a favor and try to smell the flowers along the way because as much as life can suck sometimes, there will be moments when everything is worth it. Savor those moments when they come.

You might be thinking that you have such a long way to go still, and you're right. But don't focus on the end goal because when it comes to self-improvement, there really isn't one. Don't look too far into the future either; just focus on your next step, and once you've taken it, the next one after that.

You don't have to be the best; you just have to be slightly better than you were last week.

CAREER PLANNING
FOR TEENS

How to Understand Your Identity, Cultivate Your Skills, Find Your Dream Job, and Turn That Into a Successful Career

EMILY CARTER

INTRODUCTION

> *If you can dream it, you can do it.*
>
> — Walt Disney

How many times have you looked at yourself in the mirror and thought, "What am I going to do with the rest of my life?"? Or how many times have you noticed your classmates and the people around you constantly working on themselves, leaving you feeling like you are falling behind? A certain level of panic might set in as you realize you don't have much time to prepare for the future. Fortunately, you can always turn that around – and today, you're starting to do just that!

The winds of change are coming as your secondary education ends. It is time to start thinking about career paths. As you walk through the halls of your high school, the terms career counseling and career planning become terms you meet more often. What does that mean? Do you suddenly have to think about tomorrow?

The short answer is yes. When you are a teenager, time is of the essence, and time waits for no one. Instead of starting to browse the options aimlessly, you took the logical first step and you purchased this book.

The importance of career planning during your teenage years will set the pace for how your career path will develop in the future. I am not saying that you can't thrive at a later age. However, during the crazy times of uncertainty that we live in, the best approach to the world of professional development is an early one. It is important to gain early access and exposure to help you achieve career awareness. But not only that. Through career planning in your teenage years, you enable a firmer and more harmonious career path that aligns with your wishes and goals.

Up until now, you may have used the classroom as an environment similar to the workplace. This is the perfect way to begin. It sets the tone for what you should expect in the future and helps you become more aware of your skills and interests. Nevertheless, it is still a classroom at the end of the day. It is still a closed and safe space where you can make mistakes and not be as involved as you should be.

This book can help you step out of your comfort zone. It can help you utilize the brainstorming bit and use it to your advantage. Once you take the first step, you will notice endless possibilities. The practices you get to learn and the experiences you are about to undergo will help create individualized access to a brighter tomorrow.

How does it sound so far? Convincing or not?

There is a second important aspect of choosing career planning during your teenage years, and it includes all the benefits you get from it.

Going through the process of choosing your career can help you identify your interests. It is okay if you weren't quite aware of your likes and dislikes up until now. This important aspect can help you choose the field that will make you happy in the future. Every person in the world has a "true calling," so why not figure out what yours is from an early age?

Another benefit you will gain is knowing how to make an informed decision. After all, there are all these factors to contribute; you might have difficulty navigating through it all. That is okay. That is what career advice is for. You can always rely on a mentor or a role model to help you get through the challenging period. Ultimately, they will motivate you and help you set goals that will lead you to a satisfying career option. Depending on the fields you are interested in, there is so much information to gather. Avoid losing yourself in the process. Understand the requirements, skills, and qualifications needed to succeed. Once you arm yourself with the appropriate knowledge, you will have all the power in the world!

But there is no knowledge without training, so surround yourself with the best options that can help you enhance everything you know. Training opportunities, volunteering opportunities, internships, shadowing people, and part-time jobs are all key points in your quest to thrive professionally. Consider this a two-way street – you get to advance your skills and learn many new ones, but you also get to identify the skills most employers require. I can teach you how to keep in mind all the future training that will act as a catalyst for your bright tomorrow!

Many of you have big dreams and want to achieve them but are scared of the outcome. Have no fear. All you need is to stay focused and keep working toward your goal. Considering everything, you will slowly start to enjoy the benefits of your careful career planning. Here are only a few of them to get you started:

- You will learn that this is your journey only. Being surrounded by adults, starting with your parents, teachers, relatives, counselors, etc., you might lose yourself. Starting to think that this is a decision that will affect anyone but you – meaning you need to take a step back. Instead, you will embed this in your brain – the journey is yours alone – enjoy it.

- There is a benefit to change. Change is something that will happen to you either way – why not take charge of it? Reading this book will give you exclusive insight into how to manage change and flourish every time you do it successfully.

- You will learn how to make mistakes and fix them as well. The decision-making process is the important part, but make no mistake about it, you will fail at it – at first. Every decision comes with the possibility of making a mistake. But every decision is also a valuable experience – you will teach yourself how to enjoy the good decisions and quickly fix the bad ones.

- You will learn how to make up your mind and if needed, to change it too. Career planning comes with a lot of twists and turns. You may start at one point with one goal in mind and end up in a completely different place. Your road to success will be filled with twists and turns and challenges wherever you look. It is essential to accept that, depending on everything you discover about yourself, you might need to change your plans (sometimes even completely).

- Keep learning – from everything. Every step you take comes with a lesson. The same goes for this book – every chapter is filled with lessons for you to remember. It all comes down to reinforcing your connection while seeking out new experiences.

- There is also always time to celebrate yourself. Don't forget to have fun while discovering everything you can about yourself. Above all, you are a teenager, and this is still your time to shine and have fun! Just remember to work hard during the process and celebrate every milestone you complete. This way, you will boost your confidence and maybe, some magic in the air!

Throughout this book, you will learn how to set up a system that works for you. The structure allows for being flexible and persistent and learning how to tackle every obstacle that comes your way. For starters, being true and honest with yourself is the best way to begin your journey toward professional success.

Other than that, I am also covering various topics such as how to explore career options and to broaden your horizons. Learning how to leap into the future by uncovering some potential job prospects that represent the future. But never stop working on yourself. Using your technical and transferable skills is a part of all job experiences – together, we will see how you can utilize them best.

It is not all about the technical part – you will also learn how to develop a fantastic support system filled with people you can trust. Allow me to enter a hidden part of your mind and explain the importance of role models. After doing that, you might realize you have had a role model all this time!

As the planning continues, you will also gain an understanding of what it means to have some practical experience before you dive head-first into the job world. I am covering all topics – from building the perfect portfolio and resume to successfully being a part of a job interview. Moving on, you get to discover how to recognize the available professional options. Weighing in the factors and knowing how to decide on your career is essential.

Once you understand how the market works, what types of job prospects are right there at your fingertips, and how to improve your skillset constantly, you will become an invaluable part of the force that drives the world.

Let me empower you to make an informed decision about your future. There is only one bridge between your dreams and reality, so take a walk with me. Today, we are commencing an amazing journey of career planning.

Today, your dreams are waiting – let's start chasing them together!

CHAPTER 1

UNDERSTANDING YOURSELF

> "Knowing yourself is the beginning of all wisdom."
>
> — Aristotle

Even though we live in a different era, this timeless truth continues to echo throughout the centuries. But let's be honest for a moment – finding and understanding yourself can be incredibly tricky when you are a teenager. Driven by hormones and emotion, you wander through life's corridors while external factors try to sway you from your true self. And in this modern era, where the comparison to influential people can easily seduce you to build your interests around someone else's norms – the road can become even more challenging. Top it off with family expectations and other influences from your society, and voila; you are officially in the *"I don't know what I want"* maze. Oh, and the fact that so many career choices mount while you are already overwhelmed doesn't help either.

But how can you possibly get out of that maze and come face to face with your true self?

In short, the answer is within. You just need the right tools to guide you, which is what this chapter is all about. With self-assessment and personal reflection as your compass, you will uncover your inner landscape of interests, values, and skills. In addition, you will also learn how your personality traits play a major role in making the right career choice. By understanding who you are and where your interests and passions lie, you will not only define the first step toward your career but also unleash your full potential.

Now, prepare to see yourself from a different angle. Uncover the truth within, and relish how complex, unique, and beautiful you are.

Self-Assessment and Personal Reflection

The first step towards choosing a career path that resonates with you is the act of self-assessing and reflecting. You need to be able to decide on something you will genuinely enjoy and be passionate about.

As a teenager, it is easy to be influenced and distracted by many external factors. That is why it is essential to simply find a quiet place, sit down, and think about all that makes you, YOU.

Let's start with your general values and motivations. Ask yourself, what truly matters to you? What do you value? Do you live and breathe in the name of a team spirit, or do you value a quieter and more individual approach? Is the support and presence of your family the motivation you need, or maybe you wish to become more independent and carve out your own path somewhere else? Are your relationships built on trust, and that kind of support motivates you to achieve any goal? Maybe accountability and responsibility are the pillars of your actions. Or maybe, you find that honesty and transparency are super important for progressing through life.

Whatever questions and thoughts arise, try to self-reflect and write it all down. Grab a piece of paper, a journal, or a notebook, and allow every answer to flow into it. I don't recommend typing on your phone or computer; a good old-fashioned piece of paper and a pen would do perfectly. This is because the writing process is slower on paper, and it allows you to savor every thought. It allows you time to think twice before you write something down – do you really want it or not? While composing your words, you will paint a visual image in your mind and have time to really mull things over. In addition, it is a fantastic exercise to gain clarity and open your path toward discovering yourself even further.

Only some things may be clear from the start, but by gradually working your way inwards, you will understand what shapes you as a person. Take a peek into the hidden nooks within – you just might be amazed at what you will find! Plus, by defining your values, you will gain the confidence you need to become empowered. After all, your beliefs are part of choosing a career path that reflects your principles. Slowly but surely, these principles will give you a purpose that will silence any external factor. Finally, you will see how a sketch of your persona emerges on what previously was a blank page. Trust me, as the days pass and you reflect more and more, that sketch will become more clearly defined.

The next step is to identify your talents, skills, and passions. It is the part called adding color to the sketch. But before you start pondering on that, I want you to throw aside any high expectations. Just forget about what you are supposed to be or what your society prefers. Even if you don't have the answers immediately, give yourself time. And let me assure you, not all talents revolve around being creative! You don't have to be a virtuoso to succeed in life. There is beauty and potential in everything.

That being said, in the next part, I will further help you narrow down your core values, identify your interests and skills, and even uncover some hidden talents just waiting to see the light of day.

Identifying Your Values, Interests, and Skills

Through the part of self-discovery, you find out how to best utilize your interests and skills. However, you have to define them first before you can move any further. In this part, we will put focus on your self-discovery through immersing yourself in practical activities, revealing your interests, values, and skills.

Values

Values are the pillar of every human being. A clear-cut set helps you define who you are, what your core values are, and how they help you shape yourself into a confident young person.

Values can even boost your decision-making skills. So, for the sake of your bright future, try to outline them.

Once you have your general values mapped out, it is time to dive into something more specific. As I already mentioned, what you stand for needs to be aligned with your career. You cannot be one person privately and someone entirely different when it comes to your professional progress. Not only will you be fooling yourself that it is what you want or need, but it will be draining to go against your values. Simply put, your career path should complement your personality rather than go the opposite way.

With the help of these questions, you will gain a clearer idea of what matters and motivates you the most:

- Is being a leader important to you? Or are you entirely okay doing your thing in the background?
- Are you comfortable working and expanding on someone else's ideas, or maybe you wish to cultivate and "grow" your own?
- Is creativity something you excel at and a big part of who you are?
- Are you someone who wants their actions to benefit society?
- Do you perform better when you have clearly defined rules or when you are free to experiment?
- Is gaining more knowledge a priority?
- Does being under pressure motivate you, or does it have a reverse effect?
- Do you wish to advance or thrive in your comfort zone?

For some of the questions, you might need more time to decide what to answer – which is normal! If you find yourself struggling to answer, you can do some of the interests below and then get back to answering these. Sometimes one aspect may fill in the blanks in the other.

Interests

It goes without saying that your interests should also be aligned with your career. But this is also important in the long run – your career choice should be engaging and satisfying. As a teenager, it is easy to indulge in many activities or have periods when you are entirely passive. That being said, it is not really easy to immediately think of everything that interests you. And that is perfectly okay because I have the solution for that too. Here is an interesting exercise you can do that can bring you a step closer to answering your question.

As you can see below, all you need to do is think of a few past and present experiences. Dive in!

<u>Think of experiences from your past:</u>

- List up to ten notable things that brought you some satisfaction, made you feel like you've accomplished something, or pushed you out of your comfort zone – in a challenging yet exciting and enjoyable way.
- Feel free to write one sentence that will explain why you found it satisfactory.
- Read them out loud and begin noticing some patterns.

<u>Think of current interests and activities (out of school):</u>

- Would you rather read or watch a movie? Or both?
- What are the genres that you enjoy the most?
- What was the theme of your most recent enjoyable conversation? Do you talk about that subject often, and how do you feel about it?
- Do you have a role model? If yes, who and why?
- What is your ultimate travel destination?
- What are the topics that often grab your attention – both during conversations and when watching the news?
- What entertains you the most?
- Do you feel like you are more of an outdoor or an indoor person?
- Whenever you had to choose between watching a documentary or playing a video game, which one captured your attention more?
- Have you noticed yourself unconsciously doing something (writing, drawing, or maybe playing guitar)? Is there a thing that so powerfully draws you in, you lost yourself in time and space?

Even though some of the questions may seem unrelated at this point, I promise each has its own purpose. Your favorite movie might not pass your exam or land you a job in the future, but it will open other doors like what your mind is drawn to, which genre, and how it relates to your life, etc. It provides a path towards introspective, creativity, expressing yourself, finding empathy, or maybe even confidence. Whatever you discover, it will benefit you in more ways than one.

Skills

Last but not least, the part most teenagers dread – the skillset. Now, you might be terrified by the fact that you need to show a certain set of skills (even if it is only for yourself), that you freeze. That's okay! It is okay if your mind wanders aimlessly for a little while as you compose yourself. Give it a little bit of time, and then start doing this next exercise!

For this part, we will go over the activities and skills – to draw out potential hidden talents.

<u>Think of what kind of activities you enjoy and the skills that come with them:</u>

- List up to 10 activities you enjoyed. This can be absolutely anything!
- Next to each of those activities, write which technical skills you cultivated. These can be problem-solving, organizing, writing, narrating, debating, leading, helping with a specific aspect, etc.

Did you notice that you easily came up with your list of skills?

Every skill can be an arrow pushing you in the right direction. For example, if you are a good writer, this can serve you in multiple careers like publishing, journalism, teaching, book writing, etc. If you have a knack for solving challenging problems, your future can revolve around management and other areas like social jobs or politics. If you've always been good with numbers and technology, then your future area of expertise may be in the field of math, physics, technology, or something else along those lines! In essence, even a single skill can set the sails toward your ideal goals.

After finishing all three aspects, you will have plenty to think about. As you've never approached your goals from this perspective, you might also be surprised to rediscover your passions and interests. In essence, all of them will help you carve not only your career but also your overall future academic and job satisfaction. Moreover, some of them will reflect your personality traits, which is another factor to consider. All in all, they will help you fully shape yourself.

But how can you connect these traits to your professional life choices? If you can't quite make the connection yet, allow me to elaborate.

Take a look below at how they are important for navigating your way toward what you want and need.

Personality Traits and Their Relevance to Career Choices

While your values, interests, and skills are essential to get an idea of your passions and abilities, your traits will complete the whole picture. Research shows that your future academic and job performance can be directly affected by your unique personality characteristics (Wille et al., 2010, 2012; Bakker et al., 2012). In a way, the better they complement one another, the more productive and happier you will be. For example, we can take the most general categorization of introverts and extroverts. You can easily see how an extrovert would fit in a career that revolves around being social, and an introvert would feel more comfortable doing something independently.

Simply put, by defining your traits, you can pinpoint your strengths and weaknesses, achieving better career satisfaction and maximizing your performance.

Where do you see yourself thriving the most? Naturally, you wouldn't be comfortable plunging into a career that doesn't align with your personality. No worries, I got you covered! If you need to know yourself better and highlight your personality traits, you need to look inward and do some work. For that reason, I suggest doing several tests such as the ones below. You can easily find each of them by doing a quick Google search:

- Myers-Briggs Type Indicator (MBTI) – This questionnaire is based on C.G. Jung's principles and shows the uniqueness of how your personality traits help you in your decision-making.
- The DISC test – This behavioral test dates back one century, and it was established by the psychologist William Moulton Marston. It represents four aspects: Dominance, Influence, Steadiness, and Compliance, which explain your day-to-day behavior and attitude toward others.
- The Hogan personality inventory (HPI) – I love this one as it describes the bright side of your personality. It basically shows your attitude toward others when you are at your best.
- Gallup's Clifton Strengths Assessment – Another amazing tool that will help you identify your emotions, thoughts, and how you behave. It is a fantastic way to discover your talents further.
- Enneagram Personality Test – Finally, we have the Enneagram, which will depict how you see the world and, naturally, how your emotions are shaped based on those horizons.

You can decide to do one, two, or all! If you feel like all would be too much for you, that's okay! Even getting one score can serve your purpose and enrich the journey to self-discovery and awareness.

I hope that you have started working on creating a better version of yourself because this is only the beginning! By working on this chapter's elements, you should have no difficulty doing the following:

- Self-assess your motivation and values and further reflect on them.
- Become inspired by your interests and skills.
- Acknowledge your personality traits and discover your strengths and weaknesses.

I believe that now that you have discovered so many things about yourself – both new and old – you feel excited to see where it can take you! From this point of view, yes, the possibilities are endless! So, without further ado, let's explore your career options in the following chapter.

CHAPTER 2
EXPLORING CAREER OPTIONS

> "At the center of your being, you have the answer; you know who you are, and you know what you want."
>
> — Lao Tzu

As we move on together to the second chapter, there is no bigger truth than this. You hold the power within to answer your most difficult questions. You know yourself best, and if you are honest with yourself, then you will start thriving! In this chapter, we tweak the saying from one of the greatest minds in the world – Lao Tzu, to fit our needs.

When exploring career options, it is natural to start thinking about two very important core questions; "Who am I?" and "What is my life purpose?" Answering these two questions can help you get a step closer to getting the true sense of who you are.

Don't skip this step, as it is an important process to go through. As an individual teen, it can help you better understand yourself and your place in the world. At the moment, there must already be something that appeals to you more than anything else. That is a great starting point for you. As I guide you through some steps you can take, remember that the world is your oyster! The possibilities are endless, so keep an open mind.

Broadening Horizons: Introducing a Wide Range of Career Paths

Broadening horizons or overcoming obstacles? Depends on how you look at it! It is natural for you to enjoy doing various things at your age. You may enjoy drawing, painting, writing, the news, insects, animals, technology, cakes – literally anything! At this stage, your future is bright and filled with adventures, so you first need to grasp that as a concept.

Broadening your horizons does not mean stepping into the uncomfortable but rather stepping out of your comfort zone by simply enhancing your best features. At your age, it is important to broaden your horizons and allow your opinion to change as many times as you need.

If you have been interested in, say, becoming a doctor as a young kid, that does not mean you need to keep following that path by any means necessary. Every once in a while, it is okay to stop and reflect on what you have done until now and how well you have developed.

This is where all your options come in. There is always a wide range of career paths for you to consider. In essence, broadening your horizons means growing and developing. For example, about 5 years have passed since you last said you wanted to be a doctor, and now, both your interests and perspective have shifted. You feel a little uncertain about your decision – many other driving forces pull you apart from medical school rather than push you closer.

During this period, you have developed some new skills and uncovered a few hidden talents that change everything. So then, why not change everything? Your speaking and listening skills have significantly improved, and you have sharpened your wit and are detail oriented. You started loving how society develops and want to be a part of changing it for the better. Law starts sounding like the better option with each passing day.

Here is where I empower you to go after what you want and after what your set of skills allows you to go after. There is no need to abandon your potential for anything just to complete the goal you (or your parents) set for yourself long ago.

The key is using your skills for something you will enjoy doing. Remember that your whole life is in front of you, and with a little bit of your help, it can unravel in the most magical of ways. Using the tips from the first chapter, outline the interests, values, and skills you are best at, and then take it from there!

Self-assessment is important. Ask yourself, "What do I enjoy the most?" – it is how you will identify the potential career paths that align with your personality and interests.

Researching and Gathering Information on Different Industries and Professions

Next stop, you start your research! After you have collected the information about yourself, it is time to start implementing them. One of the most critical aspects of finding your true calling is looking into organizations and companies (even entire industries) and searching for someone with your specifications. Anything from thorough research on the internet to going to some networking events will do. Research allows you to thoroughly understand a potential professional path – requirements, expectations, and further developments.

This is how you identify career options and branches that perfectly fit you.

Also, think of it as an essential part of your journey toward becoming an adult. The time and resources you invest in this end up assisting you in choosing the right career prospect for you. So, set yourself up for a bright and happy future!

There are many ways you can begin pursuing the career that suits you the best. If you have never done research until now, have no fear! I'm equipping you with a complete guide on how to do it and make the best choice for you!

Start by determining what you want – the first step toward creating a bright future for yourself is being honest. Think about establishing your preferences and goals. You can go as specific as you like! Write down everything – from working hours to whether you would relocate for a career (at a certain point in life).

Prioritize the elements you feel the strongest about. Some of them are certainly more mandatory than others. These are your starting points.

Do you have any skills? – continue with listing all the skills you deem essential to your professional life. If the list is smaller than you expect, don't be discouraged! You are young, and time is on your side. Work toward developing some new skills you find interesting. After a while, you will be amazed by how long your skill list will get.

Your potential career options – write down the potential career options you have thought about. Yes, you can add more than one! Allow yourself to browse through the vastness of options – I encourage it! Having a few options will not only give you a sense of stability but it will also help you to open up your mind to something that you haven't even thought about before.

Career requirements – when it comes to expectations, it is a two-way street. Just as you expect something from a certain field or organization, they will expect something back from you. Are you ready to meet the expectations? Sit down and do your online research. Learn as much as possible about the career prospects, including experience and educational requirements. Learn about the most common responsibilities in the workplace.

A fresh point of view – following a certain profession or industry requires taking a peek into the future too. From all the ones you have lined up, which one seems like the best option for the future? As a young adult, you should consider this too. Society progresses, and as it does, it opens up new doors to the future, and at the same time it closes the ones to the past. Make an informed decision on the right option for you – one that will blast you into the world of tomorrow!

Talk to a few experienced people – you can start with the ones closest to you. If you have any relatives, or if your parents are involved in a field that you have taken an interest in, pick their brains a little bit. Remember that your research can be as extensive as you want, but it is a good idea to get some insight directly from the field too. A job can sound complicated on paper but simple in real life, and vice versa.

Do you have the option to visit their workspace? Jump with both feet to such an occasion!

Start outlining your professional life – it is all about managing your expectations while getting what you want! Outlining your professional path can help you create a solid strategy that will last you for years to come. It can give you the freedom to revise it whenever it is needed, possibly every one, two, or maybe even five years – it is all up to you. Project your needs onto the paper and see what it comes up with!

While I am on the subject, there is another thing you can do.

Emerging Careers and Future Job Trends

I only touched upon the subject above, but I believe it piqued your interest. So far, we have determined that you might have one or several careers lined up – depending on your skills and requirements. As choosing a career is one of the most important aspects of life, young people are more and more keen on taking their time before deciding what they want (instead of jumping the gun and regretting it later on).

Yet again, we return to the question, "What do you enjoy doing?" to help you get to the desired destination. The wide range of options spans from one side to the other and keeping the future in mind is a good idea. As with every other teenager, you probably want to do a good job and enjoy doing it for a long time.

This leads me to the next section – start exploring some future job trends.

At this moment, you have little to no experience and limited knowledge of what makes the world go round. All that can change in an instant. Right now, everyone (not only young people) is in an uncertain environment where things can change just like that. Navigating through the challenge of searching for the perfect professional path in a constantly evolving society is a challenge – but not an impossible one!

There is always one good place to start, and that is beyond the voice of reason! I'm not saying that you should look for something completely unreasonable, but rather expand your horizons just a little beyond the reasonable choices you have made until now.

A factor of certainty is what you should include while doing this. Add that to your skillset, and you might end up uncovering a whole new world of emerging careers.

Just to get you started, here are a few of the most promising innovative job prospects of tomorrow.

Software developers/computer managers – the tech era as we know it is in full swing, and just at the right time! Gen Z is all about technology, paving the way for new emerging careers that will shape the world of tomorrow. For this particular one, you will become a valuable asset on the market. From writing codes to analyzing and maintaining platforms, there is nothing that you can't do with this job!

To give you an estimate, currently, the job market is open for people who have a bachelor's degree, and +5 years of experience.

Coursera has listed this as one of the most promising future jobs.

Web developer – another programming heaven for all you computer lovers! Nowadays, any brand or company needs to have its own website – and as a web developer, you can make that come true. Front-end, back-end, webmaster, and full-stack developer – these are the four main options to choose from. If programming languages are your biggest interest, then this might be the perfect option for you.

To give you an estimate, at the moment, the job market is only looking for people who have a degree, no experience is needed.

It requires a simple skillset, and since first created in the 1980s, the nature of this field has changed a few times. First, with the creation and vast use of the Internet, and then with the usage of mobile phones.

Financial manager – if numbers seem like the better choice, then achieving financial stability for a company must be a part of your dream, right? Profits and expenditures, strategizing about all the bigger decisions, and utilizing your planning and organizing skills to the fullest are what a financial manager is all about.

Are you looking into this? Companies are hiring – you need a bachelor's degree and +5 years of experience.

It is estimated that this particular job will achieve growth of about 17% in the next five years.

Medical assistant – providing support in hospitals is the dream of many young people. Do you consider yourself to be one of them? If a part of your skillset includes communicating with clients, if you have always been keen on pharmacy, and if you love helping doctors, then becoming a medical assistant is the perfect choice for you.

To become a medical assistant, you need professional training and a high school diploma. This is always a growing branch, with an estimated job growth of 18% in the next few years.

Teacher – since almost every aspect of today is moved online, why not this too? The future of teaching is online. Have you noticed you have the potential to lead a class rather than be a part of it? Spreading knowledge can be a wonderful thing and preparing the new generations to come for the world sounds like an excellent idea. So, why not add the online teacher option to your list too? Consider this a great way to utilize your abilities and grow your own business from scratch. There is a wide market for anything you are looking to offer. As it is increasing with every passing minute, you could share your knowledge with people from all over the world!

Did you know that there are more than 51 million YouTube Channels, and an average visitor spends about 40 minutes a day on this platform? That has to give you some boost to try creating something useful and uploading it there!

Personal trainer – more and more people are becoming aware of their body image, mostly due to social media. As a teenager, you must have witnessed that in your surroundings too. What you are probably not familiar with is because of the fast-paced life of today, not many people can keep up with their physical activities. This is where you come in. If your people skills are honed to perfection, if you love being active, and nurture a fondness toward the human body, have you thought about being a personal trainer?

A few things you should know here – you need certification, but not a degree, to become a personal trainer. You can choose to work inside or outside the gym. You need to nurture effective communication and an encouraging attitude. As a relatively new field, you can get as creative as you want. And finally, personal trainers are not dietitians or nutritionists.

These are some of the highest trending jobs that you can consider working toward. However unconventional it may sound, one of these might be the perfect fit for you.

When it comes to discovering more options for your future, I recommend first exploring your high school resources and what programs they offer. Plus, you can reach out to a school counselor and gather opinions.

No matter where you are in the world, I would recommend searching through various career groups on social networks, like Facebook, and connecting with other young individuals – both locally and globally. Or you don't even have to connect, just gather information and analyze the latest career trends. Not only do they share many tips and websites that can be of great help, but some may inspire you to discover your own path.

When it comes to leading global websites that can help you shape your journey and be inspired career-wise, LinkedIn should be on top of your list. Other useful sites are Indeed (one of the most popular job search engines worldwide and it is easily accessible to 53 countries), Monster (with a comprehensive database of career advice and tips), and CareerBuilder, etc.

In addition, career magazines like Harvard Business Review (HBR), Forbes, and Entrepreneur can prove to be valuable assets in your quest.

Simply Google any of these, and you will easily find them.

Considering Non-Traditional and Unconventional Career Paths

Speaking of unconventional, I can notice the slight crest around your smile once this word is mentioned. So, if you are leaning more toward the creative side, there is a solution for you too! The job market is constantly changing, and the demand for certain skills changes too.

With a non-traditional career path, you might not get the linear progression you hope for, but you are in for a treat either way. As a young mind, it may even be the more logical way to shape your brain and delve deep into the professional world by choosing an unconventional path. Many industries allow for this due to the diverse skills that you can get from it.

Here are a few reasons why you should consider this:

- The right approach can help you land unique and adventurous job opportunities.
- Exploring many options can help you create a career that fits your lifestyle like a glove.
- You get to enjoy the freedom and flexibility that many people can't.
- The satisfaction of building something from 0 is immense.
- Presenting some new options results in passions that may be worth taking a second look at.

Again, I remind you of the question, "What do I want to do?" Think about what may benefit your future that still aligns with your goals and interests. Write down your passions and think about how to incorporate them into creating a new career path for yourself.

But how do you start looking for the right opportunities? Since people overall are on the rise looking for alternative ways of making money, why not join the club? As a teenager with a fresh perspective, you have plenty to offer. Here are a few ways how you can use your skills and start building your career:

- Think about having a "side hustle." This is for those who want to take on some freelance tasks. It is a great way to start learning the tips and tricks of successful freelancers. Also, it is a great way to see how your skills have progressed and how proficient you are at finishing certain tasks.
- Look into start-up businesses. They are the perfect way to start your business venture with a little help. Create a solid business plan that is unique and shows a fresh perspective, and then start researching ways to complete it!
- Online ventures are on the list too. So far, digital ventures are considered a phenomenon in the global economy. If you have an idea you need to bring into existence, then take a leap of faith! It just might be worth it.

Remember, exploring career options does not have to be a hassle or a task. Make it as enjoyable as you can. I hope that you will consider these notes and start working toward your goal. Consider this a rewarding experience, where every step is equally important. Open yourself up to a whole new world of possibilities – but not before you've reached the end of this book!

That said, in the next chapter, we will go into detail on how to develop essential skills.

CHAPTER 3
DEVELOPING ESSENTIAL SKILLS

> "Tell me, and I forget, teach me and I may remember, involve me and I learn."
>
> — *Benjamin Franklin*

Welcome to the chapter where I help you develop some essential skills needed to succeed in the workplace. Now, these essential skills are not necessarily all the ones that you have already written down. For example, marketing, management, technical, or computer skills are all good, but you can't really use them if you don't have (or work on) your soft skills.

The difference is that, unlike hard skills, you display soft skills in each situation where you converse with another person.

These are different from the ones you can learn in school. Most of them are typically learned through life experiences and the people you see as role models. Interestingly, as you grow, before you plunge yourself into the job market, you never notice that you are learning them as you go.

The subconscious part of the entire learning process is quite interesting. You do that by mimicking the behavior of a person you admire, by rationally trying to judge a situation based on facts instead of emotions, and of course, my favorite – learning from your mistakes.

All of this means that you are growing. So, when the time comes to determine which skills you excel at and which ones need honing, this is where you become fully aware of yourself as an individual. There is a highlighted importance to these skills that can make you stand out from a crowd (if utilized properly).

Now, I am encouraging you to look upon your past experiences, every situation that has taught you something. If this confuses you, allow me to help you. Let's take a look at how to identify your soft skills.

Identifying and Enhancing Your Transferable Skills

First things first – what are transferable skills? These are the soft skills you can transfer from one job position to another. Most of them are not technical by nature, and they all help you get the job done.

They are also known as soft skills – a group of important abilities that enhance your competence in the professional field. Every employer is interested in them. Even if you want to make it out on your own, you still need them to make yourself more available, presentable, and more successful at what you want to do.

Now, determining your transferable skills requires some introspection. Answer yourself this – is there anything you are naturally better at than the people around you? As you grow, have you noticed that you are better at certain things? Each time you have worked in a group, was there a task that was consistently (and I mean always) done by none other than you?

That is your strong side.

All you need to do is start building upon that. Grab a pen and paper and start writing down every skill that you have noticed about yourself. It can be anything from a good trait (such as good communication with others) to your high levels of empathy and resilience!

Identifying these non-academic skills can help you figure out how well you can adapt to various conditions – in your professional and personal life too. Consider them the tools you need to thrive in a cultural, social, and professional setting.

At some point, while writing these down, you may start wondering what good these skills will do for you. Are these skills really that important that you should focus on them so much? Or should you just look the other way and ignore them? I'm here to nudge you in the right direction and to tell you to stick this one out! There are many reasons why this is important. Any professional setting values them because:

- By having them, you enjoy support and success in any workplace.
- You can stand out with them in an interview with an employer.
- Add them to your CV to make it worth taking a second look at.
- Whenever you apply for a promotion, having soft skills is perfect for accentuating (how it helped you navigate your position and relationships with others).
- Even if you want to make it on your own, they are much needed, especially since, all jobs include some form of communication with clients.

The best thing about transferable skills is that they are called that because you can use them at any job! That makes it essential for you to recognize and accentuate them even more!

You have probably managed to create a list of skills by now. Now, let's further break down this exercise into two bits.

The first step is to write down the competence level (it can be a number from 1-10 or 1-5, whatever suits you best) next to each of them. It is important to be realistic about yourself so you can get the best results out of this exercise. Some competencies might get a 10; some might get a six or even a two – and that's okay! Look at the numbers and note the ones with a lower number. That gives you an idea of what you need to focus on. Whether it is a time management skill, or the power to work well in a team, if it needs your attention, do everything it takes to improve it.

There are many ways to enhance transferable skills – some of those ways include:

- Taking one or even a few online courses or maybe watching YouTube channels that provide such presentations.
- Volunteering someplace that will get you a step closer to working with people in order to develop your 'people skills.'
- Put yourself in a teaching position and share your knowledge and wisdom with others.

These are just a few to begin with, but the truth is, once you start looking, you will see that there is a whole world of options that provide you with a way to hone your soft skills.

The next step is to take a good look at your list and find out what is missing. Yes, this is something you might not have thought of until this moment. But there are so many soft skills that you are bound to forget about a few of them. Does your list need to include some literacy skills? Maybe organizational skills? Or some stress management skills? Yes, there is a lot where that came from too!

Do your research and add all the ones you find on the Internet. They can help you widen your horizons and paint a new picture of what you can perfect and achieve within this section.

On that note, I have separated some of the most important ones for you – how to build and make the most out of them so they can help you thrive in a professional environment! Take a look!

Communication, Teamwork, Problem-Solving, and Critical Thinking Skills

According to the World Economic Forum report on the future of jobs, these are some of the most wanted transferable skills! Increase your value by working on enriching them with every passing moment. Here is a straightforward way on how you can do that for each one.

Communication

How you provide information to the people you work with and the clients you work for is a vital aspect of any job. Considering how they wish to receive the information you provide is one of the ways you can be proficient at this soft skill in particular. As a teenager, do you think you have what it takes to master the art of communication?

Sharing and giving information – communicating – is a vital part of life not just in a professional setting either. It is everywhere around us, and it comes in many forms. You have already encountered them – a verbal, a non-verbal, a written, or even a visual form.

The most important bit here is knowing how to give and receive clear and concise information.

As a teenager who has grown up amid the Internet and technology boom, you may know much more about communication than you think. Adults a few decades back used the telephone as a means of communication. Then along came emails, texting, and social media. Nowadays, communication is made easier in theory, but not everyone can do it.

What happened?

Ease of access meant losing the proper dialogue needed to establish a relationship with whoever was on the "other end of the line." In effect, newer generations (including you) lost the ability to communicate effectively. Communication's most essential aspects include patience, listening, understanding, and controlling your thoughts and emotions in order to get the best outcome for your situation. Because of today's culture, like many young people, you may have been neglecting this skill most of your life, it is only natural not to know how to properly establish a relationship in any setting, not just a professional one.

Thankfully, that can be fixed!

It all starts with the simplest thing – eye contact. Whenever you have the opportunity to talk to someone, there are many things you can do to make yourself more presentable and to successfully open up the lines of communication. Here are some other ways you can practice in order to improve your communication skills:

- Start paying attention when someone is talking to you. Make a scheme in your mind and pinpoint the essential things so you can reciprocate.
- Work on using clear language. You don't have to make your sentences long and complex – sometimes, the simplest answer is the most effective.
- Use body language to your advantage. Sometimes non-verbal communication says more than words do. Practice standing up straight, using a calm tone of voice, appropriate gestures, and gentle facial expressions.
- Ask for feedback whenever you can. This is an exercise best done within a circle of people you are comfortable with. Ask your parents, relatives, or teacher if they find your communication skills to be improving.
- Speak up when something is not clear. Start from the smallest thing – when you see that something is not very clear to you, asking questions about it is a great way to clear the air of any assumptions.
- Work on your confidence. Last but not least, consider your level of confidence as a driving force that pushes you forward into the professional world. Invest a small portion of your day to work on it, and soon, you will see some incredible changes.

Communication is great, but once you've mastered communicating with a single person, can you manage to do the same with more people at the same time?

Teamwork

The meaning of Teamwork is communication and navigating several relationships at the same time. It improves equality and the ability to recognize the strengths and weaknesses of each person in the group. An additional benefit is that it provides excellent opportunities to work with various types of people.

Do you consider yourself to be a team player? Do you know that being a good team player is one of the key aspects of success? Taking pride in being able to adapt to change is a good thing, so make sure to accentuate it whenever possible.

But what happens to those that don't have the high level of skills for this?

As a teenager, you might find yourself in a difficult position if you are unable to be a team player. Some of us are followers, others are leaders, but everyone can fit the model of being a team player. If you have written this down on your paper and put a low grade next to it, then it is time to take some action!

Here are some tips to get you started!

Generally, it is a bit difficult to teach a person how to become a team player from scratch, but thankfully, there are a few exercises that can help you hone this skill to perfection. Other than communication being a pillar of a good team, here are a few other things to consider exploring:

- ◇ Define the relationship by making clear everyone's role in the group. Any group at the beginning may seem like total chaos, but that is only until responsibilities are divided up. Once that happens, everyone understands their duties and tasks, avoiding confusion and repetition, and thus creating a seamless experience.

- ◇ Focus on collaborating too. If you don't know how to become an equal participant in a group, then have a discussion. Talking about it can clear the air and give you the floor whenever you want to share an idea or a thought. Also, this way, the entire group promotes compromise and encourages everyone to contribute with their valuable and unique perspectives.

- ◇ There is no group without trust. Practicing trust starts from something small and develops over time into the biggest support the group will have. If you haven't worked in a team until now, you might not have experienced this, but after working in one for a while, you will start to feel a certain level of integrity that the group exhibits. It becomes a supportive and reliable space where everyone is equal in terms of sharing concerns and ideas.

- ◇ The team shares the strike or the win together! It doesn't matter if it is a win or a loss; a team always sticks together. When the collective objectives are met because you know that you have worked hard enough as a team to reach the goal, then you also have the grounds for the celebration together as well.

- ◇ Learn as much as you can. At the end of the day, the team is comprised of many different people. All of them, along with their unique points of view, traits, and responsibilities, can give you a free platform to learn! It is the perfect opportunity for personal and professional growth, so whenever you have the chance, jump at the idea of being a part of a team!

As you can see, being in a team is a continuous process and you can't learn much after only one day. However, spending some time being a part of one may end up with you acquiring many fruitful results.

Every team has its ups and downs. What happens when you reach a low point and need to resolve a certain issue?

Problem-Solving

There is so much happening in the world right now that it is impossible to avoid stress. Unpleasant situations can stand there, waiting around every corner. As a teenager, you might have encountered a lot of them, or you may have only experienced a small amount. Either way, you must learn they are an inevitable part of our day-to-day life.

In the professional setting, a failure or a mistake can bring on a large amount of stress. I have seen this happen many times on various occasions. Sometimes, the situation escalated to become even bigger than it was, and in other cases, it was resolved almost immediately. Do you know what contributes to this outcome?

Having problem-solving skills. The ability to analyze a certain situation (and de-escalate it if needed) is a much-needed skill in every professional environment. Any teenager would be lucky to master this skill, as it is imperative for success in an individual and group setting as well. Developing and presenting problem-solving skills can help you to thrive.

For those that feel stuck...

If your problem-solving skills are not up to par, remember you can always do something about it. Nowadays, plenty of exercises and tips will get you started working on it. Here, practicality is key, so try to push yourself whenever you are in a tricky situation. The following are some practical tips for you below:

- Try to calm your mind down. If you are a person that doesn't work well under stress, do some stress relieving exercises. It can be anything from slowly breathing in and out for a few seconds, counting back from 20, or anything else that works for you. The purpose is to create a calm and collected environment within.
- Collect all the facts. If you don't know where to begin, simply follow the trail of information. Whenever you are faced with an issue, start by gathering information about it. What happened, how many people are involved, what's at stake? Look at it as if you were solving a puzzle – you need to tie all the pieces together. Once you do that, the solution usually stares you right in the face.
- Always look for a pattern. If you are wise enough, you will start looking for patterns at an early age. The mind of the average teenager might not go that far, but I am here to help you overcome that challenge. Each time you evaluate a tricky situation, try to look for a pattern of behavior. Start with yourself and expand your circle as you go, including your peers along the way. Try to find a connection to why something is happening (especially if it occurs repeatedly).
- Think outside the box. Yes, you have heard this many times before, but for a good reason. Coming up with alternative and creative solutions for challenges and issues can help you develop in unimaginable ways. Don't try to limit yourself to conventional approaches. Take up the exercise of creating a fictitious problem. Then, think of at least three ways to solve it. It is called training your mind.
- After you have come up with a valuable solution – enforce it! The sooner you take action to mend an issue – the better the results will be. This is slightly connected to the previous point. Sometimes, the first solution will backfire. And that's okay. It is why you have a few tricks up your sleeve – use them wisely!
- Don't give up. The most important thing to remember is not to give up on this. Take this as a personal note rather than a tip. Building up soft skills such as this takes time, so practice persistence. Learn how to make yourself think better with every challenge you face until your skill becomes next to perfection.

As we move on from the subject of problem-solving skills, I couldn't help but look forward to the last bit. Completing the circle with the last skill – critical thinking.

Critical Thinking

Instilling all of these key skills that scream leadership position means focusing deeply on each of them. The final one includes the art of critical thinking. Have you always found yourself to be a fairly reasonable person that is open-minded, a little bit skeptical, but always with respect toward precision and different points of view? Then, you are a valuable critical thinker.

These individuals tend to analyze any situation, observe, and evaluate it based on their information. The language of Michael Scriven and Richard Paul (2003) defines critical thinking as:

"Critical thinking is the intellectually disciplined process of actively and skillfully

conceptualizing, applying, analyzing, synthesizing, and/or evaluating information gathered from, or generated by observation, experience, reflection, reasoning, or communication, as a guide to belief and action."

What happens if you feel like you don't have it?

There is a certain discipline to learning everything – apply that in this situation as well. As a teenager, learn how to use critical thinking to your advantage. It is the last piece of the puzzle from this section that can shape you into a phenomenal professional.

Enhancing your critical thinking skills can be done with the assistance of the following tips:

- Evaluation should be the first thing on your mind. Evaluate everything from your sources, to how you filter the information into a relevant and irrelevant pile, and also, whether you challenge any assumptions or leave them hanging in the air. This is the first aspect of critical thinking. Developing a heightened sense of reasoning is key.

- Listen to the arguments and sources. As a critical thinker, you need to consider all the arguments you encounter during challenging situations, as well as the sources of those arguments. Again, an excellent exercise is to come up with a fictional issue. Develop the issue like it is a scene from a crime book. Come up with a few peers with various backgrounds and expertise and then think about their claims. Go step by step and explain your thought process to yourself. Consider multiple perspectives, however "out there" they may be. Creating such a scenario can help you develop a certain "voice of reason," where you only conclude based on facts.

- Ask the right questions. Have you ever noticed how the most difficult question to answer is… "Why?" Do you know that is the only way to fully explore an issue? You stimulate your practice-thinking abilities this way and you may be surprised by all the answers you get.

- Always, and I mean always, broaden your horizons. This is not something you can only apply in this case but in every other aspect of life too. Reading books, articles, and research papers can help you broaden your knowledge on any subject and help you feel like you are doing something to improve your critical thinking skills.

While I am on the subject of books, read as much as you can! For example, finishing this one will give you plenty of insight into what you want to do, be, and achieve in life. So, keep going!

Developing Digital Literacy and Technological Proficiency

After we have taken a good look at the most important skills together, it is time to go through another section that includes transferable skills from the 21st century. So far, I have delved into the subject of skills that have been around for a long period of time. But at this point, after you have mastered the ones above, it is time to look toward the future.

Being proficient in technology is a must for anyone these days. Whether you are a teenager, an adult, or even a senior, you are bound to adapt to the lifestyle of the world we live in now. It involves plenty of technology everywhere you turn. So, how does this apply to a professional environment?

Imagine having your own company and looking to employ a handful of people. The company can be in any sector, starting from IT and finishing up in the fashion field. As you go through the interview process, you come across an applicant with no digital literacy (almost impossible in this day and age but humor me for the sake of argument). Would you consider employing them if you knew how much time it would take to educate them on the subject of technological proficiency? Yes, it does seem like an unnecessary challenge, right?

Being skilled in digital literacy means knowing how to look for and filter relevant information precisely, quickly, and safely. This is more than just knowing how to use a computer. It is the act of browsing safely and being professional while doing it. It is a skill that will help you become a lifelong learner.

If you put your mind to it a little bit, you will realize that digital technologies are ever-changing. Nothing is constant. Even though this results in an array of flexible ways that help you to learn and work, you need to know how to keep up with the latest trends.

Being digitally literate can help you integrate into any field you want. Do you want to know what it takes to make that happen? Be mindful of the following tips:

- ◈ You should start from scratch. Yes, as a young person raised in the digital era, I know this sounds kind of weird, but hear me out. You need to familiarize yourself with the simplest of tasks, such as file management, knowing your way around all operating systems, creating spreadsheets, and knowing how to present the information. Many features might have slipped through your fingers, so take a few steps back and explore.

- ◈ Learn how to stay safe on the Internet. As beautiful a place as it can be, it is also the place of predators, information thieves, and more. Knowing how to be cautious when sharing information on the web is a part of being proficient in digital language.

- ◈ Even if you are not into coding, programming, or software development, you still need to stay on track with the latest developments in the field. That way, you can present another way of staying on top of a situation. Participating in a few courses or online forums can help you continuously build your knowledge.

- ◈ Experiment for creative freedom. Let's face it, eventually, with any work you do, you will want a little bit of freedom for your creative side to shine through. Pick the digital world as the most useful tool to make that happen. Challenge yourself – resolve issues using technology, learn through the trial-and-error process, and make the most out of it.

- ◈ Talk to people. However out of the blue this might seem, talking to peers that are as equally involved in the digital world as you may open up some fresh possibilities for you. Exchange ideas and discuss projects – it is how you can grow and deepen your knowledge.

Digital literacy will always evolve and grow. Being a teenager, it should not be difficult to adopt a growth mindset and be open to all the opportunities technology can provide you with!

Cultivating Emotional Intelligence and Adaptability

Well, well, well – we have slowly reached the topic that most teenagers avoid – emotional intelligence. But, instead of boring you with details, I am here to tell you that you can express your emotional intelligence in a healthy manner that can also help you evolve in the working arena.

Do you know what emotional intelligence means? *It is the ability to define and take control of your emotions and recognize the feelings of those around you.*

On the other hand, *adaptability is the capacity to adjust to ever-changing conditions.*

Do you know how you can develop both of these transferable skills?

The simplest answer is to create a higher level of self-awareness. The emotions you deal with as a teenager may be overwhelming at times – it is a normal process, as you are still learning how to put them under control. By being a little gentler toward yourself, you can notice which things trigger you and how you react to them, thus getting to the core of you.

Another thing – the people around you (especially in a professional setting) count on you to think on your feet and with a cool head. But that doesn't mean you should quickly dismiss all your feelings and act like a robot. Find the balance where you can validate the feelings of others and show empathy but still act professionally.

Practice active listening skills but learn how to create a barrier where it does not personally affect you or change your opinion in any way. All of this can be a handful in the beginning, so I suggest you take things slow and one at a time.

Showing a healthy and appropriate approach will only result in maturity and success. Calmly dealing with any changes that may come your way is the best way to take full control of a situation and come out on the other side like a true winner!

Did all of this seem like too much for you to handle? After all, you are still very young, and you have yet to expand your knowledge and skills, but with clear guidance, you will tackle this seemingly complex subject. That leads us to the next chapter – finding the perfect guidance!

CHAPTER 4
SEEKING GUIDANCE

> "Wisdom is the best guide and faith is the best companion."
>
> — *Dalai Lama*

But what happens in those times when you feel like you have lost any sense of direction? However hard you try, and however clear your goal may be, sometimes you might get the feeling of being stuck. You feel like all the research and theory that you have done is simply not good enough.

This is the time to start experiencing the practice bit, not only the theory bit. After all, by plunging yourself into the professional world you step into the unknown without a safety net. Deciding what you want to be when you grow up is a tough question.

Instead of putting yourself under a lot of pressure by trying to accomplish everything on your own, why not try to seek out some guidance? Take the pressure off and create a safe space for you to thrive. I am giving you some insight on how to pave the road to success with the help of others.

The Role of Mentors and Role Models

Many studies have shown the importance of mentoring. All humans learn as much as possible by watching, then mimicking someone else's behavior. It has always been the easiest way to learn. Being a teenager, it is especially important to surround yourself with people you look up to, people who can positively influence your existence, and help you develop an understanding of the professional world.

Think about what kind of learning experience you want to gain. Also, try to answer this question – who do you look up to the most? Why? The role models and mentors should be people who are active participants in the community. They should be able to thrive in a professional and/or a personal setting, and they should also be able to offer you a plateau of educational and career aspirations.

There is a slight difference between a mentor and a role model. Here is a brief explanation of both.

Mentor – a mentor is a person who has plenty of experience in a specific professional field and possesses the skillset that you lack. As a teenager and a less experienced individual, they support your transitioning process from the safe environment of a classroom to the rollercoaster of the real world.

More often, they provide you with examples of how to think and act in the most common situations. I encourage every teenager to have a mentor – it can be anyone – a teacher from school, someone you admire, someone from your workplace. Ask them if they would assist you and take it from there!

Role model – the role model is not necessarily someone who can show you how to properly act, but rather show you the importance of differentiating between bad and good. A role model often presents positive and negative examples to help you understand both and to choose the right one.

Also, role models can be people you choose unconsciously. This starts from your early childhood, as you are drawn into the behavior of the people you see most often – your parents, relatives, teachers, etc. Who is your role model? Have you noticed something about them you liked so much, you started implementing it yourself?

Both are considered equally important since they can boost both morale and motivation. Their role in shaping your future includes the following:

- ⋄ You get inspired. Whether it is a mentor or a role model, they are oftentimes more experienced than you are. Note their stories, their challenges, and the obstacles they had to overcome. Allow them to teach you how to navigate through your work with the help of the knowledge you have accumulated over the years.
- ⋄ Take the advice. Despite how much stubbornness there may be within you, give them some space to help you. A career decision is a challenging process, so once you decide to seek assistance, let them help prepare you for a particular profession.
- ⋄ Deepen your skillset. Having the proper set of skills is the jumping point that will help you stand out from the crowd tomorrow. Most of these skills include the transferable skills I talked about in the previous chapter. Mentors are especially important here, as they give you a better insight into skills such as communication, navigating through a professional environment, the power of a successful presentation, etc.
- ⋄ Write down all the contacts. Both the mentor and the role model can be of invaluable worth when it comes to getting you in touch with the right people. They can help you create a beneficial network and make you more visible to the most important people and companies in the industry.

This is only the beginning – getting a taste of what you want sounds like a dream. But there is still a lot to cover, so let's move on to the next guidance step.

Utilizing Resources Like Career Counseling and Guidance Services

You are a part of the generation that will be the driving force that moves the world forward. Having this in mind, utilizing all the available resources to be the positive change in the world takes bringing out "the big shot" resources like career counseling.

It is a beneficial step that will lead you in the right direction and to the desired career path. Getting in touch with a career counselor is the push you need. As an individual, you are in a transitioning period, because as soon as your teenage years are over, you will become a valuable asset in the job marketplace.

Career counseling and guidance are the steps you can take to identify career opportunities that you are otherwise unable to uncover by yourself. The first step to take is to talk to a teacher, your school counselor, or a career advisor and start gathering information.

All of them may provide you with various tidbits of information, so once you set up an appointment with them, get the most out of your one-on-one with them. In the previous chapter, you created a list of the strengths (your skills) and rated them. Take that list with you and discuss it with them. You won't believe how valuable their input will be.

If you want to get the proper guidance, then you also need to share all your accomplishments up until that point with them. Gather your information about your education, your grades, your hobbies, your interests, and every extra-curricular activity you have undertaken such as internships, etc. All this information can provide an insight into who you are, and can be extremely valuable to any counselor who is trying to help you.

They will give you a lot of tips and steps you can take. They will teach you how to explore job descriptions, and they will help you learn how to research multiple occupations. In the meantime, after reviewing every bit of the information you have provided them with, they will let you know if you need to obtain any additional qualifications for the field you have in mind. On top of all that, a career counselor will also guide you through any of the alternatives as well.

Last but not least, they will provide you with some online platforms to help you with your career exploration. They will help you to evaluate the potential for growth, and to teach you how to search for the best opportunities within the salary range.

Networking and Informational Interviews

Have you heard of the term networking? If your core goal includes finding the perfect job field for you, then you probably have. But not all teenagers know what it means. Networking represents getting in touch with any of the connections you have obtained during your time researching the job market. The target of networking is to build a relationship with companies and individuals who can, in the present or the future, give you plenty of advice, information, or a professional opportunity.

An informal interview is a vessel through which you deepen your relationships with the contacts from your network. Consider them as an opportunity to expand and get some useful info from a simple conversation.

Before you begin, you need to know how important this step is. As a teenager, from the informal interview, you will gain:

- Information about how you actually do a specific job. You will get the real picture of what it is like to occupy a certain position, rather than learning from your idea about it.
- Insight about how it is to work in a real environment, with real issues, and real rewards. Sometimes, the stress can be almost overwhelming, at other times, you may enjoy every second of your time spent there.
- Knowledge about how to get to where you want to be. With a few strategic steps, you can get into the field of your choosing.

Now, you have opened the doors of communication and you have set up an interview. You have done everything – from gathering information about the person you are meeting to collecting all the information about yourself. These are all proper steps but, once the interview begins, what are you going to ask whoever is on the other side?

Allow me to be of service. Below you will find a set of questions that you can consider as a starting point. Go over them, think about which answers you want to get, and how you can deepen the conversation on each question. Consider these questions as a way to take control of the interview and to get all the information you need. Here they are:

- Ask the other party to describe a day in their life. What types of situations do they encounter, and how do they deal with them?
- What are their interests? Is there something they like a lot, and something they strongly dislike? It can be anything from getting up early in the morning, to a special routine.
- The steps they took to get to where they are right now. Opportunities, formal education, expanding their skillset – everything it took!
- How many mistakes did they make along the way? Did that greatly impact their current position? Would they change something from their past?
- Why choose the field they are in at the moment? Are they planning on sticking with it for a long time, and what surprises came with the job?
- Ask them to give a piece of advice to a youngster like yourself.
- Can they recommend someone else for you to talk to? It is a great way to further expand your network.

Networking and getting information from informal interviews are great ways to get ahead on your quest for a successful professional life. Here is another extra step you can take to make that happen.

Engaging With Online Communities and Professional Organizations

There is another way to gain all the relevant data about job prospects – seeking guidance from professional organizations and online communities. Over the past few decades, these two options have become pillars of the thriving community we live in today. There are many, many options out there, all you need to do is begin your research.

- Identify the communities that can help you. It is important to locate the ones you share the same interests and goals with – it is how you will get the most out of the experience.

- Being online is easier – you are only a few clicks away from finding a community that aligns with your career goals. Once you find it, become an active member of it. Ask questions and take part in discussions. Soon you will realize you have expanded your network beyond your wildest imagination.

- Engage as much as you can. Virtual events, webinars, volunteering, taking up an internship, and sharing your journey with others – establish yourself as a knowledgeable member of the community and open up a path for further engagements and networking opportunities.

Sometimes, when you are too close to a certain situation, you might get caught up in it and set some unrealistic expectations. Guidance from a third party is the best way to tackle the situation. It is your responsibility to set up a support and guidance system for yourself. That way, you can help yourself move further along the path of creating a bright professional future for yourself.

With this, you get some help for the next step, which is planning for education and training. Let's go through the subject together.

CHAPTER 5

PLANNING FOR EDUCATION AND TRAINING

> "Education is the passport for the future, for tomorrow belongs to those who prepare for it today."
>
> — Malcolm X

Planning for your future sounds like one of the most exciting things to do. Considering this will be one of your biggest life changes, it is only fair to do it your way. At least mostly, right? However, that still doesn't change the fact that you are a teenager and might not know what you want or how to get it. But don't let this discourage you.

There will be moments when you feel doubtful about your choices. Then it is best to simply take a deep breath and try to remind yourself that you don't need to rush. Put one foot in front of the other at a pace that suits you – after all, these are major life choices, and it is best to be handled with great care and research on your part.

Concentrating on educational and vocational plans may help you identify yourself better and help you reach financial stability. When you focus on all your lists, wishes and plans, and get support from the people around you, you know you are headed in the right direction.

As a starting point, review your options. Do they require special education or simpler training? This act of evaluating the steps needed to get to a certain position is called career planning. As a teenager, you think you have all the time in the world. Be careful here, you should avoid shifting to a slower gear and letting go of your professional dreams.

Instead, it is time to delve deeper into your options. Let's go!

Exploring Post-Secondary Education Options

It is vital to understand that whichever option you choose, you should probably not do it at the last minute. Yes, choosing a career path is a challenge in and of itself, but that does not mean you need to procrastinate until the last minute. Remember, you are getting into a pretty competitive world out there, so start your engine now!

Make sure to have collected all the necessary documents and submit them before the deadline. Check the admission periods for all the schools you are interested in and underline them as important dates!

This is the importance of sticking to a plan. Do you know the answer to the question "What do I want to do after school?" – If not, then make a note of it to answer it before your final year of school begins. During that summer, you can give yourself time to think and research all the options – are you going to college, do you want to undergo vocational training, join the military, or get a job?

It helps to talk with a person that you consider close. This can be your friend, maybe a family member, or even a professional. During this period, it is important to keep focusing on improving your skills, both technical and soft.

Once you become ready to start preparing yourself for the next chapter of your life, it is time to dive deep and take some action! Once school's out, you can start doing plenty of things to prepare yourself for the next chapter. Here are a handful of things that should absolutely be a part of your list:

- Start visiting trade schools and colleges. Consider it the most important step you need to take, and that is why you are doing it earlier than expected. Planning your future means deep research, so why not start visiting universities beforehand? Explore the different campuses and see what types of degree programs they offer. It will become an invaluable experience. You can differentiate between what they offer in theory and how they achieve it in practice.
- Start job-shadowing someone. It kind of sounds like a mentor, but it's a whole other thing. Once you have decided on a particular branch you'd like to get involved in, it is important to shatter the glass ideal of what the job is supposed to look like. Rather than creating your idea of what the responsibilities and workflow will look like, take a more "hands-on" approach. Shadowing a person who works in the field of your interest is a great way to get the feel of it without actually working.
- Start volunteering. Extra-curricular activities are just as important as academic achievements when applying to a university (or anywhere else). Also, getting some valuable experience can only enhance you as an applicant and person ready to dive into the professional world. Inquire about some volunteering spots in your town. There is a high chance you'll find one that fits right with your interests and skill set. Help others and help yourself through the process as well.
- Take note of what you need to improve. A skill set is something that you can focus on and improve at all times. If you need to boost your creative thinking process – focus on that. If you need to improve your presentation skills – focus on that, and so on. I believe you get the picture on this one, so get to work!
- Brainstorm the next year. The last year of your studies will go by in a flash. Thankfully, it is time to start looking into some activities and skills you haven't tried so far. Be mindful that some of them can help you get some leadership skills, and skills to become an excellent teammate. Read about the available courses and choose one (or a few) that seem like a good fit.

Evaluating the Importance of Higher Education for Specific Career Paths

Sometimes, it takes a little bit of time to realize what you want to do in life. And that is fine. There is an undeniable stability in wanting to take the year off and explore your options a little further. Of course, it only works if you truly commit to it.

However, before you immediately jump to the conclusion that maybe taking a year off or focusing on working for a while before you get to your dream might set you back a bit. Why? In most cases, there is a certain importance in higher education, especially if your career path leads you right to it.

For many teenagers, having a higher education means getting into a specific field of work and achieving success. While there are many professions out there that require no university degree, many of them still do.

Think about this for a while - even if your preferred career choice does not require you to continue your formal education, if you have the chance to go to university, why not take it?

Are you looking for a way to enhance your learning skills? Higher education can make you more prepared, help shape you as a person and provide you with the option of career maturity, adaptability, and a sense of belonging.

Allow me to elaborate further. Some careers require a traditional approach, and here are a few to begin with:

If you are going into medicine. Do you think becoming a healthcare professional without any higher education is possible? If this is one of your choices, then you absolutely need to comb through all the universities that provide graduate programs that will get you a step closer to achieving your goal. Whether it is a nursing program or medical school, you need to be adequately prepared, especially in those cases where another life is at stake.

If you are going for a legal profession. Are you dreaming about becoming a lawyer or a judge? Your dream will only nudge you in the right direction. It requires plenty of work and studying hard. Also, it cannot be achieved without formal training. Every legal professional undergoes a graduate and even a post-graduate program. Through these programs, you get the ability to understand and learn complex legal concepts. You will also enjoy the perk of building your network while in law school.

If you are going into education. There is no way you become a part of the educational system without the proper education, because it will be you that one day shapes the minds of the future. Obtaining a degree in teaching will open up a realm of possibilities for you. It can help you make the transition from a teenager yourself to someone who helps teenagers in the future become who they want to be.

If you are going into science. There are more than a few reasons why going into the field of science requires investing in higher education. You will not only enjoy the perks of the wider network, but also you will gain expertise, guidance, and research opportunities, as well as laboratories so advanced that you'll get to learn some pretty spectacular things! On top of that, gaining better data analysis skills and using scientific methodology while obtaining your scientific research degree will make you feel even more fulfilled!

If you are going into engineering. Due to the fast advancements in technology, it is no wonder why so many young people want to be a part of this ever-growing world. Being one of them yourself is a great idea! If you have always had a knack for building and creating things and have shown a special kind of admiration toward technology, then this is the field for you. But don't be fooled into thinking that a few YouTube crash courses are the equivalent of higher education. Obtain a degree in computer science, information technology, or engineering. It is a field requiring a certain level of specialization to thrive.

These are just a handful of options that require a formal higher education. But if these are not on your list, there is no need to feel discouraged! In the next section, we go through some alternatives that you might find incredibly useful!

Considering Alternatives to Traditional Education

We live in a world where looking for alternatives to college has become increasingly popular, and it is getting more socially acceptable by the minute. Teenagers fail to realize that this practice has existed since the dawn of time. Every generation has that "revelation moment" where they realize there are many alternatives to be considered.

For some teenagers, college is still an essential and wonderful experience. But, for those who wish to take a more alternative path toward creating a bright future, many options are right here waiting for you! Does your teenage intuition tell you that maybe college is not the right choice for you? Before making a long-term commitment that you might regret, pause. Let me help you think outside the box for a bit.

Your career goal should be your main focus, and getting there is only a part of the process. So, look into some of the options that I have laid out for you and see if one of them appeals to your senses:

An apprenticeship – the delicate art of training for a career as a carpenter, an electrician, and so much more lies in the form of an apprenticeship. This is an incredible way to get the most out of your training and enter the workforce as a worker with plenty of skills! After an apprenticeship, you can easily get licensed (granted after you are under strict surveillance and training for a specified time period). Take this as an alternative to traditional education but know that it too takes a while to complete it.

Community college – you might have only heard about this option until now but don't know what it is. So far, this has been the most popular alternative to university studies, mostly because of the accessibility point of view. A community college is a fantastic option that offers various programs – one of which will surely be up to your liking. This is an excellent chance if you are considering attending a school close to your home. The perfect option if you want to take on a job while working. Do you wish to get the feel of a higher education without going through the entire four-year challenge? Community college is the answer.

Online learning – the vastness of the Internet shows no limits! All you need to do is find the right course that fits your needs. Dedicate a few hours of your day to learning what you love. After some time, you will find yourself filled with knowledge and skills that you could have only dreamt about obtaining in such a short time! What I love the most about the Internet is that anyone can use it as an educational tool. Why not do that yourself? View it as a means to improve overall performance and expertise. Take some free courses or pay for a few courses if necessary! Either way, as long as you are determined and pass the classes with flying colors, you will have a list of employers or clients waiting for you.

A vocational education – one of the fastest-growing college alternatives is the trade schools. It seems that although they cost a little less than a more formal higher education, they are still the preferred choice of many. Any teenager wanting a streamlined path toward becoming a part of the workforce should try this. Why waste your time sitting in classes you have no interest in? Instead, spend your time wisely – learning what you are interested in!

An employment – you might be one of those individuals that want to get right into building their portfolio with employment – right out of high school. In today's world, getting a job after finishing your secondary education and working your way up the ladder to a position you choose is more possible than ever. Even though, as a worker, you will encounter many challenges along the way (and during the application process, too), it might be worth your while. Many employers nowadays value the possibility of career advancement through both employment and education, so if you are up for a challenge like this one, I encourage you to take the next step.

Social media – as you can see, in today's world, there are many more options than you can think of. One of those options includes having a full-time career as a content creator or a social media personality. This is an option that was not available 10 or 15 years ago. Even though it is a relatively new field, it attracts more and more people every day. If this is your dream job, then you might want to learn something more about it. Many young people start with this, but only a few succeed. The key is having an entrepreneurial and dedicated spirit, so good luck!

Entrepreneurship – instead of getting a degree or a 9-5 job, you can always focus on building something from the ground up yourself! Turn that dream into reality with the help of some meticulous entrepreneurship. As a young mind, you have a fresh perspective of what the world needs and where it is going, so why not utilize that to create some cash flow? The invention or the business idea that you keep circling back to – focus on that, build on that, and reap the benefits once you succeed!

These are part of your options (to name a few) that can help you determine which professional path you want to take. After narrowing down your choice, we come to the next step of the planning process – finances!

Financial Planning for Education and Scholarships

Fitting your professional future into your budget can sometimes mean making a little bit of a sacrifice. Since it is only for the duration you need to obtain the proper skills or degree, this should not be a problem. As a vibrant young teenager, you have plenty of options – if you don't have the necessary means to finance your next step it does not mean you should immediately quit!

All you need is a solid plan. So, here are a few resources that could get you started:

- See how you can save some money and make the most out of it. Check the available scholarships and whether you are eligible for any of them. As a student, many benefits and grants serve the purpose of helping you achieve your goals and dreams, so use them to the fullest extent!

Planning for Education and Training

- Create a balance between focusing on your education and your work (mostly if you want to do a good job at both). Many teenagers skip this step, firmly believing that they "got this." Well, do you? Set some time to think and create a plan that can help you achieve all the deadlines, finish all the work, and complete your goals. You can help prevent spiraling down into a hole filled with missed deadlines and opportunities.
- Be mindful that things can change in a minute. Understanding that there is a specific extent to which things can go one way if you don't maintain them is key. Upgrade your flexibility and remember to prepare yourself for everything. Because, as much as you give, sometimes, things can go awry. It is in those cases that you need to have a plan B, C, and all the other letters if you need to – make sure you are prepared for the unexpected.
- Always be on the lookout for new opportunities. Every new day is an opportunity in and of itself. As much as it sounds like a solid idea to make a financial plan, that does not mean that you should completely ignore some wonderful opportunities that may cross your path. Regularly check any resources that might be of help to you, and don't give up!

Create a stable financial structure that can support your next step in the educational process. Be mindful of those bad days, as they may come easily, but they may also go easily as well.

Now, we are at a crossroads – the subject of planning for your education and the training process to become a valuable part of the workforce is complete. But we are only getting started on the practical aspect of it!

The next chapter encompasses the power of practical experience. Learn all you can about it!

CHAPTER 6

GAINING PRACTICAL EXPERIENCE

> *"You cannot create experience. You must undergo it."*
>
> — Albert Camus

Experience is not something that you can obtain by only listening to your classes or courses. For this bit, you need to dip your toes into the professional waters and find out how you can swim for yourself.

The teenage years are the best years of your life. But they are also the ones where you should work the hardest. In the beginning, it might seem like a waste of time to focus on gaining and sharpening your skills. But, if you look at the long run, you will soon notice how, with each passing day, you have a bigger need for them.

So, once you've established your plan for education and training, it is time to start gaining some practical experience. That will help you set a strong foundation for all professional curveballs that life throws at you later.

Do you know where to begin? Do you know your options? This is another confusing aspect on the road to finding the right career path. Thankfully, it is easy to overcome it! I have broken down the most popular choices for you below. Take a look at them and evaluate how they would fit into your situation – one of them will eventually work out for you!

Volunteering, Internships and Part-Time Jobs

It is easy to become a part of the enchanted circle – you need the experience to get a job, but you need a job to get experience! I have noticed that this fact can create a bit of panic for some teenagers. No worries, there are always some pretty good options that can help you get started. As long as you are dedicated to your goal, you can achieve anything!

For a beginner such as yourself, it might confuse you to notice that plenty of job opportunities require a certain degree of relevant experience. This is a normal part of the job-seeking process, but when you are at such an early stage, how can you take control of the situation?

Well, there are many ways you can contribute to building your portfolio. For starters, take a look at the most common ones – volunteering, internships, and part-time jobs.

Volunteering – these are available in almost every field. In today's world, volunteering is the act of being an active participant in the community. When you start doing this at an early age, it sets you apart from the crowd and makes you more prepared for what's to come.

Consider this as an essential activity that will open the doors to finding the perfect job opportunities for you. Are you looking for some experience in the democracy field or maybe the veterinary field? A passionate individual like yourself should only view this as the essential steppingstone into the professional world. It will give you an insight into how your community works, bring some purpose to your life, and teach you some valuable lessons about work. Fun fact – volunteering can also improve your overall well-being and self-esteem!

Why not check out a few companies in your area? Do the proper research (depending on your field of interest) and note the few distinguished establishments you find. From this point on, all you need to do is get in touch with them and start volunteering!

Internships – some of you feel the need to benefit financially as well as professionally on the road to success. That is where internships come onto the scene. As with volunteering, you get to benefit from creating a wide network, get some experience, and help yourself learn about what you want to do later in life.

Even though remote work is becoming increasingly popular, as a teenager, you have more access to an internship than ever before. Think about dedicating a summer or a few hours of the week to this cause and see how it will benefit you in the long run.

After you have completed your internship in whichever field you like, (administration, social media, fashion, graphic design, etc.) you will come out the other end thriving! You might not notice, but through the process, you will not only gain a little bit of professional and financial stability but will also expand your theoretical knowledge beyond your wildest imagination. Plus, you get to amplify your resume!

Part-time jobs – now, you are working toward getting a university degree, and that is your sole goal. So, why waste your energy with working a part-time job?

This is the mindset of a common teenager. You might feel like this would be an unnecessary distraction when in fact, it is the one thing you need! A part-time job can give you a unique insight into what makes the professional world go round. You will get to experience it for a short while and learn some valuable lessons during it.

If your soft skills are not up to par, you will certainly experience a revelation. Besides seeing how specific rules apply in the workplace, you will improve your time management, gain a sense of responsibility, and learn how to work in a team.

Last but not least, this will not only boost your resume but your confidence too!

Remember, these options are only the tip of the iceberg! There are as many options to gain experience as job choices, so buckle up because I have a lot more for you.

Summer Programs and Camps

Now, while I was on the subject of internships, I mentioned that you can spend a summer learning and expanding your skills. If this is stuck in your mind, then this next part is for you.

First of all, let me applaud you for your good thinking! Considering a summer program or a camp is an excellent opportunity to grow, learn, and figure out what you want to do with your life. While many teenagers underestimate the subject of a summer camp, (sounds geeky at first) you saw the possibility of investing in yourself! At the end of the day, that is what matters the most!

On the other hand, if you are still on the fence or strongly against it, allow me to elaborate. What have your summers been like up until now? Going out with your friends, maybe reading a book, playing video games, and spending your time idly doing nothing important. If I am correct, then you probably need a change. As much as you deserve the break after 9 months of studying hard, there is a much better way to use your time and acquire something valuable.

To those of you that have not yet realized the benefits of investing in yourself over the summer, I dedicate this next bit to you:

- Start using everything you have learned so far – even if it has only been in theory, entering a summer program will give you the platform to try all you have learned so far. Whether it is a technical skill or a soft skill, this is the best place to see if it works, as it is a safe zone that will not lead to some serious repercussions.

- ⬥ Go soft and go practical – you will be placed in a unique environment – a learning one. This is not only your time to shine but your time to also be a creator of a better self. Practicality is key here, so once you browse the plateau of available summer camps and programs, choose the one that will give you the best experience.

- ⬥ It is about all kinds of skills – you may not have thought about this until now, but entering a summer program can help you plunge into a world without any kind of safety net. Deliberately place yourself in a position where it is obligatory to learn many life skills. It all starts from the smallest and simplest skills and builds up to the challenging ones you are looking to obtain. This can be a way for you to learn both how to make your bed and practice leadership skills. Sounds like something you'd want to experience, right?

- ⬥ A summer program is not a place of anarchy – but a place of understanding and learning accountability. Yes, you will be left to your own devices, but you will be under the constant observation of professionals who know how to handle any situation. Consider them your mentors and let them guide you. These are usually a handful of counselors who are there for you to learn from them. They will hold you responsible for your actions to the fullest extent, thus giving you the trial, you need for a professional life.

- ⬥ Learn without the stress of – school, exams, talking in front of your entire class – all of which can make you feel high levels of stress and anxiety. Everything changes the minute you are a teenager, so the important thing is to give yourself time to grow. But also, the space to grow. A summer program is a great way to learn without the added stress of classmates and grades. It is about letting go of your fears and fully committing to the tasks at hand.

- ⬥ Make life-long connections – I know that expanding your network is the last thing on your mind when starting a summer program, but it is one of its most incredible benefits. When you look at it – both the counselors and your peers may end up being excellent and very valuable to you in the future – and vice versa!

I hope that I have helped you make up your mind on this one. Speaking of mind, this next one might be the perfect fit if you want to sharpen yours in a more competitive and challenging environment.

Shadowing Professionals and Job Shadowing Opportunities

At this stage, you must wonder what various jobs look like. Is the stress level the same in any field? Is there a different level of responsibility depending on the type of work? Also, how do you know you have reached a stage where you are ready to become a professional or an expert in a particular field?

If there is one thing that can help answer all of these questions, it is a job shadowing opportunity. You are a teenager, which means that most of these vacancies where you can shadow someone are designed specifically for you.

Having this opportunity to shadow a professional means you get to have someone introduce you to the vast business world and what it encompasses. Additionally, it has proven to be a successful approach to bringing successful individuals into many fields, and it has become an acceptable – no, preferable course of action.

This can help you determine your major in college, realize what you want to do after you finish high school, and give you an idea of what the rest of your life would look like. Remember that question grown-ups always asked you? "What do you want to be when you grow up?" Well, after this, you should be able to answer it satisfactorily.

Do you know what you need to do to get there? Other than being polite and professional, you need to choose a company that can provide you with one of their employees as the best example of what you want to be. Request a shadowing appointment where you introduce yourself. Share your interests, which school you're attending, why you are interested in shadow work, and whether they have someone on the dates you're available. For this last one, keep in mind that not all will have someone available for the first dates you request, so showing some flexibility is a plus.

Once you make all the necessary arrangements, it is time to start the shadow work! It is key to realize that you are in the observer role and won't have much to do. In contrast, you will have much to see and learn. Even if you don't have any background in the field, use this as the groundwork upon which you will build a better understanding of the workplace as a definition.

There are many things you will learn on your job shadowing journey. The small tasks you get will result in you gaining the following:

You will learn how the job you want works – shadowing a professional will give you direct access to your future – you will see how you should function and witness a typical day that includes all the responsibilities, challenges, and issues.

The connection with the other positions – any job you choose to take up as a career path will have a close connection to another branch. With job shadowing, you will learn how to connect with various branches and form successful relationships. You will learn how to be a part of a well-oiled machine that works impeccably.

Expand your network – however long or short your shadowing experience may be, it is crucial to start networking. You are a teenager now, but the connections you coin will be the ones that can help you spread your wings in full glory once you become a part of the workforce.

Learn how to learn – don't be afraid to ask questions and take small matters into your own hands (when possible). This is how you can develop a more accurate representation of yourself and the job you want to do.

Note that, depending on the job shadowing program you find, the tasks may vary – substantially. Making the most out of it can only mean one thing – flexibility. Keep an open mind, whatever the situation, trust your gut, and think independently. Circumstances may change at any moment, so here are a few tips to help you out during those times:

- ⬦ You don't need to focus so much on leaving a good impression, but you should always be polite and professional.
- ⬦ Keep in mind that your mentor might have some demanding responsibilities and provide the space to finish them.
- ⬦ Not everything will look interesting – a part of the experience may be incredibly dull – that is normal.
- ⬦ Appreciate everything your mentor says to you – remember, they dedicate a valuable portion of their time to teaching you how things work.
- ⬦ It is okay if, by the end of the shadowing process, you realize you don't want to pursue that particular career – consider it another lesson you have learned.

After you have gained all the necessary practical experience, you should be ready to write it all down – as a part of your resume! Do you think you got what it takes to create a successful one?

Building a Portfolio or Resume to Showcase Skills and Experiences

It takes the skillful act of putting words together and doing it in a way that accentuates your capabilities to the fullest extent. However active you may have been with all the internships, volunteering, job shadowing, etc., you may not have the proper skills to put all your experiences into words.

More often than not, teenagers get confused when they come to this section, and not only because it poses quite a writing challenge, but many need to recognize the difference between a portfolio and a resume.

Before we go much further, help yourself – learn the difference.

Portfolio – the portfolio is a visual representation of your practical work. It should be filled with examples of your work. You might think that only photographers use a portfolio (due to the visual aspect of it), but anyone can use it. A portfolio can be filled with links, videos, texts, various illustrations, and so much more.

A typical portfolio includes an originality statement (a small paragraph where you write that the work included is yours and confidential). Furthermore, it should have a summary of your career, a brief biography, and a small paragraph that will serve its purpose as a belief statement. Here, you include your motivations, values, likes, and goals.

Resume – on the other hand, a resume is a more concise and less creative way of showing a company who you are. There are many formats for you to choose from, but all in all, it should contain the following – a summary of your working experience (as a beginner, you should list all the practical experience you have gained, including starting and finishing dates and contacts, in chronological order), add your education in chronological order too, and list all the skills you have (these include soft skills and technical ones, relevant for the position you are applying).

Before you start applying for the jobs you have found, you need to create an impeccable resume and portfolio that will set you apart from the crowd. There are a few ways how to do that:

Research the role you're applying for – there is nothing worse than giving your potential employer a bunch of information they're not interested in. Put some time and effort into researching the role you are going for and customize your resume to fit their needs (to a certain point). Remember, you still need to keep the information within reasonable and truthful boundaries.

Add all your accomplishments – gather all the recommendations, achievements, extra-curricular activities, internships, and programs you have undergone. Demonstrate to your future employer that your education and investment in yourself have been your primary goal up until then.

Keep it short but include everything – I know this sounds a little complicated, but you need to keep your sentences short. Include all the info you need, and especially for your resume. Keep it within a page.

Promote yourself – language is not the only thing that matters while creating your resume and portfolio. It is imperative to know how to promote yourself too, so further enhance it with color. You can even go as far as creating an online portfolio – that's always a showstopper!

By the end of this chapter, you've made it easier for yourself to become a person that has some participation in the practical section, not just the theoretical one.

As we close the chapter on gaining some practical experience, we open the next one – deciding what you want. Toward the end of the job shadowing part, I mentioned that you might not like what you see. Have you thought about what to do if that happens? Either way, see for yourself in the following chapter.

CHAPTER 7
MAKING INFORMED DECISIONS

> *"Nothing is more difficult, and therefore more precious, than to be able to decide."*
>
> — *Napoleon Bonaparte*

Napoleon's decisions may not have always been right, but he is definitely right about this one. It is finally time for you to decide what you want. However scary it may sound, bear with me – there are ways to exclude your emotions and make a choice based solely on facts (ones you have gathered so far).

From knowing the current and future job opportunities to knowing how good or bad you would be at each of them, it is all about considering the info you have. That said, there are a few steps you can take that can help you pick a successful career alternative.

Weighing the Pros and Cons of Different Career Options

You are a teenager, so don't be surprised if you find it very difficult to exclude emotions from your decision-making process. After all, this may be the most challenging step you face. Thinking logically, you must already have a few alternatives lined up, and now, all of them seem like good options! So, which one to go for?

Start enjoying the power of making a list with pros and cons. If you are unable to do it yourself, ask for help! Get your mentor, a friend, a relative – anyone whom you trust, to assist you. Making a decision this large requires your full attention and the need to analyze all the factors. I recommend you use all the deep research you have done so far, as well as some soul-searching.

It might be difficult at the moment, but <u>picture yourself ten years from now.</u> What do you see? Do you see a role where you can thrive and constantly move up the corporate ladder, or do you maybe see yourself as running your own business, making the rules as you go? Try answering this question truthfully – you will gain an excellent starting point for your career path.

You have a very big decision to make, so get your pen and paper out and start writing! Lay out all the options in front of you. Underneath each, make a division into two sections. One will be for the pros and the other one for the cons. Remember, you are making this decision based on your priorities and needs! Start writing things down. While you do that, do some further investigation of your own – down to the last detail! Take a look at the working hours, take a look at the experience needed for each field separately, and take a look at the benefits that are mostly offered for each position. Also, see if there is a possibility for growth in every field. As an inexperienced individual, you may overlook this, but some job positions can become generic over time. That being said, after a few years, you may find out there is no room to grow. It is much better to be aware of it before you are already deep into the work.

Consider this as one of the best aspects of your decision-making process. Right now, all opportunities may seem equal – when in fact, they are not. Instead of leaving it all to your gut, you are doing the right thing by filling out the negative and positive sides of every alternative you have.

In reality, when you look at the situation on paper, you will see that some concerns you thought were incredibly large can be handled in a minute. On the other side, you may uncover some potential opportunities or new concerns that will completely shift the focus of everything.

Trust the process – that is the most important thing to do. Find the thing that is the driving force that would pull you forward into professional success and discover what your breaking points are. For some, it might be the generic work I mentioned earlier. For others, it might be the long hours or maybe, the long commute. _For you, it will be anything that does not fit your wants and needs._

The pros and cons list is just a plan where you prioritize your needs and goals and align them with the job opportunities on the market. I am explaining the market demand and how to understand it better below. Read it so you know how to make an even better and more informed decision.

Understanding Market Demand and Job Prospects

As a teenager, you might not be able to identify what skills are necessary for the job market of today. During all this uncertainty, you might be panicking and unable to take a step in any direction. However, when your future employment is at stake, you need to understand both the market demand and the job prospects.

The uncertainty that is arising in the *market demand* at the moment is due to its dynamic nature. Things progress faster than usual, and it is all thanks to the help of technology. Many job opportunities considered solid and necessary about a decade or two ago are now slowly diminishing. Contrary to that, technology paves the way for many new prospects to emerge and promises these will be the exact ones that will lead society into the future.

What you might notice here is that the job prospects for you (based on the specific and soft skills you have) vary from the market demand.

Let's talk a bit about disruptions.

In a perfect world, as soon as you finish high school, go to university, and get a degree (or not), you start working within the field you want. Everyone gets the training and fulfills the requirements during high school, with almost no extra-curricular activities, and the transition from a schoolbook to an office desk is as seamless as possible.

In reality, things cannot be further from this. Nowadays, the world is facing a global skills gap since the market is constantly looking for a vaster skillset than anyone can achieve with traditional education. I cannot imagine how it is for a teenager such as yourself to face this kind of situation.

Fortunately, however limited your skillset is, understanding the market demand and looking into future job prospects can help place you a step ahead of everyone else.

Noticing a gap or a lot of inequalities between what you want to do, and your level of expertise is the first step in the right direction. This means that you have realistically evaluated the prospects and are ready to face whatever challenges may come your way.

You are now standing on the edge of a certain change. Instead of holding back and pushing your potential down, try doing the exact opposite. Embrace change, become change. The transition from studying to working can either make you or break you. Try to focus on the making bit.

Making yourself better for future *job prospects* comes from the ability to invest in your career development. That is what we have been learning about together until now, and that is what you will continue doing long after you read this book.

Do you need some tips to help you set up for the future? On top of all you have done until now, here are a few tips that can catapult you to the top of your employers' job lists!

1st tip – it is essential to stay on top of all the recent changes in your field of interest. All the recent changes equate to adding some new skills to your resume. As long as you are aware that change is constantly happening, you can stay on top of the situation and become a life-long learner. Consider this as a primary tip that will help you increase your employability. While you regularly update your skills, you will become more in sync with what employers want and what the market needs.

2nd tip – signaling that you are the best candidate for the job in any field requires having some professional validation beforehand. I have mentioned this many times before. Consider this as an extracurricular activity. Getting an extra certification or undergoing a seminar is somewhat of a precondition for entering the workforce. Many courses vary in importance, duration, etc., which can signal to employers you have taken the extra step to become eligible for a certain job position.

3rd tip – focus on positive development (and I don't mean this in the sense of making yourself presentable). Expand your views and interests as much as you can, and always have this in mind – *you are doing this for yourself*. Yes, showing a certain level of diversity is important, especially as a young person just entering the workforce. But at the end of the day, it is you who must be happy and fulfilled by it.

That leads me to the next aspect to consider – and that is the overall quality of life based on the career path you choose.

Considering Lifestyle Factors and Work-Life Balance

Enough about technicality. Let's talk about practicality! By now, you must already have a system set in place and a certain lifestyle. You have your wants and needs, your goals, and your routines. You have your friends, your relatives, the people you are closest to. You have your hobbies and interests and things that help you pass the time. You have an entire life set up.

You have a certain lifestyle that, up until this point, has been supported by your parents/guardians. Suddenly, it is time to start thinking that you need to survive by yourself. It is time to let go of the training wheels.

Now, it is time to face the music and start thinking about how to make it on your own. Transitioning from a teenager to an adult feels like it's happening faster than a heartbeat. As soon as you turn 18, you're not a child anymore. On top of choosing a career path now, you also need to be extra careful about it so it can fit into your life and not change it as much.

Considering the balance between work and life is another one of the most important factors when choosing your preferred field of interest. It is not all about technical and soft skills and how to upgrade yourself. It is also about the overall quality of life and whether the subject you choose fits right into that.

If you are still looking at the pros and cons list you made earlier, remember to focus on choosing a career that helps you lead the life you want. Today, anyone, even a teenager, can notice that the lines between professional and personal life have become blurred, almost non-existent. The many trends, including flexible hours, working from home, being constantly available for work because of your smartphone, etc., have resulted in more of a negative response than a positive one. People who have been working for years have noticed how they bring their work home more frequently than before, and the shift in working hours is actually a shift in their entire day. That can lead to plenty of frustration and stress.

As a fresh mind who is only entering the world of work, remember that you have all the power to create the lifestyle that will suit you the best.

It is important to maintain a balance between professional and personal life.

It is important to understand how valuable of an aspect this is.

It is important to strive toward creating a life for yourself that you like.

I am hoping that I can help you reinforce this as soon as possible so you can enjoy the outcome for many years to come. If you weren't aware until now that life is full of choices, here it is. You are in front of one, a very important one. Any call you make will influence your life.

There are a few perks that come with choosing to make a balance between your work and your personal life. Take a look at them below:

- You will have some time to focus on your physical health. It is important to maintain an active lifestyle, especially if the career path you choose tends to lead to a more sedentary lifestyle. Keeping your body active can help you remain focused, happier, healthier, and thus enjoy a good work-life balance.

- Never neglect mental health too. Being a workaholic may be a challenge for you now – you are young, full of energy, and have a lust for life. But what will happen in 10 or 20 years from now? Constantly focusing on your work without having time for yourself or your family and friends can result in a significant mental decline. You should be able to work without having any difficulties, so eliminate them from the start.

- There is a lot of stress in the world, don't let it consume you. Imagine taking up a career path that requires you to be available nonstop, gives you little to no freedom to do something for yourself, and makes you constantly feel under pressure. Eventually, you will start slipping, and you will be unable to manage your workload. Being under a lot of stress for a long period will only have a negative effect. This is why you need to opt for a job that teaches you how to manage your workload within working hours and allows you to leave something for tomorrow.

- When you have the time to focus on personal activities, you are more productive at work. This is a fact that you might not be aware of yet. Having some personal time for yourself, instead of only focusing on your professional engagements, can help you feel more fulfilled, thus be more productive and present while working.

All of this sounds excellent on paper, but once you are part of the real deal, it can significantly change your viewpoint. Sticking to a schedule you have set beforehand may be more difficult than you have imagined. It is at those times you should focus on the following:

- Start your work, and then set a goal. Try to be as realistic with your goals as possible. Understand that you can work both on a personal and a professional goal at the same time and make some room for both during the day. Doing this can help you maintain a better balance.

- While you work, work productively. Come to terms with the fact that you will only have a certain amount of time in the day dedicated to work, so make the most out of it. Increase your productivity levels by managing your workload and ensure that the extra tasks you may get from your work will not affect your personal life.

- This leads me to the following – separate state and church. Work is one thing, home is another, and while you are at home, refrain from using your work laptop or checking notifications after hours. If you want to maintain a balanced lifestyle, then stick to the schedule you've prepared for yourself.

- Last but not least, put stress management as your priority. Every job comes with its obstacles and challenges. Learn that while you're still a teenager. Also, find a healthy way that helps you cope with stress. It can be anything from taking a 5-minute break to developing a new hobby such as running, writing, listening to podcasts, etc.

Achieving a balance between work and life is essential. Instead of looking for a job that has long working hours, create stability by growing and enjoying more aspects of life than just the work one. Learn how to best evaluate where the biggest potential for growth is.

Evaluating the Potential for Growth and Advancement in Chosen Fields

There is a sort of dramatic point to it all, but if you are not growing in life, then what are you doing exactly? The potential for career growth comes from the fact that you need a sense of purpose to start this journey. It is the path that separates you from the bigger picture and the career of your dreams.

Looking at that piece of paper with all you've written down on it. Can you easily spot the career paths where you'd have the biggest progress?

Important note – *career growth and career development are entirely different things. If we have focused on career development and transferable skills until now, career growth shifts the focus to entering a field that can help you thrive.*

Career growth has the option to advance in a particular field. In the long run, it helps you unlock a higher level of your potential, ultimately reaching the top! If you choose an area where, after a while, you will hit the ceiling of developing your skills and will start doing generic work, would that bring much satisfaction to your life? Contrary to that, choosing a field where one thing constantly changes will give you a plateau of options – ones you'll never be bored of.

After all, it is all about growth. Right now, the power is in your hands – you can shape your future life and add this secret ingredient in every aspect. You may not believe it, but in all cases, the possibility for career growth is the catapult that will move you forward. Essentially, it is highly beneficial to your well-being and will make you happy. So, choose career advancement, choose a better life, and choose yourself!

There is a balance in everything, isn't there? I applaud you for being able to stop and look within, weigh in all the factors, and make an informed decision. From all the steps we have gone through together, this might have easily been the most difficult one – so brava!

Consider this as a chapter where you need to take a breather from all you have done so far and rest your body for the next bit that is coming – taking some swift actions! We're going from a passive to an active exercise – let's see what you need to do there!

CHAPTER 8

TAKING ACTION

> *"Now is no time to think of what you do not have. Think of what you can do with what there is."*
>
> — Ernest Hemingway

It is time to start acquiring the career of your dreams. You have done all this planning, researching, and investing in yourself. You are more than ready. You got this. These are the last steps you will take toward creating your bright future.

Taking action does not mean aimlessly running around and doing everything you can until "something sticks." It means being strategic about your future, striving toward the achievement of your goals, and of course, having a backup plan.

Are you excited to get started? Your own chapter in life is almost ready to unfold.

Setting Short-Term and Long-Term Career Goals

There is a certain importance behind setting goals for yourself. It amplifies the importance of being a part of society, and for many teenagers, it gives the much-needed self-boost. Career goals are the motivation that can drive you forward and keep you jumping out of your bed, filled with excitement every morning.

You are a young person, so learning how to set goals properly is a skill you should possess. The trick to knowing what you want is being completely honest with yourself.

By learning how to set short-term and long-term goals, you create a mood board. Fill it up with everything you want to achieve.

It is important to note that it is not all about the destination. This is about the journey along the way as well. As a teenager, you need to stop to realize what resources you have at hand, determine that what you want to achieve is really your goal, not someone else's, and identify all the aspects where you might need some help. So, when you look at it, it is a simple thing to do. But it requires your full attention!

All of us have goals. They can be small, large, personal, or professional. Nevertheless, many teenagers confuse the action of setting a goal with the plan to achieve it. Daydreaming and thinking about what you want to achieve without doing anything about it will only get you somewhere, but not necessarily where you intended. It is a nice sentiment, though. Do you want to achieve everything you put your mind to? In that case, you need a solid plan to make it happen.

Actually, you need a **smart** plan to do it.

Are you wondering why the word smart is accentuated? SMART goals are a concept that can help you achieve wonders, especially with your career. It is the guidance many teenagers aren't aware of but find useful when they stumble upon it. This exercise can help you map out the steps to achieve your goal. It is probably one of the best exercises you will utilize, mainly because many people of all ages use it – constantly!

SMART is the acronym for the process you are about to undergo. Each letter represents a significant course of action you should take to achieve a successful career. Here is a short representation of what they mean:

S – stands for specific. By this point, you should have more than just an idea for your future self. Don't be afraid to go into a detailed plan – it might give you a clearer view of the big picture!

M – stands for measurable. This means tracking your progress. Take small steps toward achieving it, but ensure they are measurable. Take learning a new language as an example. Dedicate an hour of your time every day to understanding it – that is a quantifiable way of achieving your goal.

A – stands for attainable. Be realistic with yourself. We have covered the aspects of what you can and can't do, underlining your strengths and weaknesses. Now it is time to use that. Don't push yourself too hard – instead, create an attainable goal (one you know you can achieve).

R – stands for realistic. Just like the previous letter, a realistic goal will help you develop your skills instead of creating a cloud of insecurities around you.

T – stands for time-bound. When you set up a goal, you should have a specific timeline. This means tracking down your progress until the process is complete. Breaking down the long-term goal into smaller milestones can help you prove there is constant progress and help you easily reach your goal.

You know what SMART goals are. Do you know how they support you? During the time you dedicate to fulfilling your dreams, this exercise provides you with some silent support along the way. Regard it as your fuel.

The process of setting a goal can have a positive impact on your overall lifestyle. After putting some time and effort into the plan, it can help you become better, stronger, and more successful. Ultimately SMART goals are shaping you into the person you want to be.

Take the lead as soon as you set your plan. Create some long-term or short-term career goals. As an exercise, it can provide you with many benefits, not only because it will give you the confidence you need (and open doors for you). Also, this is ultimately a rewarding experience. Working to achieve your dream results in picking up an extra skill or two on your way there. You will start feeling more independent and will learn from all the challenges you meet along the way.

Also, every time you set up a goal (be that a short-term or a long-term one), remember it can change at any time. Keep your mind flexible at all times. Give yourself a break every time you feel like you need one. Finally, don't forget to celebrate all the little milestones! It may seem insignificant, but success is made out of a lot of the small things you do every day. Pat yourself on the back after every milestone you achieve.

However, this is only the beginning. After all, you should know how to create a proper plan filled with strategies. For that matter, I will go over all the necessary details to do that in the following section.

Creating a Strategic Action Plan

It is all about creating a professional development plan. Through this door, you will enter right into the professional world. Depending on your goal, you can outline some objectives. Create a solid plan on how to achieve them. There are numerous opportunities out there for you. You can dream of becoming an art director, a graphic designer, a party planner, someone who runs their own business, etc. You have so many available options; you just need to choose and start walking your path toward success.

That is what a strategic action plan is for.

The bottom line is - be aware of everything. When I say everything, I mean – start from yourself. Knowing where to begin means fully understanding what you are good at. This is your jumping point and the strength you hold when times get tough. There are a lot of factors that weigh in here. So, take a look at the outline I have prepared for you below – you might find it incredibly useful!

Analyze Your Strengths and Weaknesses

We have mentioned them at the beginning, but as you can see, they are such an important part of creating a career path that we are constantly going back to them. Through them, you outline who you are.

As I pointed out before, these include both the soft and the technical skills you currently have. Once you finish evaluating yourself, you start outlining which ones you excel at, and which ones need improvement. The ones you are good at are the force driving you toward achieving anything you want. The ones that need improvement are the ones that are currently holding you back.

On the other hand, the list might lack a thing or two, so you might consider adding them and working on them – that's a great option too! Think skills, think traits. Any one of them can be polished to perfection through formal education or training. You may even achieve perfection by working on them without any help!

Write Down the Values

As you start working toward making some progress on a professional level, you will see there will be many bumps in the road. Some are minor, such as tight deadlines or an argument with a colleague. But others are of a more considerable significance. These include when the workflow interferes with your decision-making process – when working under a lot of stress every day and doing a lot of work that you are maybe overqualified for, but without the proper compensation.

It is time to reconsider things when what you do interferes with your professional development plan. Before wasting 5 or 10 years at a job you don't like, outline your core values and find a workspace that aligns with that.

Think About the People Who Can Help

When creating a strategic action plan, finding your weaknesses is an inevitable part of the process. Instead of letting it put you down, rise back up. I feel like there is no such thing as too much networking. It is essential to building your professional portfolio and ensuring you are noticed in the job market.

All the connections you can make with both offline and online networking can contribute to a flourishing career. Make it a part of your action plan to attend as many events and seminars as possible. Try to make a variety of it too – some of them can be events for improving your transferable skills, and others may be informal events where you reach out to people from your chosen industry.

Either way, the networking plan can be your ultimate jumping point to where you want to be.

Work on Your Image

Another significant aspect of a successful career plan is presenting yourself in such a manner that employers can't say no to you. This means a presentable and decent style and having one all over your internet presence. Let's face it; everyone leaves a digital footprint, so make it count while you are working on yours!

What I mean is making sure your professional and personal online platforms are thriving. For example, create a LinkedIn profile, and showcase all the work you have done so far. Let future employers know that you are a dedicated and qualified individual.

Constantly add to your accomplishments. This includes everything from attending conferences and seminars to workshops and academies. In this way, you will demonstrate that you are dedicated to constant improvement.

Keep an Eye on Job Openings, and Don't Be Afraid to Make a Selection

After all, you have come all this way and worked so hard on yourself – you should not allow yourself to be swayed into a job option that does not check all the boxes for you. Being flexible about it is one thing

– completely changing your mindset, goals, and vision just to fit a profile is another thing. Appreciate all the work you've done so far and only consider possible employers who would do the same.

These are the handful of important things you should note when you are creating an action plan. Every step matters – so step into the land of opportunities with a solid plan.

At the end of the day, it is all about feeling capable and confident with who you are and confident with what you know. Once you reach that point, there is nothing you cannot overcome. The more honest you are, the more bullet-proof the career action plan you make will be.

Overcoming Obstacles and Staying Motivated

Earlier in this chapter, I mentioned that sometimes, plans can change. The teenage years are filled with challenges and obstacles. These are an inevitable part of life. In fact, they complete life and give it fullness, representing the magnificent experience of being alive.

That often translates into the professional field. When you work on a goal for a longer time, you may get caught up in the process. That can ultimately bring some dissatisfaction and lack of motivation. It is a part of the journey. It can happen to anyone.

Do you notice this starting to happen to you? In the beginning, you were doing great, but something happened, and suddenly, you are feeling lost in the whirlwind of information and the next steps you're about to take. Suddenly it all seems like too much. Suddenly, you need some time to breathe.

Sometimes, when working toward a goal, you start struggling to find motivation right before you cross the finish line. The reality of the situation is that getting motivated is the most challenging part of the process. When you transition from high school into the real world – that is the biggest change. Being a teenager, you may feel like you don't have enough time to do everything in time.

Any transition process is difficult. Every action you will take in life may come with more than a few obstacles. If looking for the motivation to continue working on you seems too much, this section is designed especially for you.

Did you know you will come face-to-face with a few snags on your way to success? Did you know that about 80% of teenagers end up not following their primary career path? Something comes in their way of achieving their dreams, and they simply give up. That does not mean that they are unhappy with their current career paths. It only means they have encountered a change.

Whatever happens in your quest for the career of your dreams, you need to remain flexible and open to all possibilities. The process can be overwhelming but remember that it's not over until you get what you want and feel accomplished, happy, and satisfied with your choice. Curveballs will come and go, but instead of giving in to the pressure and the low motivation levels, try doing the opposite. Powering through is the best way to persevere.

Here are a few tips to help you get back on track.

Remember, it is all about finding the best approach for you. When you start feeling like your motivation levels are going down, it is time to switch it up. Don't be afraid of change – that only means that you are adapting and acknowledging yourself in all your glory!

Learn to Remember Your Goal

There are so many things you need to do on your path to greatness. Starting with the big picture, then breaking it down into smaller bits, setting some short-term and long-term goals. You are constantly figuring out your next step – and that can be a lot. Any human could get caught up in the process and lose the necessary motivation to continue. When this happens, stop, take a minute to breathe. Remind yourself - what is your primary goal?

But try not to get too attached to the initial concept that you've developed. Also, do you repeat to yourself what you need to do every day? If you need to remind yourself what your daily goal is, is it the right choice for you?

It is Okay if You Slip Up

As I mentioned, change can happen at any time. Once you are working on a long-term goal, it is natural for you to feel like your batteries are drained. Even if you miss a task or two, there is no need to be disappointed in yourself. The important thing is to get right back up and recommit to your goal. Did you manage to get off track because of your grades or a hobby? No worries, you got yourself!

Think about it this way – every person on the planet who had wanted to make a change eventually slipped. Everyone who has worked on themselves have had a minor or a major setback. Don't let that make you feel discouraged. Change and fluctuations are a natural part of the process – it means you are on the right path.

Get Some Extra Support

Talk to your family, friends, or mentors and seek additional help. You would not believe how much of a difference a sound support system makes. Surround yourself with people who are familiar with your goals. These people would give anything to support you every step of the way.

This way, whenever you feel down or start feeling tired of pursuing your dream, you can turn to any one of them. Their job is to make you feel secure in yourself while reminding you to push your limits. They are here for you, so don't be afraid to share.

Visualization and a Positive Attitude

This is the power couple you need to succeed! Start visualizing yourself – how you overcome any obstacle that comes your way, how you achieve your goal, and how that makes you feel. Use the happiness you feel each time you picture yourself succeeding and allow it to be the force that moves you every time you feel like stopping.

Positive self-talk can change a lot. It is not only an excellent way to keep your self-acceptance and self-motivation up. This practice also improves your overall attitude and mood. You deserve to achieve greatness, which is what you aim at – every day.

Embrace every barrier that comes your way. Refresh your memory – you are bigger than anything that stands in your way. Losing motivation can happen to anyone. Ultimately, your goal is a constant and positive change – and that doesn't come without a few challenges!

Continual Learning and Adapting to Changing Career Landscapes

Adapting to change is just as important as overcoming obstacles. Another aspect that we have only touched upon is the subject of tomorrow. Every field – be it technology, biology, engineering, or writing – is led by experts, respectfully, and these people are improving the course of the future career paths of everyone that follows.

Right now, you are in the place of a follower – someone still learning and slowly applying the rules. Becoming a part of a workforce that is changing by the minute can feel like entering a race mid-way. Thankfully, this is not necessarily bound to happen – especially if you come prepared.

The key to becoming a part of the future is your mindset. Think as if you are already there. Up to this point, you have only been a high school student. Until you realize the best way to thrive is to become a lifelong learner, you might not get far with your career goals.

The ever-changing career landscape is what will nudge you in this direction – you weren't expecting this, right?

All of the skills that I have mentioned before are a great starting point. Your soft skills, such as time management, problem-solving, critical thinking, the ability to successfully communicate, etc., are the perfect ground upon which you will build yourself up. Combine that with the technical skills – but remember you constantly need to upgrade them too.

Ten years from now, you may have to face the fact that your career choice is now obsolete or a dying branch – what then? To avoid this from happening to you, choose a wide range of sources for improving and broadening your technical skills. If you allow this to become a continuous learning habit, you might end up as a part of a flourishing collaboration in a field you never even thought to be a part of.

Keeping an open mind when it comes to career searching can be a stretch for some, so here is a successful way to deal with it:

- Try to give some new skills a chance – you might end up liking them.
- As you do that, remember there is no need to try something extremely different from what you are doing at the moment. Be diverse but selective.
- Before entering the workforce, you have the unique position to look at things from a different perspective – from the outside. Analyze and look for weak spots – this is the commitment to lifelong learning.
- Once you become a part of the workforce, bring the outside – inside! Provide a unique point of view and help develop the creation of a steady stream of genius ideas.

Nobody can do this but you – you have the distinctive opportunity to rise to the occasion of always being a few steps ahead. Achieve that with the power of continual learning, and you will have no worries adapting to the ever-changing career landscapes.

Learning to recognize an opportunity is something you will practice for a lifetime. But, preparing to seize an opportunity you find is something you practice every day. By taking action and giving it your best to shape everything you have learned so far into an impressive representation of who you are, you will be ready to plunge deep into the next step of your life.

Finally, it is time to make the transition into the professional world. Don't worry. If you have done everything we have covered up until this point, you are more than prepared for it!

CHAPTER 9

TRANSITIONING TO THE WORLD OF WORK

> "It takes courage to grow up and become who you really are."
>
> — E.E.Cummings

Congratulations on reaching the final stage of this book! You are almost done with your secondary education, and it is time to turn over a new page! Now comes a time in your life when you will discover the endless possibilities of job professions.

Soon enough, you will have a crisp degree in your hand and a head filled with knowledge and useful information. After a successful secondary education, it is time to continue your learning process through another channel – work.

In this process, you become yourself. Now, learn how to utilize all available tools and make the most out of your working experience.

Job Searching Techniques and Strategies

There is a difference in approach every time someone thinks of a job opportunity. Some people create opportunities and grasp them with both hands. Others have a more laid-back approach and wait to see when a new job opportunity opens up. Both methods are good, but it is time to think about which group you belong to more. Are you proactive about it or are you more passive?

My advice is – to be the former instead of the latter. Yes, you can still wait for an opportunity to open up, and you will meet it with arms wide open, but in the meantime, why not put some effort into it?

There are many aspects to consider as soon as you start looking for a job. Approach the situation from any angle – see that you have made the right connections. Make sure you've undergone all the extra training and academies, and mentally prepare for when that day comes – and you are employed.

I am talking about strategies and techniques. There are multiple ways of how you can approach the job market, and some of them are known to be very effective. As soon as you spot a job opening, thoroughly evaluate it before applying for it. For those who still need a nudge in the right direction, here is a detailed list of what you can do.

1. Make a Selection

Once you get out of school, you might become overwhelmed with all the possibilities out there. This is where you need to make a selection. Review all the open options and only apply to those that made the cut. How to make the proper selection? That's easy – all you need is to ensure the job opportunity aligns with your skills and interests.

2. Digital Footprint

The digital presence is the first thing your future employer will look at. Even though, for almost every vacancy out there, you need to send out a resume and a cover letter (sometimes even a portfolio), they are bound to Google you. Your online presence is what leaves a first impression long before they contact you for an interview.

Teenagers nowadays rule the social media platform, so why not use it to your advantage? Create a profile on a job-related social media platform (such as LinkedIn) and showcase yourself as a strong candidate.

You can even take an extra step. Depending on the field you are interested in, you can create your website and show your area of expertise. Think of it as the extracurricular activity that will set you apart. Through your digital footprint, you let your employer know your area of expertise, skillset, and work.

> A tip for those just entering the workforce: for example, if you are a graphic designer – pick a few subjects and make a few templates. This is a great way to show your abilities and provide the employer with a portfolio.

3. A Specific Set of Skills

The job you will apply for will require a specific set of skills. This is why you should constantly tailor your application. Many companies out there need a particular level of expertise and knowledge, so when applying, let them know you have it. Re-evaluate your skills each time and accentuate the ones that are of the most significant importance for the vacancy. Visit the company website and see what they focus on and what they promote. You may even find another opening for a job that suits you better!

4. Referrals Are a Power Tool

As long as you remember this, you are good to go! Until now, you must have done a plateau of extra activities, including internships or part-time jobs. Ask for a referral because you are more likely to get hired for the job of your dreams once your future employer sees that you have done very well before. You can even get a letter of recommendation. This is the additional step you take toward achieving your career goal. It works like a charm!

Making a career move can be easy if you know how to use all the tools at your disposal properly. And, while we are on the subject of tools, we talked about building your resume. Did you manage to create one that would capture the attention of your future employer?

If not, the next section is dedicated to all the details that make up a successful resume and cover letter.

Crafting a Compelling Resume and Cover Letter

You may be good at many things, but writing is not one of them. The thought of sitting in front of your laptop and writing a resume and a cover letter scares you. Yet, you know that getting the job you want is right there at your fingertips. All you need to do is create a compelling cover letter and resume.

There is a certain importance to the application you send when applying for a job opening. These documents are a representation of who you are. Naturally, you want to make yours so good that they accentuate you as the best candidate. Every young professional should implement this. But gathering and writing down all your knowledge and qualifications is not enough.

So now, you sit in front of a blank page and ask yourself – how to create a successful professional resume that captures the essence of who I am?

Here is how.

Resume – it is a vessel through which you can prove you have the knowledge, skills, and expertise to tackle any challenge that comes your way. The moment you start writing your resume, you stop being a student and become a young professional. Present yourself in that light. Add all your relevant educational achievements to the position you are applying for (remember, I mentioned earlier that you need to tailor your application documents to the vacancy).

It is all about including relevant information. However, there are a few steps that are a must. Maximize the power of your resume by adding accurate information. Start by including your contact info (email, telephone number, etc.). Let your employers know that they can contact you at any time. Also, the beginning of a resume should include a summary. It can be short, only a few sentences, but make them count. Highlight your achievements that are related to the job you're applying for.

Working your way down, you should add your educational accomplishments (chronologically) and your work experience. The chronological order will reveal your age, so you can include any internships, part-time jobs, volunteering – anything you have done to accentuate your skills.

Next stop, you have the technical and transferable skills. Accentuate them. Let your future employer know you hold all relevant knowledge for the position. Use active language when describing your achievements and focus on important keywords. When tailoring your resume to a specific job, use concise language. Open their website and find a few keywords. Include them in your resume.

Prioritize the content that is relevant to the vacancy. You can exclude anything unrelated to the job you are applying for. Finally, proofread, and you're done!

Cover letter – the thing about a cover letter is that it should read like an essay, but it should be brief and to the point. A cover letter is not more than half a page, and it should speak directly to your employer about how your set of skills applies to the job you are applying for.

I advise you to avoid any fluff content. Instead of talking about what you want to achieve and how unique and original you are, talk about how you can use your skills to excel at the job. The cover letter should let your employer know you are a terrific hire. Here is how you can do that.

First off, you can use a cover letter template, but write a new cover letter each time you apply for a new job. Tailor it to the organization or company you're applying to and avoid being generic about it. At the very beginning, address the cover letter to the hiring manager. Using "to whom it may concern" or "dear Sir or Madam" does not show that you are very interested in the job, so avoid these salutations.

A good opening is everything. Make the hiring manager want to know more about you by hooking them from the first line of your cover letter. Make it snappy, passionate, and witty. Also, this is a great way to include the word "why." Why are you applying for the position? Why are you the best candidate? Let them know that you have a lot to bring to the table.

With the help of your qualifications and a few strategically placed examples, show why you are the perfect candidate for the job. This is the backbone of your resume. If you have a few experiences, accentuate the ones that present you the best.

Last but not least, finish off with a bang! The last paragraph of your cover letter is your last chance to make a memorable impression, so use it wisely. Sign off with a professional and positive attitude instead of loosely selling yourself. Create an appropriate closing, and hint to a CTA (call-to-action). Oh, don't forget to sign it with your first and last name too!

As with the resume, proofread it, make the necessary corrections, and you are done.

After you've successfully drafted and sent out your application documents, you come to the waiting period. Depending on the company, this period varies from a few days to a few weeks.

This is your chance to prepare yourself for the interview.

Navigating Job Interviews and Professional Etiquette

When the waiting period is over, and you get the call that you are invited for an interview is when it all suddenly becomes real. The interview is your chance to make a good impression and learn more about the company and its people. The interview's success depends on how you prepare for it, what you say during it, and what happens after the meeting. The three stages are essential to cover. On top of that, there is the factor of professional etiquette, so let's see how you can make the most out of it.

The first stage – the preparation stage is the process that will help you execute a flawless interview. You have a goal, and that is to show that you are the perfect applicant. Practice confidence, capability, modesty, and perseverance. Shift your focus from only leaving a good impression to presenting your true self in the best light possible. Come prepared because the interviewer can ask you some tricky questions. Know how to let them know your weak points but point out how you are working to improve them. Practice how to answer every question they have skillfully.

When I said to come prepared, that meant you should have a question for them too. Browse through their online presence and see what they are all about. If their vision and mission seem unclear, ask them what it is. It would help clear the air right from the start and leave a long-lasting impression that you are genuinely interested in the vacant position.

Work on your body language too. Remember to be polite with everyone you meet and have professional yet natural and open body language. Practice how to keep your back straight and your head up.

The second stage – the second stage is what happens during the interview. Leaving a good impression is important, so I advise you to show up on time (that means at least 10 minutes early). Through this, you show your interviewer that you respect their time and appreciate the time they've taken from their busy schedule to fit you in. Let the professional attitude shine through, both inside and out. Dress appropriately, showing that you are ready for a successful start. Right before you enter the room, turn off your phone – you should have a smooth interview without any interruptions.

Take your portfolio with you (if needed). For those job options where you have to present a summary of your work, take your portfolio with you. It shows the recruiter that you are more than prepared. Use a pleasant and positive greeting and begin. During the course of the interview, be a good listener and answer all of their questions. Allow them to finish their trail of thought and show that you can be an excellent team player.

Table manners are everything, so if your employer is conducting an interview with you over a meal, then remember the basic table manners and refrain from any alcoholic beverages.

The third stage – the interview is coming to a close, and everything went as smoothly as you expected. You have made an excellent connection with your interviewer, and now you want to express your gratitude for this opportunity. Follow up with an email and wrap up the entire experience with a positive attitude. Even though this is a small detail, it will make you more memorable than anyone else. On top of it, it says plenty about your personality and accentuates your attention to detail.

Having professional etiquette and working your way through a job interview takes a lot of work. There are many aspects to consider and look out for – curveballs are everywhere. Thankfully, with my help, you can easily overcome any challenge that stands in your way.

Embracing Continuous Professional Development

Continuous work and self-development are the only ways to keep thriving in a constantly developing professional landscape. Things evolve as quickly as possible, leaving almost no chance for workers and employers to adapt. In such an environment, it is of absolute importance to keep refreshing your skillset and elevating your experience.

That is when Continuous Professional Development takes the floor. Also known as CPD. This is a program that is specifically designed to offer benefits to everyone who is a part of the workforce. As a young individual, fresh to the job market and ready to learn, CPD provides the best benefits to help you reach higher ground in your career. The best thing about it is that you can constantly upgrade yourself through the program!

The fast advancements in the professional world mean you should be ready to improve within minutes of entering the workforce. That is why you should focus a little bit on the CPD. Once you start taking an active part, you will see how your skillset will be constantly refreshed.

Do you know what you gain through a CPD? You put a little bit of effort and time into sharpening your skills, but you come out the other end like a winner! During a short period, you have the unique chance to work on specific skills you need to hone (or learn from scratch) and advance in your chosen field. Continuous professional development acts as a platform through which you are given a safe space to learn, develop, and improve.

The main goal of a CPD is gaining a wider palette of skill sets that will ensure the profession of your career. However, it comes with many other benefits.

- You keep up with the latest trends. There are constantly new trends out there, with the latest one being working from home. The norms change from one day to the next, thus creating the need to adapt. An increase in following the working trends has developed a sense of reason, community, and the demand for a CPD.
- You create a higher value for the profession. Take up a part in a CPD that is all about your profession and see how much you are missing out on. The constant development (especially if it is a field connected to technology) requires someone who keeps up – so be a step ahead!
- A boost in morale is always appreciated. CPD holds the power to make you more effective in the workplace. Through the program, you can open the door to career advancement and finally utilize your leadership skills.
- Refresh your memory as to why you chose this career in the first place. Even as a young person, you may find yourself in a dull position with only a few years of working experience under your belt. Enroll in a CPD program and refresh your interest in your role.

It is all about staying ahead of the curve and making yourself relevant. Enrolling in CPD programs and courses is the best way to do that. Look at it as the indispensable tool that will grow your career and expand it in every direction. Make yourself the best lifelong learner, unlock your hidden potential, and remain relevant in a dynamic environment.

A high level of responsibility comes with taking up a new job. Becoming a part of the workforce has never been easier and more challenging at the same time. But, despite that, you have grown so much and developed in unimaginative ways during these chapters. This was the final chapter – the cherry on top – that helped shape you into the strong professional of tomorrow!

CONCLUSION

> "The only person who is educated is the one who has learned how to learn and change."
>
> — *Carl Rogers*

Change is an unavoidable part of life. It is the only constant thing in this life. My dear reader, my lovely teenager, you have come a long way since you started reading this book. Evolving from being a high school student to becoming an active participant in the community falls under the category of the largest shift in life – ever.

If you are still unaware of what you have done, why not look back and review the road you've traveled? After all, you have been focusing on completing the milestones one by one. Whenever this happens, every human is bound to pay attention to the task at hand, not noticing the change that happens all around.

As a teenager, so far, you have been exposed to a limited number of experiences. All of them have been great, and most have also provided a lesson you'll need in the future. But, after completing all the exercises we worked on together, you should have a clear path about how to proceed in life.

You started with your interests and your skills. You also unraveled some of the most important dilemmas of a teenager. It takes a lot of courage and self-reflection to find out the answers to questions about your future self. No wonder many of you may have even been scared about taking the next step of discovering yourself. Some of you may not have had any idea how to proceed. After all, preparing for your future career and exploring all the possibilities can be a confusing time. But thankfully, you have come out the other side shining through!

The most important thing you have extracted from your journey to discovering your future career path is reflection. Thinking twice before taking a step in any direction is better than aimlessly wandering back and forth. You learned how to harness and direct your energy toward something important to you, toward a field you'd thrive in.

Thanks to this book, you did not lose sight of all that is important to you.

Through careful planning and a few conveniently placed steps, you managed to build the future you. Now, who do you see when you look at yourself in the mirror? Do you see an accomplished individual ready to take on everyday challenges? Do you see a person who is more than capable of tackling a situation and completing tasks with flying colors? Here's to hoping for a positive answer, but either way, you have done an amazing job.

From reflecting upon your character, your strongest and weakest traits, to working toward creating a bulletproof resume, even to exploring the career options and researching the market of tomorrow – that is all you need to do to find out what you want to be.

But, most importantly, you learned two things.

The first one is pinpointing all the weaker spots using deep self-reflection. You have learned how to be honest with yourself because only a truthful approach can help you unlock your full potential. After making many lists with your interests, goals, and skills, you have learned how to differentiate them. Also, you learned how to rate them and how to improve them. You have even discovered the power of lifelong learning – something that can help you become a professional in any field you choose!

The second one is discovering what is good for you and properly researching the job market to get there. What you might not have been aware of up to this point is that exploring career options and analyzing the market in a way where it could provide some valuable information to you is difficult. Through this book, you learned how to do that with ease. Whether it was a traditional or a non-traditional approach, you marvelously tackled the act of gathering info on many industries. It is one of the greatest skills you will ever develop!

Remember, you did a lot of planning - and a lot of research too. You worked on yourself as hard as you could. Now, it is time to dive deep into the professional world.

There is one last lesson to be learned here. Throughout the book, I continuously mentioned that you need to put your dreams and needs first. Whichever path you choose to walk in life, make sure it is one you have chosen yourself. Even though you might need to manage your expectations as things unravel, I strongly advise you never to give up on your dreams.

Writing this book, even though it is filled with many logical steps and instructions, still has a very important undernote – believe in yourself and work to achieve your dreams! It would be my greatest pleasure if you use all the steps, I included here to get the career of your dreams. Manage your expectations but try to exceed them every time! At the end of the day, it is all about obtaining the career of your dreams! It is where you can make a difference! Become a part of a field that has always been your passion. That is why, throughout this book, I have constantly mentioned your beliefs and goals and their high significance. Because, in many ways, your uniqueness and all your talents make you a valuable part of this world. You need to utilize them to make the most out of it and bring some positive change into something important to you.

At last, you will feel a sense of completion – the work you've done to get to where you are right now is only a starting point, but it is still so much! Hopefully, I have helped you learn how to pursue whatever makes you feel satisfied and happy.

So go out there and start serving your purpose – I am confident you will always thrive.

EMILY CARTER

SELF-REGULATION WORKBOOK
for Teens

Coping Skills and CBT Exercises for Teens to Improve Self-Control, Master Emotions, Resist Impulsive Behavior, and Uplift Yourself When Feeling Down

INTRODUCTION

"Rule your mind or it will rule you." – Horace

Sounds like a pretty powerful saying, doesn't it? But it seems like lately, all you ever do is let go. You let go of the things that surround you; you let go of every aspect of you; you let go of your thoughts and let them wander around. You notice they're reaching places you don't really want to go, but you go there anyway.

But you've been doing this for a while. In the beginning, it didn't seem like such a scary thing to indulge in. Now, it looks like you've completely changed yourself. When you look in the mirror, you are unrecognizable – and not just physically, but emotionally and mentally too. What happened? When did you decide to hand over control over yourself completely to your mind? In retrospect, was it a good idea?

Go back to the saying, "Rule your mind, or it will rule you." Think about this for a moment. Is it really a good idea to hand everything over to your mind? I mean, it is your most powerful tool, so why not give full control to it?

But you already know the answer to this question. Do you know how I know that? Because you already gave full permission to your mind, and you noticed that it led you astray. It started going to the deepest and darkest corners, ultimately dragging you along. And you were never able to escape from its claws. You succumbed to its power, and now you feel helpless. You are stuck in a vortex of unpredictable behavior and negative thoughts. Of course, you want to step away from that – who wouldn't?

I welcome you to the beginning of the most magnificent and transformative journey you will ever walk on. There is only one project in life you will constantly need to work on – and that is yourself. I am assuming you picked up this book because somewhere deep inside you, you noticed that a change should happen. You notice how incredible you can be and that something is holding you back. That something is yourself and yourself only.

My name is Emily, and I am so glad you allowed me to be a part of your transformative journey. Over the course of these pages, I will try to transfer some of my passion for helping others to you. I have taken most of the examples, exercises, and basically everything in this book from my personal experience. Noticing that there was a gap in my life skills later in life made me realize that I had missed out on plenty. So, while I managed to learn everything I wanted and came out on the other side swinging, I still wanted to help others.

That's how this book came to be. Without giving it much thought, I sat down and started writing. I implemented everything I did and created such a bullet-proof plan that you are hardly ever challenged to make a mistake. What helped me the most during my personal journey was the Cognitive Behavioral Therapy (CBT) approach – which is the book's main topic.

Together, we will explore the CBT method, how it can help you, and how it can be the pillar upon which you will build your self-regulation goals. Whenever you felt like you needed help understanding your thoughts, feelings, and behavior, there was no one to help you – until now! Together, we will cover so much – how to identify and challenge your negative thinking patterns, how to tap within yourself and create balanced and realistic thoughts, and how to focus on building yourself up through the power of positive self-talk.

On top of that, I even touch upon the most well-known CBT behavioral techniques. As you turn the pages, you will discover them, and the best thing about them is that you can try them on your own!

How so? I have meticulously added exercises in almost every chapter. While these are small, their impact will be of great benefit to you. They will help you understand better what is written on these pages and help you to understand yourself better. This book is all about being assertive, being smart, developing the best coping skills, and understanding the core of who you are. It is about learning, constantly developing, and working on yourself. For without work, there is no change.

Last but not least, I dedicate the last chapter to you for all of you who are still doubting that this book has the power to change your life. It is all about preventing yourself from entering that swirl of negativity you're so desperately trying to get out of. It is the cherry on top of everything you will learn while reading this book!

I truly hope that what you find between these pages will empower you to develop and grow into the best and brightest version of yourself!

So don't wait any longer – turn the page and allow me to help you reinvent yourself!

PART 01

CBT COGNITIVE TECHNIQUES

CHAPTER 01

INTRODUCTION TO COGNITIVE BEHAVIORAL THERAPY (CBT)

"You have the power over your mind – not outside events. Realize this, and you will find strength." – Marcus Aurelius

Well, you're here, at the beginning of your journey, desperately trying to control everything around you – and yourself. If you have picked this book up, it probably means that you truly are struggling to find your way in this chaotic world.

I am here to tell you that it is okay – it is okay to feel what you're feeling. It is okay to think what you're thinking, and it is even okay to be surprised by everything new that comes your way. Whether you are dealing with some kind of an emotional issue, or you have noticed a behavioral pattern within you that you'd like to change, or maybe even some self-limited thinking, this book can be the answer to everything you're searching for.

In this chapter, together, we are going to start our journey filled with wisdom, and deep insight, and open the magical doors of cognitive behavioral therapy. Here, you will have the ultimate chance to get to know yourself and become a better version of you. Allow me to introduce CBT through a few subchapters.

The Principles of Cognitive Behavioral Therapy

Let's start from the very beginning. Do you know what cognitive behavioral therapy means? CBT is a skill-based psychotherapy treatment that can help people get in control of their feelings, thoughts, and emotions, so they can navigate through life easily. This approach can help you spot the negative influences on your mind and soul and the patterns that result in more harm than good. As a concept, CBT is time-based, goal-orientated, and a very well-structured treatment. Whether you are dealing with depression, anxiety, or any other type of disorder, this approach can help you subsequently change your view of yourself and the world.

By reframing your thoughts, you can improve your overall quality of life. So far, things sound appealing, don't they? Let's explain further. To get into the CBT scheme, you need to know the basic principles. These are considered to be more of "levels" rather than principles. Here they are:

1. **Your core beliefs** – you start from the very beginning – who are you? How do you view yourself? What do you believe in? Do you know that the core beliefs represent the strongest childhood experiences? If you look within yourself, you can discover a whole world filled with beliefs about your future, yourself, your environment, and so on. These beliefs are deeply rooted, and it is your task to uncover them.

2. **Wrong assumptions** – these types of assumptions can be very discouraging about your entire well-being. You are young, filled with energy and hope – but what you're probably not aware of

is that people generally hold on to the bad rather than the good. This type of action is classified as a cognitive distortion. Imagine having a lot of irrational thought patterns – seems like, over time, they might take over your perception of reality, right?

3. **A negative way of thinking** – which ultimately leads to overall negative perceptions of reality. After a while of succumbing to the negative patterns and thoughts, they will become your reality. You will start noticing that they have become a habit. The tricky part about them is that they are very short, and they can stir up negative emotions, making them difficult to recognize. However, don't mistake these automatic negative thoughts with the "common" negative thoughts. All of us are human beings after all, and it is only natural to have distorted thoughts* every once in a while. But, when this turns into a habit, that's when you should become alert.

*Distorted thoughts are also known as cognitive distortions. When this happens, you usually believe that one mistake defines your entire being and that the particular mistake makes you a failure. That leads to the belief that you should try to never make mistakes again. Finally, it all results in overgeneralization – thinking that you can never get something right and that things will never get better.

CBT can help you realize that you don't always have to believe in what you think. It will also help you realize that every time you are faced with a challenge, a difficult emotion, or a distortive thought, you have a choice. You can always be kinder, starting by sharing kindness with yourself, and then everything around you.

How CBT Can Benefit Teens

Let's put things into perspective here, shall we? I challenge you to a little thinking game – called action and reaction. You have probably noticed the ever-so-slight changes that happen when you have positive or negative thoughts. What changes did you notice happening (physically) whenever a distorted thought goes through your mind? In contrast, what kind of change do you notice happening when a positive thought overwhelms your mind?

Emotions affect behavior – that is something almost every teen is blissfully unaware of. Your thoughts, emotions, and behaviors are all linked. The first one is the thought – usually caused by a certain situation. The thought is your interpretation of an event. Then comes the emotion. The emotion is the second one in line, and it is triggered by what you thought of earlier on. In most cases, especially with teens, this emotion turns to the negative side. Finally, the behavior enters the scene. The negative emotions you feel influence your behavior, leading to you acting in a way you might regret later.

So, how can CBT help you prevent this negative vortex from further developing into a part of your personality?

CBT is known to have both short and long-term benefits. First, we tap into the short-term ones:

- ◆ This type of therapy shows fast results. Many psychologists and therapists use it to help young people overcome challenges in life. The average time it takes to get deeply familiarized with the CBT skillset is about 15 sessions. The alternative to that is reading carefully selected material with exercises that help you achieve your goal - this book!

- ◆ The activities you may encounter are engaging – meaning you won't have to sit and listen all the time, but rather take matters into your own hands. You get involved, and through a very interesting concept, you change yourself.

- ◆ You are held accountable for your own actions – but don't let this fool you, this is not a negative concept. You are empowered to take control of your life. You constantly apply the new principles you learn.

Together, we slowly approach the long-term benefits of CBT for teens. After a while of working on yourself, you will discover that this is an effective way to increase self-awareness and emotional intelligence – which is ultimately the path to living a healthy and happy life. As time passes, you will notice the following long-term benefits:

- You will start to respond to stress in a healthier way. Whenever you are faced with a negative thought or a challenging situation, you shift them toward a realistic or positive attitude and approach them the same way. Not letting anxiety, fears, and phobias take over is an excellent step forward.
- Being more compassionate – for some of you, this seems like a state you might never be able to achieve. Well, you couldn't be more wrong about that! You will find that compassion is within you, around you, and a constant part of your life.
- Reduce the unhealthy behavior you've indulged in for so long. The negative thoughts you had about yourself, the interactions with other people – all the situations in your life will become something you manage with skill and grace rather than tension and negativity.

With these goals in mind, it is time to look within – and learn the concept of self-regulation.

Setting Goals for Self-Regulation

Being a distressed teen can't be easy – you are constantly thinking that you live in a world where you don't belong anywhere, you allow these negative thoughts to overwhelm your mind, and it seems like you're failing each challenge you face. Keeping the weight of the world on your shoulders is not an easy job to do – and it is also not your job to do too. The sooner you realize that the easier it will be for you to move on and step into a more centered and powerful version of yourself.

What is self-regulation? It is a skill that many teens struggle to obtain at first – mostly because emotions play a big role in their lives. However, self-regulation means being able to manage your thoughts, your emotions, and your behavior, no matter what surrounds you. Having self-regulating skills can help you pull away from the emotional disturbance you've been experiencing, and it can help you navigate the tasks, challenges, and responsibilities more easily.

All of this seems good in theory, but when it comes to practice, how can you implement it?

Now, before you plunge head-first into making some severe changes in your life, you need to understand what kind of difference you want to achieve. Once you've determined who you are, where you are, and where you want to go, you can start utilizing the techniques and skills to complete your goal.

When you clearly know your starting point, setting up some goals can help you outline the path you want to walk to get there. The goals you will start developing will help you achieve the self-regulation act. For example, you can set a goal to react calmly in challenging situations – for instance, you can set a goal that your initial reaction to someone declining your invitation for a cup of coffee would be calm, centered, and respective of the others.

The process of setting goals will not be complete without your willpower, perseverance, and the understanding that those people who have managed to achieve this calm, is because they have made self-regulation their "default setting." Have you ever encountered someone so calm – be that a professor, your parent, or anyone else from your environment, that their calmness made you aware of yourself and your own behavior? Depending on one teen to the next, that kind of calm behavior can either lead to a reaction where you're embarrassed about your way of acting or it may make you want to act out. Needless to say, both situations are far from ideal.

Setting goals is a part of being proactive – and realizing that you want to possess that calmness that you have witnessed in others. You want to be powerful; you want to be in control, and you want to know how to handle yourself in every situation. With this in mind, how do you actually start setting goals? That's where I come into the picture to help.

If you could skip ahead in time where you've obtained all the knowledge and skills necessary to master self-regulation. How would your life be different from the one you're living today? Would anything change? If yes, what? Which are the first specific things that came into your mind – something that changed for the better? Are there some things you can do better than today?

Read through the first exercise below. See what you need to do and start working!

EXERCISE 1

GOAL-SETTING

In this exercise, you are going to set some goals that will allow you to start working on fully stepping into your power.

First step – write down your ultimate goals. While you are writing down your goal, make it well-defined. For example, you can write down "Become more in charge of my emotions." Consider these goals to be the changes you want to see happening to you.

Second step – add a description of each goal, and what it would mean to you to achieve it. Think of this as breaking down your goals into more specific pieces. Use a detailed description to get rid of a certain issue you've been dealing with or use that detailed description to describe your future self. As an addition to the previous example, you can be more specific about it, by saying something like, "Becoming more in charge of my emotions will mean dedicating more time to myself, learning how to be more centered, calm, etc".

Third step – start thinking about the actions you need to take to achieve these goals. These actions need to help you remain consistent and on the right track – something that can show you you're getting closer to reaching your goals. To continue with the same example, you can do the following - "Meditate each day, keep a gratitude journal, channel your energy to positive things, indulge in mindfulness exercises, etc." By making your goal specific you are actually creating a bullet-proof action plan.

Ultimately, each of your goal-setting points should look similar to the example below:

The ultimate goal: Become more in charge of my emotions.

The specific goal: Becoming more in charge of my emotions will mean dedicating more time to myself, learning how to be more centered, calm, etc.

Actions I take to make it happen: Meditate each day, keep a gratitude journal, channel my energy to positive things, indulge in mindfulness exercises, etc.

Now, go ahead and write down at least five goals of yours following the steps above:

_____

_____

_____

_____

_____

_____

_____

_____

Self-Regulation Workbook for Teens

_____

_____

_____

_____

_____

_____

_____

_____

_____

By doing this exercise you will be able to tap deep within yourself and uncover the core of your being – and that is the first step toward improvement.

Cognitive behavioral therapy can be fun – as long as there is someone like me who can guide you through the process, break everything down into smaller pieces, and show you that, as long as you keep putting one foot in front of the other (no matter the pace) you can get to your ultimate goal of being better.

What Did You Learn From This Chapter?

As a first chapter, it seemed pretty exciting, right? To sum up, here is what you learned from it:

- What is cognitive behavioral therapy.
- What are the three principles of CBT.
- Distorted thoughts and how they affect your quality of life.
- Thoughts, emotions, and behaviors are connected – they represent the cycle you are most likely trying to step out of.
- There are both long-term and short-term benefits of applying CBT in your life.
- Self-regulation – what it is and how you can use it to improve yourself.
- How to set goals for self-regulation.

Cognitive behavioral therapy is the key to creating a stronger and more powerful version of yourself. Now, over the course of this book, I will keep focusing on explaining every little detail that you might think we've overlooked. For example, take a look at what the next chapter is about! We discuss what I mentioned earlier – the process of thought, emotion, and behavior – how it affects your life and how it shapes you into an individual. Turn the page and discover all you need to know about it!

Introduction to Cognitive Behavioral Therapy (CBT)

CHAPTER 02

UNDERSTANDING THOUGHTS, FEELINGS, AND BEHAVIORS

"The happiness of your life depends upon the quality of your thoughts."
– Marcus Aurelius

Before we continue any further, I need you to realize one thing – no person is immune to life's challenges. No matter what has happened to you and how you experienced certain situations, this is something that will always leave an impact and slightly alter you. After every event that occurs, be that a positive or a negative one, the remains of the experience are what your mind deems important, and that's what's left – long after the event has finished.

But, to truly tap within yourself and uncover "what you're made of," you need to know how to do that first. As a most likely inexperienced young mind, you don't really know where to begin. While in the first chapter, we recognized the essential dots that need connecting, in this chapter, I am helping you delve deep within yourself, dissecting the very core of who you are.

The concepts we will cover together here will help you better understand your thoughts, feelings, and behaviors as well as how to manage them.

Identifying Automatic Thoughts

From the moment you wake up to the moment you fall back asleep, thousands of thoughts pass through your mind. Some are wonderful and happy and fill you with joy, while others are negative and make you feel bad. There are many reasons why this happens, especially when it comes to automatic negative thoughts.

Overall, automatic thoughts are what we think of instantly – kind of as a first response to anything that happens around us or to us. These thoughts are mostly triggered by an outside source, but how you manage them in your mind and what you connect them with is what matters. Let's talk about automatic negative thoughts.

These automatic negative thoughts happen for various reasons. For example, teens who are dealing with anxiety or mood swings are more prone to experience negative thinking. Now, don't get me wrong – the automatic negative thoughts are sometimes what helps us survive, but if this is your constant state of mind, then you need to change something. It is a way of "anticipating threats" in a way.

These automatic thoughts connected to a negative thinking pattern are usually a result of your core beliefs and previous experiences. So, your automatic thoughts are actually what you truly believe about yourself, your future, and the world around you.

With that in mind, it is time to start identifying the automatic thoughts (especially the negative ones). Most of the time, people have a difficult time doing this at first, and if that happens to you, remember that it's okay. That is why CBT can help you open doors of your mind you haven't even been aware of until now.

There is a key to identifying automatic thoughts: looking for what first comes to mind when an emotion arises. For example, you open your Instagram account, and you see that your friends got together for a cup of coffee but didn't invite you. How would that make you feel? The immediate response you have is your automatic thought. It can be positive – where you think, "Oh good, it's such a nice day, I hope they're having a good time," or negative – "They didn't invite me, I'm not wanted, nobody likes me."

Both of these responses are extreme, and any profound feeling you get is entirely understandable. But what you do with them later on is what counts the most. Let's face it – whatever comes first to mind is what you truly believe in. However, while we are on the subject of identifying the automatic thoughts, we get a true insight into who we are. It is a type of awareness and understanding of your thinking.

Becoming aware is a process where you can distance yourself from the response you may have and reevaluate yourself. You start looking for the meaning in the situation and ask yourself whether there truly is the worst part about it and what it is. For example, in the example I mentioned earlier, if you have the ability to identify your automatic thought, specifically the negative one, the response would be "What's the worst part of it?" thus tapping into the core reason why you believe you are mistreated.

Recognizing the Connection Between Thoughts, Feelings, and Behaviors

What I personally love about CBT is that it has a unique way of uncovering the connection between thoughts, feelings, and behaviors. If you haven't noticed that by now, allow me to explain – the main goal of cognitive behavior therapy is to connect the three main dots – and allow you to see the full picture about yourself.

Has it ever happened to you that you act in a specific way and keep repeating that behavior? Have you ever concluded that you constantly have the same feelings and don't know why that's so? Shedding a light on your entire mindset is good – it gets you a step closer to change.

So, if the thoughts are ideas, feelings are the emotions you get after a thought occurs, and the behavior is the action you take as a result of the feeling, they seem pretty connected to each other, right? But how?

It is all about discovering whether you keep making the same decision over and over again. Take the example above – if you have noticed your friends going out for a cup of coffee without you often, and your first response was always a negative one, then ask yourself what you're feeling. Give it a moment to identify the emotion. If you are angry, ask yourself why. Slow down with the pace and pay attention to that little voice that's talking. What's it saying? Because this voice is you talking to yourself. Whenever you notice an automatic thought, here are a few questions that can help you make the connection – thoughts, feelings, behaviors.

What are your beliefs?

What is your self-talk?

What are your values?

What do you think about the people in that particular situation?

By recognizing this, you can determine whether the thoughts are realistic or not. Maybe, just maybe, the connection you make is only based on past experiences rather than an objective point of view. The connection between thought, feeling, and behavior will always happen, but it is your job to challenge your thoughts to be objective, and evidence-based rather than relying solely on the emotions, without knowing where that will take you (and let's face it – it's usually a negative direction).

Exploring the Cognitive Triad

The cognitive triad was developed as a framework by the founder of cognitive behavioral therapy, Aaron Beck. He wanted to create this as a scheme that would allow individuals to identify a negative pattern in their behavior easily.

This triad is (as you guessed it) a triangle with three specific points. It suggests that individuals who usually experience emotional distress are often negatively viewing themselves. However, they view the world and the future negatively, too. These are the kinds of negative feelings that arise from a place of anxiety, depression, and low self-esteem. As a teenager, it is your task to identify all of them so you can develop a more positive and realistic approach to life. To make things a little bit more visual for you, here is a figure of the cognitive triad.

Here is a little example. The cognitive triad always starts with the self. In negative terms, it can represent a saying that you constantly use, such as "I'm never going to be good enough." The second corner of the triad is the views about the future. In negative terms, they can be something like "I will never achieve my goals." Finally, the last bit of the triad includes the views of the world. In negative terms, it goes something like this: "Everybody is out to get me."

While reading this, did one small part of your mind think these thoughts are most likely untrue? Did you find yourself in any of these statements? If that happens, you are on the right path to change. The cognitive triad is an excellent example of providing yourself with the mirror you need. It shows you how you have behaved so far, it shows you what your usual approach is, and it helps you become more aware of yourself and your negative thoughts.

With that in mind, I am giving you a moment to think. Notice your pattern of thoughts and actions, and then, identify the places where you believe you need improvement.

What Did You Learn From This Chapter?

Throughout this chapter, we went deep into the concept of self – once you made this realization that you are more than your thoughts and that there are a lot of dots to be connected, you learned the following:

- That there is a connection between thoughts, feelings, and behavior.
- How to identify the automatic negative thoughts.
- The automatic negative thoughts are normal, but only to a certain extent.
- Discovering that there is a connection between each part of who you are.
- Learning to challenge your thoughts whenever you notice it leads to a negative reaction.
- What is the cognitive triad, and why is it important.

Connecting the dots lifted a veil you didn't even know was there. You learned how everything within you works and that, just like the physical part (our bones are all connected), our thoughts are connected as well. I hope this made you feel a little bit better about yourself, yet you are still questioning how to solve this.

As I mentioned earlier in the chapter, negative thoughts happen all the time. Here, we recognized them and established a connection. In the next chapter, we will challenge them!

CHAPTER 03

CHALLENGING NEGATIVE THINKING PATTERNS

"Change your thoughts and you change your world." – Norman Vincent Peale

No truer words have ever been spoken. But, even with that in mind, people seem to neglect the fact that there is so much more to the act of challenging yourself. It takes great courage, persistence, and knowledge to stand up to probably the one person who gets in your way – yourself.

I have noticed, over my dedicated years of work, that teenagers are not aware of the power they hold within. As with every other adult on the planet, they also have the ability to control their thoughts. Yes, I am talking about you, too. I'm not sure whether the reason why they avoid doing this is because of fear they will fail or just plain laziness, but I am sure of one thing – you, and only you, are in charge of yourself. You are strong and capable, and after reading this chapter, you will know how to challenge negative thinking patterns.

Recognizing Cognitive Distortions

Here is the thing – you probably trust your mind too much. After all, is there anything else you can do? I mean, it is your brain at the end of the day, and it is probably right, right? Generally, it is a good idea to trust your brain. It is designed to look for your own good and find solutions or keep you away from dangers. But there are still situations where you might want to second-guess your trail of thought. Now, keep in mind here that your brain is not trying to trick you, lie to you, or deceive you; instead, it works this way as a result of developing some connections and beliefs that are not healthy.

This happens so often that it may surprise you. As I stated in the previous chapter, your thoughts, feelings, and behaviors are all connected, whether they make up for a good or a bad outcome. When the behavior is biased, that is how you define a cognitive distortion. The cognitive distortions are a representation of the irrational thoughts and beliefs that you constantly reinforce. As time passes, they become a part of who you are.

In the beginning, you may not notice them much – they are simply there – like a feature of your mind and your everyday thoughts. That is the reason why they are thought to be so damaging. You don't recognize them until they have completely taken over your mind. These cognitive distortions come in many forms, but they all result in inaccurate thinking patterns and false beliefs, and they have the potential to do some damage.

Now, it may be scary to admit this is happening to you – and that's perfectly normal. After all, you are human, and it is okay to fall under the spell of your own mind sometimes. We may all stumble occasionally, and some of us struggle with these challenges longer, and some don't. It is all about accepting the fact that some skills and abilities will only improve with practice, and they will help you become the best version of yourself. But let's not get ahead of ourselves.

To know exactly what to work on, you first need to understand how to recognize the cognitive distortions. Here is a list of the most frequent ones:

1. All or nothing – the polarized thinking also known as black-and-white thinking, where you go from one extreme to the next.
2. Overgeneralizing – the distortion where you generalize one example to an overall pattern.
3. Mental filter – focusing on the negative aspects of a situation, completely excluding the positive ones.
4. Removing the positive – a tricky situation where you acknowledge the positive aspects but completely reject them at the same time.
5. Jumping to conclusions – the inaccurate belief about what someone else is thinking, usually based on predictions without any evidence.
6. Catastrophizing – the act of stepping out of your perspective and exaggerating the meaning, likelihood, or importance of things.
7. Emotional reasoning – the realization that all of us have, at some point, experienced any one of these distortions.
8. Should statements – the statements you make about yourself and what you have to do.
9. Labeling – usually mislabeling – the tendency to go to extreme forms of overgeneralization, where you assign judgments of value to yourself and others.
10. Personalization – the situations where you take all things personally and blame yourself for no logical reason.

Recognizing cognitive distortions may seem a little scary at first, but it is all for the greater good. After helping these come to the surface, you can start implementing some techniques that can help you rewire your brain.

Techniques for Challenging and Reframing Negative Thoughts

Reframing negative thoughts may be challenging. Thankfully, there are many successful techniques that can help you achieve that. The techniques I'm about to share with you below can significantly change your overall outlook and mental well-being. Remember, the ultimate goal is not to completely remove the negative thoughts but to find a way to prevent them from overwhelming you.

1. Notice the negative thoughts. Pay attention to everything that pops into your mind. This could be anything – a situation, something about yourself, or something about other people.
2. Reflect and take a break. Identifying negative thoughts means taking a break and questioning whether your thoughts are accurate or not. This will not only lead you to the next step but will also prevent you from spiraling down into an unknown, dark maze of thoughts.
3. Think of the alternatives. When you realize that your thought is probably not true, consider other ways of viewing the situation. You can find both positive and neutral perspectives here and change your mind.
4. Replace the negative thought with a positive one. Once you pinpoint the initial negative thought, replace it with a positive or a neutral thought – and try to stick with it (mostly because it is probably the truth).
5. Stick with it. Any way that works for you is a good enough way to stick with a positive thought. You can be grateful for the work you've done that day, or you can write down your positive thoughts, or you can do any other thing that will help you feel empowered, and in control.

These techniques are amazing. When you start using them, in the beginning, it all may feel a little strange, but stick with it. After some time, you will see how helpful they are in the process of training yourself to be better.

The next exercises go into further detail on how to train your brain.

EXERCISE 2

REFRAMING NEGATIVE THOUGHTS

Let's play this exercise called, "Fact or opinion?" During this exercise, you will have to sit and read through a list of statements that you will write yourself. These statements can be anything. Try to write at least ten of them, but if you have more, feel free to write all of them down. The statements should be your own thoughts - something that constantly pops into your mind. Below are some examples to get you started.

Now, put your thoughts on trial. Next to each of the sentences, write down whether you think they are facts or just your own opinion.

I am a failure. _____

I suck at everything. _____

I am ugly. _____

I rejected a friend when they asked for my help. _____

I'm a bad person. _____

I yelled at my parents. _____

Nobody cares about me. _____

Everything will turn into a disaster. _____

I am overweight. _____

I am selfish. _____

I am not loveable. _____

I failed an exam. _____

Challenging Negative Thinking Patterns

After doing so, look at the list again. Has anything changed? Your perception of yourself maybe? Did you notice that when you step back and objectively analyze your thoughts, most of them seem like they are just your opinions, and not reality?

You can take a breath now because, after this exercise, you know everything will be okay.

Creating Balanced and Realistic Thoughts

Balanced thinking seems almost impossible to achieve. You either go for the best or the worst-case scenario, right? Wrong.

Balance is something that should be incorporated into all aspects of your life. I can understand that, as a teenager, you might have difficulty achieving that, but the sooner you start training yourself, the better results you will have. Earlier, I mentioned that a part of the cognitive distortions includes seeing things in only black or white without giving the possibility for all the colors to shine through. Well, creating balanced and realistic thoughts is just that – the ability to see beyond the black and white and enjoy life while looking at things as neutrally and realistically as possible. It is like learning how to appreciate all the colors in the spectrum for the very first time.

It may sound a little less interesting at the moment, but there is a reason behind that, too – extreme thoughts can be exciting – and they usually are, especially for young people. But if you get used to this kind of behavior and abide by the rules of the extreme, it will eventually become a part of who you are.

By thinking in the middle, you get to see all the sides of a situation – sometimes there are two sides, sometimes more, but there is always more than one side. Cognitive behavioral therapy has ensured you can incorporate an approach that is not based on assumptions to get to the bottom of your thought trail.

Think about it – the balanced way of thinking is a calm way of thinking. It will provide you with benefits such as making better decisions, an overall state of calmness, less anxiety, being able to see the bigger picture, and so much more. Oh, and also, cognitive behavioral therapy is so much more than this, but you will have to stick around for the next chapters to find out!

EXERCISE 3

CREATING BALANCED THOUGHTS

To create balanced thoughts is easier said than done – that's why this exercise focuses on just that. It is called "the friend exercise," and here is what you need to do. Whenever you are faced with a challenging situation, something that might make you want to spiral down into that negative pattern you've adopted, first, write down your opinion about the situation and then, think about one of your closest friends. If you share your opinions and thoughts with them, how would they reply? What would they say? Write that down too.

Here is how the exercise would go:

Your opinion	Your friend's reply
I am really unhappy.	Is there a particular reason for that?
Everyone's ignoring me.	Have you reached out and noticed they do?
I don't get any attention.	What's the reason you need the extra attention?
I'm a bad person.	No, you're not, you're just having a bad day.
I'm not beautiful.	You are extremely beautiful.
Nothing goes well in my life.	Not true - you have plenty of things to be thankful for.
I am stuck in a loop.	One you can always get out of by making small steps.
I will never get better.	Yes, you will, and I am here for it.
X person doesn't like me anymore.	Have you tried talking to them and clarifying?
My terrible past will create a horrible future.	Not true - you are the creator of your future.

Their feedback will most likely differ from what you think. You don't even have to really share this with your friend – as long as you do the exercise, you practice a different point of view. After a while, you will realize that it is not so difficult to have several points of view about a certain thing – and the freedom to choose the most positive one.

Your thoughts are not always part of reality. Sometimes, the picture they paint in your mind differs from the truth – a lot. That's why this chapter focused on that – showing you how wonderful of a thing it is to have a few different opinions and the best ways to train your brain to look for the more positive in every aspect of life.

What Did You Learn From This Chapter?
- ✧ All the power you need to change is something you already hold within.
- ✧ Cognitive distortions are all around you; it is time to learn how to recognize them.
- ✧ A list of the most common cognitive distortions.
- ✧ Negative thoughts can be managed with a few well-utilized techniques.
- ✧ The realization that thoughts can be balanced.

At the end of the day, the sole reason why you picked up this book and decided to make it your ultimate guide toward change is because you want to be better. Once you figure out how to challenge your thoughts, it is time to put that work to some good use, don't you think?

In the following chapter, I will discuss how you can make more out of your trail of thoughts and influence them in a way that will lead to some spectacularly positive thinking – ultimately challenging yourself to improve your entire life.

Shall we? After you.

CHAPTER 04

BUILDING POSITIVE SELF-TALK

"It isn't what you have, or who you are, or where you are, or what you are doing that makes you happy or unhappy. It is what you think about." – Dale Carnegie

It takes some people a long time after they are born to realize that to be happy, you just need to be. It seems like the most essential things in life are also the most difficult ones to figure out. So, I understand where you are coming from. However difficult it may be to explain it, there is a certain lightness of being when you reach that state of positivity in your life. But to get there, you need to walk the path of building and realization.

In this chapter, we will commence our journey through the magnificence of indulging in positive self-talk together. Bear with me; it's not impossible to achieve, and if you think it is, allow me to change your mind.

Importance of Positive Self-Talk

There is something called "inner voice." This is a voice that only you can hear, and it is a way of talking to yourself. In many cases, you might not even be aware that you're doing it, but you still do it. This is a voice that combines your beliefs and thoughts and creates a sort of "internal monologue" that you "hear" during the day. As a concept, self-talk is a powerful thing because it has a big impact on who you are and how you feel. By underlining this, you realize its importance – ultimately knowing that it will either be a positive thing, something that will lift you, be supportive and beneficial, or turn into a negative thing and completely undermine your confidence.

Self-talk has a great impact on your mental health – the way you see yourself, and the way you view the world (the triad that I mentioned before). But the thing is, this can quickly turn for the worse if you don't know how to focus on the positive.

Negative self-talk can have a significant impact on your health overall – from chronic pain to affecting your confidence and creating a distorted body image; negative self-talk has many consequences. That is why we are solely focusing on the positive. The importance of positive self-talk comes from the fact that the benefits are – you guessed it, plenty. Here is only a handful of them:

- Improved self-esteem and overall wellbeing.
- Improved body image and less stress.
- Motivates you enough to overcome any challenges or obstacles.
- Reduces the symptoms of personality disorders, anxiety, and depression.
- Helps you feel in control of your life.
- Calms you down.
- Diminishes chronic pain.

Now, it sounds like something you want to try, right? We are headed toward the next exercise; take a look below.

EXERCISE 4

PRACTICING POSITIVE SELF-TALK

Most people (especially the young ones) believe that practicing positive self-talk only limits your exposure to negativity. That is, to a certain extent, correct, but there is a lot more you can do in this situation. In this exercise, I am going to accentuate the power of self-care. I know self-care is something you see everywhere around you these days, especially because it is the talk of the town on social media. But have you ever stopped and wondered why that is so? Social media has a certain power; however, it is still not that great for many people. Nevertheless, the reach you can have with it makes up for a positive stamp you can leave in someone else's life. If you can do that, change the life of even one person for the better, why not try?

Now, let's see the exercise. I mentioned we're going to focus on self-care. The first thing you need to do is give yourself a small amount of time. Yes, start as small as possible – 5 minutes or 10 minutes of your day are enough to create a habit. Within this timeframe, do something for yourself. This is not a selfish act but rather a much-needed one. Engage in something that will lift your spirits and rejuvenate your entire well-being.

I can understand how the options may be plenty in this case, and viewing all of them may make you feel stuck rather than determined, so let's start from the beginning. Here are a few things you can do throughout your day:

- A little bit of physical activity.
- Focusing on a hobby of yours (painting, writing, cooking, etc.).
- Reading a book.
- Preparing a meal for yourself.
- Indulging in mindfulness meditation.

After doing any activity, the self-care bit comes later on. Take out a pen and write down three things that you liked about it below. These can be three good things you felt or thought, or whether the activity you engaged in put a smile on your face, made you forget about the time, etc.

The Activity _____

The Three Things I liked About It:

01. _____
02. _____
03. _____

The Activity _____

The Three Things I liked About It:

> 01. _____
> 02. _____
> 03. _____

The Activity _____

The Three Things I liked About It:

> 01. _____
> 02. _____
> 03. _____

The Activity _____

The Three Things I liked About It:

> 01. _____
> 02. _____
> 03. _____

The Activity _____

The Three Things I liked About It:

> 01. _____
> 02. _____
> 03. _____

The Activity _____

The Three Things I liked About It:

01. _____
02. _____
03. _____

The Activity _____

The Three Things I liked About It:

01. _____
02. _____
03. _____

The Activity _____

The Three Things I liked About It:

01. _____
02. _____
03. _____

The Activity _____

The Three Things I liked About It:

01. _____
02. _____
03. _____

The Activity

The Three Things I liked About It:

```
01. _____
02. _____
03. _____
```

The beauty of this exercise will come only if you are persistent. You won't notice an immediate difference, but after a while of indulging in this exercise, you will start noticing that positive self-talk is your "default setting." It is something your mind immediately jumps to, and it will help you train your brain to think in a healthier and stronger direction.

Identifying and Challenging Negative Self-Talk

I only scraped the surface on the topic of negative self-talk earlier. As a young mind, before we begin, what you need to understand is that negative self-talk is a part of being human. Just like positive self-talk can boost your productivity, improve your mood, and make you happier, negative self-talk has its consequences, too. It can diminish your self-confidence, it can lead to self-blame, and tear down your emotional well-being.

It is your responsibility to find the difference between having negative self-talk every once in a while, and constantly indulging in this pattern. Spotting the difference between the two is the first step toward making a change. It means you have identified the negative self-talk – and the second step is to dismiss it.

EXERCISE 5

CHALLENGE THE NEGATIVE SELF-TALK

That leads us to this next exercise. I know that you want to make a change for the better. I know that you want to challenge yourself, your views, and the core of your beliefs. And in this exercise, that is exactly what you're going to do.

All of us are constantly met with negative thoughts during the day. These thoughts are either about yourself or your environment. But most of these usually pass after a minute or two. This is the correct way to deal with negative self-talk – acknowledge it, let it pass, and do not dwell on it. Once you notice that you are doing the exact opposite, turn to this exercise for help.

Here is what you're going to do.

Every time you notice that your mind is setting on a negative thought, and you find your inner voice saying, "You're not good enough," challenge that negative self-talk with positive self-talk. Keep doing this because persistence is a must for all change to occur.

There are many good things you can tell yourself, contrary to the negative belief that keeps popping up in your mind. Here are just a handful of statements for you to repeat each time you are faced with a negative self-talk pattern:

I will do my best.
I am good at this, and I can do it.
I will be well, and I will do well.
I am good enough.
I am happy, and everything is going well for me.

Below, you can find rows where you can write down your negative self-talk, and the positive self-talk you used to challenge it. Writing them down will significantly boost your progress.

Negative Self-Talk   Positive Self-Talk

_____   _____
_____   _____
_____   _____
_____   _____
_____   _____
_____   _____
_____   _____
_____   _____
_____   _____
_____   _____
_____   _____

Developing Affirmations and Positive Coping Statements

You have probably already noticed this – we are trying to create a positive mindset and cultivate mindfulness and happiness overall. Yes, there will be such things as bad days, but it is your responsibility to prevent them from ruling your life. Affirmations and positive coping statements are more than just a way to help you cope with a stressful situation or improve your mood. It can boost your self-esteem, it can help you look on the bright side of life, and most importantly, decrease negative thinking.

By using these affirmations and statements every day, you can work toward achieving the goals you have set for yourself and work on your overall personal development and growth. All of them are helpful every time you feel insecure or worried or when you need a little push. I know it sounds strange to talk about affirmations at the moment; it may even sound silly to some of you, but that is exactly why you should try them.

Many people undermine the power of affirmations because they seem "too easy." Well, if they are too easy, why not give them a try? Positive thinking has always been effective and beneficial for improving alertness and mindset and effectively coping with every curveball life throws at you.

The idea is – when you constantly repeat these to yourself – whether they are about your body, your mind, your relationship with yourself, your environment, etc, they will become engraved in your mind. After a while, you will truly start believing them and, as a result of that, think more positively.

Not quite sure how to make that happen? I prepared two exercises below so you can differentiate between affirmations and positive coping statements so that you can learn how to implement both of them in your life.

EXERCISE 6

AFFIRMATIONS

This exercise comes in the form of journaling. While you may not be up to the idea at first, hear me out. When you put pen to paper and write down your affirmations, it will seem like they have taken a certain shape, like they make sense, that there is truth to them. That is why this exercise is an extremely powerful one.

Your first step is to take out a pen (and a notebook if you prefer writing to it rather than to the lines below). Then, you are going to choose some affirmations that "make sense" to you or some affirmations you'd like to embed in your mind. You can find some affirmations either in books or online, or you can come up with them yourself. To get you started, here are a few:

I am strong, and I always attract positivity.

I can heal, and I can only attract healthy things into my life.

I am grateful for everything in my life right now.

I am kind, and I am enough.

I see the beauty that lies within me.

I create my own future.

Only good things will happen to me.

Keep writing these affirmations – either one in a day or all of them (depending on how you feel). After some time, you will notice that your self-talk will consist of plenty of affirmations that instantly put a smile on your face.

EXERCISE 7

POSITIVE COPING STATEMENTS

This next exercise is all about focusing on positive coping statements. These are the ones that you can use every time you feel sad or down, something that will help you cope with difficult times. The difference between the previous exercise and this one is in the approach – because basically, you do the same thing – repeat positive things to yourself. But, in the previous exercise, the idea is that you approach affirmations with a neutral mindset. Here, with positive coping statements, you approach the exercise because you have noticed a negative pattern of thoughts in your mind (usually caused by an external event).

So, here is what you need to do. We have all been there – a stressful situation creating a chain of negative self-talk, and whether it is a mild or a severe reaction, it still needs to come to an end. That is when the coping mechanisms come into play. When you are faced with this kind of situation, you can remember and repeat one (or a few) of the following positive coping statements:

This is not final; it will pass.

Stop, give yourself a minute, breathe – because you can do this.

Even if I am feeling angry, I can still deal with this.

Feeling bad is a normal reaction, but I will allow it to wash over me and pass.

It is something I have done before, and I will do it again.

It will not last forever.

I don't need to rush. I can take things slowly.

My mind is not always my friend.

I feel this way because of past experiences, but I should feel okay now.

Building Positive Self-Talk

I am stronger than I think.

―――o―◇―o―――

I learn from experiences, and I see every challenge as an opportunity.

―――o―◇―o―――

Things will be easier next time.

―――o―◇―o―――

Repeating these statements to yourself each time you are faced with a challenging situation can help you easily move forward and cope with whatever comes your way in a healthier way.

What Did You Learn From This Chapter?

Having to learn a lot about positive self-talk means tapping into the core of who you are and realizing that you have a good side – something light and happy to accentuate. With that in mind, here is an overview of what you learned in this chapter:

- ✧ What is self-talk, and what is the importance of positive self-talk.
- ✧ What is negative self-talk, how to identify it, and what it can do to you long-term.
- ✧ What are affirmations and positive coping statements, and why they are important.

Positive self-talk is the pillar to creating a better and stronger you. This chapter was filled with enlightenment and richness, and it may have even put a smile on your face. However, deep down, you still feel like you can't do this... like you need something more to make this happen and change your life for the better. It seems like the catalyst you're looking for to start this process is still lost.

That's what the next chapter is all about – the catalyst you are looking for is called acceptance, and it is one you need to work on before you continue your journey through the magnificence that cognitive behavioral therapy brings. You have me by your side every step of the way, so don't even try to get discouraged! Instead, turn the page, and let's start working on that together!

CHAPTER 05

MINDFULNESS AND ACCEPTANCE

"The curious paradox is that when I accept myself just as I am, then I can change."
– Carl Rogers

When it comes to mindfulness, the beginning is always the most challenging part of it. Somehow, it seems like being present at the moment is both the easiest and the most challenging thing to do. To tell you the truth, almost everything in this book will initially feel that way. But that should not stop you from going after what you want to achieve.

Since this is the chapter where you might have the most questions, I decided to focus it on practice rather than theory – because sometimes, the best way to learn is through exercise. It is time to focus on mindfulness and acceptance.

Introduction to Mindfulness

Allow me to start answering all of your questions in this first bit. Let's start with the easiest thing – do you know what mindfulness is?

Mindfulness is the ability of an individual to be fully present and aware of the moment, where they are going, what they are doing, and refrain from being overly reactive or overwhelmed by the surroundings. Usually, mindfulness is something that everyone possesses naturally, but some people have a better grip on it than others. Do you know why that is so? It's because these people practice it daily. Now comes another question – how do you practice mindfulness daily? What can it do to make your life better?

When you bring mindfulness into your life, you start feeling it through all your senses. Mindfulness is a state of mind through which you can wake up the emotional, mental, and physical processes within you. It is available to you at all given moments; all you need to do is pause, breathe, and allow it to settle in.

There are many mindfulness techniques you can try. By utilizing the techniques below, you can improve your mental clarity and stray as far away from anxiety and negative thought patterns as possible. Some of them may seem a little strange to do at first but trust me on this one – you will find that all of them are successful in the end. But before we go directly into the techniques, let's talk a little bit about acceptance and non-judgemental awareness.

Cultivating Acceptance and Non-Judgemental Awareness

Cultivating acceptance and non-judgemental awareness is not particularly a different subject in itself but rather another aspect of mindfulness. Now, let's take things a step back. We live in a world where jumping to conclusions and judgments happens all around us. The practice of non-judgemental awareness and acceptance seems to fade away slowly. Instead of being the norm, it has become the exception to the rule. That is why it is of utmost importance to explore the significance of being calmer and centered and approach everything in life with less judgment and a more accepting mindset.

To understand non-judgment, you first need to understand the nature of judgment. This is a cognitive process through which you classify, estimate, and then form opinions about yourself, other people, ideas, situations, etc. The way you do that is through your core beliefs and morals. Judgment is a natural part of being a human, but it can easily turn into an issue when you are using too much of it.

Contrary to that, we have non-judgment. Cultivating this can help you view situations and events from multiple perspectives. When you remove judgment from the equation, you provide space for empathy and a deeper understanding. This process promotes effective communication and a healthier way of dealing with everything that happens around you.

But the best part about it by far is enhancing growth and moving in a positive direction. Approaching yourself and the people around you with acceptance and non-judgment means creating a new terrain to walk on – a terrain of growth. This means allowing yourself to move past your vulnerabilities, insecurities, and mistakes and then fostering a mindset that focuses on development and freedom of expression.

All of this may sound like the best thing you can do, but none of it would be possible without using these practical strategies and the exercises below. Let's go over the strategies together before moving on to the exercises.

1. Try to cultivate mindfulness. As I mentioned at the beginning of this chapter, mindfulness is the practice of being completely present in the moment – but you need to achieve that without any judgment. This way, you can reflect and choose a better and calmer response.

2. Challenge your opinion every time – especially if it is a hypothetical one. Judgment is often based on limited information, so every time you find yourself in this situation, challenge your thoughts. Seek out a different perspective, have an open dialogue with different people, and be open to changing your mind and broadening your horizons.

3. Empathy is key. This shows the ability to understand the people around you without immediately turning to judgment. You put yourself in their shoes, and you show genuine compassion.

4. You avoid using stereotypes – about yourself and the people around you. Stereotypes are conceptions (or misconceptions) about a certain individual based on a larger group of people. Stereotypes can limit your understanding and lead to judgment rather than acceptance.

5. Reflecting upon your past self is like challenging your beliefs, impulses, and judgments. See how your behavior history has developed and what you want to change about it. By examining your own impulses, you can work toward creating a less judgmental approach.

6. Indulge in non-comparison. You don't need comparison in your life. Not because it frequently leads to judgments but because it is an arbitrary way of examining yourself. Instead of comparing yourself to others, why not concentrate on your growth? You will get a lot more out of it by doing so.

EXERCISE 8

FIVE SENSES MINDFULNESS

We are starting with the exercises, with the five senses of mindfulness being the first one. As an exercise, it has proven to be incredibly helpful, especially in cases when you want to completely feel like you are present at the moment. This is a practical way to practice mindfulness fast in any situation. All you need to do is follow the instructions. Here they are:

5 Notice five things you can see. Take a good look at your surroundings and bring to your attention five things that you can see. Out of everything that you see, choose something that you normally wouldn't pick.

4 Notice four things you can feel. No matter what your surroundings look like, try to find four things you can feel. This can be anything from the texture of your clothes to the surface of a chair, a table, a sofa, or anything you can find.

3 Notice three things you can hear. Take a moment to shut down all your other senses and notice three things you can hear. These, too, can be anything that surrounds you – from the traffic outside on the street to the birds chirping, to a clock ticking, to someone talking loudly in the background, to the sound of the rain.

2 Notice two things you can smell. This is an important one, as it needs a lot of concentration. No matter what is inside the room, you need to isolate the other senses and focus on the things you can smell – be these pleasant or unpleasant smells. Maybe it's a nice perfume, maybe it's the food from the next room, maybe it's the smell of the rain.

1 Notice one thing you can taste. This is when you can go for the food you've smelled a few minutes earlier. If that is not the case, focus on anything else you can taste – a beverage, a taste in your mouth, a piece of gum – anything.

This is a very easy way to achieve a state of mindfulness. You don't need a lot of time to do it, but you can still be aware of yourself and the current moment.

EXERCISE 9

BODY SCAN MEDITATION

This exercise is like doing an x-ray on your entire body. Get started and sit in a comfortable position. Focus on that, and then shift your focus to your breath. Notice the sensation you have each time your lungs fill with air and each time you exhale. Then, choose one part of the body from which you can start. It can be either the top of your head or the bottom of your body (left or right foot). Be careful, pay attention, and focus on that particular spot. Spend about 20 seconds to a minute focusing on that particular spot before you move on to the next part of your body. Acknowledge the sensation that is happening when you focus on each individual part, and don't forget to breathe in and out through each step in the process. The deep breaths can help you relax and release the tension in your mind and body.

During this exercise, it is okay for your mind to drift a little. Notice that, and when it happens, slowly return your thoughts and focus to the present moment. Remember, if this happens, you haven't failed or anything because you can always bring the thoughts back to your body and move on. If it helps, visualize how you get the thoughts back before continuing.

This awareness exercise can help you maintain your focus on a certain thing, thus helping you be more present in the moment.

EXERCISE 10

BOX BREATHING

This is a very quick and easy way to get yourself into a calmer state. As an exercise, it is something that anyone can practice, especially in cases when you want to bring back your thoughts and keep your concentration. Here are the steps you need to take:

1. First, breathe in through your nose, and count slowly to four while you do. Focus on the present moment and feel how the air fills up your lungs.
2. Then, hold your breath for about 4 seconds. Avoid inhaling or exhaling during this time.
3. Then, slowly exhale through your mouth for a duration of 4 seconds.
4. Wait 4 seconds until you inhale again.
5. Repeat this process 4 times - that's enough to help you to center yourself.

Mindfulness and Acceptance

EXERCISE 11

MINDFUL WALKING

There is a certain awareness that happens each time you walk. This awareness can help you observe your impulses, emotions, and thoughts, as well as sensations that run through the body. As an exercise, mindful walking can help you develop positive behavioral change and develop coping skills. Here are the three steps of this exercise:

- Prepare yourself to go out for a walk. Before you start walking, try to stand still for a few moments and focus on your breathing. Notice how every part of your body feels.
- When you begin your walk, try to notice every movement of each part of your body. Notice how everything feels - your arms, your legs, your head, your skin, every part of you. Notice how you carry your body around.
- Once you've done that, start paying attention to everything around you. If you feel like your thoughts are getting distracted, slowly bring them back to the present moment. In the end, how did the walk make you feel?

EXERCISE 12

ACCEPTANCE PRACTICE

The highs and lows in life are unavoidable things, and the sooner you understand that, the better grasp you will have of yourself. I can understand that, as a young person, you don't quite know how to handle situations where you just have to accept yourself, a situation, or a moment. That is why I am proposing this acceptance practice exercise. You'll find this to be especially useful in situations where you're not particularly satisfied with an outcome. Here is what you need to do:

1. Describe the situation you're in right now to yourself. Now answer this - what about that situation makes you unhappy or dissatisfied?
2. Has this situation happened before? If so, how did you react to each time it happened? Did you look for help, did you look for acceptance, or were you angry and hopeless?
3. If you could do something to change the situation, what would that be? What do you think is holding you back to make this change? Or, if you have no other choice but to accept the situation as it is, what do you think is holding you back from surrendering to it?
4. The final question you're going to ask yourself is connected to the future. To remain present, how will you approach this situation from now on?

Take this as an example - you're feeling helpless, like you are in a vortex, and you want to get out of it immediately. Start answering the questions above (honestly and truthfully) and see where they lead you. To help you start thinking in the right direction, here are a few starting points. When you have found yourself in one of the situations below, this is the best exercise to use.

Situation: A grade on a test

Reaction: _____

Can you change the situation? How? _____
_____
_____

How will you approach this the next time? _____
_____
_____

Situation: A grade on a test

Reaction: _____

Can you change the situation? How? _____
_____
_____

How will you approach this the next time? _____
_____
_____

Situation: A grade on a test

Reaction: _____

Can you change the situation? How? _____
_____
_____

How will you approach this the next time? _____
_____
_____

Mindfulness and Acceptance

Situation: A grade on a test

Reaction: _____

Can you change the situation? How? _____

_____

_____

How will you approach this the next time? _____

_____

_____

Situation: A grade on a test

Reaction: _____

Can you change the situation? How? _____

_____

_____

How will you approach this the next time? _____

_____

_____

Situation: A grade on a test

Reaction: _____

Can you change the situation? How? _____

_____

_____

How will you approach this the next time? _____

_____

_____

Self-Regulation Workbook for Teens

Situation: A grade on a test

Reaction: _____

Can you change the situation? How? _____
_____
_____

How will you approach this the next time? _____
_____
_____

Situation: A grade on a test

Reaction: _____

Can you change the situation? How? _____
_____
_____

How will you approach this the next time? _____
_____
_____

Situation: A grade on a test

Reaction: _____

Can you change the situation? How? _____
_____
_____

How will you approach this the next time? _____
_____
_____

Mindfulness and Acceptance

Situation: A grade on a test

Reaction: _____

Can you change the situation? How? _____
_____
_____

How will you approach this the next time? _____
_____
_____
_____

EXERCISE 13

GRATITUDE PRACTICE

Feeling bad is pointless – someone had to say it. I figured, why not me? This last exercise for this chapter focuses on how to do more than accept a situation in your life but rather celebrate it. I know it seems a bit strange to do that, especially if you find yourself in a situation you don't like, but this exercise can help you realize one thing. That even if you are in an unwanted spot at the moment, in the grand scheme of things, you are right where you're supposed to be – and you should be thankful for that.

Let's simplify it – here's what you need to do for this exercise:

- ◇ Describe yourself as you are at the moment or a situation you're in at the moment that you don't really like.
- ◇ Think about this for a while – even if you are not in a particularly good situation, how can you benefit from it? There has to be something good about it, but you never gave it much thought. So, in this case, give it a moment and give it the thought.
- ◇ Before you wrap up this exercise, find one (or a few) different perspectives from the one you have. Remember – feeling pointless about something is normal, but to a certain extent. As a young person, you have the power to appreciate the opportunities and benefits of every thought, feeling, and situation and use them to feel better and act on something.
- ◇ Finally, what can you do to express gratitude for the situation you're in at the moment? (there has to be something)

Let me give you an example of this. You wake up in the morning, and everything seems okay. You're making yourself a good breakfast and you want to savor it before your day begins. But you burn the breakfast and make a mess out of the kitchen. You start thinking that everything always goes wrong, that you're good for nothing, and that everything is a mess. Once you feel the onset of these thoughts coming, just pause for a while and allow them to pass through you. Among the chaos, find at least one thing you're grateful for - the sun, the cold, the fact that you're standing in the kitchen, still learning how to cook, apparently, the fact that you're alive and well, and these things happen to anyone - it can be anything. Give power to that rather than giving power to the momentary negative feelings you have.

Situation: _____

How can I benefit from it?:

1. _____

2. _____

3. _____

Things I am grateful for:

1. _____

2. _____

3. _____

Situation: _____

How can I benefit from it?:

1. _____

2. _____

3. _____

Things I am grateful for:

1. _____

2. _____

3. _____

Mindfulness and Acceptance

Situation: _____

How can I benefit from it?:

1. _____
2. _____
3. _____

Things I am grateful for:

1. _____
2. _____
3. _____

Situation: _____

How can I benefit from it?:

1. _____
2. _____
3. _____

Things I am grateful for:

1. _____
2. _____
3. _____

Situation: _____

How can I benefit from it?:

1. _____

2. _____

3. _____

Things I am grateful for:

1. _____

2. _____

3. _____

Situation: _____

How can I benefit from it?:

1. _____

2. _____

3. _____

Things I am grateful for:

1. _____

2. _____

3. _____

Mindfulness and Acceptance

Situation: _____

How can I benefit from it?:

1. _____
2. _____
3. _____

Things I am grateful for:

1. _____
2. _____
3. _____

Situation: _____

How can I benefit from it?:

1. _____
2. _____
3. _____

Things I am grateful for:

1. _____
2. _____
3. _____

Situation: _____

How can I benefit from it?:

1. _____
2. _____
3. _____

Things I am grateful for:

1. _____
2. _____
3. _____

These exercises are more than just a mechanism to help you cope with yourself and your environment – they are the arsenal you need to become better, stronger, and healthier.

What Did You Learn From This Chapter?

This is a chapter where you managed to reach deep within – and uncover a calmer and more centered side of you. Other than realizing that every one of us has it, you learned the following:

- What is mindfulness and an introduction to a few techniques.
- What is acceptance and how to cultivate non-judgemental awareness.
- Learned an exercise about the five senses of mindfulness.

Mindfulness and acceptance should be a core part of who you are. They can help you walk the path of calmness and control of your life. Speaking of control, it still feels like you haven't reached that point where you can have complete control of your behavior patterns, right? Fear not, because, in the next chapter, I am starting the subject of understanding those behavior patterns – taking a step toward grasping the steering wheel of your life. Turn the page, and I hope you're ready because you're in for a wild ride!

Mindfulness and Acceptance

PART 02

CBT BEHAVIORAL TECHNIQUES

CHAPTER 06

UNDERSTANDING BEHAVIOR PATTERNS

"Small daily improvements are the key to staggering long-term results." - Anonymous

No matter what you do in life – be that personal development, professional development, or any other aspect of your life – it can be improved if you are consistent and work on it daily. Cognitive behavioral therapy is here to show you just that. With me as the vessel, you get to learn new things about yourself with every new chapter.

We all have certain behavior patterns. These affect us in a certain way and are our personal characteristic traits. It is a chain of thoughts and actions that have happened in certain patterns within your life, and they have often repeated themselves over and over. In this chapter, you will notice that I am focusing on two specific aspects – the ABC model and the triggers that lead to impulsive behaviors. Finally, we will wrap up this chapter by learning how to identify behavior patterns.

Exploring the ABC Model – Antecedents, Behaviours and Consequences

The ABC model is a perfect example of how CBT works – focusing on the present rather than the past. This basic CBT technique assumes your beliefs based on how you react to certain events. As a model, it challenges cognitive distortions and irrational thoughts. That, in turn, allows you to reconstruct these thoughts or beliefs into healthier ones.

This model has many benefits for your mental and emotional health. By using the ABC model, you can identify inaccurate thoughts and beliefs and learn how to let go of them. The process itself teaches you how to notice your automatic thoughts. However, instead of immediately acting upon them, you get to give yourself a break and explore different options. Once you see how it works, you will notice that you can use it in many situations – be that with yourself and your private thoughts, in a professional environment, or whenever you come face to face with a challenging situation.

Before I move on to the exercise where you can see the ABC model in motion, remember one thing about it – it can help you develop positive emotions and rational thoughts. So, each time you're faced with anxiety, anger, embarrassment, guilt, fear, or sadness, this is the model to turn to.

EXERCISE 14

THE ABC MODEL IN USE

This model's beauty is that you can pinpoint a negative thought whenever you have it. Things immediately make more sense when you try to shape them in a certain way. In this case, they are shaped into letters. Before you begin this exercise, you should know the components of this model. Here they are:

- **A** – means the activating event or adversity
- **B** – means your beliefs about that certain activating event. These beliefs include both obvious and underlying thoughts about yourself, others, or a certain situation
- **C** – means consequences. These consequences usually include your emotional or behavioral response

Now, when you start the exercise, you work under the assumption that the letters A, B, and C are connected, and B is the most important component. CBT as a concept focuses on B to change the thinking patterns and create new ways of viewing yourself, the people around you, and situations.

Think about it this way - A is the activating situation or moment, B is your beliefs and thoughts about this moment, and C is the consequences of those beliefs.

For example, (A:) your friend agrees to have lunch with you, but they don't follow up on the initial agreement. Your mind immediately jumps to a conclusion (B:), thinking that they don't care about you, and then (C:) you start blowing things out of proportion with the thoughts that nobody cares about you, pick a fight with your friend, and so on.

Your exercise is to think of a situation when something similar to this happened to you and analyze how you reacted to it. When you come up with the situation, start from the very beginning - point A. Only this time, you will try to come to a different outcome. What happened at point A? Sit with that for a while and try to think of exactly what happened.

To come to point B, recognize your thought patterns and all the irrationality around them. Recognize that they make you have negative feelings and are part of a vortex you thought you couldn't get out of – until now. Come up with different approaches and different patterns of thoughts - more positive ones - that will lead you to different conclusions. Abandon the thought you originally had at the moment when the situation occurred and look for alternatives.

When you finally arrive at point C, it means you've done everything to explore other options for your specific situation and have managed to shift your thoughts. They are now neutral or positive, realistic, and don't make you feel angry or sad as a response to them.

Sit with this for a little bit. Learn how you can apply this exercise in various situations. Here are a few examples you can get started with:

1. Instructions given to you by your parents. They do that a lot and you don't really like it.
2. The feeling of peer pressure. It feels like everyone is doing much better than you.
3. Having an exam in the near future. The pressure of the "deadline" before the exam is too much to handle.
4. A reminder that you need to come back home before X o'clock. You don't need a reminder that you're still a teenager.
5. A warning from a teacher. This can lead to the school contacting your parents.
6. Social media. Either too much of it or not enough of it can make you feel anxious.

Antecedent (**A**):

Behavior (**B**):

Consequences (**C**):

Antecedent (**A**):

Behavior (**B**):

Consequences (**C**):

Antecedent (**A**):

Behavior (**B**):

Consequences (**C**):

Antecedent (**A**): _____
_____

Behavior (**B**): _____
_____

Consequences (**C**): _____
_____

Antecedent (**A**): _____
_____

Behavior (**B**): _____
_____

Consequences (**C**): _____
_____

Antecedent (**A**): _____
_____

Behavior (**B**): _____
_____

Consequences (**C**): _____
_____

Self-Regulation Workbook for Teens

Antecedent (**A**): _____

Behavior (**B**): _____

Consequences (**C**): _____

Antecedent (**A**): _____

Behavior (**B**): _____

Consequences (**C**): _____

Antecedent (**A**): _____

Behavior (**B**): _____

Consequences (**C**): _____

Understanding Behavior Patterns

Antecedent (**A**): _____
_____

Behavior (**B**): _____
_____

Consequences (**C**): _____
_____

Antecedent (**A**): _____
_____

Behavior (**B**): _____
_____

Consequences (**C**): _____
_____

Antecedent (**A**): _____
_____

Behavior (**B**): _____
_____

Consequences (**C**): _____
_____

Antecedent (**A**): _____
_____

Behavior (**B**): _____
_____

Consequences (**C**): _____
_____

Antecedent (**A**): _____
_____

Behavior (**B**): _____
_____

Consequences (**C**): _____
_____

Antecedent (**A**): _____
_____

Behavior (**B**): _____
_____

Consequences (**C**): _____
_____

With those newfound thoughts and emotions, how would your behavior change? Do you notice it taking a turn for the better?

Understanding Behavior Patterns

Recognizing Triggers for Impulsive Behavior

Many people believe that impulsive behavior is a disorder. I am here to tell you that just because you've been stuck in the maze of your mind doesn't mean you are dealing with a disorder. However, you should still know how to manage your impulse control and avoid impulsive behaviors.

An impulsive behavior is every time you act quickly on something without any thought about the consequences. In your mind, only the present moment exists (which is a good starting point), but there is no thought about the future whatsoever. What young minds such as yourself fail to notice here is that we all act on impulses sometimes. It is a part of who we are, and it is an important part of the human experience. But, if you indulge in this behavior for a longer period, instead of only engaging in it from time to time (until you become an adult and learn how to control it), then it means you are walking a thin line.

When you are acting on impulse, it means you are acting spontaneously. You don't consider how it could affect you later on or how it could affect others. You never wonder what might happen because you only think about the here and the now.

Before I move on to the exercise, I am sharing a few examples of impulsive behavior. You may recognize yourself in some, and that's okay because here, I have created a safe space for you to learn and develop at your own pace.

Here are the examples:

- You have frequent outbursts
- You overshare details of your personal life with everyone you meet
- You overindulge in things, showing binge behavior
- You tend to make all situations a lot scarier and more urgent than they actually are
- You turn to hurting yourself, physically, mentally, or emotionally, every time you are faced with disappointment.

EXERCISE 15

COMMON TRIGGERS

Every day, you experience a wide range of emotions – be those positive, neutral, or negative. Almost all of them relate to a certain event, something that happens to you that day. However, it is your response to these events that matters. These events are your triggers, and you act on them based on a similar previous experience. It encompasses your state of mind based on past memories, experiences, or events, and it usually results in an intense emotional reaction, no matter what your current mood is at the moment.

This exercise can help you know your common emotional triggers and how to deal with them so you can create and maintain good emotional health.

Take out a pen and dedicate some time to sit with yourself. Think about some situations that made you feel bad. Which part of those situations triggered you? Was it some kind of disapproval, rejection, or exclusion, or maybe you felt ignored, critiqued, unwanted, smothered, insecure, and like you were losing control? These situations are known as common triggers, where you lose your independence and turn to something you're not. Once you pinpoint the feeling, listen to your mind and body. Your mind is probably loud and filled with negative thoughts, and your body also shows symptoms – a pounding heart, shakiness, and sweaty palms.

Some of the most common triggers young people face are fear of rejection, stress, being ignored, negative memories, being ridiculed, conflict, psychological trauma, being vulnerable, helpless, having a lack of socializing, etc.

Now go ahead and write everything down below:

Situation	The Trigger of Bad Feeling

Understanding Behavior Patterns

This is when you need to take a step back and acknowledge your current state, but remember, that you know the root and know how to get there and change the reaction. Remind yourself that it is okay to feel whatever you feel, but let it pass through you. Own your feelings, but do so with compassion for yourself, not judgment. Give yourself some space, take a short break to regroup, and return to the situation with a calmer mindset.

Identifying Patterns of Behavior

At the end of the day, you started reading this book so you can not only improve yourself but learn how to accept yourself. For without acceptance, there is no change. It can be difficult to accept that you are dealing with something that is a core part of who you are, but by identifying that part of you, you give yourself the unique chance of improving the situation – improving yourself.

It all comes down to being self-aware and acknowledging a pattern. In this case, whatever happens, I would suggest one thing – that you commit honesty toward yourself. Be honest about every feeling and every thought because you need a certain recognition to strengthen your mind. Identifying your pattern of behavior will do just that – push the subconscious act into the realm of consciousness, where you are fully aware of what is happening to you. Apply logic to this case, and you know that you can shift or tone it down whenever you notice a behavior pattern with a negative frequency. By doing this, you create new opportunities for self-reflection and growth.

What Did You Learn From This Chapter?

It is important to realize that you have so much power within you – and that you can easily take control of yourself. But everything seems so much easier once you find out the perfect steps to make that happen. In this chapter on understanding behavior patterns, you learned precise ways to deal with yourself, among other things, as pointed out below:

- What is the ABC model and how it can influence your thinking patterns.
- What is impulsive behavior and its triggers.
- How the common triggers are connected to your behavior patterns.

When you understand your behavior patterns, that's when all things start to put themselves into perspective. With this, you go through the process of opening up to yourself, right down to your core, to find out what you're truly made out of. When you get that out of the way, only one thing remains: start building yourself up! To do that, you will need to develop a few skills, the first of which is coping skills. I am here to help you achieve that – turn the page because the next chapter is all about it!

Self-Regulation Workbook for Teens

CHAPTER 07

DEVELOPING COPING SKILLS

"We cannot solve our problems with the same thinking we used when we created them." – Albert Einstein

What does it mean to cope? It seems like, every day, you are coping with something, and everything feels like it is out of the ordinary. Each experience gives you a different thought, each action creates a reaction within you, and each feeling you have, comes with a set of consequences. The thing is, you noticed that you focus more on the negative rather than the positive. You start feeling like your mind and spirit are both tumbling down. You know, throwing a pebble down the side of the hill will ultimately nudge larger and larger rocks along the way. By the time it all reaches the end, some large rock formations would have fallen.

If you are coping with some emotions and thoughts that cannot be explained any other way than this, it is time for you to learn how to put them aside. In this chapter, I am teaching you all there is to know about effectively managing yourself. The best way to do that is by developing strong coping skills.

Learning Effective Coping Strategies for Managing Stress and Emotions

Negative emotions and stress can sometimes get the better of you. That's understandable to a certain extent, given the lifestyle most of us lead. Even for a young person such as yourself, things can feel a little too much sometimes. But noticing that you have more stressors in life than good feelings is the first step in the right direction. The second is implementing some effective coping strategies.

The main purpose of these strategies is to learn how to tolerate negative events and realities while keeping your positive self-image and emotional control intact. You implement coping strategies each time you face a life challenge. This challenge is usually a negative situation and requires some sort of adaptation on your end. Other times, some positive changes may make you feel stressed, too. All of them require you to adapt and adjust to a certain new environment or situation, and for a brief moment, until you do that, you might feel like you don't have control over the situation. That may make you feel bad, panicked, anxious, or depressed. In some cases, it can even go to extremes. You are here because of that – so we can push the negative aside and learn how to deal with it. By learning these coping strategies, you will learn how to glide smoothly through life rather than trip and fall every time.

To manage your emotions and stress every time, here are some effective coping strategies for you:

- ⬥ When faced with a situation, instead of jumping to conclusions, try to find as much information about it as you can. If necessary, include the people in your support group and find a solution.
- ⬥ Any problem can be broken down into small parts. That way, instead of dealing with it as a whole, you deal with smaller, more manageable chunks.
- ⬥ Practice breathing and relaxation techniques. They will automatically regulate your nervous system and keep you calm.

- ⟡ Don't underestimate the power of a creative outlet. Anything from art, music, or dance can help you healthily process your emotions and be a productive way to spend your time.
- ⟡ Get in touch with a friend who makes you feel like you are loved for who you really are.
- ⟡ Reach out to a mentor, parent, or teacher – anyone who can guide you further.
- ⟡ Work on reframing your negative thoughts and shifting your mindset. Remember, it is all about looking at a situation from a different point of view.
- ⟡ The power of journaling is no joke. When you write things down, you put them into perspective, and they start making sense in terms of what you're going through. But they are also easier to handle once you physically see them in front of you.
- ⟡ Dedicate your time to helping someone else. When you indulge in such an activity, you can help lower your overall stress levels and connect to others. Ultimately, you work on your well-being and health.

Whenever you feel like you want to react negatively in a given situation, remember that there will be consequences to that. Once you start gathering these consequences, one by one, they will come up to be the core of your personality - since you would be reacting to them, thinking about them, and so on. Since both positive and negative behaviors are repetitive patterns, it is high time you've learned the coping skills for each situation. The next step is building a "toolbox" of the coping skills you've mastered the most.

Building a Toolbox of Coping Skills

Okay, so let me ask you something – what do you do when you're emotionally activated? We all indeed have different ways of coping with stress, but what are your "go-to" tools that you take to deal with an unwanted or stressful situation? If you're reading this book, that means you either want to update your skills or you want to change them completely. As a young adult, trying this on your own may be difficult because you don't have a starting point.

But now, with this book, you can easily focus on building a toolbox of coping skills.

What is a toolbox of skills? These are the skills you have up your sleeve and you use them each time you are faced with a challenging situation. However, before you build your own toolbox, you need to learn something. The key to developing new skills and knowing how to use them is practicing them even when you're not emotionally activated. Once you develop that ability to think clearly in any situation, things will seem a lot easier to cope with. This is something you can rely on each time you move forward and overcome a curveball.

To move on and try to implement those skills in your daily life, you need to decide what you're going to put in your emotional toolbox first. As you are starting from scratch, here are a few suggestions to get you started. You can use these skills every time you feel like you need soothing.

1. **Distract yourself** – there is nothing wrong with distracting yourself every time you feel upset. If you start feeling like you can't keep control over a certain situation, and you don't want to let go of control, then it is most likely best if you step back. Distract yourself with something until the strong emotions pass. This is only the first skill you can implement, so try to combine it with some of the other skills that I mention below. Here, you can watch a movie, listen to music, get into a hobby of yours, do some puzzles, etc.

2. **Mindfulness exercises** – whenever you're feeling emotionally overwhelmed, it is difficult to focus on the present moment. Your mind wanders all over the place, and it is challenging to stay put in the present. That is why mindfulness exercises are a perfect thing. These exercises can help you shift the attention back to yourself and to where you are right now and how you're feeling right now. The exercises can be anything you want – from a breathing exercise to meditation exercise, journalling, coloring, or maybe even progressive muscle relaxation exercises.

3. **Move your body** – by moving your body, you keep the mind active in the present, so this is another skill you should keep up your sleeve. You don't have to do extreme exercises here; all you need to do is listen to your body and go at your own pace. Sometimes, intense movements

are what you need. Other times, you can focus on slow movements. This can be anything – from stepping onto your yoga mat to running, gardening, stretching, or doing some exercise videos.

4. **Calming sensory objects** – using your senses to calm down is a great way to keep yourself grounded and in the present moment. In this case, you can, for example, touch something or engage a few of your senses at the same time. If you are faced with a challenging situation, look around you – that's the first thing that will keep you in the present. Find some sensory objects. These can be a soft blanket, a candle, a lotion, a pen, a toy, a fidget spinner, a warm or cold beverage, a piece of gum, photos of people – it can be anything.

It is such a happy feeling to create a palette of coping skills and keep them up your sleeve just in case a challenging situation arises. This so-called toolbox can help you stay more calm and centered - because you know that, at any given moment, you have something to fall back on rather than falling into a hole of negativity. After this, it is time to learn how to implement these coping skills in day-to-day situations.

Implementing Coping Skills in Daily Life

It is all about dedicating some time out of your day to give something to yourself. Working on yourself is very important, and since you picked up this book, you're already on the right path. But you still need to put in some effort.

For most young people, time management is a challenging concept in itself. Every day has 24 hours, and how you divide your time and attention is what matters the most. Once you subtract the time for rest, time to finish your daily obligations, and time spent with your friends and family, there is rarely some time to focus on yourself, right? Well, the first thing you're going to do is learn how to manage your time and give at least five or ten minutes during the day to yourself. Even in those times when you feel like you are racing with the clock, pause for a second, breathe, and start over.

When you look at it from a different perspective, it is about priority management more than time management. If you want to put in the work and create a better version of yourself, then you need to dedicate minutes, if not hours, to yourself only.

Be careful though, your mind may trick you into believing that self-care is selfishness. That dedicating time to yourself is a bad thing. Don't trust that voice. You are being kind and compassionate to people and yourself. You are working to achieve a certain goal. You are starting a journey to self-care and self-revelation.

So, create a schedule first. You already have the coping skills listed above, and you know you need to work on them every chance you get, not only in a situation where you're emotionally challenged. Now, all you need to do is begin. Implement the coping skills we uncovered in your daily life. Soon enough, you will notice yourself exhibiting a different pattern of behavior. A better one.

What Did You Learn From This Chapter?

The purpose of this chapter was to open your eyes to the world of possibilities. To teach you about all the things you can do and be and how to cope healthily with everything life throws at you. To summarize, here is what you learned from it:

- Some effective strategies that can help you manage your emotions and stress levels.
- A set of coping skills you should have in your arsenal.
- How to implement those coping skills in your everyday life.

Coping skills are easy to master. I know that after the end of each chapter, you are baffled by all the new information you learn, but as you can see, the next chapter always completes the previous one. Using that logic, things will seem a lot easier once you delve into the next chapter – which is all about behavioral activation. Turn the page and learn all about it!

CHAPTER 08

BEHAVIORAL ACTIVATION

> *"Do not wait, the time will never be 'just right.' Start where you stand, and work with whatever tools you may have at your command, and better tools will be found as you go along." – George Herbert*

There is an idea that focuses on enhancing a sort of positive behavior. Behavioral activation is just that – deliberately practicing certain behaviors to activate a positive emotional state. The concept depends on the fact that as long as you engage in good and healthy activities, you will feel good.

How does this seem to you? Is it something you would try? When I was young, I thought this would never work for me. But, despite my doubts, I still gave it a go. After a few failed attempts, I focused on enhancing my behavioral activation. So you see, this is something anyone can do. And I bet that you would be better at it than I was! Do you want to know why I think that? Because you have this book in your hands!

Understanding the Connection Between Behavior and Mood

Remember that I mentioned the relationship between thoughts, emotions, and behavior in the previous chapters. Now, in order to change that, you need to acknowledge and recognize it first.

I want us to begin by distinguishing between emotions and feelings. These are often confused with each other, yet they are pretty different. Now, don't get me wrong; they are still connected, but they come with different time limits and labels. By understanding the difference, you will be able to better control your behavior and make healthier choices in life.

Emotions. They are not conscious. These reactions happen within your body, and they often come as a consequence of thoughts, memories, and experiences. Some of the most common emotions include happiness, anger, sadness, fear, surprise, and disgust. Also, emotions are often associated with facial expressions.

Feelings. On the other hand, feelings happen in the mind. They are conscious. They are a reaction to the emotions you are experiencing. Feelings are based on the reaction to the emotions you are experiencing, as well as the perception of any events and thoughts.

Emotions and feelings are two separate things because emotions happen due to a physical response within the brain, and feelings are a response to the emotional reaction.

So, how can these two impact your behavior?

Because the emotions create a physical response, and the feelings are conscious, they impact your overall behavior. However, in such situations, people tend to believe that their behavior is justified because of their emotions. The thing is, as long as they believe this, they may struggle to understand that behavior is a choice. Behavior does not have to be impacted by your mood. Behavior can be healthy. Once you start noticing this, you can make a change. If your mood often dictates your behavior, you can react in three ways – positively, negatively, or refuse to respond at all. If you allow your emotions to control your behavior, then you live on so-called "autopilot." That kind of behavior may lead to you making choices you will regret later. As long as your behavior is based on your feelings, it can lead you astray.

EXERCISE 16

MOOD AND ACTIVITY DIARY

Let's do an exercise here. Get a pen and locate the worksheet below. Have them handy at all times during the next week or so. Within this timeframe, try to notice your mood every time – when you get up in the morning, before you go to bed, at each time during the day, and every time you come face to face with any type of situation.

Always take a minute to reflect and write down your mood and behavior. As I have already mentioned, when you put anything on paper, it takes a form of its own and becomes more real. Think of you writing down how you felt as a sort of diary. Once the week has passed, you can go back to your notes and see how your mind has gradually shifted for the better, even if it is a little bit.

Activity: _____ Mood: _____

Activity: _____ Mood: _____

Activity: _____ Mood: _____

Activity: _____ Mood: _____

Activity: _____ Mood: _____

Behavioral Activation

Activity: _____ Mood: _____

Activity: _____ Mood: _____

☺ ☺ ☺ ☹ ☹

Activity: _____ Mood: _____

☺ ☺ ☺ ☹ ☹

Activity: _____ Mood: _____

Setting and Achieving SMART Goals

The reason why I'm adding this as a segment into this book is because it is important to know how to work on your goals, not just to have them. In your case, you are working on creating a better, calmer, and happier self. But, sometimes, everyone needs a little push in the right direction. That's why I am including the SMART goals.

Whatever you put your mind to, you can achieve. Think of the SMART goals as your guide that will help you get to where you want in a specific timeframe. For those of you who are already familiar with this concept, let's revisit it. And for those of you who don't know it, take a look at it below:

SMART is an acronym that can help you determine your goals – make them reachable and clear, as they should be. Here is what every letter stands for:

- **S** – stands for specific, significant, simple, and sensible
- **M** – stands for measurable, motivating, and meaningful
- **A** – stands for achievable, attainable, and agreed
- **R** – stands for relevant, realistic, result-based, and reasonable
- **T** – stands for time-bound, time-based, timely, and time-sensitive

While this sounds simple and straightforward enough, you probably still need some guidance on how to practice it. That's why we are moving on to the next exercise.

Self-Regulation Workbook for Teens

EXERCISE 17

SMART GOAL-SETTING

The goal you want to achieve now is to adhere to positive behavior and change a certain aspect of yourself that will affect the quality of your overall lifestyle. With that in mind, here is how to set a SMART goal.

This approach is based on certain criteria. Take a pen and write down your goal. Then, find the SMART letters in a vertical line below it. Add your answers to the following questions next to each letter – see below.

S > be specific. What will you achieve? How will you do that?

M > be measurable. What will you use as a pointer to show you that you've met your goal?

A > be achievable. Do you possess the right skills to achieve this?

R > be relevant. How important will the results be?

T > be time-bound. What is the deadline for you to achieve your goal?

MY GOAL

S > _____

M > _____

A > _____

R > _____

T > _____

Behavioral Activation

MY GOAL

_____

| S |_____
|___|_____

| M |_____
|___|_____

| A |_____
|___|_____

| R |_____
|___|_____

| T |_____
|___|_____

MY GOAL

_____

| S |_____
|___|_____

| M |_____
|___|_____

| A |_____
|___|_____

| R | _____ |
| | _____ |

| T | _____ |
| | _____ |

MY GOAL

_____
_____

| S | _____ |
| | _____ |

| M | _____ |
| | _____ |

| A | _____ |
| | _____ |

| R | _____ |
| | _____ |

| T | _____ |
| | _____ |

MY GOAL

_____

| S | _____ |
| | _____ |

Behavioral Activation

M _____
_____

A _____
_____

R _____
_____

T _____
_____

MY GOAL

_____
_____

S _____
_____

M _____
_____

A _____
_____

R _____
_____

T _____
_____

Self-Regulation Workbook for Teens

MY GOAL

_____
_____

> **S** _____
_____

> **M** _____
_____

> **A** _____
_____

> **R** _____
_____

> **T** _____
_____

By learning that the SMART goal will provide you with clarity, motivation, and focus, you can soon learn to implement it with every other goal you have – not just this one.

Increasing Engagement in Positive Activities

Science has always suggested that positive thinking is a skill everyone can learn. It is also the main focus of this book. But when it comes to actually doing the work, a lot of people shy away from it. Before thinking that it "takes too much work" to do it, think about the near future. Visualize yourself doing things you want, things that make you feel complete and happy. Just the thought of it makes you happy, doesn't it?

Well, think about how much better you will feel if you actually increase your engagement in positive activities. Just stop and think about what makes you happy. Do you have a hobby that makes you feel fulfilled? Do you have an interest that makes you lose track of time? It can be anything – as long as it puts a smile on your face. It can be drawing, going out with people, watching a movie, reading a book, meditating, running, or photography – all cards are on the table!

By increasing engagement in positive activities, you learn how to stay present in the moment. Your mind does not wander around, creating negative scenarios and falling into the same depressing vortex over and over again. Rather, it instead focuses on what you can do better. As insignificant as this may sound in the beginning, indulging in such activities can help you shift your mindset after a while.

EXERCISE 18

BEHAVIORAL ACTIVATION WORKSHEET

I have found that the most successful way to indulge in behavioral activation is by making a worksheet. Trust me, it is as simple as it can get. There is not much complexity to it, and you don't even have to dedicate a lot of time to it. A few minutes of your day is enough.

Take a pen and write down all the things you love. I mean, things you truly love. They can be of any area of your life. For example, you can write the following.

I love my pet.

I love that I get up early every morning.

I love that I work on myself at least once a week.

I love that it's summertime.

I love watermelon.

You see? This can be anything as long as you focus on the good things. There is always something good and something to be thankful for, and by indulging in this exercise, you accentuate it.

EXERCISE 19

ACTIVITY EXPERIMENT

The next exercise for today is focused on the question – *what would you do if you knew the <u>outcome</u> would be the best possible scenario?*

Experiment with a particular activity. Say you want to improve your mood and focus; running three times a week is an excellent way to do that. But you feel like you're going to fail as soon as you begin. Well, I am all up for changing your thoughts, so let's do it. I know that if you've never run before, your mind will immediately go to thinking you'll fail. Let's entertain that thought for a minute. Why do you think you will fail? Because if you never ran before, how would you know? True, you need to have a certain level of physical preparedness to run, but you also need to run to have physical preparedness. It is a circle, and one cannot go without the other.

Once you realize this is the same for all activities you want to indulge in, you will start looking at it a bit more positively. For the sake of this exercise, let's look at the best possible scenario. You will start running three days a week. You will feel incredible, you will look better, and while you're thinking about your future self, you always picture yourself with a smile on your face. That's the best-case scenario I want you to focus on every time you want to start something new. It doesn't have to be running exactly – it can be anything you want as long as it is an activity that will make you happy.

Behavioral Activation

Activity: _____

The Best-Case Scenario: _____
_____
_____
_____
_____

Activity: _____

The Best-Case Scenario: _____
_____
_____
_____
_____

Activity: _____

The Best-Case Scenario: _____
_____
_____
_____
_____

Self-Regulation Workbook for Teens

Activity: _____

The Best-Case Scenario: _____

_____

_____

_____

Activity: _____

The Best-Case Scenario: _____

_____

_____

_____

Activity: _____

The Best-Case Scenario: _____

_____

_____

_____

Activity: _____

The Best-Case Scenario: _____

_____

_____

_____

EXERCISE 20

POSITIVE ACTIVITY CATALOG

This last exercise for this chapter is connected to the previous one. After you do your best with the smallest positive activity and you see the results, you will want to do another activity and then another one. As you stack these up, one at a time, you end up creating a catalog of everything you're doing to improve yourself.

All you need to do here is to remember to write everything down. Write down the activity, how it made you feel, and how often you indulged in it. This is sort of a journalling process except we call it a catalog of positive activities. Give it a few months to really see the results. Let's say you've indulged in several activities in the past period, and then you stopped to look back on how far you've come. Everything you've written down will be the catalog you refer to – each time you need inspiration or a little boost to move ahead in life.

Activity: _____

How it Made me feel?: _____

_____

Times done: ☐   ☐   ☐   ☐   ☐   ☐   ☐   ☐   ☐   ☐

Self-Regulation Workbook for Teens

Activity: _____

How it Made me feel?: _____

_____

Times done: ☐   ☐   ☐   ☐   ☐   ☐   ☐   ☐   ☐   ☐

Activity: _____

How it Made me feel?: _____

_____

Times done: ☐   ☐   ☐   ☐   ☐   ☐   ☐   ☐   ☐   ☐

Activity: _____

How it Made me feel?: _____

_____

Times done: ☐   ☐   ☐   ☐   ☐   ☐   ☐   ☐   ☐   ☐

Activity: _____

How it Made me feel?: _____

_____

Times done: ☐   ☐   ☐   ☐   ☐   ☐   ☐   ☐   ☐   ☐

Behavioral Activation

Activity: _____

How it Made me feel?: _____

_____

Times done: ☐   ☐   ☐   ☐   ☐   ☐   ☐   ☐   ☐   ☐

Activity: _____

How it Made me feel?: _____

_____

Times done: ☐   ☐   ☐   ☐   ☐   ☐   ☐   ☐   ☐   ☐

Activity: _____

How it Made me feel?: _____

_____

Times done: ☐   ☐   ☐   ☐   ☐   ☐   ☐   ☐   ☐   ☐

Activity: _____

How it Made me feel?: _____

_____

Times done: ☐   ☐   ☐   ☐   ☐   ☐   ☐   ☐   ☐   ☐

Activity: _____

How it Made me feel?: _____

_____

Times done: ☐   ☐   ☐   ☐   ☐   ☐   ☐   ☐   ☐   ☐

Activity: _____

How it Made me feel?: _____

_____

Times done: ☐   ☐   ☐   ☐   ☐   ☐   ☐   ☐   ☐   ☐

Activity: _____

How it Made me feel?: _____

_____

Times done: ☐   ☐   ☐   ☐   ☐   ☐   ☐   ☐   ☐   ☐

Activity: _____

How it Made me feel?: _____

_____

Times done: ☐   ☐   ☐   ☐   ☐   ☐   ☐   ☐   ☐   ☐

Behavioral Activation

Activity: _____

How it Made me feel?: _____

_____

Times done: ☐   ☐   ☐   ☐   ☐   ☐   ☐   ☐   ☐   ☐

Activity: _____

How it Made me feel?: _____

_____

Times done: ☐   ☐   ☐   ☐   ☐   ☐   ☐   ☐   ☐   ☐

What Did You Learn From This Chapter?

Slowly but surely, you are learning so much about yourself and how you can improve. This chapter was probably a true revelation that there is always a flip side to everything. By learning this now, you keep in mind how to be more assertive and engage in positive behavior.

Let's review what we've learned from here:

- ✧ Explaining what behavioral activation is.
- ✧ What are emotions and feelings, and how they differ from each other.
- ✧ Behavior can be a consequence of feelings, but behavior is always a choice.
- ✧ Setting SMART goals.
- ✧ Increasing engagement in positive activities makes you more present.

It is very easy to let negative emotions and feelings control your behavior. That's probably the reason why most people indulge in it. It takes perseverance, control, and determination to get to the other side – where the grass is greener. I am breaking down the journey into small steps to make things a lot easier for you, and I hope you can already feel the difference! But, as much as I like to say that we're almost there, you still need to do a few things. The next chapter is all about assertiveness training. With it, you will unlock a whole new level of yourself. What are you waiting for? Turn the page!

CHAPTER 09

ASSERTIVENESS TRAINING

"The only limit to our realization of tomorrow will be our doubts of today." – Franklin D. Roosevelt

Train your brain – that's all you ever need. In the previous chapters, I focused on the importance of looking at thoughts, feelings, and behavior as one. But now, it is time to focus only on the aspect of assertiveness. This will be the tool that will keep you in check every time life gets complicated.

Before we delve into the chapter together, let's talk about assertiveness – do you know what it is? Assertiveness is the quality of being confident and self-assured without being hostile or aggressive. Many people think this is a part of personality, which is why some people have it while others don't. The truth is that this is a skill that you can train yourself to possess. The assertiveness skills can help you respond to any situation better and help you build yourself up into a stronger version of yourself.

Importance of Assertive Communication

Since this is our subject for the chapter, and I have dedicated an entire one to it, why is it so important? Assertiveness, in itself, is something quite a lot of people struggle with. As a young person, you may feel like you fear hurting someone else, appear selfish, show aggression, etc. All of these are reasons why you feel afraid to be confident, to stand up for yourself, and to voice your needs.

In many situations, these fears come from a lack of understanding about assertiveness. To clear things up right from the start, assertiveness is not to be mistaken with aggression – even though both include showing your point of view. The difference is that aggression has a hostile and demanding approach, and assertiveness includes calm and respectful communication.

By explaining them, you can see how important assertive communication is. You will show stability to yourself first and then to the people around you. Then, you will know how to ask for something with confidence and clarity. Finally, you will stop feeling subjugated and powerless and instead step into your full force.

Learning Assertiveness Skills

Rather than boring you with details and theory, I want to focus on practice within this chapter. You are fully aware of what assertiveness is. Now, it is time to start learning how to implement it in your life. Learning assertiveness skills is one of the most effective ways for you to get your message across. Here is how to learn assertiveness:

- ⋄ **Think about your style** - are you a more active person, someone who wants their voice to be heard, or are you a more passive person, and tend to stay in the background? Once you determine this, it is time to apply the next steps.

- **Use first person singular** - whenever you want to talk about something, use "I" as much as you can. This will give off the feeling that you're using statements that connect you, meaning you are ready to take on responsibilities or consequences.
- **Learn how to say no** - this is very self-explanatory. If you don't want to do or say or feel something, just say no.
- **Rehearse** - if you have something to say, and you're afraid you're not going to sound right, rehearse it.
- **Body language** - at all times, you need to be aware of your body language - for it speaks even when you keep quiet. Notice yourself in front of the mirror - and practice poses that are calm and radiate certainty.
- **Check on yourself** - the last step and the biggest one is checking in on yourself. Your emotions and your thoughts are what matter the most, so at all times, keep them in check. There's no need for you to give off what you think and feel all the time. Instead, take a deep breath, take a step back, and calmly approach every situation.

Actually, learning assertiveness seems easy, right? But why would you learn it if you don't know what you're gaining from it? Understandable. I wouldn't want to abide by anything if I didn't know how it would help me. With that in mind, here is what you will gain from learning assertiveness skills:

- Better communication – when you are being assertive, you have the best chance to successfully deliver a message across. If you are too much on the aggressive side, then you are more likely to lose the message in the process, as the receiving party will only focus on the aggression they see. It is all about being honest about what you want.
- Increased confidence and self-esteem – when you truthfully communicate your feelings and thoughts, you stand up for yourself, your rights, and the core of who you are. This naturally boosts your confidence and self-esteem.
- Improved relationships – starting from the relationship you nurture with yourself, moving on to your relationships with the people around you. Assertive communication is usually based on mutual respect and trust, and that is why it is an important aspect of every relationship. Communicating directly and being honest can eliminate any resentment or underlying negative feelings that come from a point of unmet needs.
- Less stress – this is my favorite benefit. We are all aware that stress is an unavoidable part of life. But did you know that not putting yourself first can elevate your daily stress levels to uncomfortable heights? A lot of stress for a prolonged period leads to significant changes within your mind and body for the worse. Also, learning to be assertive can make you feel stressed. However, while being more assertive may make you feel discomfort and tension initially, knowing that you are open and straightforward in your communication while considering all parties involved will significantly decrease your stress levels long-term.

Improving your communication abilities does not have to come with a high cost. Sometimes, all it takes is to focus on yourself and learn a few new skills.

Role-Playing Assertiveness Response

Before I go into the exercises, one last bit. Being able to communicate assertively is a skill you need to develop so you can maintain healthy relationships, both with yourself and the people around you. It also helps build up your self-esteem.

Role-playing assertiveness response is assertiveness training. Through it, you get to experience all sorts of things – how you initially want to react when you're met with an uncomfortable situation and how to train your brain to react in a more assertive way.

To understand this in-depth, take a look at the exercises below.

EXERCISE 21

ASSERTIVE COMMUNICATION ROLE-PLAY

This exercise is focused on role play. Learning how to communicate assertively is best done by switching sides. Let's say you are talking to your parents or guardian, and they say that you need to focus on yourself and start standing up for yourself. While this seems reasonable for a parent to say, you act out. You begin to shout and say that you don't want to do anything, that you constantly feel pressured, and you don't know where to begin so you can make yourself better.

With the assertive communication role-play, you switch the roles any way you want. You can either be the parent and understand their point of view and why they are discussing this with you. Or you can indulge in assertive feedback rather than aggression. Either way, this assertive communication exercise is developed to help you change your point of view and teach you how to react more calmly in such challenging situations.

EXERCISE 22

ASSERTIVE COMMUNICATION SCENARIOS

The last exercise for this chapter is connected to assertive communication scenarios. In these scenarios, try to think of something that already happened just to see if you could have reacted better in that situation. Assertive communication scenarios can be truly helpful if you want to retrace your steps back and see how far you've come, or to see how much more you need to work on.

Let me give you a few examples of these assertive communication scenarios.

- ◇ For example, you can start with the feedback you received. It can be anything from feedback at home to feedback at school etc. Something that made you have negative feelings.
- ◇ Or you can move on to declining something you don't want to do. Maybe there has been a situation where you have felt pushed into doing something you didn't want to do, which made you act out later on. We are all human, and when we're cornered, aggression can quickly surface.
- ◇ Criticism is next. You can see it everywhere you go. Sometimes, you even feel it deep down. But oftentimes, it happens that criticism is something we don't take lightly. This especially goes for young people. It can make you feel helpless, and it can make you act out.

These are only a handful of situations where you might have felt like you are doing less than optimal work, or that you're cornered, or you simply feel attacked, and you have the need to fight back. Well, let's turn that around.

Here are 10 scenarios for you to practice. Some of these situations may have already happened to you, while others may not have. For those that you've already experienced, you could try practicing how you would have altered your behavior. Also, for those you haven't experienced, try to think of how you would react in the best possible way.

1. You felt cornered by your classmates for who you are.
2. You had a verbal altercation with someone.
3. Your parents looked at you at dinner, and it felt like there was disappointment in their eyes.

4. You woke up from a bad dream feeling terrible, and that feeling persisted throughout the day.
5. You find yourself thinking that you'll never be good enough.
6. Your teacher confronted you for a lousy job you've done on your homework.
7. People make fun of you because of a certain hobby you have.
8. Every time you look in the mirror you don't like what you see.
9. You voiced out an opinion with your friends, and they laughed at you for it.
10. The feedback you got for a project you worked on was not what you expected it to be.

Now, think of how you already reacted earlier, or think about how you would react in each one of these situations (it was probably not optimal). The next step is to replay that scenario in your mind, but this time, try to turn your reaction around. Instead of bursting out, what would you say to make your response assertive?

Looking back on these types of communication encounters and how you could have improved them will help you better understand the great role assertiveness has in your life. It will also help you look at any situation with a clear mind and readiness to communicate and solve anything that comes your way!

What Did You Learn From This Chapter?

Assertiveness is a skill that will serve you throughout your life. A little bit of theory and a lot of practice can go a long way. Let's review what we learned from this chapter:

- ✦ What is assertive communication.
- ✦ The importance of assertive communication.
- ✦ What you will get by learning assertiveness skills.
- ✦ How to role-play an assertiveness response.

By looking at the logical order of things, once you know how to approach a certain situation in life, you should know how to solve it, too, right? Life gives us challenges every day, and the best way to deal with them is to go toward them – head-on. So, the following chapter will focus on that. I know that you probably already possess some problem-solving skills, but it is time to take a deeper look into it. Let's turn the page and continue learning.

CHAPTER 10

PROBLEM-SOLVING SKILLS

"A problem is a chance for you to do your best." – Duke Ellington

I love that you have picked up this book in your hands because, by this stage, you are pretty much aware of the power within you and how you can do your best at any given moment. We talked about the many challenges you might face and how to identify them, and I added many exercises that can help you get back on the right track.

This chapter offers an entirely different insight into yourself. While I helped you tap into your emotions and feelings in the previous chapters, we will discuss matters of the mind here. Your true power comes from your thinking patterns – if you focus on reshaping them, you focus on creating a better you.

Now, we're delving deep into the subject of problem-solving and how it can help you reform yourself.

Steps for Effective Problem-Solving

The problem-solving skills are an absolute must when it comes to skills you should work on. Once you step out in the world, you will see that having these skills will make the difference between success and failure in everyday situations. These skills can help you navigate the complexities and challenges of life and get accustomed to the ever-changing environment.

But what encompasses effective problem-solving? Is this something you are born with, or something that you can develop over time? You're just in luck because these skills can be developed at any point in life – but as I say, the sooner, the better. Whenever you find yourself in a situation that requires a solution and you don't know where to begin, turn to problem-solving. This can be anything that happens during your day. It can also be anything that happens within you. As we work together to get you up and running, learning the steps that will help you get there is important. Now, I will only mention these steps, and we will discuss them in detail below.

I like to consider these the ultimate five steps to tackling any challenge in your life. These five steps consist of:

1. Identifying the issue
2. Generating all kinds of possible solutions
3. Evaluating those solutions
4. Implementing the chosen solutions
5. Adjusting as necessary

Now, let's break these down and talk about them, one step at a time, starting from the top.

Identifying Problems and Generating Solutions

The first step in the problem-solving process is to have a clear definition of the challenge, issue, or setback. You don't need to do this in an instant. Remember, some situations are a little more complex and require a longer time to decipher them. That's okay. During that period, collect as much information as you can. Because the more information you have, the better and easier it will be for you to identify the cause of the issue at hand. For example, if you constantly succumb to negative thoughts, it is essential to identify where it comes from and how it affects you. Also, it is necessary to underline that it all comes from a lack of training. Once you clearly understand the root cause, you can start developing a solid action plan to address it. It is highly important to include all available information – gather first, act on it later.

By doing this step, you are doing yourself a favor – as you are directly affected by the situation.

By doing this, you take a step back to gain a different perspective and insight.

The second step is all about brainstorming. Finding a few possible solutions to a challenge can sometimes be more difficult than you can imagine. I urge you to stay on course and be persistent, as it is worth it in the end. I would advise that, as soon as you come to this second step, you try to come up with as many solutions as you can. It doesn't matter if they are very unrealistic or not. The point of this step is to teach yourself how to stray from your regular mindset. Brainstorming and generating all sorts of possible outcomes can help you bounce off ideas. Once you delve into deep thinking, you can create such a session that the ideas you generate will be amazing, and you can just keep them in the back of your mind without any judgment or critique. Coming up with a list of possible solutions may take a while or a bit. It all depends on your specific way of functioning. Consider all the options you have thought of and weigh the pros and cons of each option. Given the information you gathered, what seems like the most effective solution to you (out of all the things you came up with)?

Evaluating and Implementing Solutions

The question leads us to the third step, which is evaluating the solutions. Within this step, it is crucial to keep an open mind and always consider a different perspective. Try to step out of your usual way of thinking as much as you can. Take all the time you need during this process, especially in the beginning, because you will need some time to train your brain anyway. While you are on this step, it is important to consider the consequences of all the options you have in mind. Some of the long-term effects may not be up to your liking. That is why you are in the process of evaluating each possible option. Prioritize them based on their feasibility and the impact they may have. While they sound nice in theory, their execution may be more challenging than you can imagine, while other solutions may be instantly implemented. That is why choosing a solution that addresses the challenge directly and effectively is essential. If you need some help in this section, you can always go back to the SMART concept to help you out. The last thing to remember here is that not all may work according to plan, and you should always keep this in the back of your mind – but more on that later.

The fourth step is implementing the solution. Here is when you need to start planning carefully. Everything needs to go as smoothly as possible, and you must know your responsibilities. Designing a layout plan with everything in front of you will give you a better idea of how to execute it. You can see this below in the exercise 25, solution implementation practice.

Monitoring, Adjusting, and How the Overall Process Will Make You Feel

Last but not least, it is always important to track the implementation process. As this is the last step of your problem-solving skills, you can only truly complete this process once you realize that regular check-ins are a must. While you are implementing a solution to any of life's challenges you're faced with, it is vital to address them from time to time to prevent them from becoming bigger or creating an additional challenge. Adjusting the solution is imperative to ensure that whatever you want resolved is on the right track. Sometimes, plans don't go as they're supposed to, and you may end up with a problem that is not fully resolved. The thing is, you need to be flexible while you approach a challenge or an issue. Monitor how your chosen solution works, and if you feel like something could be done better, don't be afraid to make any adjustments. It all comes down to the feedback you get – both from yourself and your surroundings. The solution should completely resolve the issue and fulfill your hopes. Once you notice this is not happening, it is time to take actionable steps. Take a few steps back. If necessary, go to the brainstorming step, and see what else you've come up with. Maybe things will change when you look at the solution from a different perspective. And you will find that something else may work better instead.

It is important to be fully invested in the process. This five-step problem-solving process can help you overcome any obstacles you face. Remember that it is all about defining the problem, analyzing it,

Self-Regulation Workbook for Teens

and getting all the necessary information – those are the first steps. Then, by understanding the root of the issue, you come up with a few solutions and go for the one that seems the most logical at the moment. If by any chance something doesn't work out, back to the drawing board you go!

I love it when people are being practical about something. That's why I tend to focus on creating the ultimate mind-spirit balance. But, to do that, we always need exercise. The following exercises you see will provide you with an incredible way to get in touch with yourself and activate that problem-solving part of your mind.

EXERCISE 23

PROBLEM-SOLVING STEPS PRACTICE

Another way to name this exercise is "a real-life example." You need to practice the problem-solving steps over and over again. In this first exercise, I encourage you to start doing this whenever you are faced with a challenge because there is no better way to master problem-solving skills than to begin utilizing them right there – on the spot!

Depending on your situation, you may have to wait a little longer for such a situation to arise. If that's the case, then give this practice a nudge. Think of any past situation that has been haunting you for a while now. Write it down. From this perspective and this point in time, how would you approach it? Write that down too. Now that you have more knowledge in your arsenal, would it be easier for you to tackle it? Why? Also, once you've settled it in your mind, how did that make you feel? Follow the problem-solving steps below and start practicing.

1. Identifying the issue.
2. Generating all kinds of possible solutions.
3. Evaluating those solutions.
4. Implementing the chosen solutions.
5. Adjusting as necessary

1. The Problem: _____

2. Possible Solutions: _____
   _____
   _____
   _____

3. What is Good/Bad in Each of the Solutions?: _____
   _____
   _____
   _____

4. The Solution I Will Implement: _____
   _____

Problem-Solving Skills

1. The Problem: _____

2. Possible Solutions: _____
   _____
   _____
   _____

3. What is Good/Bad in Each of the Solutions?: _____
   _____
   _____
   _____

4. The Solution I Will Implement: _____
   _____

———o—◇—o———

1. The Problem: _____

2. Possible Solutions: _____
   _____
   _____
   _____

3. What is Good/Bad in Each of the Solutions?: _____
   _____
   _____
   _____

4. The Solution I Will Implement: _____
   _____

———o—◇—o———

1. The Problem: _____

2. Possible Solutions: _____

_____

_____

_____

3. What is Good/Bad in Each of the Solutions?: _____

_____

_____

_____

4. The Solution I Will Implement: _____

_____

—o—◇—o—

1. The Problem: _____

2. Possible Solutions: _____

_____

_____

_____

3. What is Good/Bad in Each of the Solutions?: _____

_____

_____

_____

4. The Solution I Will Implement: _____

_____

—o—◇—o—

Problem-Solving Skills

EXERCISE 24

SOLVING COMMON PROBLEMS

Practice makes it perfect. Instead of pulling yourself down into the vortex of negative behavior, realize there are many ways to train your brain. One of those ways is to keep posing small challenges for yourself every day. These challenges do not have to be ones of the past or ones you have to make up. But rather, these could be challenges you can find anywhere you turn.

What do I mean by this? Well, more than mere puzzles, of course! Solving common problems such as puzzles or brain teasers can help you challenge your mind. But the real thing to incorporate here is a small scheme that can help you get out of your negative thought pattern every time. If you are unsure that you are thinking "out of the box" to the widest extent, then these teasers can help you out.

Here are a few common issues that every teenager faces:

1. A face filled with spots or pimples.
2. Feeling left out in social situations.
3. Feeling overwhelmed with school.
4. Not wanting to do homework every day.
5. Having very low self-esteem and a bad body image.
6. Difficulty connecting with friends.
7. Difficult connecting with siblings and/or parents.
8. Struggling at school.
9. Struggling to fit in in social situations.
10. Feeling unmotivated.
11. Not knowing what to do with yourself and your future.
12. Frequently arguing, with everyone.

Now, let's elaborate on one of these in this exercise. Let's go with number 3 - feeling overwhelmed with school.

The first step you're going to take is to identify the issue - which we have.

The second step is thinking about possible solutions. In this case, you can try to limit your distractions or ask for help.

The third step is to evaluate the solutions. For example, if you ask for help, you may learn more, and become better (one of the pros), but you may feel like you are losing your independence (one of the cons). Limiting your distractions seems like a pretty good idea so far.

The fourth step is to choose the best solution - which is in this case limiting the distractions.

The fifth and final step is to implement the solution. Always start small but do this every day. Start with 10 minutes or half an hour a day and work your way up - as long as you feel good and are comfortable with the process.

Now, go ahead and do some practice yourself.

1. The Problem: _____

2. Possible Solutions: _____

   _____

   _____

   _____

3. What is Good/Bad in Each of the Solutions?: _____

   _____

   _____

   _____

4. The Solution I Will Implement: _____

   _____

---

1. The Problem: _____

2. Possible Solutions: _____

   _____

   _____

   _____

3. What is Good/Bad in Each of the Solutions?: _____

   _____

   _____

   _____

4. The Solution I Will Implement: _____

   _____

1. The Problem: _____

2. Possible Solutions: _____
   _____
   _____
   _____
   _____

3. What is Good/Bad in Each of the Solutions?: _____
   _____
   _____
   _____
   _____

4. The Solution I Will Implement: _____
   _____

———o—◇—o———

1. The Problem: _____

2. Possible Solutions: _____
   _____
   _____
   _____
   _____

3. What is Good/Bad in Each of the Solutions?: _____
   _____
   _____
   _____
   _____

4. The Solution I Will Implement: _____
   _____

———o—◇—o———

1. The Problem: _____

2. Possible Solutions: _____
   _____
   _____
   _____

3. What is Good/Bad in Each of the Solutions?: _____
   _____
   _____
   _____

4. The Solution I Will Implement: _____
   _____

―――――o―◇―o―――――

1. The Problem: _____

2. Possible Solutions: _____
   _____
   _____
   _____

3. What is Good/Bad in Each of the Solutions?: _____
   _____
   _____
   _____

4. The Solution I Will Implement: _____
   _____

―――――o―◇―o―――――

Problem-Solving Skills

1. The Problem: _____

2. Possible Solutions: _____
   _____
   _____
   _____

3. What is Good/Bad in Each of the Solutions?: _____
   _____
   _____
   _____

4. The Solution I Will Implement: _____
   _____

———o—◇—o———

1. The Problem: _____

2. Possible Solutions: _____
   _____
   _____
   _____

3. What is Good/Bad in Each of the Solutions?: _____
   _____
   _____
   _____

4. The Solution I Will Implement: _____
   _____

———o—◇—o———

Self-Regulation Workbook for Teens

1. The Problem: _____

2. Possible Solutions: _____
_____
_____
_____

3. What is Good/Bad in Each of the Solutions?: _____
_____
_____
_____

4. The Solution I Will Implement: _____
_____

———o—◇—o———

1. The Problem: _____

2. Possible Solutions: _____
_____
_____
_____

3. What is Good/Bad in Each of the Solutions?: _____
_____
_____
_____

4. The Solution I Will Implement: _____
_____

———o—◇—o———

Problem-Solving Skills

Try to do this with every issue you face in life. It is mind-altering how useful these steps can be.

You can still indulge in daily crossword puzzles, sudoku, chess, or anything you find interesting. These games are a fantastic way to enhance your logical thinking. But this exercise is the one thing you need to pull yourself back up. Sure enough, after a while, you will notice yourself thinking outside the box constantly.

EXERCISE 25

SOLUTION IMPLEMENTATION PRACTICE

This last exercise is all about implementing a little bit of everything you've learned so far. The practice of implementing a solution includes understanding the challenge or issue, setting some clear objectives, designing the solution, and allocating the necessary resources to make it happen.

To solve a problem, you need to know how to approach it in a way that would result in a successful resolution. The thing is, as I mentioned earlier, you can't always be sure if what you have in mind as a potential solution would work or not. As the last exercise, this is the simplest one of them all – just try. Give it a go! I know that there may be many things blocking you from making a decision or thinking clearly, but as we are nearing the end of this book, you have to be honest – we did cover almost all of them, right?

So, what I want you to do is to choose one single problem you currently have in your mind. Then go through all the problem-solving steps. Once you have the solution you want to implement, then go and give the solution you have in mind a try. Even if it fails, today's chapter taught you that you can always go back to the brainstorming step and assess the situation from the beginning. Because the solutions you may come up with could be the best ones, but nothing will really happen if you never act on them.

What Did You Learn From This Chapter?

In this chapter, I am hoping to have given you the liberty to think positively with your mind. To challenge yourself every single time and hopefully to have nudged you in the right direction. Without challenges, there is no growth.

Let's make a short recap of what you've learned here:

- You learned the five steps of problem-solving skills.
- You had an exercise on how to implement the problem-solving practice.
- An exercise you need to implement daily – solving common problems.
- The last exercise that simply nudges you to begin.

So far, this book has been about uplifting you and pushing you forward in life. I can imagine what it must be like for you right now. You finally started believing that you can do anything you set your mind to, and you can create a better and more positive version of yourself. But what will happen if you fall back to your old self? Is there still a voice in the back of your mind telling you that you have a chance of failing, that everything would have been for nothing?

The book's last chapter is about permanently cementing everything you've learned so far. It is about preventing a relapse (should you get to that point). You see – I really did think of everything. I have been where you are and know what you're going through. So, turn the page, and let's take the final steps toward creating a better you – together!

CHAPTER 11

RELAPSE PREVENTION

"Life is very interesting. In the end, some of your greatest pains become your greatest strengths." – Drew Barrymore

With this lovely quote, I open up the book's last chapter. To be honest, Drew Barrymore could not have said it better – turning the pain into your strong side is one of the many joys in life. It is what makes you stronger, more resilient, calmer, more centered, and happier overall.

While all of this is true, word for word, you are still a human and a young one at that. You're still learning. Who knows how many times you're going to fall in life before you lift yourself back up? Each time that happens, you will probably want to get right back into the negative mindset, completely dismissing the CBT approach and everything you've worked so hard for. I understand – you may be faced with extremely challenging situations, which can damage all the progress you've made.

But that doesn't mean you should give up. On the contrary, it means that you should have something to fall back on. I understand where your fear is coming from. Maybe that little voice still tells you that you can never improve, even if you went through this entire book and completed all the exercises with flying colors.

Even if your conscious mind notices the change, your subconscious mind may still make you believe that you are not worthy of anything good. This is known as the turning point in the process, and it is when most people relapse.

Because your progress is important, I decided to dedicate this last chapter to relapse prevention. Let's discuss how to handle yourself in tough times.

Recognizing Warning Signs of Relapse

When you have undergone a program or have used an approach where your sole focus has been yourself, you may feel encouraged once you step out into the world. However, some of you may hesitate about everything because of fear. You may be scared that you will fail and return to your old self. I know that no one wants to have an immediate fear of failure once you step out into the unknown. That is why it is essential to create a relapse prevention plan. It will help you learn how to avoid relapse and will help you gain even more skills on how to handle yourself. Ultimately, it will be the final trick you will have up your sleeve that will keep you in check.

When you've worked so hard to make a better person out of yourself, you walked a long and challenging journey. With each step, you got out of your comfort zone, and you assessed the situation over and over again. The level of self-awareness increased, and everything about you unfolded in stages – right before your eyes. The unfolding part gives you a part of the answer. This is the first thing you need to look into if you have the fear of relapse. The more acute the self-awareness is, the easier it will be to spot any issues.

Ultimately, there are a few signs that can apply to anyone when we talk about relapse. They are:

- **Emotional relapse** – the denial tends to be strong here. Emotional relapse is the most serious form of relapse here because, after all, we are focusing on thoughts, feelings, and behavior. You may notice feeling isolated and being emotionally reclusive as the first signs. Other than that, you start not being involved in any day-to-day activities, having negative views about yourself and others around you, having difficulty sleeping, and having a reduced concern for personal hygiene.
- **Mental health** – you start lacking the resistance you worked so hard to obtain. Instead of focusing on the good, taking a step back, and assessing every thought and situation that needs your attention, you stop doing this. You slowly start going back to your old habit of immediately jumping to the wrong and negative conclusions. You notice how the exercises and knowledge you've gained over the past period of time slowly start to slip away from you. Your mental health stops being your priority, and you abide more and more by your past thinking patterns.

Noticing the warning signs of relapse can make you both aware and unaware at the same time. How come? Well, the unaware part is that voice that keeps telling you everything will go wrong, and you're not worth it. The aware part is that you know that you can do better, but you feel like you are constantly pulled under the surface.

Developing a Relapse Prevention Plan

Observing the warning signs I just mentioned is a step in the right direction. To fully prevent yourself from stepping back into your old habits means taking the warning signs seriously. The thoughts that cross your mind don't always need your attention or action. A part of developing a relapse prevention plan means controlling your levels of stress.

Learn to recognize each time when your stress levels go up and are unchecked – especially if you are dealing with anxiety issues. Experiencing anxiety means that you are dismissing the path of dealing with stress healthily.

The main part of your relapse prevention plan should be lowering stress levels. Thankfully, there are a few ways you can naturally achieve this. Here are some examples:

- Regularly exercising or indulging in physical activity of your liking.
- Keeping in touch with your friends and family and giving them a little bit of your time.
- Making a list of feel-good movies and songs that you can turn to every time you feel an onset of negativity creeping up on you.
- Always focusing on the positive mindset rather than the negative.
- Maintaining a healthy diet, filled with nutrient-dense foods.
- Journaling, or any other way of writing down the good things that come to your mind.
- Celebrating all the milestones you achieve in life, be those small or large.

Since I am ending this list on a celebratory note, I think it is high time to start looking into the strategies, right? The other biggest part of creating a solid relapse prevention plan is creating strong strategies that will help you maintain success. In other words, let's give the spotlight to the bright side of life!

Strategies for Maintaining Progress Over Time

Over time, it is critical to maintain effectiveness and progress. It is not just about reaching a certain point and then remaining there. No. You will develop as a person throughout your life. During this time, you will keep discovering new things about yourself. You will push your limits and strengthen your boundaries. You can't remain in the same spot your entire life – and you won't.

A part of relapse prevention is the list of strategies that can keep you on the right track every single time. And I am talking about much more than open and honest communication with yourself and with others. I am talking about seeing the good, focusing on the good, and achieving the good.

The trick is to keep yourself motivated. Why are you doing all of this? To create a better version of yourself. Do you want to keep working on this? Yes. Why? Because it makes you feel better and achieve more. Do you need to feel pressured about it? Absolutely not!

Find something that will truly motivate you. At this point, I can give you a little nudge in the right direction. Below, you will find a list of a few techniques or strategies that I have learned about along the way that have helped me remain on track. In order to keep on going, try implementing at least a few of them. That way, you'll know you will have done everything for yourself.

All of these are very easy to do. See for yourself below!

1. **A reward** – reward yourself for all the times you have overcome a certain challenge. As you work on yourself and your goals, you will constantly step out of your comfort zone. You will face an increasing number of challenges and give much effort to overcome them. As that happens, reward yourself each time you make it through. Whether it is a milestone you've set for yourself or the consistency you've maintained, never forget to treat yourself.

2. **Relax** – in all fairness, you can't constantly work on yourself. Everybody needs some time to relax, and you are no exception. You may have just gone through an emotional rollercoaster – that means you did quite a demanding job keeping yourself up! So, when you notice that a calmer period is coming, or you just feel like you need to recharge, give yourself that time. This type of recharging can be anything – from drawing yourself a bath to enjoying a hot beverage – anything that can relax you.

3. **Prepare for the day** – the best way to tackle things is not only one at a time but also one day beforehand. By creating a list of the things you need to do the following day, you can have a clear picture of your responsibilities and divide them into smaller sections. By doing this, you can overcome them very easily. Once you know success is guaranteed, nothing is stopping you!

4. **Be realistic and own yourself** – as I mentioned in the SMART goal frame, your goals should always be realistic. You need to be honest with yourself about how much time you would need to achieve or complete something. What I didn't mention is that you should always own your goals. Do whatever you want to carry out because something might constantly push you back or tell you not to do anything. Take responsibility for your actions and carry them out to the very end – you will be glad you did so.

5. **Indulge in a power hour** – when you feel like you have a lot more energy, focus it on something you've been putting on the back burner for a while. This could be any type of tedious task or something you didn't want to face yet. By putting things in the front line while you have energy, you take advantage of the perfect situation. Instead of doing nothing and then beating yourself up because you've done nothing at the time when you felt you could be active, you're doing something productive. This task could be anything – because you'll see that you will feel lighter as soon as you complete it.

These are only a handful of strategies you can implement to lift any remaining weight off your shoulders. They will slowly pave the way for progress. Before I wrap things up, remember this – progress is still progress, no matter how slow you move. And before you know it, time has passed, and you will look back only to see you've come a long way.

What Did You Learn From This Chapter?

As the last chapter of this book, its goal was to complete the circle – and give you the last bits of information you need to help you on your journey to reinventing yourself. Here is what you learned from it:

- ✧ The progress you make is as important as you say it is.
- ✧ Relapse can happen to anyone – there are a few warning signs that point to it.
- ✧ It is your responsibility to stop the relapse from happening by utilizing the relapse prevention plan.
- ✧ Other than prevention, you can always focus on the good – try using the strategies for maintaining progress over time.

I can only hope that the biggest thing you learned from this chapter is not to beat yourself up every time. Life will happen to you, whether you want it to or not, and you will not be prepared for what it gives you most of the time. However, you must remember how strong you are through all the challenges and especially, the curveballs. You can achieve anything you set your mind to and easily become the best version of yourself. There is no need to fear what's yet to come because whatever it is, through the power of this book, you can overcome it.

CONCLUSION

"I am the master of my fate; I am the captain of my soul." – William Henley

With this wonderful quote in mind, I would like to bid you one final adieu. As we reach the end of our journey together, I want to reflect on everything we've learned. Now, I am not going to do the regular "let's review what we've learned" since we did that at the end of each chapter. No. I will help you reflect on these lessons, as they will be the most valuable life lessons you will ever learn.

Through this book, you realized there is a way for you to shape your future and yourself, and you learned about all the different strategies you can implement to make that happen. Together, we highlighted the importance of self-control and accentuated your potential for continuous personal development. What you learned here is more than just another skill set. It is the cornerstone of creating a successful, fulfilling, and happy life. Once you realize that you have no trouble mastering self-control and that the CBT approach is the most successful one, you will have gained complete power over your life.

Making deliberate choices that align with your goals and values and what you aspire to be is important.

Managing your time is important.

Resisting falling back into your old ways is important.

Pushing through the most challenging times is important.

Self-control and CBT have helped you achieve just that. By utilizing the tools you found in this book, you will commit to life-long learning and self-improvement. I can only imagine the feeling you got while reading this book – that feeling comes from realizing that we are constantly evolving. There was always room for improvement and development. You just had to find a way to do that. At the end of the day, it is all about abiding by a growing mindset and opening yourself up to all life can offer. Through all the steps you made while reading this book, you noticed that they are still significant, no matter how small they are.

Being a teenager is difficult. Being a teenager in the 21st century seems like the biggest challenge – especially when you're the teenager in question. I can understand that. I did understand that. That's why this book was filled with information that was helpful to you. You learned how to create new habits and keep yourself away from a life that was difficult and negative.

Before we part ways, I leave you with this – always surround yourself with people who are good for you. Always try to look on the bright side. Remember that the choices you make today pave the way for the person you will become in the future. Having full control over yourself and constantly learning is not something you achieve once – but rather something you work on every day. You are willing to make a change, and I know you have both the patience and the determination to make that change possible. Cultivate your mind and move forward through life. Carry the lessons from this book with you and allow them to guide you to create and control the life you've always wanted!

EMILY CARTER

DBT WORKBOOK
for Teens

Easy & Proven Ways to Manage Anger, Anxiety & Stress, Improve Communication Skills, and Develop Healthy Coping Skills for Better Emotional Regulation Using Mindfulness & DBT

INTRODUCTION

"Life is a balance of holding on and letting go."

– Rumi

You are about to begin a journey of self-discovery. I know you. You've come from a challenging place and want to see how to deal with whatever life throws at you differently. Being a teenager is one of the most challenging things you have gone through in life so far. As you navigate this exciting phase, you notice changes happening all around you – the dynamic in your family changes, your friendships grow and change, you enter a new school environment, and you also change and grow as a person, as well. You've probably even felt lost and insecure at times. That's why I'm here to give you a hand.

Don't think of this book as another self-help book. Think of it as a friend – one who will guide you through this exciting chapter of your life designed specifically for you. Here, you will learn what it takes to be a teenager in this world and how to find yourself, center yourself, and to simply – be yourself. The skills I focused on in this book are based on Dialectical Behavior Therapy (DBT). This powerful approach can help you manage your emotions and build your entire life from the ground up.

Understanding Dialectical Behavior Therapy

Dialectical Behavior Therapy, or DBT, is a type of cognitive-behavioral therapy that was originally developed to help people manage their intense emotions. Nowadays, it is the perfect tool for young people like you to develop some strong skills. DBT is built on the idea that two things can coexist and be true at the same time. A good example of this would be, accepting yourself for who you are but also wanting to change yourself. The balance between these two is what DBT is all about.

Right now, you feel like there is a rollercoaster of emotions – one minute, you feel like you are on top of the world, and the next minute, you feel like all is falling apart. The good news is that DBT will help you navigate these highs and lows even when you're struggling with stress, sadness, anxiety, or just the regular changes that happen within you while growing up. The DBT skills can help you collect all the tools you need at your disposal to tackle anything that comes your way.

Before we begin, it is crucial for you to understand that DBT consists of four concepts. These concepts are - mindfulness, distress tolerance, emotional intelligence, and interpersonal effectiveness. We are going to go through all of these concepts together. Just to give you an idea of what each of these represent, here are some brief explanations.

Mindfulness is the art of being fully focused and present in the moment. It consists of observing, describing, and participating without any judgement. It is considered the foundation of DBT. Through it, you can enhance your awareness and allow yourself to recognize your own thoughts.

Distress tolerance is knowing how to survive and cope with difficult situations. Here, it is all about soothing yourself and accepting the situation as it is. Life can deal you with some tough cards sometimes, and distress tolerance is important so that you can learn how to survive during these moments without engaging in harmful behaviors.

Emotional regulation is the ability to manage your emotions in what is considered a healthy way. Identifying and managing your emotional responses is crucial if you want to maintain emotional balance. This way, you can enhance your overall well-being.

Finally, interpersonal effectiveness is knowing how to communicate with other people in a way that exudes confidence and respect. As an aspect of DBT, it can help you navigate social situations and build long-lasting relationships.

All of these concepts tie together to create a comprehensive framework that will help you deal with any kind of emotional challenge that comes your way. As you go through this book, you will notice how strong and important they are.

How to Use This Workbook?

Using this workbook to your advantage will be easier said than done in some situations. But, looking at the bigger picture, you will realize that this book is meticulously divided into sections that focus on the core DBT skills. Every section comes with incredible explanations, is easy enough to understand and implement, and is filled with exercises and examples. These can help you apply what you've learned in real-life situations. To answer your question of how to use this workbook, the best way to do that is through the exercises. They are extremely beneficial, and all you need to do in most of them is to take notes, and sometimes have a partner to talk to (depending on the exercise).

Through the book, you will find many ways to use DBT skills to overcome the challenges you're faced with in life every day. Some of the examples can be your reassurance – you're not alone, and you've never been alone in this.

Before we dive right into the subject, let me tell you something important – you already are as capable and strong as you wish. Just think about this – you are here, reading this introduction, getting ready to read the book that will ultimately shape your life. You are ready to take control. The path is filled with obstacles. It will not be easy. Sometimes, you may want to give up, but I am here to help you power through and make it to the other side. This book is designed to help you every step of the way.

Work through these skills, make mistakes along the way, and allow yourself to grow. Be patient, as change takes a lot of time. Count all small steps you take as victories and get ready to start the journey – because now, it is time for you to turn the page and begin!

Part 1

MINDFULNESS

"To a mind that is still, the whole universe surrenders."

– Lao Tzu

There is a certain connection between your mind and your relationship with yourself and everything else around you. This certain kind of connection you have is special. It is unique, and depending on how well you nurture it, it will either flourish or perish.

In this first part, we will talk about mindfulness and how to stop whatever you are doing and start focusing on yourself. Because remember, the star of this book is you. The work you will be doing while reading is unmatched – and you will only get to realize that once you are done with the last page. I will have managed to describe every aspect you should focus on. Now, it is yours to accept and grasp the term mindfulness with both hands.

But that's not all. In this part, I will help you explore a few other important aspects of DBT - these include the wise mind, the what skills, and the how skills. You might see them as confusing terms now. However, as we delve deeper into the book together, you will notice how all of them are connected. There is not one without the other. It is all about getting a better understanding of what lies ahead for you. While you want to paint the big picture now, remember that any big picture consists of small things. From mindfulness, to the how skills, these are the small, yet significant things you are going to explore.

What Is Mindfulness?

Mindfulness. This word signifies an incredible concept of being fully present in the moment. It elaborates on the fact that your mind is completely present. Whether you are doing something, moving through a certain space, or you are fully invested in what is going on.

For a young mind such as yours, this may seem like a strange concept. You may even ask, "Well, isn't my mind present all the time?" and you are right to do so. It may even sound illogical as a statement, except it isn't. The mind works all the time, and often, it can steer us away from the moment we're currently in. You've probably felt it before – it simply takes off in the middle of a situation, and you start to lose touch with your senses, your body, and so on. As soon as you know it, this is something that can make you feel absent in an instant.

Sit with this for a while, has this ever happened to you? It must have at some point by now. That is why I am starting this book with the concept of mindfulness. Because everything you will ever learn from this point on connects back to it. Mindfulness is more than the human ability to be fully present in the moment – it is the pillar upon which this book is based.

The good thing about mindfulness is that you already have it within you. This is not something you need to work to obtain (like a degree), it is already present. All you need to do is learn how to access it and nurture it.

Are you still feeling a little bit confused? I've created a small list of things that can help you understand the concept of mindfulness. Think of them as facts, something that cannot be changed.

- Mindfulness is a familiar thing. You already do this every day, but up until now, you haven't been aware of it.
- Mindfulness is not some special thing you can be or do. You hold a spectacular power to be present within yourself, and you do not need to change to harness it. All you need to do is cultivate it.
- Mindfulness recognizes your full potential. Every solution that requires change from you should not be implemented. Mindfulness helps you cultivate the best of who you are as a human being.
- Anyone can do mindfulness – specifically because it has the potential to grow into a transformative phenomenon. You can really benefit from it, and it is an easy thing to focus on.
- You can easily turn mindfulness into a lifestyle. It is more than just a practice. By doing that, you will slowly implement a caring and an awareness approach to every aspect of your life.
- It will spark up your entire life. Mindfulness comes with many benefits, including happiness, improved relationships, better work, wilder imagination, and innovation, as well as effectiveness and resilience.

But of course, you are not here to learn just about mindfulness. We both know that this is only the beginning. Next, you are going to delve a little bit deeper into your mind.

WISE MIND

Wise mind - more famously known as the "aha" moment in DBT. I already mentioned that DBT is an abbreviation for dialectical behavior therapy. It is kind of like a talk therapy that can help you understand your emotions as well as your behavior. Within this book, you are going to learn how to incorporate that into your everyday life. Remember that the whole purpose of DBT is to help you accept the reality of your life and your behavior as well as to help you enjoy it to the fullest extent.

I am aware that until this point, everything sounds completely new to you, but you will soon find out that everything serves its own purpose. And the wise mind is only the first concept for you to understand. Well, a wise mind is not something you have. It is a technique. The wise mind is the core aspect of DBT, and it is based on the concept that there are three states of mind – a reasonable mind, an emotional mind, and a wise mind.

The wise mind represents the absolute optimal state. This is the place where emotions and rational thinking come together. The wise mind allows an individual to make a solid and sound decision based on both, so it is something that aligns with their goals and values. As a technique, the wise mind is very successful and powerful because it can help you strengthen your mind, especially when you are feeling a little distressed. It includes mindfulness exercises so you can make the most out of any situation.

The good thing about the wise mind is that it comes with many qualities and characteristics. By cultivating it, you can navigate many challenges that come your way. Here are some of them:

- You get to work on your intuition. The wise mind technique can help you get a better understanding of what comes within you and can guide you toward taking the appropriate action.
- After using it for a while, your ability to clearly see any situation or issue is improved. You are objective and don't allow strong emotions to overwhelm you.

- ✧ The wise mind is the perfect way to incorporate some balance into your life. The reason behind this is to incorporate both the rational and the emotional aspects, helping you find the exact middle between them.
- ✧ As you incorporate the wise mind technique into your life, you open yourself up to an authentic experience. Instead of being led by external factors, you delve deep into your true, authentic self.
- ✧ A life of compassion is what follows. Cultivating the wise mind means you will foster a feeling of empathy, understanding, and compassion – both toward yourself and others.

It seems that navigating challenges will be easy after reading this, right? We are only at the beginning, so let's move on to discovering how to integrate both the reasonable and the emotional mind.

As a concept, the wise mind relies on the merging of the reasonable and the emotional mind. The reasonable mind is the analytical one, the one that looks at every situation logically, while the emotional mind represents the intuitive aspect of it all. When you combine the two together, you can make sound decisions.

EMOTIONAL MIND — **WISE MIND** — **REASONABLE MIND**

There is an importance behind doing this. By balancing the reasonable and the emotional mind, you can start effectively solving problems and making decisions. Why is that so? Well, think about it. Say you need to make a decision. A large one. If you only look at it from a logical point of view, you may come to a very robotic and detached solution. But on the other hand, if you only include your emotional side in it, you might make an impulsive and irrational decision.

That's why I love to focus on both aspects. While doing that, you discover a whole new part of yourself too – a balanced one. Using the wise mind means you consider your goals and values, but also your well-being. And once you find it – you never go back.

You learn that when emotions are the only thing driving your decisions, you may become moody and reactive and act in a way that is not really typical for you. As you are a teenager, I can understand how emotions can get in the way sometimes. That's probably the main reason why you started reading this book in the first place. Without the help of a little bit of logic, you will only rely on your impulsivity.

It is time to take a look at the first exercise.

EXERCISE 1
IDENTIFYING AND ACCESSING THE WISE MIND

The first of the many exercises you will find throughout this book is identifying and accessing the wise mind. As you can see, we already explored the topics of reasonable and emotional mind – now it is time to put them both to good use!

As you can see, cultivating mindfulness is a crucial thing if you want to access the wise mind. You need to be present in the moment and be attentive – fully aware of your feelings, thoughts, and body. I mentioned earlier that it is all about balance – the perfect combination between emotion and reason. Here is how you can identify and access your wise mind.

It is all about using mindfulness. Find a space where you feel comfortable and do the following (you can either sit down or do this standing up):

- Take a minute to pause and take a deep breath.
- Clear your mind from everything, and focus on you, both physically and mentally, in that moment.
- Focus on the current thing that constantly occupies your mind. This can be anything - an idea, a plan, or maybe an emotion.
- Sit with it for a minute and recognize it fully. Allow yourself to recognize the sensations you have with that idea or thought in your mind.
- Now, it is time to access the wise mind.
- Ask yourself, "How can I benefit from this plan/idea/action/thought? Is this connected to my wise mind?"
- Allow yourself to listen to both the emotion and the logic. The answer is somewhere in between. If it helps, take notes.
- Before you finish this thought process, check if the decision you are making causes you any imbalance of emotion or reason. Remember, the wise mind should also give you peace of mind.

If you don't know how to check in with yourself, it is always good to follow the breadcrumbs – your body. I have noticed that many people, especially young people, experience the wise mind in the center of their body or between the eyes. To complete the process, try to allow yourself to enter a meditative state. Try to intentionally bring awareness to these body parts and see how you feel. Notice the thoughts and the feelings. If you are making the right decision, you will feel calmer, centered and ready to get back into reality.

_____

_____

_____

As you continue reading, you will discover a lot of new things about yourself. And I will be there every step of the way, making it easier for you to understand the process of balancing yourself and your emotions. The next thing we're going to look into is the mindfulness skills. These are considered the foundation of all DBT skills. They are also known under a different name – the what skills and the how skills. Remember earlier in the chapter, when I mentioned this? Well, first off, we are going to start with the what skills, and then we are going to move on to the how skills.

WHAT SKILLS

The issues that are addressed with these mindfulness skills can help you know who you are, what you want to do with your life, and how to obtain it. These skills can even help you control what's going on in your mind. The "what" part from the what skills refers to the ways of practicing your thinking – what you do to take control over yourself. The three ways that I'm about to share with you are important, and all of them can help you whenever you are dealing with an issue or need a change. They are - observing, describing, and participating. I will go into detail for each of them below.

01.
Observing

Observing is about being present in the moment and opening up all of your senses to every experience - your touch, sight, smell, taste, and hearing. The lens of your senses can be extremely powerful, and during the observation of the present moment, you utilize all of them. When you observe, you experience without ever labelling the experience. In the beginning, you may find yourself struggling with this, and that's okay. After a while, you will notice the quiet benefits of this skill. You will learn how to observe without your mind talking as much.

It will be difficult for you to watch thoughts go by, as there is always a little bit of temptation included, which is also something that can help you get "caught up" in the experience. When you get caught up, this may mean you are becoming obsessed, where you preoccupy yourself with something, and you can't stop thinking about it. With the power of observation, the goal is to stand back a little bit. I do not want you to detach from the situation entirely but rather take a step back and try to view it objectively.

Another thing here – I know it is tempting for you to react to every thought you have in this situation – especially to the negative ones. These thoughts can make you want to leave a specific situation. But the challenge of being observant means experiencing something without judging whether it is good or bad. In this situation, you let all the thoughts go by.

EXERCISE 2
BODY SCAN

Let's make two exercises connected to this observing skill. In this first exercise, I advise you to sit down, or even lay down on a yoga mat or a carpet. Try to completely relax and feel yourself, your entire body. Focus on your breath and notice how your body inflates and deflates with every breathing cycle. Now, you should do a body scan. Start from the top (or from the bottom) and work your way through every part of your body. Really feel and pay attention to every part of your body - arms, legs, torso, hair, neck, everything.

Now, notice your thought pattern. You are a teenager, so chances are – there is something about yourself that you don't like. Say, for example, you don't like your legs. As soon as you think about them, you immediately have negative feelings. By using the power of observation, notice these thoughts –

but allow them to flow through you rather than being stuck with them. It may take you a while to get there, so I recommend you practice this whenever you get a chance.

When I want to connect with myself, I always start from the bottom and work my way up. If you don't know where to begin, this is a good starting point. Start from the feet and feel them (one at a time). Consider this to be almost of a spiritual practice. While you observe, you also connect on the highest possible level. The goal here is to be connected with every part of your body, know all its edges and how they make you feel. Now, we were talking about the feet. Start with whichever one you like, and really feel it. Is it in pain, is it pulsating (maybe if you've walked for a longer time before you did this exercise)? Acknowledge any sensations you feel around it - is it cold, hot, or incredibly comfortable? Do you have a sock on your foot? How does that feel too? This exercise is all about becoming more aware of sensory experiences - and ultimately, more accepting of them. This exercise is about training the mind rather than relaxing it. After a short while, you will see how it makes you feel a little more centered, and helps you connect to any sensations you're feeling without judging them.

EXERCISE 3
OBSERVING THE SURROUNDINGS

It is interesting to see how many things surround us. These things are incredible – just take a look at what surrounds you at the moment. It seems almost incredible, right? In this exercise, it is about observing your environment. For example, if you are at home, during the day, or in the office, find a sunny spot. Give it a minute and notice the sun's rays penetrating through the windows and illuminating the room. Allow the opinions to wash over you once again, and to let them flow.

On the other hand, if you are outside, try to be even more observant. Do the surroundings change often (meaning – are you a part of a crowd)? Or maybe you're in a park? Observe with all of your senses, and allow the feelings to sink in.

02.
Describing

The next skill we're talking about is describing. This, in simple terms, means putting into words what you have observed. However, it still means describing an experience without any judgment.

This act of describing the responses and the things that happen around you (or to you) can provide you with the ability to label events and behaviors. When you start describing a situation that makes you feel a certain way (either good or bad), it helps you observe it more objectively and make a clear connection between yourself and what surrounds you or what is happening.

The goal here is to use the skills of observation and description together to help you stay in the present moment. Together, they will provide you with the focus you need.

EXERCISE 4
DESCRIBING THOUGHTS, FEELINGS, AND SENSATIONS

It is important to learn how to describe everything you think and feel – and not consider those things as facts. Your state will constantly change, and for example, if you feel afraid, it does not necessarily mean that there is a real danger around you. So, in this exercise, you will learn how to describe your thoughts, feelings, and sensations.

Pick one thing that you do every day – your morning or night routine, cooking a meal, walking, or playing with your pet – yes, this can be anything. Start by observing the experience while you are doing it. As you notice every single detail (even some details you have missed before), start describing the experience without judging it. For example, you might be one of those people who don't close the toothpaste after using it – and you might associate that with a feeling of laziness or indifference. Try to remove these "obstacles" and just describe to yourself what you are doing. Describe the experience, the sensations, every little thing.

_____
_____
_____
_____
_____
_____
_____
_____

It is quite a revelation when you look at what you have described. This will give you a sense of who you are, what interests you, and what you notice the most, as well as give you an insight into your thought pattern. Except in this situation, it will look as if you have taken a step back and you are looking at the situation objectively – meaning you're on the right path.

EXERCISE 5
"I FEEL" STATEMENTS

Now, take things a step further – and feel.

During this exercise, we are going to label emotions. There are probably at least a handful of times in life when you felt disappointed, happy, sad, angry, content, etc. In this fifth exercise, you will learn how to verbally describe your feelings in a given moment.

This is an exercise you can do next time you find yourself in a situation that makes you feel a certain way. Until now, you have most likely relied on the factor of the emotional mind, leading to a possible outburst in many situations. But now, try to do this exercise. Something happens to you – maybe a friend or a sibling tells you something you don't like, or a situation starts making you feel uncomfortable. Rather than an outburst and creating an even bigger situation, try to step back and – use the wise mind. Observe whatever you think and feel during that given moment, and then state it. Make the "I feel" statement. Say, "I feel sad you acted that way", or "I feel disappointed in you."

Let's try to put this into perspective by examples. The "I feel," statements would be ones that reflect your present state, but they should be ones you realize will pass and will be resolved with time. So, here are a few examples of when a bad scenario presents itself before you. This is the best time to use these statements. You can also use the following for practice.

1. When you get caught up in a verbal altercation with a friend.
2. When you notice that your parents are pushing you to your limit.
3. When you have a misunderstanding with your sibling.
4. When you expected someone to do something for you, and they failed to deliver.
5. When someone promised you something, but they didn't fulfill it.
6. When you feel cornered by a teacher or educator because of a certain thing you did or didn't do.
7. When you are all alone with yourself, and you have this surge of negative feelings coming on.
8. When your romantic interest is not interested in you anymore.
9. When you feel trapped in a social situation.
10. When your best friend does something to you, intentionally (or not).

These sayings come from a valid point – but saying them out loud not only helps you create a better communication channel with someone else but also with yourself. These sayings are also a reflection of what is happening at the moment. They are not facts; they are just thoughts or feelings, so there is no need to cling to them like facts. I would encourage you to put them on paper as this is the easiest way to exercise them. Write down the "I feel" statements and keep doing that until you feel comfortable with yourself to communicate them with the people around you.

Situation: _____

I feel... _____

_____

_____

Situation: _____

I feel... _____

_____

_____

Situation: _____

I feel... _____

_____

_____

_____

Situation: _____

I feel... _____

_____

_____

_____

Situation: _____

I feel... _____

_____

_____

_____

Situation: _____

I feel... _____

_____

_____

_____

Situation: _____

I feel... _____

_____

_____

_____

Situation: _____

I feel... _____

_____

_____

_____

Situation: _____

I feel... _____

_____

_____

_____

Situation: _____

I feel... _____

_____

_____

_____

Situation: _____

I feel... _____

_____

_____

_____

Situation: _____

I feel... _____

_____

_____

_____

Situation: _____

I feel... _____

_____

_____

_____

Situation: _____

I feel... _____

_____

_____

_____

Situation: _____

I feel... _____

_____

_____

_____

Situation: _____

I feel... _____

_____

_____

_____

Situation: _____

I feel... _____

_____

_____

_____

03.
Participating

The final "what" skill we're going to dissect is the participating skill. It means completely immersing yourself in a certain activity. It means jumping head-first and allowing yourself to be involved in the moment. Doing this helps you to let go of self-consciousness and be completely present in whichever activity you're indulging in. When you participate with awareness, you can completely enjoy the moment without having to overthink every step of the way or be "half-present" in the moment. Participating is an excellent skill to use if you are feeling stressed.

In order to participate, all you need to do is actively practice the other skills and then immerse yourself in this one. Instead of closing this cycle with dissociation and not really remembering or enjoying something, do the opposite. Participate. This is the perfect way to start actively practicing these DBT skills until they become a part of who you are.

EXERCISE 6
MINDFUL PRACTICE

That leads us to the sixth exercise. Mindful practice means being active and aware. For this exercise, try to do something that you do often (like washing the dishes, eating, or something else). But this time, try to pay full attention to everything. Concentrate as hard as you can and notice every single thing you're doing. Then, try to do every single thing as well as you can. Take washing a piece of fruit as an example. Take the fruit (let's say it's a pear), go to your kitchen sink, and turn on the faucet. This is something you unconsciously do every time - but in this case, try to feel the whole process. Do you turn the water all the way to the coldest or the hottest point? Or do you maybe rinse your piece of fruit with lukewarm water? How does it feel? Notice the water going through your hands and between your fingers, onto the skin of the pear. Notice how gentle you are so you don't damage the fruit. Be as specific as you can while doing this task. Then, take a pen and write down how this made you feel - being mindful and completely present in the moment.

Activity: _____

How being mindful made me feel: _____

_____

_____

_____

Activity: _____

How being mindful made me feel: _____

_____

_____

_____

Activity: _____

How being mindful made me feel: _____

_____

_____

_____

Activity: _____

How being mindful made me feel: _____

_____

_____

_____

Activity: _____

How being mindful made me feel: _____
_____
_____
_____

Activity: _____

How being mindful made me feel: _____
_____
_____
_____

Activity: _____

How being mindful made me feel: _____
_____
_____
_____

Activity: _____

How being mindful made me feel: _____

_____

_____

_____

As I mentioned earlier, the basis of everything in this book revolves around the concept of mindfulness. The skills we're looking into together are all connected to it, and they are considered the foundation of DBT. After reading through the what skills, you are probably aware of what I'm talking about. You've probably noticed that the issues addressed by these skills will help you realize who you are and what you want out of life. These skills will also help you control what's happening in your mind, resulting in you living in the moment and focusing on the now.

HOW SKILLS

The second set of skills we will tackle are the how skills. These are just as important as the what skills, and their focus is helping you practice mindfulness. DBT has truly paved the way for any person to develop themselves into the form they want, and these skills are the perfect beginning to that adventure! To deepen your practice, you should follow these three skills that I have outlined for you below. They are – nonjudgmentally, one-mindfully, and effectively.

01.

Nonjudgmentally

The first one is being nonjudgmental. As people, all we do is judge – especially teenagers. But if you are a person who is constantly judged for your behavior, looks, or anything else – you will probably understand this the most. After all, you are in the middle of those teenage years where, frankly – kids can be mean.

I am sorry to be the bearer of bad news, but judgment continues throughout your entire life. You judge others, but mostly, you judge yourself. The thing is, you need to understand that judgment as a form can possibly lead to the creation of a highly hostile environment – both inside and outside your body. It can lead to guilt, shame, sadness, and so much more.

That's why I would like to dedicate some time to learning how not to judge. The point here is to allow yourself to observe everything you've observed until now but open up to a different kind of thinking. It is not about withholding your judgment but rather understanding it. Observe your thoughts as if you are observing a different person. Treat yourself more gently. The judgemental thoughts will slowly start to fade away because, at given moments, you will begin practicing the most powerful act – of letting go.

EXERCISE 7
PRACTICING SELF-COMPASSION

I mentioned that the most judgment you are ever going to receive in your life is judgment from yourself. As human beings, we are all flawed, but it seems like we keep forgetting that at times. That is why I designed this exercise – to remind you that, if you want to make sure you're viewing the world with compassion, you need to begin with yourself.

Say you're trying to observe a situation, and it is just not working out for you. You keep getting distracted, and other things keep popping up in your mind. You start to spiral, and before you know it, you blame yourself for your entire behavior without ever giving yourself the benefit of the doubt.

The exercise is as follows – you notice that you are starting to go down that rabbit hole, but you don't know how to stop. Start by noticing every sentence that goes through your mind and every negative thought about yourself. With each sentence, take a step back and analyze it. Here's a small example of it. You start thinking about that friend who let you down or said something mean to you. Then, you start thinking about whether they actually don't like you (or maybe they never did?). This is the time when you need to stop going down the rabbit hole, because you are practically spiralling - you start thinking you don't have any friends, or that this particular friend doesn't care about you, and so on. Bring yourself back to the surface by reminding yourself that anyone can have thoughts and feelings that do not coincide with yours at some point.

Then, ask yourself this – are each of those spiralling thoughts true? Or is it something that is derived from the emotional mind (which is usually activated when we don't have full control over a situation)? Remember to do this every time you feel like your self-compassion levels are low. Below, you can find some lines to take notes.

_____

_____

_____

_____

_____

_____

Part 1: Mindfulness

_____
_____
_____
_____
_____
_____
_____
_____
_____
_____
_____

EXERCISE 8
CHALLENGE JUDGMENTS

Challenging yourself about yourself is one thing – but challenging yourself about judgments towards the outside world is a whole new thing. In this exercise, let's try to do that together, shall we?

Say you're in a situation where you're meeting a new person – and you instantly start to judge them. Once you notice yourself doing this, it means you are on the right path of mindfulness. Notice all the thoughts going through your mind and witness how they form. Question them. Why are you thinking this? Is the person standing opposite you really that bad? Or is it something that may have derived from another experience you've had with another person in the past – that reminded you of them? It is important to start recognizing these thoughts in your head. Don't forget to take notes of your observations.

02.
One-Mindfully

The second one is one-mindfully. This is a skill that will come up as you are reading this book in one way or another. The idea behind it is that whatever you are doing, you should be doing one thing at a time. It is about finding mindfulness in everything you do. For example, if you are learning, reading, or working, do that. Don't play music in the background. Try not to turn the TV on or have some kind of other noise happening. Or when you're with someone else, say a friend, try to be with them, present in the moment, instead of constantly looking at your phone.

The idea behind this is that you can give your full attention to something and do your best to maintain it. Doing this will help you stay in the present moment rather than having your attention divided all over the place. So, you see, mindfulness truly has a lot to do with the level of awareness you bring into your life. Focusing on being present in the moment, giving your undivided attention to what you are doing – there is no greater feeling than that. Most of us, all through our lives, are distracted. Whether it is by images, feelings, thoughts, or even worries – we constantly try ways to steer clear of the present moment. Once you get used to this, it's a little challenging to put everything away and focus on only one thing.

Being one-mindfully is an excellent way to pull your attention to what is happening at the moment. With it, you can absorb the information and take part in the present.

However, the most important thing to remember here is that you always need to be patient with yourself. It takes time to master this skill, and while some of you may achieve this in a shorter time period, others may need some more time. In the beginning, if you're having trouble focusing on a task, try to remove all the distractions from your surroundings. Observe everything that surrounds you and pinpoint the things you need to remove. Choose one thing that you'd like to focus on and start doing it slowly. With time, this will become an unconscious process.

EXERCISE 9
FOCUS YOUR ATTENTION ON ONE THING AT A TIME

That is precisely why I have chosen this to be an exercise as well. In life, sometimes you need to stand still and let go of every thought and emotion. It is with this exercise that you're going to do just that. Let's try focusing your attention on one thing at a time.

Stand in the middle of a room. You don't even have to do anything – just watch. Now, choose a couple of objects around the room. Then, try to focus on one subject (say, a chair). Take a deep look at the chair and try not to think of anything else. Notice the materials, the patterns, the shapes – pay full attention to the chair. At that moment, you should completely forget about the other items you've chosen or that there is anything else in the room. After you've observed one thing, try to shift your focus to another thing. Do this process with a few objects just to get started. Before you know it, you will be able to do this in a heartbeat, with everything.

03.
Effectively

The third one is effectively. As a word, effective is something you're going to hear a lot. The goal here is to know you're effective every time you focus on what works. Instead of thinking whether something is right or wrong, you should focus on understanding how to accept and work with a situation as it is. Effectively means allowing yourself to let go of the need to be right. When you are determined to be right, it may cloud your judgment and make you come to the wrong conclusion or decision. Being determined to be right all the time can be a very challenging thing.

Effectiveness is knowing how to tolerate and accept a situation or a person you don't really like. Effectiveness is knowing you are right but still letting go because fighting something and proving how right you are don't really align with your values anymore. You are simply – better than that. By accepting a situation where you know you can't change things, you show the actual signs of growth.

EXERCISE 10
ALIGNING ACTIONS WITH VALUES AND GOALS

For the last exercise of this chapter, you are going to need a pen. The goal is to access your values, and then make goals based on them. But, to assess your values, you need to start somewhere, right? Well, start by thinking about the values that you hold in your life. Now start writing. Let's go step by step.

Think about what matters most to you in life. Write down 5-10 values that come to mind. These can be anything. Here are some examples:

- I value respect for myself and others.
- Gratitude for what I have is important to me.
- I believe in the strength to overcome challenges.
- I value honesty and being true to myself.
- I care deeply about kindness and helping others.

MY VALUES

1. _____
2. _____
3. _____
4. _____
5. _____
6. _____
7. _____
8. _____
9. _____
10. _____

Based on the values you wrote down, create goals that reflect them. Here are a few examples:
- ✧ If you value respect, a goal could be to strengthen your relationships.
- ✧ If you value success, you might set a goal to achieve something specific in your studies.
- ✧ If you value gratitude, your goal could be to practice it daily.
- ✧ If you value honesty, a goal could be to communicate more openly with people.
- ✧ If kindness matters to you, a goal might be to volunteer or support a cause regularly.

MY GOALS

1. _____
2. _____
3. _____
4. _____
5. _____
6. _____
7. _____
8. _____
9. _____
10. _____

Now, write down actions you can take to reach your goals. These should be small, specific steps that align with your values. For example:
- ✧ Respect - make an effort to listen more in conversations.
- ✧ Success - break your big goal into smaller tasks and tackle them one by one.
- ✧ Gratitude - start a gratitude journal and list three things you're thankful for each day.
- ✧ Honesty - practice expressing your thoughts clearly, even when it's difficult.
- ✧ Kindness - offer help to someone in need or do something nice for a friend or stranger.

ACTIONS

1. _____
2. _____
3. _____
4. _____
5. _____
6. _____
7. _____
8. _____
9. _____
10. _____

It is important to answer this truthfully as it can help you align your actions with your beliefs and values. In most cases, the answer is straightforward. You either take some action that aligns with these values, or you don't. The exercise is to create goals that align with what you believe in. The action should match your value. If it doesn't, think about what you need to change in order for that to happen. Write that down, and then remind yourself that you have a goal every time your mind feels like it starts to go down a rabbit hole.

What Did You Learn in This Chapter?

This is a chapter that only opened the doors for you toward a whole different world. Out of everything you've read, here is a summary of what you learned in part 1:

- ✧ The concept of mindfulness.
- ✧ The power and the characteristics of the wise mind.
- ✧ The importance of what skills – observing, describing, and participating.
- ✧ The importance of the how skills – non-judgmentally, one-mindfully, and effectively.

As we close the part on mindfulness, we embark on an adventure – and right into the second part! There, we are going to discuss everything connected to distress tolerance – what it is, learning how to refine it – everything. So, turn the page – and let's discover some wonderful new things together!

Part 2

DISTRESS TOLERANCE

*"The real man smiles in trouble, gathers strength
from distress, and grows brave by reflection."*

– Thomas Paine

In the first part of this book, we began by highlighting mindfulness. I did mention that mindfulness will be the foundation upon which you will build yourself up. So, this second part is about something that is closely connected to the topic of mindfulness. It is a sort of an extension of mindfulness.

Let's start from the very beginning. If you have never heard or thought about it until today, we will discuss distress – and everything connected to it. Later on, as the chapter unravels, we will also include much more information linked to it. All of this will help you regulate your emotions and increase your interpersonal effectiveness.

What Is Distress Tolerance?

Have you ever asked yourself if you are a person that gets agitated quickly? I mean, you are a teenager, so this is kind of "a given". But how do you perceive yourself? Considering we have removed the factor that you are in your teen years?

Distress tolerance is your ability to manage perceived emotional distress. It includes making it through an emotional episode without worsening the situation. People who are dealing with low distress tolerance may become a little overwhelmed whenever they come face to face with a stressful situation. Sometimes, when this happens, they may even turn to a very unhealthy or destructive outlet that would help them cope with it.

But the thing is – everyone experiences stress every once in a while. You've probably found yourself experiencing stress, too. You can experience stress over everything – a fight at home, bad grades, lost romantic interest, etc. No matter how small or large this stress is, it can affect your ability to manage that particular situation. Sometimes, you can notice how it's more difficult for you to manage strong negative emotions such as guilt, anxiety, fear, shame, anger, and sadness. The stronger the emotion is, the more difficult it is to control it.

Poor distress tolerance can be a very challenging thing. The first thing you need to do in this situation is to identify the emotions you're experiencing. However, as a teenager who doesn't have that much experience on the topic, identifying such strong emotions may be terrifying. The relief you may get from a self-destructive measure is only a short-term one. The truth is that every distressing emotion can make matters worse and pile up feelings of guilt and shame, ultimately leading to you being even more upset.

Thankfully, there is some good news behind all this! After all, that's why we're here. There are many techniques we can work on together to help you cope with the intense emotions you have. These healthy distress tolerance outlets are perfect! With their assistance, you can create a long-term outlook on dealing with every challenging thing in your life.

Increasing your distress tolerance can be an effective way to help yourself regulate your impulsivity and anger. This can come with many other benefits, ultimately leading to you living a calmer, happier, and more serene life.

Before we go into the techniques to work on, let's look at the factors a bit. Oftentimes, you need to realize that what you are feeling is okay, but it has not been within your control because you were not aware that such a background exists with emotions in the first place.

For example, there may be biological influences on distress tolerance. The temperament you have may just be the indicator of the level of difficulty you're met with each time you face a challenging situation.

Another example is distorted beliefs. Suppose you are intolerant when it comes to challenges. In that case, you may find yourself thinking you're always upset about something, that you will never feel better, and that everything is terrible, or you hate everyone – or everyone hates you. These types of thinking patterns can make it more challenging for you to come up with upsetting events. While these are automatic thoughts, they often result in avoidance, withdrawal, and even self-harm.

I know that, while reading this, you already felt a little bit distressed, but don't worry. The reason why we go deeper into this subject together is to help you come out the other side better, stronger, and happier. With that in mind, let's move on to the distress tolerance techniques.

Distraction

The first one is distraction. This can be a very easy way to take action and thus increase your distress tolerance level. It usually includes various methods that can help you take your mind off of things. The different methods can be as follows:

- Distract yourself by doing something you like – when times get tough, turn your attention to something you really like to do. It can be anything, as long as it is an activity that will help you become fully present in the moment.

- Distract yourself by focusing your attention on someone else – it is about realizing that sometimes, more than just one person goes through a difficult period. Depending on your situation, there will often be other people involved. Some of the distractions you can indulge in include people watching (sitting outside on a bench and quietly observing people), calling someone (a friend or a relative, just to check on them, and see how they are), or going outside and physically meeting someone.

- Distract yourself by doing chores – probably the most effective (and used) approach of all is distracting yourself by throwing yourself into work. There is a certain satisfaction in completing a task, something you cannot feel with anything else. So, when you're facing a difficult situation, it is time to find all the things you've put on the back burner and complete them. The chores can be anything – from rearranging your clothes to doing your dishes, redecorating – anything that will make you feel like you are doing something important – because you are.

While we discuss these simple yet effective distraction methods, it is important to realize that they are here not only to help you cope but to help you in the long run as well. Consider utilizing them whenever you feel stuck or have a strong sense of negative emotions washing over you. I must warn you – it will be challenging in the beginning! You may not be able to focus on one thing at a time or anything because you still haven't completely succeeded in controlling your emotions, but don't worry! Practice makes it perfect, and the sooner you start, the better!

And while we are on the topic of practicing, it is time to move on to the next exercise.

EXERCISE 11
IDENTIFYING HEALTHY AND UNHEALTHY DISTRACTIONS

This one is connected to how you perceive things as good and bad. We already learned that distractions are coping mechanisms – but some can have a positive effect, while others can negatively influence your overall life. In this exercise, I am going to help you differentiate between them and pay close attention to what is good and what is bad.

Take out a pen and paper, or use the worksheet below, and imagine a scenario where you are challenged in a certain way. You've faced a difficult situation, and now you need to know how to healthily cope with it. But also, before you start writing things down, consider everything you've read so far in this chapter.

Now begin – divide your piece of paper by drawing a vertical line down the middle of it. On the left side, write healthy; on the right, write unhealthy distractions. Keep that scenario in your mind. It may even help more if you have multiple scenarios or past events just to compare your behavior. In some cases, you may have turned to things such as sleeping a lot, avoiding the issue, shutting down, overeating (or not eating enough), and so on. These are all the unhealthy distractions you've participated in – so you can put them in the right section. Now think about all the cases where you faced the issue at hand; be understanding, indulge in physical activity, or talk to someone about it. All of these things are healthy distractions, and they can actually help you cope.

Healthy Distractions	Unhealthy Distractions
_____	_____
_____	_____
_____	_____
_____	_____
_____	_____
_____	_____
_____	_____

Healthy Distractions	Unhealthy Distractions
_____	_____
_____	_____
_____	_____
_____	_____
_____	_____
_____	_____
_____	_____
_____	_____
_____	_____
_____	_____

Even though these might not have necessarily been the things you wrote down, you get the idea. To know which of all the responses should go in the left and which ones should be in the right section, think about this – there is a certain result that comes with every little thing we do. This is an essential thing to remember when it comes to distractions. The result may be you end up feeling better – or worse. That's how you know what is healthy and what is an unhealthy way to cope with things. Out of all the things that crossed your mind, how many of them have truly made you feel calm and better? Focus on them because these are the good things, the productive distractions.

Radical Acceptance

Has it ever happened to you to face a situation that is so difficult you thought it would be impossible to accept it? Maybe you had a falling out with your best friend, or a very bad grade, or a fight with your parents. This can be anything that has made you feel like everything around you is falling apart, and you can't really deal with it. This is where the second skill comes in handy – and it is radical acceptance.

Sometimes, trying to cut out all the unnecessary drama in life is advisable. It is also advisable to accept a situation as it is. After all, there is a lot of relief behind that, so why not try it? Things are not in your control anyway, and there is no harm in letting go. By doing this, you practice radical acceptance.

Think of it this way – you are not accepting the pain or approving of it in any way. On the contrary, you simply allow yourself to focus on what is in your control and what you can do. It is all about creating a shift in your energy. Rather than preparing for war and leading with your emotions, you start to plan your next move and do that with a calm and clear mind.

You should accept radical acceptance if you're willing to go through life's challenges stronger than ever. As a part of DBT, it is a technique that includes embracing the present moment. The situations you may find yourself in the middle of during your life can be highly challenging. Some of them may even be borderline unbearable. Radical acceptance comes into place when things seem almost impossible. I'm talking about situations where most people would run from. Radical acceptance means facing all these challenges without trying to avoid or change them.

So, how does radical acceptance function?

The thing you need to realize here is that it is not about acceptance. You cannot just be okay with a situation that is obviously far from optimal, right? Radical acceptance is just acknowledging a situation – as it is, without any judgment. At that moment, you stop fighting reality. I know that this is a lot easier to read about than to do in actual life, but the more of it you accept, the more resilient you become. This technique is created to help you build some tolerance against distress. Because this is where the real magic happens, radically accepting reality, with all its painful parts, can help you open the door to personal transformation and growth.

Radical acceptance comes with many benefits. All you need to do is truly commit to it. The few reasons why you are developing this as a skill, are to start cultivating self-compassion, increase your tolerance to distress, to no longer fight what cannot be changed, to improve your ability to cope and solve issues effectively, to stay away from harsh judgment, and deepen your capacity to accept things in all areas of your life. Picture radical acceptance as a threshold you need to cross to get to the other side happier. But, in order to achieve this, you will need to practice it. I have prepared a couple of exercises for you to try. But before that, let's talk a little about how to practice radical acceptance.

All of this may seem simple in theory, but it can be quite challenging in practice. But, to master it, you still need to practice it. To do that, here are a few steps I always like to incorporate. These steps have helped many other people as well as myself, so I am sharing them with you so that after much practice, they can become your "second nature".

- ⬦ You may discover you are constantly fighting against your reality (complaining or wishing that everything was different).
- ⬦ Then, you start acknowledging what reality is, even if you don't really like it. You notice that you can't change anything about the situation.
- ⬦ You make the choice to accept the situation as it is and breathe into the discomfort of it all.
- ⬦ You start embracing self-compassion. There are many painful emotions as you go through the process, but you suddenly realize that beating yourself up about it will only make things worse, not better.
- ⬦ Finally, you start to shift your focus. At that exact moment, you ask yourself what the next thing you can do to be effective and take better care of yourself is.

The trick with radical acceptance is that you need to start small and know how to cope properly. The change process is long, so you also need to be compassionate and patient with yourself. If you need some more time to master this – take the time. Don't put pressure on yourself. Go through the exercises I have prepared for you and guide yourself toward the new realm of acceptance and understanding.

EXERCISE 12
ACCEPTING DIFFICULT EMOTIONS

This exercise is about embracing change and accepting the things that cannot be changed. Radical acceptance is not always easy, but that doesn't mean you can't incorporate it into your life – starting today. Think about it this way – there are a few statements you can say whenever you are faced with a challenging situation. After all, the most difficult part of radical acceptance is to go through and feel the emotions, no matter how hard it is.

Take a pen and paper, or use the worksheet below, and sit down. Think of a situation where you felt like your entire world was turned upside down. Think of the most difficult situation you've ever been in and the feelings that you have. If you haven't gone through the process, you might still notice the negative emotions surfacing. Accepting difficult emotions is about knowing how to handle them. Now, you're going to start handling them by using coping statements.

To get you started on this, here are a few examples:

- I am able to accept the present moment as it is.
- I know I will get through this no matter what.
- I will survive, and this feeling will pass.
- I can't change what happened in the past, but I can learn to let go and focus on the present.
- Fighting my negative emotions only makes them stronger. I now allow them to wash over me and pass.
- I can choose to create my own path despite the negative history.
- I don't need to judge, just to take the appropriate action toward the future.
- I can get through all the complex emotions, even though they seem like the most difficult thing to do at the present moment.

You can either use these, create your own coping statements that would work best for you, or make a mix of both. Some of the examples you can take from your own experience include:

- My fallout with my friend does not define me as a person.
- When I look in the mirror, I choose to see the good.
- My bad grade does not mean that I will fail at everything.
- I love myself no matter what.
- My romantic interest may not be interested in me anymore, and that's okay.

Either way, these can be an excellent reminder that tomorrow will be better than today and that you already have all the tools to accept difficult emotions.

Situation: _____

Coping Statement: _____

_____

_____

Situation: _____

Coping Statement: _____

_____

_____

Situation: _____

Coping Statement: _____

_____

_____

Situation: _____

Coping Statement: _____

_____

_____

Situation: _____

Coping Statement: _____
_____
_____

Situation: _____

Coping Statement: _____
_____
_____

Situation: _____

Coping Statement: _____
_____
_____

Situation: _____

Coping Statement: _____
_____
_____

Situation: _____

Coping Statement: _____

_____

_____

Situation: _____

Coping Statement: _____

_____

_____

Situation: _____

Coping Statement: _____

_____

_____

Situation: _____

Coping Statement: _____

_____

_____

Situation: _____

Coping Statement: _____

_____

_____

Situation: _____

Coping Statement: _____

_____

_____

EXERCISE 13
DIFFICULT SITUATIONS

As you can realize, radical acceptance is a skill that gets better the more you practice it. In this exercise, together, we are learning how to cope with difficult situations. To improve your engagement in radical acceptance, you need to know how to take the proper steps in a difficult situation. Here are the steps – all you need to do is memorize them and try them out next time you come face to face with an almost impossible situation.

1. Think about resistance. Certain cases act like triggers; notice them. It is only in those situations that you cannot accept something.
2. When something difficult happens, remind yourself that you cannot change the situation.
3. Then, remind yourself that things are absolutely out of your control.
4. Think about what would happen if you started to accept the situation as it is. Imagine what it would be like to receive the problem.

5. Suppose it is not possible to do that. In that case, you can always utilize some relaxation strategies such as journalling, self-reflection, and mindfulness practices to help you understand your emotions and what you're going through.
6. Allow yourself to feel safe in your skin and feel all the emotions.
7. Observe what kind of an effect they have on your body. Does your chest feel tight? Do you need to breathe deeply? Is there any pain?
8. Always remember that life is still worthwhile, even with a lot of pain in it.
9. Practice this acceptance process whenever you feel like you have some issues with a particular situation.

These magnificent steps can help you stop thinking about how things could have been and help you start thinking about the things that are at the moment. These steps will help you stay present. To know when these steps are best used, here are a few example situations for you. These include situations that you might have already been in by now. If not, they will give you a perfect starting point so you can brainstorm some situations that actually have happened to you. As you read them, think about something similar happening to you. You can also use the lines below to make some notes.

- When you have an argument with a friend at school, and you feel a lot of emotions.
- When you want to explain something to someone, and it looks as if they don't understand you - and you get frustrated about it.
- When something you see happening reminds you of a certain situation that happened to you.
- When it looks like you may need some help to repair something.
- When you come face to face with a challenge.

_____
_____
_____
_____
_____
_____
_____
_____
_____
_____

Self-Soothing

In life, you're always going to face some ups and downs. There will be plenty of moments of happiness, but also there will be some tough times too. Before I go into the following technique, this is a gentle reminder for you – you live in a very fast-paced world. As humans, we are not created to endure as much as we do. So, when you're feeling emotionally distressed, just keep in mind that it is okay.

That leads me to the topic of self-soothing. DBT is designed in such a way to help you navigate tough situations with so much ease. It teaches you how to be constructive and deal with every situation healthily. Out of all the tools and techniques we're going to cover in this book together, this one is both the most effective and the most challenging. The self-soothing means using all the senses you have to bring calmness into your existence. It comes with a set of sensory strategies (the two exercises in this section will help you with that), so let's get started.

The interesting thing about self-soothing is that it is connected to the distress tolerance. When you are in the middle of a situation that causes some intense emotions, the one helpful thing is to try to relax in the moment using your senses. In these moments, self-soothing can help a lot because you feel highly overwhelmed, and you need a pleasant sensation to calm down. Self-soothing skills focus on the five senses of taste, hearing, smell, sight, and touch. In those moments when you feel incredibly distressed, you might find it difficult to navigate through this and get back to your senses. However, you can always rely on self-soothing skills.

Get ready to go through some trial and error while you practice this. Still, in the end, you will experience the ultimate stress relief from it. The goal here is to practice this for as long as you need until you are confident you can turn to them whenever you need them.

Since it is about engaging the five senses, let's take a look at each of those senses individually, shall we? Below, I am sharing some suggestions with you. These can be your starting point as you go through your soothing journey.

- Let's start with sight. Whenever you feel distressed, turn to something that means a lot to you – for example, take a look at a picture of your partner (if you already have one), your family, or your pet – as long as you feel the love overflowing you while you look at it.
- Move on to the sound. In a stressful situation, all people, especially teenagers, have found sound to be the most soothing thing they can turn to. Put on some music and allow the feeling of calmness to wash over you.
- Taste something. A simple thing such as chewing your favorite gum can help you recenter and feel much better instantly. Your favorite meal may just help you bring yourself back to yourself again.
- Try using your smell. Another incredible thing about different scents is that they remind us of different things. To calm yourself down at a given moment, you can always turn to your favorite perfume, lotion, or spray. There is a certain mindfulness to smelling something that reminds you of good times.
- The final one is touch. A soft blanket, a favorite toy, or your most comfortable clothes – touching something that feels comfortable is one of the best ways to calm down in a stressful situation.

Self-soothing as a concept seems relatively straightforward, but when the time comes for you to actually utilize it, it may feel like it's a little more than just challenging. That's why I've created two excellent exercises where you can get the most out of this skill.

EXERCISE 14
RELAXATION

There is a little bit of science behind the relaxation exercise, specifically because it is paired with muscle relaxation. Allow me to explain this a little more. Lay down, or sit down comfortably in a chair, and completely relax your entire body. Now, to fully relax your muscles, try to breathe in and out deeply and slowly, and slow down your heart rate with it, too.

Focus on one group of muscles and try to tighten them. Hold for a few seconds, and then relax. Allow them to rest for a few seconds before doing that again. Each time you tighten and relax your muscles, you slowly release the tension. Go into detail, and as you inhale and exhale through the process, feel your muscles relaxing, one at a time. Once you notice that one group of muscles is relaxed (for example your arms), you can move on to the next group of muscles and so on. As soon as you know it, your entire body will feel completely relaxed.

EXERCISE 15
BUILDING A SELF-SOOTHE KIT

Before I moved on to the exercises, I mentioned the five senses – touch, sight, hearing, smell, and taste. This exercise can help you combine them in order to create a self-soothing kit that is a perfect fit for you. Let's put the words into action!

Take a pen and a piece of paper (or use the worksheet below), and on one side, write all the five senses. Now, with the help of the examples I presented above, start to brainstorm. Dedicate some time to each sense and think about what calms you down. Try writing down a few things next to each sense. For example:

Sound – the sound of waves crashing on the shore, the sound of my favorite playlist, etc.

As soon as you're done writing this and brainstorming about each sense, take a look at what you've written. Right now, you have, in your hands, your own self-soothing kit. It is designed by you, for you, and as long as you are completely honest while writing it, this can help you every time you feel distressed. Think of this as your first-aid kit. Whenever you find yourself in a challenging situation, simply go back to it, open it up, and use all the power that is placed inside of it.

Sight _____

_____

_____

_____

_____

Sound _____

_____

_____

_____

_____

Taste _____

_____

_____

_____

_____

Smell _____

_____

_____

_____

_____

Touch _____

_____

_____

_____

_____

Pros and Cons

Moving on to the pros and cons. I know the thought that crossed your mind right now – the pros and cons are relatively easy to do, and you already know what they are. But not in DBT terms. The pros and cons of DBT are very different from the mainstream pros and cons we all know. *The way DBT views pros and cons is by focusing on tolerating vs. not tolerating or coping vs. not coping.* In other words, pros and cons in a distressing situation using DBT means looking at all the consequences of all the potential actions you may take.

Since the exercise here would be a little bit larger, we can move on to it together. Study the method and discover how to make the most of this DBT skill.

EXERCISE 16
PROS AND CONS WORKSHEET

The best way for me to describe this skill is by putting it in motion. Picture a difficult situation – it can be something you make up as you go or a past situation that stuck with you. It can be anything – a challenge at home, school, or friends. Now, think about your initial response to that situation. Is it filled with outbursts, with a lot of emotions, and with a response that you could barely control? This is something we're trying to change through this exercise.

Write down the initial response that automatically came to your mind. Now, it is time to create the pros and cons worksheet. Divide your piece of paper into two sections and write the pros in one and the cons in the other section. You can also use the worksheet below.

Now, when you write the pros and cons of this specific situation, you will do that by utilizing DBT. Answer these questions:

- How can you step out of this situation with success?
- Can you get what you want out of it?
- Are you used to being in distress?
- What would happen if you spoke up?
- How can you tweak the initial response to get better results?

Write all the answers down and separate them into the cons or the pros section. As you look at the piece of paper with all the emotional and logical things included, you end up realizing that there may be more to the story (taking a look at things from the other side's perspective) and that you can always choose what you act on (emotions, logic, or both).

Here are a few example situations for you:

10. You have a fight over different opinions with a friend.
11. You get scolded by your parents for something you did or didn't do.
12. You failed to deliver a project at school.
13. You bailed on your friends without explanation.
14. You had a fight with your sibling.

Let's take one of these situations as an example for our answers. For example - failing to deliver a project at school. How can you respond to that? Let's take a look at a few example answers:

1. You may come up with a constructive answer that shows the reality of the situation.
2. You may panic and start crying.
3. You may communicate with your teacher and ask them if you could finish the project and deliver it at a later date.
4. You may blame someone else for you not being able to complete the project on time.
5. You may break down completely and argue with your teacher.

Now, think of the consequences of each one of these answers. For some answers, the consequences are good, and for some, they are bad. You can easily categorize them. To make the most out of every situation in the long run, you need to respond calmly and honestly. That way, you can act on both logic and emotion.

Situation: _____

Initial Response: _____

Pros: Cons:

_____   _____

_____   _____

_____   _____

_____   _____

Situation: _____

Initial Response: _____

Pros: Cons:

_____   _____

_____   _____

_____   _____

_____   _____

Situation: _____

Initial Response: _____

_____

Pros: Cons:

_____   _____

_____   _____

_____   _____

_____   _____

Situation: _____

Initial Response: _____
_____

Pros: Cons:

_____   _____

_____   _____

_____   _____

Situation: _____

Initial Response: _____
_____

Pros: Cons:

_____   _____

_____   _____

_____   _____

Situation: _____

Initial Response: _____
_____

Pros: Cons:

_____   _____

_____   _____

_____   _____

Situation: _____

Initial Response: _____
_____

Pros: Cons:
_____   _____

_____   _____

_____   _____

_____   _____

Situation: _____

Initial Response: _____
_____

Pros: Cons:
_____   _____

_____   _____

_____   _____

_____   _____

Situation: _____

Initial Response: _____
_____

Pros: Cons:
_____   _____

_____   _____

_____   _____

_____   _____

Part 2: Distress Tolerance

Situation: _____

Initial Response: _____
_____

Pros: Cons:

_____   _____

_____   _____

_____   _____

_____   _____

What Did You Learn From This Chapter?

As we slowly close this chapter, this is the part where we reflect upon everything we've discovered together so far. While your journey is just getting started, you have done an amazing job up to this point. Let's see what you can take away from this part with you:

- ♦ What is distress tolerance, and how to increase it.
- ♦ Distraction as a powerful distress tolerance technique – and how you can utilize it.
- ♦ Radical acceptance – one of the pillars of DBT and a skill that can serve you the most.
- ♦ How to come to terms with difficult situations by incorporating the self-soothing skills – what are they, how powerful are they, and how easy it is to use them.
- ♦ The magnificence of making a pros and cons worksheet – they are very different from the pros and cons you're used to.

As the mind becomes stronger and healthier, so does the body. Until now, we have focused on bringing together all aspects of DBT and utilizing them in your mind. In the following section, we will shift our focus and gain a whole new perspective on things. Turn the page and start the next chapter – because it is all about properly dealing with your emotions!

Part 3

EMOTIONAL REGULATION

"I don't want to be at the mercy of my emotions. I want to use them, to enjoy them, and to dominate them."

– Oscar Wilde

It is always important to keep your emotions in check. As you can see from what you read so far, you can't really shut them out. Emotions are important, and they are a healthy way to express yourself. But when is it "enough" of emotions? Until now, we have talked about matters of the mind, but now we get to talk about matters of the soul.

You communicate with yourself and with other people through emotions. It is an excellent way to create relationships and approach situations. But as a teenager, you may not always know how to control your emotions. Sometimes, they come in large shipments, and you don't know what to do with them all. So, you unload them. You unload them on yourself, and on the people around you. At the moment, while you're doing that, it even feels like a storm is happening inside of you. But once the moment has passed, you look at things differently, from another (calmer) perspective, and you may notice that you've created chaos.

It is just as challenging to control your emotions as it is challenging to control your thoughts. That's why, in this part, you will uncover everything you need to know about your emotions. I will start from the very beginning, so get ready – because it is quite an interesting process to go through!

What Is Emotional Regulation?

Emotional regulation means taking action to alter the intensity of any emotional experience. Many of you may think that this is a way to hide and suppress your emotions when it cannot be farther from it. Emotional regulation means having the ability to have full control over your emotions through many approaches.

As you go through your life, you will notice that some people are better at regulating their emotions. These people seem to have a higher emotional intelligence, and it may seem like they are fully aware of their experiences within and the experiences of those around them. These people seem naturally calm.

While this is true – these people are calm – they still experience a fair share of negative emotions. They have just managed to regulate their emotions properly. Emotional regulation is not something you have or don't have – it's something you improve and master over time. In life, you will face many challenges and difficulties, which can take their toll on your physical and mental health.

This is why emotional regulation is so important. Slowly, you are reaching the stage of adulthood, and as an adult, you are expected to regulate your emotions that fit with the "socially acceptable way of handling them". It is known that when emotions get the best of us, sometimes they lead to issues.

The thing is, there are many things that can influence emotional regulation. Every stressful situation you've ever had to deal with provoked powerful emotions from within. I have mentioned this a few times throughout the chapters.

Now, you are aware that you may hurt relationships by not taking charge of your emotions. It is the kind of emotional volatility that can make a change for the worse. You may end up saying or doing things you never meant to do in the first place.

Other than having an overall negative impact on any relationship, feeling overwhelmed can cause unnecessary struggles and suffering. If you don't start dealing with it, then you will have to deal with a lifetime of not having new opportunities and experiences.

It is all about maintaining a positive reaction - that's what this chapter will delve into. The thing we're learning here is how to properly respond to a challenging situation, and together, we are going to cover a few important things.

First, we're going to start with opposite action, and a few exercises that can help you develop it. Then, we are going to move to learning how to focus on the positive. Finally, we are going to focus on ourselves, and our physical health as well.

Opposite Action

Putting those words into action is something you will start doing now! It is time to fully control your emotions and discover the power of emotional regulation! Opposite action will teach you how to do just that!

When all emotions are activated, they make us respond in a certain way. It seems like we are almost pre-programmed to do that with all of them. The opposite action is a skill that can help you respond completely the opposite of how you normally would. This is how you get ready to act and take control over yourself. Of course, this means focusing on the negative emotions only whenever you want to take the opposite action.

That leads me to the first exercise of this part. Here it is below.

EXERCISE 17
RESPONDING OPPOSITE TO INTENSE EMOTIONS

It is all about learning how to recognize and deal with your emotions. Yes, it will take a lot of practice to make this happen, but this exercise is an excellent starting point. Once combined with the other ones from this chapter, they bring together all the aspects of emotional regulation you need to know and practice.

For this exercise, think of five emotions you feel most of the time. Keep in mind that they should be negative emotions. Write them down on a piece of paper, or on the worksheet below, and write how they make you act. Now, after you're done with that, write down the opposite reactions of these emotions. It is a kind of role-playing where you think of the opposite reaction to your intense emotions. For example:

When you feel shame, you have the need to hide.

But the opposite of shame is keeping your head up and facing anything head-on.

When you feel depressed, you feel like you want to curl up and stay away from the world.

But the opposite of that is going out, getting active, and staying in touch with everything and everyone.

When you feel anger, you want to attack or defend yourself.

But the opposite is to show concern and kindness – or simply walk away.

Create this list and stick to it – especially if you want the negative emotions to go away and for you to feel less uncomfortable. This is the perfect skill – along with the belief you hold within that this kind of exercise will work!

Emotion: _____

Action: _____

_____

Opposite Action: _____

Emotion: _____

Action: _____

_____

Opposite Action: _____

Emotion: _____

Action: _____

_____

Opposite Action: _____

Emotion: _____

Action: _____
_____

Opposite Action: _____

Emotion: _____

Action: _____
_____

Opposite Action: _____

Focusing on the Facts and Problem-Solving

Problem-solving seems like a relatively easy thing to do. Once you are met with an issue, you need to figure out the best course of action and then proceed to resolve it. The thing is, while it all sounds good "on paper", it's not that easy to do in life. Sometimes, you may find yourself in situations where there isn't really a way out – at least, that's how it seems in the beginning. I am here to tell you that problem-solving, as a technique, cannot truly exist if it is not connected with the former one – and that is focusing on the facts. Fact-checking and problem-solving skills as a part of DBT are essential and should be looked into immediately.

The main goal of this skill is to help you manage and regulate your emotional response by looking at the facts and the facts only. It is about examining the facts supporting your feelings, assumptions, and thoughts. This process can help you differentiate between judgments and interpretations. And if you haven't been aware of it by now – these two can often distort emotions. Focusing on the facts as a DBT skill can help you both with emotional regulation and with distress tolerance. You will see, once you finish this book, that all of the skills and techniques you will uncover here are connected.

Now, let's do some work! Here are the steps you need to take in order to check the facts when it comes to DBT:

- ✧ Identify the emotion. Look within yourself to find out what you are feeling and why you are feeling that particular emotion.
- ✧ Identify the event next. What happened to you that triggered the emotion you're dealing with at the moment? Can you pinpoint that?
- ✧ Clarify your thoughts. A certain chain of thoughts started roaming around your mind as you felt those emotions. Identify those thoughts –they could definitely be connected to a belief you hold on to.

- ⬥ Start looking at the facts – and checking them. Evaluate the situation and whether the emotion and intensity match the facts of your situation.
- ⬥ Create a new response. After you look at the emotions and the facts, it is time for you to check if they align. If they don't (which will probably be the case), you need to change your emotional reaction and create one that suits the facts better.

As you can see, this is the perfect DBT skill for a teenager – because you are the ones who struggle with emotions the most! Also, you are the ones who have the most difficulty distinguishing between the reality of a situation and your thoughts. Fact-checking means improving your emotional intelligence. Fact-checking can help you draft healthier responses to any kind of situation.

And, if you think that this is not something that's created for you – think again. This DBT skill can be used by anyone who needs some assistance managing their feelings, emotional responses, negative thoughts, or anything else. While this is an incredibly powerful tool for adults who want to improve their emotional intelligence, teenagers can benefit from it in the same way. After using this skill for a while, you will notice that you can resolve conflicts better, you can improve your overall well-being and enhance your mental strength. While I am on the topic of how this skill can help, why not look at all the benefits that come from it? Here, I am sharing some of the best ones with you, hoping to get you practicing this skill as soon as possible!

- ⬥ Your emotional intelligence will improve. As a skill, fact-checking can help you better understand your emotions and the triggers behind them, thus resulting in improved self-awareness on an emotional level.
- ⬥ You will stop reacting as impulsively. Granted, your parents probably say this will happen to you once you step out of the teenage era and into adulthood, but this is not always the case. It is all about analyzing if the emotions fit the facts. Doing this can help you reduce any overreactions and emotional responses that are not adequate for the situation you're dealing with.
- ⬥ You will improve your problem-solving skills. A clever approach once means a clever approach again. After some time, this kind of clever approach will help you get a clearer scope of the situation and will give you the assistance to make rational decisions and seek effective solutions.
- ⬥ You will improve your relationships with the people around you. Once you have a better understanding of your emotions, you will lead not only with your mind but also with empathy. As you understand that, your connections with the people around you will grow stronger and better.
- ⬥ You will enjoy improved mental health. Nowadays, it seems like mental health is a topic often communicated among people – and for a good reason. By implementing this approach, you can strengthen your overall mental health and maintain it at an optimal level.
- ⬥ Your self-confidence will skyrocket! Yes, I do mean this! When you do good, you see good, and you are good, you will end up feeling good! Gaining control over your emotions will lead to increased self-esteem and much more confidence when you handle a challenging situation in your life.

So, you see, the sole act of focusing on the facts will help you go a long way, especially because it will help you become a little more rational and turn to that corner of your mind that we mentioned earlier – the wise mind. Speaking of which, let's move on to the exercises connected to the fact-checking aspect of DBT.

EXERCISE 18
CHALLENGE IRRATIONAL THOUGHTS

When you're focusing on the facts, it means that you are challenging everything you believe in. It's true – this is when your entire belief system is being broken down. So, in order to start that up, you will need to challenge every irrational thought that goes through your mind. Let's talk about checking the facts.

Sit down and think of a situation where you had arrangements with people, and you've been looking forward to spending time with these people. Now, imagine that, in that particular situation, the people you were supposed to meet cancelled on you at the last moment. Now, think about how that would make you feel. Would you feel nervous, sad, or angry? Or maybe some other feeling you associate with when facing such an event? As soon as the emotions surface, it is time for you to do that fact-checking. Here are the steps you're going to take.

1. Identify the emotion first. For example, in this case, you might feel very angry.
2. Identify what caused you to feel that way. The cancelation of plans.
3. Start describing the event. How did you feel when you initially heard that? What was the first thing that crossed your mind? Did you start thinking that they don't appreciate your time, or they're just pulling your chain, or they don't care about you, and they never have?
4. Start with your interpretation. Go deeper into what you thought and felt. Why does this make you feel this way? Go deeper and find the reason.
5. Now check the facts. Has this been the first time these people have cancelled on you? Or maybe you've cancelled them a few times before, and they seemed fine with it? Did they apologize to you?
6. Come out with the facts. After you start rationalizing a little bit, things will easily start to put themselves into perspective. It is completely understandable to feel annoyed, disappointed, or even sad about the entire new situation, but the situation is really not that important to be that angry about it. You slowly start to realize that the extreme response you have does not match the severity of the situation – especially if there is a reasonable explanation behind it.
7. Start formulating a new response. How would you react the next time such a situation happens to you? Would you know how to properly formulate your response? Remember that while it is always okay to feel slightly disappointed, that is not an excuse to blow the situation out of proportion. It is all about checking the facts and then comparing them to your current emotions, thoughts, and feelings.

This exercise of checking the facts will help you rationalize and will help you calm yourself down every time you feel like a strong surge of emotions is coming to the surface. Here are a few situations when you can use this:

1. Whenever you feel anxiety about a social event.
2. When you are having an argument with a friend (or just had one).
3. When a crush rejects you.
4. Whenever you feel like your parents are criticizing you a lot.
5. Whenever you fail an exam.

Emotion: _____

Reason for the Emotion: _____

Describe the Event: _____
_____

Go Deeper: _____
_____

Facts: _____
_____

Your New Response: _____
_____

Emotion: _____

Reason for the Emotion: _____

Describe the Event: _____
_____

Go Deeper: _____
_____

Facts: _____
_____

Your New Response: _____
_____

Emotion: _____

Reason for the Emotion: _____

Describe the Event: _____

_____

Go Deeper: _____

_____

Facts: _____

_____

Your New Response: _____

_____

Emotion: _____

Reason for the Emotion: _____

Describe the Event: _____

_____

Go Deeper: _____

_____

Facts: _____

_____

Your New Response: _____

_____

Emotion: _____

Reason for the Emotion: _____

Describe the Event: _____
_____

Go Deeper: _____
_____

Facts: _____
_____

Your New Response: _____
_____

EXERCISE 19
PROBLEM-SOLVING TECHNIQUES

The second exercise is connected to the aspect of problem-solving. The truth is that how you feel about a problem is more important than the actual problem. This is a saying you will learn to be true after this exercise. Sometimes, when you come face to face with a certain situation, you may feel insecure and unable to solve the issue at hand. Whenever you don't know how to proceed, you need to come back to this exercise. Well, this is not particularly an exercise but more of a set of techniques you can use to find yourself on the other side – with any situation or issue solved. Take failing an exam as an example:

1. Feel better about it – to start feeling better about failing the exam, you need to know how to regulate the emotions that surface. This may look like the opposite of what your gut is telling you, but it works. By exposing yourself to an uncomfortable situation, you may start to regulate your emotions better.

2. Tolerate it – here, I'm not talking about keeping quiet about the situation and turning a blind eye, but rather tolerating a situation you probably cannot change at the moment. This is the time to identify the problematic feelings and thoughts you have and try to bring yourself back to the present moment.

3. Stay in the current position – this may come as a shocker, mainly because we are working toward creating an attitude that will help you control your thoughts and emotions, but it is true. Sometimes, you may need a minute to deal with the shock of a certain situation. In this case, if the situation happens to be that serious or shocking, think of it this way – give it a minute. If you are not ready to rationalize and shift your perspective, then simply don't. Allow yourself the time you need to become calm and collected.

There are many people out there who believe that solving an issue can only have two outcomes. Sometimes, things are not as black and white as they seem, so whenever you feel like it, give yourself the time to calm down before you start exploring the right solution. Here are a few situations when you can make that happen:

1. Whenever you're coping with some friendship issues.
2. Whenever you feel like you have peer pressure.
3. Whenever school is starting to get to be too much for you.
4. When you have a conflict with a teacher.
5. When you struggle to properly manage your time.

Focus on the Positive

Easier said than done, right? But the thing is, increasing positive emotions is an essential part of creating an overall good life. Thankfully, there is an aspect of DBT that focuses just on that. Other than teaching you how to regulate and deal with negative emotions, it encourages you to focus on the positive ones. Focusing on the positive means providing you with more skills to help you manage emotions rather than the alternative – being managed by them. By doing this, you will even reduce your chances of negative emotions (and vulnerability caused by them) and will start building a positive emotional experience.

You need to understand here that you are not trying to put the positive emotions in place of all the negative feelings you've had. You are learning how to put them both in the same place. They should coexist, and as long as they do, it means you understand that sometimes the negative emotions will rule, and sometimes the positive emotions will rule – but no feeling is final.

That means building up the positive emotions does not mean you completely dismiss or remove the negative ones. You are simply expanding your experience. Now, in the beginning, this may be very challenging for you, especially if you have learned to focus on the negative for a long time. Thankfully, everything can be undone, and with the help of this DBT skill, so can the constant negative thinking.

To help you out, just so you can get started, there are a few ways to build positive emotions – both by including emotional experiences in your life. The first is focusing on short-term experiences, and the second is focusing on long-term experiences.

Let's try to differentiate them, shall we?

Short-term experiences are positive ones that are usually already a part of your everyday life. You may not give that much attention to them because they are something you do every day, but they make you feel good. This could be anything from walking in a park, watching your favorite TV show, talking to a friend, going for a run or a swim, or taking a bite out of your favorite meal. It is in these small things that we tend to find the true joy of life. When you do something you love, it fills you up with positive emotions. And no matter how difficult life may be for you, these positive emotions that come from short-term experiences mean a lot and can make a big change. The more you do them, the more positive energy you will create around you.

Long-term experiences are usually made up of positive things that have a long-lasting impact on the quality of your life. These are the things that are considered to make life worth living. For example, one of the things you can say to be the biggest positive long-term experience is your list of goals. Think about it – no matter what you do in life, you have a goal every day when you wake up. A driving force that gets you out of bed. For some people, this may be a combination of a few smaller goals, and for others, it may be one big goal that they have set their heart on. Your goals can be anything – from developing a new skill to learning how to craft something to moving to a different city or country, learning a new language, getting into college, getting the job of your dreams, etc. Here, the possibilities are endless. Think carefully about what would make your life more pleasant and happier. After you have the answers, turn those answers into goals and start working toward a better and brighter future.

Another thing that I'd like to include here is the relationships. Out of all the long-term experiences you may have in life, relationships are one of the most impactful things you can count on. Starting from a relationship with yourself and moving on to a relationship with the people around you, this is an important area of your life to work on. It can help you create a more positive future for yourself. You have probably seen this happening to some of your classmates at school – they have no issue developing any kind of relationships – whether they are personal or professional. This sometimes comes easy for some people, but for others, it can be a little challenging. Chances are, if you are reading this book, you are probably a part of the latter group – but that's okay! That's why I am here – to help you work through all the troubles you have and create a better version of yourself, as well as a happier life.

You can do both – reach out for new friendships and work on the existing ones. While both can be difficult at times, both are worth it. For example, working on the current relationships you have may be connected to anyone – from a friend to a sibling to a romantic interest. These are the people you spend a lot of time with. After working on maintaining a strong relationship with them, you can notice how your feelings improve. As this is a long-term commitment, you get a long-term positive experience out of it. Instead of letting your happiness depend on one person, try to cultivate many different relationships.

The second example is when you're trying to create a new relationship. This can be extremely difficult. The trick here is to find a place where you can do a joint activity with other people, such as dancing, bowling, singing, etc. Once you visit that place often, you will find yourself in the middle of a familiar crowd. Spark up a conversation with someone you think you can "click" with as a friend and make your way from there.

By this time, you should know what cultivating a positive emotion and experience means. In addition, we will turn to some fantastic exercises I've prepared for you to set you up for success!

EXERCISE 20
POSITIVE AFFIRMATIONS

When times get tough, it is all about focusing on the positive. For this exercise, you are going to do just that – try to focus on the positive. Only in this case, you will start with no one other than yourself. If you have not noticed this by now, all negative emotions come from a place of negative belief about ourselves. Once you realize that and try to shift your perspective, your environment and you will change as well. I have found that, with the power of positive affirmations, you can do anything you set your mind to – including changing your entire mindset from a negative to a positive one.

Look at yourself in the mirror as you do this. The first time you stand in front of your mirror is going to be a difficult one. Why? Because you will need to think of ten good things to say about yourself. These can be good things in terms of your mind, smile, energy–anything you can think of. Talking positively to yourself is an excellent way to start focusing on the positive. It can help you reprogram your mind and start looking for the good things everywhere you turn.

Now, while you stand in front of the mirror, talk about some things about yourself – some positive things. Say them out loud as if they are already a part of your reality – even if they are not. Here are a few examples just to get you started:

1. My mind is wonderful.
2. My energy is addicting and fantastic.
3. All good things come my way without exceptions.
4. Whatever I attract, I become.
5. I feel constantly happy and fulfilled with my life.

You have the creative freedom to add anything you want to this list – the longer and more specific you make it, the better. Do this exercise every day so you can start feeling the results very soon!

MY POSITIVE AFFIRMATIONS

_____

_____

_____

_____

_____

_____

_____

_____

_____

_____

_____

_____

_____

_____

EXERCISE 21
GRATITUDE JOURNALING

For the second exercise, you are going to need a journal. This can be a regular notepad, a real journal, or even the notes app on your phone. As long as it is something where you can write constantly and go back to see what you've written, you're good. To get started, you can also use the worksheet below.

Take a pen and start writing. I suggest you do this every day. Notice everything happening around you and to you - and accentuate the positive each time. Even on those uneventful days where nothing really happens, it is your task in this exercise to find something for which you are grateful. At the end of each day, write down all the things you're grateful for that day. Allow this to become a practice. Try not to skip a day. Remember that being grateful doesn't necessarily mean something good has happened. You should always be grateful for the things you already have and who you already are.

For example, you can be grateful for another good day where you learned how to master your negative emotions. You can be grateful for everything you already have in life – a healthy body, mind, family, friends, etc. Or you can even be grateful for the small things in life that actually make a lot of difference – like a sunny day or if someone holds an elevator door for you. This gratitude journaling exercise can help you look at all the positive things in life. By writing them down, you focus on them so much more that, before you know it, this will become your default way of thinking.

Date: _____

Today I am Grateful for... _____

_____

_____

Date: _____

Today I am Grateful for... _____

_____

_____

Date: _____

Today I am Grateful for... _____

_____

_____

Date: _____

Today I am Grateful for... _____

_____

_____

Date: _____

Today I am Grateful for... _____

_____

_____

Date: _____

Today I am Grateful for... _____

_____

_____

Date: _____

Today I am Grateful for... _____

_____

_____

Date: _____

Today I am Grateful for... _____

_____

_____

Date: _____

Today I am Grateful for... _____

_____

_____

Take Care of Your Body

A healthy mind requires a healthy body. These are words to live by. As someone who has invested so much into dealing with your emotions, realizing how to keep them going is the most challenging thing. What not many young people realize is that exercise does you a lot of good – not just for the body, but for the mind as well. There are a few things in life that are always a recommended option, and physical activity is one of them.

To take care of your body means to treat it with caution. Listen to it every time it tries to tell you that it's full when it comes to food, that it needs a stretch when you've been sitting down for too long, and that it is time for a little bit of pampering after a long day of studying. DBT focuses mostly on the mind, but it is always important to keep up with your body too. And to get into that, it is important to follow the next exercise.

EXERCISE 22
BUILDING AN EXERCISE ROUTINE

As soon as you start thinking about getting active, here is an exercise that can help you get in the right mindset. Start by looking into some options. When it comes to working out, think about what you like – is it cardio exercises, weightlifting, running, yoga, pilates, swimming, or something completely different?

Pick something that you want, something that you enjoy, something you feel good about. Then, just start doing it. I know it sounds pretty simple, but when you come to think of it, it really is! Dedicate at least 10-15 minutes at first, just to get into the routine, and then start dedicating some more time from your day to it.

After a while, you will start feeling like you have support – something that helps you be even more focused on the positive. Taking care of your body instantly puts you in a good mood, and after a while, you can see how that reflects on the outside, too. Write down every exercise you do, write down how many times a week you've exercised, and write down how it made you feel to work out to such an extent that you now feel spectacular!

This exercise is designed to help you exercise and give you the most out of your journey to create the most spectacular version of yourself!

_____

_____

_____

_____

What Did You Learn From This Chapter?

It is time to close another chapter filled with extremely powerful DBT skills! I know that this one was a tad longer and a little denser with information, so let's try to take out the best from it. Here is a little summary of what you learned in this chapter:

- ✦ What is emotional regulation, and how does it affect your overall quality of life.
- ✦ Opposite reaction and how to take control of yourself.
- ✦ Solving issues by focusing on the facts – giving yourself clarity in situations when your judgment seems clouded.
- ✦ The power of positivity.
- ✦ The power of exercise on your overall emotional and mental state.

In this chapter, I covered everything about managing your emotions and keeping up with the positive things in life. After you turn this page, a different world awaits! The next part is all about interpersonal effectiveness – from social skills to boundaries. It is time for you to discover the final aspect of DBT so you can shine! Let's go into the details and round up our incredible journey together!

Part 4

INTERPERSONAL EFFECTIVENESS

"To effectively communicate, we must realize that we are all different in the way we perceive the world and use this understanding as a guide to our communication with others."

– Tony Robbins

Together, we have come to the last part of this book. So far, DBT has taught you plenty, but now, it is time to take all that knowledge that was always within you and turn to the final bit – interpersonal effectiveness and how to use it. During this part, you will notice what it is like to work on some aspects of your personality you might not have thought about until now. It is time to focus on what you can improve –yourself. Through the power of interpersonal effectiveness, you will become the version of yourself you're striving toward.

But for now, maybe one thing is on your mind only – what is interpersonal effectiveness? I took the liberty of explaining that to you before we go into further detail.

What is Interpersonal Effectiveness?

When it comes to relationships, everyone can be tricky. Even when considering the relationship, you are developing with yourself, you need to work hard – because you can be tricky, too. The trickiness part comes from the fact that not everyone knows how to use the power of the wise mind. Because as soon as it becomes a part of a relationship, you know you are in for constructive communication. Constructive communication is the key to success in all your relationships – with yourself, your family, friends, etc.

With this in mind, interpersonal effectiveness is about asking what you want or even saying no to someone while keeping your self-respect and the relationship intact. It is all about having a conversation (a relationship) with someone; no matter the outcome, you still feel good about yourself. Interpersonal effectiveness does not mean you need to twist your words and be diplomatic every time until you get what you want. It does not even mean you should get what you want every time. But it means that you should be happy with the outcome and yourself every time. It is about being proud of how you communicated things to that point where you feel good about yourself but still see the situation objectively. After all, you should not applaud yourself if you mishandle a communication or a relationship issue, right?

Essentially, interpersonal effectiveness means that you have found a calm yet strong way to express your needs while maintaining your integrity. In this case, the most important thing you can do is ask what you want or need and say no to a situation that doesn't suit you.

This entire section is an integral part of DBT because it can show you exactly how you affect your relationships. By now, you know that all communications and relationships are important. But did you know that the outcome of those communications and relationships is important as well? The outcomes affect your well-being, your self-esteem, and your sense of purpose. Now that you know all this, would you still be able to continue your relationships as you did until this point?

Social Skills

A lot of young people don't know how to ask for something, but rather make demands about it. Some adolescents even ask for things in a way that is confusing or don't ask at all. Interpersonal effectiveness skills are helpful here – they can make you focus on the most effective way to create and maintain a relationship. That is why I love this section; it is dedicated to the power of social skills.

Social skills are something everyone has. Some of you may have more of them, some less – but it is ultimately something embedded in our systems as human beings. We all need to communicate and create relationships with other people. This is something that cannot be done without some strong and healthy social skills. Let's explain this a bit better.

Think of any relationship you have as a tree. The better the relationship is, the bigger the tree grows. The stronger it is, the more incredible it looks. But this tree needs a system to support it while it is growing. The roots grow just as much as the leaves! Think of this every time you create or try to maintain a relationship with someone. For that relationship to grow, you need to focus on the roots. DBT, including the social skills, helps you with that. It can help you realize how to build strong roots, maintain relationships, and be effective at it.

The goal is to develop these social skills to help you become a better person. While I would love to get into the DBT interpersonal effectiveness skills right away, let's just look at it from a different angle – from the benefits point of view. Once you develop the social skills you need, here is what you will experience:

1. Improved communication

Considering interpersonal effectiveness means considering another method of communicating your feelings and thoughts clearly and respectfully. When you learn how to express them effectively, you can reduce any misunderstandings you have with the people around you, and you can build stronger and better relationships with everyone. How to do this? Don't worry; this is the part that I decided to focus on the most, and the three exercises cover the three aspects of this. They are *active listening* (when you fully concentrate on the other person and what they are saying, understanding their perspective and all), *resolving conflicts* (this is when you can be assertive and address an issue in a way that is constructive and helps you focus on finding a solution), and *empathy* (this is the part where you are respectful of both yours and the other party's feelings, thoughts, and emotions).

2. Boundaries

Teaching yourself how to establish boundaries in your personal and professional life will help you go a long way in the future. It will also help you understand other people's boundaries as well. This will help you come to terms with yourself and will prevent you from getting into conflicts in interpersonal relationships.

3. Improved self-respect

The DBT skills you will learn here will enhance your self-respect, as you will notice that you make choices that align with your values and self-worth. This will give you the ability to stand up for yourself in tough situations.

4. Less stress, more emotional intelligence

I mentioned empathy just a few sentences before this, and while I have created an entire exercise about it, you need to understand how deeply this will impact you. When you use interpersonal skills and strengthen them, you can navigate through relationships with ease, which will lead to less emotional strain and less anxiety. In turn, this will show great empathy and higher emotional intelligence. You learn how to understand and recognize your emotions and those of the people around you, so don't be afraid to open up!

Let's move on to the exercises for this part.

EXERCISE 23
ROLE-PLAYING – ACTIVE LISTENING

One of the key components of DBT is practicing active listening. Since the exercises here have the objective of helping you create the best version of yourself, I suggest you do some role-play for all the exercises for today. You will need a few materials for this particular one – a quiet space, another person who can help you with the exercise, a timer or a stopwatch, and a scenario (but this is optional).

Before you go into the exercise, it is important to accentuate how helpful active listening is in any relationship. It is more than just hearing the words; it is remembering and responding to them accordingly. This is an essential skill in every DBT aspect, and it can ensure that all misunderstandings are minimal. Active listening includes asking clarifying questions and letting the other person speak while you give them your full and undivided attention.

For this exercise, choose to be the listener, while the person sitting across from you would be the speaker. Then, they will start talking about an issue with you. This can either be an imaginary issue or a real-life issue. Here is an example scenario:

You were organizing a party, and you didn't invite them. Now, you get to hear how they feel and what they think about it. Listen to them talk, but really hear what they have to say. Answer their questions and share your opinion on the topic, too. Talk about your initial responses (especially yours) and note how everything made you feel. Talk about the challenging parts of active listening and what you learned. Also, think about how you can apply this exercise in real life. *Time your responses to a minute or two just so you can avoid getting stuck in unnecessary info.*

There are more scenarios such as this one - here are a few examples just to get you going:

1. You wanted to talk about your feelings, but you got shut out in the middle of the conversation.
2. They felt like you didn't listen to them when they were talking.
3. You were supposed to go to school together, but you forgot to pick them up.
4. You asked them if they wanted to go shopping with you, and they declined.
5. You asked for help from them for a school assignment, and they didn't help you.

They did a favor for you, but never even got a thank you from you.

EXERCISE 24
ROLE-PLAYING – ASSERTIVENESS

The second exercise has a different objective. Assertiveness is something you need to develop if you want to learn how to express your thoughts and feelings directly, respectfully, and honestly. This exercise is about refraining from being aggressive or passive while doing so.

Again, for this exercise, you will need another person who will actively participate. You will need a space where you can do the exercise and a timer so you can time your responses.

Assertiveness is the middle ground in communication. It means setting clear and respectful boundaries. It also means maintaining a steady tone of voice and manner, maintaining eye contact, and being honest yet respectful.

In this situation, you can be both the speaker and the listener. The scenario can be anything you like – from a fictional one to a real-life one. If you are the listener, then you will have to respond to the reaction of the speaker (they choose a scenario where they express a need or stand up for themselves). After you're done, you can switch the roles.

As an example scenario, let's say you borrowed something from them and didn't return it. In this role-playing exercise, you will need to understand the needs of the speaker. Listen to their, "I" statements, where they express their needs and feelings, and adhere to the clear boundaries they set. If you feel like you cannot do the last one, then it is okay to talk about it until you find a middle ground. Throughout the exercise, try to maintain a calm and steady voice and keep eye contact at all times.

Note that, during this exercise, you and the person sitting across from you may not be able to see eye to eye. This role-playing exercise has a goal to provide a realistic response – which may be one of three things – acting positively, asking for further clarification, or acting negatively. But no matter the response, you should maintain the assertiveness.

To make the most out of this exercise, I recommend you be both the listener and the speaker. Here are a few sample scenarios:

1. Trying to refuse a request from the person sitting opposite you.
2. You talked about them behind their back, and they found out, now they're confronting you with it.
3. They treated you unfairly, and now you are confronting them.
4. You try to set boundaries with them.
5. You ask them for help with a certain assignment or homework.
6. They pressured you into staying out later than you were supposed to.

Once the exercise is done, look within and note how you felt when you expressed yourself. Did you learn something about your communication style? How challenging was it for you to maintain your assertiveness at all times? Finally, think about how you can apply assertiveness to your life because you may have just learned something new and positive about yourself through this exercise.

EXERCISE 25
ROLE-PLAYING – EMPATHY

The last exercise from this part is all about empathy. Some of you may already know what empathy is – it is the ability to feel what the other person is feeling. It is the ability to put yourself in their shoes and understand their origin in a certain situation. Empathy is a very important skill that every teenager should develop. That's why I recommend a role-playing exercise here – so you can get the most out of it.

You know the drill – you need another person, a quiet space for the exercise, a partner, and a timer so you can measure your responses. But in this case, the first thing you will do is start discussing the concept of empathy. Empathy is the ability to understand another person's feelings. Also, it is not about fixing an issue or a concern. It is not even about giving advice! Empathy is a part of a healthy relationship and the base for effective communication. It can help a person feel understood and supported.

The components of a conversation filled with empathy include reflecting emotions back to the speaker, avoiding being judgmental or critical, offering validation about their feelings, and listening to them actively. Empathy is an important part of every relationship you form in life, and it can help you in many social interactions.

Create a scenario where the speaker needs support. For example, let's say that the person opposite you is upset because they had an important exam, and they failed it or didn't perform as they expected. This is an emotional thing for them, and it is your job as the listener to hear what they have to say – whether that is anxiety, frustration, anger, sadness, or something else.

It is your job to listen to them attentively while they are speaking. They describe the situation in detail, and it is your job to reflect back to them what they say and offer support. Try to avoid giving them advice as this is not a very good approach. After the time has passed and you shared some empathy with them, switch the roles. It is important for you to understand what it's like to be on both sides of the situation. This way, you will know how it feels, you will know what the most challenging bit was, and you will learn something about yourself – how you handle these kinds of situations and in which areas you can improve. Finally, you will learn how to apply empathy in your real-life relationships.

To get you started, here are a few example scenarios how you can practice that:

1. You failed a test, and you want to talk about it.
2. They are being bullied and they just want you to hear them out, because it is a difficult time for them.
3. You are anxious about a presentation and want to talk about it.
4. They are struggling with body image issues.
5. You simply want to talk about your day and your challenges.

You felt left out in a certain situation and want to be understood.

Setting and Maintaining Boundaries

Boundaries are the limits we set for ourselves in relationships and interactions with others. They define what is acceptable and unacceptable behavior towards us, helping to protect our emotional well-being and maintain healthy relationships. Setting and maintaining boundaries is crucial for everyone, but it can be especially important for teenagers as they navigate friendships, family dynamics, and the pressures of school life.

In DBT, boundaries are seen as essential for emotional regulation, self-respect, and effective interpersonal relationships. Learning how to set and maintain boundaries can help you feel more in control of your life, reduce stress, and prevent feelings of resentment or frustration.

Boundaries can be divided into several categories, each of which plays a vital role in maintaining healthy relationships:

Physical boundaries: These relate to your personal space and physical comfort. They determine how close others can get to you physically and what kind of physical contact is acceptable. For example, you might feel uncomfortable with hugging someone you don't know well or prefer to have your own space when studying.

Emotional boundaries: These involve your feelings and emotions. Emotional boundaries protect your emotional well-being by helping you avoid being overwhelmed by others' emotions or taking on their problems as your own. For example, you might set a boundary by telling a friend that you're not comfortable discussing a certain topic that triggers anxiety for you.

Intellectual boundaries: These involve your thoughts, ideas, and beliefs. Intellectual boundaries protect your right to have your own opinions and beliefs and to respect those of others. For example, you might set a boundary by asking someone not to criticize your ideas or beliefs in a disrespectful way.

Time boundaries: These involve how you manage your time and prioritize your activities. Time boundaries protect your time by helping you balance different aspects of your life, such as school, extracurricular activities, and social life. For example, you might set a boundary by saying no to a social invitation because you need to study or rest.

Material boundaries: These involve your personal belongings and financial resources. Material boundaries protect your possessions and money by ensuring that they are used or shared in ways that you're comfortable with. For example, you might set a boundary by not lending your favorite book to someone who tends to lose things.

Setting these boundaries is essential for several reasons:

Self-respect: Boundaries help you show respect for yourself by acknowledging your own needs and limits. When you set boundaries, you say your comfort and well-being matter.

Emotional protection: Boundaries protect you from being overwhelmed by others' demands or emotions. They allow you to take care of your own emotional needs first, so you don't burn out or become resentful.

Healthy relationships: Boundaries are the foundation of healthy relationships. They help ensure that both you and others know what is expected and what is off-limits, reducing misunderstandings and conflicts.

Stress reduction: Clear boundaries reduce stress by preventing you from taking on too much responsibility or feeling pressured to meet others' expectations. This can lead to a more balanced and fulfilling life.

Since boundaries are an important part of life, it is imperative to know how to implement them. These can help you grow into the person you want to be. Let's move on to the exercise bit.

EXERCISE 26
BOUNDARY-SETTING

The first exercise is all about creating healthy boundaries. If you do not know how to properly place them in your life, let me remind you that you are not the only one. Many people, such as yourself, are probably struggling to do the same. But the difference is that you have this book in your arsenal – one you can easily pass on to someone you notice is in need of it. In DBT, setting and maintaining healthy boundaries is an essential part of becoming a strong version of yourself. That is why this exercise is crucial.

You will need a pen and paper to write things down, and other than that, you're good to go! Before you start writing things down, understand that boundaries are exceptionally important. They are the limit that can help you protect yourself from any emotional, mental, and physical damage. They can help you manage your relationships with yourself and the people around you – mostly because they are based on mutual respect and understanding.

Write down all the times you felt like someone challenged you to do something that is out of your comfort zone – for example, when you hung out with your friends, and they dared you to do something you didn't really like doing. That is your boundary. You probably didn't want to say no to that just because you didn't want to look like a coward or a weak person at the moment, but deep down, you knew that it was not something you liked doing. Write about how you would react if you knew that you could set a boundary at the moment. Would anything be different?

Reflect on that – how would it feel to set a boundary? Would it feel like something you can gain confidence from? Or would it feel like a big challenge? Remember that the good thing about challenging yourself, in this case, is that you not only learn new things about yourself but also learn how you may handle a situation in which you are expected to do one thing but would prefer to do the complete opposite.

Think about the aspects of your life for which you want to set boundaries. For example, these aspects may be connected to school, to your friends, or even to yourself. Setting a boundary is not an action you do only once – it is a continuous process you will keep doing – it requires ongoing attention. While you write down the things you are setting boundaries to keep a note that you will constantly need to remind yourself how to practice them, and basically focus on taking care of yourself.

_____

_____

_____

_____

EXERCISE 27
BOUNDARY COMMUNICATION

It is one thing to set boundaries for yourself, but it is a completely different thing to try to communicate those boundaries with the people around you. If you want to practice effectively communicating these boundaries, DBT suggests you practice that. Because no matter what you do in life, practice makes it perfect. You need to know how to empower yourself and clearly express your boundaries at every given moment. That is why this exercise is created solely for that intention.

For this exercise, I recommend that you sit down with someone (maybe a parent or an older sibling) so you can fully grasp the scope of what it is you are trying to do. The exercise is a conversation with them where you express your feelings. Try to sit them down and explain what is happening – how you feel, what makes you uncomfortable, or what awakens some negative emotions or thoughts within. Stay focused on the topic and be assertive. Let them know that your final goal is to know how to communicate your boundaries.

Now, think about an aspect of your life where you want to set a boundary. This could be anything – something that has been bothering you, something that has been making you uncomfortable, or something you've wanted to change. Talk to them and explain the entire situation. For example, this can be trying to stop someone at school from bullying you. While you are explaining, use a calm tone and a steady voice. I know this may be difficult for you at first but think about what you may gain from it. These exercises are designed solely for your consideration and are here to help you improve. And in time, after practicing them, you will.

Now, after you've communicated your issue, I recommend grabbing a pen and paper and writing down how the conversation made you feel. Did you feel confident about it? What was the most challenging part of the process? Would you think that, in real life, when you communicate this, you might get a response that would put you back to square one? If so, how would you react to prevent yourself from going back? It is through these questions of self-reflection that you will be able to learn how to better stand up for yourself and know how to deal with future situations.

_____

_____

_____

_____

_____

The DBT interpersonal effectiveness skills are the final part we are going to cover in this book. They are specifically designed to help you get what you need from a relationship while being respectful of yourself and the people around you. Relationships can be very challenging and tricky, and at any point, you might come face to face with some unstable and extremely negative emotions.

That is why I am sharing the effectiveness tools: DEAR MAN, GIVE, and FAST.

Objectives Effectiveness: DEAR MAN

Starting from the first one, DEAR MAN is something that can help you achieve a certain goal or objective – no matter what that is. As you can probably notice, DEAR MAN is an acronym, and it stands for:

Describe the current situation

Express your feelings

Assert yourself

Reinforce

stay **M**indful

Appear confident

Negotiate

When it comes to the use of DEAR MAN, you first need to make sure of what you want. The clarity of your argument will be based on the clarity of your thoughts. So, if you want to start determining what you want or need, give some time to your priorities. It's okay that, at certain times in life, you feel overwhelmed. But this feeling of being overwhelmed can help you remove all the low-priority demands. Start considering doing things only because you want to do them, not because you *should* do them.

Also, consider asking for help when you need it. At the end of the day, you need to come to terms with the fact that you don't have to do everything yourself. You can even use the DEAR MAN to ask someone else for help – it all depends on your goals. Here are some goals that you might have in mind:

1. You want to stand up for your rights and want to be taken seriously.
2. You want to resolve a conflict.
3. You want to have your opinions and thoughts to be taken seriously.
4. You want to request something from someone in a way that they will do it.
5. You want to refuse to be a part of an unreasonable situation and refuse a certain request.

However, there is something to remember here. Even with the DEAR MAN technique, note that you can't have it your way all the time. You can't get everything from people constantly. Sometimes, your techniques will be put to the test, and you will need to increase your interpersonal skills; other times, they will fail completely. That's okay. In these situations, it is important to go back to distress tolerance because you know that what you want is impossible to get.

While this is a little bit tricky to understand right now, I have created an exercise for each of these techniques. That will give you the clarity you need.

EXERCISE 28
DEAR MAN

What's interesting about all these exercises is that no matter what you want to achieve, you always go back to the wise mind I mentioned at the beginning of the book. There is no better mindset than the wise mind, so whenever you want to do this exercise, go into that state and then begin.

For this exercise, you will need a pen and paper and a friend, sibling or parent – someone you completely trust. Take the pen and paper and write out the acronym vertically. Each letter represents a certain aspect you're going to focus on. This way, you will have the opportunity to spend as much time as you need on the most challenging letter. Before you begin, make sure you are comfortable.

Sit down with the person you've chosen to be your partner and think of a situation you want to discuss. Start from the beginning – here is an example of how the conversation should flow:

Let's say you sat down with a friend who gave you a hard time and maybe even made fun of you in front of other people. Now, start going through the letters.

D – Describe the situation from your point of view and clarify what you are asking them. In this case, you're asking them not to do that to you anymore. But, since you are wise, try to only state the facts. That means you have to limit yourself to not judging the situation, who and what caused it, and whether it is good or bad.

E – Express your feelings about the situation. Avoid transferring the blame to them but let them know how you feel. Go from the assumption that they don't know how you feel (because that is usually the case). Think of this as your opportunity to openly tell them how you feel.

A – Assert yourself – tell them what you want. In this case, you want to stop being made fun of in front of other people. Be clear and concise so that there is no misunderstanding. Do not assume that the person sitting across from you is able to read your mind.

R – Reinforce your statement. That way, you will make sure there is a positive outcome to your request. I recommend that you reinforce there would be a positive outcome if they agree with you and a negative outcome if they don't – that way, you are more likely to get an affirmative response.

M – Mindfulness of your goal. The person sitting across from you will not be mindful of your goal – that's why you should do that yourself. Don't get distracted from the conversation and, if you need to, start repeating things – be just like a broken record. If they attack you, ignore their attacks. Repeat yourself until you make your point and notice they have understood you.

A – Appear confident, as if you are in charge of the situation. You may not be at first, but you will lean into it as time passes. Exude confidence in your posture, your tone of voice, and your words.

N – Negotiating is key. You can be as confident as you want, but you also need to be flexible. If you want to get something, you need to be willing to give something, too. Focus on your goal but be practical about what will work. Make way for communication and find a mutual solution to the issue.

Just to help you get going, here are 5 example scenarios:

Asking to spend some more time together.

Ask them for some extra help on something.

Ask to spend less time together.

You feel like you need to raise a particular subject with them and talk about it.
Ask them to include you more in their social activities

Describe the Situation _____

_____

_____

Express Your Feelings _____

_____

_____

Assert Yourself _____

_____

_____

Reinforce Your Statement _____

_____

_____

Mindfulness _____

_____

_____

Appear Confident _____

_____

_____

Negotiate _____

_____

_____

D _____

_____

_____

E _____

_____

_____

A _____

_____

_____

R _____

_____

_____

M _____

_____

_____

A _____

_____

_____

N _____

_____

_____

D _____
_____
_____

E _____
_____
_____

A _____
_____
_____

R _____
_____
_____

M _____
_____
_____

A _____
_____
_____

N _____
_____
_____

D _____

_____

_____

E _____

_____

_____

A _____

_____

_____

R _____

_____

_____

M _____

_____

_____

A _____

_____

_____

N _____

_____

_____

_____

D _____

_____

_____

E _____

_____

_____

A _____

_____

_____

R _____

_____

_____

M _____

_____

_____

A _____

_____

_____

N _____

_____

_____

D _____

_____

_____

E _____

_____

_____

A _____

_____

_____

R _____

_____

_____

M _____

_____

_____

A _____

_____

_____

N _____

_____

_____

Relationship Effectiveness: GIVE

Let's move on to the second exercise, which is all about relationship effectiveness. I cannot remind you enough how challenging it can be to deal with unstable emotions. During these times, one wrong step in communication can damage a relationship beyond repair. That is why the technique GIVE will provide you with the help you need to keep your relationship intact, even in those times when you have an argument.

GIVE is another acronym that will help you obtain some skills that are important for all those times when you don't know how to act in an argument but still want to meet your goal or objective. Each letter represents a certain aspect you're going to focus on. Here is what GIVE stands for:

Gentle

Interested

Validate

Easy manner

To provide you with a little more clarity on this one, think of the GIVE as a how skill and of DEAR MAN as a what skill. DEAR MAN is more about what you do, and GIVE is more about how you do it (the same thing will apply to FAST, but more on that later on. However, since all these skills are connected, you will subconsciously improve your DEAR MAN skills by using the GIVE skills.

A part of the relationship effectiveness is to tend to your relationships as regularly as you can. You should not allow any issues or troubles to pop up and should remain there – like an elephant in the room. Instead, GIVE is your opportunity to address them as soon as they happen. By doing this, you use all the skills you've learned from this book to prevent any issues from becoming bigger and eventually blowing up. This technique also helps you end any toxic relationships because it shows you it is not necessarily a good thing to continue doing something you don't want and give a person the attention they probably don't deserve.

GIVE is, just like DEAR MAN, all about goals. Before you start your communication, it is important to be clear about what you want. Sometimes, you may want a person to accept you more. You may want to stop them from rejecting or criticizing you as much. Some of the goals you may have in mind include the following:

1. You want to act in a certain way so the other person will give you what you want.
2. You want to act in a certain way so the other person will not feel wrong about you rejecting their requests.
3. You want to act in a certain way to balance the good of the short-term goals with the good of the long-term goals.

So, you see – this one is all about balancing your relationships with the goals you have for yourself and your life. You should not sacrifice who you are just to get the respect of others – which, at the end of the day, you probably don't even need. The only time you should commit to something is when you want to. As we lean into GIVE and learn the FAST technique, you will see how these three techniques should be used at the same time and balanced effectively.

EXERCISE 29
GIVE

For this exercise, think about how you want to be treated in a situation during a discussion. Do you want to be yelled at, or do you want to be treated with kindness? How would you imagine the conversation will flow if you want to be treated with kindness? This exercise consists of you getting a pen and paper, as well as someone to discuss with. Here is how you can use the acronym.

First, write it down on your piece of paper.

G – Remind yourself that people respond in a gentle manner better than they do to yelling. That's why, no matter what you want to discuss, as long as you present it well and approach them with kindness and respect, you know you have opened a steady line for communication. Avoid being snarky, making threats, and passing judgment on them. Tolerate it if they want to say no to you and give them time to respond to what you said to them.

I – Being interested is another thing you should focus on. Has it ever happened to you that sometimes someone doesn't listen to a word you say? You see their attention is being pulled to a different side, and you get a little angry about it. Well, you should give as much as you get. Being interested may be a challenging thing for you, but in this case, it is only fair to listen to their point of view, too. Maintain eye contact, don't interrupt them, and carefully listen to what they have to say.

V – Show the other person that you've listened to their side of the story by completely understanding them. Validate their point of view and try to put yourself in their shoes. Even in those times when you think they aren't making much sense, try to find the grain of truth and reason for what they are saying. Be non-judgmental and be that in a loud way. Validate their feelings, wants, opinions, and difficulties (which, remember, does not mean you have to accept them). Oftentimes, someone just needs to feel heard and seen, and that paves the way for a potentially solid relationship.

E – Easy manner means trying to be as friendly and as easy-going as you possibly can be. You can even use humor to ease into the conversation and relax the other person. You should not guilt-trip them but rather have a good attitude, especially if the other person may feel hurt by your request. Give your best to accept their response and maintain calmness.

Here are a few scenarios to get you started:

1. Support your friend when they're having a bad time.
2. Resolving a conflict you may have with them.
3. Comforting them after they get a bad grade.
4. Talking about a sensitive issue.
5. Helping them whenever they feel anxious about something.

Gentle _____

_____

_____

Interested _____

_____

_____

Validate _____

_____

_____

Easy Manner _____

_____

_____

G _____

_____

_____

I _____

_____

_____

V _____

_____

_____

E _____

_____

_____

G _____

_____

_____

I _____

_____

_____

V _____

_____

_____

E _____

_____

_____

G _____

_____

_____

I _____

_____

_____

V _____

_____

_____

E _____

_____

_____

G _____

_____

I _____

_____

V _____

_____

E _____

_____

_____

G _____

_____

I _____

_____

V _____

_____

E _____

_____

G _____

_____

_____

I _____

_____

_____

V _____

_____

_____

E _____

_____

_____

Self-Respect Effectiveness: FAST

The last technique is FAST. It is very easy to get lost in the moment and lose yourself in the whirlpool of emotions while you are having a conversation or an argument with someone. And before you know it, you have bent to their will without ever having the intention of doing that. This is where the last technique – FAST, comes into the picture. As you can see, it is a self-respecting effectiveness skill, and it is one we will dissect together in depth. FAST can help you maintain your self-respect during a discussion, conversation, or argument with someone.

Yes, you guessed it, this is an acronym as well. It will teach you how to act every time you are faced with a challenging situation, yet you are determined to meet your goals without sacrificing yourself in the process. Here is what FAST stands for:

be **F**air

no **A**pologies

Stick to values

be **T**ruthful

I mentioned earlier that FAST is just like GIVE – it is a part of the how skills that will help you have an objective and successful discussion. For this technique, you must remember that nobody can take away your self-respect – unless you give it up willingly. I noticed something, especially with young people such as yourself, that self-respect is based on the quality of your relationships with other people. By using this skill, you learn how to tend to your relationships skillfully.

As with the two previous techniques, before you begin your conversation, you need to keep your goal in mind. Doing this will help you remain focused and clear on what you want. And remember, the focus here is maintaining your level of self-respect. With that in mind, here are a few goals as an example for you:

1. You want to like yourself.
2. You want to feel effective and capable.
3. You want to act in a way that makes you feel moral, respected, and valued.

Before we move on to the exercise, I would like to share the wise words of Eleanor Roosevelt – *"No one can make you feel inferior without your consent."*

EXERCISE 30
FAST

We have made our way to the last exercise of the book – and boy, is it a good one! For this final exercise, you will need to practice in the same way you practiced with the other two exercises – you need a pen and paper and someone to talk to. Again, you can choose anyone you want – it can be a sibling, a parent, or a friend. Only this time, note that it's helpful to practice FAST when you're not in the middle of an argument so you can first get used to it. Then, as you do, you can start using it in real-life situations when things get a little more intense.

Take out your pen and paper, write the acronym vertically, and go through the letters one by one.

F – it is all about being fair. When you think of a situation you want to discuss with the person sitting opposite you, you need to be fair when describing it. After all, while you still want to put whatever it is you feel or think about the situation on the table, you still need to be mindful of their wants and needs, too. Stick to the facts and avoid judgment but remain fair to yourself.

A – if you don't have to, don't apologize. Putting yourself in a position when you want to ask for something is not a reason to apologize. Having a different opinion or a point of view is also not a reason to apologize. It is okay for you to take up space. The only situation where you need to apologize is when you have made a mistake and want to get things right. Apologizing means you are wrong. Taking up space and having an opinion is not wrong. Apologizing for doing all this will only make you lower your self-worth and self-respect. Also, it gets on other people's nerves.

S – stick to your values as much as you can. I know that it can be scary to ask for a change (or to ask for anything, for that matter). At the time, it might feel like the person you're talking to may stop liking you if you ask them for something. Through my years of experience, I have noticed that this is often the case, especially with young people – and that is why I am accentuating it now. Don't let fear be the overwhelming feeling, and don't compromise just to avoid conflict or to please the other person. Doing this will only make you like yourself less in the long run.

T – lastly, make sure you are always truthful to yourself. Stick to the facts and avoid stretching them out too thin. If you start noticing a dishonesty pattern within yourself, remember to cut it out. In the long run, this pattern will make you like yourself less and less and will diminish your self-respect. There is no need to make judgmental statements – only the facts are enough. Also, being truthful means being grounded and not acting helpless. Even in those times when you feel insecure and scared, try to stand firmly on the ground with both feet.

Here are a few example scenarios to get you started:

1. Trying to say no to peer pressure.
2. Make your voice heard in a group project, where you only know the person sitting opposite you.
3. Asking more time to finish a task.
4. Dealing with unwanted criticism.
5. Setting boundaries with the person sitting opposite you.

With FAST, there are some instances where being truthful may be a destructive thing for the relationship. To guide yourself through this tricky process, I suggest you include a wise mind to guide you whenever you feel like it is appropriate to do so.

It is incredibly interesting to learn that these techniques are part of what makes you an incredible, stable, calm, and happy person. I would love to see you give them all a go because there is so much you can learn about yourself from them!

Be **F**air _____

_____

_____

_____

No **A**pologies _____

_____

_____

_____

Stick to Values _____

_____

_____

_____

Be **T**ruthful _____

_____

_____

_____

F _____
_____
_____

A _____
_____
_____

S _____
_____
_____

T _____
_____
_____

F _____
_____
_____

A _____
_____
_____

S _____
_____
_____

T _____
_____

F _____
_____
_____

A _____
_____
_____

S _____
_____
_____

T _____
_____
_____

F _____
_____
_____

A _____
_____
_____

S _____
_____
_____

T _____
_____

F _____

_____

A _____

_____

S _____

_____

T _____

_____

What Did You Learn From This Chapter?

As the final chapter in the book, I believe that things are wrapping up quite nicely. I know this was a long one and that we had a lot to cover here, so let's do a short recap of everything you learned through this chapter, shall we?

- ✧ What is interpersonal effectiveness.
- ✧ Social skills and the power of creating and maintaining relationships.
- ✧ What you will gain by developing your social skills.
- ✧ The power of boundaries; different types of boundaries – why setting them and maintaining them is important.
- ✧ The first of the three techniques – DEAR MAN – is all about the effectiveness of objectives.
- ✧ The second of the three techniques – GIVE – is all about the effectiveness of relationships.
- ✧ The third of the three techniques – FAST – is all about the effectiveness of self-respect.

This chapter may have been the longest one, but it was essential to go through it together so I could help you go through this wonderful journey to yourself. All of the techniques you've learned here are something that will soon become invaluable to you. I know it will be difficult to deal with them at first – it may have seemed like the more you read this book, the more challenges you will have. But there is nothing better than stepping out of your comfort zone when you know it is the path toward creating the best version of yourself.

That being the case, I can't wait for you to turn the page so we can complete our time together on a high note!

CONCLUSION

Congratulations! You've made it to the end of this book! I am happy to say, however, that your journey to your true self is something that will continue long after you've completed reading this. I wouldn't even be surprised if you come back to the book every once in a while. By exploring and practicing the skills of DBT, you will take a significant step toward understanding yourself better, managing your emotions more effectively, and building healthier relationships (with yourself and the people around you). This is no small feat—learning and applying DBT skills takes courage, dedication, and a willingness to grow. You should be incredibly proud of yourself.

Take a moment to reflect on everything you learned in this book. Think back to when you first started reading this book. Do you feel like you can face some life challenges better now? Do you think you have a better scope of your emotions? How have you changed through this book? How can you manage your life better from now on?

Up until this point, you may have been faced with times when you didn't know how to react or hoped for a different outcome than the one you got. That's okay. Learning how to get through these situations equals growth. What matters here is that you are committed to learning and applying these skills, every time things are hard.

The skills you've learned in this book are tools that you can carry with you for the rest of your life. They're not just for times of crisis or extreme emotion; they can be integrated into your everyday routines, helping you to live more mindfully, manage stress, and communicate more effectively. But, to make the most out of them, you need to know how to make that happen.

Try to practice these skills as often as you can. For them to become a part of who you are, you need to practice them as often as possible. Set some time aside every day and revise the techniques you've learned here. The more you practice them, the easier they will be for you.

Practice with mindfulness. As you learned in the book, mindfulness is the foundation of DBT, and to take full advantage of this, you need to keep being fully present and remove judgment from your thoughts and feelings. Use the toolbox of skills you've taken from this book every time you face a challenge. Consider how you can make the most out of each situation.

Reflect on your past experiences and notice how you start to use the DBT skills in your life. Put some finishing touches and keep moving forward while constantly evaluating your progress. Also, don't forget to ask for help when needed. If you feel like you need some assistance in overcoming a challenging situation, remember that you are not alone. You can always come back to this book and revisit a chapter or a segment alone, or with a friend, sibling or anyone you like.

As you continue to grow and develop, remember that the skills you've learned in this book are just the beginning. Life is full of opportunities for learning and self-improvement. By staying open to new experiences and challenges, you'll continue to build resilience, deepen your self-awareness, and strengthen your relationships.

DBT is not about perfection; it's about progress. It's about finding a balance between accepting yourself as you are and striving to become the person you want to be. It's about understanding that you have the power to shape your own life, even in the face of adversity.

You've embarked on a journey that many never take — self-improvement and emotional growth. You've shown that you're willing to face your challenges head-on, learn new coping methods, and build a life that reflects your values and aspirations. This is a remarkable achievement, and it's something you can carry with you as you move forward in life.

As you close this book, know that the skills you've learned are yours to keep. They are tools that can help you navigate the many twists and turns that life will inevitably bring. Whenever you face a new challenge or feel uncertain about the future, remember the progress and strength you've discovered within yourself.

You are capable, resilient, and worthy of the life you want to create. Keep believing in yourself, practicing your skills, and moving forward. The journey doesn't end here — it's just the beginning. Your future is full of possibilities, and you have the tools to make the most of them.

Thank you for allowing this book to be a part of your journey. Wishing you all the best as you continue to grow, learn, and thrive.

COPING SKILLS WORKBOOK
for Teens

How to Manage Anger, Anxiety & Stress, and Use CBT and DBT Exercises for Lifelong Emotional Regulation

EMILY CARTER

INTRODUCTION

In today's day and age, it can be quite challenging to be a teen. The interesting bit is that, while you are young, you can't wait to get to those crazy teenage years. But once you do, it's not exactly what you expected - I know, we've all been there. You have a lot of freedom and a lot of opinions, and you want to express every little thing that pops into your head. However, you can still feel something within you, like something's not right.

You feel like you don't have enough space to process all kinds of emotions. It starts to feel like your teenage years are about to be a rollercoaster. One minute, you feel like everything is great, and the next, you are overwhelmed by everything surrounding you. You have to meet certain expectations from your family (in terms of how you should behave, what grades you should get, etc) When you go to school, the same expectations happen there as well. Then, of course, there is also peer pressure (which somehow always seems to be present). At the end of the day, life starts to feel like it is too much for you to handle. You feel stressed, anxious, and just unable to process everything around you, especially when things sometimes happen too fast.

Well, I am happy to tell you that you are not alone in this.

I am even happier to tell you that I will help you get through this!

I designed this book with the sole purpose – for you to have a practical guide that can help you navigate life's challenges. You will do that using Cognitive Behavioral Therapy (CBT) and Dialectical Behavior Therapy (DBT)**.** These two evidence-based approaches have helped millions of young people gain control over their emotions, build resilience, and improve their relationships. These techniques aren't just for therapy sessions. They are also skills you can use in everyday life. They can help you handle stress, anxiety, sadness, and anger and even help in those moments when everything just feels like it's too much.

CBT helps you recognize and change unhelpful thought patterns. If I take a wild guess here, these negative thoughts probably make you feel worse. Ever notice how one negative thought can spiral into a full-blown bad day? Well, CBT gives you tools to catch those thoughts and reframe them - so they don't take over. DBT, on the other hand, will help you work on balancing emotions, improving communication, and learning to stay calm in difficult situations. Basically, these skills help you handle life.

I am happy to share this workbook with you - mostly because it isn't about a series of lectures or just a bunch of unrealistic advice. I made it interactive, practical, and for real life – your life. Each chapter includes exercises, techniques, and activities that will help you apply these coping skills in a way that makes sense for you (I know this may sound confusing now, but once you start the chapters, it will make much more sense). So, no matter what you deal with – anxiety, self-doubt, or you just want to build healthier habits, here you will find a step-by-step guide that will help you be more in control.

Oh, and one last thing before we begin – you don't have to be in a crisis to benefit from these skills. In fact, the best time to learn these healthy coping strategies is before things get out of control. But, even if you do feel like you are on the verge, remember this – as long as you have this book in your hands, everything will be alright. Think of this workbook as a toolkit for your mental well-being. You can turn to it every time you need support, clarity, or just a reminder that you have the power to navigate through whatever comes your way.

No one expects you to have life figured out. As a teenager, I felt the same way, but as soon as I grew up, I realized that most of the things were just a result of not knowing how to control myself. But with the right skills (the ones I included in this book), you can learn to handle stress and regulate emotions. You can build a balanced and fulfilling life. You can work through this book on your own or with a supportive adult – just know that every small step you take is a step toward emotional strength and a better you.

Are you ready to take control of your emotions, develop better coping strategies, and build the skills to handle whatever life throws at you? Let's begin together!

UNDERSTANDING CBT AND DBT

"You have power over your mind – not outside events. Realize this, and you will find strength."
– Marcus Aurelius

We all learn, grow, and understand. It is a part of the wonder called life, and we are all aware that there are always some ups and downs. We embrace every challenge and overcome every obstacle that comes our way. But what happens when things become a little too much for us? Does it mean that we cannot cope with anything anymore? Does it simply mean we're tired?

As a teenager, I can fully understand how you feel. You already deal with all these kinds of feelings, thoughts, and emotions, and it feels like it is bad enough that you can't regulate them on a daily basis. The thing is, as soon as anything happens to you, you start to feel like you're spinning out of control! This may have happened to you once, twice, or more than a few times, and after each time, you feel disappointed in yourself.

Well, I am glad you're here because, from this point on, I will help you embark on a journey of self-discovery. However, to properly do that, let's break things down – one at a time. This first chapter is all about easing you into the process.

We will start by explaining some basic terms.

What is CBT?

The first thing we're going to do is explain the concept of CBT. Yes, you have probably guessed it already – there is a difference between CBT and DBT. Before you go much further into detail and exercises, I believe this is the right way to start learning things.

CBT is like a therapy session – one that can help you manage all your symptoms by helping you change how you think and how you behave. Basically, it is based on the concept that your thoughts, feelings, and emotions are all connected – and that too much negativity can make you feel trapped. The goal of CBT is to help you deal with any issue you may have, and just help you cope with life overall in a more positive way. CBT can help you break down the larger issues into smaller tasks. It constantly looks for practical ways to help you make that happen.

This approach has been proven effective in treating many issues and even mental health conditions. You may be dealing with anything from anxiety, OCD, panic attacks, and phobias to PTSD, insomnia, and even chronic pain – CBT can help you cope, even handle whatever it is you think is unresolvable.

In terms of emotional regulation, CBT works in such a way that it helps you break down everything about your problems into three sections – your feelings, your thoughts, and your actions. As you analyze every single section, you try to work out whether all of what you're experiencing (or at least a part of it) seems unrealistic. You realize the effect this has on you. By doing this, you work out how to change your thoughts and the behaviors that are not of much help to you. Also, you learn how to manage the problems you have and prevent them from having a negative effect on your life (especially your emotions).

The funny thing about CBT is that we all do this at some point in our lives. Some of us focus on this without putting too much thought into it. Others put a lot of energy into it. Whatever the case, CBT is an approach that can help anyone with any kind of issue – especially because the techniques used are very easy! Some of the most popular examples of CBT techniques include journaling. Writing down what you feel, think, and experience throughout the day can help you step back and look at whatever is happening from a different, calmer perspective. Some other quite popular techniques include breathing exercises, role-playing, mindfulness, setting goals, and doing certain physical activities. Do any of these sound familiar? That's because CBT is based on putting the focus on yourself and pulling away from negativity while focusing on logic.

That did not sound bad, right? I know that this is still uncharted territory for you, but don't worry – I am here to guide you every step of the way.

What is DBT?

On the other hand, DBT is somewhat of an altered CBT approach. While it focuses on the same goal (to make you feel better and become a better version of yourself), the approach is a little bit different here. DBT's main goals are to help you live in the present moment, fully embrace it, and develop a healthy way of coping with stress. It also helps you learn how to regulate your emotions and improve your relationships with the people around you.

DBT is very well known among people who need help with emotional regulation. This approach relies on a certain set of principles, including distress tolerance, interpersonal effectiveness, acceptance and validation, behavior change, biosocial theory, and emotional regulation. These principles have the power to help you create a certain core mindfulness and regulate your emotions.

Now, what is the difference between CBT and DBT? It seems like I have talked plenty about it. But, at this point, it still sounds like the same thing, right? It is okay to be a little confused right now, especially because there is so much for you to learn!

The difference between CBT and DBT is what you learn during the process. The other difference is knowing how the treatment is delivered. Both of them are equally powerful approaches. Here, the thing is – it all comes down to your personal needs. There are many differences between these two, but the approach is the main one. With CBT, you focus on your behavior and your patterns of thinking. And on the other side, with DBT, you focus on your relationship with yourself and the people around you.

The bottom line is that both of them can help you deal with different mental challenges. Again, it all comes down to the approach you prefer. In some cases, you can even go as far as to focus on both of them and use both approaches – if you feel like you could benefit from both. And that is exactly why we're here! These two approaches (when combined) can help you work out wonders!

Benefits of Using CBT and DBT

Both Cognitive Behavioral Therapy and Dialectical Behavior Therapy stand out as powerful, evidence-based approaches. Believe me when I say – these approaches offer hope and healing, but what makes them the pillar of modern mental health care is that they can adapt to each individual need. Sounds fascinating, doesn't it? I would love to talk about their effectiveness for a little bit (bear with me on this one), but also share some real-life success stories with you, and finally, how both these approaches can transform your everyday life.

CBT is recognized as a gold standard that can help treat a variety of mental health issues. As I mentioned earlier, this includes anxiety, depression, and post-traumatic stress disorder (PTSD). Now, if you need some actual reassurance that this works, this next part is for you. Research shows that CBT is highly effective if you want to minimize the symptoms. It can help you identify and challenge unhelpful thought patterns and behaviors. According to a meta-analysis by Hofmann et al. (2012) published in *Cognitive Therapy and Research*, CBT significantly outperforms other therapeutic approaches (in the treatment of depression and anxiety disorders).

On the other hand, DBT was originally developed to treat borderline personality disorder. However, it also expanded its reach to address issues such as substance use, eating disorders, and other mental health challenges. Because of its dual focus, you get to experience the most results. Here, you combine acceptance strategies (mindfulness) with change strategies (emotion regulation, distress tolerance, and interpersonal effectiveness). A 2023 study by Vijayapriya and Tamarana published in *Research in Psychotherapy* journal showed how DBT may lead to significant improvements in emotional regulation and interpersonal development in individuals who have higher mental health needs.

Both therapies offer structured, actionable tools that empower individuals to take charge of their mental health, making them highly effective for a wide range of challenges.

While statistics and studies are compelling, it's the personal journeys of those who have embraced CBT and DBT that truly bring their impact to life. Here, I would like to remind you to view these with an open mind and heart and to try to understand that their journey has been just as challenging as yours. Also, as you can see from these success stories, these are all shared by people who are well into their adult lives. This is another positive thing for you – because you start to comprehend and work on your issues from an earlier age. I am here to remind you that you are bound to succeed.

Take a look at the success stories.

Emma's Story – Overcoming Anxiety with CBT

Emma, a 32-year-old marketing professional, had struggled with debilitating anxiety for years. Social situations, once joyful, became sources of dread, and her career began to suffer. Through CBT, Emma learned to identify her automatic negative thoughts such as "I'll embarrass myself" – and challenge them with evidence. By practicing gradual exposure to anxiety-inducing situations, she rebuilt her confidence. Amazingly enough, Emma now leads presentations with ease and actually enjoys a thriving social life.

Mark's Journey – He Found Balance with DBT

Mark, a 24-year-old college student, battled emotional dysregulation and impulsive behaviors. DBT taught him mindfulness techniques to stay present and recognize his emotions without judgment. He also mastered distress tolerance skills, such as using grounding exercises during moments of high stress. With consistent practice, Mark's relationships improved (significantly, if I may add), and he found stability in both his academic and personal life.

These stories highlight how tailored interventions in CBT and DBT can lead to profound, life-changing results.

How These Therapies Can Be Applied to Everyday Life

The beauty of CBT and DBT lies in them being the most practical ones. They're not just for therapy sessions. Honestly, they offer tools you can carry into your daily life and handle challenges with resilience and clarity. And at the end of the day, isn't that why you are here? There are a few ways you can include both CBT and DBT into your everyday life. While I have some ideas for you below, I recommend that you use at least one of the CBT and one of the DBT ones (for starters). I will share many techniques with you here. These techniques here, as well as many other ones will be presented in detail, just for you. They span throughout the entire book. Familiarize yourself with the exercises, one at a time, and try to do them once a day. Then, you can try some of the other ideas I've shared. Compare and combine to get the best results. Once you get the hang of it, you will have no trouble doing them every day – even subconsciously.

CBT in Daily Life

- **Challenging Negative Thoughts** – If you find yourself thinking, "I'll never be good at this," pause and ask, "What evidence supports this thought? What evidence contradicts it?" This shift can help reframe your mindset.
- **Behavioral Activation** – Struggling with motivation? Break tasks into smaller, manageable steps and commit to action. The act of doing often reignites motivation.

DBT in Daily Life

- **Mindfulness –** Practice being present during everyday activities, such as eating or walking. Notice the sensations, smells, and sounds around you without judgment.
- **Distress Tolerance –** When faced with overwhelming emotions, use grounding techniques like the 5-4-3-2-1 method (identify five things you can see, four you can touch, three you can hear, two you can smell, and one you can taste).
- **Interpersonal Effectiveness –** Use the DEAR MAN framework (Describe, Express, Assert, Reinforce, stay Mindful, Appear confident, and Negotiate) to navigate difficult conversations with assertiveness and respect.

These strategies not only improve mental health but also enhance overall well-being and strengthen relationships. And I'm happy to say – these strategies are only the beginning.

What Did You Learn in This Chapter?

Before we leap into the next chapter (where the true excitement begins), let's take a look at what we learned from this one. After all, this is the basis on which you will only continue to build yourself up as a person.

In this chapter, you learned:

- What is CBT, how does it work, and some of its most popular techniques
- What is DBT, how does it work, and its principles
- What is the difference between the two
- The benefits of using these two approaches
- How you can use the approaches in everyday life

Now, turn the page, and let's move on to the next chapter!

②

UNDERSTANDING YOUR EMOTIONS

"Emotion can be the enemy, if you give into your emotion, you lose yourself. You must be at one with your emotions because the body always follows the mind." – Bruce Lee

There is so much happening behind the screen that you are (currently) unaware of. The wonderfulness behind the complexity of being human shines bright and illuminates everything. Yet somehow, as individuals, we sometimes remain in the dark. But this is not a bad thing. Without darkness, there cannot be light – and without knowing that something is wrong, you would never know you need to work on it or improve it.

This chapter is all about addressing your emotions. Let's learn together how you can help them work for you instead of controlling you. It is an interesting process to dive deep into yourself and uncover the real truth about yourself. It is such a liberating feeling – you'll see.

The Science of Emotions

Have you ever thought about your emotions as a concept? Do you know where they come from? Some of you may answer this question with the heart, some with the head, and some of you may just shrug without answering. Sometimes you feel sad, and other times you feel happy – this is how all our bodies work. It may come as a surprise but there is some science behind all of this, so stay with me.

In essence, your emotions come from your brain. To be more precise, they come from the limbic system, which is a very complex structure found in the cerebral cortex. This part of the brain is responsible for your emotions, your behavior, and your level of motivation. Think of this as somewhat of the control center of your body. It can interpret various emotional stimulations.

Basically, your limbic system is your EQ (emotional intelligence). It includes the amygdala, hypothalamus, and hippocampus. When all these aspects are combined together, they work to help you regulate your emotions in any given situation. One of the most important structures of the limbic system is the amygdala. Its responsibility is to help you process emotions like anger, fear, anxiety, and aggression (the reason why we're here). What happens is that when you feel threatened, the amygdala sends a signal to the hypothalamus, and this makes you act in a certain way.

So far, this all seems like a relatively logical explanation, but where are the hormones and emotions? There is more to the limbic system than you think. Hormones also play a very important role in how you feel – especially because you are a teenager. All the hormones that you're probably already aware of (dopamine, oxytocin, cortisol, etc) that either make you feel good or not.

But, there is also one final point, where you might suddenly feel angry or scared or even snap at someone – without knowing why. You just can't explain it. Well, in this case, it is all about the environment. Sometimes, your emotions can be ruled by an external factor. This can be anything from your genetics to your surroundings. This is the last bit of the science equation regarding what can influence your emotions and response.

Emotions are complex, and there is no easy way to explain all of them. That is probably why you feel the way you feel right now. But fear not – there is always light at the end of the tunnel. There is no one explanation for your emotions because there is no one answer that could fit everyone. For now, all you need to remember is that emotions are an essential part of what makes you a human. They can help you navigate through life and connect with yourself and with those around you.

Emotional Brain Development

Of course, there is no science behind emotions without emotional brain development. These topics go hand in hand. But, for a teenager, it seems like you have a long way to go in terms of brain development. No, don't take this the wrong way, it's just that science says that the brain of a teen is not fully developed until they reach the age of about 25. So, to get there, you need to first understand how your brain works.

How does the teenage brain process emotions? This is a question your parents or guardians have probably asked themselves many times. Even though they have been teenagers at some point in their lives, this concept seems like a completely unfamiliar one to them. The thing is, the brain of every teenager works differently – and this differs a lot from an adult's brain. Adults tend to think with their prefrontal cortex, which is the rational part of the brain. This part of the brain responds to situations with reasonable judgment and is fully aware of any long-term consequences.

As mentioned earlier, you, as a teen, process everything with your amygdala – which is the emotional part. In every teenager's brain, the connection between the emotional part of the brain and the center for making decisions is still developing – and sometimes, this doesn't happen at the same time. This is why you tend to get emotional at times, and later, you cannot really explain why you acted the way you did. You still feel more than you think.

But why does understanding brain development help in managing emotions? Why would this book help you? If it is normal to feel this way, then isn't the best course of action to just wait it out? Well, no. The thing is, a lot of things can happen to you before you reach the age of 25 or so. You don't have to wait and succumb to the pressure of emotional irregularity until that moment comes. What you can do in the meantime is to try to understand your brain and thus manage your emotions. Yes, the rest of this chapter will be all about that.

Identifying and Differentiating Your Emotions

Identify, differentiate, and manage – these are the three things you will learn over the course of this book. These are considered quite important if you want to learn all there is to know about emotional development. Strong emotional development leads to skills such as social awareness, self-awareness, responsible decision-making, the ability to build relationships, and emotional regulation. These are the skills you may struggle with at the moment. In order to conquer this, you will need to know your emotions – you can do this by acknowledging the three major stages in emotional development.

1. **Identify emotions** – at first, since you are born, it is believed you only have three emotions – happiness, fear, and anger. However, as you grow, so does the palette of emotions you feel. The first thing you need to do whenever you find yourself in a situation that needs extra attention from your end is to recognize the emotions you feel.

2. **Differentiate emotions** – as you grew, up until this point, you probably realized that there is a way to experiment with emotions – at least, with how you express them. While this is a healthy way of growing up and developing into a healthy adult, this is your time to figure out how to differentiate between knowing how to express emotions healthily rather than in an unhealthy way.

3. **Manage emotions** – we all grow and enter into various social environments where we need to be in control of our emotions. Of course, that doesn't mean you need to act like an animal when you are alone and restrain yourself in public. It means you need to know how to manage your emotions and support your further development in life.

Differentiating Between Primary and Secondary Emotions

Indeed, there is such a thing called primary emotion. Then there is secondary emotion, too. These are very well known by therapists everywhere in the world, but not by the common people – especially not by teenagers. So now I'm going to share them with you so you can get a better idea of what it is that I'd like to teach you.

Primary emotions are the ones that teens typically think about when they think about feelings. These are a kind of emotional response – so-called pure reactions to anything that happens around us or to us.

Secondary emotions are traced to the core emotions, but these are a little bit more complex. Here, you may use a lot of words to describe these feelings. The secondary emotions are the emotions of the primary emotions. While these vary from one situation to the next, they are always a reaction to whatever the first feeling was.

But why do these two matter? Emotional awareness is an essential part of the work that could promote emotional and mental well-being. The concept of secondary emotions can give you the opportunity to understand them better – and use them to your advantage. Differentiating is essential if you want to truly become aware emotionally. This will give you the space to explore yourself over and over and to also explore what you do with your feelings.

And now, let's go into the techniques for naming and understanding your feelings. Some techniques are better than others, but again, it all boils down to what you find to be most useful to you. Let's start unwrapping the exercises!

EXERCISE 1

EMOTION WHEEL

Sometimes, emotions can feel overwhelming or confusing, but this exercise will help you understand and manage them better. You'll use an *Emotion Wheel* – a chart with basic emotions at the center that branch out into more specific ones.

First, take a moment to figure out how you're feeling. Take a look at the Emotion Wheel and pick the main emotion that stands out, like sadness, anger, or fear. Then, dive deeper into the outer parts of the wheel to pinpoint exactly what you feel, like lonely or frustrated.

Once you know what you feel, think about what triggered it. What happened? What are you telling yourself about the situation? How is your body reacting – like a tight chest or shaky hands? Then write this down to get it out of your head.

Understanding Your Emotions | 419

Then, ask yourself, "Is this thought accurate? Could I be making assumptions?" Just remind yourself that emotions aren't bad – they're just signals. It's okay to feel what you feel. You tell yourself, "It makes sense I feel this way because…" Validation can help you calm down.

Now, you should decide what to do with the emotion. If it's helping you, then go with it. If it's not, try something different, like doing the opposite of what the emotion urges you to do. For example, if you feel angry and want to yell, take a deep breath and speak calmly instead.

Finally, reflect on how the process worked. Did your emotions feel less intense? Did it help you handle the situation better? The more you practice, the easier it gets to handle emotions healthily.

EXERCISE 2

FEELINGS JOURNAL

Keeping a feelings journal is a simple way to make sense of emotions and learn how to handle them better. All you need is something to write with and a bit of honesty.

First, write down how you're feeling right now. Don't overthink it – just one or two words like "anxious" or "excited." Then, think about what happened today that might've made you feel this way. Was it something someone said? Something you did? Write that down, too.

Next, ask yourself what thoughts are connected to this feeling. What are you telling yourself about the situation? Are these thoughts helpful, or are they making you feel worse? Try to challenge anything that doesn't feel true or fair by asking, "Is there another way to look at this?"

Lastly, write what you can do to feel better or to healthily handle the emotion. Maybe you need to take a break, talk to someone, or just let yourself feel it for a while without judging it.

Writing in your feelings journal will help you understand yourself better. The more you do it, the easier it gets to notice patterns and figure out what you need.

The Impact of Emotions on Behavior and Health

Emotions might feel like these big, uncontrollable waves sometimes, but they actually have a lot of power over how we think, act, and even feel physically. Let me break it down.

How Emotions Influence Thoughts and Behavior

Have you ever noticed how being in a bad mood can make everything feel 10 times worse? That's because emotions influence how you see the world. If you're feeling sad, you might start thinking, "Nobody cares about me," even if that's not true. On the flip side, when you're happy, everything feels easier, and you notice the good stuff more. Your emotions shape your thoughts without you even realizing it.

Now, those thoughts affect how you behave. For example, if you're angry, you might snap at someone or say something you will regret later. If you're anxious, you might avoid doing things that scare you, even if they're important. But you can make better choices when you take a second to understand your emotions. Instead of letting them control you, try to pause, think, and decide how you want to act.

The Connection Between Emotions and Physical Health

Here's something wild: emotions don't just live in your head – they also show up in your body. When you're stressed or scared, your heart beats faster, your muscles tense up, and sometimes you may even get headaches or stomachaches. That's because your brain is telling your body, "We're in danger!" – even if the danger is just an upcoming test.

If you stay in those intense emotional states for too long, your body starts to feel the effects. Constant stress, for example, can mess with your sleep, make you feel tired all the time, and even weaken your immune system. On the other hand, positive emotions like joy or gratitude can actually boost your health. They help you relax, sleep better, and feel more energized.

EXERCISE 3

MIND-BODY CONNECTION MAPPING

This exercise can help you notice how your emotions show up in your body so you can understand and manage them better. All you need is a quiet moment and something to write with.

First, pause and think about how you're feeling emotionally. Are you happy, sad, stressed, or something else? Write that down. Then, focus on your body. Do you feel tension anywhere, like tight shoulders or a heavy chest? Is your breathing fast or slow? Write down everything you notice.

Next, think about how your body and emotions might be connected. For example, if you feel nervous, your stomach might hurt, or if you're angry, your jaw might feel tight. Draw a quick outline of a person (stick figures work!) and mark where you feel these sensations.

Finally, decide what to do with this information. If your body feels tense, you might stretch or take deep breaths. If your emotions feel overwhelming, simply remind yourself it's okay to feel this way and try something calming, like listening to music or going for a walk.

Mapping the connection between your mind and body can help you feel more in control and show you how to care for yourself better.

_____

_____

_____

Common Emotional Challenges for Teens

Before we wrap this chapter up with a nice bow, let's talk about some of the most common emotional challenges you face. Don't think that I haven't noticed why you're here. You feel stressed. You feel angry. You feel like you carry the weight of the world on your shoulders. You don't know what to do with it. It seems like everything is falling apart at times, and you can't always make sense of it all.

There are a few common emotional challenges for teens – let's go through them together.

Stress and Its Effects

Stress can hit from all angles. For you, it might be schoolwork piling up, arguments with friends or family, or pressure to meet everyone's expectations. Even stuff like social media or figuring out your future can feel overwhelming. Sometimes, it feels like everything is happening all at once.

When stress gets out of control, your body and mind let you know. You might feel constantly tired, have trouble sleeping, or even get headaches or stomachaches. Your mood can swing wildly, and little things might make you cry or snap. It's like carrying a weight you can't put down.

If you don't deal with stress, it doesn't just go away. It can pile up. Over time, it can make you feel burned out, anxious, or even depressed. It can also mess with your health, causing issues like constant fatigue or a weaker immune system. Learning to handle stress now can help you avoid bigger problems later.

Anxiety in the Teenage Years

Anxiety is that nagging feeling like something bad is about to happen, even when everything's fine. For you, it might be triggered by things like tests, social situations, or big changes like starting at a new school. Sometimes, there's no obvious reason – it just shows up out of nowhere.

When you're anxious, your body reacts. Your heart races, your hands get sweaty, and you might feel shaky or dizzy. Mentally, your thoughts spin out of control, and it's hard to focus on anything else. It's like your brain is stuck in the "what if" mode.

It is common knowledge that everyone worries sometimes. But anxiety is different. While worry usually fades after the stressful thing is over, anxiety can stick around and show up even when nothing is wrong. It feels bigger and harder to shake off.

Understanding Anger

Anger can come from feeling misunderstood, treated unfairly, or not having control over things. For you, it might be someone breaking a promise, being ignored, or feeling overwhelmed by responsibilities. It's that hot, frustrated energy that can bubble up quickly.

When you're angry, your body reacts fast. Your face feels hot, your fists might clench, and your heart starts pounding. Emotionally, you might feel like yelling, crying, or just wanting to smash something. It's like a storm brewing inside you.

Anger isn't always bad – it can help you stand up for yourself or fix something unfair. But unhealthy anger happens when you let it control you, like lashing out or bottling it up until you explode. Healthy anger means expressing it in a way that solves problems without hurting others or yourself.

What Did You Learn From This Chapter?

You probably started to feel like everything you thought you knew about yourself just went right out the window. Everything you read here felt like kind of an eye-opener, right? This chapter was filled with some new info for you, and just to sum it all up before we move on to the next one, here is what you learned today:

- ✧ You learned that emotions need to be understood
- ✧ You discovered the science behind emotions
- ✧ You learned how emotional brain development happens (and why it hasn't happened to you yet)
- ✧ You learned how to identify and differentiate your emotions – especially the primary and secondary ones
- ✧ How emotions impact you in more ways than you can imagine
- ✧ Some of the most common emotional challenges for you – anger, anxiety, and stress

We may be putting this chapter to a close, but we turn a new leaf, and we open up a new chapter. I have talked plenty about emotions, and now it is time to dedicate an entire chapter to emotional awareness. Don't worry. The more you read, the more you learn! Let's start the next chapter together!

③

BUILDING EMOTIONAL AWARENESS

"Emotion, which is suffering, ceases to be suffering as soon as we have a clear picture of it."
– Benedict Spinoza

Emotions have a way of influencing our lives in the best and worst ways. However you look at it, we cannot fully enjoy life without emotions. They are an essential part of our being. Being a teenager only amplifies the feelings already within you, which has probably made you feel awkward. The thing is, emotions (and being aware of them) are an important part of who you are – and how you react to situations.

I am sure that many of you can relate to this: There have been many times when you wished you had reacted differently because you could not control your emotions at that moment. I may not have a time machine to return you to those past moments where you can create memories that could have unfolded differently, but I can send you to the future well aware of your emotions and ready to tackle anything. In this chapter, I will help you build emotional self-awareness.

Developing Self-Awareness

Emotions come from inside us, and they impact the way we view ourselves, the people around us, and the world, too. Emotions influence how we live, how we spend our time, whether we are motivated or not, and even the career we choose. In a way, they create guidance and meaning for us.

But when you are not aware of your emotions, things can easily turn for the worse. You could become trapped in a vicious cycle and not be able to break free. This is basically what I call life without emotional awareness.

Developing emotional awareness (or self-awareness) is important if you want to keep making the decisions that are right for you and help you move forward in life. This is how you can maintain your interest, take chances, and continue being curious in life. In order to do all of this, you need to know how to recognize and develop your emotional self-awareness.

The key to all learning in life (no matter what you try to learn) is monitoring yourself. By doing this, you correct your behavior and mistakes, and you try again until you get it right. If you want to increase your self-awareness and be more in tune with your emotions (but not let them control you), you need to first keep a few strategies in mind. I am sharing them with you below so you can see how easy it is to master yourself.

- **Use the emotion wheel** – this is the feeling list (or a wheel) which I introduced earlier that includes a lot of words that describe feelings. These words can be anything you want – from the best to the worst ones. Have this at hand so whenever you feel like you are lost for words, you can immediately find how you feel thanks to this list.

- **Your feelings send you a message** – every single time. The message is usually that you are safe (or not), and it is usually about something that impacts your motivation and/or values. It is all about using this message wisely.

- **Develop resilience** – there are a lot of emotions out there that can make you feel less than what you're truly worth. These can also be very difficult to cope with. It is imperative for you to know a few exercises on how to build this resilience (exercises are just below) to help you cope with these negative emotions better.
- **Mindfulness is important** – Yes, if you want to get the most out of life, of whatever aspect of it, mindfulness is key. It is all about training where your focus and attention go. Once you're able to do this, you can work on it until you perfect it.
- **Don't forget self-compassion** – when you lean into it, you will quickly notice that whenever you feel overwhelmed, it is the act of compassion that can help calm you down. Give yourself the credit you deserve along the way, and accept that, to see things objectively, you will need some time to practice. We are all human, and we all make mistakes from time to time, but that does not mean you have a deep wound that cannot be healed. Trust yourself and the process, and give yourself some time.
- **Pause** – as funny as this may sound to a teenager like you, to take full control over your emotions, sometimes you need to pause for a moment. While you do this, observe what you feel and identify the one (or the many) feelings that burst inside of you. Each day, you have the opportunity to work on this because each day, every one of us is faced with different challenges and situations.
- **Feel your body** – and listen carefully to what it has to say. It takes a lot of patience and practice to do this. Try to start a conversation with your body. How does it feel when you have these intense emotional episodes? Scan your body and see what it has to say.
- **Notice the pattern** – there is always one. In a variety of settings, sometimes you feel things, and they lead to a certain behavior. The thing is, that behavior is usually a pattern (because it's always a specific one). Identify this emotional path because it can interfere with your judgment and lead to a lot of sadness and suffering.

I have a list of a few exercises I would like to share with you in terms of developing self-awareness. These are specifically created to suit your needs, and they can help you turn inward and discover the hidden chambers within yourself – the ones filled with awareness and control.

EXERCISE 4

SELF-REFLECTION JOURNAL

A self-reflection journal is like having a conversation with yourself. It's a way to check in, explore what's going on in your head, and better understand yourself. All you need is a notebook, your thoughts, and a few quiet minutes.

First, think about your day and write down something that stood out – maybe something you're proud of, something that upset you, or just something random that felt important. Let yourself be honest, even if it's messy or doesn't make much sense.

Next, ask yourself questions like: *Why did this moment matter to me? How did it make me feel? What does it tell me about what I want or need?* Try to dig a little deeper, connecting your thoughts to your feelings.

Finally, write down one thing you can take away from this. Maybe you learned something about yourself or realized what you'd do differently next time. Even if you just feel lighter from getting your thoughts out, that's enough.

This journal isn't about being perfect or always having answers - it's about giving yourself space to listen to what's going on inside. The more you practice, the clearer things become.

Date: _____

Something That Stood Out Today: _____
_____

Why is it Important?: _____
_____

Takeaway: _____
_____

—o—◇—o—

Date: _____

Something That Stood Out Today: _____
_____

Why is it Important?: _____
_____

Takeaway: _____
_____

—o—◇—o—

Date: _____

Something That Stood Out Today: _____
_____

Why is it Important?: _____
_____

Takeaway: _____
_____

Date: _____

Something That Stood Out Today: _____

_____

Why is it Important?: _____

_____

Takeaway: _____

_____

Date: _____

Something That Stood Out Today: _____

_____

Why is it Important?: _____

_____

Takeaway: _____

_____

Date: _____

Something That Stood Out Today: _____

_____

Why is it Important?: _____

_____

Takeaway: _____

_____

Building Emotional Awareness

Date: _____

Something That Stood Out Today: _____

_____

Why is it Important?: _____

_____

Takeaway: _____

_____

EXERCISE 5

WHO AM I? WORKSHEET

The "Who Am I?" worksheet is like a personal scavenger hunt to figure out what makes you *you*. It helps you understand your values, interests, and what's important in your life.

Start by writing down answers to a few simple prompts:

What do I love doing?: _____

_____

_____

What's something I'm really good at?: _____

_____

_____

What makes me feel happy or excited?: _____

_____

_____

Who are the people that matter most to me?: _____

_____

_____

What's something I'd like to improve or work on?: _____

_____

_____

Next, think about how these things connect. For example, if you love helping people and feel happiest when you're around friends, maybe you value connection and kindness. If you enjoy art or sports, it might mean creativity or physical activity is important to you.

Finally, write a short statement about who you are based on your answers, like: *"I'm someone who values creativity, helping others, and spending time with people I care about."* It doesn't have to be perfect - it's just a way to see yourself more clearly.

_____

_____

_____

_____

_____

This worksheet is a great reminder that you're unique, and knowing yourself better helps you figure out where you want to go in life.

EXERCISE 6

EMOTIONAL SELF-AWARENESS QUIZ

This quiz can help you figure out how well you understand your emotions and what you can do to feel more in control. It's not about getting the "right" answers - it's about learning more about yourself.

Just grab a pen and answer these questions honestly:

	Yes	No
1. When I feel upset, can I name the emotion I'm experiencing?	☐	☐
2. Do I notice how my emotions affect the way I treat others?	☐	☐
3. Can I tell when I'm starting to feel overwhelmed or stressed?	☐	☐

Building Emotional Awareness

4. Do I ever take time to figure out why I'm feeling a certain way?	Yes ☐	No ☐	
5. How often do I feel like my emotions control me instead of the other way around?	Often ☐	Sometimes ☐	Rarely ☐

Once you've answered, think about what your responses tell you. If you struggle to name your emotions or notice their effects, maybe it's a sign you need to slow down and check in with yourself more often. If you feel like your emotions take over a lot, you could try calming techniques like deep breathing or journaling.

This quiz is just a starting point. The more you practice paying attention to your emotions, the better you'll get at understanding and managing them. It's like building a muscle - one step at a time.

EXERCISE 7

REFLECTION ON A RECENT EMOTIONAL EXPERIENCE

This exercise will help you look back on a recent emotional experience to understand it better. It's like replaying a moment in your head to figure out what happened and why it mattered.

First, pick a recent moment when you felt a strong emotion - maybe you were angry, happy, sad, or excited. Write down what happened, just the facts, like you're telling a story: *"I got into an argument with my friend because they cancelled our plans at the last minute."*

What Happened?: _____

_____

_____

Next, ask yourself: *What was I feeling at that moment?* Write down all the emotions you can think of – sometimes, there's more than one. Then, ask yourself: *What triggered that emotion? Was it the situation itself or what I thought about it?*

What Did I Feel?: _____

_____

_____

What Was the Trigger?: _____

_____

_____

Finally, reflect on how you reacted. Did you say or do something you're proud of? Or maybe it's something you'd handle differently next time? Write down one takeaway, like: *"I felt hurt because I value my time with friends. Next time, I want to tell them how I feel instead of keeping quiet."*

Takeaway: _____

_____

_____

_____

This reflection isn't about judging yourself – it's about learning. Each time you do this, you will understand your emotions a little more and figure out better ways to handle them in the future.

Techniques for Gaining Insight into Your Behavior

To make your life more meaningful, you need to use these exercises and think of them as techniques. For example, in every reflection you do, realize that there is a technique there. Ask yourself – is this something that is in line with my values and who I want to be as a person or not? This can help you step back and see the bigger picture.

Recognizing Triggers and Patterns

You experience a lot of emotions during the day. Some of them are bad, some of them are good. Most of them (if not all) relate to specific events that happened. But your response to these events is your starting point.

A trigger (specifically an emotional one) can be anything – from a memory to an experience or an event. This is something that sparks up an emotional reaction. It does not care for your current mood. Emotional triggers are associated with PTSD. To control and overcome yours, you need to know how to identify them first.

Think back on some situations in your life where you felt excluded, ignored, challenged, etc. Or maybe you felt betrayal, rejection, insecurity, loss of independence, helplessness, criticism, disapproval, or simply lost control. These events that have embedded themselves into your mind, soul, and body are the triggers. The way you respond to them (the same way every single time) is the pattern. These two are connected. To recognize and move past them, you need to do three things:

1. **Retreat** – take a step back whenever you feel yourself getting heated, and stop to think about what just happened – and why you acted the way you did.
2. **Go back** – this has happened to you before, hasn't it? Go back to the roots and find the origin – when was the first time you felt that way? Keep in mind – you may need some time to get to the bottom of this.
3. **Curiosity is key** – yes, when I say you need more time, this is what I think. Dedicate some time if the connection is not clear, and try to get as much insight as you can on what triggered you and what made you repeat the patterns you do.

Identify what sets off your emotions. Remember that it is all about finding out what triggers your bursts of emotion. Think hard and dig deep. This is how you can get to the core and thus break the patterns you have been repeating for a very long time.

EXERCISE 8

TRIGGER IDENTIFICATION WORKSHEET

This worksheet can help you identify what triggers your emotions, allowing you to better understand your reactions and feel more in control.

First, think about a time when you felt a strong emotion - maybe you were angry, sad, or anxious. Write down what happened, like: *"I got really mad when someone interrupted me during class."*

What Happened?: _____

_____

_____

Next, ask yourself: *What triggered that emotion?* Was it the situation itself, what someone said or did, or how you interpreted it? For example: *"I felt like they didn't respect what I had to say."*

What Was the Trigger?: _____

_____

_____

Then, dig a little deeper: *Was this about something bigger?* Maybe the trigger reminded you of another time you felt ignored, or maybe you were already stressed, and this made it worse.

Dig Deeper: _____

_____

_____

Finally, contemplate how you reacted and how you might handle it next time. Did your reaction help or make things harder? If you face the same trigger again, what could you do differently? For example, *"Next time, I'll calmly ask for a chance to finish speaking instead of snapping."*

Reflection: _____

_____

_____

By identifying your triggers, you're not just reacting. You're learning to pause, understand, and choose how you respond. It's like uncovering the map of your emotions!

Patterns in Emotional Reactions

As I mentioned earlier, the patterns are the ones you need to look out for whenever you want to deal with emotional triggers. You may have acted the same way for a very long time without noticing it.

EXERCISE 9
EMOTION-TRIGGER LOG

This exercise will help you track your emotions and what triggers them so you can start spotting patterns and understand yourself better. It's like keeping a journal, but it is focused on emotions.

Whenever you notice a strong emotion, write it down. Include:

- **What happened** - Describe the situation, like: *"I got a bad grade on my test."*
- **How I felt** - Name the emotion(s) you experienced, like: *"Disappointed, frustrated, and embarrassed."*
- **What triggered it** - Think about what specifically set off the emotion. Was it the event itself or how you thought about it? For example: *"I felt like I didn't try hard enough, and now my teacher will think I don't care."*
- **How I reacted** - Write down what you did next, like: *"I avoided my teacher and didn't talk to my friends about it."*

Then, look back at your log at the end of the day or week. Are there certain triggers that keep coming up? Do you notice any patterns in how you react? This reflection helps you figure out what you might want to work on, like handling a situation differently or changing how you think about it.

The more you use your emotion-trigger log, the better you get at understanding what's really going on inside you – and that's a powerful skill to have.

Develop strategies to manage triggers – the triggers can be easily overridden. All you need to do is have a solid plan and a lot of exercises (just like the ones here) that will help you along the way.

What Happened? _____

_____

How I felt? _____

_____

What Triggered It? _____

_____

How I reacted? _____

_____

_____

What Happened? _____

_____

How I felt? _____

_____

What Triggered It? _____

_____

How I reacted? _____

_____

———o–◇–o———

What Happened? _____

_____

How I felt? _____

_____

What Triggered It? _____

_____

How I reacted? _____

_____

———o–◇–o———

What Happened? _____

_____

How I felt? _____

_____

What Triggered It? _____

_____

How I reacted? _____

_____

---○-◇-○---

What Happened? _____

_____

How I felt? _____

_____

What Triggered It? _____

_____

How I reacted? _____

_____

---○-◇-○---

What Happened? _____

_____

How I felt? _____

_____

What Triggered It? _____

_____

How I reacted? _____

_____

What Happened? _____

_____

How I felt? _____

_____

What Triggered It? _____

_____

How I reacted? _____

_____

———o—✧—o———

What Happened? _____

_____

How I felt? _____

_____

What Triggered It? _____

_____

How I reacted? _____

_____

EXERCISE 10

TRIGGER MANAGEMENT PLAN

This exercise helps you create a plan for dealing with triggers so you can respond to tough situations in a way that feels calmer and more in control.

First, pick one trigger that keeps coming up – something that often sets off strong emotions. For example: *"When someone criticizes me in front of others."*

Next, write down:

- ◇ **What usually happens** – Describe how you feel and react when this trigger happens, like: *"I feel embarrassed and angry, and I usually shut down or snap back."*
- ◇ **What I want to change** – Think about how you'd prefer to respond. For example: *"I want to stay calm and respond without making it worse."*

Then, make a plan for the next time this trigger shows up:

- ◇ **Pause and breathe** – remind yourself to take a few deep breaths before reacting.
- ◇ **Check my thoughts** – ask yourself, *"Am I making this worse by assuming the worst?"*
- ◇ **Choose my response** – decide what you can say or do to handle the situation better, like: *"I'll calmly say, 'I'd appreciate feedback privately.'"*

Finally, write down how you'll take care of yourself after dealing with the trigger. Maybe it's talking to someone you trust, journaling about it, or doing something that helps you relax.

This plan gives you tools to handle tough situations instead of just reacting to them. The more you practice, the easier it gets to manage your triggers!

Trigger: _____

_____

What Usually Happens: _____

_____

_____

What I Want to Change: _____

_____

Plan for the Next Time: _____

_____

_____

Trigger: _____

_____

What Usually Happens: _____

_____

_____

What I Want to Change: _____

_____

_____

Plan for the Next Time: _____

_____

_____

———o—◆—o———

Trigger: _____

_____

What Usually Happens: _____

_____

_____

What I Want to Change: _____

_____

_____

Plan for the Next Time: _____

_____

_____

Trigger: _____

What Usually Happens: _____

What I Want to Change: _____

Plan for the Next Time: _____

Trigger: _____

What Usually Happens: _____

What I Want to Change: _____

Plan for the Next Time: _____

Emotional Vocabulary

Your emotional vocabulary is what will help you develop better emotional skills. Expanding your emotional vocabulary will leave you with a list of free emotions that you can use, recognize, and learn from each way you feel them. This can feel like a book that offers you brand new sentences every time you open it. Because the more you understand every nuance of every emotion, the deeper understanding you will have of yourself. Creating a rich emotional vocabulary can help you understand yourself, the world around you, and why you feel what you feel.

EXERCISE 11
EMOTION VOCABULARY BUILDING

This exercise is an amazing one if you want to expand your "feelings vocabulary" so you can describe your emotions better. When you can name what you're feeling, it's easier to understand and deal with it.

First, grab a notebook and write down a few basic emotions like happy, sad, angry, scared, or calm. Then, challenge yourself to think of more specific words for each one. For example:

- ✧ Instead of just "happy," you might write "excited," "grateful," or "proud."
- ✧ For "sad," you could add "disappointed," "lonely," or "heartbroken."

Next, think about recent situations where you felt something strong. Try to match the emotion you felt to a more specific word. For example: *"When my friend cancelled our plans, I wasn't just mad - I felt let down."*

If you get stuck, you can look up a feelings chart online, take a look at the emotion wheel or think about how you might describe the feeling to someone else.

The more you practice; the more words you'll have to explain your emotions with. Having the right words makes it easier to communicate what you're feeling - and to figure out what you need. It's like building a toolbox for your emotions!

Practice emotional expression – it is not all about how you feel on the inside. It is about what you show on the outside, too. Remember that no matter what, it is always a good rule of thumb to appear calm and collected. Whatever you're feeling, try to articulate it with words.

_____

_____

_____

_____

_____

_____

EXERCISE 12

EXPRESSIVE WRITING ACTIVITY

This activity should be your go-to for letting emotions out on paper. It's not about perfect writing - it's about expressing how you feel without holding back.

Simply grab a notebook or open a document and pick a recent experience that made you feel something strong, like frustration, happiness, or sadness. Then, set a timer for 5–10 minutes and write freely about:

- ✧ **What happened -** Describe the situation in your own words.
- ✧ **How I felt -** Write about the emotions you experienced, like: *"I felt hurt and ignored when my friend didn't text me back."*
- ✧ **Why it mattered -** Explore why this event affected you, like: *"It made me feel like they didn't care about our friendship."*

Don't worry about grammar or making it sound good. Just let your thoughts flow, even if they're messy or random.

When the timer goes off, take a deep breath and read what you wrote (if you want to). Then, ask yourself: *"What did I learn from this? Do I feel lighter after writing it down?"*

This activity helps you process emotions and better understand them. Sometimes, just getting things out of your head and onto paper is enough to make you feel a little more in control.

Language can either make or break something. The expressiveness you feel you need to articulate is excellent, but in order to avoid being overly harsh in a certain situation and avoid hurting yourself or someone around you in the long run – *choose your words carefully.*

What Did You Learn From This Chapter?

This chapter was all about learning how to regulate your emotions. If you want to move forward and create a better version of yourself, then take the most out of this chapter by remembering the following:

- ✧ Develop self-awareness with the help of some incredible techniques
- ✧ What are triggers, and patterns, and how can you recognize and control them
- ✧ The usefulness of an emotional vocabulary

Before we move on to the next chapter, I want to say that I am so proud of you! You have truly come a long way. These exercises I have prepared for you, as well as the fantastic outline are my way of saying that I am here for you – and we can do this together! Now turn the page and let's continue!

4

COGNITIVE BEHAVIORAL STRATEGIES

"The only limit to our realization of tomorrow will be our doubts of today." – Franklin D. Roosevelt

In this chapter, I am focusing my attention on all the strategies that can bring you a step closer to being the most powerful version of yourself. These strategies are a part of CBT, and all of them have proven to be quite effective. They are based on all the connections that happen between your emotions, thoughts, and behaviors.

I have talked plenty about how CBT focuses on giving you the tools to solve all of your issues, but for you, it may have felt a little chaotic. Well, this chapter is filled with exercises and strategies – so buckle up!

Identifying and Challenging Negative Thoughts

Negative thoughts are a part of our lives. The thing is, sometimes we can really get caught up in them and allow them to overflow us. This has probably happened to you many times. Through the exercises you are going to learn today, you will discover multiple ways to identify and challenge your negative thoughts. You may find some of these exercises challenging – but that's the point! Maybe you have assumed that the worst is about to happen for too long. Maybe, just maybe, it is time for you to let yourself go a little bit and focus on yourself, on what's important – on what's good. That is why we will start with one of the most important exercises.

Recognizing Cognitive Distortions

Cognitive distortions are thoughts that may cause you to perceive reality in a much worse way than it actually is. Most of these thoughts are irrational or exaggerated. These are mental fillers that stuff your brain with incorrect assumptions and deductions and create a vicious cycle that can be hard to get out of.

Here is an exercise that can help you tame these thoughts.

EXERCISE 13

COGNITIVE DISTORTION IDENTIFICATION

This exercise helps you catch those tricky thoughts that can mess with how you see things. Sometimes, your brain jumps to conclusions or exaggerates situations, and this helps you spot when that's happening.

Start by thinking about a recent moment when you felt upset, stressed, or anxious. Then, write down the thoughts you had at that moment, such as: *"I'm going to fail this test, and everyone will think I'm stupid."*

_____

_____

_____

Next, ask yourself:

Is this thought realistic? For example, "Is it true that one bad test means I'm a failure? Probably not."

_____

_____

_____

Am I using a cognitive distortion? Check if your thought fits any of these patterns:
- **All-or-nothing thinking:** Seeing things as only good or bad.
- **Catastrophizing:** Assuming the worst will happen.
- **Mind-reading:** Thinking you know what others are thinking.

If you notice a distortion, rewrite the thought in a more balanced way. For example: "Even if I don't do great on this test, I can learn from it and do better next time."

_____

_____

_____

The more you practice, the better you get at catching unhelpful thoughts and replacing them with ones that are more realistic and kinder to yourself. It's like training your brain to see the bigger picture!

Thought Records

I always love it when there is a practical way to make use of everything that happens within you – that is why this strategy of recording your thoughts is one of my favorite ones. It can help you pencil in your thoughts and feelings about a certain situation and even add some evidence for it so you can approach every scenario and every event calmly and logically. Take a look at the exercise below – you'll see what I'm talking about.

EXERCISE 14

THOUGHT RECORD WORKSHEET

This exercise helps you break down your thoughts and emotions so you can understand them better and respond in a healthier way.

Start by writing about a situation that made you feel upset or stressed. For example: *"I argued with my friend because they cancelled our plans at the last minute."*

_____

_____

Then, fill in the following steps:

1. **Emotion:** Write down how you felt in that moment, like: *"Angry and disappointed."*

_____

_____

2. **Thoughts:** Jot down what you were thinking, like: *"They don't care about me."*

_____

_____

3. **Evidence for your thought:** List reasons why your thought might feel true, like: *"They've cancelled plans before."*

_____

_____

4. **Evidence against your thought:** Then, write reasons why your thought might not be true, like: *"They said they had an emergency."*

_____

_____

5. **Balanced thought:** Come up with a more realistic way of seeing things, like: *"Maybe they cancelled because they really couldn't make it, not because they don't care about me."*

_____

_____

Cognitive Behavioral Strategies

Finally, check in with yourself. Ask: *"How do I feel now compared to before?"* Writing things out can often help you feel calmer and more in control. The more you practice, the easier it gets to think through situations instead of just reacting.

Reframing Negative Self-Talk

Oh my, there are so many strategies here that it can be hard to keep track at first, right? Well, don't worry. That is why I have created a section at the end of each chapter – something that will remind you of everything you've learned. And this next one will take you by storm!

If you have indulged in negative self-talk for a while now, it may be possible that you feel the effects of it – you feel worthless and incapable. There is a way to reframe all these statements of negative self-talk that you have inflicted upon yourself so deeply. Take the exercise number 15 as a guideline on how to do that.

EXERCISE 15

REFRAMING STATEMENTS

This exercise helps you turn negative or unhelpful thoughts into more balanced and positive ones. It's like flipping a switch in your mind to see things differently.

Start by writing down a negative thought you've had recently, like: *"I always mess things up."*

_____

_____

_____

Then, go through these steps:

1. **Check the facts:** Ask yourself, *"Is this 100% true? Do I really always mess up?"* Usually, the answer is no. Yes ☐   No ☐

2. **Look for another perspective:** Think about what you'd say to a friend in the same situation. For example: *"Everyone makes mistakes sometimes, but that doesn't mean they're a failure."*

_____

_____

_____

3. **Reframe the thought:** Rewrite the negative thought in a more realistic and encouraging way, like: *"I made a mistake, but I can learn from it and do better next time."*

_____

_____

_____

Keep practicing with different thoughts until it feels natural to catch and reframe them. Over time, this will help you feel less stuck in negativity and more focused on what you can do to grow and improve.

_____
_____
_____
_____
_____
_____
_____
_____
_____

Goal Setting and Problem-Solving

I can only assume this is something you've probably already seen somewhere. Let me guess – you thought it was a ridiculous idea. Well, it's not. The SMART approach can help you formulate a plan to achieve a certain goal. It works every time – as long as you dedicate yourself to it.

EXERCISE 16

SMART GOALS WORKSHEET

This exercise will assist you in creating goals that are clear and doable. Instead of saying *"I want to be better at school,"* you will learn how to break it down into a plan you can actually follow.

Start by picking one thing you want to work on. Then, use the SMART formula to write your goal:

1. **Specific:** What exactly do you want to do? For example: *"I want to improve my math grade."*
2. **Measurable:** How will you know you've achieved it? Like: *"I'll aim to get at least a B on my next math test."*
3. **Achievable:** Is this realistic for you? If not, make it smaller. Instead of *"Ace every test,"* you might say, *"Study for 30 minutes a day."*
4. **Relevant:** Why does this goal matter to you? For example: *"Doing better in math will help me feel more confident."*
5. **Time-bound:** When will you complete this? Like: *"By the end of the next test week."*

Once you've written your SMART goal, create a small action plan. For example: *"I'll review notes every day, ask for help if I'm stuck, and use practice tests to study."*

When you follow this process, you can track your progress and feel proud when you hit your goals. It's all about taking small, clear steps toward what you want!

S _____

M _____

A _____

R _____

T _____

Action Plan: _____

_____

S _____

M _____

A _____

R _____

T _____

Action Plan: _____

_____

S _____

M _____

A _____

R _____

T _____

Action Plan: _____

_____

S _____

M _____

A _____

R _____

T _____

Action Plan: _____

_____

S _____

M _____

A _____

R _____

T _____

Action Plan: _____

_____

EXERCISE 17
PROBLEM-SOLVING STEPS

This is an exercise that will help you tackle problems step by step instead of feeling stuck or overwhelmed. It's like building a map to find a solution.

First, think of a problem you've been dealing with – big or small. Then, follow these steps:

1. **Describe the problem:** Write down what's going on, keeping it clear and simple, like: *"I keep forgetting to turn in my homework on time."*

2. **Brainstorm solutions:** List as many ideas as you can, even if they seem silly. For example: *"Set reminders, ask a friend to check in with me, or create a homework checklist."*

3. **Pick the best solution:** Choose the one that seems most realistic and helpful. For example: *"Set reminders on my phone for each assignment."*

4. **Make a plan:** Write down what you'll do step by step. Like: *"After school, I'll set reminders for each assignment and check them off when they're done."*

5. **Try it out:** Put your plan into action and see how it works.
6. **Review:** After a few days, check in with yourself: *"Is this helping? If not, what can I tweak?"*

This process helps you feel more in control and less stressed about problems. It reminds you that there's almost always a way forward, even if you have to try a few different things to find it!

Relaxation Techniques

Any relaxation technique is an excellent way to lower your levels of stress, anger, anxiety – anything that you feel building up inside you. But it is about so much more than that. This is an excellent way to help you cope not only with day-to-day stressors but also with long-term stress.

Deep Breathing Exercises

Has it ever happened to you that you find yourself taking a deep breath and then slowly exhaling in the middle of a certain situation? Trust me, your body knows itself, and when it comes to this breathing technique, it is the best one that can calm you down.

EXERCISE 18
DEEP BREATHING PRACTICE

This exercise helps you calm down whenever you feel stressed, angry, or overwhelmed. It's a simple way to help your body and mind feel relaxed.

Find a quiet spot where you can sit down. Close your eyes or just focus on something in front of you. Then, all you need to do is follow these steps:

1. **Breathe in:** Slowly inhale through your nose for a count of four. Your belly should fill up like a balloon.
2. **Hold:** Then, gently hold your breath for a count of four while your body feels still.
3. **Breathe out:** Finally, exhale slowly through your mouth for a count of six.

Repeat this process for a few minutes and only focus on your breath. If your mind wanders, bring it back to the feeling of the air moving in and out of your body.

Afterward, check in with yourself: *"Do I feel calmer or more focused?"* Deep breathing can easily become your go-to when you need a quick way to reset.

Progressive Muscle Relaxation

Progressive muscle relaxation is something you have to feel yourself. As a teenager, I believe you're already intrigued, so here is the exercise.

EXERCISE 19
MUSCLE RELAXATION

This exercise helps release tension in the body. You focus on relaxing each part of you. This way, you can feel calmer and more in control. For example, all you need to do is find a comfortable place to sit or lie down, close your eyes if you want to, and take a deep breath. Then, you need to do this:

1. **Tense a muscle group:** Start with your feet. Squeeze the muscles in your toes and feet as tightly as you can for about five seconds.
2. **Relax:** Then, let go of the tension and notice how your muscles feel looser. Imagine all the stress leaving that part of your body.
3. **Move up my body:** After that, slowly work your way up, repeating the same process for each muscle group.

Remember to take your time. Notice the difference between tension and relaxation in each area.

When you're done, take a deep breath and let your whole body feel heavy yet calm. This exercise helps you let go of physical stress. It can make your mind feel more peaceful.

Visualization

The power of visualization is a concept that people have been turning to for a long time now. What makes it so good is that you can go as deep and as detailed as you want with it – and the more you do it, the calmer you become.

EXERCISE 20
GUIDED IMAGERY

This exercise is the perfect way to relax. All you need to do is imagine a peaceful place in your mind. All you need to do is follow this example to get it right – sit or lie down somewhere comfortable. Close your eyes and take a few deep breaths. Then, begin to imagine a place where you feel completely safe and happy. It could be a beach, a forest, a cozy room, or anywhere else.

As you picture this place, focus on the details:

- **What do you see?** Maybe the ocean waves, trees, or soft lights.
- **What do you hear?** Like birds, water, or a gentle breeze.
- **What do you smell?** Fresh flowers, salty air, or something like baked cookies.
- **What do you feel?** Warm sand under your feet, soft grass, or a cozy blanket.

Let yourself stay in this place for a few minutes and enjoy the calm and safety it brings. If your mind starts to wander, gently bring it back to your peaceful scene. When you feel ready, take a deep breath, open your eyes, and carry that calm feeling with you. Try this exercise and reset when you feel stressed or overwhelmed.

Building Resilience Through Positive Thinking

Last but not least, never forget the power of positive thinking and affirmations. These can help you turn your life around! A teenager should have at least one of these exercises in their arsenal – so here is the last exercise for this chapter for you.

EXERCISE 21
POSITIVE AFFIRMATIONS

This exercise can help you build confidence and feel better. All you need to do is focus on positive thoughts. It's like you try to give your mind a pep talk. In this case, start by thinking about something you struggle with or want to feel more positive about. Then, create a simple, somewhat encouraging statement to repeat to yourself. For example:

- If you feel like you're not good enough, you should say: *"I'm doing my best, and that's enough."*
- If you feel nervous about something, you should say: *"I am strong and capable."*
- If you're having a bad day, you should say: *"This moment is tough, but I can handle it."*

Look in the mirror and repeat your affirmation out loud or in your head several times. Focus on the words and how they make you feel. As time passes, the more you practice, the more natural it feels to think positively about yourself. Over time, these affirmations will help you replace negative thoughts with kinder, more supportive ones.

What Did You Learn From This Chapter?

This chapter was filled with interesting techniques and exercises. And I am so happy you got to where you are! Before we move on to the next chapter, let's take a quick look at what you learned from this one:

- ✧ It is important to challenge your negative thoughts, especially through thought records and cognitive distortions
- ✧ You reframe the way you talk to yourself and focus on solving issues – one at a time
- ✧ A few relaxation techniques
- ✧ How to train your brain to think more positively

Now, let's turn the page and jump into the next chapter together!

DIALECTICAL BEHAVIOR THERAPY STRATEGIES

"Feelings are just visitors, let them come and go." - Mooji

It seems like the perfect quote to start this chapter with. DBT usually focuses on people who feel a lot. These may be people who have been struggling with PTSD or just people who often have deep and intense feelings. But, what you're here for, and what I'm here for, is a way to find out how to move past this stage and into a stage of a lighter sense of being. Noticeably, things have been a little difficult for you lately – but that's why I'm here. To make things a lot lighter for you.

In this chapter, I am going to uncover the most useful and powerful techniques that can help you master DBT and, thus, master yourself.

Mindfulness Techniques

A lot of people want to include a little bit of mindfulness in their lives overall. The thing is, most of them believe that this is a very time-consuming process, and they get discouraged before they even begin. I am happy to tell you that they could not be more wrong! As someone who has been dealing with this topic for a long time, I have created the perfect blueprint that can help you add some mindfulness techniques to your life. Trust me, it is a lot easier than you can imagine.

You're already past that stage where you meet everything with anger, stress, rage, or even impatience. You are here to learn, and I am here to show you how to learn and what you need to learn.

Mindful Breathing

Let's start from the beginning – what's the first thing that comes to mind when you think of mindful breathing? Is it breathing for the mind, or is it just being more aware of the present moment? Mindful breathing is actually a very powerful meditation practice. It focuses on paying attention to the natural flow of your breathing cycle. All you need to do is simply – inhale, exhale, and feel the moment.

EXERCISE 22

MINDFUL BREATHING

This exercise can help you stay in the moment and calm your mind. You need to focus on your breath. It's simple, but it can make a big difference, especially if you feel overwhelmed.

To give you a little bit of a pointer, here is what you should do – find a quiet spot where you can sit down. Close your eyes. Then, follow these steps:

1. Take a slow, deep breath in through your nose. Feel the air fill your lungs.
2. Hold your breath for a second and notice how it feels.
3. Breathe out slowly through your mouth (just like you're blowing out a candle).

As you breathe, focus on how the air feels as it moves in and out - cooler when you breathe in, warmer when you breathe out. If your mind starts to wander, instead of becoming frustrated about it, gently bring your focus back to your breath.

Do this for a few minutes and let your breath guide you. Each time you practice, it gets easier to find a sense of calm and stay present, no matter what's happening around you.

Body Scan

This is a very interesting mindfulness technique that can help you connect with yourself. Considered another powerful meditation practice, it can help you relax your body, mind, and soul within a very short period.

EXERCISE 23

BODY SCAN MEDITATION

This exercise will help you relax and connect with how your body feels. It will make you pay attention to each part of yourself, one area at a time. It's like checking in with yourself from head to toe. Here is what you need to do – find a quiet place to sit or lie down and close your eyes. Take a deep breath in, let it out slowly, and start the scan:

1. Begin at the top of your head, noticing whether it feels tight, heavy, or relaxed. Try to let go of any tension as you exhale.
2. Move to your face – your forehead, eyes, cheeks, and jaw. and check if you're clenching anything and relax those muscles.
3. Next, focus on your neck and shoulders. Let them drop if they feel tight.
4. Work your way down to your arms and hands. Notice any sensations like warmth, coolness, or tension.
5. Then, pay attention to your chest and stomach. Feel the rise and fall of your breath.
6. Finally, continue down to your legs, all the way to your feet and toes, and let go of any tension you notice.

If your mind starts to wander, gently bring your attention back to the part of your body you currently want to focus on. When you're done, take one last deep breath. Once you do this, you will notice how much calmer and more connected you'll feel. This exercise will help you tune in and relax when life feels too much.

Grounding Exercises

The strong emotions you feel come with an overwhelming sense of wanting to calm them down. I get that. You're a teenager, everything feels like it's too much, and sometimes you don't know what to do to calm yourself down. It feels like nothing works, and that makes you even more frustrated. One of the most incredible exercises you can do in the case when you feel like nothing is working is this – a simple grounding exercise. Grounding means bringing your focus back to yourself and your senses – all of them. Just for that purpose, I have prepared the next exercise for you.

EXERCISE 24
5-4-3-2-1 GROUNDING TECHNIQUE

This exercise will help you feel calm and present when you're overwhelmed, anxious, or stuck in your head. It uses all the senses to bring you back to the moment. As an example – take a deep breath, then look around you and do the following:

5 things you see: Name five things you can see around you. They can be anything, like a chair, a window, or even the way sunlight hits the wall.

4 things you feel: Notice four things you can physically feel, like the texture of your clothes, the floor under your feet, or the cool air on your skin.

3 things you hear: Listen for three sounds, like birds outside, your breathing, or faint background noises.

2 things you smell: Focus on two scents, like the smell of your shampoo, food nearby, or even just fresh air. If you can't smell anything, try to think about smells you like.

1 thing you taste: Pay attention to one taste, like gum, a sip of water, or just the natural taste in your mouth.

Take another deep breath when you finish, noticing how much more grounded and in control you feel. It's a quick and easy way to get through stressful moments.

Emotion Regulation Skills

Skills that can help you navigate your emotions are imperative to possess because they can help you navigate all life's challenges. These can help you control and manage your overall emotional state. Now, of course, sometimes, when you have an emotional response to something, it is normal, but as soon as you notice that regulating your emotions becomes a challenge in many cases, it is time to start working on it. Emotion regulation matters if you want to lead a balanced and happy life.

Identifying and Labeling Emotions

While this is something that is done at the beginning of this book (remember, we already talked about this), I decided to look back and revise this. As you can imagine, this is a very important aspect to focus on (since I mention it more than once). Identifying emotions is the proper way to approach yourself before you address any situation you're in. Take the exercise below as your starting point.

EXERCISE 25
EMOTION LABELING WORKSHEET

This exercise is about understanding and naming what you feel. When you can label your emotions, it's easier to figure out what to do with them. What you should do here is start by thinking about a recent situation that made you feel a strong emotion. Then, write or think about these steps:

1. **What happened?** Describe the situation briefly - who was there, what happened, and how it made you feel.

_____

_____

2. **What did you feel?** Try to name the emotions you experienced. Was it anger, sadness, happiness, frustration, excitement, or something else? If you can't think of the exact word, use phrases like "a mix of…" or "kind of like…" to describe it.
_____
_____

3. **Where did you feel it?** Notice how the emotion showed up in your body. Did you feel butterflies in your stomach, a lump in your throat, or tension in your shoulders?
_____
_____

4. **What made it stronger or weaker?** Think about what made the emotion increase or decrease during the situation.
_____
_____

Writing it down or even just going through the steps in your head helps you make sense of your feelings. The more you practice, the better you get at understanding yourself and what you need at the moment.

_____
_____
_____
_____
_____
_____
_____
_____
_____

Opposite Action

The opposite action is quite an interesting skill. As a teenager (someone who most likely goes against everything they're being told – don't worry, we've all been there), you may find this incredibly intriguing. The focus of this is to act the opposite of the urge to act on the emotions you feel at the moment.

The exercise below can give you more clarity.

EXERCISE 26

OPPOSITE ACTION PLAN

Through this exercise, you can manage intense emotions. All you need to do is the opposite of what the emotion makes you do. It's a way to stay in control when your feelings start to take over. In this case, start by thinking about a situation where you felt an emotion that pushed you to act in a way that didn't really help. Then, follow these steps:

1. **What's the emotion?** Name the emotion you're feeling – like anger, sadness, fear, or frustration.

2. **What does it make you want to do?** Figure out what the emotion is pushing you to do. For example, when you're sad, you might want to isolate yourself. When you're angry, you might feel like yelling.

3. **What's the opposite action?** Choose to do something opposite of what the emotion is telling you. If you feel like isolating yourself, reach out to a friend instead. If you feel like yelling, try to speak calmly or walk away.

4. **What happens?** After trying the opposite action, notice how it changes your mood or the situation.

_____
_____

By practicing opposite actions, you learn that you don't always have to follow your emotions blindly. You can take charge and respond in a way that's more helpful to you.

TIPP Skills

This is another handy skill that can help you regulate yourself in "times of trouble". It is all about learning how to act quickly, on your feet, and effectively regulate your emotions. As you can see, it consists of a few aspects – and I have described all of them in the exercise below.

EXERCISE 27

TIPP SKILLS PRACTICE

This is an exercise that will help you calm down quickly when your emotions feel out of control. TIPP stands for *Temperature, Intense Exercise, Paced Breathing, and Progressive Relaxation* – four steps that can bring you back to a calmer state.

Here's how to practice it:

Temperature: Cool yourself down by holding something cold, like an ice pack or a cold drink, or by splashing cold water on your face. It helps your body and mind reset.

Intense Exercise: Do something physical to burn off energy, like jumping jacks, running in place, or even just shaking your hands and legs. This helps release tension.

Paced Breathing: Slow your breathing by inhaling deeply for four seconds, holding it for four seconds, and then exhaling slowly for six seconds. Repeat this until you feel more grounded.

Progressive Relaxation: Tense and then relax each muscle group in your body, starting from your toes and moving up to your head. This helps you release any leftover physical stress.

You can use these steps all together or just pick the one that works best at the moment. Practicing TIPP helps you handle big emotions and stay in control.

Distress Tolerance

Distress tolerance is closely connected to ACCEPTS skills, as shown below. Distress tolerance means having the skills to accept and perceive the environment as it is and not try to change it or demand it to be different in any way.

ACCEPTS Skills

The ACCEPTS skills outline the perfect strategy you need whenever you want to distract yourself from distress or negative emotions. By doing this, you give them time to settle and lower their intensity.

EXERCISE 28

ACCEPTS WORKSHEET

This exercise helps you distract yourself when your emotions feel too overwhelming. ACCEPTS stands for *Activities, Contributions, Comparisons, Emotions, Pushing Away, Thoughts, and Sensations* – different ways to take your mind off tough feelings.

Here's how to work through it:

Activities: Do something that keeps you busy, like drawing, listening to music, playing a game, or going for a walk.

Contributing: Help someone else, like doing a chore, helping a sibling, or texting a friend to check in on them. Helping others should make you feel better, too.

Comparisons: Remind yourself of other tough times you've gotten through or think about people who've overcome similar challenges.

Emotions: Do something that sparks a different emotion, like watching a funny video, listening to uplifting music, or looking at cute pet pictures.

Pushing Away: Imagine putting the problem in a box and locking it away for now. It's not about ignoring it forever, just giving yourself a break.

Thoughts: Focus on something else entirely, like counting backward from 100 or trying to name all the countries you can think of.

Sensations: Use your senses to distract yourself - holding something cold, lighting a scented candle, or listening to calming sounds.

By practicing ACCEPTS, you remind yourself that you have the tools to manage tough moments. It gives you space to cool down and think more clearly.

Self-Soothing Strategies

Oh, I know – your eager-to-learn teenager eyes have just started to read this over and over again, thinking, "How can I self-soothe myself?" Believe me, there is a perfectly good way to do this, and it all boils down to whether you want to try the exercise below or not. My suggestion – give it a go – you will be surprised.

EXERCISE 29

SELF-SOOTHING ACTIVITIES LIST

As a part of this exercise, you need to create a go-to list of things that make you feel calm and safe when you're overwhelmed or upset. It's all about using your senses to take care of yourself.

Just to give you a little guidance, here's how you should do it:

1. **Sight:** Think of things that are relaxing to look at, like sunsets, calming videos, or fairy lights. Then, write those down.
2. **Sound:** List sounds that calm you, like your favorite music, nature sounds, or even humming softly to yourself.
3. **Touch:** Include comforting things you can feel, like wrapping up in a cozy blanket, holding a stuffed animal, or taking a warm shower.
4. **Taste:** Add foods or drinks that feel comforting, like hot chocolate, tea, or your favorite snack.
5. **Smell:** Think of scents that relax you, like candles, essential oils, or the smell of fresh rain.

Write these all down in a list so that the next time you feel stressed, you will have ideas ready to help you feel better. Practicing self-soothing will remind you that you can take care of yourself in tough moments.

Sight _____

_____

_____

_____

_____

Sound _____

_____

_____

_____

_____

_____

_____

Touch _____

_____

_____

_____

_____

_____

_____

Taste _____

_____

_____

_____

_____

_____

_____

Smell _____

_____

_____

_____

_____

_____

_____

Distracting Techniques

It is all in the name – if you want to keep yourself calm, you need a distraction. It is okay to need a distraction every time you feel overwhelmed or distressed – it's normal! But, with that in mind, you need a good **distraction plan.**

EXERCISE 30

DISTRACTION PLAN

Come up with a plan to distract yourself when your emotions feel too big or overwhelming. It's about giving yourself space to calm down before you deal with what's bothering you.

This is what to do:

1. **Make a list of activities:** Think of things you enjoy, or that keep you busy, like watching a show, playing a game, reading, drawing, or going for a walk.

_____

_____

_____

_____

_____

2. **Choose a focus task:** Pick something that takes your full attention, such as solving a puzzle, organizing your room, or trying a new recipe.

_____

_____

_____

3. **Set a time limit:** Decide how long you'll distract yourself - for example, 20 minutes. After that, check in with how you're feeling.

4. **Have it ready:** Make sure you have easy access to your distraction tools, like books, games, playlists, or art supplies.

Distraction isn't about ignoring your problems forever - it's about giving yourself a break so you can come back to them with a clearer mind. Having a plan means you're ready whenever you need it.

Interpersonal Effectiveness

Lastly, for this chapter, I am about to nudge a topic that is just as important as the topic of you. It is the topic of how you present yourself in front of everyone in the world and how you communicate with people around you. Remember that a balanced life comes from the need to look within when you have to, but also to find the balance outside of you. Interpersonal effectiveness focuses on just that – it gives you the skills and strategies to communicate your needs, maintain excellent relationships with the people around you, and constructively resolve any conflicts or challenges that arise along the way.

EXERCISE 31

DEAR MAN WORKSHEET

This exercise is all about the need to ask for what you need or stand up for yourself in a respectful and confident way. DEAR MAN is an easy-to-remember strategy for communicating effectively.

Here's what you need to do:

1. **Describe:** First, start by clearly describing the situation without adding emotions or blame. For example, "When you cancel plans at the last minute…"
2. **Express:** Then share how you feel about the situation. "I feel hurt and disappointed when that happens."
3. **Assert:** After that, say what you need or want. "I'd like you to let me know earlier if you can't make it."
4. **Reinforce:** Explain why it's worth listening to you. "It'll help us avoid misunderstandings and keep things fair."
5. **Mindful:** Stay focused on the goal and don't get distracted by arguments or emotions.
6. **Appear confident:** Speak in a calm and steady voice, even if you feel nervous inside.
7. **Negotiate:** If needed, be open to compromising or working together to find a solution that works for both of you.

Write out a practice conversation using the DEAR MAN steps, so you feel more prepared. This helps you handle tough situations and get your point across without being aggressive or passive. And honestly, you will immediately feel calmer as soon as you write this down.

_____

_____

_____

_____

_____

_____

_____

Dialectical Behavior Therapy Strategies

What Did You Learn From This Chapter?

Wasn't this a fun chapter? I understand if you need some more time to go through it – you can go as slowly as you need, trying one exercise a day and comparing exercises and techniques until you see what works best for you. But all in all, you can see how DBT helps you create a healthier and calmer version of yourself. Through these exercises, you have gathered a lot of information about yourself (you probably didn't even think about it until now), and before we move along to the next chapter, I'd just like to touch upon what you learned here:

- ⬥ There are many mindfulness techniques you can use.
- ⬥ Emotion regulation skills and identifying emotions are a big part of who you are and who you want to become.
- ⬥ There are many distress tolerance strategies you can choose from – ACCEPTS skills, self-soothing, and even distracting.
- ⬥ It is just as important to present yourself well in front of others as it is in front of the mirror.

We covered the ground here, and I believe it is time to move on to the next chapter. There is still a lot more to conquer, so turn the page, and let's go over the next chapter!

6

BUILDING HEALTHY COPING SKILLS

"Believe you can, and you're halfway there." – Theodore Roosevelt

There will always be some difficult times in life. As you move forward in life, the things that may have an effect on you may be bigger and bigger. Once you become an adult and are well into your 30s and 40s, you will look back at this time right now and appreciate it. Not just because every new stage of life comes with its own challenges but also because you have found the perfect coping skills to deal with any curveball life throws at you – and it all starts here and now.

Coping skills are a way for you to deal with any kind of stressful situation. It is all about managing your stress. This, in the long run, can help you function better both physically and mentally. There are many ways to make this happen (to deal with an issue). All you need to do is remember the techniques and remember that, in the long run, you are looking for ways to eliminate your stress. This may mean making or altering a plan you've already had. Whatever you do, keep the techniques and exercises from this chapter in mind so you can successfully overcome any situation in life – not just now but overall!

Effective Communication

Whenever you interact with others, you need to know how to listen to them and communicate effectively. These two are the basis of a functional communication channel between yourself and another person. This is something you can benefit from in the future, especially career-wise. But it is also something that can help you deal with any kind of situation or negative feelings and thoughts you may have.

Effective communication also means staying focused and consistent – and offering something valuable to the table, too. When there is communication, there is a focus and a purpose. In itself, the concept allows everyone to get a point across.

Take a look at the techniques and exercises connected to effective communication below.

Assertiveness Training

If you've never come face to face with this phrase before, allow me to explain. Assertiveness training is the right to express everything you want – your thoughts, feelings, and needs to another person, but you need to do it in a respectful way. That being said, instead of being angry, aggressive, or anxious, you need to be calm and articulate yourself in a neutral way. The following exercise can help you do just that.

EXERCISE 32

ASSERTIVE COMMUNICATION PRACTICE

This exercise can help you practice speaking up for yourself clearly, respectfully, and confidently. There is no need to be aggressive or passive-aggressive. Assertive communication can help you express your thoughts and needs while still considering others.

Here's how you can practice it:

1. **Identify a situation:** Simply think of a time when you struggled to speak up - maybe asking for help, setting a boundary, or disagreeing with someone.

   _____
   _____

2. **Write out what you want to say:** Just make sure your message is clear and direct. Instead of saying, "Whatever, it's fine," try, "I'd like to talk about this because it's important to me."

   _____
   _____

3. **Use 'I' statements:** Focus on your feelings instead of blaming. Instead of "You never listen to me," say, "I feel unheard when I don't get a chance to share my thoughts."

   _____
   _____

4. **Practice a strong but calm tone:** Say your statement out loud, and make sure your voice is steady, and your body language is open.

5. **Prepare for responses:** Think about how the other person might react and how you can stay assertive without the need to back down or get defensive.

   _____
   _____
   _____
   _____

The more you practice, the easier it gets to stand up for yourself and keep your relationships healthy. Don't worry, I will discuss this again later, in the next chapter, and even have another exercise connected to this made just for you.

Active Listening

Another aspect you need to consider is the part where you actively listen, and you are actively being listened to. As a communication skill, this is the act of going beyond the words that the other person utters at you (or in your presence). To succeed in this case, you need to be alert and present in the moment – just be focused on the entire act of communication.

EXERCISE 33

ACTIVE LISTENING EXERCISE

This exercise will help you practice really listening when someone is talking instead of just waiting for your turn to speak. Active listening makes conversations better and can help you understand people more.

Here's how to do it:

1. **Pick someone to practice with:** A friend, family member, or even a video or podcast works.
2. **Focus fully on them:** Put your phone down, make eye contact, and show that you're paying attention with nods or small responses like "Yeah" or "I see."
3. **Repeat or summarize what you hear:** After they finish, restate what they said in your own words: "So, you're saying that…" or "It sounds like you feel…"
4. **Ask follow-up questions:** Instead of jumping in with your own story, ask something like, "What happened next?" or "How did that make you feel?"
5. **Check your body language:** Always keep an open posture, avoid crossing your arms, and face them to show you're engaged.

Afterward, think about how it felt to listen without interrupting or shifting the focus to yourself. The more you practice, the better you get at making people feel heard and understood. If you feel like you need some assistance with honing your communication skills, I got you covered on that in the next chapter.

Setting Boundaries

Boundaries are designed to protect your mental and personal space. These are the fences we all put up to make ourselves feel safe. Think of them as the limits of the other people's behaviors toward you (how far they can go). These types of boundaries define where you end and where another person begins. With their help, you can get a true sense of who you are and what you want and need in life. They can help you build your self-esteem, your self-control, and your overall well-being.

But what happens when you don't know how to set boundaries? Don't worry. It is not the end of the world – it is simply something you have to work on and tweak a little bit to get what you deserve – peace of mind. I have prepared an exercise that can help you do just that.

EXERCISE 34

BOUNDARY SETTING WORKSHEET

With the help of this exercise, you can figure out your personal boundaries and practice how to set them in a clear and respectful way. Boundaries protect your energy, emotions, and personal space.

These are the best ways how you can make that happen:

1. **Identify your boundaries:** Think about what makes you uncomfortable or stressed in relationships, school, or daily life. Do you need more personal space? More respect for your time? Less negativity from others?

   _____
   _____
   _____
   _____

2. **Write a boundary statement:** Here, you need to use clear, direct language. Instead of "I don't like when you do that," say, "I need you to ask before borrowing my stuff."

   _____
   _____
   _____
   _____

3. **Practice saying it:** Repeat your boundary out loud, and make sure your tone is calm and firm.

4. **Expect pushback:** Some people might not like your boundaries. In such cases, remind yourself that you have a right to set limits, even if others don't agree.

5. **Decide on consequences:** If someone keeps crossing your boundaries, plan your response. "If you keep texting me late at night, I'll have to mute my notifications."

   _____
   _____
   _____
   _____

Write down a few boundaries you want to set and how you will communicate them. Practicing them will help you feel more confident about standing up for yourself in a healthy way. Boundaries are important to have if you want to lead a happy and healthy life. I will talk more about them in the next chapter.

Seeking Support

Sometimes, you just don't know where to begin, or you may feel like you are all alone, trapped in a vicious cycle. You might even feel like you are not doing enough for yourself. This book is here to remind you that no matter how strong or weak you think you are, you don't have to do this alone. When you start to feel like things are getting too much for you (and there will be such moments), you need to remember that you can always reach out to someone else for support. After all, progress is not linear, and even with all the techniques at your disposal, there may still be moments when you find yourself thinking you can't do this. I am always here to remind you that it is okay to feel that way from time to time but that it is also okay to seek out help whenever you feel that way. This is one of those techniques that will amaze you – the power of other people in your life.

Identifying Supportive People

Needless to say, there are always some people who make you feel good, while others make you feel bad. This happens to everyone in life, but in your case, you need to carefully select those people that make you feel amazing. That is why I have created the perfect exercise to help you make that happen.

EXERCISE 35

SUPPORT NETWORK MAP

Through this exercise, you can figure out who you can turn to when you need help, advice, or just someone to listen. When you know your support system, it makes it easier to reach out when you're down.

Take a look at what you need to do:

1. **List your support people:** Write down the names of people you trust - friends, family, teachers, coaches, or even online communities.

_____

_____

_____

_____

_____

_____

2. **Organize by role:** Group them based on how they support you. Who gives good advice? Who cheers you up? Who helps you feel safe?

_____

_____

484 | *Coping Skills WorkBook for Teens*

_____

_____

_____

_____

_____

_____

3. **Identify gaps:** If you notice areas where you don't have enough support, think about ways to build stronger connections.

_____

_____

_____

_____

_____

_____

4. **Make a plan to reach out:** Write down one or two people you can check in with this week, even if it's just a quick message.

_____

_____

_____

_____

_____

_____

5. **Keep it updated:** Your support system might change over time, so revisit it when needed.
6. Once you see your support system written down, it reminds you that you're not alone, even when things feel tough.

Building Healthy Coping Skills

Expressing Needs and Asking for Help

Now comes the more challenging bit. You may find your support group, but you need to let them into your life, too. The need to express your feelings, be vulnerable, ask for help – that is all a part of being a human. The thing is, not a lot of people know how to really do this. This is all normal, especially for a teenager. You have all these feelings and thoughts inside you; it constantly feels like your blood is boiling, and sometimes, it may even feel like you can't articulate your message. Thankfully, I have designed an exercise that can help you make that happen in a very short period.

EXERCISE 36

ASKING FOR HELP ROLE-PLAY

Sometimes, asking for help feels awkward or uncomfortable, but practicing it makes it easier. In this exercise, simply imagine a situation where you need support – maybe you feel overwhelmed with school, struggle with a friendship, or deal with stress at home.

First, choose someone you trust to practice with or say your words out loud to yourself. Start with a clear and direct statement, like "I've been feeling really anxious about my grades, and I don't know how to handle it. Can we talk?" or "I need help setting boundaries with a friend, but I'm not sure how to do it."

If you practice with someone, pay attention to their response. Do they seem supportive? Do they understand? If you practice alone, imagine different ways the conversation could go and how you might respond.

Afterward, try to reflect on how it felt to ask for help. Did you feel nervous? Relieved? The more you practice, the more confident you become when you truly need to reach out when you need support.

_____

_____

_____

_____

_____

_____

_____

_____

_____

_____

_____

_____

_____

_____

_____

Self-Care Practices

No matter what you do, nothing in the world can help you – not my techniques or exercises, anything – if you don't properly take care of yourself. I know that this may seem strange to read, but taking care of yourself is just as important as learning how to communicate your needs to someone else in a healthy way. Self-care has always been important. This is how you make sure your needs are met.

Good self-care will keep any imbalance, stress, and burnout at bay. Some of the best practices that I mention below will help you reconnect with yourself, relax, and have some fun. These are the things you should enjoy the most.

Importance of Sleep, Nutrition, and Exercise

Need I say more? These three aspects are the main ones when it comes to taking care of your physical self. There is a connection between the mind and the body, and you can nurture it through proper nutrition, exercise, and sleep. I know this may initially seem like too much. Take a look at the exercise below and take it as your starting point on your journey.

EXERCISE 37

SELF-CARE ASSESSMENT

If you want to take care of yourself, this isn't just about relaxing – it's about making sure you meet your physical, emotional, and mental needs. This exercise can help you figure out where you do well and where you might need to focus more on self-care.

Go through the categories below and rate how often you do each one: **Often, Sometimes, or Rarely.**

	Often	Sometimes	Rarely
1. **Physical Self-Care:** Am I getting enough sleep? Eating foods that give me energy? Moving my body in ways that feel good?	☐	☐	☐
2. **Emotional Self-Care:** Do I let myself feel and process emotions instead of ignoring them? Do I have healthy ways to cope with stress?	☐	☐	☐

3. **Mental Self-Care:** Do I challenge negative thoughts? Do I give myself breaks when I need them? Do I spend time doing things that help me grow?	Often ☐	Sometimes ☐	Rarely ☐
4. **Social Self-Care:** Do I spend time with people who make me feel good? Set boundaries when I need to? Do I reach out for support when I'm struggling?	Often ☐	Sometimes ☐	Rarely ☐
5. **Fun & Relaxation:** Do I make time for hobbies, creativity, or things that bring me joy?	Often ☐	Sometimes ☐	Rarely ☐

After you finish, look at the areas where you answered **Rarely** and pick one small step you can take to improve. Self-care isn't about being perfect - it's about making sure you take care of yourself in ways that actually help.

Hobbies and Activities for Stress Relief

After you take care of the physical, there comes the mental aspect of your self-care process. What you decide to do with your mind results in whether you stay mentally fit or not. So, choose the former, and start investing yourself in activities and hobbies that keep your mind sharp. Trust me, this will go miles in improving your overall well-being.

EXERCISE 38

STRESS-RELIEF ACTIVITY PLAN

When you're stressed, it helps to have a plan, so you don't get overwhelmed. This exercise can help you create a go-to list of activities that actually help you feel better. First, think about what kind of stress you have – school pressure, friendship drama, feeling exhausted, or just too many emotions at once. Then, choose activities that match what you need.

- ◆ **If you need to calm down:** Take deep breaths, listen to music, take a warm shower, or do a body scan.
- ◆ **If you need to release energy:** Go for a walk, stretch, dance, or squeeze a stress ball.
- ◆ **If you need a distraction:** Watch a funny show, play a game, read, or do a hobby.
- ◆ **If you need support:** Talk to a friend, journal, or write down what you'd say to someone if you could.

Write down at least five activities that help you overcome each kind of stressor you can think of, so when stress hits, you don't have to think too hard - just pick one and do it.

_____

_____

_____

_____

Developing a Coping Toolbox

Everyone has different ways of dealing with stress – even you. These are the things you probably developed at a very early stage when you weren't quite aware of yourself as much as you are right now. That is okay. These are all skills that can be honed and improved as time passes. Sometimes, they are supportive, sometimes, you just realize that you can do better – and find new ones.

No matter what the case, it is important to have a toolbox of coping skills that can help you each time you feel upset or emotionally activated. Think of it as literally a box – one you can open every time you need help with something. Every time you feel like your tolerance level is low, or you feel anger, sadness, and just too much of everything, you can turn to this toolbox. Simply open it and take what you need.

But how do we build this toolbox? The following exercise explains just that.

EXERCISE 39
COPING TOOLBOX CHECKLIST

To have a coping toolbox means you have go-to strategies ready when you feel overwhelmed, stressed, or upset. This checklist helps you figure out what works best for you so you can build your own personal toolkit.

✓ Calming Techniques
- Deep breathing exercises
- Listening to music that relaxes you
- Taking a warm shower or bath
- Doing a body scan or progressive muscle relaxation
- Using grounding techniques (like 5-4-3-2-1)

_____

_____

_____

_____

✓ Emotional Release
- Journaling your thoughts and feelings
- Talking to someone you trust
- Cry if you need to
- Draw, paint, or create something
- Write a letter (even if you don't send it)

_____

_____

✓ Physical Activities
- Taking a walk outside
- Stretching or yoga
- Dancing to music
- Squeezing a stress ball or fidget toy
- Doing any movement that feels good

_____

_____

_____

✓ Distractions
- Watching a favorite movie or show
- Reading a book or comic
- Playing a game
- Doing a hobby (crafts, puzzles, baking, etc.)
- Organizing or cleaning a small space

_____

_____

_____

✓ Comfort Items
- A soft blanket or stuffed animal
- A scented candle or essential oils
- A playlist of songs that make you feel safe
- A photo or memory that reminds you you're loved

A note to yourself with encouraging words

Check off the ones that already work for you and add any new ideas you want to try. When you feel overwhelmed, you can look at the list and pick something that helps.

What Did You Learn in This Chapter?

Another chapter successfully finished – I am so proud of you! You have come such a long way in this challenge, and it feels like you are conquering your thoughts, feelings, and emotions one step at a time! I cannot imagine how strong you feel right now. We covered a lot of ground in this chapter, let's do a little summation of what you learned:

- It is important to build healthy coping skills for long-term success in life
- Learn how to communicate your needs with others
- It is always okay to ask for help when you feel like you need it
- Self-care as a pillar of your overall well-being
- Having a coping toolbox handy can be quite beneficial

Now, it is time to move on to the next chapter – one filled with many new and exciting things for you. I have carefully prepared each exercise so far, and this continues in the following pages – so turn the page around, and let's focus on our journey together!

7

BUILDING HEALTHY RELATIONSHIPS

"Don't walk in front of me – I may not follow. Don't walk behind me – I may not lead. Just walk beside me and be my friend." – Albert Camus

A beautiful quote, isn't it? But sometimes, it feels like the only thing you can reply to this is – easier said than done. In those exact cases, you need to be more patient and daring – in a good way. The foundation of every relationship you will have in your life is based on your relationship with yourself. Yes, I know, this entire chapter will be food for thought. But also, in this chapter, you will learn how to build healthy relationships – both with yourself and with the people around you.

It seems like this is a two-way street, so this is your queue to invest your side of the effort.

Communication Skills

Let's start from the very beginning. Communication skills are the things you apply whenever you receive any kind of information. You may not have noticed this until now, but you already have a certain set of communication skills developed. You use them every time you interact with someone. The thing is, there is a difference between having communication skills and honing them to perfection. As I mentioned in the last chapter, here we are going to (again) focus on making your communication skills exceptionally sharp. And yes, we are going to do this together.

I have covered the communications skills (and subskills) that you need to work on, so you will have no trouble expressing yourself and giving feedback to anyone, ever.

Active Listening

The first one is active listening. As you can imagine, this is being mindful when you listen to someone else. It means you pay close attention to what they have to say, ask them things that are not clear to you, and give them proper feedback.

Active listening is a very important technique you should practice. When someone notices you have it, it builds both respect and understanding. This is a skill that will help you build yourself up and climb the societal ladder with ease.

It is not difficult to engage in active listening. Some of the most popular techniques include paying attention to the facial expressions of the person you're speaking to, their body language, and their tone. Another popular technique includes shutting out all technology while you're talking to someone (or rather listening to them); this way, you remove all distractions and give them your full attention.

If you're still unsure how to approach this skill, don't worry – you can always refer back to exercise 33 in the last chapter to practice this skill.

Assertive Communication

The second one is assertive communication. Basically, this is learning how to clearly and respectfully state what you need. When you are assertive when doing so, you show other people where you stand, and you show them that you know where they stand too. To succeed in assertive communication, you need to focus on your feelings, avoid being judgemental, and just be honest when you say what you need or want. I know this seems like a practice that can take up a lot of time – and it will. But as time passes, you will notice that assertive communication is one of the pillars when it comes to strengthening your relationships. You promote growth, reduce conflict, and easily overcome any difficult situations.

Differentiating Between Passive, Aggressive, and Assertive Communication

You just learned what assertive communication means. But if you're here, that means you probably don't use this. So, what kind of a communicator are you? There are two other cases where you might stand on this one (of course, not being fully aware of them). While assertiveness is considered to be the middle ground when it comes to communication, you are probably at one or the other end of the spectrum at the moment. What does this mean?

It means you are either passive or aggressive in communication. Let's explain so you know the difference. Passive communication is when you feel stressed, depressed, and tense for a long period, and you start to feel resentment. Passivity leads to you being constantly quiet for a long time and then suddenly lashing out.

On the other side, aggressive communication is when you're actively (and constantly) dissatisfied with everything that surrounds you. In this case, you force your needs onto someone else, you cross all boundaries and disrespect others (even bully them), and you weaken all the relationships you have.

At the end of the day, it is all about knowing how to communicate your needs, wants, and rights while being respectful and understanding of the other side's needs and wants. There are many ways to practice assertiveness and excel at it, but the following exercise is probably one of my personal favorites. Once you go through it, you will realize that it is the perfect fit for you.

EXERCISE 40
ASSERTIVENESS ROLE-PLAY

Being assertive means to stand up for yourself and still respect others. This exercise will help you practice speaking up in a clear, confident way. With this exercise, you will avoid being aggressive or passive. Find a friend or family member, or even practice in front of a mirror. Pick a situation where you need to be assertive - maybe when you ask a teacher for extra help, set a boundary with a friend, or say no to something you're uncomfortable with.

Follow these steps:

1. **Use "I" statements.** Instead of blaming or accusing, focus on your feelings and needs. Example: "I feel frustrated when I don't get a chance to speak. I'd like to share my thoughts too."
2. **Keep your tone calm and steady.** Speak clearly, make eye contact, and stand with confidence.
3. **Be direct but respectful.** Say what you need without apologizing unnecessarily or backing down. Example: "I can't help with that today, but I hope it goes well."

After you practice, ask yourself: Did I stay calm? Did I get my point across? How did it feel to speak up? The more you practice, the easier it becomes to be assertive in real-life situations.

Nonverbal Communication

The third one of the communication skills has actually nothing to do with communication. But also, it has everything to do with it. In many cases, when we speak (or when other people speak) and are fully invested in the topic, the body follows. Nonverbal communication means conveying a message without the use of words. Here, a speaker may use their hands to make a gesture, use their face as they make eye contact, or even use their entire body to express something.

It has probably happened to you many times – you met someone who is excellent at nonverbal communication, and you either felt happy that you could completely understand them, or you felt a little bit intimidated by their skill. Whatever the case may be, you can easily learn how to communicate without using your words – and I am here to teach you just that. Let's cover the most important aspects of it.

You can get a lot of information just by looking at someone's posture and movement. Think about it, you have probably already noticed this. When someone is mad or defensive, they cross their hands. When someone wants to explain something, and they're really invested in it, they do a lot of gestures and so on. Body language can show you when someone has strong feelings and attitudes about something (be that positive or negative). All you need to do is observe.

Facial expressions are probably responsible for the largest portion of nonverbal communication. You can say so much by making a simple face. For example, think of how many things have been communicated only by a smile or a frown. It's amazing, right? Sometimes, when you see the look on someone's face, you immediately know what they want to say or what they think. Because the face is the first thing we see, even before someone speaks to us, it is the first form of communication before you actually utter any words.

When you focus on improving your nonverbal communication skills, you focus on adding importance to your conversations. A big portion of the communication that happens among people is nonverbal, so you need to be fluent in that too. This exercise I've created for you focuses on that.

EXERCISE 41

NONVERBAL COMMUNICATION PRACTICE

Communication isn't just about words - your body language, facial expressions, and tone of voice can say just as much (or more) than what you actually say. This exercise helps you become more aware of how you communicate without words and how to read nonverbal cues from others.

Step 1: Observe Yourself

Stand in front of a mirror or record yourself while saying a simple sentence like, "I'm fine." Try saying it in different ways:

- With a smile and relaxed posture
- With crossed arms and a frown
- While you avoid eye contact and mumbling

Notice how each version sends a completely different message, even though the words don't change. Ask yourself: What emotions come across in my expressions and body language? Do they match my words?

Step 2: Practice with a Friend

Ask a friend or family member to talk briefly with you about anything. Focus on using positive nonverbal cues, like:

- Making eye contact
- Nodding or using small reactions to show you're engaged
- Keeping an open posture (not crossing your arms or looking away)

Then, switch roles and try the opposite. Cross your arms, avoid eye contact, or fidget. See how it changes the way the conversation feels.

Step 3: Reflect

Think about a time when you misread someone's body language or when yours didn't match what you were saying. How can being more aware of nonverbal communication help you express yourself better and understand others more clearly? Nonverbal cues are powerful, and being mindful of them can make a big difference in how you connect with people.

Building Empathy

It is time to move on to the next skill, which is kind of an important one. Before I begin, I must say this – there is a little bit of empathy in every one of us. While some people know how to express it better, and others may not, empathy is always there – entwined in the core of our being.

In your instance, empathy can be a true game-changer when it comes to building the best version of yourself. This is how you can cultivate connection and openness. This is how you can help yourself and the people around you feel less alone. Through building empathy, you can improve your commitment to creating a better life for yourself, your overall well-being, mindfulness, and willingness to do better.

You may have mistaken empathy for compassion or sympathy, but these are not the same things. They seem like they are, but empathy is something a lot deeper. When we talk about empathy, we talk about our feelings with people – not just for them. For example, when you are empathetic toward someone, you don't just guess how they feel. You feel the same feelings they have, and you are there for them.

Practicing Empathy

This sounds a little bit tricky, but no worries – I am here to guide you every step of the way. Think of building empathy as building a muscle. The longer you work on it, the better it gets. You can do many exercises to make this happen – and of course, I have included the best ones here. The only thing you need to be mindful of before you begin is that you need to be patient with yourself. There is no need to put some stress on yourself through your journey. All you need to be is calm and trustworthy in the process.

It is all about being curious about other people's experiences. These can tell you a lot. They can also help you deepen your understanding of them and their journey. So, when you want to practice empathy, start by giving them your full attention. Pay attention to the nonverbal communication as well, and ask them questions that will help you clarify their situation. Try to avoid making assumptions, and with every word, step out of your comfort zone and into a kinder, more mindful one.

I believe the best way to learn empathy is to take on a few roles. The role-playing exercises I created for this book are an amazing starting point. They can help you see your own perspective more clearly and the perspective of the person or people standing opposite you. Here is the next exercise.

EXERCISE 42

PRESCRIPTIVE-TALKING ROLE-PLAY

Seeing things from someone else's point of view can help you understand their feelings, strengthen relationships, and avoid unnecessary conflict. This exercise will help you practice how to step into someone else's shoes and consider their perspective before you react.

Step 1: Pick a Scenario

Choose a situation where two people might see things differently. Here are some ideas:

- A friend cancels plans at the last minute, and you feel annoyed.
- A teacher gives you extra homework, and you think it's unfair.
- A sibling takes something of yours without asking, and you feel disrespected.

Step 2: Play Both Roles

First, take your own perspective. Say out loud how you feel and why. Be honest about your frustration, disappointment, or confusion.

Next, switch roles. Pretend you are the other person. Why might they have acted the way they did? What might they be feeling? For example:

- **Friend's perspective:** "I know I cancelled, but I had a really stressful day and needed time alone."
- **Teacher's perspective:** "I assigned extra homework because I want my students to be fully prepared for the test."
- **Sibling's perspective:** "I didn't think borrowing it would be a big deal, and I meant to put it back."

Step 3: Reflect and Adjust Your Response

Now that you've considered both sides, think about how this changes your reaction. Do you still feel as upset? How would you handle the situation differently now?

Try responding in a way that acknowledges both your feelings and theirs. For example:

- "I get that you needed a break, but I was looking forward to seeing you. Next time, just let me know earlier."
- "I still don't love having extra homework, but I understand why you assigned it."
- "I'd appreciate it if you ask before borrowing my stuff. That way, we can avoid any misunderstandings."

Step 4: Apply It in Real Life

The next time you feel frustrated with someone, pause for a moment and ask yourself: *What might be going on from their perspective?* It doesn't mean you have to agree with them, but understanding their side can help you respond more patiently and confidently.

Reflective listening

Reflective listening means both hearing and understanding what the other person is trying to say to you, but in the meantime letting them know that they are heard and understood by you. This takes active listening (which we already talked about) and giving them feedback too. Here, your attention needs to only focus on the person you're talking to at the moment – no one and nothing else. Here is an exercise that can help you do that.

EXERCISE 43

REFLECTIVE LISTENING PRACTICE

Listening isn't just about hearing words – it's about making the other person feel understood. Reflective listening helps you stay engaged in conversations, show empathy, and avoid misunderstandings. This exercise will guide you through practicing reflective listening so you can improve your communication skills.

Step 1: Find a Partner

Ask a friend, family member, or classmate to have a conversation with you. Let them choose a topic – something they care about, whether it's a recent experience, a problem, or something exciting happening in their life. Your goal is to listen actively and reflect on their words.

Step 2: Listen Without Interrupting

As they speak, focus on:
- Making eye contact
- Nodding or using small verbal cues like "I see" or "That makes sense"
- Avoiding distractions (no phone-checking or thinking about what you'll say next)

Resist the urge to give advice, correct them, or share your own story. Just listen.

Step 3: Reflect What You Heard

Once they finish speaking, summarize what they said in your own words to check if you understood correctly. Use phrases like:
- "So, what I'm hearing is..."
- "It sounds like you're feeling..."
- "You're saying that..."

For example, if they say, "I'm so stressed about my exam. I feel like no matter how much I study, I'll still mess up," you could reflect:
- "It sounds like you're really worried about the exam and feel like studying isn't helping as much as you'd like."

If they agree, great! If not, ask, "Did I get that right?" and let them clarify.

Step 4: Validate Their Feelings

Even if you don't fully understand or agree, acknowledge their emotions. You might say:
- "That sounds really frustrating."
- "I can see why you'd feel that way."
- "That makes sense."

Validation doesn't mean you have to fix their problem—it just shows that their feelings are real and important.

Step 5: Switch Roles and Reflect

Now, let your partner practice reflective listening while you talk about something on your mind. Notice how it feels when someone truly listens to you.

Step 6: Apply It in Real Life

Try using reflective listening in daily conversations. Whether a friend is venting, a teacher is giving instructions, or a family member is sharing something important, take a moment to listen, reflect, and validate. It can make a huge difference in how people connect with you.

Empathy in Conflict Resolution

Empathy can go a long way, especially when you want to resolve a conflict with someone. It can help you understand the other side's perspective and feelings. In terms of conflict, it can act as a bridge both parties need to cross to get to a mutual understanding (or meet halfway, whatever works for you). Suppose you utilize empathy whenever you try to resolve a certain issue. In that case, you will have a unique opportunity to understand the other person's emotions and point of view and find a common ground where you can both agree on something. By doing this, you will be able to diffuse any tension and reach an understanding. Allow me to further explain how you can do this.

It is all about the ability to humanize the person standing across from you. When tensions arise and a situation gets heated, it is easy to forget that you are speaking to another human being. Emotions get the best of you, and you may act out – quite impulsively. In this case, whenever you feel like you need to calm yourself down and get to the bottom of the conflict, it is important to stop and remind yourself that the other person is human too. They have their own thoughts and feelings, and they want to express them too. Step into their shoes for a moment and see what it is like from the other side. Use empathy in such cases so you can get the best results.

When it comes to techniques for empathetic communication, we have covered most of them during the course of this book. The best ones that I can mention here include active listening and validation of the other person's point of view. Also, bring them a sense of safety by showing them you will understand them rather than lash out at them. Furthermore, you can identify the points where miscommunication may happen and try to bridge that gap. By doing all of this, you will create a sense of safety and start to engage in a constructive conversation. It is indeed easier to lash out at someone, but this will by far have the better result.

EXERCISE 44

EMPATHY IN CONFLICT RESOLUTION SCENARIOS

Conflict happens. It's part of life. But how you handle it can make a huge difference in your relationships. This exercise will help you practice using empathy to resolve conflicts in a way that strengthens connections rather than damages them.

Step 1: Understanding Empathy in Conflict

Empathy means putting yourself in someone else's shoes and trying to see things from their perspective. In a conflict, this doesn't mean agreeing with everything the other person says – it just means acknowledging their feelings and making them feel heard.

When conflict arises, people often focus on proving they're right instead of understanding the other person's emotions. But if you listen with empathy, you're more likely to find a solution that works for both of you.

Step 2: Choose a Scenario

Pick one of these situations (or think of your own) and imagine how you would normally react:
- A friend snaps at you for no reason, and you feel hurt.
- A classmate takes credit for something you did in a group project.
- Your parent or guardian keeps telling you to do something you don't think is fair.
- A sibling borrows your stuff without asking and doesn't return it.

_____

_____

_____

_____

Now, instead of reacting with anger or frustration, you will work through the situation with empathy.

Step 3: Pause and Identify Emotions

Before responding, take a deep breath and ask yourself:
- What emotions am I feeling? (Hurt? Frustration? Annoyance?)
- What might they be feeling? (Stressed? Overwhelmed? Misunderstood?)
- Is there something deeper going on for them?

For example, if a friend snaps at you, your first reaction might be to snap back. But if you stop and think, you might realize they've had a rough day, and their response isn't actually about you.

Step 4: Respond with Empathy

Now, rewrite how you would handle the situation using empathy. Instead of saying, "Why are you being so rude?" you might say, "Hey, you seem upset. Did something happen?"

Here are a few empathy-based responses you can use in conflicts:

- **Acknowledging feelings:** "I get why you're frustrated."
- **Asking open-ended questions:** "Can you help me understand why this upset you?"
- **Validating their perspective:** "I see why that would bother you."
- **Offering a compromise:** "What if we tried this instead?"

Take your chosen scenario and write out both an instinctive reaction (without empathy) and an empathetic response. Compare the two. Which one is more likely to lead to a resolution?

Step 5: Reflect and Apply

Think about a recent conflict in your life. Could empathy have changed the outcome? How will you handle a future conflict differently now that you've practiced responding with understanding?

Next time you're in a tough situation, pause and use this strategy. You might be surprised at how much smoother things go when people feel heard and understood.

Managing Relationship Challenges

By this stage in your life, you probably already have your own idea of what your relationships with other people should look like. Whether you think of a relationship with yourself, a partner, your family, your friends, or your teachers, there is a clear idea of what that should look like. The thing is, not everybody thinks the same way you do. When you're young, this idea usually comes from what surrounds you and what you see – the relationship between your family, movies you watch, series, and even books you read – oh, and the media, too! But, these are not always realistic ideas of what relationships overall should look like. That is mostly the reason why young people like yourself get in conflict in the first place (yes, not everything is your fault).

To manage a challenge in a relationship takes effort – and it takes two. However, no matter what the case is, start from yourself, work on yourself, and you will immediately see how things will get better. There are two main things you can focus on, and I've covered both of them – let's see them together.

Building Healthy Relationships

Handling Peer Pressure

There is always a desire to fit in – society, with classmates, with any type of group. But, when you want to enter a new group, there is always something called peer pressure hanging over your head. Handling peer pressure is not always challenging, especially when you are among people who share the same thoughts, opinions, and values as you do. But if that isn't the case, the peer pressure is strong.

Do you know how you can recognize peer pressure? I call this trusting your gut. You are most likely put in a situation you don't really like (deep down), and you need to do something that you wouldn't normally do or something you know is wrong. All of this has one goal – to become accepted into a certain group.

You probably came up with some ideas on your own while you were reading this, but just in case you didn't, here are a few techniques you can use to resist any negative influence. First things first, remember that you don't have to please anyone and that you are enough. Then, try to avoid situations and people who make you feel uncomfortable. If someone is pushing your boundaries, stand firm on your feet and decline. Focus on spending time with people who make you feel supported, loved, and understood. It may be difficult to understand, but not everyone will like you – and that's okay. And if all else fails, you can always turn to someone for support or help.

Having a little confidence in yourself can go a long way. It can teach you how to act better in such situations. You will not succumb to the pressure you're faced with and will come out the other side a winner. All you need to do is remember that you are good enough just as you are and that you are doing everything you can to become better with each passing day.

EXERCISE 45

PEER PRESSURE RESISTANCE SCENARIOS

Peer pressure can be tough. Sometimes, it's obvious – like someone daring you to do something risky. Other times, it's more subtle, like feeling you have to dress a certain way or agree with something just to fit in. This exercise will help you practice standing up for yourself and making choices that align with what *you* truly want.

Step 1: Recognizing Peer Pressure

Before you can resist peer pressure, you have to recognize it. Think about situations where you might feel pressured to do something you're not comfortable with. It could be:

- ✧ A friend pushing you to try something you don't want to (drinking, smoking, skipping class).
- ✧ Classmates making fun of someone and expecting you to join in.
- ✧ A group convincing you to spend money on something you don't need.
- ✧ Friends pushing you to post something online that doesn't feel right.

Peer pressure can be direct (someone telling you what to do) or indirect (feeling like you have to do something to fit in). Take a moment to think about a time when you felt pressured. What did it feel like? How did you respond?

_____

_____

_____

Step 2: Choose a Scenario

Pick one of the scenarios below (or come up with your own) and imagine you're in that situation:

- **Scenario 1:** Your friends are sneaking out at night and expect you to join them. When you hesitate, they tease you for being "too scared."
- **Scenario 2:** A classmate offers you a vape and says, "Come on, it's not a big deal. Everyone's doing it."
- **Scenario 3:** Your friends are making fun of someone online and want you to comment something mean to fit in.
- **Scenario 4:** You're at a party where people are drinking. Someone hands you a drink and says, "Just one sip won't hurt."
- **Scenario 5:** A friend is pressuring you to let them copy your homework. When you refuse, they act annoyed and say, "I thought we were friends."

Step 3: Identify Your Feelings and Values

Before responding, pause and ask yourself:

- How do I feel about this? (Nervous? Annoyed? Stressed?)
- What are my values in this situation? (Honesty? Safety? Self-respect?)
- Will doing this make me feel good about myself later?

Knowing your values makes it easier to stand your ground. If something doesn't align with what *you* want, it's okay to say no.

Step 4: Practice Saying No

Now, rewrite how you would respond to your chosen scenario in a way that's firm but respectful. You don't have to make a big scene – you just need to make it clear that you're not interested.

Here are some ways to say no:

- ◆ **Be direct:** "No thanks, I'm not into that."
- ◆ **Use humor:** "Yeah, I don't feel like getting grounded today."
- ◆ **Suggest an alternative:** "Let's do something else instead."
- ◆ **Blame something else:** "My parents would get mad at me if they found out."
- ◆ **Walk away:** If they won't take no for an answer, remove yourself from the situation.

Now, write out your response for the scenario you picked. How do you feel about your response? Would you be able to say it in real life?

_____
_____
_____
_____
_____
_____
_____
_____

Step 5: Reflect and Apply

Think about how peer pressure affects your life. Have there been times when you said yes to something you didn't want to? How did it feel afterward?

Now that you've practiced, challenge yourself to notice peer pressure when it happens and use these strategies to stand up for yourself. Remember – real friends respect your choices, even if they're different from theirs.

Healthy Boundaries

The other thing you can always focus on to get the best results in terms of managing relationship challenges is to set healthy boundaries. Now, even though we already discussed them in the last chapter, I feel like it is worth it to mention them again. These can help you define what appropriate behavior means to you – especially in a healthy relationship. This is called healthy because it is based on keeping both parties involved safe. It is also a crucial step if you want to create a foundation for a long-lasting and positive relationship – with anyone.

As I mentioned, these boundaries differ from person to person and are usually governed by culture, social context, and personality. They are interpersonal limits that help us function better as individuals and as members of society.

When you set boundaries for yourself, it means you are aware of yourself. It means that you have expectations set in place which can help you determine whether you are comfortable or not in a certain situation. But also, as the importance of setting boundaries is always present, so is the ability to communicate clearly. As you mature and grow up, you will see that these two are actually intertwined – one cannot go without the other.

It is easy to set and maintain boundaries if you know how to approach this topic right. It all comes down to being assertive. Assertiveness means you need to know how to openly and respectfully share what it is you want, need, and feel. Think of your priorities as a form of self-care. Just be clear in what it is you want to articulate, try not to raise your voice, and accept that, sometimes, there may be a little discomfort on both ends (when you state what you want) – and all of that is a normal part of the process.

Finally, as much as you'd like other people to respect your boundaries, you need to respect theirs as well. This is something that can help you overcome any challenge you have in life, especially when communicating with another person. Just take a look at the exercise below, and things will get a lot clearer for you.

EXERCISE 46

BOUNDARY-SETTING PRACTICE

Setting boundaries means knowing what makes you feel comfortable and standing up for yourself when someone crosses the line. Boundaries help you protect your time, energy, emotions, and personal space. This exercise will help you practice recognizing when boundaries are needed and how to enforce them in a way that is clear and confident.

Step 1: Understanding Boundaries

There are different types of boundaries:

- ⬦ **Physical boundaries** – Deciding who can touch you, how close people can get, and when you need personal space.
- ⬦ **Emotional boundaries** – Protecting your feelings and not taking on other people's emotions as your own.
- ⬦ **Time boundaries** – Managing your time so you don't feel overcommitted or pressured.
- ⬦ **Digital boundaries** – Deciding who can contact you, what personal information you share, and how much time you spend online.

Think about a time when someone made you feel uncomfortable by ignoring one of your boundaries. What happened? How did you react? If you need some help with this, I suggest you reflect on the boundary-setting worksheet from the previous chapter. This can be an excellent starting point for you.

Step 2: Recognizing When a Boundary is Needed

Boundaries are needed when:

- ⬦ Someone pressures you to do something you don't want to do.
- ⬦ A friend or family member disrespects your feelings.
- ⬦ People constantly ask for your time or energy, leaving you exhausted.
- ⬦ Someone invades your privacy, like reading your messages or touching your belongings without permission.
- ⬦ A person crosses a personal or emotional limit that makes you uncomfortable.

Choose one situation from above (or one from your own life) and write down how it made you feel.

Step 3: Practicing Boundary Statements

The best way to set a boundary is to be **clear, calm, and direct**. Boundaries are not about being rude or controlling—they're about respecting yourself.

Here's a simple formula:

"I feel [emotion] when [behavior] happens. I need [boundary]."

For example:
- "I feel overwhelmed when I get too many messages late at night. I need people to text me earlier in the day."
- "I feel uncomfortable when people touch my stuff without asking. I need you to ask before using my things."
- "I feel stressed when my time isn't respected. I need to leave by 9 PM, so I can't stay later."

Now, write your own boundary statement for the situation you picked in Step 2. How does it feel to say it?

___

Step 4: Handling Pushback

Sometimes, people don't like hearing "no." They might:
- Guilt-trip you ("Come on, don't be like that!")
- Ignore your boundary ("You're being too sensitive.")
- Keep pushing ("Just this one time?")

If someone doesn't respect your boundary, you can:

- **Repeat your boundary**: "I already said I can't stay late. Please respect that."
- **Offer an alternative**: "I can't hang out tonight, but let's meet up tomorrow."
- **Walk away**: If they refuse to respect you, you don't have to stay in the conversation.

Write down ways you could respond if someone pushes against your boundary.

_____
_____
_____
_____
_____
_____
_____
_____

Step 5: Apply It in Real Life

Think about one area in your life where you need stronger boundaries. How will you start enforcing them? Who do you need to communicate with?

Practice saying your boundary statement out loud. If setting boundaries feels uncomfortable, remember: You are allowed to protect your space, energy, and emotions. The people who respect you will respect your boundaries.

What Did You Learn From This Chapter?

Congratulations on completing the longest chapter of this book! Before we move on to the final chapter, let's just make a small recap of everything you've learned here.

- Communication skills, especially active listening, assertiveness, and nonverbal communication, are incredibly important in creating a better and stronger version of yourself.
- Empathy has a big role in the process.
- Learn how to practice empathy and use it whenever you come in contact with someone.
- Every relationship in life comes with its own set of challenges – but now you have the tools to overcome anything that comes your way.
- You can easily become who you want to be as long as you set healthy boundaries.

Your magnificent mind is filled with plenty of useful information – but it still feels like something is missing. Well, it is time for me to say this for the last time – turn the page, and let's discover the last bit of what you need to step into the most powerful version of yourself!

Building Healthy Relationships | 505

8

LONG-TERM EMOTIONAL REGULATION STRATEGIES

"We don't know where we're going, we don't know what's going to happen, but no one can take away from you what you put in your own mind." – Edith Eger

We've talked about the good things, and we've talked about the bad things. We've covered how to identify and regulate your emotions and deal with negative thoughts. But now, you may start to wonder – how long can you keep this up? Is this really working on yourself, or are these just techniques that will help you patch things up for just a little while?

It's okay to have these questions. These are a part of growing up. And honestly, you don't know what's going to happen tomorrow, but you do want to see that you can cope with whatever comes your way. That is why I am dedicating this chapter to long-term emotional regulation strategies. While you now know how to deal with any kind of situation, you also need a little bit of support so you can easily handle anything and everything in the future.

Developing Consistent Habits

As you go through life, you will notice the power of consistency – especially the part where you show up for yourself, day after day. I have divided this chapter into two sections you need to focus on – and this is the first one. Developing constant habits is a very easy thing to do – it only takes a few weeks to become consistent in anything. But, deep down, when it comes to your core, remember that you can choose to be whoever you want every day. This is where your consistency should come from. If you want to become the best version of yourself, it is all about focusing on the right habits. And what are these "right habits"? Well, they are all the things I mentioned in all the previous chapters – the techniques, the exercises – everything!

So you see? This kind of goes full circle – one cannot go without the other.

Daily Emotional Check-Ins

The emotional check-in is the time in your day when you need to stop for a minute and assess how you feel. This is a very important thing to do because it can help you become more honest about yourself. It can bring you calmness (knowing that you can identify your feelings), it can help you talk about them more openly, and it can help you cope with them better. Also, doing this is a proactive problem-solving tool, it can help you build self-awareness skills and help you create a connection between your thoughts and feelings.

There is a lot of importance in checking in with yourself on a regular basis. As humans, we are constantly preoccupied with many things, and sometimes, it can be very easy to stray away from our path. In these situations (and yes, they are very likely to happen), you need to be gentle with yourself rather than harsh. You need to give yourself a break but remind yourself that you have a goal, you have something quite attainable, and you are going for it every day.

I found the best way to check in with yourself is through the worksheets I designed for the next exercises. They are probably the best techniques, and as you can see, they can also be helpful tools.

I'm presenting these techniques to you in the form of worksheets. Now, for your keen teenager eye, it will seem like they are extremely similar (and you're right about it, sort of). The worksheets are quite similar, though as soon as you delve a little deeper into them, you will notice that they are focused on different things. Take a look for yourself and see.

EXERCISE 47

DAILY EMOTIONAL CHECK-IN WORKSHEET

Checking in with your emotions every day helps you better understand yourself, recognize patterns, and build emotional awareness. Instead of letting emotions control you, this practice gives you the power to notice how you feel and respond in a healthy way. This worksheet will guide you through a simple emotional check-in that you can do daily.

Step 1: Pause and Notice

Take a deep breath. Close your eyes for a moment and check in with yourself. How do you feel right now? Don't rush – just notice. Are you calm? Stressed? Excited? Tired? Write down the first words that come to mind.

Today, I feel: _____

_____

Step 2: Identify the Cause

Think about what might be influencing your emotions today. It could be something that happened at school, a conversation with a friend, upcoming responsibilities, or even how much sleep you got last night. Try to name the main reason behind how you're feeling.

I think I feel this way because: _____

_____

Step 3: Rate Your Emotions

On a scale of **1-10**, where **1** is "not intense at all" and **10** is "overwhelming," rate how strong your emotions are.

My emotional intensity is: _____ / 10

If your number is **7 or higher**, it might help to use a coping skill (like deep breathing, journaling, or talking to someone). If it's **3 or lower**, you might be in a good place to focus on goals and productivity.

Step 4: Check Your Body

Emotions don't just exist in your mind – they show up in your body too. Where do you feel your emotions physically? Do you have tension in your shoulders? A tight chest? A headache? Maybe your stomach feels weird, or you feel extra energetic.

Right now, I notice in my body: _____

_____

Step 5: Respond to Your Emotions

Now that you've identified how you feel and why, think about what you need. Do you need to calm down, cheer up, take a break, or talk to someone? What action can you take right now that would be helpful?

One thing I can do to take care of myself today is: _____

_____

Step 6: Set an Intention

End your check-in by setting a small intention for the rest of the day. It can be something like:
- ✧ "I will take deep breaths when I feel overwhelmed."
- ✧ "I will focus on things I can control."
- ✧ "I will remind myself that my feelings are valid."

My intention for today is: _____

_____

Final Reflection

Doing this check-in every day helps you stay connected to your emotions and respond in a healthy way. Try it for a week and see how it affects your mood, stress levels, and decision-making. If you notice patterns in your emotions, you can start making changes that help you feel better.

Today, I feel: _____

_____

I think I feel this way because: _____

_____

My emotional intensity is: _____ / 10

Right now, I notice in my body: _____

_____

One thing I can do to take care of myself today is: _____

_____

My intention for today is: _____

_____

Today, I feel: _____

_____

I think I feel this way because: _____

_____

My emotional intensity is: _____ / 10

Right now, I notice in my body: _____

_____

One thing I can do to take care of myself today is: _____

_____

My intention for today is: _____

_____

———o—◇—o———

Today, I feel: _____

_____

I think I feel this way because: _____

_____

My emotional intensity is: _____ / 10

Right now, I notice in my body: _____

_____

One thing I can do to take care of myself today is: _____

_____

My intention for today is: _____

_____

Long-Term Emotional Regulation Strategies

Today, I feel: _____

_____

I think I feel this way because: _____

_____

My emotional intensity is: _____ / 10

Right now, I notice in my body: _____

_____

One thing I can do to take care of myself today is: _____

_____

My intention for today is: _____

_____

---o-✦-o---

Today, I feel: _____

_____

I think I feel this way because: _____

_____

My emotional intensity is: _____ / 10

Right now, I notice in my body: _____

_____

One thing I can do to take care of myself today is: _____

_____

My intention for today is: _____

_____

Today, I feel: _____

_____

I think I feel this way because: _____

_____

My emotional intensity is: _____ / 10

Right now, I notice in my body: _____

_____

One thing I can do to take care of myself today is: _____

_____

My intention for today is: _____

_____

EXERCISE 48
DAILY MOOD TRACKER

Keeping track of your mood each day helps you notice patterns, understand what affects your emotions, and make better choices for your well-being. This exercise will guide you through tracking your mood and identifying factors that influence how you feel. The more you pay attention to your emotions, the easier it becomes to manage them in a healthy way.

Step 1: Record Your Mood

Think about how you've felt today. Try to sum it up in one or two words. You don't need to overthink it—just write down what feels right.

Today, I feel: _____

Step 2: Rate Your Mood

On a scale of **1-10**, where **1** is the lowest (really bad) and **10** is the highest (really great), rate your overall mood for today.

My mood rating for today is: _____ / 10

Step 3: Identify the Main Emotion

Write down the main emotion that stood out today. You might have felt many emotions, but choose the one that was strongest.

- ◇ Happy
- ◇ Excited
- ◇ Calm
- ◇ Confident
- ◇ Angry
- ◇ Frustrated
- ◇ Sad
- ◇ Lonely
- ◇ Overwhelmed
- ◇ Anxious
- ◇ Bored

My strongest emotion today was: _____

Step 4: What Affected Your Mood?

Think about what influenced how you felt today. Did something specific happen? Maybe a conversation, an event, or even just how well you slept? Choose or write down the biggest factors that impact your mood.

- ✧ **School:** Tests, homework, classes, teachers
- ✧ **Friends:** Conversations, conflicts, fun moments
- ✧ **Family:** Support, tension, time together
- ✧ **Sleep:** Well-rested or tired
- ✧ **Food & Drink:** Healthy eating, too much sugar, caffeine
- ✧ **Social Media:** Positive or negative experiences online
- ✧ **Weather:** Rainy, sunny, cold, warm
- ✧ **Physical Activity:** Exercise, lack of movement
- ✧ **Personal Thoughts:** Overthinking, self-doubt, confidence

The biggest factors affecting my mood today were: _____
_____
_____

Step 5: How Did You React to Your Mood?

Now, think about how you responded to your emotions. Did you cope in a healthy way? If you were stressed, did you do something that helped? If you were happy, did you share it with others? If you reacted in a way you'd like to change, what could you do differently next time?

Today, I responded to my emotions by: _____
_____
_____

Step 6: What's One Thing You Can Do Tomorrow?

No matter what kind of day you have, you can always make small changes to improve your mood for tomorrow. You may want to get more sleep, take deep breaths when stressed, or spend time with someone who makes you feel good.

One thing I will do tomorrow to take care of my mood is: _____
_____
_____

Final Reflection

Tracking your mood every day helps you see patterns over time. Are there days of the week when you feel better or worse? Do certain activities improve your mood? If you do this for a week or more, you might start to notice connections between your emotions and your daily choices. The more you understand your mood, the more control you have over how you respond to it.

Today, I feel: _____

My mood rating for today is: _____ / 10

My strongest emotion today was: _____

The biggest factors affecting my mood today were: _____

_____

_____

Today, I responded to my emotions by: _____

_____

_____

One thing I will do tomorrow to take care of my mood is: _____

_____

———o–◆–o———

Today, I feel: _____

My mood rating for today is: _____ / 10

My strongest emotion today was: _____

The biggest factors affecting my mood today were: _____

_____

_____

Today, I responded to my emotions by: _____

_____

_____

One thing I will do tomorrow to take care of my mood is: _____

_____

Today, I feel: _____

My mood rating for today is: _____ / 10

My strongest emotion today was: _____

The biggest factors affecting my mood today were: _____

_____

_____

Today, I responded to my emotions by: _____

_____

_____

One thing I will do tomorrow to take care of my mood is: _____

_____

Today, I feel: _____

My mood rating for today is: _____ / 10

My strongest emotion today was: _____

The biggest factors affecting my mood today were: _____

_____

_____

Today, I responded to my emotions by: _____

_____

_____

One thing I will do tomorrow to take care of my mood is: _____

_____

Today, I feel: _____

My mood rating for today is: _____ / 10

My strongest emotion today was: _____

The biggest factors affecting my mood today were: _____

_____

_____

Today, I responded to my emotions by: _____

_____

_____

One thing I will do tomorrow to take care of my mood is: _____

_____

––––––o–◇–o––––––

Today, I feel: _____

My mood rating for today is: _____ / 10

My strongest emotion today was: _____

The biggest factors affecting my mood today were: _____

_____

_____

Today, I responded to my emotions by: _____

_____

_____

One thing I will do tomorrow to take care of my mood is: _____

_____

EXERCISE 49

STRESS LEVEL LOG

Tracking your stress levels helps you understand what triggers your stress, how it affects you, and what you can do to manage it better. Stress isn't always bad – sometimes it pushes you to get things done – but it can take a toll on your mind and body when it builds up. This log will help you check in with yourself and make small changes to reduce stress before it overwhelms you.

Step 1: Rate Your Stress Level

Think about your overall stress level today. On a scale of **1-10**, where **1** is completely relaxed, and **10** is extremely overwhelmed, choose a number that best represents how stressed you felt.

My stress level today was: _____ / 10

Step 2: Identify Your Stress Triggers

What caused your stress today? Stress can come from many sources, and sometimes you may not even realize what's overwhelming you. Take a moment to think about what might have contributed to your stress.

- **School:** Homework, tests, deadlines, difficult subjects
- **Friends:** Arguments, feeling left out, peer pressure
- **Family:** Expectations, conflicts, responsibilities
- **Social Media:** Comparison, negativity, overwhelming news
- **Health:** Lack of sleep, poor diet, feeling sick, not enough exercise
- **Future Worries:** College, career, and life decisions
- **Other:** Unexpected events, feeling unmotivated, too much on your plate

The biggest stressors for me today were: _____

_____

_____

Step 3: How Did Your Stress Show Up?

Stress doesn't just stay in your mind; it also affects your body and behavior. Think about how your stress showed up today. Did you notice any of these signs?

Physical Signs:
- Headache or stomach ache
- Tired but unable to relax
- Fast heartbeat or shallow breathing
- Muscle tension or clenched jaw
- Restlessness or fidgeting

Emotional Signs:
- Feeling frustrated or irritable
- Anxiety or constant worrying
- Lack of motivation
- Feeling overwhelmed or helpless
- Mood swings or wanting to isolate yourself

Today, my stress affected me in these ways: _____

_____

_____

Step 4: How Did You React to Your Stress?

When you felt stressed today, how did you handle it? Did you use a healthy coping strategy, or did you react in a way that made things harder? Think about what you did when stress hit.

- ⋄ **Healthy Responses:** Deep breaths, exercise, journal, listen to music, take breaks, talk to someone
- ⋄ **Unhelpful Responses:** Shut down, avoid responsibilities, lash out, procrastinate, overeat, doom-scrolling on social media

I responded to my stress today by: _____

_____

_____

Step 5: What Can You Do Differently Next Time?

Stress will always be a part of life, but how you handle it can make a big difference. Next time you feel stressed, think about one thing you can do differently. For example, take a deep breath before reacting, ask for help, or step away from the situation to clear your mind.

Next time I feel stressed, I will try to: _____

_____

_____

Final Reflection

Keeping a stress log helps you see patterns in what stresses you out and how you respond. If you track your stress for a week or more, you might notice certain things that trigger it or ways to manage it better. Stress isn't always avoidable, but with practice, you can learn to handle it in a way that protects your mental and physical health.

My stress level today was: _____ / 10

The biggest stressors for me today were: _____

_____

_____

Today, my stress affected me in these ways: _____

_____

_____

I responded to my stress today by: _____

_____

_____

Next time I feel stressed, I will try to: _____

_____

Long-Term Emotional Regulation Strategies

My stress level today was: _____ / 10

The biggest stressors for me today were: _____
_____
_____

Today, my stress affected me in these ways: _____
_____
_____

I responded to my stress today by: _____
_____
_____

Next time I feel stressed, I will try to: _____
_____
_____

My stress level today was: _____ / 10

The biggest stressors for me today were: _____
_____
_____

Today, my stress affected me in these ways: _____
_____
_____

I responded to my stress today by: _____
_____
_____

Next time I feel stressed, I will try to: _____
_____
_____

My stress level today was: _____ / 10

The biggest stressors for me today were: _____
_____
_____

Today, my stress affected me in these ways: _____
_____
_____

I responded to my stress today by: _____
_____
_____

Next time I feel stressed, I will try to: _____
_____
_____

My stress level today was: _____ / 10

The biggest stressors for me today were: _____
_____
_____

Today, my stress affected me in these ways: _____
_____
_____

I responded to my stress today by: _____
_____
_____

Next time I feel stressed, I will try to: _____
_____
_____

My stress level today was: _____ / 10

The biggest stressors for me today were: _____
_____
_____

Today, my stress affected me in these ways: _____
_____
_____

I responded to my stress today by: _____
_____
_____

Next time I feel stressed, I will try to: _____
_____
_____

It is important to integrate these check-ins into your routine as they will give you a better insight into yourself. As time passes, you will notice many more patterns that you have (and you have broken) just because you decided to use these exercises.

Creating a Balanced Life

When life comes at you hard, you may find yourself facing challenges you never knew you'd be facing before. The responsibilities can easily pile up, leaving you unable to figure out where to begin if you want to start creating a healthier lifestyle. Well, as funny as it sounds, it is all about balance. Of course, not just balance by itself – but one achieved with the right strategies, exercises, techniques, and mindset.

Balance your life, and you will balance your emotions. It is as simple as it sounds. This will increase your productivity, it will improve your overall well-being, and it will help you nurture yourself at one point and focus on doing something at another point.

Of course, I will once again mention the self-care routines as they are an inevitable part of your life. Through them, you give yourself the break you need, you listen to your body, mind, and soul, and answer their calls every time. That will inspire you to create harmony – both within and outside of you.

Adapting to Life Changes

I dedicated the second part to adapting to the changes in life. At times, you may find yourself challenged – where it seems easier to lash out and burst in the moment rather than take a step back and assess the situation. Well, I'm here to tell you that the latter is the right choice – every time. I'm not saying it's easy, but it is imperative if you want to continue moving ahead in life.

Coping with Major Life Events

The only thing you need to do in this instance is to acknowledge that change is happening. Now, most people either lash out at the moment or retreat and just ignore that a major life event is happening.

Either way, you know this is a wrong approach. Coping with major life events takes time and effort and here is how you can do that.

First things first, acknowledge what is happening, and write down everything positive you can about it. You may not find it at first, but that is why you take a step back and objectively look at the situation. Quiet your mind and prepare yourself for the change. Be kind to yourself through the process, and if you feel like it, turn to someone for support. Talk it out on time.

As you can look at the last exercise for this chapter (and this book), you can see that it all comes down to coping with change. This change will vary from one period to the next – all you need to do is adapt it to your current situation and make the most out of it.

EXERCISE 50

COPING WITH CHANGE

Change can be exciting, scary, or overwhelming – sometimes all at once. Whether it's switching schools, making new friends, dealing with family changes, or adjusting to unexpected life events, change can shake up your emotions and make you feel uncertain. This exercise will help you understand how you react to change, recognize your emotions, and find ways to cope with change in a healthy way.

Step 1: Identify a Recent Change

Think about a recent change in your life – big or small. It could be something personal, social, academic, or even something within your family. Change doesn't always have to be negative; sometimes, even positive changes can bring stress.

Describe a recent change in your life: _____

_____

_____

Now, reflect on how this change has affected you. Ask yourself:

- Was this change expected or unexpected?
- Did I have any control over it?
- How did I feel when it first happened?
- How do I feel about it now?

This change made me feel: _____

_____

_____

Step 2: Recognizing Your Reactions to Change

When change happens, you might experience a mix of emotions – excitement, fear, frustration, sadness, or even relief. Your thoughts and behaviors may shift as well. Take a moment to reflect on how you reacted.

Which of these reactions do you relate to?

Long-Term Emotional Regulation Strategies

Emotional Reactions:
- Feeling anxious or worried
- Feeling excited but nervous
- Feeling overwhelmed or stressed
- Feeling sad or disappointed
- Feeling frustrated or helpless

Behavioral Reactions:
- Avoiding the situation or ignoring it
- Trying to control everything
- Talking to someone about it
- Finding ways to adjust to the new situation
- Dwelling on the past or wishing things would go back to the way they were

My reaction to this change was: _____

_____

_____

Are there any reactions you'd like to change next time you experience something new?

Step 3: What Helps You Cope With Change?

Not all change is easy, but there are ways to handle it so that it doesn't feel so overwhelming. What strategies have helped you in the past when you've gone through significant changes?

Healthy Coping Strategies:
- Talking to a trusted friend or family member
- Writing down your thoughts and feelings
- Breaking things into smaller steps to feel less overwhelmed
- Focusing on what you can control instead of what you can't
- Practicing mindfulness, deep breathing, or relaxation techniques
- Reminding yourself that change can lead to growth

Unhelpful Coping Strategies:
- Avoiding the situation or pretending it's not happening
- Isolating yourself from friends or family
- Letting negative thoughts take over
- Ignoring your emotions instead of acknowledging them
- Lashing out or taking frustrations out on others

One healthy coping strategy I will try moving forward is: _____

_____

_____

Step 4: Finding the Silver Lining

Even difficult changes can lead to personal growth, new opportunities, or important life lessons. Think about the change you wrote about earlier – can you find anything positive that has come from it?

Ask yourself:
- What have I learned from this experience?
- Has this change helped me grow in any way?
- Have I discovered new strengths or skills because of it?
- Is there anything good that has come from this situation?

One thing I have learned from this change is: _____

_____

Final Reflection: Your Personal Growth Plan

Change will always be a part of life, but you have the power to decide how you respond to it. Take a deep breath and remind yourself that you are strong, adaptable, and capable of handling challenges.

Next time I face a big change, I will: _____

_____

_____

By understanding your reactions, recognizing your feelings, and practicing healthy coping strategies, you can build resilience and confidence for the next time you face whatever comes your way.

Building Future Resilience

Last but not least, before I wrap this chapter up, I am here to remind you that everything is about resilience. This is something that you build over time, not in a week or two. It takes a lot of courage, focus, investing your time in it, and adapting to changes through the process. Resilience means being strong enough to withstand and cope with life's challenges.

This is the first thing you need to do. Constantly remind yourself that you have a set of values and skills you have learned from this book that can help you overcome everything. This is a growth mindset, where you know you can always learn something new from every experience you have. That is how you rebound from any situation. And, of course, stay calm through the process.

The one technique I would like to mention here (in addition to everything else I have mentioned in this book) is establishing what you want to achieve. Recognize your strengths and work on your weaknesses. Manage your time effectively and do your best to excel.

There is a certain importance in lifelong learning. By doing this, you commit to a forever-growing mindset. The advantages that come from that are plenty. You get to see and enjoy yourself growing with each passing day. You get to advance in your career, increase your confidence, and work on yourself every day. And in the middle of everything, you will see that you have created a versatile life that you enjoy so, so much!

What Did You Learn From This Chapter?

Well, as this chapter comes to a close, the end of your journey is near. You have grasped the concept of what it means to focus and work on yourself your entire life, and now you have all the tools you need to make that happen for you. But just before we say our final goodbyes, let's recap what you learned in this chapter:

- ✧ There are some habits you need to make consistent – those are the ones that lift you up in life
- ✧ The power of a balanced life helps you create a happy life
- ✧ Change is inevitable. It's how you react to it that is important
- ✧ Resilience of the future is the right way to go – it will set you up on a path of lifelong learning

I am so happy that you have finally come to this chapter. Turn the page, and let's give ourselves the proper sendoff!

CONCLUSION

You've made it to the end of this workbook. That alone is something to be proud of! Through the 50 exercises I've created, you learned how to recognize your emotions. You also learned how to challenge negative thoughts and develop healthier coping strategies. With my help, you explored how Cognitive Behavioral Therapy (CBT) can help you change your negative thought patterns. Oh, and also - how Dialectical Behavior Therapy (DBT) can help you regulate your emotions, manage stress, and build stronger relationships. But most importantly, you stumbled upon something even more valuable here. That is a deep understanding of yourself.

And for that, I'll repeat it – I am so much proud of you!

Just think back to when you started this workbook. At the time, your emotions probably felt like too much to handle. All the stress, self-doubt, or anxiety took over in ways that made your life harder than it should have been in the first place. I get that.

But now, you have a whole set of tools to help you handle those moments. You understand how your thoughts influence your feelings and behaviors. Also, you have the skills to challenge and reframe unhelpful thoughts. Together, we practiced CBT techniques. Because of that, you now have the ability to shift your perspective every time things get out of control. Now, you don't believe every negative thought but question it, challenge it, and replace it with something more balanced and realistic.

Also, you learned about the power of DBT strategies, too! You saw firsthand how these skills can help you manage your emotions. They don't control you anymore. From distress tolerance techniques like the TIPP method and ACCEPTS to emotion regulation exercises – you discovered practical ways to calm yourself when emotions try to get the best of you. Along with my help, you practiced mindfulness as well. Now you know how to stay present and not get lost in worries about the past or future.

Let me remind you of another thing you did – you developed interpersonal effectiveness skills. These will allow you to communicate your needs, set boundaries, and build healthier relationships in the future.

But your journey wasn't just about understanding CBT and DBT. It was about learning how to apply these strategies in real life. Through the exercises, you discovered how to Identify and manage stress before it becomes too much to handle. You can now challenge self-criticism and build a more positive inner dialogue. You can happily say that you can also recognize emotional triggers and respond calmly rather than with an outburst. Moreover, you have a set of healthy coping skills (that can actually help you avoid all the different kinds of unhealthy behavior).

You even managed to strengthen your relationships. Now, you express yourself clearly and listen with empathy. Last but not least, you learned some emotional regulation strategies that will support your mental well-being.

Now, the question is – what comes next?

The end of this workbook doesn't mean the end of your growth. The skills you learned here are tools you can use throughout your whole life. You can turn to them when you need support, clarity, or emotional balance. The more you practice these strategies, the more natural they'll become to you. I know that some days will still be tough, but now you have a solid foundation to help you handle anything with confidence.

I'd like to address another thing – one of the biggest shifts you made is in your emotional awareness. You learned that emotions aren't something you need to fear or avoid. On the contrary, you need to think of them as signals, messages from your mind and body that help you understand what's going on. Now you know how to recognize and accept your emotions. Now, you have the power to respond in ways that align with your goals and values.

I have also helped you build healthy coping skills. You don't need to rely on quick fixes anymore. I mean, you saw it yourself – they can make you feel worse than before. You know that true self-care isn't just bubble baths and relaxation (even though this can be nice every once in a while). It is all about the right choices. They will support your well-being. By that, I mean how to set boundaries, practice gratitude, and challenge negative self-talk.

Finally (and most importantly), you took control of your emotional health. Suddenly, you don't feel stuck in old patterns anymore. This is all because now you have the knowledge and skills to navigate through life with resilience.

You can build stronger relationships. You know how to communicate effectively and set healthy boundaries. You're sure that no matter what life throws at you, you have strategies to manage it.

So, as you close this workbook, always remind yourself that you did all the work and learned the skills. I know that now, you can do anything! Practice and grow – do it constantly. And remember that every step forward (no matter how small) is a step toward a healthier, more balanced you. This isn't the end of your journey – it's only the beginning.

THANK YOU

Thank you so much for purchasing my book.

The marketplace is filled with dozens and dozens of other similar books, but you took a chance and chose this one. I hope it was well worth it.

So again, THANK YOU for getting this book and for making it all the way to the end.

Before you go, I wanted to ask you for one small favor.

Could you please consider posting a review for my book on the platform? Posting a review is the best and easiest way to support the work of independent authors like me.

Your feedback will help me to keep writing the kind of books that will help you get the results you want. It would mean a lot to me to hear from you.

Leave a Review on Amazon US →

Leave a Review on Amazon UK →

ABOUT THE AUTHOR

Emily Carter is an author who loves helping teens with their biggest turning point in life, adulting. She grew up in New York and is happily married to her high school sweetheart. She also has two of her own children.

In her free time, Emily is an avid volunteer at a local food bank and enjoys hiking, traveling, and reading books on personal development. With over a decade of experience in the education and parenting field she has seen the difference that good parenting and the right tips can make in a teenager's life. She is now an aspiring writer through which she shares her insights and advice on raising happy, healthy, and resilient children, teens, and young adults.

Emily's own struggles with navigating adulthood and overcoming obstacles inspired her to write. She noticed a gap in education regarding teaching essential life skills to teens and young adults. She decided to write comprehensive guides covering everything from money and time management to job searching and communication skills. Emily hopes her book will empower teens and young adults to live their best lives and reach their full potential.

To find more of her books, visit her Amazon Author page at:

https://www.amazon.com/author/emily-carter

REFERENCES

The Big Book of Adulting Life Skills for Teens

Adulthood quotes (546 Quotes). (n.d.). Www.goodreads.com. Retrieved May 18, 2023, from https://www.goodreads.com/quotes/tag/adulthood?page=2

AdventHealth. (2019, March 19). *Don't wait: 15 reasons to head to the emergency room*. AdventHealth. https://www.adventhealth.com/hospital/adventhealth-new-smyrna-beach/blog/dont-wait-15-reasons-head-emergency-room

Allen, S. (2022, June 2). *10 ways to save time every day that most people ignore*. Grammarly. https://www.grammarly.com/blog/save-time/

ASI Hastings. (2021, August 1). *The most effective way to clean a p-trap*. ASI Hastings. https://www.asiheatingandair.com/info/the-most-effective-way-to-clean-a-p-trap/

Ates, K. (2021, April 7). *Normal wear and tear vs. property damage: a landlord's guide*. Rentspree. https://www.rentspree.com/blog/normal-wear-and-tear

Bank of America. (2022). *Saving money tips - 8 simple ways to save money*. Better Money Habits. https://bettermoneyhabits.bankofamerica.com/en/saving-budgeting/ways-to-save-money

Banton, C. (2023, March 28). *Interest rate*. Investopedia. https://www.investopedia.com/terms/i/interestrate.asp

Better Health. (2014). *Relationships and communication*. Better Health Channel. https://www.betterhealth.vic.gov.au/health/healthyliving/relationships-and-communication

Boogaard, K. (2021, December 26). *Write achievable goals with the SMART goals framework*. Atlassian. https://www.atlassian.com/blog/productivity/how-to-write-smart-goals

Boundaries: What are they and how to create them. (2022, February 25). University of Illinois Chicago Wellness Center. https://wellnesscenter.uic.edu/news-stories/boundaries-what-are-they-and-how-to-create-them/

Brown, T., & Finch, S. (2022, September 27). *How to rent your first apartment: apartment guide and checklist*. Apartment List. https://www.apartmentlist.com/renter-life/first-time-renter-apartment-guide-checklist

Businessman with an affliction quotes by Anas Hamshari. (n.d.). Www.goodreads.com. https://www.goodreads.com/work/quotes/85599385-businessman-with-an-affliction

CDC. (2017). *CDC - How much sleep do I need? - sleep and sleep disorders*. CDC. https://www.cdc.gov/sleep/about_sleep/how_much_sleep.html

CDC. (2021a, March 1). *Healthy eating tips*. CDC. https://www.cdc.gov/nccdphp/dnpao/features/healthy-eating-tips/index.html

CDC. (2021b, May 16). *Benefits of healthy eating*. CDC; U.S. Department of Health & Human Services. https://www.cdc.gov/nutrition/resources-publications/benefits-of-healthy-eating.html

CDC. (2022a, June 2). *How much physical activity do adults need?* CDC. https://www.cdc.gov/physicalactivity/basics/adults/index.htm

CDC. (2022b, September 13). *Sleep hygiene tips - sleep and sleep disorders*. CDC. https://www.cdc.gov/sleep/about_sleep/sleep_hygiene.html

Chen, J. (2020, April 9). *Lease definition and complete guide to renting*. Investopedia. https://www.investopedia.com/terms/l/lease.asp

Clear, J. (2014, January 23). *The marshmallow experiment and the power of delayed gratification*. James Clear. https://jamesclear.com/delayed-gratification

Collins, C. (2020, April 21). *The importance of self confidence for your success*. Mom's Got Money. https://www.momsgotmoney.com/the-importance-of-self-confidence/

Compound interest calculator. (n.d.). Www.investor.gov. https://www.investor.gov/financial-tools-calculators/calculators/compound-interest-calculator

Cuncic, A. (2022, November 9). *How to practice active listening*. Verywell Mind. https://www.verywellmind.com/what-is-active-listening-3024343

Davenport, B. (2020, May 31). *21 examples of healthy boundaries in relationships*. Live Bold and Bloom. https://liveboldandbloom.com/05/relationships/healthy-boundaries-in-relationships

Davis, T. (2018, December 28). *Self-care: 12 ways to take better care of yourself*. Psychology Today. https://www.psychologytoday.com/us/blog/click-here-happiness/201812/self-care-12-ways-take-better-care-yourself

DeNicola, L. (2023, January 11). *Miss a credit card payment? Here's what you can do*. Intuit Credit Karma. https://www.creditkarma.com/credit-cards/i/what-happens-if-you-miss-a-credit-card-payment

Dieker, N. (2022, January 18). *What credit score do you start with*? Bankrate. https://www.bankrate.com/personal-finance/credit/what-credit-score-do-you-start-with/

Do other countries have credit scores? (n.d.). Chase. https://www.chase.com/personal/credit-cards/education/credit-score/do-other-countries-have-credit-scores

Dweck, C. (2016, January 13). *What having a "growth mindset" actually means*. Harvard Business Review. https://hbr.org/2016/01/what-having-a-growth-mindset-actually-means

Feuerman, M. (2017, November 9). *Managing vs. resolving conflict in relationships: The blueprints for success*. The Gottman Institute. https://www.gottman.com/blog/managing-vs-resolving-conflict-relationships-blueprints-success/

Field, B. (2022, November 16). *7 surprising ways to make your relationship even better*. Verywell Mind. https://www.verywellmind.com/7-surprising-ways-to-make-your-relationship-better-5094212

Folger, J. (2022, December 10). *Tips for successful retirement investing*. Investopedia. https://www.investopedia.com/articles/personal-finance/111313/six-critical-rules-successful-retirement-investing.asp

Fontinelle, A. (2018). *8 financial tips for young adults*. Investopedia. https://www.investopedia.com/articles/younginvestors/08/eight-tips.asp

Fontinelle, A. (2021, May 17). *10 reasons to use your credit card*. Investopedia. https://www.investopedia.com/articles/pf/10/credit-card-debit-card.asp

Food for teenagers: meal plan on the cheap! (2021, January 18). Shelf Cooking. https://shelfcooking.com/food-for-teenagers/

Freer, J. (2022, July 1). *Apartment maintenance - what is it and who is responsible for it*? ApartmentAdvisor. https://www.apartmentadvisor.com/blog/post/apartment-maintenance-what-is-it-and-who-is-responsible-for-it

Georgiev, D. (2023, February 28). *How much time do people spend on social media in 2023*? Tech Jury. https://techjury.net/blog/time-spent-on-social-media/#gref

Glowiak, M. (2020, April 14). *What is self-care and why is it important for you*? SNHU. https://www.snhu.edu/about-us/newsroom/health/what-is-self-care

Gomstyn, A. (2019). *Food for your mood: how what you eat affects your mental health*. Aetna. https://www.aetna.com/health-guide/food-affects-mental-health.html

Gould, W. R. (2021, November 9). *10 red flags in relationships*. Verywell Mind. https://www.verywellmind.com/10-red-flags-in-relationships-5194592

Gupta, S. (2021, December 27). *How to build trust in a relationship*. Verywell Mind. https://www.verywellmind.com/how-to-build-trust-in-a-relationship-5207611

Harvard School of Public Health. (2019, June 3). *Potassium*. The Nutrition Source. https://www.hsph.harvard.edu/nutritionsource/potassium/

Health care for young adults findings and recommendations from the report investing in the health and well-being of young adults. (n.d.). https://nap.nationalacademies.org/resource/18869/YAs_Health_Care_brief.pdf

Healthwise Staff. (2022, February 9). *Time management for teens: care instructions*. Myhealth.alberta.ca. https://myhealth.alberta.ca/Health/aftercareinformation/pages/conditions.aspx?hwid=ug6046

Healthy boundaries for teens. (n.d.). Crime Victim Center of Erie County. Retrieved May 13, 2023, from https://cvcerie.org/healthy-boundaries-for-teens/

Hill, L. (2021, April 22). *Breakfast: is it the most important meal*? WebMD. https://www.webmd.com/food-recipes/breakfast-lose-weight

Holly. (2020, July 23). *Creating a house cleaning schedule that works*. Simplify Create Inspire. https://www.simplifycreateinspire.com/daily-weekly-monthly-cleaning-schedule/

How are FICO scores calculated?. (2018, October 19). MyFICO. https://www.myfico.com/credit-education/whats-in-your-credit-score#:~:text=FICO%20Scores%20are%20calculated%20using

How health insurance works. (2020, April 13). Blue Cross NC. https://www.bluecrossnc.com/understanding-health-insurance/how-health-insurance-works

How to change a home air filter. (n.d.). The Home Depot. https://www.homedepot.com/c/ah/how-to-change-a-home-air-filter/9ba683603be9fa5395fab906a15a05f

How to clean the inside of your washer and dryer. (n.d.). Www.appliancewhse.com. https://www.appliancewhse.com/Content.aspx?ID=25

How to improve communication skills in your relationship. (n.d.). The Jed Foundation. https://jedfoundation.org/resource/how-to-improve-communication-skills-in-your-relationship/

How to make a meal plan. (n.d.). Safefood. https://www.safefood.net/how-to/meal-plan

How to understand your costs and key health insurance terms. (2018, March 8). HealthCare.gov. https://www.healthcare.gov/blog/understand-health-insurance-definitions/

How to use a plumbing snake and when it's necessary. (2021, September 28). WM Buffington Company. https://wmbuffingtoncompany.com/blog/plumbing/when-and-how-to-use-drain-snake/

In and Out Express Care. (2019, March 3). *Top 9 reasons to go to urgent care - common urgent care complaints.* In and out Express Care. https://inandoutexpresscare.com/top-9-reasons-for-an-urgent-care-visit/

Keech, D. (2022, October 31). *15 home maintenance tasks and repairs everyone should know how to do.* Military by Owner. https://blog.militarybyowner.com/15-home-maintenance-tasks-and-repairs-everyone-should-know-how-to-do

Kellogg, K. (2021, February 10). *How to clean a dishwasher (quickly!).* Architectural Digest. https://www.architecturaldigest.com/story/how-to-clean-a-dishwasher-with-vinegar

Kilkus, J. (2022, March 27). *Is the mind-body connection real?* Psychology Today. https://www.psychologytoday.com/us/blog/navigating-cancer/202203/is-the-mind-body-connection-real

Lake, R. (2023, April 28). *How do credit cards work?* Investopedia. https://www.investopedia.com/how-do-credit-cards-work-5025119

Lawler, M. (2022, August 26). *How to start a self-care routine you'll follow.* EverydayHealth. https://www.everydayhealth.com/self-care/start-a-self-care-routine/

Lawler, M. (2023, March 17). *What is self-care, and why is it so important for your health?* Everyday Health. https://www.everydayhealth.com/self-care/

Lyons, M. (2021, December 9). *How to ground yourself: 14 techniques you need to try.* Www.betterup.com. https://www.betterup.com/blog/how-to-ground-yourself

Making an appointment. (2014, August 21). HealthCare.gov. https://www.healthcare.gov/blog/making-an-appointment/

Manolas, K. (2022, October 25). *Rental scams: how to spot them & what to do.* Avail. https://www.avail.co/education/guides/a-tenants-guide-to-finding-an-apartment/how-to-spot-a-rental-scam

McQuitty Hindmarsh, L. (2023, March 1). *20+ freezer essentials for a well stocked freezer.* Mums Make Lists. https://www.mumsmakelists.com/freezer-essentials/

Medcalf, A. (2022, August 2). *How to be honest and build trust in a relationship.* Abby Medcalf. https://abbymedcalf.com/how-to-be-honest-and-build-trust-in-a-relationship-2/

National Institute of Mental Health. (2021). *Caring for your mental health.* National Institute of Mental Health. https://www.nimh.nih.gov/health/topics/caring-for-your-mental-health

O'Shea, B. (2022, August 30). *What is a good credit score?* NerdWallet. https://www.nerdwallet.com/article/finance/what-is-a-good-credit-score

Pant, P. (n.d.). *How much should I save? 50 30 20 Rule.* TIAA. https://www.tiaa.org/public/learn/personal-finance-101/how-much-of-my-income-should-i-save-every-month

Parker-Pope, T. (2019). *How to have a better relationship.* The New York Times. https://www.nytimes.com/guides/well/how-to-have-a-better-relationship

Parrish, M. (2022, May 13). *How to help students develop a growth mindset.* Good Grief. https://good-grief.org/ways-to-develop-a-growth-mindset/

Peddicord, K. (2020, October 2). *12 rules for renting a home oversees.* U.S. News & World Report. https://money.usnews.com/money/retirement/baby-boomers/articles/rules-for-renting-a-home-overseas

Petersen, L. (2019, January 24). *Strengths of compromise as a conflict resolution.* Chron. https://smallbusiness.chron.com/strengths-compromise-conflict-resolution-10502.html

A quote by Eleanor Brown. (n.d.). Www.goodreads.com. Retrieved May 13, 2023, from https://www.goodreads.com/quotes/9752464-self-care-is-not-selfish-you-cannot-serve-from-an-empty

A quote from Nineteen Minutes. (n.d.). Www.goodreads.com. Retrieved May 13, 2023, from https://www.goodreads.com/quotes/75688-everyone-thinks-you-make-mistakes-when-you-re-young-but-i

Ramsey Solutions. (2023, March 15). *How to save money: 22 simple tips.* Ramsey Solutions. https://www.ramseysolutions.com/budgeting/the-secret-to-saving-money

Robinson, L., Segal, J., & Smith, M. (2019). *Effective communication*. Help Guide. https://www.helpguide.org/articles/relationships-communication/effective-communication.htm

Rose, G. (2023, April 6). *Buying life insurance as an investment*. NerdWallet. https://www.nerdwallet.com/article/insurance/life-insurance-as-an-investment

Rosen, T. (2021, January 22). *Tips for going to the doctor by yourself as a college student*. Bwog - Columbia Student News. https://bwog.com/2021/01/tips-for-going-to-the-doctor-by-yourself-as-a-college-student/

Rudd, L. (2017, April 12). *How to change a light bulb. Living - Your Home, DIY and Life*. HomeServe. https://www.homeserve.com/uk/living/how-to/how-to-change-a-light-bulb/

Ryan, A. (2020, May 28). *Tips for your young adult and their 1st apartment*. Simply Family Magazine. https://simplyfamilymagazine.com/tips-for-your-young-adult-and-their-1st-apartment

Saraev, N. (2022, May 19). *The top 10 most common time wasters & how to avoid them*. Day.io. https://day.io/blog/the-top-10-most-common-time-wasters-how-to-avoid-them/

Saving and investing for your future. (2022). University of Minnesota Extension. https://extension.umn.edu/personal-finances/saving-and-investing-your-future

Security deposit laws by state. (n.d.). Rocket Lawyer. Retrieved May 13, 2023, from https://www.rocketlawyer.com/real-estate/landlords/property-management/legal-guide/security-deposit-laws-by-state

Segal, J., Robinson, L., & Smith, M. (2019, March 21). *Conflict resolution skills*. HelpGuide. https://www.helpguide.org/articles/relationships-communication/conflict-resolution-skills.htm

17 relationship communication quotes every couple will love. (2021, February 16). The Healthy. https://www.thehealthy.com/family/relationships/relationship-communication-quotes/

Sharp Emerson, M. (2021, August 30). *Eight things you can do to improve your communication skills*. Professional Development | Harvard DCE. https://professional.dce.harvard.edu/blog/eight-things-you-can-do-to-improve-your-communication-skills/

Sheldon, R., & Wigmore, I. (2022, September). *What is pomodoro technique?*. WhatIs.com. https://www.techtarget.com/whatis/definition/pomodoro-technique

Sheppard, S. (2021, October 25). *How to build a respectful relationship*. Verywell Mind. https://www.verywellmind.com/respect-is-vital-to-building-a-healthy-relationship-5206110

Simeon, D. (2014, March 6). *Want your teen to be more organized? 10 ideas that actually work*. Your Teen Magazine. https://yourteenmag.com/teenager-school/teenager-middle-school/help-your-teenager-get-organized

Soukup, R. (2020, July 7). *How to stock your first kitchen*. Living Well Spending Less®. https://www.livingwellspendingless.com/how-to-stock-your-first-kitchen/

Srinivasan, H., & 2021. (2022, October 21). *When to use a debit card—and when to use a credit card instead*. Real Simple. https://www.realsimple.com/work-life/money/debit-vs-credit-card

Stickley, A. (2022, September 28). *The most effective ways to clean a garbage disposal*. The Spruce. https://www.thespruce.com/cleaning-a-garbage-disposal-2718863

Stretch your protein budget — nourish and exercise your body. (n.d.). Www.ag.ndsu.edu. Retrieved May 13, 2023, from https://www.ag.ndsu.edu/nourishyourbody/stretch-your-protein-budget

The importance of investing early and often. (n.d.). Associated Bank. https://www.associatedbank.com/resource-center/saving/investing-early-and-often

20 biggest time wasters for college students – college girl smarts. (2020, December 9). College Girl Smarts. https://www.collegegirlsmarts.com/biggest-time-wasters-for-college-students/

Types of abuse. (n.d.). The Hotline. https://www.thehotline.org/resources/types-of-abuse/

Vega, M. (2022, March 23). *Do you need an apartment co-signer? Apartment Living Tips*. ApartmentGuide.com. https://www.apartmentguide.com/blog/do-you-need-an-apartment-co-signer/

Wallender, L. (2022, June 17). *How to unclog any drain*. The Spruce. https://www.thespruce.com/how-to-unclog-a-drain-2718779

Washington state's mandatory auto/motorcycle insurance law. (n.d.). Office of the Insurance Commissioner Washington State. https://www.insurance.wa.gov/washington-states-mandatory-automotorcycle-insurance-law

Wells Fargo. (2022). *Why invest?* Wells Fargo. https://www.wellsfargo.com/goals-investing/why-invest/

What is a credit score? (2020, September 1). Consumer Financial Protection Bureau. https://www.consumerfinance.gov/ask-cfpb/what-is-a-credit-score-en-315/

What is renters insurance and what does it cover?. (2021, October). Allstate. https://www.allstate.com/resources/renters-insurance/what-does-renters-insurance-cover

Williams, R. (2019, March 28). *10 spiritual self-care tips to be happy.* Chopra. https://chopra.com/articles/10-spiritual-self-care-tips-to-be-happy

Wooll, M. (2022, January 11). *Why face-to-face communication matters (even with remote work).* BetterUp. https://www.betterup.com/blog/face-to-face-communication

Money Skills for Teens

Allinson, M. (2023, January 18). *Why is money important in our lives? Robotics & Automation* News. https://roboticsandautomationnews.com/2023/01/18/why-is-money-important-in-our-lives/59144/

Bank of America. (2019). *Creating a budget with a personal budget spreadsheet. Better Money Habits.* https://bettermoneyhabits.bankofamerica.com/en/saving-budgeting/creating-a-budget

Bell, A. (2022, April 7). *What are the 5 purposes of budgeting?* Investopedia. https://www.investopedia.com/financial-edge/1109/6-reasons-why-you-need-a-budget.aspx#:~:text=Having%20a%20budget%20keeps%20your

Blinka, D. (2023, February 2). *How to calculate and compare unit prices at the store.* WikiHow. https://www.wikihow.com/Calculate-and-Compare-Unit-Prices-at-the-Store

Bowling, L. (2019, February 22). *How much should i spend on clothing?* Financial Best Life. https://financialbestlife.com/how-much-should-i-spend-on-clothing/

Braverman, B. (2022, May 10). *Big purchases need major planning. here's where to start* | CNN business. CNN. https://edition.cnn.com/2022/05/10/success/save-for-a-big-purchase/index.html

Drury, P. (2022, January 25). *25+ jobs for teens (with job search advice).* Resume.io. https://resume.io/blog/jobs-for-teens

FarmWell. (n.d.). Financial wellbeing: *Developing a healthy money mindset.* FarmWell. https://farmwell.org.uk/wp-content/uploads/sites/2/2022/03/Financial-Wellbeing-Developing-a-Healthy-Money-Mindset.pdf

Fernando, J. (2023, March 9). *Bond: Financial meaning with examples and how they are priced.* Investopedia. https://www.investopedia.com/terms/b/bond.asp

Frankenfield, J. (2019). *Online banking.* Investopedia. https://www.investopedia.com/terms/o/onlinebanking.asp

Ganatra, M. (2022, September 27). *How to analyze your options before buying an insurance policy.* Forbes Advisor INDIA. https://www.forbes.com/advisor/in/life-insurance/how-to-analyze-your-options-before-buying-an-insurance-policy/

Gongala, S. (2014, July 25). *21 essential life skills for teens to learn.* MomJunction; MomJunction. https://www.momjunction.com/articles/everyday-life-skills-your-teen-should-learn_0081859/

HappyBank. (n.d.). *Financial tips: Six steps to creating a positive money mindset.* Happy State Bank. https://www.happybank.com/resources/six-steps-to-creating-a-positive-money-mindset

Hasty, A. (2023, April 5). *Bank accounts for teens. Compare the Market.* https://www.comparethemarket.com/current-accounts/content/kids-teens-current-accounts/

Hayes, A. (2020, October 3). *Mutual fund.* Investopedia. https://www.investopedia.com/terms/m/mutualfund.asp

Hayes, A. (2022, July 6). Stock. Investopedia. https://www.investopedia.com/terms/s/stock.asp

Jordan, T. (2019, January 14). *The 7 best budgeting methods.* Atypical Finance. https://www.atypicalfinance.com/7-best-budgeting-methods/

Kagan, J. (2023, April 4). *What is an ATM and how does it work?* Investopedia. https://www.investopedia.com/terms/a/atm.asp#:~:text=To%20use%20an%20ATM%2C%20you

Lahunou, I. (2022, June 14). *How to shop smart: 30 ways to make smarter decisions.* Monetha. https://www.monetha.io/blog/rewards/how-to-shop-smart/

Lake, R. (2020, February 4). *How to protect your online banking information.* Forbes Advisor. https://www.forbes.com/advisor/banking/how-to-protect-your-online-banking-information/

Lake, R. (2021, April 9). *What are the different types of bank accounts?* Forbes Advisor. https://www.forbes.com/advisor/banking/what-are-the-different-types-of-bank-accounts/

Langager, C. (2022, August 23). *A beginner's guide to stock investing.* Investopedia. https://www.investopedia.com/articles/basics/06/invest1000.asp

PSECU. (2020, June 5). *How to make good purchasing decisions.* Blog.psecu. https://blog.psecu.com/learn/financial-tips-for-every-stage-in-life/2020/06/05/how-to-make-good-purchasing-decisions

Resnick, N. (2017, July 25). *The 6 best jobs for teenage entrepreneurs.* Entrepreneur. https://www.entrepreneur.com/starting-a-business/the-6-best-jobs-for-teenage-entrepreneurs/296365

Step Change Team. (n.d.). *Credit card debt. what to do if you can't pay*. stepchange. Www.stepchange.org. https://www.stepchange.org/debt-info/credit-card-debt.aspx

Waugh, E. (2022, January 31). *Why is credit important? - experian*. Www.experian.com. https://www.experian.com/blogs/ask-experian/why-is-credit-important/

Which Team. (2023, May 16). *17 ways to save money on your household bills and living costs in 2023* - which? News. Which? https://www.which.co.uk/news/article/how-to-save-money-on-your-household-bills-aiTGN6b5jZ2N

Wu, A. (2023, May 2). *How to compare prices online (with pictures)* - wikiHow life. Www.wikihow.life. https://www.wikihow.life/Compare-Prices-Online

Social Skills for Teens

A Little Dose Of Happy. (2022, August 15). *9 Tips for cultivating relationships that last - a little dose of happy*. Aldohappy. https://aldohappy.com/cultivating-relationships

Abrahamsen, S. (2019, August 28). *5 Easy ways to track your personal growth*. Little Coffee Fox. https://littlecoffeefox.com/track-your-personal-growth/

Allen, R. (2011, April 1). *How to challenge your beliefs*. https://www.rogerkallen.com/how-to-challenge-your-beliefs/

Angel, D. (2016, December 28). *The four types of conversations: Debate, dialogue, discourse, and diatribe*. https://davidwangel.com/the-opportune-conflict/2016/12/28/the-four-types-of-conversations-debate-dialogue-discourse-and-diatribe

AZ Quotes. (n.d.). *Top 25 first impression quotes (of 109)*. Retrieved July 4, 2023, from https://www.azquotes.com/quotes/topics/first-impression.html#:~:text=You%20never%20get%20a%20second%20chance%20to%20make%20a%20first%20impression.&text=You%20only%20have%20one%20first

Baller, E. (2016, May 27). *10 Ways to cultivate a positive mindset and change your life*. Tiny Buddha. https://tinybuddha.com/blog/10-ways-cultivate-positive-mindset-change-life/

Barclays Life Skills. (n.d.). *What are your strengths? - 5 ways to find out*. https://barclayslifeskills.com/i-want-to-choose-my-next-step/school/5-ways-to-find-out-what-you-re-good-at/

Barrier, J. (n.d.). *8 Strategies for meaningful conversations - improve your skills*. Preach It, Teach It. Retrieved July 6, 2023, from https://preachitteachit.org/articles/detail/eight-simple-strategies-to-have-meaningful-conversations/

Baulch, J. (2016, September 5). *Thought challenging when negative*. Inner Melbourne Psychology. https://www.innermelbpsychology.com.au/thought-challenging/#:~:text=Break%20your%20thoughts%20down%20into

Carnahan, L. (2022, June 2). *How to hold a conversation and build deeper connections*. Vector Marketing. https://www.thevectorimpact.com/how-to-hold-a-conversation/

Cherry, K. (2017). *Understanding body language and facial expressions*. Verywell Mind. https://www.verywellmind.com/understand-body-language-and-facial-expressions-4147228

Cherry, K. (2022, November 8). *How our brain neurons can change over time from life's experience*. Verywell Mind. https://www.verywellmind.com/what-is-brain-plasticity-2794886

Cherry, K. (2023a, February 22). *What are the 9 types of nonverbal communication?* Verywell Mind. https://www.verywellmind.com/types-of-nonverbal-communication-2795397#:~:text=Nonverbal%20communication%20means%20conveying%20information

Cherry, K. (2023b, March 10). *What is self-awareness?* Verywell Mind. https://www.verywellmind.com/what-is-self-awareness-2795023

Cuncic, A. (2019). *Things to start doing if you have social anxiety disorder*. Verywell Mind. https://www.verywellmind.com/social-anxiety-disorder-tips-3024209

Cuncic, A. (2023, February 15). *10 Best and worst small talk topics*. Verywell Mind. https://www.verywellmind.com/small-talk-topics-3024421

Davenport, B. (2022, July 1). *75 Confidence-boosting positive affirmations for teens*. Live Bold and Bloom. https://liveboldandbloom.com/07/mindfulness/positive-affirmations-teens

Davis, T. (2019, April 11). *15 Ways to build a growth mindset*. Psychology Today. https://www.psychologytoday.com/za/blog/click-here-happiness/201904/15-ways-build-growth-mindset

Drillinger, M. (2020, February 25). *6 Ways to make friends when you have social anxiety*. Healthline. https://www.healthline.com/health/anxiety/how-to-make-friends-when-you-have-social-anxiety#2.-Fight

Eatough, E. (2022, January 12). *25 Toxic personality traits to spot in yourself and others.* Betterup. https://www.betterup.com/blog/toxic-traits

Eisler, M. (2019, April 19). *15 Ways to declutter your mind.* The Chopra Center. https://chopra.com/articles/15-ways-to-declutter-your-mind

Elcomblus. (2020, December 18). *Elements of verbal communication.* https://www.elcomblus.com/elements-of-verbal-communication/

Gordon, J. P. (2019, November 7). *Low self-esteem and social anxiety.* Counselling Directory. https://www.counselling-directory.org.uk/memberarticles/low-self-esteem-and-social-anxiety#:~:text=This%20very%20low%20self%2Desteem

Gupta, S. (2022, September 14). *What is self-acceptance?* Verywell Mind. https://www.verywellmind.com/self-acceptance-characteristics-importance-and-tips-for-improvement-6544468

Hailey, L. (2022, November 9). *15 Effective ways to connect with absolutely anyone, anytime.* Science of People. https://www.scienceofpeople.com/how-to-connect-with-others/#:~:text=A%20struggle%20to%20connect%20could

Holland, K. (2018). *Positive self-talk: Benefits and techniques.* Healthline. https://www.healthline.com/health/positive-self-talk

Hull, R. H. (2016). *The art of nonverbal communication in practice.* The Hearing Journal, 69(5), 22. https://doi.org/10.1097/01.hj.0000483270.59643.cc

Incledon, N. (2018, April 11). *How low self-esteem affects relationships.* Peacefulmind.com.au. https://peacefulmind.com.au/2018/04/11/how-low-self-esteem-affects-relationships/#:~:text=Low%20self%2Desteem%20can%20give

Kentucky Counselling Center. (2021, May 14). *How to build mental resilience.* https://kentuckycounselingcenter.com/how-to-build-mental-resilience/

Kottke, J. (2018, May 17). *The respect of personhood vs the respect of authority.* https://kottke.org/18/05/the-respect-of-personhood-vs-the-respect-of-authority

Kropf, J. (2023, May 15). *50 Easy ways to get out of your comfort zone.* Healthy Happy Impactful. https://healthyhappyimpactful.com/ways-get-out-comfort-zone-quotes/

Lawler, M. (2022, August 26). *How to start a self-care routine you'll follow.* Everyday Health. https://www.everydayhealth.com/self-care/start-a-self-care-routine/

Liles, M. (2021, February 21). *101 Uplifting confidence quotes for days you're struggling with low self-esteem.* Parade. https://parade.com/989608/marynliles/confidence-quotes/

Lindberg, S. (2020, November 26). *Self-Improvement goal setting tips.* Verywell Mind. https://www.verywellmind.com/tips-for-goal-setting-self-improvement-4688587

Lumen Learning. (n.d.). *Effective communication.* Lumen Learning.com. Retrieved July 7, 2023, from https://courses.lumenlearning.com/suny-monroecc-hed110/chapter/communication/

Manson, M. (2019, April 11). *5 Skills to help you develop emotional intelligence.* https://markmanson.net/emotional-intelligence

Matthews, D. (2020, January 9). *How to identify your limiting beliefs and get over them.* Lifehack. https://www.lifehack.org/858652/limiting-beliefs

Mayo Clinic. (2020, April 22). *A beginner's guide to meditation.* https://www.mayoclinic.org/tests-procedures/meditation/in-depth/meditation/art-20045858#:~:text=%22Meditation%2C%20which%20is%20the%20practice

Melinda. (2019, June 3). Social anxiety disorder. Help Guide. https://www.helpguide.org/articles/anxiety/social-anxiety-disorder.htm

Merabet, L. B., & Pascual-Leone, A. (2009). *Neural reorganization following sensory loss: The opportunity of change.* Nature Reviews Neuroscience, 11(1), 44–52. https://doi.org/10.1038/nrn2758

Merriam-Webster. (n.d.). *Definition of respect.* https://www.merriam-webster.com/dictionary/respect#:~:text=%3A%20high%20or%20special%20regard%20%3A%20esteem

Merriam-Webster. (2020). *Definition of self-confidence.* https://www.merriam-webster.com/dictionary/self-confidence

Mindtools. (n.d.). *Empathy at work.* https://www.mindtools.com/agz0gft/empathy-at-work

Morin, A. (2022, July 28). *5 Ways to start boosting your self-confidence today.* Verywell Mind. https://www.verywellmind.com/how-to-boost-your-self-confidence-4163098

Nemours Kids Health. (n.d.). *5 Ways to (respectfully) disagree (for teens).* Kids Health. https://kidshealth.org/en/teens/tips-disagree.html

Nguyen, S. O. (2023, January 31). *88 Daily journal prompts on life, love, and gratitude*. Parade: Entertainment, Recipes, Health, Life, Holidays. https://parade.com/1308069/steph-nguyen/journaling-prompts/

NHS. (2021, February 1). *Raising low self-esteem*. https://www.nhs.uk/mental-health/self-help/tips-and-support/raise-low-self-esteem/

Nigam, D. (2023, April 13). *Elements of verbal and non verbal communication*. https://www.linkedin.com/pulse/elements-verbal-non-communication-divakar-nigam

Perry, E. (2022, June 7). *20 Personal values examples to help you find your own*. Better Up. https://www.betterup.com/blog/personal-values-examples

Perry, E. (2023, March 14). *How to build confidence: A guide to doing it right*. Better Up. https://www.betterup.com/blog/how-to-build-confidence

Peterson, T. J. (2022, March 25). *What is self-confidence?* Healthy Place. https://www.healthyplace.com/self-help/self-confidence/what-is-self-confidence

Pollack, J. (2021, April 19). *Tip #7: Challenge your beliefs*. Pollack Peace Building. https://pollackpeacebuilding.com/blog/tip-7-challenge-your-beliefs/

Portland Community College. (2020, March 11). *What are the five conflict resolution strategies?* Climb. https://climb.pcc.edu/blog/what-are-the-five-conflict-resolution-strategies#:~:text=Identify%20specific%20points%20of%20disagreement

Price, C. (2018, January 8). *Strengthening your teen's social and conversation abilities*. Hey Sigmund. https://www.heysigmund.com/strengthening-teens-social-conversation-abilities/

Pyramid Psychology. (2021, June 14). *4 Conversation tips for teens: Getting past the shy*. https://pyramidpsychology.com/how-to-get-past-the-shy-4-conversation-tips-for-teens/

Quizzclub. (2017, April 7). *"You never get a second chance to make a first impression" was an ad slogan for which company?* https://quizzclub.com/trivia/you-never-get-a-second-chance-to-make-a-first-impression-was-an-ad-slogan-for-which-company/answer/152271/

Rao, S. T. S., Asha, M. R., Rao, J. K. S., & Vasudevaraju, P. (2009). The biochemistry of belief. *Indian Journal of Psychiatry, 51*(4), 239. https://doi.org/10.4103/0019-5545.58285

Ratey, J. J. (2019, October 24). *Can exercise help treat anxiety?* Harvard Health Blog. https://www.health.harvard.edu/blog/can-exercise-help-treat-anxiety-2019102418096#:~:text=How%20does%20exercise%20help%20ease

Raypole, C. (2019, February 25). *How systematic desensitization can help you overcome fear*. Healthline Media. https://www.healthline.com/health/systematic-desensitization

Raypole, C. (2020, February 27). *Self-Actualization: What it is and how to achieve it*. Healthline. https://www.healthline.com/health/self-actualization

Reach Out. (2019). *Self-esteem and teenagers*. https://parents.au.reachout.com/common-concerns/everyday-issues/self-esteem-and-teenagers

Reynolds, N. (2020, October 12). *10 Important social skills you need to teach your teen now*. Raising Teens Today. https://raisingteenstoday.com/10-important-social-skills-you-need-to-teach-your-teen-now/

Sander, V. (2021, August 18). *How to improve your social skills - the complete guide*. SocialSelf. https://socialself.com/blog/improve-social-skills/

Sander, V. (2023, January 4). *16 Ways to respond when someone is disrespectful to you*. SocialSelf. https://socialself.com/blog/someone-disrespectful/

Schultz, K. (n.d.). *Self-Image: Definition, issues, & tips*. The Berkeley Well-Being Institute. https://www.berkeleywellbeing.com/self-image.html

Segal, J., Robinson, L., & Smith, M. (2019, March 21). *Conflict resolution skills*. Help Guide. https://www.helpguide.org/articles/relationships-communication/conflict-resolution-skills.htm

Segal, J., Smith, M., Robinson, L., & Shubin, J. (2020, October). *Improving emotional intelligence*. Help Guide. https://www.helpguide.org/articles/mental-health/emotional-intelligence-eq.htm#:~:text=Emotional%20intelligence%20(otherwise%20known%20as

Shah, M. (2022, January 8). *Challenges are what make life interesting and overcoming them is what makes life meaningful*. Set Quotes. https://www.setquotes.com/challenges-are-what-make-life-interesting/

Skills You Need. (2011). *What are social skills?* https://www.skillsyouneed.com/ips/social-skills.html

Smith, J. (2020, September 25). *Growth vs fixed mindset: How what you think affects what you achieve*. Mindset Health. https://www.mindsethealth.com/matter/growth-vs-fixed-mindset

Smith, S. (2018, April 10). *5-4-3-2-1 Coping technique for anxiety*. University of Rochester Medical Center. https://www.urmc.rochester.edu/behavioral-health-partners/bhp-blog/april-2018/5-4-3-2-1-coping-technique-for-anxiety.aspx

Social Skill Center. (2021, February 19). *The difference between verbal and nonverbal communication.* https://socialskillscenter.com/the-difference-between-verbal-and-nonverbal-communication/#:~:text=There%20are%20two%20primary%20forms

Sonder Wellness. (2022, August 22). *Healthy friendships: 6 Key ingredients.* https://www.sonderwellness.com/blog/2022/08/22/healthy-friendships/

Stenvinkel, M. (2016, October 3). *13 Things to do instead of comparing yourself to others.* Tiny Buddha. https://tinybuddha.com/blog/13-things-instead-comparing-others/

Suni, E., & Dimitriu, A. (2020, September 18). *Anxiety and sleep.* Sleep Foundation. https://www.sleepfoundation.org/mental-health/anxiety-and-sleep#:~:text=Sleep%20deprivation%20can%20worsen%20anxiety

This Way Up. (n.d.). *How to deal with social anxiety.* https://thiswayup.org.au/learning-hub/social-anxiety-explained/

University of Texas. (2020, November 3). *How much of communication is nonverbal?* https://online.utpb.edu/about-us/articles/communication/how-much-of-communication-is-nonverbal/#:~:text=It%20was%20Albert%20Mehrabian%2C%20a

Voss, P., Thomas, M. E., Cisneros-Franco, J. M., & de Villers-Sidani, É. (2017). Dynamic brains and the changing rules of neuroplasticity: Implications for learning and recovery. *Frontiers in Psychology, 8*(1657). https://doi.org/10.3389/fpsyg.2017.01657

Wallis, L. J., Virányi, Z., Müller, C. A., Serisier, S., Huber, L., & Range, F. (2016). Aging effects on discrimination learning, logical reasoning and memory in pet dogs. *AGE, 38*(1). https://doi.org/10.1007/s11357-015-9866-x

Warley, S. (n.d.). *How to practice self-awareness.* Life Skills That Matter. https://lifeskillsthatmatter.com/podcast/how-to-practice-self-awareness/

Waters, S. (2021, November 15). *How to carry a conversation — the art of making connections.* Www.betterup.com. https://www.betterup.com/blog/how-to-carry-a-conversation

Westside DBT. (n.d.). *The neuroscience of change—or how to reset your brain.* Retrieved June 28, 2023, from https://westsidedbt.com/the-neuroscience-of-change-or-how-to-reset-your-brain/

Yeager, D. S., Hanselman, P., Walton, G. M., Murray, J. S., Crosnoe, R., Muller, C., Tipton, E., Schneider, B., Hulleman, C. S., Hinojosa, C. P., Paunesku, D., Romero, C., Flint, K., Roberts, A., Trott, J., Iachan, R., Buontempo, J., Yang, S. M., Carvalho, C. M., & Hahn, P. R. (2019). A national experiment reveals where a growth mindset improves achievement. *Nature, 573*(573). https://doi.org/10.1038/s41586-019-1466-

Career Planning for Teens

Boys & Girls Clubs of America. (2022, January 19). The Importance of Goal Setting for Teens. Great Futures. https://www.greatfutures.club/the-importance-of-goal-setting-for-teens/

Carlsson, A. (2023, June 16). Embracing Continuous Professional Development: Unlocking Career Growth and Success. LinkedIn. https://www.linkedin.com/pulse/embracing-continuous-professional-development-career-growth-carlsson/

Columbia University. Connecting Your Self-Knowledge to Career Options. Columbia University Center For Career Education. https://www.careereducation.columbia.edu/resources/connecting-your-self-knowledge-career-options

Columbia University. What to Know Before You Go: Researching Organizations. Columbia University Center For Career Education. https://www.careereducation.columbia.edu/resources/what-know-you-go-researching-organizations

Corhn, D. (2022, June 28). 5 Tips For Helping Teens Plan Ahead For A Sizzling Future Learning Coach Success. Connections Academy by Pearson. https://www.connectionsacademy.com/support/resources/article/5-tips-for-helping-teens-plan-ahead-for-a-sizzling-future/

Crown copyright Province of Nova Scotia (2012, branding update 2015). Guide to Career Planning With Your Teenager, Explore Careers Nova Scotia. https://explorecareers.novascotia.ca/sites/default/files/2018-06/16-44875%20Post-Secondary%20Guide%20Teenager%20English%20SPREADS%20FINAL-s_1.pdf

D'Monte, A. (2023, February 16). How Industry Mentors & Role Models Impact High School Students. LinkedIn. https://www.linkedin.com/pulse/how-industry-mentors-role-models-impact-high-school-students-d-monte/

Dr. Akos, P. (2020). STARTING EARLY: Career Development in the Early Grades Association for Career and Technical Education. School of Education, University of North Carolina at Chapel Hill. https://files.eric.ed.gov/fulltext/ED610366.pdf

Feder, M. (2022, August 26). 5 Steps to Making a Financial Plan for Your Education. University of Phoenix. https://www.phoenix.edu/blog/5-steps-to-making-a-financial-plan-for-your-education.html

Government of Alberta. (2023). Career Paths and Your Lifestyle. Alberta Alis, maintained by Alberta Seniors, Community and Social Services. https://alis.alberta.ca/look-for-work/career-paths-and-your-lifestyle/

INSIGHT REPORT MAY (2023, April 30). Future of Jobs Report 2023. World Economic Forum. https://www.weforum.org/reports/the-future-of-jobs-report-2023/

Kovacs, S. (2020, January 2). TEENAGE EQ AND ADAPTABILITY. Ambassador Leaders. https://ambassadorleaders.com/toolkit/eq-adaptability

Medically reviewed by: KidsHealth Behavioral Health Experts. Motivation and the Power of Not Giving Up. TeensHealth. https://kidshealth.org/en/teens/motivation.html

MIT. Network & Conduct Informational Interviews. Career Advising & Professional Development. https://capd.mit.edu/channels/network-conduct-informational-interview/

Page, M. team. (2021, November 16). Setting Personal Development Goals in 2022. Jobs and Recruitment Agency in Australia. Michael Page. https://www.michaelpage.com.au/advice/career-advice/career-progression/setting-personal-development-goals-2022

Pearson. (2020, December 10). Leading Students Through a Changing Career Landscape. Pearson. https://www.pearson.com/ped-blogs/blogs/2020/12/leading-students-through-changing-career-landscape.html

PWC, UNICEF, GENERATION UNLIMITED (2021, December). Reaching YES Addressing the Youth Employment and Skilling Challenge. Generation Unlimited. https://www.generationunlimited.org/reports/reaching-yes-addressing-youth-employment-and-skilling-challenge

Thompson, H. Make Your Action Plan. A Part of the Youth Advocates for Community Health Program. Community Youth Development Division of Extension. University of Wisconsin-Madison. https://youth.extension.wisc.edu/articles/make-your-action-plan/

U.S. DEPARTMENT OF LABOR. Soft Skills to Pay The Bills. United States Department of Labor. https://www.dol.gov/agencies/odep/program-areas/individuals/youth/transition/soft-skills

UNICEF (2022). The 12 Transferable Skills - UNICEF's Conceptual and Programmatic Framework. © United Nations Children's Fund. https://www.unicef.org/lac/media/32441/file/The%2012%20Transferable%20Skills.pdf

Self-Regulation Workbook for Teens

Ackerman, C. (2017). *21 Mindfulness Exercises & Activities For Adults (+ PDF)*. Positive Psychology. Available at: https://positivepsychology.com/mindfulness-exercises-techniques-activities/#mindfulness-interventions-techniques-worksheets

Ackerman, C. (2017). *Cognitive Distortions: 22 Examples & Worksheets (& PDF)*. Positive Psychology. Available at: https://positivepsychology.com/cognitive-distortions/#common-cognitive-distortions

Apex Recovery. (2023). *Relapse Prevention: Coping Skills And Warning Signs*. Available at: https://apex.rehab/relapse-prevention-coping-skills-warning-signs/

Ayushka. (2023). *The Art Of Non-Judgment: Cultivating Compassion And Empathy*. Medium. Available at: https://medium.com/@ayusingh2506/the-art-of-non-judgment-cultivating-compassion-and-empathy-158f038c6f2a

Behavioral Therapy? Healthline. Available at: https://www.healthline.com/health/abc-model#benefits-and-examples

Better Help. (2024). *Behaviors, Emotions, And Feelings: How They Work Together*. Available at: https://www.betterhelp.com/advice/behavior/behaviors-emotions-and-feelings-how-they-work-together/

Bonfil, A. & Wagage, S. (2020) *A Course in CBT Techniques: A Free Online CBT Workbook*. Available at: https://cogbtherapy.com/introduction-to-cbt

Calm. (2024). *Reframing Negative Thoughts: How To Challenge Negative Thinking*. Available at: https://www.calm.com/blog/reframing-negative-thoughts

Carroll, D. (2019). *The Relationship Between Thoughts, Feelings, And Behaviors*. Debbie Woodall Carroll. Available at: https://debbiewoodallcarroll.com/the-relationship-between-thoughts-feelings-and-behaviors/

Classroom Mental Health. (2024) Helping Students Connect The Dots: Thoughts, Feelings, & Behaviors. Available at: https://classroommentalhealth.org/in-class/thoughts/

Cleveland Clinic. (2024) *Stress: Coping With Life's Stressors*. Available at: https://my.clevelandclinic.org/health/articles/6392-stress-coping-with-lifes-stressors

Counselling Life Coaching. (2024). *Understanding The Cognitive Triad In Cognitive Behavioral Therapy (CBT)*. Available at: https://counselling-lifecoaching.com/understanding-the-cognitive-triad-in-cognitive-behavioral-therapy-cbt/

Darcy, A. (2023). *Balanced Thinking – What Is It, And How Can You Benefit?* Harley Therapy Mental Health Blog. Available at: https://www.harleytherapy.co.uk/counselling/balanced-thinking-benefits.htm

Davis, T. (2021). *Ultimate Positive Thinking Exercises (+ 3 Great Techniques)*. Positive Psychology. Available at: https://positivepsychology.com/positive-thinking-exercises/#techniques

Delaware Psychological Services. (2021). *10 Ways To Practice Positive Self-Talk*. Available at: https://www.delawarepsychologicalservices.com/post/10-ways-to-practice-positive-self-talk

Get Self Help. (2024) *Positive Coping Statements*. Available at: https://www.getselfhelp.co.uk/positive-coping-statements/

Great Expectations. (2024) *Quotes About Problem-Solving*. Available at: https://www.greatexpectations.org/resources/life-principles/problem-solving/quotes-about-problem-solving/

Grouport. (2024) *Empowering CBT Techniques Quotes: Words Of Wisdom For Personal Growth And Cognitive Mastery*. Grouport Therapy. Available at: https://www.grouporttherapy.com/blog/cbt-quotes

Health Direct. (2022). *Self-Talk*. Available at: https://www.healthdirect.gov.au/self-talk

Hope + Wellness. (2024). *How To Make A Coping Skills Toolbox*. Available at: https://www.hope-wellness.com/blog/how-to-make-a-coping-skills-toolbox

IIENSTITU. (2023). *Mastering Problem Solving: Daily Exercises To Elevate Your Skills*. LinkedIn. Available at: https://www.linkedin.com/pulse/mastering-problem-solving-daily-exercises-elevate-your-skills/

Indeed. (2022). *What Is Assertiveness Training? Definition, Benefits, And Steps*. Available at: https://www.indeed.com/career-advice/career-development/what-is-assertiveness-training

Kara. (2019). *How To Develop And Implement Healthy Coping Skills Into Your Daily Routine*. Hartzell Counseling. Available at: https://hartzellcounseling.com/how-to-develop-and-implement-healthy-coping-skills-into-your-daily-routine/

Kitazawa, E. (2022). *Behavioral Patterns In Psychology: Learn To Accept Yourself*. Shortform. Available at: https://www.shortform.com/blog/behavioral-patterns-psychology/

Loving Roots Project. (2019). *Using Positive Affirmations To Create A Good Mindset*. Available at: https://www.lovingrootsproject.com/allblogposts/using-positive-affirmations-to-create-a-good-mindset

Maini, N. (2023). *5 Simple Steps To Effective Problem Solving*. Synergogy. Available at: https://synergogy.com/5-simple-steps-to-effective-problem-solving/

Mind Tools. (2024) *Smart Goals*. Available at: https://www.mindtools.com/a4wo118/smart-goals

Mindful. (2024) *Getting Started With Mindfulness*. Available at: https://www.mindful.org/meditation/mindfulness-getting-started/

Mitchell, K. (2017). *15 Positive Thinking Exercises & Activities To Transform Your Life*. Thoughts Catalog. Available at: https://thoughtcatalog.com/kathy-mitchell/2017/03/15-positive-thinking-exercises-activities-to-transform-your-life/

My Self Help Habit. (2020). *Ten Tips For Maintaining Progress Towards Your Goals*. Available at: https://www.myselfhelphabit.co.uk/2020/01/24/ten-tips-for-maintaining-progress-towards-your-goals/

Newport Academy. (2022). *CBT For Teens: How Cognitive Behavioral Therapy Works*. Newport Academy. Available at: https://www.newportacademy.com/resources/mental-health/cbt-treatment/

Newport Academy. (2022). *The 5 Types Of Coping Skills For Teens, Plus 10 Healthy Coping Strategies*. Available at: https://www.newportacademy.com/resources/empowering-teens/coping-skills-teens/

NHS. (2024) *Reframing Unhelpful Thoughts*. Available at: https://www.nhs.uk/every-mind-matters/mental-wellbeing-tips/self-help-cbt-techniques/reframing-unhelpful-thoughts/

Nunez, K. (2020). *What Is The ABC Model In Cognitive*

Pelzer, K. (2023). *Looking Ahead – 100 Quotes On Strength And Resilience To Help Get Us Through Tough Times*. Parade. Available at: https://parade.com/1012592/kelseypelzer/quotes-for-tough-times/

Pietrangelo, A. (2020). *Is Impulsive Behavior A Disorder?* Healthline. Available at: https://www.healthline.com/health/mental-health/impulsive-behavior#causes

Positive Mind Works. (2023). *The Importance Of Assertive Communication*. Available at: https://www.positivemindworks.co/the-importance-of-assertive-communication/

Problem Solving (2024) How Do You Implement Your Solution? LinkedIn. Available at: https://www.linkedin.com/advice/0/how-do-you-implement-your-solution-skills-problem-solving

Raypole, C. (2020). *How To Identify And Manage Your Emotional Triggers*. Healthline. Available at: https://www.healthline.com/health/mental-health/emotional-triggers#finding-yours

Raypole, C. (2022). *How To Do A Body Scan Meditation (And Why You Should)*. Healthline. Available at: https://www.healthline.com/health/body-scan-meditation#how-to-do-it

Rice, A. (2021). *How To Challenge Negative Self-Talk*. Psych Central. Available at: https://psychcentral.com/lib/challenging-negative-self-talk

Shawn, B. (2009) *61 Self-Control Quotes That Can Change Your Life*. Happy Publishing. Available at: https://www.happypublishing.com/blog/self-control-quotes/

Sutton, J. (2021). *How To Perform Assertiveness Training: 6 Exercises*. Positive Psychology. Available at: https://positivepsychology.com/assertiveness-training/#assertiveness

Vallejo, M. (2022). *Automatic Negative Thoughts (Ants): How To Identify And Fix Them*. Mental Health Center Kids. Available at: https://mentalhealthcenterkids.com/blogs/articles/automatic-negative-thoughts

Vogel, K. (2022). *The Basic Principles Of Cognitive Behavioral Therapy*. PsychCentral. Available at: https://psychcentral.com/pro/the-basic-principles-of-cognitive-behavior-therapy#basic-principles

WebMD. (2023). *What Is Box Breathing?* Available at: https://www.webmd.com/balance/what-is-box-breathing

Whitworth, E. (2023). *8 Radical Acceptance Exercises To Help You Be Fully Present*. Shortform. Available at: https://www.shortform.com/blog/radical-acceptance-exercises/

DBT WorkBook for Teens

Barila, A. (2020) *How To: Effectively Set Boundaries*. Therapy With AB. Available: https://www.therapywithab.com/blog/2020/10/12/how-to-effectively-set-boundaries

Bariso, J. (2019) *28 Emotional Intelligence Quotes That Can Help Make Emotions Work For You, Instead Of Against You*. Inc. Available: https://www.inc.com/justin-bariso/28-emotional-intelligence-quotes-that-can-help-make-emotions-work-for-you-instead-of-against-you.html

Butler, A. (2024) *How To Access Your Intuitive Knowing, Or "Wise Mind"*. Available: https://www.sagetherapy.com/post/how-to-access-your-intuitive-knowing-or-wise-mind

Center Stone. (2024) *Healthy Vs. Unhealthy Coping Mechanisms*. Available: https://centerstone.org/our-resources/health-wellness/substance-use-disorder-healthy-vs-unhealthy-coping-mechanisms/

Charlie Health. (2023) *Check The Facts DBT*. Available: https://www.charliehealth.com/post/check-the-facts-dbt

Counceling Center. (2024) *DBT Skill Radical Acceptance: For Mental Health Healing*. Available: https://counselingcentergroup.com/dbt-skill-radical-acceptance/

Cuncic, A. (2024) *How To Embrace Radical Acceptance*. Very Well Mind. Available: https://www.verywellmind.com/what-is-radical-acceptance-5120614#toc-how-to-practice-radical-acceptance

Da Costa, J. (2023) *Self-Soothe DBT Skills: Sensory Strategies For Distress Tolerance*. Center For DBT. Available: https://centerforcbt.org/2023/11/06/self-soothe-dbt-skills/

DBT Tools. (2024) *Emotional Regulation Skills*. Available: https://dbt.tools/emotional_regulation/index.php

DBTSelfHelp.com. (2024) *How Skills: One-Mindfully, Non-Judgmentally, Effectively*. Available: https://dbtselfhelp.com/how-skills-one-mindfully-non-judgmentally-effectively/

DBTSelfHelp.com. (2024) *Objectives Effectiveness: Dear Man*. Available: https://dbtselfhelp.com/objectives-effectiveness-dear-man/

DBTSelfHelp.com. (2024) Pros And Cons. Available: https://dbtselfhelp.com/pros-and-cons/

DBTSelfHelp.com. (2024) *Relationship Effectiveness: Give*. Available: https://dbtselfhelp.com/relationship-effectiveness-give/#google_vignette

DBTSelfHelp.com. (2024) *Self-Respect Effectiveness: Fast*. Available: https://dbtselfhelp.com/self-respect-effectiveness-fast/

DBTSelfHelp.com. (2024) *What Skills: Observe, Describe, Participate*. Available: https://dbtselfhelp.com/what-skills-observe-describe-participate/

Dialectical Behavior Therapy. (2024) *DBT Distress Tolerance: Exercises, Videos, And Worksheets*. Available: https://dialecticalbehaviortherapy.com/distress-tolerance/

Grouport Therapy. (2024) *Inspiring Quotes To Live By: Embracing DBT Skills For Personal Growth And Transformation.* Available: https://www.grouporttherapy.com/blog/dialectical-behavior-therapy-quotes

Iraheta, N. (2023) *Four DBT Problem-Solving Techniques.* Health And Healing Therapy. Available: https://www.healthandhealingtherapy.com/dbt-problem-solving-techniques/

Klynn, B. (2021) *Emotional Regulation: Skills, Exercises, And Strategies.* Better Up. Available: https://www.betterup.com/blog/emotional-regulation-skills

Lagace, M. (2024) *91 Mind Quotes To Make You Wiser.* Wisdom Quotes. Available: https://wisdomquotes.com/mind-quotes/

Mindful. (2020) *What Is Mindfulness?* Available: https://www.mindful.org/what-is-mindfulness/

Modern Recovery Services. (2023) *Boundary Setting: Definition, Benefits, And Techniques.* Available: https://modernrecoveryservices.com/wellness/coping/skills/social/boundary-setting/

My Cleveland Clinic. (2022) *Dialectical Behavior Therapy (DBT).* Available: https://my.clevelandclinic.org/health/treatments/22838-dialectical-behavior-therapy-dbt

Psychiatric Associates. (2024) *How Interpersonal Effectiveness Improves Your Relationships.* Available: https://psychassociates.net/how-interpersonal-effectiveness-improves-your-relationships/

Resource Group. (2024) *The Wise Mind Technique In DBT.* Available: https://resourcegrp.org/blog/what-is-the-wise-mind-technique-in-dbt/

Sunrise. (2017) *DBT Interpersonal Effectiveness Skills: The Guide To Healthy Relationships.* Available: https://sunrisertc.com/interpersonal-effectiveness/

Sunrise. (2017). *DBT Distress Tolerance Skills: Your 6-Skill Guide To Navigate Emotional Crises.* Available: https://sunrisertc.com/distress-tolerance-skills/

Zencare. (2024) *Distract, Relax, And Cope: Distress Tolerance Skills.* Available: https://blog.zencare.co/distract-relax-and-cope-distress-tolerance-skills/

Coping Skills WorkBook for Teens

Asicrecovery. (2024, March 18). DBT Principles — The Complete Guide - ASIC Recovery. ASIC Recovery. Available at: https://www.asicrecoveryservices.com/post/dbt-principles-the-complete-guide/

Bariso, J. (30 September 2019). 28 Emotional Intelligence Quotes That Can Help Make Emotions Work for You, Instead of Against You. Inc. Available at: https://www.inc.com/justin-bariso/28-emotional-intelligence-quotes-that-can-help-make-emotions-work-for-you-instead-of-against-you.html

Better Health. Every Mind Matters. (2025). nhs.uk. Available at: https://www.nhs.uk/every-mind-matters/mental-wellbeing-tips/self-help-cbt-techniques/thought-record/

Beyond The Shop Door. (10 September 2020). 35 Powerful Quotes on the Importance of Emotional Intelligence!. Beyond The Shop Door. Available at: https://beyondtheshopdoor.com/2020/09/10/35-powerful-quotes-on-the-importance-of-emotional-intelligence/

Bogers, N. (13 February 2024). The Science Behind Your Emotions. Noldus. Available at: https://www.noldus.com/blog/science-of-emotions

Brooten-Brooks, M. (16 July 2024). How to Set Healthy Boundaries With Anyone. Very Well Health. Available at: https://www.verywellhealth.com/setting-boundaries-5208802

Buckner, L. (29 January 2025). What Is Effective Communication? (With Benefits and Tips). Indeed. Available at: https://www.indeed.com/career-advice/career-development/effective-communication

California Prime Recovery. (2025). 10 Motivational Quotes for Well-Being and Resilience. California Prime Recovery. Available at: https://californiaprimerecovery.com/10-motivational-quotes-well-being-and-resilience/

Centerstone. (2025). 6 Tips to Adjusting to Change: How to Adapt and Overcome. Centerstone. Available at: https://centerstone.org/adjusting-to-change-adapt-and-overcome/

Cherry, K. (30 January 2025). 9 Types of Nonverbal Communication. Very Well Mind. Available at: https://www.verywellmind.com/types-of-nonverbal-communication-2795397

Connections Child and Family Center. (02 October 2023). TIPP Skill: Turning the Temperature Down on Emotional Intensity. Connections Family Center. Available at: https://connectionsfamilycenter.com/tipp-skill-turning-the-temperature-down-on-emotional-intensity/

Edis, N. (2023, February 2). 30 best quotes about Emotional Intelligence. ThinkPsych. Available at: https://thinkpsych.com/blogs/posts/30-best-quotes-about-emotional-intelligence?srsltid=AfmBOorCRS2SXNZGI7yU9ru43j-OhutWOdsljAw4P-CrjBzU49NeNw-c

Golden, B., PhD. (2023, October 9). Emotional awareness is essential for our emotional and social well-being. Psychology Today. Available at: https://www.psychologytoday.com/intl/blog/overcoming-destructive-anger/202310/10-ways-to-increase-your-emotional-awareness

Grinspoon, P. (04 May 2022). How To Recognize And Tame Your Cognitive Distortions. Harvard Health Publishing. Available at: https://www.health.harvard.edu/blog/how-to-recognize-and-tame-your-cognitive-distortions-202205042738

Grouport. (2025). Empowering CBT Techniques Quotes: Words of Wisdom for Personal Growth and Cognitive Mastery | Grouport Journal. Grouport. Available at: https://www.grouporttherapy.com/blog/cbt-quotes

Grouport. (2025). *Empowering DBT Skills Quotes: Words of Wisdom for Personal Growth and Emotional Resilience | Grouport Journal.* Grouport. Available at: https://www.grouporttherapy.com/blog/dbt-quotes

Hofmann, S. G., Asnaani, A., Vonk, I. J. J., Sawyer, A. T., & Fang, A. (2012). The Efficacy of Cognitive Behavioral Therapy: A Review of Meta-analyses. *Cognitive Therapy and Research, 36*(5), 427–440. https://doi.org/10.1007/s10608-012-9476-1

Karla McLaren. (2024, May 17). Your emotional vocabulary list | Karla McLaren | Karla McLaren. Available at: https://karlamclaren.com/emotional-vocabulary-page/

Klynn, B. (28 November 2024). Emotional Regulation: Skills, Exercises, And Strategies. Better Up. Available at: https://www.betterup.com/blog/emotional-regulation-skills

Martin, S. (30 January 2017). 16 Quotes To Inspire Healthy Relationships. Psych Central. Available at: https://psychcentral.com/blog/imperfect/2017/01/16-quotes-to-inspire-healthy-relationships#Quotes-to-Inspire-Healthy-Relationships

Mayo Clinic. (24 January 2024). Relaxation Techniques: Try These Steps To Lower Stress. Mayo Clinic. Available at: https://www.mayoclinic.org/healthy-lifestyle/stress-management/in-depth/relaxation-technique/art-20045368

Meinke, H. (30 December 2019). Understanding the Stages of Emotional Development in Children. Rasmussen University. Available at: https://www.rasmussen.edu/degrees/education/blog/stages-of-emotional-development/

Miller, C. (06 October 2021). Primary And Secondary Emotions. Optimum Joy. Available at: https://optimumjoy.com/blog/primary-and-secondary-emotions-clair-miller/

Moore, M. (2022, September 21). What's the Difference Between CBT & DBT? Psych Central. Available at: https://psychcentral.com/lib/whats-the-difference-between-cbt-and-dbt

Morgan, S. (07 August 2023). The Power of Empathy in Conflict Resolution. LinkedIn. Available at: https://www.linkedin.com/pulse/power-empathy-conflict-resolution-sarah-morgan/

Morin, A. (03 novemvber 2023). Healthy Coping Skills for Uncomfortable Emotions. Very Well Mind. Available at: https://www.verywellmind.com/forty-healthy-coping-skills-4586742

Nash, J. (05 January 2018). How to Set Healthy Boundaries & Build Positive Relationships. Positive Psychology. Available at: https://positivepsychology.com/great-self-care-setting-healthy-boundaries/

NHS. (2022, November 10). Overview - Cognitive behavioural therapy (CBT). nhs.uk. Available at: https://www.nhs.uk/mental-health/talking-therapies-medicine-treatments/talking-therapies-and-counselling/cognitive-behavioural-therapy-cbt/overview/

Northup, G. (02 August 2023). 10 Communication Skills For Your Life And Career Success. Indeed. Available at: https://www.indeed.com/career-advice/resumes-cover-letters/communication-skills

Pal, P., Hauck, C., Goldstein, E., Bobinet, K., Bradley, C. (14 October 2024). 5 Simple Mindfulness Practices for Daily Life. Mindful. Available at: https://www.mindful.org/take-a-mindful-moment-5-simple-practices-for-daily-life/

Pietrangelo, A. (12 December 2019). 9 CBT Techniques for Better Mental Health. Healthline. Available at: https://www.healthline.com/health/cbt-techniques

Quino, M. (22 February 2024). Creating Harmony: 9 Tips for a Balanced Lifestyle. D&V Philippines. Available at: https://www.dvphilippines.com/blog/tips-for-a-balanced-lifestyle

Raypole, C. (13 November 2020). How to Identify and Manage Your Emotional Triggers. Healthline. Available at: https://www.healthline.com/health/mental-health/emotional-triggers

Schimelpfening, N. (2023, November 2). Dialectical Behavior Therapy (DBT): definition, techniques, and benefits. Verywell Mind. Available at: https://www.verywellmind.com/dialectical-behavior-therapy-1067402

Scott, E. (06 March 2024). 5 Types of Self-Care for Every Area of Your Life. Very Well Mind. Available at: https://www.verywellmind.com/self-care-strategies-overall-stress-reduction-3144729

Scott, E. (26 September 2023). How to Use Assertive Communication. Very Well Mind. Available at: https://www.verywellmind.com/learn-assertive-communication-in-five-simple-steps-3144969#toc-assertive-vs-aggressive-vs-passive-communication

Tura, N., MA. (2024, December 5). How to Develop Insight Into Your Own Life (with Pictures). wikiHow. Available at: https://www.wikihow.com/Develop-Insight-Into-Your-Own-Life

University of Rochester Medical Center. (2025). URMC. Encyclopedia. Undersranding the Teen Brain. Available at: https://www.urmc.rochester.edu/encyclopedia/content?ContentID=3051&ContentTypeID=1

Vijayapriya, C., & Tamarana, R. (2023). Effectiveness of dialectical behavior therapy as a transdiagnostic treatment for improving cognitive functions: a systematic review. *Research in Psychotherapy: Psychopathology, Process and Outcome, 26*(2). https://doi.org/10.4081/ripppo.2023.662

Printed in Dunstable, United Kingdom